Political Parties
and Political Development

D0068810

STUDIES IN
POLITICAL DEVELOPMENT

1. *Communications and Political Development*
Edited by Lucian W. Pye

2. *Bureaucracy and Political Development*
Edited by Joseph LaPalombara

3. *Political Modernization in Japan and Turkey*
Edited by Robert E. Ward and Dankwart A. Rustow

4. *Education and Political Development*
Edited by James S. Coleman

5. *Political Culture and Political Development*
Edited by Lucian W. Pye and Sidney Verba

6. *Political Parties and Political Development*
Edited by Joseph LaPalombara and Myron Weiner

7. *Crises and Sequences in Political Development*
by Leonard Binder, James S. Coleman, Joseph LaPalombara,
Lucian W. Pye, Sidney Verba, Myron Weiner

◈

Political Parties
and Political Development

Edited by Joseph LaPalombara
and Myron Weiner

CONTRIBUTORS

LEONARD BINDER   LUCIAN W. PYE

WILLIAM N. CHAMBERS   STEIN ROKKAN

HANS DAALDER   DANKWART A. RUSTOW

RUPERT EMERSON   GIOVANNI SARTORI

MORTON GRODZINS   ROBERT E. SCOTT

OTTO KIRCHHEIMER   IMMANUEL WALLERSTEIN

PRINCETON, NEW JERSEY
PRINCETON UNIVERSITY PRESS

Printed in the United States of America
by Princeton University Press, Princeton, New Jersey

First Princeton Paperback Printing, 1969
Second Princeton Paperback Printing, 1972

FOREWORD

IN THIS sixth volume in its "Studies in Political Development," the Committee on Comparative Politics of the Social Science Research Council has turned to a subject which was vital in inspiring the emergence of modern political science. Once scholars of comparative government examined what lay behind the formal constitutions and governmental structures of Western states, they were usually first impressed with the role of political parties. Thus it is understandable that the study of political parties and party systems and of interest groups provided the focus for the growth of dynamic political science.

The contemporary study of the new states in Asia and Africa owed much to this new tradition in political science, and indeed some pioneering studies, such as those of Weiner in India, Ward and Scalapino in Japan, Coleman and Rosberg in Africa, have focused on parties and party systems. In the light of these traditions the Committee felt that the time was propitious for a study which would explicitly treat the relationship of party systems to political development and which would be worldwide in scope.

In the tradition of political science it has been conventional to see political parties and party systems primarily in terms of their representative functions, their adaptive capabilities, and their stabilizing roles. In this study the editors and authors have sought to raise new questions about the potential roles of parties and party systems for initiating, managing, and consolidating dynamic political change and development.

This study is also unique in the series in the degree to which it seeks to relate European and American experiences with current developments in the emerging areas of Asia and Africa. All of the members of the Committee on Comparative Politics have vivid memories of how Sigmund Neumann bade us in our enthusiasm for examining contemporary problems of political development not to break our link with the tradition of studying Western politics. Initially this study was to have been the vehicle for Neumann himself to have demonstrated the relevance of European comparative party studies for understanding the whole wide phenomenon of political development. Had it not been for his untimely death Sigmund Neumann would have been the senior editor of this volume.

He participated vigorously in the preliminary planning of the study and as one of the great pioneers in the comparative study of political parties his wisdom and experience guided the design of the entire enterprise.

In keeping with the spirit of seeking to link European and American studies with work on the contemporary developing areas the authors of the chapters in this volume met at Villa Falconieri at Frascati from January 6 to January 9, 1964. The work of the authors was furthered by the presence at the meeting of: Franz Ansprenger, Otto-Suhr-Institut, Free University Berlin; Dennis Austin, Royal Institute of International Affairs, London; David Butler, Nuffield College, Oxford; Szymon Chodak, University of Warsaw; Mattei Dogan, Centre d'Etudes Sociologiques, Paris; R. P. Dore, The London School of Economics and Political Science; Aldo Garosci, University of Turin; Colin Leys, Makerere College; W. J. M. Mackenzie, University of Manchester; Serif Aref Mardin, Ankara University; W. H. Morris-Jones, University of Durham; Guglielmo Negri, University of Rome; and Alberto Spreafico, University of Florence.

The editors wish to express particular thanks to their colleagues on the Committee on Comparative Politics for continued encouragement; to Professor Giovanni Gozzer and Guglielmo Negri for facilitating the holding of the conference at the Villa Falconieri; to Sidney Tarrow and Gloria Pirzio Ammassari for their recording of conference proceedings; to Harry Eckstein, Giovanni Sartori, Robert Ward, and the editors' graduate students at M.I.T. and Yale for their frank and valuable criticisms and suggestions; to Mrs. Coleen Bellmard at Rome and Mrs. Eleanor Mamber at M.I.T., who provided exceptional secretarial services as well as managed the complex logistics of international communication and organization; and to Pendleton Herring and Bryce Wood of the Social Science Research Council, whose cooperation and encouragement were essential to the successful completion of this project.

The editors and authors of this volume also join with others who have previously appeared in this series in expressing their gratitude to Richard Hatch at M.I.T., who did such a brilliant job in improving the organization and style of significant portions of this manuscript. The index of this volume represents the patient and dedicated work of Gail Mau.

LUCIAN W. PYE

CONTENTS

Foreword   v

PART I: THE ORIGIN AND DEVELOPMENT OF PARTIES

1. The Origin and Development of Political Parties
    by Joseph LaPalombara and Myron Weiner   3

2. Parties, Elites, and Political Developments in Western
    Europe by Hans Daalder   43

3. Parties and Nation-Building in America
    by William N. Chambers   79

4. The Development of Parties in Turkey
    by Dankwart A. Rustow   107

PART II: PARTY SYSTEMS AND THEIR TRANSFORMATION

5. European Political Parties: The Case of Polarized
    Pluralism by Giovanni Sartori   137

6. The Transformation of the Western European Party
    Systems by Otto Kirchheimer   177

7. The Decline of the Party in Single-Party African States
    by Immanuel Wallerstein   201

PART III: PARTIES AND THE CRISES OF POLITICAL DEVELOPMENT

8. Political Recruitment and Participation in Egypt
    by Leonard Binder   217

9. Electoral Mobilization, Party Competition, and
    National Integration by Stein Rokkan   241

10. Parties and National Integration in Africa
    by Rupert Emerson   267

11. Political Parties and the Crisis of Succession in the United
    States: The Case of 1800 by Morton Grodzins   303

PART IV: PARTIES AND GOVERNMENTAL PERFORMANCE

12. Political Parties and Policy-Making in Latin America
     by Robert E. Scott   331

13. Party Systems and National Development in Asia
     by Lucian W. Pye   369

CONCLUSION

The Impact of Parties on Political Development
     by Myron Weiner and Joseph LaPalombara   399

A Selected Bibliography, prepared by Naomi E. Kies   439

Contributors   465

Index   471

Part I: The Origin and Development of Parties

CHAPTER 1

The Origin and Development
of Political Parties

JOSEPH LAPALOMBARA AND MYRON WEINER

THE POLITICAL party is a creature of modern and modernizing political systems. Whether one thinks of Anglo-American democracies or totalitarian systems such as the Soviet Union, Fascist Italy, and Nazi Germany; emergent African states in their earliest years of independent evolution or Latin American republics that have hobbled along for over a century; a mammoth ex-colonial area such as India groping toward democracy or an equally mammoth Communist power such as China seeking to mobilize a population through totalitarian methods, the political party in one form or another is omnipresent.

Wherever the political party has emerged it appears to perform some common functions in a wide variety of political systems at various stages of social, political, and economic development. Whether in a free society or under a totalitarian regime, the organization called the party is expected to organize public opinion and to communicate demands to the center of governmental power and decision. Somehow too the party must articulate to its followers the concept and meaning of the broader community even if the aim of the party leadership is to modify profoundly or even to destroy the broader community and replace it with something else. Moreover, whether the country is relatively democratic India or relatively undemocratic Ghana, a long-established democracy like Britain or a thriving totalitarian state like the Soviet Union, the party is likely to be intimately involved in political recruitment—the selection of the political leadership in whose hands power and decisions will in large measure reside.

These similarities of function—and they could be further multiplied—suggest that the political party emerges whenever the activities of a political system reach a certain degree of complexity, or whenever the notion of political power comes to include the idea that the mass public must participate or be controlled. Thus one might argue that, just as bureaucracy emerged when public administration could no longer be adequately handled in the prince's household, the political party materialized when the tasks of recruiting political leadership and making public policy could no longer be handled by a small coterie of men unconcerned with public sentiments. The emergence of a political party clearly implies that the masses must be taken into account by the political elite, either out of a commitment to the ideological notion that the masses have a right to participate in the determination of public policy or the selection of leadership, or out of the realization that even a rigidly dictatorial elite must find the organizational means of assuring stable conformance and control.

It is not a matter of historical chance that dictatorial regimes in the modern world rely heavily on the political party. For, if the power dam or steel mill is conceived of by political elites in the developing areas as a symbol of economic modernity, the political party is similarly seen in the popular mind as a symbol of political modernity. Thus political elites may create parties (or give the name of party to some other political grouping) when in fact the conditions for the establishment and maintenance of political parties are absent and when what has been created is not in fact a political party. Political development implies among other things a measure of political participation by large numbers of people who do not belong to the dominant political elite. In the broadest sense participation may refer only to a psychological involvement in the political process: a measure of identification with the nation-state as distinct from parochial groupings, a capacity to empathize with those who make political decisions,[1] a readiness to give support to the political system and perhaps even to the policies pursued.[2] A portion of the public may be alienated, but alienation implies deviations from a norm or from a prior identification. In some political systems, particularly those which are authoritarian or totalitarian, participation may be primarily psychological and only in a minor degree substantive. But in all democratic regimes and even in some totalitarian systems participation is often substantive as well. Individuals may vote, participate in voluntary associations seeking to influence public policy, or be members of political parties concerned with affecting the selec-

---

[1] On the concept of "empathy" as an index of modernity, see Daniel Lerner, *The Passing of Traditional Society*, Glencoe, Ill.: The Free Press, 1958, pp. 47-54.

[2] On the importance of support for the system in modern political systems, see Gabriel A. Almond and Sidney Verba, *The Civic Culture*, Princeton: Princeton University Press, 1963, Ch. 4.

tion of candidates to public office.³ In non-democratic regimes of a
plebiscitarian nature there may be attendance at political rallies and
mobilization for systemic goals such as economic development or
the conduct of war.⁴

Political development also implies a political complexity which
requires a high degree of organization. Indeed one view of development suggests that in a modern society people have the capacity
to establish and maintain large, complex but flexible organizational
forms capable of carrying out the new or enlarged functions which
modern societies are called upon to perform. Thus the capacity to
utilize energy and technology for exercising control over nature
involves not merely technical skills but also the capacity to create
corporate forms for the large-scale management of men and materials in modern industries. Similarly, a modern society requires a
complex school system and universities capable of innovating or of
adapting themselves to innovation; bureaucracies capable of carrying on the complex tasks of modern governments; and intricate institutions designed to run the mass media and mass transportation net-
works to facilitate the flow of ideas, information, and personnel.⁵
These developments suggest not only that man is capable of forming purposive complex organizations but also that at certain stages
of historical development man is indeed compelled to form such
organizations.

It should be clear therefore that when we speak of parties we do
not mean those cliques, clubs, and small groups of notables that can
be identified as the antecedents of the modern political party in most
Western countries. In England, for example, it is possible to trace
incipient parties back to the early seventeenth century; in France
the development of small groups that were embryonic parties mate-

³ This function or activity, however, is often artificial when performed by parties.
A good illustration is Leonard Binder, *Iran: Political Development in a Changing
Society*, Berkeley and Los Angeles: University of California Press, 1962, pp. 221-226.

⁴ The plebiscitarian use of parties in totalitarian systems such as Nazi Germany,
Fascist Italy, and the Soviet Union is well known. See, for example, William Eben-
stein, *The Nazi State*, New York: Farrar and Rinehart, Inc., 1943, pp. 43-44;
Denis Mack Smith, *Italy: A Modern History*, Ann Arbor: University of Michigan
Press, 1959, pp. 389-402; and Merle Fainsod, *How Russia is Ruled* (rev. ed.),
Cambridge: Harvard University Press, 1963, Part II and pp. 381-382.

⁵ The problem of defining modernity is treated by other authors in this series
published by Princeton University Press. See, for example, Lucian W. Pye, ed.,
Communications and Political Development, 1963, pp. 14-20; Joseph LaPalombara,
ed., *Bureaucracy and Political Development*, 1963, pp. 9-14, 35-48; Robert E. Ward
and Dankwart A. Rustow, eds., *Political Modernization in Japan and Turkey*,
1964, pp. 3-13.

rialized somewhat later but clearly precedes the Revolution of 1789. To be sure, the cliques, clubs, and groups of notables sought to capture and control the exercise of political power and in this sense manifested one of the salient characteristics of political parties. However, when we speak of political parties in this essay, we do not mean a loosely knit group of notables with limited and intermittent relationships to local counterparts. Our definition requires instead (1) continuity in organization—that is, an organization whose expected life span is not dependent on the life span of current leaders; (2) manifest and presumably permanent organization at the local level, with regularized communications and other relationships between local and national units; (3) self-conscious determination of leaders at both national and local levels to capture and to hold decision-making power alone or in coalition with others, not simply to influence the exercise of power; and (4) a concern on the part of the organization for seeking followers at the polls or in some manner striving for popular support.

Given this definition, it is obvious that political parties are primarily phenomena of the last century. In England the modern party really got underway with the organization of the local registration societies favored by the Liberals after the Reform of 1832.[6] In France and other places on the continent the transformation of legislative cliques or political clubs into mass-oriented organizations is associated with the revolutionary year of 1848. In the United States, although modern parties with substantial following and stable structures appeared in the 1790's with the Federalists of Hamilton and Adams and the Republicans of Jefferson and Madison, it was not until the era of Andrew Jackson in the 1830's that party organization developed to include strong centers of local power on a substantial mass base.[7] In Japan, the first of the Asian countries to transplant major Western political institutions, parties in the sense that we are using the term did not emerge until after the Meiji restoration of 1867 and perhaps not even until the First World War.[8]

[6] See Samuel H. Beer, "Great Britain: From Governing Elite to Organized Mass Parties," in Sigmund Neumann, ed., *Modern Political Parties*, Chicago: University of Chicago Press, 1956. Also, R. T. McKenzie, *British Political Parties*, New York: St Martin's Press, 1955.

[7] V. O. Key, *Politics, Parties and Pressure Groups*, New York: Crowell Publishers, 1958; William N. Chambers, *Political Parties in a New Nation: The American Experience, 1776-1809*, New York: Oxford University Press, 1963.

[8] Robert Scalapino, "Japan: Between Traditionalism and Democracy," in Sigmund

6

The small oligarchical groups which take the name of party in some countries of Latin America, Africa, and Asia are more akin to the factions of notables in the Roman Republic or in some instances to the revolutionary clubs in late eighteenth-century France than they are to political parties concerned with winning or maintaining popular support in modern democracies or totalitarian states. The disappearance of what were often called political parties in some new states of southern Asia and Africa may suggest only that the conditions necessary for the establishment and maintenance of parties were absent, or that the groups which disappeared were not political parties in our sense of the term.

If, as we suggest, the emergence of political parties is a useful institutional index of a level of political development and its emergence is related to the modernization process, then we must ask what in the modernization process facilitates this development. To understand the conditions necessary for the establishment and maintenance of modern political parties we must first turn to an examination of the historic circumstances under which they arose.

I. Origins of Parties

The creation of parties has been a continuous process. The historical graveyards are cluttered with parties which dominated the political scene but which subsequently failed to adapt to new circumstances and therefore died, were absorbed by new more active movements, or withered into small marginal parties. Nonetheless the circumstances under which parties first arise in a developing political system—together with their initial tone and configuration—clearly have an important effect on the kinds of parties which subsequently emerge. We shall briefly survey three types of theories which have been suggested concerning party origins: institutional theories focusing on the interrelationship between early parliaments and the emergence of parties; historical-situation theories that focus on the historical crises or tasks which systems have encountered at the moment in time when parties developed; and, finally, developmental theories that relate parties to the broader processes of modernization.

Neumann, *op.cit.*, pp. 305-315. Also Robert Scalapino, *Democracy and the Party Movement in Prewar Japan: The Failure of the First Attempt*, Berkeley and Los Angeles: University of California Press, 1953.

PARTIES AND PARLIAMENTS

It is customary in the West to associate the development of parties with the rise of parliaments and with the gradual extension of the suffrage. One broad historical formulation of this gradual process is Max Weber's division of party evolution into the stages of aristocratic cliques, small groups of notables, and plebiscitarian democracy.[9] Duverger notes too that parties are related to the evolution of national parliaments and the growth in the size of the electorate. Parties, he suggests, grew out of political assemblies as their members felt the need of a group to act in concert. As the vote was subsequently extended these committees began to organize the electors. Duverger's theory thus postulates stages in party development: First the creation of parliamentary groups, then the organization of electoral committees, and finally the establishment of permanent connections between these two elements.[10]

Both Weber and Duverger indicate that the cliques and the elite political clubs, though often the precursors of modern parties, were not political parties as we have been using that term. The famous "Breton Club," which met in pre-revolutionary France and which later became the nucleus of the Jacobins, was little more than a legislative clique based on a specific geographic region; similarly the political clubs and aristocratic salons that persisted in England into the nineteenth century were essentially makeshift arrangements for electing notables to parliament and, more rarely, for bringing together lawmakers who might share similar views.

To speak of political parties in Europe, then, before the middle of the nineteenth century is to speak very loosely indeed. It is not until the suffrage is broadened and the notables feel the need for some sort of party organization at the local level that we find the first significant prototypes of what we today know as the mass party. Duverger is quite correct in his insistence that it is of great importance to know whether parties were initially created internally or externally. An internally created political party is one that emerges

[9] Max Weber, "Politics as a Vocation," in Hans Gerth and C. Wright Mills, eds., *From Max Weber: Essays in Sociology*, New York: Oxford University Press, 1946, pp. 102-107.

[10] Maurice Duverger, *Political Parties*, New York: John Wiley and Sons, Inc., 1955, pp. xxiii-xxxvii. Among the best critiques of Duverger are Aaron B. Wildavsky, "A Methodological Critique of Duverger's *Political Parties*," *Journal of Politics*, Vol. 21 (1959), pp. 303-318, and Harry Eckstein, "Political Parties," in *The International Encyclopedia of the Social Sciences*, forthcoming.

gradually from the activities of the legislators themselves. As the need for creating legislative blocs and of assuring the re-election of members of these blocs is increasingly felt, political organization at the local level or in the electoral constituency occurs. As Duverger observes, such local level organization may be simply the result of the fact that certain legislative blocs or factions share nothing more than origins in the same geographic section of the country. This was the case with legislative groups that emerged in eighteenth-century France;[11] it was similarly and strikingly the case with the first political parties to emerge in Japan in the 1870's and 1880's.[12] Likewise in Italy, which achieved unification late, the first party organizations reflected the geographic proximity of certain legislators who sought coordinated action and some semblance of local organization as a means of assuring control over governmental policy on the one hand and re-election to office on the other.[13]

The real impetus for the creation of some form of party organization at the local level in the West is generally thought to be the extension of the suffrage. The major steps in the creation of party organization in Great Britain can be clearly associated with the electoral reforms of 1832, 1867, and 1884. Where the suffrage is greatly restricted, local electoral committees are simply not needed; where it is expanded, the need to woo the masses is strongly felt. What was once a struggle limited to an aristocratic elite or small groups of notables now becomes a major drama in which large segments of the citizenry play an active role.

To the extent that entrenched parliamentary groups recognize the implications of an expanded suffrage, an effort to create local electoral committees can be detected. Thus, in much of Europe at least, the modern political party began when a working and continuous relationship was established between such committees and legislative groups. Where the local organization and the local parliamentary connection is established as the result of initiative exercised by those who are already in the legislature or who hold national public office, we can speak of political parties as having been created internally. This is not to imply, of course, that the local units are necessarily simply the creations of the legislators for there are often some local groups which provide the basis for a mass organiza-

[11] Maurice Duverger, *op.cit.*, pp. xxiv-xxv.
[12] Robert Scalapino, "Japan: Between Traditionalism and Democracy," in Sigmund Neumann, *loc.cit.*
[13] Denis Mack Smith, *op.cit.*, pp. 27-35.

tion. Some striking cases of internally created parties would be the Conservative and Liberal parties in Great Britain and Canada, the Democratic and Republican parties in the United States, the first conservative parties to emerge in Scandinavia in the middle of the last century, the National Liberal and Progressive parties in Bismarckian Germany, the Liberal and Progressive parties in post-Tokugawa Japan, and the Liberal party in nineteenth-century Italy.

Externally created parties are those that emerge outside the legislature and invariably involve some challenge to the ruling group and a demand for representation. Such parties are more recent phenomena; they are invariably associated with an expanded suffrage, strongly articulated secular or religious ideologies, and, in most of the developing areas, nationalistic and anti-colonial movements. Such parties may receive their original organizational impetus from such varied sources as trade unions, cooperatives, university students, intellectuals, religious organizations, veteran associations, and so on. In the West the most notable examples of externally created parties were the many Socialist parties that emerged late in the nineteenth century and the Christian or Christian Democratic parties that were created in the early twentieth century partly in response to the threat of proletarian political movements. The role of the trade unions in the establishment of the British Labour party and of several continental socialist parties, of agricultural cooperatives in the creation of strong agrarian parties in Scandinavia, of religious organizations in the creation of political parties in Belgium, Austria, Germany, France, and Italy is too well known to require elaboration here. Similarly, most of the political parties now functioning in Africa and Asia were formerly nationalist movements, messianic and chiliastic movements, and caste, religious, or tribal associations that developed outside of and in some instances hostile to whatever parliamentary framework had been created by colonial governments.

Duverger says of the externally created parties that they tend to be more centralized than those that are internally created, more ideologically coherent and disciplined, less subject to influence from the legislative contingents of the parties, and generally less willing to ascribe major importance to or be deferential toward parliament. This may well be the case,[14] and, if so, it would explain in part why many constitutional orders that reflect the values and the relative

---

[14] One should guard against sweeping generalizations, however, as witness, for example, the great importance of the parliamentary contingent in the British Labour party.

power alignments of the eighteenth century are clearly threatened by some of the mass parties of external creation and of more recent vintage. It is not merely that the externally created parties are more ideological, more disciplined, or more aggressive in making demands on the system. It is also that, largely as a result of the circumstances under which they arose, they have frequently not developed a vested interest in existing political (and in most instances social or economic) institutions. This observation is equally valid in the developing areas where nationalist movements typically take complete control of the governmental framework when the colonial rulers withdraw from the political system. While Socialist parties in Europe often had to make peace with those who ran the parliamentary framework—or risk civil war—the nationalist movements which took power had as it were a *tabula rasa* on which to operate and could, if they chose, abolish the parliamentary system itself. Nationalist parties often found it relatively easy to establish one-party systems and place extraordinary restrictions on civil liberties precisely because no organized group in the society with any measure of popular support was committed to the maintenance of a competitive framework.[15] The leaders of many governing parties in Africa, in their attempts to establish central authority, or, alternatively, to utilize an opportunity to concentrate power for the purposes of self-aggrandizement, have often banned other political parties and abolished free elections. On the other hand, the Socialist parties of Europe that rejected the parliamentary framework were often ultimately socialized into the democratic constitutional order. The post-Second World War parties, particularly of Austria and Germany, recalled the bitter days of the 1920's and early 1930's when militancy resulted not in the rise of socialism but in the rise of totalitarian regimes; the moderation of parties in these countries today, not to mention their support for the parliamentary order, is in part related to the memories of an earlier unforgettable era.[16]

While some scholars have, as we have seen, stressed the importance of parliament and the expansion of the suffrage as a critical variable in the emergence of parties, others, particularly historians of European intellectual history, have stressed the role of ideology. Thus the emergence of parliaments, adult suffrage, and parties

[15] See David Bayley, *Public Liberties in the New States*, Chicago: Rand McNally and Co., 1964.
[16] Kurt Shell, *The Transformation of Austrian Socialism*, New York: University Publishers, 1961.

themselves is related to the gradual emergence of democratic ideologies. The notion of popular sovereignty and the earlier medieval notion of tyrannicide are viewed as efforts to restrict autocratic power. R. R. Palmer, in his study of the way in which the "lower classes" entered the European political process,[17] has forcefully argued that the concepts which justified placing limitations on the authority of kings and the notions which facilitated the creation of parliaments, the expansion of the suffrage, and the establishment of civil liberties predated these developments. Insofar as the emergence of parties, or political organizations or movements which antedate parties, is concerned one can effectively show that a wide variety of ideologies have in fact served as vehicles for their justification. Indeed some parties were created as the instrumentalities of counter ideologies, in sharp disagreement with dominant political values. It has frequently been pointed out, for example, that the republican doctrines which underlay the American constitution did not conceive of parties as an institution of democratic society; similarly British liberal thought of the nineteenth century paid little attention to the parties that were rapidly emerging. Socialist doctrine saw parties as instruments of classes, to wither away along with the state when class struggle came to an end. Indeed most of the mass parties extant in the West would probably not have emerged had there not developed, in addition to an extended suffrage, direct challenges to prevailing ideologies.

There were really no systematic attempts either to study parties empirically or to place them in the context of democratic theory until the beginning of the twentieth century with the writings of Michels and Ostrogorski. Moreover the rapid development of mass parties in Asia and Africa—at least as far as non-Communist parties are concerned—appears to have taken place without the benefit of systematic theorizing. The Congress party in India, the Kuomintang in China, and the parties of Meiji Japan emerged, as it were, out of local situations in the midst of great historical developments which affected them and which in turn were affected by them.

Greater theorizing is needed, however, because Duverger's attempts to trace the early development of parties to the emergence of parliaments and electoral systems could hardly be applied to most of the developing areas. There are of course some colonial regimes which created representative bodies and even established

[17] R. R. Palmer, *The Age of the Democratic Revolution*, Princeton: Princeton University Press, 1959.

limited suffrage. But even in those instances the nationalist movements often refused to work within the parliamentary system. In India, for example, the nationalist movement developed before central and state parliaments were created and in principle refused to work within legislative councils until the mid-1930's, some fifty years after the movement first began and some fifteen years after it assumed a mass character. Moreover many colonial regimes were so hostile to nationalist attempts to establish independent countries that the nationalist movements had to function in a clandestine fashion. In Algeria and in Indonesia, for example, nationalist movements had to assume a military character to defeat colonial regimes that refused to grant independence; similar situations exist in the areas of Africa still under Portuguese domination and in the apartheid regime of South Africa. Finally, there are situations in which mass parties materialize where there is neither a colonial regime nor a parliamentary system. In Latin American republics there have occasionally emerged political parties aimed at breaking the monopolistic power of military and/or landed elites in control of the government. In China of the 1920's the Kuomintang was organized by a section of the intelligentsia with the express purpose of creating military force and political support aimed at establishing centralized control over the various regions of the country. And, finally, even in the European cases it is not always clear that the first mass parties materialized in societies in which parliamentary systems had already been established. In Italy, for example, the Mazzinian group that emerged early in the nineteenth century was, as in China, of a striking quasi-military nature and concerned primarily with bringing about the unification of the Italian states.[18]

The parliamentary circumstances under which some European parties emerged might more usefully be viewed as simply one type of historical circumstance, not as the general case from which all others are deviants. However, the European cases do call our attention to the fact that parties often grow out of crisis situations. Under some circumstances they are the creatures of a systemic political crisis, while in other circumstances their emergence itself creates a crisis for the system. For frequently a crisis occurs that the established political elite—whether kings, aristocrats, or colonial bureau-

[18] For an interesting discussion of the Mazzinian movement as a prototype for parties arising out of colonialist conditions, see Guglielmo Negri, *Three Essays on Comparative Politics*, Milan: 1964, pp. 45-54.

crats—is either unwilling or unable to handle in a manner that would inhibit the establishment of oppositional political organization. These historical crises thus place a "load" on the traditional political system that either results in the organization of political parties or is actually caused by the emergence of parties. It is to this concept of "crises" or "loads" that we now turn.

CRISES IN POLITICAL SYSTEMS

Elsewhere in this series[19] there has been suggested the concept of crises as historical-situational developments that political systems typically experience as they move from traditional to more developed forms. It has been suggested that the way in which political elites cope with such crises (and in some instances prevent them from assuming serious proportions) may determine the kind of political system which develops.[20] The point we shall stress here is that such historical crises not only often provide the context in which political parties first emerge but also tend to be a critical factor in determining what pattern of evolution parties later take. They are often historical turning points in political systems. New institutions are created that persist long after the factors which precipitated their creation have disappeared; and memories are established in the minds of those who participated or perceived the events that have subsequent effects on political behavior. These internal political crises may be precipitated by a wide variety of parametric changes, sometimes occurring simultaneously: wars, inflation, depression, mass population movements, a demographic explosion; or less dramatic changes in the educational system, occupational patterns, agricultural or industrial development, or the development of mass media. Of the many internal political crises which nations have experienced during the period in which political parties were being formed, three strike us as most salient in their impact on party formation: legitimacy, integration, and participation. Though these crises may be analytically distinct, it is commonly noted that in most of the late-developing countries they are frequently telescoped so that political leadership has the extraordinary burden of simultaneously attempting to cope with political problems

[19] See Lucian W. Pye and Sidney Verba, *Political Culture and Political Development*, Princeton: Princeton University Press, 1965.

[20] Our formulation is in keeping with the important observation of Max Weber that salient events in a nation's history may have an enduring impact on the type of system that develops and that differences among systems can often be explained on the basis of these experiences. Max Weber, *The Methodology of the Social Sciences*, Glencoe, Ill.: The Free Press, 1949, pp. 182-185.

which historically in other societies had been spread over relatively long periods of time. Moreover there is no logical temporal sequence to these crises though, as we shall see, their sequence has important consequences that must be borne in mind. Finally, not all changes need occur in crisis proportions. Changes may occur imperceptibly, and leadership may prove to be so adept in handling "loads" as to move a system from one state to another with minimal strain.

Of these three crises, legitimacy is the issue around which some of the earliest parties both in Europe and in the developing areas were first created.[21] The internally created parties of which Duverger speaks appeared to arise at a time when the issues of legitimacy (or constitutional order) were much debated. But Sir Lewis Namier, in his now classic study, *The Structure of Politics at the Accession of George III*,[22] has forcefully argued that the politics of mid-eighteenth-century England can be analyzed without using the party denomination of Whigs and Tories. Namier suggests that MPs entered parliament for a wide variety of reasons; that there was no party organization to bring these men together in support of policies or programs, but that whatever groupings existed were based largely on personal loyalties; that government could not count on the loyalty of members of parliament because of any party affiliation; and, most important from our point of view, that parties did not exist at the local level. Dankwart Rustow, in his study of Swedish political parties,[23] similarly argues that the early Ruralist and Ministerial aristocratic parties that developed within parliament during a time when the legitimacy of representative institutions was first being established were confined to parliament with limited and unstable membership and not at all engaged in mass organization. On the other hand, though parties did not exist in the sense we have used the term, there was at least a vague feeling in the minds of some individuals that political differences could be labeled by "party." As Herbert Butterfield has stressed,[24] parties in Britain (and in Sweden) were first created in the minds of men; their expansion into modern

[21] S. M. Lipset discusses the "crisis of legitimacy" in the evolution of the United States as a nation-state. He also details empirically for the American experience several of the problems we discuss in this section. See his *The First New Nation*, New York: Basic Books, 1963, pp. 16-23.

[22] Sir Lewis Namier, *The Structure of Politics at the Accession of George III*, London: The Macmillan Company, 1959.

[23] Dankwart A. Rustow, *The Politics of Compromise: A Study of Parties and Cabinet Government in Sweden*, Princeton: Princeton University Press, 1955.

[24] Herbert Butterfield, *George III and the Historians*, London: Collins, 1957, Book 3.

political parties took place when the political system experienced a crisis of participation.

The legitimacy crisis has, however, been more central to the early formation of parties when the existing structure of authority failed to cope with the crisis itself and a political upheaval ensued. Insofar as the revolutionary groups that pressed for the abolishment of royal authority in late eighteenth-century France assumed a popular character we may speak of the beginnings of political parties in France. Similarly, nationalist movements that emerge to change the existing governmental system and the rules which determine who shall govern and how they shall be selected are products of a legitimacy crisis. Nationalist movements frequently begin as small coteries of men concerned with increasing their influence on colonial government and administration and increasing their opportunities for participating in administrative office. They are initially, at least, not concerned with eliminating foreign rule and establishing a totally new governmental framework. But typically, as these leaders feel that they are denied adequate opportunities to participate, they are provoked to reach out for popular support and convert their small associations into mass nationalist movements. In countries in which the small nationalist elite is relatively satisfied with the steps taken by colonial government no such effort to create a mass movement need necessarily occur. In Ceylon, for example, the Ceylon National Congress, though moderately critical of the constitution which the British provided in 1932, was prepared to work within the new framework.[25] Compared with nationalist organizations in other countries, it was relatively satisfied with the steps the British were taking to increase opportunities for self-government. In Ceylon therefore no mass movement emerged before independence. It was not until the British established elections that any major effort was made to involve a large public. Similarly, many of the patron-parties of French Africa have made limited efforts to establish local party units and to involve individuals who do not belong to the governing elite.

One can argue that when governmental leadership fails to cope adequately with a crisis in legitimacy—whether it be the monarchy in eighteenth-century France or the French colonial government in Algeria in the 1950's—a crisis in participation may occur and with it the creation of parties concerned with establishing local organizations

[25] See Howard Wriggins, *Ceylon: Dilemma of a New Nation*, Princeton: Princeton University Press, 1960.

16

or some measure of local support. Where the legitimacy crisis is adequately resolved—where parliaments are established and the power of the monarchy diminished, or colonial regimes establish a measure of self-government acceptable to the indigenous elite—then the "parties" formed may not involve a broader public and may be more appropriately conceived of as incipient parties.

A crisis in integration has also provided the milieu in which parties have first emerged. Here we are concerned with the problem of territorial integrity and more broadly with the process by which ethnic communities previously divided come to accommodate themselves to each other. In Europe the emergence of parties in Germany and Italy took place in the midst of integration crises. In Germany the Bavarian-based Center party developed in the context of a struggle between Bavaria and Prussia as the Bismarck Liberals pressed for the establishment of a greater German state under terms that were unacceptable to the Center party. In Italy the mass movements of Garibaldi and Mazzini, as well as the internally created Historical Liberal groups, were directed at the unification of the Italian states.

Though the nationalist parties which have emerged throughout Asia and Africa are typically integrationist parties, it is rare that they were organized primarily to achieve national integration. On the other hand, integrationist crises are manifest—indeed often created —by anti-integrationist groups. In pre-independence India the Muslim League was organized with a view toward protecting an ethnic minority against what the leadership of the League felt were threats from the Hindu majority. The expansion of the League into a mass movement was clearly associated with an integrationist crisis that ultimately resulted in the partition of the subcontinent. Elsewhere in Asia religious, linguistic, and tribal minorities have often organized political parties in opposition to the nationalist movement and advocated special protections within the framework of an accepted colonial rule, or else favored the creation of several nation-states where there had previously been one.

While in some places the crises of legitimacy and integration have often been accompanied by the creation of political parties—and particularly of incipient political parties—the earliest parties in most countries have typically been associated with what we might call the "crisis of participation." Great social and economic transformations have resulted in enormous changes in existing stratification systems.[26] The break-up of Western feudalism was accompanied by demands for political representation by the entrepreneurial and middle class; industrialization carried with it not merely the promise of economic well-being but also the many conditions that caused working masses to follow in the footsteps of the middle classes in the demand for a more meaningful role in the determination of public policy.

We are concerned here with the first crisis of participation—the crisis which occurs before parties have been established and where the target of participation efforts is a non-party elite. This early crisis of participation—which occurred in Europe in the eighteenth and nineteenth centuries and in Asia and Africa in the twentieth century—involves a subjective change in the relationship between the individual and authority. Once a number of subjects cease, for whatever reason, to accept the authority of their rulers, then closed political systems are placed under stress and, except in very rare instances, cannot remain closed. This is true whether the rulers be hereditary monarchs, tribal chieftains, ascriptively selected bureaucrats, or colonial masters. A rejection of existing authority as wholly legitimate will result in individuals banding together to change the rules of the system so that they can gain a share in the control of the state apparatus. The earliest participation crisis may thus also involve a crisis in legitimacy.

The very changes which lead to the growth of new social groups and elites may also weaken the authority of those who traditionally hold power. With the growth of economically modernizing groups, landed power is reduced in importance; the development of secularism facilitates the growth of professional classes and reduces the importance of traditional elements whose status and authority rest on their capacity to appeal to sacred symbols and beliefs. The growth of the mass media strengthens the political potential of the experts in communications and diminishes the importance of traditional communication specialists. It is in this context of an erosion of traditional belief patterns, particularly as they affect the individual's relationship to authority, that political parties and other types of politically relevant organizations emerge.

[26] For an elaboration of the thesis that most pressures of groups on existing governmental institutions are fundamentally attempts to change the prevailing stratification system, see David E. Apter, "A Comparative Method for the Study of Politics," *American Journal of Sociology*, Vol. 64 (November 1958), pp. 221-237.

Historically speaking, traditional elites have reacted differently to the crisis of participation, with, as we shall note below, profound consequences for subsequent political development. One obvious type of reaction is for the traditional elite to accommodate emergent demands for participation. The classic example of this accommodation would be the British case. A shorthand way of depicting the attitudes of the British aristocracy toward the participation crisis is to note that peerages were eventually extended to members of the rising mercantile classes. By way of contrast, the textbooks note that the French aristocracy never accepted the Revolution and became a rigidly closed elite early in the nineteenth century.

MODERNIZATION AND THE EMERGENCE OF PARTIES

Though the concept of crises is useful for understanding the circumstances under which parties first emerged and therefore the factors likely to affect their subsequent development, we still do not have an adequate notion of the conditions which must be satisfied for parties to emerge. Political systems have, after all, experienced these and other crises in pre-modern times when parties did not exist at all; moreover crises of legitimacy or integration may be accompanied by the development of parties in some political systems but not in others.

We have already suggested that parties emerge in political systems when those who seek to win or maintain political power are required to seek support from the larger public. There are at least two circumstances under which such a development occurs: (1) A change may already have taken place in the attitudes of subjects or citizens toward authority; individuals in the society may believe that they have the right to influence the exercise of power. (2) A section of the dominant political elite or an aspiring elite may seek to win public support so as to win or maintain power even though the public does not actively participate in political life. A non-participant population may thus be aroused into politics. But whether a process of change has already been at work which propels and even compels the public to participate, or politicians arouse the public, this suggests that there must be fundamental conditions which precede political participation. Why this change in public attitudes, which appears to transcend cultural and national boundaries, takes place is worthy of considerably more systematic reflection than is possible here.

It is obvious that one must consider the appearance of new social groups as a consequence of larger socio-economic changes, and in particular the appearance or expansion of entrepreneurial classes and the proliferation of specialized professional classes. One may well ask whether a measure of political and perhaps occupational autonomy is not a factor in the capacity of such social classes to participate in politics and take part in political organization.[27] Increases in the flow of information, the expansion of internal markets, a growth in technology, the expansion of transportation networks, and, above all, increases in spatial and social mobility appear to have profound effects upon the individual's perception of himself in relation to authority.

One might also ask whether a certain level of communication is not necessary in a society if people are to band together in political organizations. How much of a transportation system is essential if individuals in different portions of a country are to assemble and if there is to be a continuous relationship between a national and local unit? In India, for example, though small nationalist groups were created in various parts of the country—especially in urban areas—in the 1860's and '70's, it was not until 1885, sometime after the country had a reasonably well established mail and telegraph system, railroads, and widely circulated English-language newspapers, that the Indian National Congress was created.

One might ask too whether the secularizing effects of an educational system and the homogenizing effects often associated with urbanization are stimulants to the creation of political organization. Does the shift from a subsistence to a money economy, involving as it so often does the destruction of patterns of local authority and greater individuality and independence in the marketplace, spill over into political organization? Does the growing expansion of state power, involving the establishment of legal controls, greater administrative penetration into a larger number of individual decisions, and in general an expansion of governmental functions, lead individuals to organize either to prevent "encroachments" by the state (a phenomenon of the late mercantilist era) or to channel state

[27] The question of why people participate politically has received extensive research treatment in the West. The relevant literature is reviewed by Robert E. Lane, *Political Life: Why People Get Involved in Politics*, Glencoe, Ill.: The Free Press, 1959. Cf. the essay by John H. Kautsky, ed., *Political Change in Underdeveloped Countries*, New York: John Wiley and Sons, 1962, pp. 13-29. Also important as an effort to explain the preconditions for political participation is Daniel Lerner, *op.cit.*

permanently set the party development process; subsequent conditions and events continue to shape the configuration of parties. Indeed, it is one of our central theses that the nature of political parties will continue to be strongly conditioned by the manner in which historical crises, subsequent to the onset of parties, materialize and are responded to.[29] This point can best be illustrated by a discussion of the kinds of parties and party systems that can be identified empirically.

NON-PARTY POLITICAL SYSTEMS

Political parties as we conceive them are not an essential feature of a political system. Obviously political systems managed to function over many centuries without the presence of parties, and indeed we have argued that the emergence of parties requires the presence of certain preconditions. Even if these latter are present, however, parties may fail to materialize or, once having developed, may actually be repressed.

We thus find in the modern world oligarchical, authoritarian political systems dominated by military and/or civil bureaucracy that deny any legitimate place in the political process to political parties. In some of the post-colonial areas where this pattern occurs the first post-colonial regimes were formed out of nationalist movements dominated by one or more parties: the Muslim League in Pakistan, the Nationalist Union party of Sudan, the Anti-Fascist People's Freedom League (A.F.P.F.L.) in Burma. In other post-colonial areas the dominant oligarchies succeed in keeping political parties from coming into existence in the first place. This occurred under Mba's rule of Gabon (with French help) and in effect took place in Vietnam under Diem.

Where the emergence of parties is deliberately impeded by a dominant elite, the rationale will usually be that the country is not yet "ready" for parties (which may or may not be the case), or that some overriding national problem, such as security, requires that the development of political parties be consciously delayed. The argument against an open party system may be so telling that opponents of the dominant oligarchy may limit their demands to

[29] In saying this we do not mean to exclude the possibility that parties and party systems will subsequently also be shaped by political institutions and political leaders. It is clear that how the polity is actually managed has a continuing bearing on the parties. On this point, see below, Ch. 5, "European Political Parties," by Giovanni Sartori. Cf. S. M. Lipset, *op.cit.*, pp. 286-295.

that of participating in the ruling clique or of finding a place in a coalition of oligarchs ruling through the instrumentality of a single party.

Where parties have actually existed for a time the attack on them—designed to limit their powers or remove them from the political system—will generally be based on the claim that the nation's problems grow out of or are intensified by party activities. This occurred in Pakistan when the military regime under Ayub outlawed political parties. This has also been the thrust of Charles DeGaulle in France, who clearly abominates parties and who sought a Fifth Republic in which the parties would play a minor role. While parties are more difficult to repress in countries such as France, where they have existed for many decades, the recent history of Europe shows that a competitive party system can be subjected to enormous setbacks.

Concerning situations where genuine political parties have existed but are subsequently repressed, there are two important observations to bear in mind. The first of these is that oligarchical or dictatorial regimes may find that they cannot function adequately without the existence of at least one party. As we noted earlier, it is striking that regimes ranging from the most democratic to the most totalitarian seem to find it necessary to operate in part through the agency of one or more parties. The party may be ideologically justified as the elite vanguard of the proletariat, as in the Soviet Union, or merely viewed as a convenient or necessary means of mobilizing public support, as in Egypt. It is this ubiquitous tendency for parties to emerge in one form or other that leads us to think that there do exist conditions of technology, communication, and organization that make the political party itself a strong probability in the contemporary world.

Second, it is apparent that, once political parties have emerged in a political system, their repression does not necessarily terminate their activities. Where parties are outlawed, they will usually continue to operate underground. This occurred under both German Nazism and Italian Fascism. It is also evidently the case in Franco Spain. The one possible exception is the Soviet Union, where there is no evidence available suggesting the presence of an organized underground opposition. But there is in the Soviet Union a single party, which leads us to suggest that the presence of the party itself—and the opportunities it may provide for internal differences of opinion and of opposition maneuvering—tends to satisfy the propensity of the party to emerge at certain points in a nation's history.

Totally repressed parties tend to take on a clandestine and conspiratorial character that profoundly affects the long-range political evolution of a society even when parties reemerge from the shadows of illegality. To cite the most conspicuous examples from the West, it is generally agreed that the Bolshevik party in Russia and the Communist parties of such countries as Italy and France were strongly conditioned in their attitudes toward the political process and significantly influenced in the degree of appeal they have for the masses by the long periods during which they were compelled to operate outside the pale of legality. Similarly, many of the parties of the post-colonial nations—the Federation of National Liberation (F.L.N.) in Algeria comes readily to mind—were strongly molded in their orientations to society, other groups, and the political process by the years during which they were driven underground by colonial authorities.

We assume therefore that in almost all places where parties are totally suppressed the ruling military and/or bureaucratic oligarchies have created conditions of great potential political instability. This instability applies not only to volcanic pressures in the existing regimes but, more important, also to the patterns of action that parties are likely to manifest once they do acquire the mantle of legitimacy. Such parties are likely to apply to their own future opponents the same standards and patterns of repression to which they were subjected. For this reason it is necessary to look carefully at the varying ways in which different societies respond to the historical crises of political participation.

Turning to political systems in which parties do exist, we note that they are either of the one-party or competitive-party variety, with several subtypes in each category which we shall discuss below. However, it is necessary to say something first about the circumstances that seem to give rise to one or the other of the major types.

CONDITIONS FOR COMPETITIVE PARTIES

It is striking that one-party situations did not develop in Western countries until sometime after modern parties had materialized and usually only after some major crisis had occurred in competitive-party systems. That is, wherever one can note a one-party situation in the West, it is associated with the following conditions: a previously existing competitive-party situation; serious conflict among existing parties; a catalytic crisis such as war, revolution, depression, or policy paralysis; the emergence of a strong externally created party with an explicit mission to "discipline" (i.e. to repress) all other political parties.

The historical trend in Western Europe—though with many interruptions—seems to have been toward a competitive-party system. One important reason for this is that the earliest parties were primarily the extension of those legislative cliques, clubs, and groups of notables who differed among themselves somewhat, who competed for control over policy, and who found it convenient or necessary to shore up their own loosely structured groupings with more cohesive organization. Some movement in the direction of tighter organization would probably have occurred in any event simply as an impelling logic governing the interaction among the cliques.

In any case, the initial onset of modern parties in the West simply continued or reproduced a degree of open competition over the exercise of power which had accompanied the development of the legislature and the extension of the suffrage. Previous struggles between monarchs and bourgeoisie were replaced by competition among segments of the bourgeoisie itself. The process was a gradual one, involving the formulation of a complicated set of rules concerning the competitive process. It gave rise to important values and expectations regarding the rights of the opposition. Since men could differ over issues of public policy and since these differences could no longer be expressed merely by a limited group of gentlemen interacting in parliament, it was natural that each parliamentary group sought to mobilize its supporters through a form of organization—the party—more complex than anything hitherto existing and more adequately attuned to effecting the necessary linkage between parliamentary groups and new voters.

As noted above, into this previously established framework came the externally created parties of the late nineteenth and early twentieth centuries. Most of these provided aggressive opposition to the entrenched bourgeois parties and indeed compelled many of the latter to intensify their efforts to modernize party organization. The newer parties were based on a direct and open appeal to the masses. Their stock in trade was not merely appeal based on articulated differences over policy but a frank effort to use the modern means of psychology and communication to mobilize mass support at the polls.[30] Willingly or not, the traditional, internally created parties were compelled either to imitate both the organization and manipulative patterns of the newer mass parties (and thereby to become mass parties themselves) or to risk going completely out of existence. It should be noted, however, that the very system of proportional representation strongly advocated by Socialist parties on the Continent later served to preserve—even as vestiges of what they once were—bourgeois parties that failed to adapt to modern organizational and ideological requirements. Such parties can be found in Italy, France, and Belgium. They have been driven out of West Germany, where the electoral law requires that a party receive at least 5 per cent of the vote before gaining representation in the Bundestag.

The rise in prominence of the political parties in Western competitive systems placed the parties at the center of the political process. On the one hand, this transformation was healthy in the sense that it indicated that the political system was adjusting to the requisites of modernity. On the other hand, the very prominence of the political parties in such systems made them the most obvious and immediate targets of all those who, for whatever reasons, sought to make fundamental changes in the systems themselves. Thus the Bolsheviks felt impelled to remove all other party competition; the foremost and earliest targets of the Nazis were the parties that had been prominent during the Weimar period; the Italian Fascists moved quickly and systematically to suppress party organizations with which they had competed up until 1924. The Communist parties in Eastern Europe following the Second World War were equally assiduous in removing all parties except those whose continued existence did not pose a real problem of substantial opposition. Moreover the current attacks on alleged failures of parliamentary government in Western Europe center on the political parties. This is true not merely of France, where the parties suffered a major setback with the onset of the Fifth Republic, but also of Italy, where

[30] Lipset cites T. H. Marshall for the observation that the origins of extreme ideologies are to be found in the crisis of participation, that is, the effort by the bourgeoisie or working class fully to participate socially and politically. See S. M. Lipset, "The Changing Class Structure and Contemporary European Politics," *Daedalus*, Vol. 93 (Winter 1964).

antagonism toward parliamentary government has picked up considerable momentum in recent years.

It is possible, then, to say that competitive-party systems seem to materialize naturally and logically in societies where the pressure to create party organization was initially felt in the legislature. However, in these same societies the development of externally created parties poses a major threat to the continuation of a competitive system for several important reasons. First, externally created parties, precisely because they do not "naturally" come into existence within the context of parliamentary institutions, tend not to be strongly identified with these institutions themselves. Indeed, some of the external mass parties not only reflect deep social fissures within the societies but may actually emerge in the teeth of legal and other repressive obstacles placed in their way by the dominant elites. Leaders of such parties do not necessarily subscribe to the gentlemanly rules of political competition and do not necessarily share an interest in keeping the political process operating within historically prescribed patterns.

Second, the advent of externally created mass parties tends toward a radicalization and intensification of the competitive process itself. Political survival seems to dictate that the most extreme tactics be duplicated and that all parties to the conflict adopt the kinds of voter manipulation and mobilization patterns that promise to bring the most dramatic pay-offs. This snowballing effect in party organization and behavior is often criticized in the West as contradicting the democratic presumption that appeal should be made to the voter's reason and that the vote itself should be a matter of rational choice. The snowballing effect also often leads members of traditional or dominant elites, who fear that they cannot compete on equal terms, to conclude that the only formula for political (and social and economic) survival dictates a serious restriction on the activities of parties, or even political party abolition.

Third, externally created mass parties often develop a total formula for the society, or an ideology that excludes a willingness to tolerate opposition. The grave instabilities of some existing competitive-party systems can clearly be traced in part to the existence of such political parties. Total formulae or exclusive ideologies are incompatible with the continuation of free and open competition. The struggle for power in such systems implies not merely that the victory of such groups will bring an opportunity to defend their interests through public policy; it also implies that the continued even if peaceful opposition from competing parties will not be tolerated. As a minimal strategy, the opposition can be subjected to varying forms of harassment that place them at an electoral disadvantage; as a maximal strategy, steps can be taken actually to outlaw or otherwise to repress the opposition.

As we reflect on the history of the Western nations, it is apparent that only some countries have managed adequately to cope with the problems that circumstances such as these create. Where the newer, externally created mass parties have been substantially incorporated into the prevailing system, and therefore socialized into the central political values of parliamentary government, we generally see reasonable stability and a strong possibility that competitive parties will persist. Where the incorporation has been relatively imperfect, where the central values concerning the political process are not adequately shared, we often find unstable political systems in which a continuation of competitive parties is somewhat problematical.

The degree of incorporation into the prevailing system and adequate socialization into the values of parliamentary government are directly and strongly related to the manner in which the salient historical crises have been handled. This is not intended as a novel formulation but merely as a means of focusing our attention on aspects of a nation's history and circumstances that seem to be of prime relevance for the relationship of political parties to political development. Thus it is a commonplace to note that France is still having to cope with a crisis of legitimacy which has continued to gnaw at the fabric of French society for over 150 years. A century after unification it is apparent that Italy has still to resolve the crisis of national integration. In both of these countries the crisis of participation persists in the sense that for large segments of society there is neither psychological nor substantive involvement[31] in the making of public policy. The frustration, the lack of a sense of political efficacy that many Frenchmen and Italians feel, adds to the radicalization of political party interaction and tends to lead to the advocation of extreme solutions that would entail the abolition of com-

[31] From the standpoint of political stability, the important dimension here seems to be not substantive (from the view of the outside observer) but psychological, that is, a sense of political efficacy. See, for example, Angus Campbell, *et al.*, *The American Voter*, New York: John Wiley and Sons, 1960, Ch. 18. For very important comparative data on this point, see Almond and Verba, *The Civic Culture*, Ch. 7.

petitive parties. All of this is compounded of course by the crisis of distribution, which typically takes place after parties have been established. Mass externally created parties ideologically committed to a greater satisfaction of distributive demands continue to exert magnetic attraction for millions of voters. On the other side, forces unwilling to accede to distributive demands tend to protect what power they have by recommending the suppression of opposition parties. Thus in France and Italy the persistence of critical unresolved problems continues to endanger the survival of open competitive-party systems.

CONDITIONS FOR NON-COMPETITIVE PARTIES

When we turn to the developing areas, and particularly to Africa, it is evident that the emerging pattern is the one-party situation. The reasons for this pattern are varied and can be outlined here only in a highly generalized manner. The first consideration is that many of the so-called political parties in Africa are not political parties as we are using the term. The fact that a small group of oligarchs may create a paper organization of which they are members does not thereby make the organization a political party; it is something else, however important or marginal it may be to the development of the political system. If it makes sense to distinguish, with Weber, Duverger, and others, eighteenth- and nineteenth-century cliques, clubs, and groups of notables from the organizations called parties that emerged in the West largely in the late nineteenth century, it seems equally logical not to think that a small band of African oligarchs constitutes a political party. If we bear this caveat firmly in mind, we can better understand why and how it is possible in many post-colonial nations for so-called "political parties" both to materialize and to disappear with rapidity. It is important to recall that when we speak of a political party, we are referring to an organization that is locally articulated, that interacts with and seeks to attract the electoral support of the general public, that plays a direct and substantive role in political recruitment, and that is committed to the capture or maintenance of power, either alone or in coalition with others.[32]

[32] We acknowledge that not all writers are as concerned about this problem of definition as we are. Thus, Rupert Emerson, in his contribution to the present volume (Ch. 10, "Parties and National Integration in Africa"), favorably cites the view of Thomas Hodgkin that one should accept as parties all those African groups which regard themselves as such. This is clearly a looser definition than we follow in this chapter.

It is of course possible to repress or to abolish such organizations even after they have been firmly implanted in a society over a relatively long period. Repression or abolition will naturally be easier where political parties are relatively young, but we would repeat that, if what is suppressed or abolished is really a party, it is likely to continue to exert pressures to re-emerge. Once the historical conditions that give rise to political parties have been reached, and particularly if real parties have actually materialized, they will tend to survive no matter how long they have been in existence or how intense repressive measures may be. We do not say that competitive parties will materialize but merely that societies that satisfy the conditions for political party organization will tend to have at least one party.

Thus in looking at the emerging nations it is necessary to ask both whether the conditions for party development exist and whether the extant organizations are in fact political parties or something else. If the pre-conditions we have discussed are lacking, these states are likely to be governed by one or more "political parties" that may be nothing more than limited cliques or oligarchies. This was the way in which most Western countries were governed over many centuries, and no one would presume to analyze palace cabals, coups d'état, alternations in power of rival families or rival segments of a small aristocracy as the emergence or disappearance of political parties in one-party or competitive-party states. The political party is both a manifestation and a condition of the thrust to modernity; it is unlikely that we shall shall find it in societies where all other attributes of modernity are almost utterly lacking.

A second central observation is that the pattern of change in the developing nations differs from the patterns of institutional evolution which preceded and conditioned party development in the West. The most obvious difference in many colonial areas was the absence of an indigenous parliamentary framework out of which internally created parties might gradually emerge. Naturally, most of the genuine political parties in these areas were externally created parties, manifesting many of the characteristics we have associated with such parties above. Thus the drive for power will be much more raw and untempered by the restraining influence of long-established participation in a competitive parliamentary framework. Moreover, while in Europe the aristocracy remained and continued to limit the scope of power of the new groups, in the colonial areas one party to the competition—the colonial rulers—physically withdrew. These factors, when placed alongside the propensity toward extremism of externally created parties, constitute a strong impetus toward one-party solutions in many of the emerging countries.

Many other factors, however, encourage one-party patterns in the developing nations. The most obvious of these may be described generically as pre-independence conditions. Pre-independence nationalist movements often confronted the colonial elite with a serious crisis of participation. The nationalist elite, and through them their followers, sought to share in the exercise of power. Colonial responses to their pressures can be compared to responses to emergent political parties in most of the West and in Japan in the nineteenth century. In places such as Tunisia and Algeria—as well as in Portuguese Africa today—the nationalist movements were compelled to develop under clandestine conditions when the right to organize for the purpose of achieving independence was limited or denied by colonial rulers. Nationalist groups subjected to such repressive measures and compelled to operate underground are not adequately socialized into the art of political compromise and responsible leadership. Once such groups emerge either as cliques or political parties after independence, they are likely to manifest an overly strong identification with the state, view opposition as illegitimate, and be dogmatic, uncompromising, and monolithic in their orientation.

In some colonial territories, particularly those under British rule, a system of sharing power (known in British territories as dyarchy) was established. This permitted nationalist groups actually to exercise some governmental authority prior to independence. Such patterns were established in Kenya, Uganda, Nigeria, India, Burma, and Ceylon, as well as in the American colony of the Philippines. In these territories nationalist groups or political parties could share public power before they gained total control of the governmental structure. We have here something analogous to the gradual way in which emergent groups were permitted to participate in the political and governmental processes in Britain itself. While such gradual socialization is obviously no guarantee against the emergence of one-party patterns, it has increased the probability that the political parties that developed would tend to be more pragmatic, adaptive, internally competitive, and externally tolerant of opposition than in colonial areas where repression was the standard.

Equally important in assessing the impact of pre-independence conditions is the nature of colonial rule itself. Regardless of what differences involving colonial policy may have been debated in the legislatures of imperial powers, colonial administration tended to be monolithic, with a single bureaucratic service responsible for the management of governmental affairs in subject territories. Even in those instances where dyarchy was practiced, or where indigenous persons were recruited to some roles of public administration, those practices alone did little to inculcate the ideas of competition among political parties or of the necessity or utility of an organized opposition to the ruling powers. Indeed, the colonial experience in many places created bureaucracies of overriding power that in a post-independence situation tend to support not only unbending bureaucratic as opposed to political control but also the monolithic exercise of political power by a single party.

Another factor that tends to support one-party solutions in the developing areas may be called "accelerated history" or a piling up of the historical crises discussed earlier. Accelerated history means that the developing nations will attempt a quantum jump to economic modernity, leaping over or telescoping developmental stages which required many decades in the West. The leaders of such modernizing movements often believe that they cannot afford the luxury of a pluralistic democracy that enthrones competing centers of power and influence in several political parties and secondary organizations.

Newly active social groups may demand greater political participation for economic improvement or for a more equitable distribution of goods and services. Simultaneously the new political elites may be confronted with the crises of legitimacy and national integration. The accumulation of these pressures is an impelling force leading to single-party solutions. As Emerson asserts,[33] the African leader confronted with such overwhelming problems is likely to be both hostile and disdainful toward those who suggest that party competition be encouraged. Moreover in many of the new nations the amount of power available to governing political elites is limited, and the leadership is disinclined to share it. That is, both the scope and the intensity of power that can be exercised are extremely circumscribed. The reasons for this include the primitive state of technology, the great scarcity of essential human resources, the nagging persistence of traditional power centers, and the unrefined state of adminis-

---

[33] Rupert Emerson, *Political Modernization: The Single Party System*, Denver: University of Denver Press, 1963.

trative organization. This striking limit on the amount of power that can be wielded must be viewed alongside the great clustering of crises that demand the exercise of power. Given this disparity between ends and means, those who intimately understand the limits of powers available shy away from any formulation that points to a sharing—and, in the elite view, a dispersion—of power.

Lastly, there is some evidence that one-party patterns may be viewed as an intergenerational problem. The first-generation post-colonial elites may deliberately attempt to impede the recruitment to political power of young men. One reason for this may be simply the conservatism of greater age or the fear of the superior abilities of younger educated leaders who may be able to displace the older generation if permitted to compete on equal terms. Another reason may be that the supply of potential political leadership far exceeds the positions available. Where this is the case, entrenched elites understand that the price of upward mobility for others is their own displacement. Rigid one-party solutions become the most immediately available means of responding to this threat to status and perhaps to economic livelihood.

We have thus far discussed the two major party patterns and tried to suggest historical and other conditions that seem to bring one or another pattern into existence. Within each category, however, there are subtypes which might be established. The subtypes which we suggest here are empirically extracted. We offer them not out of any firm conviction that these types satisfy the criteria of neat taxonomic construction but simply because we believe that we might better understand the relationship of parties to political development if we arrange existing patterns within the following categories.

III. Types of Party Configurations

COMPETITIVE SYSTEMS

In many political systems the dominant party or coalition in control of government must struggle to maintain power in a competitive atmosphere. Such an atmosphere requires that it be theoretically and legally possible for the "outs" to replace the "ins" without resorting to violence. A wide variety of political systems fit this category. In Asia we would include India, Malaysia, Ceylon, and the Philippines; in Africa one might include Nigeria, Kenya, and Uganda, although the latter two countries display some tendencies toward one-party patterns; a number of Latin American republics fit this category, even if somewhat imperfectly; and the most obvious and enduring examples of such political systems are to be found in the Anglo-American democracies, in Scandinavia, and on the West European continent.

Some of these countries are so large in scale (such as India and Nigeria, which together in size and population constitute a major part of the underdeveloped world) that a competitive party pluralism appears as the most feasible mode of political organization. Others are so ethnically fragmented (the above two countries, plus Uganda, Kenya, Ceylon, and Malaysia) that party competition is in substantial measure an expression of ethnic rivalry. Thus far, at least, factors such as these seem successfully to have repelled one-party solutions. Nevertheless it would be hazardous to predict that the competitive-party pattern is safe in all of these countries.

It will be observed that we have included in this first major category all of the two-party and multiparty systems. We take this step primarily on the assumption that the traditional distinction between two-party and multi-party patterns has not led to sufficiently meaningful insights. It is more than a little perplexing, for example, to be reminded that we have multi-party systems that "work," such as those in Scandinavia, and others that do not "work," such as the parties under the Third and Fourth Republics of France. We also have two-party configurations that have remained essentially unchanged for a century (as in the United States) and other so-called two-party systems that have seen the near demise of one major party and the rise of another (the British case). As Sartori notes in his contribution to this volume, the number of parties in a particular political system is essentially irrelevant.

Our concern in this volume is to facilitate the fascinating and important task of trying to relate political parties to the phenomenon of political development. We know that some parties encourage and facilitate change while others tend to impede it and in the process to create serious tensions. We know that some parties adapt very easily to open competition and the peaceful transfer of political power while others are exclusive and seem unable to react to power alternations except on the basis of violence. We know too that some parties develop great skill in the pluralistic management of a nation's affairs while others remain either incompetent in this regard or tend to suppress pluralism. It seems to us that as a long-range goal a classification system based on dimensions such as these will permit us more meaningfully to relate parties to the processes of political change.

For competitive situations we suggest a fourfold classification that is based in part on internal characteristics of the parties and in part on the way political power is held. This latter dimension refers to the political system and the terms we use to describe them are *turnover* and *hegemonic*. A hegemonic system would be one in which over an extended period of time the same party, or coalitions dominated by the same party, hold governmental power. Hegemonic systems involving one party in exclusive control of governmental machinery would include the United States during the years of the New Deal and Fair Deal; postwar Japanese politics dominated by the liberals; Norway until recently under the continual control of the Democratic Socialists; and Indian politics dominated since independence by the Congress party. These are situations typical of what Sartori would call predominant party systems.

However, we believe it is also possible to speak of hegemonic systems in some instances where the power-holding situation involves coalition. The two major examples of this configuration would be West Germany and Italy since the Second World War, where co-alition governments have clearly been dominated by Christian Democratic parties. To be sure, a coalition implies that the dominant party will be somewhat more circumscribed than would be the case were it able to rule alone. Nevertheless, the examples cited clearly suggest that, where the major party in a coalition approaches an absolute majority of the popular vote and where it succeeds over a long period in putting together coalitions which it largely controls, we should include these party system arrangements in the hegemonic rather than the turnover category. In situations where the components of a coalition change relatively often, and where one cannot speak with confidence about a dominant party in the coalition, we would have turnover rather than hegemony. This was the case for the shifting coalitions of the French Fourth Republic even though the shifts occurred within the limits of a broad center rather than from center to extreme left or right.

Turnover situations, then, would be those in which, even where there may have been hegemonic periods, there is relatively frequent change in the party that governs or in the party that dominates a coalition. Canada, for example, would be a turnover system, even though the Liberals have been in power for long periods during the present century. The Fourth Republic, as we have suggested, would also fit this category, as may the Italian Republic now that the Christian Democrats have been compelled to move away from the center coalition that characterized Italian politics during most of the postwar years. Needless to say, Britain is perhaps the most striking example of a major power with a firmly established turnover pattern.

The second dimension along which we classify competitive systems is the *ideological-pragmatic*. These characteristics refer to the parties themselves, and we believe it is of vital importance to be able to judge parties in terms of where they fall along this continuum. Obviously in multiparty systems there may be considerable variation among parties in this regard. However, despite such differences it should be possible to identify for any nation state what the central tendencies of the parties are.

In terms of central tendency, then, we can conceive of the following four subcategories: 1) hegemonic-ideological; 2) hegemonic-pragmatic; 3) turnover-ideological; and 4) turnover-pragmatic. Where the central tendency of the parties is ideological and there is frequent turnover, we may expect a great deal of turmoil. Such situations suggest that the society is so evenly divided along two or more ideological dimensions that frequent turnover on the one hand makes it impossible for any one group to implement the policy implications of its ideological orientation and, on the other hand, assures that succeeding groups in power will seek to undo whatever may have gone before.

However, it should not be thought that where the combination is ideological-hegemonic great changes will take place. In this situation much will depend on the specific content of the ideology. For those ideological parties that are committed to social, economic, and political change the hegemonic dimension would appear to be essential. To illustrate this, we might note that an Italy dominated by a conservative Christian Democratic party sought not to move too far from the status quo. However, the same party in the hands of a Fanfani or even a Moro may be expected to bring about change more rapidly—but only if the essentially hegemonic character of the party is maintained. Similarly, it might be pointed out that the kind of commitments to socio-economic transformation manifested by India's Congress party in a sense requires that the hegemonic quality of the party persist over a considerable period.

Pragmatic parties will tend to move more slowly when they are hegemonic and more rapidly when exposed to frequent turnover. The hegemonic control over American politics that the Republicans maintained from 1896 to 1932 staved off radical demands for change by the Populist movements in the West and the South. It required an electoral turnover of unprecedented proportions, as well as the development of a considerable degree of ideological content in one of the parties, to bring about the socio-economic revolution that occurred at the hands of the New Deal.

Although it is likely that the particular combination of hegemony or turnover ideology or pragmatism that a party pattern manifests may tell us something about how the parties relate to social, economic, and political development, these dimensions are not causally related to each other. A competitive-party situation with high ideological content may manifest either hegemony or frequent turnover; the same is true of a political system whose central party tendency is pragmatic. It does seem true, however, that while the drive for hegemonic control is endemically present, it is likely to be much more strongly felt by those parties that show a high ideological content. If this is true, it would seem to have important implications for probable lines of political development in the newer nations of areas such as Africa. That is, where some of the African parties tend to be ideologically monolithic, we can expect to find great pressures tending toward one form or another of the one-party pattern. It will be of interest to note the three subtypes of patterns that these one-party situations fall into.

NON-COMPETITIVE SYSTEMS

A one-party pattern is by definition hegemonic and not turnover. It is of course possible that existing one-party situations may eventually become competitive. With the achievement of national integration, the development of a relatively modernized economic system, and the solution of other pressing problems and demands the "natural" forces of political modernization may involve the substitution of competitive parties for single-party situations. Although this possibility is not to be excluded, the probability for this particular direction of political development depends in large measure on the type of one-party situation that develops. Empirically speaking, there are three of these.

One-Party Authoritarian. These are authoritarian political systems dominated by a single, monolithic, ideologically oriented but non-totalitarian party. The classic example would be Spain under Franco and the Falange; others are Mali, Ghana, and Guinea. In Asia a good example would be South Vietnam, where, while Diem still lived and ruled, the dominant "party" tried to work out an ideology of "personalism" centering on the president. Similarly, we would include Castro's Cuba here, although it seems that the intention of the Communist elite there is to turn the system into a one-party totalitarian type.

It is typical of this pattern that members of the opposition are defined as traitors to revolutionary or nationalistic causes and as threats to security. The developmental aspirations and mission of the nation, if they exist at all, are identified with a single party. Very often the party and nation are led by a single dominant figure (e.g. Nkrumah, Diem, Franco, Castro) who is supposed to personify the goals of the nation.

As the example of Spain will attest, such political systems need not necessarily be committed to social and economic change. Indeed, the ideology of the dominant party may actually be that of defending the status quo and of impeding changes that are inconsistent with its maintenance. Moreover the general response of dominant parties to demands is to repress them, thereby creating the kinds of tensions in the system that impel the dominant parties toward more and more totalitarian forms of control. An overriding concern with security leads to a great emphasis on police methods and tends to make the preservation of the power of the entrenched elite the most constant concern.

In general systems such as these are relatively ill-equipped to manage the process of economic or political modernization. They lack the advantages of planned control characteristic of totalitarian systems and the advantages of innovation and experimentation made possible by pluralistic systems. If we turn to Spain and some Latin American states for illustration, it is possible to say that a long-term persistence of one-party authoritarianism tends to mean relative stagnation rather than development. On the other hand, impelling drives toward development will almost certainly require that such systems move either in a competitive-pluralistic or totalitarian direction.

One-Party Pluralistic. These are quasi-authoritarian systems dominated by a single party which is pluralistic in organization, pragmatic rather than rigidly ideological in outlook, and absorptive rather than ruthlessly destructive in its relationships to other groups. A prime example would be Mexico's Republican party (P.R.I.) over most of the years since the Mexican Revolution. A considerable number of the new African states also fall into this category, including Senegal, Ivory Coast, Sierra Leone, and the Cameroun.

Distinguishing between this and our previous category of one-party authoritarian systems in Africa, James Coleman and Carl Rosberg offer the following explanation:

"The dominant parties in African states representative of the revolutionary-centralizing trend are heavily and compulsively preoccupied with ideology, the content of which is programmatic and transformative regarding the socioeconomic modernization of contemporary African society, and militantly neutralist, Pan-Africanist, and nationalistic regarding relationships with other African states and with the external world. They tend also to be ultrapopulistic and egalitarian, with heavy stress upon direct commitment to and participation in the party and the state. Organizationally the parties tend to be monolithic and strongly centralized, achieving a monopoly over—frequently, indeed, a complete fusion with—all other associations, as well as an assimilation of party and governmental structures throughout the society. In contrast, leaders of the dominant parties of the pragmatic-pluralistic type place far less emphasis upon ideology; they are far less concerned over the persistence of traditional elites and structures within their societies and over continued dependence upon the former colonial power. The degree of popular mobilization and commitment is substantially less than in revolutionary-centralizing states, and although unitary and hierarchical, the pragmatic-pluralistic states permit a looser relationship between the party and other associations, in a climate of 'tolerated but controlled pluralism.' One or the other of the foregoing two tendencies is manifest in all African uniparty or one-party-dominant states."[34]

The most significant difference between the two types of parties lies in the degree to which a pragmatic rather than ideological approach is pursued. As we have several times repeated, a strong commitment to ideology will almost certainly lead to a form of one-party state which is either authoritarian or totalitarian. The one-party

[34] James S. Coleman and Carl Rosberg, eds., *Political Change and Integration In Tropical Africa*, Berkeley: University of California Press, 1964, p. 6.

pluralistic situation appears to be one in which rapid regimented development is not an overriding consideration. To encourage pluralism, even within the one-party context, does not mean that change is impossible. Indeed, it may be that by seeking to accommodate the conflicting interests that exist within a society the one-party pluralistic arrangement may demonstrate a superior capacity to bring about effective economic and perhaps political development. States such as these may very well serve to destroy the widely held myth that totalitarian systems are the most efficient means of effecting rapid economic change.

The one-party pluralistic pattern may also suggest a fruitful means for dealing with the persistence of traditional values and the problem of traditional elites in many of the emerging nations. There is now considerable evidence that despite repressive measures traditional structures have amazing staying power. The one-party pluralistic alternative may suggest the ways and means whereby these structures can be peacefully harnessed to the tasks of economic development and in the process contribute to the entrenchment of some newer but nevertheless vigorous form of democratic pluralism.

One-Party Totalitarian. In these political systems the state itself is an instrument of a monolithic party which has as one ideological goal the total use of power for the restructuring of the society's social and economic system. The obvious candidates for inclusion here are Communist China, the Soviet Union, North Vietnam, North Korea, and several of the East European states. The dominant parties in these countries are truly the parties of "total integration"; they fully intend to leave untouched no facet of the individual's existence. The arsenal of instruments for political control includes everything from mild persuasion to organized terror. Germany under Hitler and, to a somewhat lesser extent, Italy under Mussolini provide historical examples of such party patterns.

Obviously systems such as these have much in common with the category of African states that Coleman and Rosberg identify as "ideological-monolithic," and which we call one-party authoritarian. Thus some may wish to include Ghana, Mali, and Guinea in this category. However, it is certain that none of these countries has yet achieved the degree of totalitarian control that is true of the other countries we include in this sub-type. Moreover, apart from the actual degree of control and various differences in party ideology, we may note two other important differences: first, the Communist, Fascist, and Nazi parties manifest an ideological commitment to use the total power of the state apparatus to achieve their various goals; second, quite unlike the African states, the Communists (and to some extent the Italian Fascists and the German Nazis) worked into their ideologies prescriptions regarding specific stages in the developmental process. There is thus an ideological rigidity to totalitarian parties which by comparison makes the "ideological-monolithic" type seem relatively flexible. Moreover, as we have noted previously, the creation of a genuinely totalitarian system may require a degree of economic and technological modernization that these African states have not yet achieved.

Where this type of party develops it is most unlikely that a pluralistic competitive-party pattern can emerge short of a major upheaval such as war or revolution. It is easy enough to say that the Nazi or Fascist systems were built on sand, but it is not nearly as easy to suggest how they might have been transformed had not war intervened. Nevertheless, events in the Soviet Union and in Eastern Europe since the death of Stalin suggest that totalitarian states are capable of changing. The Polish experience seems to confirm our previous surmise that a once vigorous pluralism cannot be permanently suppressed. Experiences in the Soviet Union may also suggest that at certain stages in economic, technological, and cultural development the pressures working against continued totalitarian control reach considerable magnitude. Opposition itself has a way of re-emerging no matter how pervasive the repressive measures, and it is this fact, among many others, that forces us to consider quite seriously whether some form of pluralism is not only the most desirable arrangement politically but also the most efficacious from the standpoint of orderly and salutary economic change.

Conclusion

Parties can be viewed from at least two alternative perspectives as far as political development is concerned. From one point of view parties are the outgrowth of a development process—the culmination as it were of processes of social, economic, and political change. Parties are thus seen as dependent variables or as the effects of other developments. From another point of view parties can be seen as an independent institutional force affecting political development itself. Thus the capacity of a society to cope with the crises of integration, participation, or distribution—crises which systems may encounter more than once in the course of development—may in large measure be affected by the kinds of parties which have materialized. Parties may thus be seen here as independent variables which have profound effects on the process of political, social, and economic change.

In this introductory chapter we have focused on parties as a consequence of the development process and attempted to suggest the conditions that give rise to political parties, the various kinds of parties that emerge or are suppressed, and the range of conditions that appear to support particular party patterns. This discussion was meant to be suggestive rather than exhaustive, but it aimed to take into account a world-wide phenomenon of political change which is giving rise to the development of various kinds of political organizations. We have attempted to see European developments in a world-wide context, for by doing so we may not only gain a greater understanding of an international development process but also see the history of European political development in a new and broader context.

We have said little in this chapter about the impact which different types of parties have had on the developmental process itself, the second dimension along which parties may be viewed. The chapters that follow were written with a view toward illuminating this particular aspect of political parties. In the concluding chapter of this volume we shall try to pull together what we consider to be the most salient findings and problems contained in the individual contributions. Our hope is that the following discussions will help to clarify not only how various kinds of parties emerge from the broad process of political development but also what probable lines of future political development we can expect to witness given certain party configurations.

CHAPTER 2

Parties, Elites, and Political Developments in Western Europe[*]

HANS DAALDER

~~~~~~

THIS PAPER is in many ways an exercise in the impossible. It treats exceedingly complex social phenomena that are tacitly reduced to a common denominator by the use of deceptively simple concepts such as "party," "elite," and "political development." It threatens to fall victim to what someone once called the "propinquity fallacy": because Europe is one geographic area, it is supposed that its political experiences can be lumped together in one general treatment. This study deals, not with *one* political system at a *given* time, but with widely *different* systems *through* time—a somewhat strange exercise for one who is thoroughly sceptical of such over-general constructs as the "European continental political system,"[1] or of the superficial assumption that European societies followed a similar political course. The addition of the *s* after "political development" in the title is therefore deliberate. It is my profound conviction that true analysis will pay detailed attention to variation in political developments between European states as well as within each of them.

At the same time, this recognition makes the task for a single political scientist well nigh hopeless. He has intimate knowledge of a few systems of government at the most, and is likely to read his own rather than true conclusions into those systems he does not know so well. What follows here consists therefore mainly of a series of eclectic remarks—usually termed hypotheses, but more honestly called impressions. At the outset of the journey I seek refuge

[*] I am grateful to the late Otto Kirchheimer, Val R. Lorwin, and Joseph LaPalombara, who criticized an earlier draft of this paper.
[1] Gabriel Almond's analysis in "Comparative Political Systems," *Journal of Politics*, Vol. 18 (1956), is a considerable advance over earlier writings that ascribed "continental" politics to such institutional factors as proportional representation and assembly government. Even so, his statement: "The Scandinavian and Low Countries stand somewhere in between the Continental pattern and the Anglo-American," *ibid.*, still betrays a similar attitude. Why should France, Germany, and Italy be more "continental," than Holland, or Switzerland, or more "European" than Britain? One wonders whether the description of the smaller European democracies as "mixed" is not in fact an elegant way of saying that they apparently have some Anglo-Saxon virtues in addition to a number of "continental" vices.

in that excellent, if worn-out, defense that it is up to those who really know the individual political systems concerned to test, prove, or more likely to disprove, my generalizations.

The starting point of this paper is the proposition that European states fall *prima facie* into at least three distinct groups: (1) countries which developed slowly from oligarchies into consistently stable democracies: e.g. Britain, the Scandinavian countries, The Netherlands, Belgium, and Switzerland; (2) countries which have undergone serious reversals in political regime, whereby democratic constitutions have given way to autocratic or even totalitarian systems of government: e.g. France, Germany, Austria, and Italy; and (3) countries which continue to have authoritarian regimes of a somewhat traditional nature, and in which democratic groups tend to form at most an underground or exiled opposition: i.e. Spain and Portugal.[2]

It is much easier to say what factors are *not* responsible for these differences in political development than to indicate their actual causes. Obviously there is no immediate relationship to differences in stages of economic development. In the group of stable democracies there are countries that underwent the industrial revolution relatively early (Britain, Belgium) and countries which entered the modern industrial era late (e.g. Norway and The Netherlands). Similarly, German industrial development came relatively early and in full force; yet here the lapse into totalitarian dictatorship was the most gruesome ever. Moreover rapid economic development did not save the French Fourth Republic, nor does it stabilize political conditions in Italy.

Consequently it will be necessary to probe deeper and to seek for other factors that are often of an historical nature. The main variables on which this paper will center are: (1) the importance of the earlier elite setting; (2) the degree of coincidence or disparity between political and economic developments; (3) the "reach" or "permeation" of (democratic) parties as against other power holders in various European societies; and (4) the cleavage lines of the party system itself.

It is not suggested that these factors are sufficient to give a satisfactory explanation of the very complex and diverse processes of development which European countries underwent, whether gen-

---

[2] As the main focus of this paper is on problems of political development, I shall not deal further with the latter group in the pages that follow.

erally or individually. They have been selected primarily because of their interest for comparative purposes in accordance with the terms of reference set for the papers in this volume.

I. The Importance of the Earlier Elite Setting

DIFFERENCES IN POLITICAL DEVELOPMENT BEFORE THE
NINETEENTH CENTURY

The great complexity of the relationships among various social classes and status groups in European society, as that between state and society generally, has tended to be confused by the cliché assumption (found typically in college textbooks as well as the *Communist Manifesto*) that there was a "natural" evolution in Europe from feudalism through absolutism and bourgeois revolution toward modern democracy. This view is an egregious simplification for a variety of reasons.

First, it pays far too little attention to the fact that the term "feudalism" is used to describe fundamentally different structures in medieval Europe. The political relationships among king, aristocracy, clergy, cities, and peasantry as well as the economic relationships among landowners, burghers, artisans, peasants, and serfs showed great variation. If the starting point differs how can one expect linear or even parallel developments afterwards?

Second, present-day European states originated in very different ways. Roughly speaking, one can divide these states, according to the manner in which political unification came about, into four groups: (1) those in which effective centralization came early and with relatively little tension (e.g. Britain, Sweden); (2) those in which centralization came early but against considerable resistance (e.g. France); (3) those in which centralization came late but fairly gradually (e.g. The Netherlands, Switzerland); and finally (4) those in which central political power was established only as a consequence of considerable political violence in the nineteenth century (Germany, Italy).

Of these four groups, (1) and (3) had eventually rather similar characteristics. There was at no time a violent clash between political and social realities. Central power enmeshed itself gradually into the social system, and both regional and social groupings in turn achieved a growing influence on the center, thus making for a society which was both truly integrated and fairly pluralistic in nature.

Things were different in France, Germany, and Italy. There central control tended to be imposed by military and bureaucratic power. Hence the state came to some degree to hover above the society; the ruled came to feel themselves subjects rather than citizens, and to regard authority with a mixture of deference and distrust rather than as a responsive and responsible agency in which they had a share.[3]

Third, differences in the manner of social and economic development, even before the nineteenth century, tended to strengthen this contrast. In Britain and The Netherlands economic development ever since the middle ages was relatively free from state intervention. Autonomous economic development tended to make the newly rising bourgeoisie a much more powerful challenger of the powers that were than equivalent groupings could be in, say, Colbertist France or Cameralist Prussia. In the latter countries the state took a much more active hand in economic development, and in the process bureaucrats tended to become more managerial while the bourgeoisie tended to become more officialized than was true in Britain or the Low Countries. In the latter case, civil freedoms and a measure of responsible government preceded the establishment of a powerful central bureaucracy; in France the new social forces were eventually powerful enough to revolt, but in the process they succeeded only in building up safeguards against the bureaucracy rather than absorbing it or making it fully accountable; in the German Reich, finally, liberal groups failed to seize power and fell prey to the stronger hold of the *Polizei-* or *Beamtenstaat*.

Finally, European societies experienced different effects from the religious wars and their aftermath. In some countries the religious composition of the population remained homogeneous (whether Roman Catholic or Lutheran). There the church often remained for long an appendage of the upper classes; if this assisted them in their bid for the support of more traditionally oriented lower-class elements, it also tended eventually to provoke both fundamentalist and anticlerical protest. In other countries (notably in Switzerland, The Netherlands, Britain, and parts of Germany)

[3] In Germany most political forces submitted fairly rapidly to the existence of the new *Reich*, in contrast to the situation in Italy, where Church resistance and regional opposition continued for a much longer time. This made the existence of the new Italian state for a long time more precarious but may, on the other hand, have provided a safety valve that prevented nationalist unifiers from going to the extremes experienced in Germany.

various religious groups contested with one another until they finally reached some measure of tolerance or accommodation. In this way religious pluralism[4] and religious dissent often provided the spearhead of political resistance against entrenched elites, ultimately forcing a recognition of the limits of state power and of the justice of individual and corporate rights.

THE TRANSITION TO MODERN DEMOCRATIC POLITICS

Through such factors (and others such as the incidents of geography and war)[5] some political systems in Europe had hardened along autocratic lines by the eighteenth century, while others had maintained or even strengthened a pluralist setting that, however oligarchical, allowed a measure of political influence to a variety of political and social groups. This vital difference was to affect the establishment of political parties during the nineteenth century in at least two respects: in the ease with which they became a recognized part of the political system, and in the role which they came to assume within it.

In Britain, the Low Countries. Switzerland, and Sweden, conciliar forms of government, whether in cities or in the center, had a long and honorable tradition. The style of politics tended to be one of careful adjustment, of shared responsibility, of due respect for ancient privileges. Attempts at absolute kingship eventually broke on the concerted strength of particularist interests, whether corporative,

[4] The fact of religious pluralism seems more important than the particular religion in question. Whereas the Catholic Church in the Latin countries identified closely with vested social interests and alienated large sections of the population in the process, Dutch Catholics turned into a distinct protest group that pleaded for a separation of church and state, represented a considerable challenge of the outs against the dominant Liberal bourgeoisie, and maintained an effective hold on lower-class groups. Similarly, Lutheranism tended to be much more an instrument of vested authority in Germany than in Switzerland, while in Scandinavia it played the dual role of both maintaining an official religion and inspiring fundamentalist protest against a too modernist sphere in the central cities. Calvinism too was in practice much more nonconformist in some societies than in others, depending on whether its hold was strongest on existing elites or on lower-class elements.

[5] Geographic factors made certain European societies more secure from foreign attack than others: the insular position of England, the mountains of Switzerland, the rivers and canals of The Netherlands made these countries to a large extent immune against invasion on land. Consequently there was no urgent need for them to develop large standing armies. This had profound consequences for domestic political and administrative structures. In Lord Esher's telling phrase, the Navy often proved "a constitutional force," while an army was more readily "a royal force" (*Journals and Letters of Reginald, Viscount Esher*, London, 1934, Vol. I, p. 269). Similarly, the early development of a citizen-militia in Switzerland was a great deal removed from the compulsory militarization of Prussian *Untertanen*.

regional, or social. As the political order was in a very real sense built upon parts, the idea that men could reasonably be partisans found ready recognition even before the age of formalized party politics. There never was a "monochromatic, unicentric world," in Sartori's sense, to form an obstacle to the formation of parties.[6]

In these countries the view that government was somehow a trust toward the governed had old roots, however elitist actual systems tended to be until late in the nineteenth century. Intra-elite competition, being a recognized and even institutionalized phenomenon, made it easier to weather what the editors have called the crisis of participation. Conflicts between towns, between town and country, or among various religious groups created certain links between clashing oligarchies and sub-political groups below them. Competing elites sometimes sought lower-class support to strengthen their position, thus granting the lesser orders a political title and whetting their political appetites. Conversely, new claimants could exercise some influence on an oligarchical system simply by the threat of potential support to one or other side within it. Once some social groups were granted a measure of influence, this tended to provoke further demands from those yet further down until, finally, the burden of proof in the suffrage debate came to rest on those who defended restriction rather than on those who advocated extension of suffrage. Some upper-class groups came to doubt their own title, while most came to realize that fighting democracy might be more dangerous to their social position than democracy itself. Thus both pressures from competing elites downward and concomitant pressures from sub-elites upward made for a competitive gradual extension of democratic rights.

This process was facilitated by the circumstance that it came about in slow, evolutionary ways. Neither in political theory nor in actual behavior was there an abrupt transition from elite politics to mass politicization. Political newcomers were slowly accommodated. At any one time they tended to be given at most only part-power— enough to give them a sense of involvement and political efficacy but not enough to completely overthrow the evolving society. Older political styles that had been developed to guarantee the rights of aristocrats or *hauts bourgeois* were thus more easily transferred. The

[6] Giovanni Sartori, *Parties and Party Systems*, New York, Harper and Row, forthcoming.

"political domain," to use Neumann's term,[7] expanded only slowly. Since at any one time the political stakes were relatively modest, the upper classes were less afraid and the lower classes less threatening. Older and newer elites were thus held more easily within the bounds of one constitutional, if changing, political system that neither alienated the one into reactionary nor the other into revolutionary onslaughts on it. In time, however, the over-all political order could thus become more truly responsive to the demands of a wide variety of political groups within it. In 1867 Bagehot thought "dignified parts of government" necessary to keep the masses from interfering with the "efficient government" of the few; a century later the many were efficiently using those very same "dignified parts of government" to secure substantial concessions to themselves.[8]

Developments were very different in those societies where power was heavily concentrated by the end of the eighteenth century. In France royal absolutism provoked truly revolutionary resistance of a much more drastic and upsetting character than appeared in the English Civil War of the seventeenth century, let alone in the Glorious Revolution of 1688. If the king called on the *droit divin* to claim absolute power, so did liberal thinkers of the Enlightenment on the basis of the nation or the people. From the outset a leading strand of French democratic thought became therefore "totalitarian" in Talmon's sense,[9] becoming highly suspicious, for instance, of *corps intermédiaires* between the individual and the state. If in the countries described earlier pluralism seemed the natural corollary of liberty, in the latter it was often regarded as the prolongation of inequality and privilege. The traumas of the French Revolution created lasting and bitter divisions in French society. Articulate political groups continued to harbor fears and suspicions of one another, doubting one another's intentions and having different views of the legitimacy of past regimes and present institutions. Paradoxically, in that European country where popular sovereignty was proclaimed first and most explicitly no governmental system ever rested on a universal basis of popular support and respect. Traditionalist groups

[7] Sigmund Neumann, *Modern Political Parties*, Chicago: University of Chicago Press, 1956, p. 404.
[8] Walter Bagehot, *The English Constitution*, London, 1867, World's Classics ed., Oxford, 1952, pp. 4ff. The fact that most of the countries here treated have remained monarchies would seem to have been a consequence more than a cause of these developments.
[9] J. L. Talmon, *The Origins of Totalitarian Democracy*, London, 1952, *passim*.

continued to be politically strong, and the newer bourgeoisie and the rising working classes came to be divided in their respective allegiances. Democratic regimes met with a continuous threat from the right. Democratic groups suspected the state even when they were nominally in control of it. This in turn made it more difficult for successive regimes to achieve their goals or to capitalize on their positive achievements and to gain legitimacy and lasting adherence throughout the nation.

In Prussia, and later in the German *Reich*, the bureaucratization and militarization of the society had gone much further than in France before the existing power division was challenged. In France democratizing forces generally triumphed, however precariously. In Germany the Kaiser-*Junker*-Army-Bureaucracy[10] complex was for a long time strong enough to manipulate the new social forces rather than to have to adjust to them. From the outset large sections of the new industrial capitalist classes were drawn into the existing power cluster; this left the fate of German liberalism to the faltering hands of mainly professional and intellectual groups rather than to a strongly unified economic class. In most European countries bourgeois elements had triumphed sufficiently to occupy key positions in the political system before the real onslaught of the working classes was felt. In Germany, on the other hand, the existing power groups were powerful enough to maintain themselves against both, even offsetting bourgeois demands for responsible parliamentary government with a careful weaning and manipulation of the new working classes. Typically, a democratic breakthrough came not of its own strength but only in the aftermath of lost wars. The explicit democratic articles of the Weimar Constitution were to become the hallmark of success of democratic forms on paper at the expense of social substance.

THE DIFFERENT ROLE OF PARTIES

The role of parties in European countries varied considerably with such substantial differences in actual political development.

In countries where modern mass democracy evolved slowly from a preexisting pluralist society various regional, social and ideological

[10] For a sophisticated analysis of the way in which the Prussian *Junkers* maintained their social position and lost their political independence by their submission to the "new social factor . . . the state power" see Joseph Schumpeter, "Social Classes in an Ethnically Homogeneous Environment," in *Imperialism and Social Classes*, Meridian Books ed., 1960, pp. 144ff.

groupings tended to form what might be called "proto-parties" at a rather early stage. Consisting of informal groupings seeking to obtain preferential treatment for themselves and the definite interests which they represented, they tended to fill certain functions of the modern political party (such as interest aggregation and to a lesser extent political recruitment), but not others (such as political socialization and political mobilization). As the increasing power of parliamentary assemblies tended to bring such groupings nearer to the effective decision-making centers, organization came to be at a premium. Similarly, when new social claimants came to exert pressure for representation, organization outside the parliament became not only profitable but essential for political survival. The process of party formation tended to spread therefore from existing competing elites downwards, but this very process also facilitated a reciprocal movement. Party organization itself created many new elite-posts even if only at sub-parliamentary levels. Second-rung leaders who provided an essential link with important elements in the expanding electorate had to be accommodated, and some in time fought their way to the top. Party competition for various groups in the electorate made some existing parties more responsive to new demands, while new social groupings came to imitate and expand existing forms of party organization.

In countries where autocratic regimes prevailed longer the development of parties showed different characteristics.

Autocracy in its more explicit forms was incompatible with free party organization. Instead factionalism and a limited measure of interest representation tended to predominate. Democratic stirrings could take form only in intellectual protest movements or outright conspiratorial activity. Thus even some of the earlier democratizing movements, both on the liberal and on the socialist side, showed strong influences of secret societies.[11]

In the more limited autocracies that the constitutional lawyers of another day used to call constitutional monarchies (as distinct from parliamentary monarchies) a measure of party organization could come about more easily. Even traditionalist political forces had eventually to resort to at least nominal electoral processes; but in their case parties were not so much the cause as a symp-

---

[11] Note, for example, the role of the Free Masons in building up early Liberal and Radical parties, and the influence throughout Europe of Mazzini's *La Giovane Italia*. See Guglielmo Negri, *Three Essays on Comparative Politics*, Milan, 1964, pp. 5off.

tom of effective political power. Certain bourgeois and professional groups sought to use the parliamentary benches for a measure of oppositional politics that was often ineffective for lack of courage and organization. Further to the left, certain *Weltanschauungsparteien* showed tighter organizational forms and ideological programs; their verbal fervor tended to be symptomatic, however, of their weak position in the present. They made up for their lack of current influence with the vista of an utopian future, and could be "wholistic" in their ideological claims precisely because they had little chance ever to be confronted with the compromises that partial power entails; only a more basic political and social revolution could change their role in a fundamental fashion.

Finally, under conditions of more democratic rule the political role of parties became more important. But often past divorce from active political power continued to hinder them in the exercise of their nominal functions, while at the same time their somewhat timid hold on governmental power was endangered by the hidden sabotage or open competition from anti-democratic groups. We shall return to this point in section III, when we shall discuss the "reach" or "permeation" of democratic party systems.

II. Coincidence or Disparity between Political and Socio-Economic Development

The complex processes which we have come to denote in shorthand as the Industrial Revolution exercised a massive influence on political developments throughout Western Europe. Everywhere the self-contained political life of separate small communities was broken up, a development which freed the individual from older political bonds and allowed for the growth of wider, if often less compendious, political loyalties. Social and economic changes created considerable turmoil, which furnished the raw material for new political alignments. State and society grew more closely together as the scope of central power expanded, while simultaneously many new social forces came to exercise strong pressures for specific government action. In the process many new links were forged between the state and its citizens through the expansion of administration and the establishment of a great number of new political groups. The modern political party itself can be described with little exaggeration as the child of the Industrial Revolution.

It would be a mistake, however, to draw conclusions too easily about specific causal determination, for in practice socio-economic changes differed greatly from one country to another and within different regions of a single country. Furthermore the political effects of seemingly similar socio-economic changes varied according to the specific political settings in which they made themselves felt.[12] It seems useful therefore to consider the effects of economic development according to at least three criteria. When did economic development start? How fast did it come? What political effects did it have on various social strata?

TIME AND TEMPO OF SOCIO-ECONOMIC DEVELOPMENT

The criteria of time and tempo give four logical possibilities according to the following scheme:

FIGURE 1: MODES OF SOCIO-ECONOMIC DEVELOPMENT

		Timing	
		Early	Late
Tempo	Gradual	I	III
	Rapid	II	IV

Of these four possibilities, II is not a real one; early European economic development germinated slowly. I is more representative for European experience. Without further proof it may generally be postulated that political strains were comparatively easy to cope with in this case: the very slowness of the process of socio-economic change gave the political system considerable leeway in meeting social and economic changes and in adjusting itself to them; these changes themselves were at any one moment also less drastic, hence less upsetting.

Somewhat similar considerations apply to III, but here a new factor enters. While in I social, economic, and political changes tended to move concurrently, a certain disparity between political

[12] Cf. supra, pp. 45-46.

and socio-economic changes could arise in countries in which economic change came late. Once new political ideas, new institutions, and new political techniques had developed in certain countries (like the United States or Great Britain), they could not but influence similar groupings in economically less developed societies as well. Political factors could therefore acquire a much greater autonomous momentum in the latter case. Thus the attempt was made to transfer certain institutional devices long before social realities showed corresponding changes. Ruling elites might deliberately concede the forms rather than the substance of democratic institutions to divert political unrest and maintain their own positions virtually intact. An elected parliament might be allowed, but not responsible government. Or a wide franchise might be granted, but only after adequate care was taken that this conveyed little power—the weighting of votes, the refusal of the private ballot, and slated apportionment of seats being particularly useful expedients in this respect. Rather than providing an effective lever in the hands of the masses, such "democratic" reforms could paradoxically develop into a measure of plebiscitary control over them. This could result in an enduring alienation of sizable sections of the population rather than in their permanent integration in an effectively responsive political system.

France provides the classic case in Western Europe of such a disparity between political and socio-economic changes. At a very early moment the country was caught in the whirlpool of mass politics. The principle of popular sovereignty was recognized long before a politically articulate people could make its will felt. Hence almost a century after the French Revolution the country could still live up to Laboulaye's description of France as "a tranquil people with agitated legislators.[13] Agitation in the *Carrousel de Paris*, not being very meaningful in terms of a large number of social and economic variables in France, could not but prematurely disillusion French citizens with politics as such. To quote Philip Williams' description of the situation that prevailed in France until quite recently, "her atomized, small-scale structure promotes political individualism, strong local loyalties, and a political psychology more adapted to resistance than to positive construction. It reinforces the old tendency to 'incivisme,' the lack of civic consciousness which makes so many Frenchmen regard the state as an enemy personified in

[13] John E. C. Bodley, *France*, New York, 1900, I, 57.

the tax-collector and the recruiting sergeant."[14] But this in turn
meant also a lack of sufficient incentive for political change. To quote
Williams again, "It was because there was no majority for action in
the country that there was no pressure strong enough to overcome
the resistance which found so many points of advantage in the constitutional framework."[15] When finally massive social and economic
changes did come, these were consequently not easily channeled along
earlier established institutional and political lines.

Finally, IV, in which economic changes are both fast and late,
offers the greatest political difficulties of all; all the problems of
III are repeated and compounded by the state of insecurity and
flux which is inherent in rapid social and economic development itself. In Europe such conditions are found only in certain regions
and usually within the bounds of a more comprehensive, stable,
articulated political system. Not so in the developing countries,
where politicization far outstrips socio-economic changes, and where
these social and economic changes themselves, if forthcoming at all,
only add to the discomfort of a body politic already weakened in
other ways.

SOCIAL CLASSES AND ECONOMIC DEVELOPMENT

What were the political consequences of economic development
(or the lack of it) for the various social classes in Europe? Obviously
such a question can in the context of this paper be answered only
in the most general, that is, misleading, terms. Even the concepts
we use, such as *aristocracy, bourgeoisie, peasantry, middle classes,
working classes*, are not really satisfactory; they are indefensible (but
necessary) simplifications of social categories and social divisions that
are in reality very complex. The following discussion contains therefore, only a very rough sketch, and a highly impressionistic one at
that.

First then, the effect of economic development on the nobility:
In certain countries (e.g. The Netherlands[16] and Switzerland) the
position of the nobility as against that of burghers and independent
peasants tended always to be weak and to grow weaker as capitalism
expanded. In other countries, notably in Britain, and to a more

[14] Philip Williams, *Politics in Post-War France*, London, 2nd ed., 1958, p. 3.
[15] *Ibid.*, p. 8.
[16] In the Province of Holland the Estates consisted in the seventeenth century of
19 members: one representative of the nobility, and 18 delegations of cities, manned
by burghers.

limited extent Germany, old aristocracies adapted themselves relatively successfully to the new facts of industrialization. This assisted them in their bid for continued political influence (even though other factors made for different attitudes toward democracy). A positive stance in favor of economic development and a paternalistic rejection of the extremes of Manchester Liberalism by both Tory squires and Prussian *Junkers* made it easier for the conservatives of both countries to maintain a measure of liaison with a significant section of the rising working classes (as well as to retain considerable rural support), which in turn facilitated the establishment of conservative mass movements in both countries.

In contrast, French and Italian aristocracies did not excel in economic initiatives and so tended to be anachronistic, their remaining political power resting more exclusively on traditional resources like their hold on the church, the land, the military, or administration. The gap between them and the rising bourgeoisie tended to grow wider than in either England or Germany. Or, to be more precise, the continued influence of the aristocracy divided the new bourgeoisie into those who adjusted themselves to the style of living of their continuing "betters"[17] and another section that sought to fight such influences. The bourgeoisie as a whole was therefore less easily credited with political ability or economic skills than were their Dutch or Swiss or English counterparts.

This fact influenced the political reactions of other groups in the population. For one thing, it helps to explain the large influence of professional and intellectual groups in these societies (considered by some observers to have been the outstanding characteristic of the politics of the French Third Republic)[18] which could not but strengthen the tendency toward the highly ideologized politics that seems typical of political societies in which political claims outstrip underlying socio-economic realities.

It also had an unfavorable effect on the relations between bourgeois and worker. In the Latin countries the patriarchal family firm

---

[17] In Prussia the same phenomenon occurred, much to the distress of Max Weber, who was angered by the tendency of "an amalgamation between a landed aristocracy corrupted by money-making and a capitalist middle-class corrupted by aristocratic pretensions." See Reinhard Bendix, *Max Weber—an Intellectual Portrait*, New York: Anchor Books ed., 1962, p. 40. The greater political and economic prestige of the German upper classes presumably lessened revolutionary resistance to them, contrary to the situation in France and Italy, where revolutionary sentiment may have been fanned by the low prestige accorded to traditionalist political and economic elites.

[18] Cf. T. B. Bottomore, *Elites and Society*, London, 1964, pp. 64ff.

long remained the characteristic form of economic enterprise. The *Patron* was a far cry from the revolutionary bourgeois of the *Communist Manifesto*. A low esteem for his economic qualities reinforced the defeatist outlook of the proletariat,[19] already skeptical of politics for reasons which we discussed earlier. A vast gap tended to develop not only between employer and worker but also between the professional socialist politicians who took part in the parliamentary game and the generally syndicalist masses who rejected all party action. This weakened both. It eventually assisted the Communist *encadrement* of the French and Italian working classes; and it goes far to explain the checkered results of both democratic institutions and social reform policies in France and Italy.

The evolution of working-class politics in most other European countries stands in considerable contrast. There the industrial revolution generally developed more thoroughly and effectively. At the earlier stages, social dislocations tended to produce a "hump of radicalism." But the rapid growth of large-scale industries and urbanization soon laid the foundation for well-organized trade unionism and concurrent social-democratic action, quickly shifting from empty revolutionary phraseology to more immediate short-term goals within the existing socio-economic systems.[20] If this strengthened democracy in systems which were already democratizing themselves, it weakened the incipient stirrings of democracy in those societies in which modernization took place largely under continued autocratic auspices (as in Germany).

Somewhat similar factors influenced the political position of the peasantry. In all European countries the relative importance of the agricultural sector declined as economic development proceeded; but whereas in some countries this process caused relatively little political tension, in others it provoked violent conflict. In some countries strong protectionist policies both symbolized and maintained the power of certain agricultural groups; whether these were large landowners (as the Prussian Junkers) or a large mass of generally inefficient small farmers (as in France) depended on earlier developments in land tenure and social organization generally. In other countries the reduction of the agricultural sector went on at a much

---

[19] See Val Lorwin's already classic "Working Class Politics and Economic Development in Western Europe," *American Historical Review*, Vol. 63 (1958), pp. 338-351; and S. M. Lipset, "The Changing Class Structure of Contemporary European Politics," *Daedalus* (Winter 1964), pp. 271-304, *passim*.

[20] *Ibid.*

faster pace. But simultaneously foreign competition, self-help, and government policies facilitated modernization. Thus Danish and Dutch farmers[21] managed well. Typically, Scandinavian agrarians often cooperated with socialist parties, in contrast to France, where sizable blocs of peasant votes turned to rightist or Communist extremists; their mood was mainly one of apolitical malaise instead of one of definite expectation of positive action.

Speaking more generally, economic development has caused the decline of some groups and the rise of others. The specific nature of the complex underlying processes has often been confused by the facile use of the hazy notion of the "middle classes." One should at least distinguish between more traditional elements, like the *artisanat*, the retail traders, and small-scale employers who form the residue of social and economic developments, and the "new" middle classes of technical, managerial, administrative, and professional people, who are rather their result. Political attitudes have tended to differ correspondingly. While in France, for instance, Poujadism tended to find its main support among the earlier groups, Gaullism has tended to appeal more strongly to the "new" middle class. The rise of the latter has tended to make for a new dimension in the political controversy between right and left also in other countries, forcing both traditional socialists and traditional conservatives to take note. Otto Kirchheimer deals brilliantly elsewhere in this volume with the far-going political transformations that seem to result from this situation in European politics.

III. The "Reach" or "Permeation" of the Party System

Partly as a consequence of historical factors European parties have differed greatly in the extent to which they have permeated and enveloped other political elites. In some countries the role of parties has become all-pervasive; in others the parties have penetrated far less successfully to the mainsprings of political power. Substantial differences are also encountered in the extent to which parties have become true integrating agencies between political elites on the national and on the local scene. In this section the "reach" of a party system is briefly analyzed along the following three dimensions:

---

[21] Dutch peasants, though split among the religious parties and the Liberal party, have nevertheless formed a powerful interest group across party lines. In addition, in the interwar period, and again since 1963, a small Poujadist-oriented Peasant Party has represented a more extremist protest-vote.

the extent of involvement of traditional political elites in the party system; the measure of absorption of new political claimants; and the degree of "homogenization" which parties provide between national and local political elites.

PARTY SYSTEMS AND TRADITIONAL ELITES

In European societies the relationship of traditionally powerful political elites and the party system seems to have taken one of three forms: they have participated from the outset, slowly learning to share power with newer groups; they have participated in the party system but only half-heartedly and with reactionary intentions; or they have stayed outside altogether, seeking to maintain their influence through other power structures (notably the military, the bureaucracy, business, or the church). The precise developments depended greatly on the way parties originated and the specific nature and extent of the democratizing process.

As we have noted, some European parties were in many ways the outcome of earlier institutionalized conflict on the elite level; factions hardened increasingly into substantial political organizations as these conflicts spread from the elites downward into an ever widening circle of political actors. Though older elites were eventually confronted with new parties outside their control, they never came in immediate conflict with the party system. This facilitated the transition from oligarchical to polyarchical forms of government.

In other European countries parties were first established in opposition to autocratic regimes that forbade or at least restricted the scope of party conflict. Eventually in these countries too older elites found it necessary to participate in electoral processes. But parties established under their auspices tended to remain little more than outward appearances, democratic figleaves, so to speak, for entrenched power positions that had their real basis elsewhere. Consequently right-wing parties in various European countries came to assume basically different attitudes toward the rules of the game of democratic party politics. The acceptance of the substance of democratic ideals and practices is still the clearest criterion with which to distinguish Scandinavian or British Conservatives from, say, the right in France, Weimar Germany, or present-day Italy.[22]

[22] These differences are apparent in the European Assemblies. Many Northern and Western Liberals have been hesitant to join the "Liberal" caucus. Many Northern "Conservatives" have stayed outside any grouping, finding it impossible to

In the latter the constant presence of potentially or actually anti-democratic parties within the party system has hindered the effective working of democratic politics; it has narrowed the range of democratic rule; it has caused disillusionment to spread to other potentially more democratic groups; and it finally eroded the very existence of democratic regimes.

The "reach" of the party system over against other traditional political elites is revealed most clearly in its relation to the permanent bureaucracy. Bureaucracies have been far more responsive to the party system in some countries than in others. Much has depended on historical relations and the specific characteristics of the ensuing party system.

Thus it was of profound significance whether an articulated party system developed before, after, or concurrently with the rise of a bureaucracy. In France and Germany powerful bureaucracies were built up as social control-mechanisms long before non-bureaucratic social groups had learned to use the weapon of political organization to secure influence. Ever since, parties have had difficulty in obtaining full control, and to this day bureaucracies have tended to enjoy a distinct political existence.[23] In Britain, on the other hand, the build-up of a modern civil service occurred after non-official social groups were securely in political control; ever since, the civil service has loyally accepted control by party ministers. Many other European countries would seem to fall between these two cases. State bureaucracies developed earlier than in Britain, but non-state groups were strong enough to make their weight felt simultaneously, and ultimately to prevent them from becoming uncontrollable elements in the body politics. To use a somewhat simple metaphor, the British Civil Service was from the outset below party; the French and German bureaucracies were to a very real extent above it; in other cases parties and bureaucracies tended to be on one line. In

---

join the right, the left really being somewhat nearer to their beliefs, though not their label.

[23] Bottomore, *op.cit.*, p. 82, quotes a letter from the founder of the French *Ecole Libre des Sciences Politiques*, Emile Boutmy, dated 25 February 1871, in which he points to the need for an administrative elite in the following terms: "Privilege has gone, democracy cannot be halted. The higher classes, as they call themselves, are obliged to acknowledge the right of the majority, and they can only maintain their political dominance by invoking the right of the most capable. Behind the crumbling ramparts of their prerogatives and of tradition the tide of democracy must encounter a second line of defence, constructed of manifest and useful abilities, of superior qualities whose prestige cannot be gainsaid."

systems where certain parties tended for long to have a hegemonic position they often staffed the bureaucracies after their own image; thus Liberal dominance made the Dutch bureaucracy long a Liberal perquisite, and in somewhat similar fashion the *Democrazia Cristiana* is at present heavily represented in the Italian bureaucracy. Alternation between parties could lead to an attempt to take the bureaucracy out of politics (as in Britain), but also to competitive politicization by rival parties. Coalition politics has often led to a careful distribution of administrative "fiefs" to rival parties, as in present-day Austria and Belgium, or to balanced appointments of rival partisans not only at the ministerial level but also in *cabinets du ministre*, or even in established administrative posts.[24] Generally speaking, bureaucratic traditions, fortified by political and legal doctrines, have prevented such devices from degenerating into the full excesses of the American nineteenth-century spoils system. Contrary to traditional belief, they have worked not too badly in those systems in which the party system itself was reasonably cohesive and effective. In a segmented society like the Netherlands, carefully balanced political appointments would even seem to have smoothed the relations among the parties and between politicians and bureaucrats. They have given parties the certainty that their views were taken into consideration at the beginnings of policy formation and in the details of policy execution; they have provided officials with a new avenue by which to obtain political support for administrative concerns; they have thus acted as brokers between officials and politicians and between various parties, softening political conflict in the process.

THE PARTY SYSTEM AND NEW CLAIMANTS

As in their relation toward older elites, party systems have differed in their responsiveness to the claims of new groups seeking political representation. In European history the outs at the lower end of the scale have been either lower-class groups (notably the working classes and the peasantry) or religious protesters (e.g. Dutch Calvinists and Catholics, English Non-Conformists, the Norwegian Left). Again, the relation between these new claimants and the party system took any of three forms: their absorption into a pre-existing party system which gradually came to widen its appeal; the

[24] See Val R. Lorwin, *The Politicization of the Bureaucracy in Belgium*, Stanford: Center for Advanced Study in the Behavioral Sciences, 1962.

formation of special parties; or their continued exclusion from the party system.

Robert Dahl[25] has suggested in the case of the United States that the non-appearance of a special working-class party was due to a considerable extent to the fact that representative government and a wide franchise were introduced before an urbanized proletariat came to exert new demands on the system. Hence parties and political techniques suitable to the operation of parties were evolved in time to grapple with this new challenge and to accommodate labor in the existing system. In contrast, in Britain representative government came early, the urban proletariat next, and general suffrage only at the end. While developments were such as to keep new rising groups within the constitutional order, the existing parties were not elastic enough to accommodate the rising demands of the working classes. In Germany, urbanization and the general suffrage preceded representative government, thus sterilizing political party activity into necessarily ineffective attitudes. With somewhat similar ideas in mind, Stein Rokkan has asked for further study of the interesting relationship between franchise extension, special electoral arrangements (such as weighting of votes, privatization of electoral preferences, proportional representation versus other electoral systems), and the mobilization of new groups into the political system.[26] These studies must then be further related, I suggest, to such factors as the earlier elite-setting, and the extent of disparity between political and social and economic development (also in their regional variations) to account for the measure of actual involvement of the out-groups in one political framework.

Generally speaking, then, not the establishment of special parties representative of the lesser groups of society but only their psychological identification with the political order and the responsiveness of that order, in turn, to new demands can serve as the true measure of the relation between the party system and new claimants. A responsive political order may ensure an effective political participation of new claimants without the establishment of special parties. Special parties, on the other hand, can both integrate and isolate according to the reaction of other parts of a party system. Thus Dutch Calvinists and Catholics established highly segmented political

[25] See Robert A. Dahl, ed., *Political Opposition in Western Democracies*, New Haven, 1966, Ch. 13.
[26] See his "Mass Suffrage, Secret Voting and Political Participation," *European Journal of Sociology*, Vol. 2 (1961), pp. 132-152.

and social organizations but jointly rose to power and in the process ensured the integration of their clienteles into the political system, actually making it more integrated, responsive, and democratized.[27] The same cannot be said, it seems to me, of the Norwegian Christians or of various parties composed of nationality interests in the Austrian-Hungarian Empire. The uncritical use of the term "fragmentation," thus, does not bring the analysis much further if attention is not paid at the same time to the question whether a division of a political system into a number of quite distinct spiritual and political groups ultimately means the break-up of one society, or rather the growing of roots of very different groupings in one constitutional order. To use Sartori's terms, seemingly fragmented systems can in practice be centrifugal or centripetal,[28] and only exact sociological analysis can reveal which is ultimately the case.

Just as older elites in certain cases stayed outside (if not above) the party system, so various groups of society remained outside or below it even after the general franchise was introduced. As suggested earlier, one cause may have been a disparity between a strong politicization of the working classes and the granting to them of the means of effective political action. In the Latin countries anarchism and syndicalism were strengthened by the acute feeling that party and parliamentary activity could achieve little in practice. Vested interests may so continue to dominate the parliamentary scene that even their nominal voters may feel manipulated rather than active participants. This has been for long true of Italy, for instance, and still is to a lesser extent of most European countries.

If we combine the first and the second paragraph of this section, the "reach" of a party system in relation to various groups in the society might be visualized as follows. Most removed (though not necessarily antagonistic) would be those political groups which are outside or below the system altogether; by definition they are politically unorganized. Following them are conscious anti-system groups that reject the existing political order but have some measure of group identification (e.g. the syndicalists, even though they rejected party organization and put their trust in spontaneous rather than institutional leaders). A somewhat closer participation is found among those who organize in political anti-system parties but with

[27] See H. Daalder, "The Netherlands: Opposition in a Segmented Society," in Dahl, *op.cit.*, Ch. 6.

[28] Giovanni Sartori, *op.cit.*, and "European Political Parties: The Case of Polarized Pluralism," Ch. 5, below.

the deliberate aim of participating in order to destroy; in practice, however, the very act of participation tends to create certain vested interests in the system (cf. Robert de Jouvenel's famous *dictum* that there is more in common between two deputies one of whom is a revolutionary than between two revolutionaries one of whom is a deputy). Anti-system parties may therefore show a wide range between outright rejection and near-acceptance, and their influence may become so great that their presence becomes a significant variable within the system. Somewhat further on the road to involvement are those isolationist parties that have no chance to gain even part-power but continue to organize definite subcultural groups that wish their voices to be heard (even if with little chance of their being taken into account). Next in the scale would come opposition parties that effectively compete for office, proximity to power being the criterion with which to measure real involvement. Here again there is considerable scope for variation; whereas some are natural "outs," others are semi-government supporters. Finally come governing parties, tied most closely to the existing system, the extent of their dominance being the measure of their effective control. A simplified representation of this scheme is given in Figure 2.

PARTY SYSTEMS: THE CENTER AND LOCAL REALITIES

The central-local axis provides yet another dimension by which to measure the permeation of party systems. Increased interaction between the center and the localities greatly affected the formation and organization of parties. Generally speaking, a two-way process took place: political forces in the center sought to extend their political bases by mobilizing political support over wider geographic areas, while political groups in the periphery organized to promote regional interests with the center.

This two-way movement resulted in very different situations. In some cases, a fundamental nationalization of politics led to a far-reaching "homogenization" between politics at the center and in regional areas; such a movement was facilitated by the absence of strong economic or cultural regional cleavages, by good communications, and by the entry of issues that helped to nationalize politics (e.g. class). In other cases ethnic, linguistic, religious, or geographic barriers prevented such an osmosis from taking place. Politicization tended to strengthen centrifugal rather than centripetal tendencies (separatist political movements like that of the Irish in nineteenth-

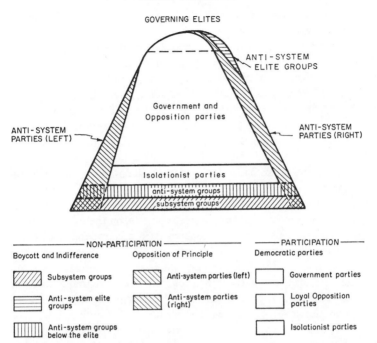

GOVERNING ELITES

ANTI-SYSTEM ELITE GROUPS

Government and Opposition parties

ANTI-SYSTEM PARTIES (LEFT)

ANTI-SYSTEM PARTIES (RIGHT)

Isolationist parties

anti-system groups

subsystem groups

——————— NON-PARTICIPATION ——————— · ———— PARTICIPATION ————
Boycott and Indifference   Opposition of Principle   Democratic parties

Subsystem groups   Anti-system parties (left)   Government parties

Anti-system elite groups   Anti-system parties (right)   Loyal Opposition parties

Anti-system groups below the elite   Isolationist parties

The area of effective democratic party government is restricted to that of the Government and loyal opposition parties—hence the "reach" of a democratic party system is measured by its total proportion of the political pyramid. This proportion is very different in various European societies: while in some it is nearly coterminous with the whole (England, Sweden) in others it occupies only a relatively small area (present-day Italy, Weimar Germany, French Fourth Republic). Proportions are far from stable moreover. On the one hand, isolationist and anti-system parties may gradually be domesticated into the system (e.g. the Nenni Socialists). On the other hand, increasing opposition to the system (as measured by a proportionate increase in the strength of anti-system groups and anti-system parties), and mounting indifference (as apparent in an increase of subsystem groups) may narrow the area of democratic politics. Anti-system parties may seek deliberate involvement to discredit democratic politics and thus to increase both anti-system and subsystem groups. This is the reasoning behind traditional Communist tactics and seems to reflect fairly accurately the situation in France before 1958, when anti-system parties, anti-system groups, and political malaise made the area of democratic politics shrink to such an extent as to make it practically ineffective.

century Britain, or of nationality groupings in the Austrian-Hungarian Empire, forming their logical extreme). In yet different cases politics at the center and in the localities tended to remain highly differentiated spheres, with only minimal linkages between them. Although this did not threaten national existence, it complicated national politics. Again, a comparison between Britain and France offers an instructive contrast.

In Britain leaders and labels penetrated relatively early from the center into the constituencies, thus drawing national and local elites into one reasonably unified system. Although certain regional sentiments and interests continued to have some importance, to this day providing British parties with distinct pockets of regional strength, they were not such as to fragment the decision-making process at the center. The essence of British politics is therefore national politics, and British parties are above all national political organizations. In France, on the other hand, local concerns long continued to dominate the choice of national parliamentary personnel. This caused a curious paradox: provided the local representative showed due respect for local sensitivities and interests, he was, on the national scene, as far as his constituents were concerned to a considerable extent a free agent. The French Chamber became therefore very much "*La Maison sans Fenêtres,*" a meeting place of local interests and individual personalities rather than of cohesive, integrated national political parties. Nationalization of politics occurred therefore more easily on the level of ideological debate than of political will, of political oratory rather than of effective national political organization. For the rest, the French Chamber tended to be more highly sensitive to interest groups (pressuring M.P.'s in their local base) than to issues of more national importance. This accentuated the cleavage between the French bureaucracy (feeling itself the self-appointed guardian of France in a truly Parisian way) and the Chamber, stronger in resisting the executive than in dominating it, more ready to veto than to formulate national policies.

The "homogenization" of politics between the center and the localities is therefore an important factor in the politics of both. An effective linkage helps to legitimize the national political order. Where links are absent, alienation is likely to ensue. The character of the party system is an important variable in this process. Parties can be agencies of both integration and disintegration. They assist national integration if they serve as genuine brokers between disparate regional or social interests (without losing their national existence in the process). They are likely to strengthen centrifugal forces, on the other hand, if they become the passive tools of sectional interests. Paradoxically, synthetic unifiers who seek to identify their own sectional interests with that of the one and indivisible nation can contribute as much to such disintegrating tendencies as those who deny the existence of one political community from over-particularistic concerns.

IV. The Cleavage Lines of the Party System

European countries reveal considerable differences according to the character and the intensity of the cleavage lines that form the basis for political conflict and political organization. These differences are partly due to objective differences in social structure; certain social cleavages did exist in some countries but not in others (e.g. ethnic diversity). They depend further on the circumstance of whether and to what extent particular cleavages were effectively politicized; factors such as religion or class have been much more exploited in some political systems than in others. Finally, considerable variations also exist in the persistence of cleavage lines in the party system. Whereas some issues have been of only passing importance and have subsequently fallen out of the political domain, others have remained characteristic dividing lines long after their original *raisons d'être* has been forgotten. In this way the particular history of past political controversy has continued to exercise a substantial influence on political loyalties and on the way in which new issues are focused and processed. Therefore only careful historical, sociological, and political analysis can do full justice to the distinct qualities of any given political system. It follows that it is much easier to categorize a number of cleavages that seem to have been historically important in European political development than to evaluate their importance for political stability or effective decision-making.

In early days David Hume considered "factions from interest" and "factions from affection" as the most normal cases, proclaiming, unlike Burke, the rise of a new category of "factions from principle": "the most extraordinary and unaccountable phenomenon that has yet appeared in human affairs."[29] Generally speaking, the most important dividing lines in Europe have tended to be: class or sectional interest (the landed versus the moneyed interests; parties representative of sections of industry or commerce, labor, or agriculture); religion (Modernists versus Fundamentalists, Catholics versus Protestants, Clericals versus Anticlericals, Anglicans versus Non-Conformists); geographic conflict (town versus country, center

[29] See David Hume, *Political Essays*, ed. Charles W. Hendel, New York, 1953, pp. 80-81.

versus periphery); nationality or nationalism (ethnic minority parties, extreme-nationalist movements, and parties having their real allegiance to another national state, etc.); and regime (status quo parties versus reform parties, revolutionary, or counterrevolutionary parties).

The difficulty of qualitative analysis of the importance of cleavage structures comes out in the exaggerated attention paid to quasi-mechanical factors, such as the number of cleavages, or whether they run parallel to or cut across one another. Both English and American literature seem to be based often on the *a priori* notion that the political universe is by nature dualistic, so that two-party systems are the self-evident political norm. This view is reinforced by Duverger's analysis, which attempts to reduce the explanation also of multiparty systems to a "superposition of dualisms,"[30] to the non-coincidence of dividing lines in the body politic. While "bargaining parties" in a dualist system are likely to ensure both stability and the orderly solution of successive issues, so the standard argument goes, a multiparty system leads perforce to fragmentation and *immobilisme*.

This view is based on a slender empirical basis. Britain and the United States have two parties, their politics are apparently satisfactory to the theorist, *ergo* a two-party system is good. In contrast, France, Weimar-Germany, and Italy had many parties, their politics were unsatisfactory, hence a multiparty system is a lesser if not an outright degenerated form. This type of reasoning then leads to the curious term of "working multiparty systems"[31]—phenomena that are apparently somewhat akin to "the boneless wonder" of Barnum's Circus. Such a view testifies to an insufficient awareness of the political experience of a host of smaller European countries (such as Belgium, The Netherlands, Denmark, or Switzerland) that have successfully governed themselves for generations under complex multiparty systems. Would it not be possible on the basis of the politics of these countries as confidently (but equally subjectively) to assert that the best political system is one in which all important social groupings have occasion to have themselves politically represented in separate parties, which can then use the forum of parliament and coalition government to reach the politics of compromise?

The confusion is clearly revealed by our tendency to hold two conflicting theories with equal conviction. On the one hand, we argue

[30] M. Duverger, *Political Parties*, London, 1954, pp. 229ff.

[31] Cf. Gabriel A. Almond, in *The Politics of the Developing Areas*, Princeton: Princeton University Press, 1960, and Dankwart Rustow, "Scandinavia: Working Multiparty Systems," in Sigmund Neumann, *op.cit.*, pp. 169ff.

that politics is best served by a constant dualistic regrouping of political forces in distinct majority-minority positions. On the other hand, we hold with equal conviction that a political system can quickly be brought to the breaking-point if a number of cleavages come to run parallel to one another—for instance, if conflicts about religion, nationality, and class each make for the same division of society. Whereas we point at one time to the crisscrossing of cleavage lines as the main source of political inefficiency, we assert at another moment that only adequate cross-pressures, which offset tendencies toward increased polarization, can make for a working political community. It is to this variable that we look to explain why Flemish and Walloons, why Capital and Labor, why Clericals and Anticlericals can continue to cooperate in feasible political systems. I suggest that this paradox cannot be explained unless new variables are also taken into account.

Of crucial importance are not only the severity and incidence of conflicts but also the attitudes political elites take toward the need to solve them by compromise rather than combat. Such attitudes are deeply rooted in political culture, itself the product of complex historical factors that differ greatly from one country to another. Traditional leadership styles, the traumatic memory of past conflicts (which may either perpetuate conflict, or cause parties to draw together), a realistic sense of what can be reached through political action and what not, the presence of substantial or imaginary common interests, the extent to which party leaders are more tolerant than their followers and are yet able to carry them along—all are important. Unfortunately they are evasive of systematic analysis except in a specific context.

V. Parties and Political Elites at the Present Time

The relation between parties and political elites in present-day Europe may now be briefly discussed in three steps of increasing generality: parties and the "Iron Law of Oligarchy"; the differences in influence among different party elites; and the influence of party elites (as a genus) over against other political elites.

PARTIES AND THE "IRON LAW OF OLIGARCHY"

The "Iron Law of Oligarchy" is both an analytical statement and a somewhat emotional political theory. In the following paragraphs we shall discuss each of these two aspects in relation to European experience.

From the analytical point of view the oligarchy model of political parties is generally buttressed by what seem to me to be three false arguments: first, the confusion of inequality of influence (as among leaders, militants, and voters) with oligarchy; second, the determinist fallacy which sees too direct a link between the social origins of politicians and class bias, in their politics; and third, the delusion of indispensability, which wrongly deduces an exclusive power position for those who fulfill functions that are socially indispensable. A short word on each of these:

Robert Michels' analysis of the various factors (both technical and psychological) which give leaders in mass organizations considerable power over their followers has rightly become a classic in political science literature. The real proof of oligarchical domination is, however, in other directions. Are leaders always unified when they are subject to pressure from below? Are they virtually unaccountable and unremovable? Are they free agents instead of brokers seeking to reconcile various conflicts in society? To what extent and under what circumstances can they dispense with considerations of mass interest or political objection? Oligarchy consists not in the taking of many decisions by few men, but in the taking by few men of any decisions they care to take.[32]

Unfortunately European political science is richer in noisy debate on such issues than in concrete research. Consequently it engages all too often in "yes" or "no" arguments rather than in careful enquiry as to the actual degrees of influence exerted by leaders as against followers. Research proper[33] would presumably uncover great differ-

[32] See Robert A. Dahl, "A Critique of the Ruling Elite Model," *American Political Science Review*, Vol. 2 (1958), pp. 463-469, and *Modern Political Analysis*, Englewood, N.J.: Prentice-Hall, 1963, Ch. v. To break away from the tautology: "an elite is present when there is inequality of influence; there is inequality of influence, hence we live under an elite," Raymond Aron has proposed (in his paper *La Classe Dirigeante: Mythe ou Realité?*, rapport introductif, Association Française de Science Politique, November 1963), to distinguish between *"classe dirigeante,"* defined as "une minorité délimitée, cohérente, consciente d'elle-même, qui prend les décisions majeures, use et abuse de sa situation privilegée pour exploiter ou opprimer les masses" and *"catégories dirigeantes,"* for "les minorités, qui dans la société, occupent des positions telles ou exercent des fonctions telles qu'elles détiennent un pouvoir dans leur sphère propre et ont chance d'avoir une influence sur la minorité qui exerce le pouvoir politique au sens étroit du terme (le pouvoir central ou étatique)," *op.cit.*, pp. 5-6.

[33] There is great need in Europe for studies along the lines of Dahl's *Who Governs?*, New Haven: Yale University Press, 1961.

ences from one party to another and from one party system to another. It would reveal, one suspects, that leaders have far greater
freedom in some matters (as foreign policy) than in other fields that
impinge more directly on the daily lives of vast numbers of people.
Furthermore, relations cannot be static; whereas at certain moments
leaders will dictate policies, at others they will bend to explicit or
even implicit demands from lower down. Parties, in other words, are
almost certainly agencies of elite-recruitment and elite-maintenance,
but they also serve as transmission belts for pressures from lower
down. Most European parties would seem to be comparatively open
agencies that allow for a great deal of intra-elite conflict as well as
for the rise of new elite groups in competition to older ones. Parties
work, moreover, generally in a democratic environment that permits
publicity and criticism by competitors and outsiders and that forces
actual accountability to independent electoral groups; this cannot
but blunt oligarchical proclivities.

As to the second false test of oligarchy, a rapidly growing series
of publications on the social background of parliamentarians, ministers,
and party members[34] has confirmed that great inequalities continue
to exist between various social classes. Upper- and middle-class
elements are highly over-represented in all parties (including the
explicitly working-class ones). In some countries there are signs
that inequalities persist (or even increase) rather than decline. It
seems an *a prioristic* sociological determinism, however, to conclude
much more from this than the obvious—that European society is still
far removed from equality of opportunity as among various classes
(notably in matters of education). Social origin may but need not
determine political sympathies. On the contrary, many politicians of
working-class origin have been more conservative than socialist
renegades from the upper classes. Politics is an autonomous process
that certainly is affected by class factors but is not causally dependent
on them. Theoretically a political elite (and above all competing political elites) composed almost exclusively of a large number of upper-
class persons can still be fully responsive to pressures from below.

Lastly, elitist theory is often marred by what might be termed the
delusion of indispensability. It is proved to the satisfaction of a

[34] E.g. the studies of J. F. S. Ross and W. L. Guttsman on Britain, Mattei Dogan
on France, Kaufmann *et al.* on Germany, Pesonen on Finland, Sartori on Italy,
etc., as well as the interesting symposium edited by Jean Meynaud on "The Parliamentary Profession," *International Social Science Journal*, Vol. 13 (1961), pp.
513-619.

theorist that a certain social group fulfills an indispensable function in society. It is concluded from this that the group has (or could have) sole control; for instance, that by withdrawing its services it could bring society to a standstill. In this way different observers have pointed to entrepreneurs, finance capitalists, bureaucrats, the military, the working class, or even the peasantry (in the physiocratic sense) as the true elite of any given society. Little attention is paid to the question whether such groupings are ever sufficiently cohesive to exploit the full power resources of their seemingly strategic social position, and what actual countervailing powers there are to stop them from even considering this. Similarly, many observers have jumped all too readily from the correct view that leadership is indispensable in large organizations (as in society at large) to the incorrect one that this gives a monopoly of power to any particular leadership circle.[35]

The "Iron Law of Oligarchy," then, is defective as an empirical theory or even as an heuristic tool. But the extent of its popularity is at the same time a significant yardstick by which to measure differences in democratic realities in Western Europe. Most elitists have come from societies where democratic politics has had an uneasy life. Mosca and Pareto reasoned mainly from the precarious background of Italian politics before 1914. Michels wrote on the basis of a German Social Democracy whose lack of power caused them to envy as well as to try to emulate Prussian rulers. Sorel's anti-parliamentary writings on the need for a spontaneous elite mirror above all the frustrations of a French intellectual banking on a mythical working class. And even Ostrogorski wrote as much to bring a message as to study scientifically the processes of caucus politics in Birmingham or in American cities. Neo-elitists are, again, most frequently found in postwar France (M. Waline's *Les Partis contre La République*, 1948, being an early specimen, later followed in far more subtle terms by Duverger[36] and many others) and among certain social scientists in the United States who feel increasingly disenchanted with traditional eager hopes for democratic reform. Against this, very

---

[35] An early trenchant criticism of Michels is contained in a book by the Dutch Socialist and criminologist, W. A. Bonger, *Problemen der Demokratie*, Amsterdam, 1934.

[36] It is interesting to note that in 1947 Duverger described Michels' *Political Parties* still as "a rather superficial little book" (in: "Die Politische Parteien und die Demokratie," *Der Wähler*, Schriften der Deutschen Wählergesellschaft, Erstes Heft, 1947), but in 1951 as "an excellent little book," *Les Partis Politiques*, Paris, 1951, p. x.

few thinkers in stable democracies, such as England, Switzerland, the Low Countries, or the Scandinavian countries, can be identified with those illustrious names. Even R. T. McKenzie's *Political Parties* does little but pay lip service to Michels and Ostrogorski.

Why this connection between elitism and societies with uneasy democratic institutions? As a political theory it is pervaded by an atmosphere of despair in political action. Elitists have a low opinion of politicians; according to Ostrogorski they are worse than either Cain or Harpagon. Elitists look at parties with equal distaste; according to Waline no self-respecting Frenchman could honestly subscribe to any of the French political parties before 1940.[37] Such pessimism about the present is reinforced by the use of the absolute yardstick of democracy as direct popular rule. Proof that even in generally accepted democratic systems men are far from equal comes therefore as a moral shock, still traceable in the grim delight that disappointed idealists, now turned "realists," continue to show at every new piece of evidence of obvious fact. In countries where the political order is effectively responsible to a wider range of political forces there is hardly the same temptation to engage in powerless invective against politicians and uncritical adulation of non-party elites; people can act and deem this sufficient.

DIFFERENCES IN INFLUENCE AMONG VARIOUS PARTY ELITES

The political power of party elites differs according to the internal structure of each party and its power in the party system.

Duverger has provided what is by far the most detailed and re-fined analysis of differences in internal party structure; he has carried the work as far as can be done short of further detailed analysis of particular parties. It would be invidious therefore in the context of this short paper to seek to add to his rich exposition except for one comment. It seems to me that his distinction between "internally" and "externally" created parties, however valuable as a starting point for analysis, is in danger of being overworked.

In the first place, not all "internally" created parties answer to Duverger's implicit model of the French Radicals; in the process of time many middle-class parties have greatly extended their organization outside parliament. They could do so—unlike the French middle-class parties—because the nationalization of politics had pro-

[37] M. Ostrogorski, *Democracy and the Organization of Political Parties*, London, 1903, Vol. II, p. 632; Waline, *op.cit.*, p. 34.

action into activities beneficial to those who organize (a typical phenomenon of the twentieth century)?

One may well ask whether there are elements in some traditional cultures, societies, and polities that seem to facilitate or hasten the development of an associational capacity in individuals. Insofar as mutual trust, for example, is a feature of ordinary human relations individuals may have a greater capacity to create durable, as distinct from episodic, political organizations than would a traditional society in which human beings typically distrust one another unless they belong to the same parochial group.[28] There may be traditional forms of voluntary or quasi-voluntary organizations—such as guilds, secret societies, philanthropic and religious associations—that provide individuals with the experiences and will to organize more modern associations.

Lastly, does not political organization presume that sufficient secularization has occurred so that individuals come to believe that through their actions they are capable of affecting the world in ways which are favorable to their interests and their sentiments?

This list by no means exhausts the variables which may condition the emergence of parties. Nor are we able to specify at this point which variables are critical under certain conditions, how one measures their relative impact, or, most fundamentally, how such variables affect political attitudes. Some tentative answers to questions such as these will be offered in the chapters that follow. For the moment, our purpose is to suggest that the origin of political parties, while deeply associated historically with what we call "crises," is also closely bound up with the general process of modernization. Thus, while the presence of one of the historical crises may be a catalyst for the organization of parties, it seems clear that parties will not in fact materialize unless a measure of modernization has already occurred.

II. Conditions for Types of Parties

It would thus appear that it is the occurrence of political crises of systemic magnitude at a point in time when sufficient modernization has taken place to provide conditions for party development that causes parties to emerge. This convergence of course does not

[28] The issue of trust or distrust and its impact on political organization is treated by Edward C. Banfield, *The Moral Basis of a Backward Society*, Glencoe, Ill.: The Free Press, 1958.

ceeded much further in other European countries than in France. Thus the Dutch Catholics and Calvinists (and Christian-Democratic parties generally) have put on increasingly effective organizational drives that have intensified reciprocal action between parliamentary and extra-parliamentary elites. Secondly, many "externally" created parties have tended to loosen up as they have approached office. Coalition tactics have often required a high degree of discretionary authority for party leaders; this has decreased the freedom of action of party segments outside the immediately dominant circle and has therefore reduced the difference from "internally created" parties. Thirdly, it seems that in Europe "parties of social integration" (in Neumann's sense)[38] are losing ground under the impact of the manifold social processes responsible for the process of de-ideologization that now occupies so much of our attention. Therefore in the short run at least the importance of the distinction seems to be declining. Whether the professionalization and the de-ideologization of politics will ultimately lead to a resurgence of irrationalist "parties of total integration" is another matter.

Following earlier writers, Neumann has considered a party in office or in opposition the basis for his distinction between "parties of patronage" and "parties of principle."[39] Whereas office gives party elites access both to the traps and the trappings of power, opposition encourages the posture of uncommitted principle. *Ceteris paribus*, the value of this distinction would increase with the measure of "predominance" (in Sartori's terminology) or "hegemony" (in the words of LaPalombara and Weiner) that particular parties have. Long tenure has made certain parties almost indistinguishable from the formal state apparatus. Conversely, remoteness from office has increased the ideological element in those parties which we termed earlier isolationist parties.

The influence of the leaders of opposition parties stands *prima facie* in inverse ratio to the strength of their governmental opposite numbers. This simple statement, however, covers relations of great complexity. Government parties have differed considerably in their willingness or ability to exploit even nominally hegemonic positions. Lack of conviction, expediency, and internal conflict have often posed serious obstacles in the way of doing so fully. The same factors have given opposition leaders a wedge with which to penetrate a seemingly solid government front. They have sometimes not been

[38] Neumann, *op.cit.*, pp. 404-405.   [39] *Ibid.*, p. 400.

satisfied to play only the parliamentary game and have used other power resources, like bureaucratic connivance, interest group pressure, or mass propaganda campaigns, to thwart government action. At other times and places government and opposition parties have often formed a tacit condominium; certain issues are removed from the party game by mutual consent, but on the condition of regular consultation. The political process, in other words, is considerably more complex than a simple opposition or juxtaposition of political parties suggests, and consequently the analysis cannot stop with parties, as we have to do here.

THE INFLUENCE OF PARTY ELITES AS AGAINST THAT OF OTHER POLITICAL ELITES

Perhaps the best measure to distinguish the relative hold of party elites on a political system as against that of other elites is to ask how far positions of political influence can be obtained through, as compared to outside, party channels. So defined, this question is the obverse of the earlier one relating to the "reach" of a party system. Where party systems are comprehensive, safely anchored in the main power positions of a society, and reasonably stable over time the role of the party in the recruitment of political elites or at least in their legitimation is by definition considerable. In contrast, where parties operate on a narrow focus, where their position toward other groups in society is precarious, where the party system is generally unstable— there party elites occupy positions of doubtful permanence, other elites finding different *loci* of power and threatening to replace parties by whatever means at their disposal (e.g. the *bouleversement* of the French elite of the Fourth Republic in 1958).

Even in systems where the reach of the party system is wide and its stability considerable it would be wrong to conclude, however, that party elites enjoy a monopoly of political influence. In the first place, the stability of particular parties does not necessarily mean a stability of their elites; internal change-overs may considerably affect their personnel and their policies even though clienteles and labels remain much the same. In the second place, the wider the scope of party-controlled political activity, the more likely it is that elements of a very diverse nature will enter into it, thus introducing institutional, personal, and interest conflicts within the life of each party.[40] The

---

[40] It is interesting to note that the amount of direct interest-representation in parliamentary parties seems to differ considerably from one country to another

superficial image of a tight elite breaks down when intra-party as much as inter-party conflicts provide the arena in which the most disparate political conflicts are being fought out.

Perhaps this is one key with which to explain seemingly contradictory developments in present-day Europe. In many countries, especially the more settled ones, we may witness, on the one hand, an increasing penetration of party activities in society (e.g. by a further politicization of the bureaucracy, by an increase in party-tied interest groups, a closer control of the mass media, etc.). On the other hand, there are equally definite signs of a lowering of the temperature of party conflict, a de-ideologization of party life, a professionalization of party activity, and a bureaucratization of organized politics. Stein Rokkan has spoken in this context of "an intriguing process of historical dialectics":

"the extension of the suffrage increased the chances for a status polarization of national politics [thus raising the temperature of politics and increasing the role of party], but this very polarization brought about a proliferation of sectional and functional organizations which in turn tended to soften the overall strains in the system and reduce the level of polarization. What we tend to find is a cumulation of forces making for a narrowing of the alternatives for national politics, a fragmentation of the net-works of policy-influencing organizations, and a consequent decline in the importance of the decisions of the electorate-at-large. This may tend to lower the level of general political participation and to alienate from politics sizable sections of the once enfranchised citizenry, leaving the basic decisions to a bargaining process between interest organizations, parties and agencies and departments of the national bureaucracy."[41]

(e.g. the studies on "The Parliamentary Profession" in *International Social Science Journal*, Vol. 13 [1961], pp. 513-619). While in some countries interest groups become increasingly involved in internal party politics, in others they seem to keep consciously at arm's length. Perhaps the reason for such differences may be sought in differences in the political role and power of various assemblies, the measure of direct access interest groups have to the administration, the power and specific structure of individual parties, and differences in formal nomination procedures. The increasing importance of government action for interest groups has inevitably raised their concern with politics. But at the same time their need for constantly satisfactory relations with government, of whatever party, has put a premium on avoiding too close involvement with any one of them.

See on this point Kirchheimer's subtle analysis elsewhere in this volume.

[41] Rokkan, *op.cit.*, p. 152.

This seems an exceedingly interesting *aperçu*; but alas, we must also underwrite the author's final lines:

"We know far too little about the dynamics of these developments and we need to do much more to facilitate co-operation and co-ordination of studies of these problems in different countries."[42]

[42] *Ibid.*

CHAPTER 3

PARTIES AND NATION-BUILDING IN AMERICA

WILLIAM N. CHAMBERS

POLITICAL PARTIES emerge out of certain sets of conditions, confront certain problems or loads in the political system, and perform inter-related functions which may include functions contributing to polit-ical integration. What the conditions are determines in part the shapes party structures will take, the functions they will perform, and how they will perform them. Yet the way in which political elites and party leaders handle political loads also determines the result in part and the impact parties may have on political develop-ment in general. In short there is a reciprocal relationship between political development and loads on the one hand and the effects of party action on the other. This relationship carries profound conse-quences for the political system, particularly in the era of national formation or nation-building.[1]

Once political parties emerge, they may take on stable structures and establish stable patterns of interaction which constitute party systems. It is probably more useful for analysis to think in terms of develop-ing party systems rather than simply of parties. For the United States it is certainly true that the relationship between parties and national integration can be understood only in terms of the party system and the net balance of integrative and malintegrative con-sequences of that system as a whole. Approached in this way, early American experience provides a useful laboratory. The United States constituted the first modern "new nation" in the sense that the American people were the first to throw off colonial rule, estab-lish an independent polity, and achieve a fresh national identity. It was also the United States that brought into being the first modern political parties and party system with the emergence of the Federal-ist and Republican formations within two decades of the assertion of independence.[2] In short, American development presents a case

[1] See the introductory chapter to this volume by Joseph LaPalombara and Myron Weiner, *passim.*

[2] Cf. Seymour Martin Lipset, *The First New Nation: The United States in His-torical and Comparative Perspective,* New York, 1963, pp. 16-98; and William N. Chambers, *Political Parties in a New Nation: The American Experience, 1776-1809,*

study of nation-building and party-building of great potential use in general and comparative political analysis.[3] The address to these phenomena here will be to discuss the context and conditions out of which early American parties arose, the shape parties took and the functions they performed, the character of the party system, and the net impact that system had on national integration. The effect of parties on integration was a kind of end-product of the totality of functions the parties performed and of their relationships with one another.

The discussion will focus on the Federalists and Republicans in the 1790's, the crucial party-building decade. Neither of these formations survived beyond the period around 1820, and the first American party system was followed by a second system in the Jacksonian era in the 1830's. Yet the parties of the 1790's marked the way for later Democrats, Whigs, and second Republicans and for the party systems they evolved. These parties and systems showed important similarities to their predecessors as well as some differences.

I. Basic Conditions in Party Development

Political parties in America did not spring from growing resistance to colonial rule from 1763 to 1776 in a manner that is familiar in many new nations in Asia and Africa today. In the revolutionary struggle sharp divisions did develop between Patriots and Loyalists. The Patriots established committees of correspondence in the thirteen colonies or states, formed the Continental Congress as a coordinating agency for the revolutionary effort and as a quasi-government thereafter, and undertook other means of agitation, cooperation, and action. Yet the Patriots did not become a party in the full sense and did not persist as a distinct political formation past the period of the struggle for independence. Cleavage between so-called Federalists and anti-Federalists appeared in the controversy over the ratification of the new Constitution in 1788-1789. Yet once again these alignments did not take on party form, and the actual contest over ratification was waged among a pluralistic congeries of leaders and groups that varied significantly from place to place

New York, 1963, pp. 1-169. Substantially all of the data concerning American party development on which this paper rests is presented in the latter work, particularly in instances when other citations do not appear here.

[3] See Karl W. Deutsch and William J. Folz, eds., *Nation-Building*, New York, 1963, p. 3, for concepts of "national growth," "national development," and "nation-building."

in the thirteen state arenas involved. In the internal politics of the several states, moreover, the contest for power was waged by a variety of factional formations rather than by parties. Only relatively advanced Pennsylvania developed something like a party system.[4]

Thus the first American parties, or national parties, emerged out of new conflicts only in the 1790's. In terms of economic groups, what distinguished Federalists from Republicans were cleavages between mercantile, investing, and manufacturing interests and certain segments of agriculture on the one side and most planting and agrarian interests on the other. Differences also arose out of disagreements over the degree to which power should be consolidated in the new national government; over proposed policies to promote economic growth and capitalist development through government action; and over the extent to which foreign policy should be oriented toward traditionalist-monarchist England or revolutionary-republican France. Lastly, conflict grew out of contentions between leading personalities such as the Federalists Alexander Hamilton and John Adams on the one hand and the Republicans James Madison and Thomas Jefferson on the other, contentions that were sometimes as petty as they were colorful; and out of cleavages among a variety of other group, sectional, religious, local, and personal interests and persuasions. The whole story does not require retelling in its historical detail.[5] The Federalists and Republicans also developed out of a set of basic conditions, which are more to the point here.

[4] Among other sources, see Elisha P. Douglas, *Rebels and Democrats*, Chapel Hill, 1955; Allan Nevins, *The American States During and After the Revolution*, New York, 1924; Frederick W. Dallinger, *Nominations for Elective Office in the United States*, New York, 1903, Ralph Volney Harlow, *The History of Legislative Methods in the Period Before 1825*, New Haven, 1917; Forrest McDonald, *We the People: The Economic Origins of the Constitution*, Chicago, 1958. In particular, McDonald gives a careful, long-term account of politics in each state as it led up to the politics of ratification. See also George D. Luetscher, *Early Political Machinery in the United States*, Philadelphia, 1903; other monographs and studies cited in Chambers, *op.cit.*, pp. 211-212, 214-215.

[5] Valuable monographs on early American party development and related phenomena include Joseph Charles, *The Origins of the American Party System*, Williamsburg, 1956; Noble E. Cunningham, Jr., *The Jeffersonian Republicans: The Formation of Party Organization, 1789-1801*, Chapel Hill, 1957, and *The Jeffersonian Republicans in Power: Party Operations, 1801-1809*, Chapel Hill, 1963; and Manning J. Dauer, *The Adams Federalists*, Baltimore, 1953; which covers far more than its title suggests. See also the early classic by M. Ostrogorski, *Democracy and the Organization of Political Parties*, New York, 1902, and the histories by Edgar E. Robinson, *The Evolution of American Political Parties*, New York, 1924; Wilfred E. Binkley, *American Political Parties: Their Natural History*, 4th ed., New York, 1962; and Herbert Agar, *The Price of Union*, Boston, 1950.

As a general theory or hypothesis, the most basic conditions associated with the development of political parties in the modern sense may be summarized under four major headings:

1) The emergence or prospect of a significant national or common political arena, within which influence or power may be sought with reference to the decision-making centers and the offices of a common political system.

2) The development of differentiation or complexity within the political system in terms of divergences in group structures and conflicts of interest and opinion and in terms of governmental structures and functions.

3) The emergence of social structures and of ideologies or utopias which permit or encourage some form of popular or mass politics and a substantial electorate.

4) A sense of felt need to develop political structures to establish relationships between leaders and popular followings if leaders are to win and hold power and governmental functions are to be performed.

This statement of conditions can readily be related to the American instance by mediating the general theory through statements of particular sets of conditions which, taken together, constitute an immediate-conditional or relative-historical explanation for the emergence of the first American parties. The recital of American conditions will be summarized[6] as a set of middle-range generalizations about American political development.

1) A national political arena was opened with the ratification of the new Constitution and the establishment of the national government in 1789.

Even in the colonial years a considerable degree of intercolonial communication and what might be called continental consciousness, or proto-national identity, had begun to emerge on the American scene.[7] This development at once helped to sustain and received new impetus from the Revolutionary War effort and the Continental Congress of 1775-1789. The limited powers of this Congress, however, together with the fact that it could not exercise direct power

---

[6] For another statement of these conditions and some of the methodology involved in the analysis, cf. William N. Chambers, "Party Development and Party Action: the American Origins," *History and Theory*, Vol. 3, No. 1 (1963), pp. 111-117.

[7] Richard L. Merritt, "Nation-Building in America: the Colonial Years," in Deutsch and Folz, eds., *op.cit.*, pp. 66-72.

over citizens but was only a quasi-government which depended on the states, and the fact that the Congress consisted of delegates appointed by state legislatures rather than of representatives chosen by the voters, kept it from providing a truly national political arena. The new general government with its single indirectly elected executive and its representative two-house Congress did become the center of a rapidly developing national arena. It was in and around this government that groups, leaders, and parties struggled and the great issues of the day were fought out.

2) *The indigenous pluralism within the American nation produced a high degree of differentiation among groups, social strata, and states or sections and a complex interplay of interests, loyalties, sentiments, and opinions; and most of these forces quickly found expression in politics and turned increasingly to the national scene.*

The cross-currents which the pluralism of early American life threw up were complex indeed. There were small-freehold farmers and great planters owning thousands of slaves; merchants, shippers and shipbuilders, importers and exporters, investors, and struggling manufacturers; artisans or "mechanics"; varied ethnic stocks and different religious faiths; would-be "aristocrats" and nascent "democrats," and sanguine "Gallomen" and sober "Anglomen"; states competing with one another; and a host of subgroupings, such as near-subsistence farmers or farmers who looked to the market. There extended across the new nation a congeries of interests that had to be given expression and accommodated if the system was to sustain itself and perform its functions; and parties developed in considerable part as a response to such felt needs. Certain interstate comparisons are also revealing in connection with this condition for party formation. Indices are difficult to assign, but Pennsylvania exhibited a particularly high degree of differentiation in the interplay of interests, which helps to explain the fact that Pennsylvania alone developed a state party system in the 1780's and also moved rapidly toward shaping local units of the national parties in the 1790's. A significant degree of complexity might also be attributed to New York, for example, where the pace of national party development was second only to that of Pennsylvania; but in New York old patterns of domination by great families and clique politics, characteristics which were much less in evidence in Pennsylvania, impeded party development.[8] It may be suggested as a hypothesis that the higher the degree

[8] For aspects of political development in Pennsylvania in the early years and

of differentiation of group and other relationships is in a political system, the greater is the probability for the development of political parties, though this probability may be reduced by the presence of other impeding conditions. Such differentiation certainly existed in American national politics by the 1790's, as various group interests took on nation-wide form and sought national expression.

Substantial differentiation also characterized the national government. It was not only formally separated into executive, legislative, and judicial branches with distinct prescribed powers but the two houses of Congress had different electoral foundations and constituencies and somewhat different functions. The Constitution also provided among the various organs of government an intricate set of checks or reciprocal relationships that in effect constituted a further differentiation of functions. Again, parties arose in part in response to the problems leaders faced in trying to operate this complex governmental machinery effectively.

3) Social structures and basic perspectives in the American experience provided a strong impetus for popular involvement in politics, demands for representation and mechanisms of consent, and the emergence of a substantial electorate.

In comparison with contemporary European societies American society was remarkably open, atomistic, affluent, and fluid. It was not bound to feudal traditions, graded structures of estates or classes, or old corporate configurations. Most men owned a piece of farm land or other property as a foundation for individual independence; a vast continent and its wealth of resources offered unprecedented opportunities; distances between rich and poor were not so great as they were in Old World societies; social distinctions and deference patterns were not so sharp or rigid, and there was no genuine aristocracy or fixed hierarchy; and social mobility was a frequent fact as well as a hope. Distinctions there were, particularly between great planters and lesser farmers and Negro slaves in the South; and where social gradations were particularly sharp and persistent, patterns of deference held on longer than they did elsewhere. Yet distinctions were generally on the wane, partly as a result of economic

into the nineteenth century, see Harry Marlin Tinkcom, *The Republicans and Federalists in Pennsylvania, 1790-1801*, Harrisburg, 1950; Russell J. Ferguson, *Early Western Pennsylvania Politics*, Pittsburgh, 1938; Sanford W. Higginbotham, *The Keystone in the Democratic Arch: Pennsylvania Politics 1800-1816*, Harrisburg, 1952, and other sources cited in Chambers, *op.cit.*, pp. 214-216, 218.

opportunity and partly because of the democratization that had accompanied the Revolution and swept many states in the 1780's. This development was furthered by the impact of the social outlook, *ethos*, or mood that Hartz has aptly called the American "liberal tradition." This fundamental perspective, with John Locke as its ideologue, was to develop steadily in American conditions from a utopia to an increasingly common general ideology and foundation for emerging consensus; and in drafting the Declaration of Independence, which became the basic statement of the American creed, Jefferson drew on Lockian ideas as "the common sense of the subject." The liberal tradition placed heavy stress on such important if sometimes conflicting values as free individualism, opportunity, individual achievement, equalitarianism, and liberal democracy.[9] It is not surprising that movement toward democratic participation, representation, and consent was rapid, and it is also not surprising that these forces brought the emergence of an extensive electorate in state after state. In terms of interstate comparisons all of these forces and particularly the stress on equalitarianism and a mass base for politics were especially pronounced in Pennsylvania, where party action developed most rapidly. On the other hand equalitarianism and the extension of suffrage took hold more slowly in the Southern states, where full-scale party structures and action came comparatively late, although even there the impact of remaining tax or property qualifications on suffrage has been exaggerated by older historians.

It may be suggested as a further general hypothesis that the greater the degree to which equalitarian political ideologies and extended suffrage obtain, the greater is the probability that political parties will develop in the absence of other, impeding factors. Recent research findings for the American case indicate that after the Revolution the great majority of white adult males in an era of widely held agricultural property could vote. Not all of them did, but the democratic impulse and keen party competition brought voting participation in the period 1799-1802 and after to the substantial proportion of 39 per cent or more of white adult males in important elections, a level that was not to be exceeded until new party rivalry appeared in the Jacksonian era.[10] Moreover access to other avenues

[9] Louis Hartz, *The Liberal Tradition in America*, New York, 1955, pp. 17-22, 35-96, *passim*; see also Lipset, *op.cit.*, *passim*.
[10] Cf. Edmund S. Morgan, *The Birth of the Republic, 1763-1789*, Chicago, 1956, pp. 93-94; Chilton Williamson, *American Suffrage from Property to Democracy*

to the political arena was comparatively open. Freedom of political belief, expression, and action was also generally accepted, despite important uncertainties and exceptions in the early years.

4) *Within the context of these conditions, a sense of felt need gradually arose for efficient means to represent and combine interests, amass power, conduct elections, and manage government.*

Innumerable obstacles stood in the way of party development, and no one set out to construct parties with a blueprint in mind. Men thought in terms of devices to meet immediate needs, or bickered about immediate interests; many important political figures including George Washington spoke out against the idea of parties. The process of party-building was one of groping expediencies as well as brilliant innovations, and it was some time before leaders came to think consciously in party-building terms. Yet in the space of a few years after the ratification of the Constitution in 1789 stable structures were evolved, and the Federalist and Republican formations emerged as parties.

This analysis is hardly unique in its basic terms. It is consistent with suggestions contained in the classical work of Ostrogorski, with the emphasis Weber puts on the relationship between popular or mass politics and "parties of politicians," and with many of the ideas offered by Duverger.[11] Yet the summary here is based primarily on investigation of the American instance. Circumstances will certainly reveal variations from context to context in the significance of any one condition in the development of political parties even though the general pattern of relevant conditions may remain constant. Indeed it may be argued that generic conditions as they affect the development of parties can be firmly established only in terms of comparative historical processes carefully analyzed through a theoretically oriented historiography or time-oriented science of political development. As V. O. Key puts it: ". . . a conception of the party system must take into account its dimension of time. It may be useful to think of the party system as an historical process rather than as patterned and static institutional behavior. . . . if the party process is viewed through time, additional aspects of the working of

---

1760-1860, Princeton, 1960; Richard P. McCormick, "New Perspectives on Jacksonian Politics," *American Historical Review*, Vol. 65 (1960), pp. 288-301.

[11] Max Weber, "Politics as a Vocation," in H. H. Gerth and C. Wright Mills, eds., *From Max Weber: Essays in Sociology*, New York, 1946, pp. 99-104; Maurice Duverger, *Political Parties: Their Organization and Activity in the Modern State*, New York, 1955, *passim*; Ostrogorski, *op.cit.*, *passim*.

party [systems] may be identified."[12] This, presumably, is the task of developmental political science or analytical history.

A possible factor in party development as it has operated in many new nations today should be noted. This is the effect of external influences on the peoples of developing areas who are seeking to achieve the modernization that most Western societies have already accomplished. The adaptation of foreign ideas or models as part of the European legacy, including general models for political parties, has played a significant part in political development in Asia and Africa today, although of course local conditions continue to have profound effects.[13] Such mimetic elements were virtually absent in the early American experience. The terms "Whig" and "Tory" had been in use in England for a century or more, but they denoted broad persuasions and shifting alliances of factions or personal clique-"connexions," in the old spelling and the old style, rather than parties as such; suffrage remained extremely narrow; and these early English political formations did not develop continuing and pervasive structures to provide stable links between leaders at the parliamentary center and substantial popular followings in the nation as a whole. It was not until the rise of the Liberal and Conservative formations after the limited first Reform Act of 1832 that England may be said to have arrived at genuine political parties. Nor were modern party models available in the 1790's in other European countries. In short the Federalist and Republican formations in the United States had to find their own way toward party structure and party action.

II. Political Development, Party Structures, and Party Functions

The argument that American parties in the 1790's were the first modern parties is more than a mere historiographical contention. It involves conceptions of what a political party is and does and of how American parties were related to the whole question of political development, and a conceptual distinction between party politics and faction politics. Political development may be understood as a move-

[12] V. O. Key, Jr., *Politics, Parties, and Pressure Groups*, 5th ed., New York, 1958, p. 222.
[13] See, e.g., John H. Kautsky, *Political Change in Underdeveloped Countries: Nationalism and Communism*, New York, 1962; Gabriel A. Almond and James S. Coleman, eds., *The Politics of Developing Areas*, Princeton, 1960; Immanuel Wallerstein, *Africa: the Politics of Independence*, New York, 1961, pp. 63-79; Thomas Hodgkin, *African Political Parties*, London, 1961, pp. 38-48.

ment toward a political system which is capable of handling the loads it confronts, characterized by significant differentiation of structures and specificity of functions, increasingly centralized and able to maintain itself. It may not be as easy to measure political development as it would be to measure economic development, for example, yet one might argue that a highly developed political system is characterized by some measure of rationalized political efficiency, defined as a substantial degree of coherence in policy output and a capacity for innovation in the face of new problems.[14] Parties and party systems may have an important impact on the course of such development.

In the American case the emergence of parties marked a significant elaboration of structures and a movement toward relative political efficiency. Before the advent of parties politics was a pluralistic, kaleidoscopic flux of personal cliques like those that gathered around the great magnate families in New York, caucuses of the sort that came and went in many New England towns, select and often half-invisible juntas in the capitals or courthouse villages in the Southern states, or other more or less popular but usually evanescent factions. All of these political formations in their pluralistic variety may be brought under the general heading of faction politics. With few exceptions such old-style "connexions" or multiple factions were characterized by lack of continuity from election to election, by tenuous or shifting relationships between leaders in government on the one hand and the electorate on the other, by comparatively narrow ranges of support from interest groupings, and thus by a confusing degree of raw, unaggregated pluralism in politics. One result was that it was difficult for the voters to hold any one group of men responsible for the direction of public policy. Another was that policy-making was generally erratic or incoherent except where it was under the control of a dominant "connexion," clique, or junta.

The advent of the Federalists and Republicans as comprehensive parties, on the other hand, brought a new dualistic order into politics. The parties emerged as durable, differentiated, visible, rationalized formations which developed stable operating structures. Continuing relationships were evolved between leaders and cadre at the center of government and between lesser leaders and cadre in the states,

---

[14] See Samuel H. Beer, "New Structures of Democracy: Britain and America," in William N. Chambers and Robert H. Salisbury, eds., *Democracy in the Mid-Twentieth Century: Problems and Prospects*, St. Louis, 1960, pp. 30-59.

counties, and towns; and in turn between this structure and broad popular followings in the electorate. It is appropriate in the American instance to consider the structure of leaders and cadre as "the party," or party proper, and its supporters or adherents in the public as its following. At the beginning American parties accomplished little toward organization strictly construed as a regularized differentiation of internal functions and corresponding division of labor. Indeed the Federalists never achieved significant organization, although the Republicans by the late 1790's and early 1800's devised party caucuses, conventions, and committees in several states which foreshadowed the full development of organization proper in the Jacksonian era. Yet both party structures in the 1790's did reach out to amass stable popular followings of considerable range and density that carried them well beyond the fluid and limited support preparty factions had enjoyed. Lastly, both parties developed distinctive sets of in-group perspectives with emotional overtones, or ideologies, that helped to bind party structures together and popular followings to the parties. In short the first American parties can be described as developing historical patterns of stable structures linked to broad popular followings, with distinguishing ideologies, and as structures that were able and ready to perform crucial political functions. It is in terms of this general idea of what a party is that the Federalists and Republicans may be thought of as the first modern parties.[15]

In the functions they came to perform the first American parties exerted an important influence on the course of political development in general. In the process of nation-building any people is likely to face a number of interrelated problems which impose significant loads on the political system. Among the most salient of these we may list the following:

1) Establishing and maintaining a national authority, or the operating political system itself.

2) Expressing and aggregating interests as essential functions and, if possible, containing conflict within a spectrum which will prevent immobilism or disruption.

3) Meeting the "crisis of participation" and meeting related problems of coordinating political action in a politics of popular participation.

[15] For a fuller elaboration of the distinction between faction politics and party politics, and of the concept of party as durable structure and rationalized performance of key functions, see Chambers, *Political Parties in a New Nation*, pp. 17-33, 39-51, and pp. 97-98, 106-110.

4) Recruiting and training at all levels new leaders who are capable of managing the problems or loads at hand.

5) Effecting a "pay-off," in Lipset's terms, or meeting the "crisis of distribution" in order to maintain the political system by convincing at least substantial segments of the population that it is an instrument through which they may accomplish their objectives.

6) Arriving at a position with reference to possible opposition to governing elites within the polity.

Each problem noted here certainly does not carry the same weight in every emerging nation, but the loads are sufficiently universal in political development to give an analysis of their impact a general relevance. How political parties affected the way each was met in the American instance can be recounted briefly.

First, although parties did not establish the national constitutional authority in the United States, they did much to assure its effective operation. Despite controversy over the balance of federal and state powers in the new political system, both Federalists and Republicans worked within it. Both parties also discountenanced periodic eruptions of violence for political purposes; thus, for example, party spokesmen did not take up the violence of the Whisky Insurrection of 1794 or the Fries Rebellion of 1799 as a weapon of opposition but condemned it instead. As time passed, parties and party leaders also came to manage the structures of the central government, establish informal connections between its separated agencies, and staff its offices. In short, the parties filled gaps in the constitutional structure of national authority in a constitutional manner and thus performed a crucial constitutional function.

Second, parties dealt effectively with one of the major problems of the new American polity in expressing and aggregating conflicting interests. Given the manifold pluralism and sectional divisions on the American scene, and given a continuation of the politics of raw group pressures and of factions, conflicts of interest might have brought immobilism in the political system along with severe strains or social disruption. Both the Federalists and the Republicans amassed followings which included national coalitions or combinations of interests and opinions, however, held together by working formulas of agreement or compromises, and the Federalists enjoyed at the outset a far wider range of group support than early historians were willing to attribute to them.[16] Conflict continued in party channels, but within viable limits.

Third, early American parties helped to meet the load of popular participation and related problems. Many Federalists were far from happy at the prospect of having to curry votes in order to hold power, but they adjusted at least in part to the imperatives an increasingly open, liberal society imposed. Their Republican opponents meanwhile actively encouraged popular involvement in politics and made the emerging general ideology of liberal democracy a particular ideology for their party, thereby winning an increasingly large following that helped to make them a dominant party after 1800. Indeed the Federalists tended to remain a "party of notables," in Weber's phrase, maintained a condescending tone, and were inclined to view elections as referenda on the policies they had already forged in government. On the other hand the Republicans, partly a "party of notables" but also and increasingly a "party of politicians," revealed a responsiveness to sentiments and opinions among their followers and in the electorate which made them what may be called a "popular party," a party highly sensitive to such currents. Yet both parties turned to general propaganda to inform voters and influence public opinion, most significantly through partisan media at the capital like the *Gazette of the United States* (Federalist) and the *National Gazette* (Republican) and satellite newspapers in the states, although the Republican *Gazette* was soon replaced by the Philadelphia *Aurora* as a national party organ. Moreover both parties gradually evolved procedures to coordinate action in the nomination of candidates and the conduct of election campaigns, and to appeal to and bring out the vote.

Fourth, the parties brought up leaders or enlisted new cadres who helped to manage political business throughout the political system. The roster of major leaders includes such brilliant figures as Hamilton, Adams, Jefferson, and Madison at the party "point," in the capital; editor-politicians like John Fenno, Philip Freneau, Benjamin Franklin Bache, or Noah Webster; such Congressional leaders as Fisher Ames, Theodore Sedgwick, James Monroe, or Albert Gallatin; and scores of prominent local leaders like John Jay in New York or Alexander Dallas in Pennsylvania. Yet the parties, partic-

[16] Dauer, *op.cit.*, *passim*; for the decline of Federalist support, Shaw Livermore Jr., *The Twilight of Federalism: the Disintegration of the Federalist Party, 1815-1830*, Princeton, 1962; also Binkley, *op.cit.*, pp. 29-51.

ularly the Republicans, also developed national behind-the-scenes cadre figures like John Beckley, who served the Republicans as a kind of informal national chairman, and untold legions of lesser cadre in the supportive echelons of the party phalanx, in the states, counties, and towns. Most early American party managers were young, and many were intellectuals to a greater or lesser degree. The average age of nine representative Federalist leaders in 1792, when incipient parties were beginning to take recognizable form, was 44, and the average age of thirteen representative Republican leaders was 36. Nearly all had attended college at a time when higher education was not common, and most had significant intellectual talents as writers or in other areas. One of the most remarkable devices for bringing forward political leadership came with the growth of indigenous Democratic or Republican societies as formal political associations in several states and cities. These societies had a short life and never became mass-membership units in the Republican party as such;[17] but they provided a useful training ground for new political elites.

Fifth, parties also provided mechanisms to assure that the new political system produced a pay-off. They not only quickly developed to the point where they could provide representation for important interests, but as each party partly emerged out of controversy over important national issues each maintained different positions on these issues. On economic policy, for example, Hamilton and the Federalists advocated government measures to encourage hothouse capitalist development even at the expense of economic inequality within the society, while Jefferson and most Republicans were content to speak for a predominantly agricultural economy as the foundation of an equalitarian simple-republican order even at the cost of a slow pace of national economic growth. In the positions they took on these and other issues the two parties in effect provided the electorate with a choice. In the coherence and innovation they brought into government they also helped to shape reasonably consistent courses for public policy. A comparison of Congressional behavior before and after the development of national parties makes clear the transition from confusion to some measure of order and coherence in policy decisions.[18] No group perhaps got all it wanted, but all important

---

[17] See Eugene Perry Link, *Democratic-Republican Societies, 1790-1800*, New York, 1942; and Cunningham, *The Jeffersonian Republicans*, pp. 49-55.

[18] [William Maclay], *The Journal of William Maclay*, New York, 1927, con-

groups had some means to express their demands; and serious dysfunction was avoided.

Sixth, American parties arrived at the acceptance of opposition. To be sure, not only Hamilton but also many other Federalist leaders were suspicious or impatient of opposition, and the Alien and Sedition Acts of 1798, which Adams as well as extreme Federalists supported, were aimed at Republican critics. Yet no general program of repression was undertaken, and when the Republicans won the presidency and both houses of Congress in 1800 the Federalists yielded power in 1801 without recourse to force. Despite overheated rhetoric in the campaign and later Congressional maneuvers to make Aaron Burr president instead of Jefferson, it was the first instance of such a peaceful transition in modern politics.[19] Meanwhile the Republicans in opposition had followed a wholly peaceful course, had carefully avoided overtones of disruptive separatism in the Kentucky and Virginia Resolutions of Jefferson and Madison that censured the Alien and Sedition Acts, and had come rather more readily than the Federalists to the acceptance of opposition after they won power. American parties achieved a *modus vivendi* of adjustment to opposition and peaceful rivalry instead of repression or violence.

In short, parties helped to meet many of the loads the new nation faced and did so in an ideological spirit of open, innovative, and pragmatic accommodation.[20] Parties moreover contributed to political development as a whole by providing mechanisms for the rationalization of politics through the party structures and by helping to introduce a measure of political efficiency which faction politics could scarcely have achieved. Within the general scheme advanced by Almond and Coleman for the analysis of non-Western or underdeveloped as well as Western or developed societies,[21] the first American parties may be said to have undertaken important aspects of the crucial functions of socialization, recruitment, interest articulation, interest aggregation, communication, and rule-making. The intricate machinery of the Constitution could scarcely have functioned as it did without the role parties and the party system played.

---

tains interesting material from the pen of an inside observer; also, Dauer, *op.cit.*, where useful tables of voting behavior are set forth, Appendix III; and Charles, *op.cit.*, p. 94.

[19] Lipset, *op.cit.*, pp. 36-45.

[20] Cf. Chambers, *Political Parties in a New Nation*, pp. 117-119, for a more detailed exposition of the role of ideology in general and party ideology in particular.

[21] Almond and Coleman, *op.cit.*, pp. 16-17, 26-58, *passim*.

It is possible to offer a conceptual generalization based on the American experience. The American parties of the 1790's took the form of cadre structures rather than mass-membership parties, in Duverger's terms; and they did not perform as comprehensive a range of internal functions as many parties in new nations in Asia and Africa have undertaken today, or at least not so intensively point by point.[22] Other differences in specific structure and function could be pointed out from party system to party system. Yet it may also be argued that the American experience lays bare useful generic aspects of the process of party development. If this is the case, all modern parties may be thought of, in a conceptual hypothesis, as historical instances of social formations directed toward the acquisition of governmental power whose definitive characteristics are stable structures, stable relationships linking leaders and popular followings, performance or an offer to perform a wide range of crucial functions in the political system, and the generation of in-group perspectives or ideologies. The specific shape of parties will vary with conditions, loads, and responses, but all modern parties seem likely to exhibit at an irreducible minimum the four general characteristics suggested by the American case.

III. Party Systems and Party Roles

The ultimate impact parties have depends on the party system. Whether there is one party or more than one makes a difference; the kinds of relationships that exist between parties where more than one appears also count; and so does the kind of leadership that develops within the parties. Thus one-party systems will have their own consequences; the impact of plural party systems may differ in societies characterized by widely-shared agreement as compared with societies riven by the centrifugal forces of bipolarized pluralism,[23] and a party system marked by intransigence is likely to produce quite different results from one in which pragmatic adaptation is the mode. Few if any of these matters can be taken as wholly foreordained, at least in the early stages of political development.

Continuing competition between the Federalists and Republicans in the 1790's produced the first modern two-party system. The American experience suggests that the defining characteristic of stable competitive two-party systems is continuing interaction between the

---

[22] See, e.g., Hodgkin, *op.cit.*, pp. 125-148, 155-165.

[23] See Giovanni Sartori, "European Political Parties: the Case of Polarized Pluralism," below, Ch. 5.

parties in which each must take the other into account in its conduct, particularly as it touches on their relations with the electorate in their bids for power and their relations to the centers of government authority. The character of this interaction may be put in terms of four interrelated criteria:

1) The existence of continuing conflict between parties, at once based on and implying the development of policy positions and ideologies which appear as "we-they" perspectives. Differences between parties in policy and ideology may be relatively broad or relatively narrow.

2) The provision of stable links or connections between elements in the public or electorate on the one hand and government on the other as the parties contend with one another.

3) The conduct of party conflict short of social disruption, with at least some degree of acceptance of the idea of a loyal opposition. If party conflict passes beyond the bounds of the spectrum suggested here, it is difficult to conceive of the parties as operating within a stable system, because the seeds of the breakdown of the system or its transition to a different kind of system would always be present. In a stable competitive party system there must at a minimum be some kind of agreement to disagree without recourse to repression or disruption.

4) The existence of a reasonable chance for "out" parties to win governmental power and become "in" parties, and therefore the possibility of the alternation of parties in power. Where one party holds an unassailably dominant position even though opposition exists, we can scarcely speak of a genuinely competitive system.

In the United States the first parties established a pattern of dual party competition. This pattern gave way in the 1800's to a period of Republican ascendency in which the Federalists grew less and less able to provide a significant national challenge to the governing party of Jefferson, Madison, and Monroe; and this pattern of one-party dominance in turn gave way to a new period of faction politics as the Republicans themselves suffered disintegration. In the Jacksonian era, however, new parties revived the pattern of dual party competition, and it has persisted in America despite periodic third-party challenges in the national arena and variations in state arenas. In its broad form the model of a stable competitive party system derived from the early-American experience and suggested here may serve as a basic model of such systems in general,[24] within which variations in particular characteristics may be taken into account.

Political parties may also be thought of as tending toward democratic or plebiscitarian poles in their behavior and roles in the party system. The issue hinges on the different ways parties respond to the load of participation in the course of political development. On the one hand the attitude of political elites may be that mass involvement in politics is something to be contended with through manipulation or control. This may be accomplished through parties as directing and mobilizing but not responsive structures; by molding interests and opinions rather than by giving them open expression; and by elections as formal referenda rather than effective choices. On the other hand elites may adjust to or stimulate patterns of effective participation in the power structure, assume attitudes of responsiveness to a variety of freely expressed interests and opinions in the party system, and view elections as open choices on broad policy options, which in turn should have an effect on public policy. Given their inclination to look upon elections as referenda on policies they had already forged, the Federalists tended toward a plebiscitarian outlook—or a restricted plebiscitarian outlook if one includes their additional inclination to view with misgivings the emergence of a sizable electorate—while the Republicans moved toward an increasingly democratic response. Yet the bent of social structure, Lockian ideology, and the polity tended to push the party system as a whole along a democratic course. The fact that parties developed in a competitive system in which each party had to appeal to a substantial electorate if it was to gain power also provided an internal dynamic in the party system itself which moved it still further in a democratic direction. The existence of open and continuing Federalist and Republican rivalry at virtually all levels of government meant that the party system provided a choice for the public or electorate. This opportunity for choice became the fulcrum of democratic consent and control in the American experience.

Variations in structure between the Federalists and Republicans are also relevant to the question of democratic and plebiscitarian patterns. The Federalists persisted in their notabilistic structure; they were internally created, in Duverger's phrase, originating as they did

[24] For a more detailed elaboration of this schema and some of its implications, and also for the decline of the Federalists and the disintegration of the Republicans, cf. Chambers, *op.cit.*, pp. 143-147ff., 191-208.

in and building out from a powerful nucleus at the center of government; and they never developed great sensitivity to popular demands. Because the Republicans were relatively free from such notabilistic characteristics, they developed more and more as a "popular party." Although they too built out from the center of government, they were also in an important part externally created, out of indigenous elements in the states and localities, in a manner Duverger finds unusual for cadre parties; and they were inclined to see elections as expressions of the popular will even to the point of investing them with a Lockian mystique. In the relationships the Republican party evolved with its popular following important patterns of two-way communication emerged, and what was said at either end of lines of communication was likely to be heard and considered at the other, at the top as well as at the bottom. In part such relationships emerged out of the fact that the Republicans grew up in opposition and were faced with the necessity of mobilizing support to counter the advantages in power the Federalists enjoyed as a government party. The result, however, was a further impetus toward democratization of the American party system.

Lastly, the democratic bent in the development of American parties found expression in the manner in which the parties performed political functions. Their style was more specific than diffuse, more instrumental than affective, and their appeal more general than particular, although personal ties continued as an important undercurrent in party life; and American parties developed in a direction that stressed mass appeals and popular mobilization in elections. Moreover the fact that the parties had a comprehensive governmental structure to work through meant that they enjoyed significant opportunities to carry popular choices in policy into effect once they had won office. Indeed the Federalists and Republicans probably achieved a higher degree of efficiency on this count than later American parties have done when internal factionalism has worked against coherent translation of national electoral choices into governmental decisions.[25]

[25] For a particularly vigorous critique of this aspect of American party and governmental action, see James MacGregor Burns, *The Deadlock of Democracy: Four Part-Politics in America*, Englewood Cliffs, N.J., 1963, *passim*; for other views see William N. Chambers, *The Democrats, 1789-1964: A Short History of a Popular Party*, Princeton, 1964, for a brief case study of America's oldest party, and George Mayer, *The Republican Party, 1854-1964*, New York, 1964, for the Democrats' durable rival; also, the general histories by Agar and Binkley, already noted.

For the democratic and plebiscitarian alternatives the crucial point is the role party systems as a whole play. They may provide channels for open recruitment, effective participation, and effective representation, or they may not; if they do, they may exhibit a substantial measure of intraparty democracy. They may provide meaningful, relatively orderly, continuing options on policy as well as leaders among which the public or electorate can choose, or they may not; if they do, they offer choices as the operative meaning of interparty democracy. It may be argued as a general hypothesis that competitive dual-party systems carry a stronger probability not only of democratic consent but of democratic control than do pluralistic multiparty systems, in the sense of the translation of broad popular choices into public policy; whereas multiparty systems or dual systems with a high incidence of intraparty factionalism are less efficient in promoting democratic control because the clarity of either-or alternatives is lacking and parties or factions must enter into *ad hoc* coalitions to govern. Yet these features and problems of consent and control are not involved at all in any effective sense in plebiscitarian systems, where domination replaces meaningful consent and manipulation replaces free choice.

IV. Parties and National Integration

In an important sense nearly every aspect of the discussion of American nation-building and party-building here is related to the question of integration. It remains, however, to isolate and analyze the elements involved from the point of view of this particular aspect of political development.

Most broadly, national integration may be taken as a process of incorporating various parts of a society into a functioning whole. Where a relatively high degree of integration obtains, a political system can perform essential functions with a substantial measure of acceptance, order, and efficiency. Integration also tends to proceed by phases, meeting various problems, so to speak, as it moves from lower to higher stages. Among these we may note the growth of obedience and loyalties to the nation which transcend loyalties to its parts; the reduction of barriers between various parts of the whole, the opening of communication, and ultimately the toleration of differences within unity; the emergence of faith in the political system; and the emergence of shared values and perspectives, or consensus. Where norms or promises of democracy exist, integration appears to require general access to effective participation in the processes of the political system. Successful integration in a society of any complexity also appears to require some rationalization of political processes so that the variety of elements in the nation may be related effectively to a single government. These aspects of political development will be taken here not as integration itself, or as "participation integration" and "process integration"; but as requisites for national integration, construed as the process of incorporation of parts into a whole. This notion of integration in general has been put suggestively by Deutsch in a summary of possible stages: "Open or latent resistance to political amalgamation into a common national state; minimal integration to the point of passive compliance with the orders of such an amalgamated government; deeper political integration to the point of active support for such a common state but with continuing ethnic or cultural group cohesion and diversity; and, finally, the coincidence of political amalgamation and integration with the assimilation of all groups to a common language and culture. . . ."[26]

National integration may be found in different dimensions at different junctures in time. Much also depends on the sequence and clustering of issues. If a developing polity faces all at once the loads of establishing legitimacy and achieving some measure of integration and also the problems of participation and distribution and of rationalizing political processes, serious strains are likely to occur.[27] In the American case the timing of issues was fortunate. It was no easy task to amalgamate thirteen previously separate, often squabbling states into a single nation. Yet the emergence of communication among the colonies and various sections even before the Revolution, the development of a continental consciousness, the Revolutionary experience and American tribulations after 1783 as a lonely republic in a generally hostile world, the existence of a substantial measure of cultural as well as linguistic identity, the rise of economic interdependence, and the increasing sway of the liberal tradition all helped toward the development of national identity in a way that few new nations in Asia or Africa today have enjoyed.[28] The federal character of the new national political system under the Constitution, with its explicit recognition of diversity within unity, marked another important step. Finally

[26] Deutsch, "Nation-Building and National Development: Some Issues for Political Research," in Deutsch and Foltz, eds., *op.cit.*, pp. 7-8.

[27] LaPalombara and Weiner, Ch. 1, above.

[28] Merritt, *op.cit.*, pp. 6-72; Lipset, *op.cit.*, pp. 23-35, 61-66; Almond and Coleman, *op.cit.*, pp. 149-152, 239-246, 366-368, *passim*; Wallerstein, *op.cit.*, pp. 85-101.

the charismatic legitimacy George Washington brought to the new government, and his refusal to allow his personal appeal to be converted into a foundation for perennial power, also did much to smooth a transition from personal foundations for legitimacy to rational foundations in a legal-constitutional order. It was only after most of these phases in the process of integration had been passed through or were underway that other loads came to the fore in the nation as a whole. There was already a significant development toward integration before national political parties appeared.

Many aspects of party action did more to hinder this development than to advance it. The Federalists and Republicans not only expressed but even exacerbated cleavage in their representation of conflicts of interest in the society and in their maneuvering for office and power; in the way in which they helped to pit men against one another "like two cocks," as Jefferson put it in describing his relations with Hamilton in the cabinet; and by contributing to a general heating-up of the political atmosphere. Indeed conflict is inherent in competitive party systems as they have been described here because such systems provide open channels for the clash of interests, sentiments, and opinions which already exist in the population and introduce new elements of antagonism on their own in their continuing rivalry for power. The we-they perspectives of parties, the stress on the virtues of "our" leaders and policies and symbols and the evil of "theirs," are all likely to stir strident outcries among rival partisans. Moreover early American party cadres were not always above sharp dealing and even occasional fraud in elections in the scramble for power; there was at least one occasion in the 1790's when invective between partisans in the American Congress came to blows; the suspicion and partisan motives which spawned the Alien and Sedition Acts carried over into the partisan strains of the election of 1800; and party conflict exacerbated personal dislikes, leading Burr and Hamilton to a duel in which the latter was killed. It was such aspects of political rivalry that Washington condemned when he spoke out against "the spirit of party" as a spirit sure to "distract the public councils." There is no discounting the malintegrative impact of such aspects of party rivalry in the American case.

Yet it is important to note two additional elements in this connection, which may be expressed as general hypotheses. First, it may be that parties of the general American type, by channeling the conflicts which already exist within the society and subjecting them to mediating structures, reduce on the whole the amount of conflict that would otherwise occur even though they generate distinctively partisan cleavages on their own. Second, it may be that such parties by expressing conflict openly in a patterned manner within the rules of the political system promote integration by facilitating rhetorical modes of expression as channels of social and psychological catharsis, thereby drawing off potential strains in the political system as a whole. In any case the American polity weathered the storms of its formative period and has weathered all such storms but one that blew up over the most continually divisive issue in American life, the place of the Negro in the national community—and in that one the loosing of the national and integrative ties of the party system in 1860 was the prelude to civil war in 1861.[29] Although parties in the 1790's scarcely ushered in a millennium of harmony, conflict was kept within peaceful bounds.

In this connection the place of ideology requires some specification. Federalists and Republicans were divided ideologically on many questions of domestic policy. Issues of world politics such as the Jay Treaty with England in 1795 touched off frenzies of logomachy in which each party hinted that the other verged on treason, and Washington thought that the Jay Treaty controversy agitated the public to a point that equaled the excitements of the revolutionary era itself. Extreme or "High" Federalists in the late 1790's could scarcely stomach the thought of the Republicans gaining power, and a few of them in the early 1800's even toyed with abortive schemes for the secession of New England from the union as an answer to Republican ascendency. Yet by and large ideology among party leaders took the form of giving vent to emotional release in rhetoric; and as a controlling element in behavior it did not reach the point of ultimate intransigence. Extremist Federalists remained a minority in the party as a whole, and John Adams as a party leader as well as President insisted on following a moderate course in foreign policy; Jefferson's conduct in office has been described as a triumph of practical adaptation over ideological inflexibility—"what is practicable," he himself commented, "must often controul what is pure theory." On the whole ideological divisions between Federalists

<hr/>

[29] See Roy Franklin Nichols, *The Disruption of American Democracy* (New York, 1948), *passim*, for a valuable analysis of the breakdown of parties as the precursor of the Civil War; also, Arthur Schlesinger Jr., *The Politics of Upheaval*, Boston, 1960, for the political strains which followed the Great Depression of 1929 and the role of party politics.

and Republicans were sharper than they have usually been between major American parties, but not sharp enough to produce disruptive consequences in the polity.

In their competition, meanwhile, early American parties made significant contributions to some of the crucial requisites for national integration. They helped to fulfill the democratic promises of the American liberal tradition by providing effective channels for popular participation. They assisted in meeting the problem of distribution by their transmission to government of the demands of important groups across the nation and in the states and localities. They contributed to solving the problem of orderly management in a complex polity by their conduct of nominations and elections and by helping to manage the agencies of the national government. In short, parties helped to realize a measure of political efficiency which could never have been achieved through faction politics.

As integration was involved in the problem of establishing constitutional legitimacy and the evolution of a viable national consensus, parties also performed directly integrative tasks in their relation with the public in several ways:

1) By supporting the new constitutional order in its hour of uncertainty and testing, even in the face of disagreements over specific interpretation of the Constitution itself.

2) By strengthening and maintaining communication and a sense of shared stakes among different groups in the several states. Thus, for example, both Massachusetts men and Virginians could join across state lines in being either Federalists or Republicans, though there were more of the former in Massachusetts and more of the latter in Virginia. Without national parties malintegration among the several states might have persisted far longer than it did.

3) By undertaking recruitment and socialization, or bringing up and training new elites to man posts in the political system and providing popular education in politics on an informal basis.

In these ways parties helped to promote a sense of political community and efficacy and thereby further strengthened the new government. If they did not perform a range of directly integrative functions comparable to those that parties have undertaken in many new nations today, this was in part because the American problem of integration was less demanding by the time parties appeared.

In the final analysis, however, the effect of parties on national integration depends on the role of the party system as a whole.

The fruitful issue for analysis appears to be not a general either-or question of whether parties integrate or don't integrate. The question is: Under what conditions do party systems of what kinds promote a net balance of integration or of nonintegration, and in what ways? It is the contention here that the first American party system, despite the malintegrative results of certain aspects of party action, produced a net balance of integrative results. This was the case in large part because of certain salient features of the system itself and their consequences.

First, there is the fact that the Federalists and the Republicans took on the form of stable, broad-gauge parties as contrasted with shifting, narrow factions. Thus the parties and their followings operated as broadly inclusive combinations of interest groups. In the long-term interaction of the parties in competition for support these combinations could be held together only by political brokerage and compromise in the party structures and in their relations with their followings. The net result was that the party system turned group conflict from unlimited pluralistic into manageable dualistic channels before it reached the decision-making centers of government. As compared with the tensions of deadlock that might have ensued if indigenous pluralism had continued unchecked, party dualism reduced malintegrative strains.

Second, because the parties developed as formations given more to the practical pursuit of power and office than to ideological intransigence, they tended to conduct conflict within a moderate range. They did so in part as a result of the moderate bent of American politics generally and in part out of the exigencies of their interaction in the party system itself. Yielding too much to the views of extremist groups or leaders threatened the loss of important blocs of votes that were essential to political success. The result was a tendency to push the party system toward moderation or centralism and to limit the ambit of extremist elements. All of these forces combined to produce a net balance of integrative results, particularly as compared with the degree of malintegration that would have followed from constant extremes in party policy or action. In this context the party system also arrived at the acceptance and legitimization of a coordinated political opposition.

Third, by providing instruments for electoral consent and democratic choice the party system helped to drain off dissatisfaction before it reached the point of serious dissaffection. It opened avenues of expression for those who were at the moment out of power as well as in, gave hope to the "outs" that they might become "ins" as a result of electoral choices, provided concrete mechanisms through which the far-flung national electorate could hold someone responsible for the conduct of government, and offered working tools for a peaceful change of elites if the electorate wished it. It is hard to imagine how major national elections could have been managed in a satisfactory manner without the machinery of operating democratic choice the party system made available. By 1800, for example, widespread dissatisfaction with Federalist leaders and policies had built up within many important groups in the population, however much parties intensified it. If the party system had not existed to help effect a transfer of power to the Republicans in a way the dispersed mechanisms of faction politics could scarcely have done, dissatisfaction might have grown to seriously disruptive proportions or turned to violence, as earlier antagonisms toward ruling elites and their policies had done in the Regulator movement in North Carolina, in Shays' Rebellion in Massachusetts, or in the Whisky Insurrection and the Fries Uprising. On balance again, the party system may be said to have reduced potential disaffection and disruption, with a net gain for integrative over malintegrative consequences.

Lastly, parties in the party system operated within the rules of the developing polity as a whole, with the obvious integrative results which this fact entailed.

This analysis of the American experience suggests as a general hypothesis that a democratic two-party system can produce a net balance of integrative impacts on political development if the parties embrace a wide range of interests and opinions in their followings held together by pragmatic adjustment, if they keep conflict within moderate bounds, and if they are ready to operate within a larger basic agreement or an accepted set of fundamental rules. The hypothesis contains a substantial set of "ifs," however; and they raise a final important question.

V. Leadership, Purposes, and Political Styles

The net impact of early American parties on national integration was what it was to an important degree because of key features which the party system came to exhibit as a whole—notably the features just outlined here, and its pragmatic development in general. It remains to explore why, or how, the American party system took on these particular characteristics; why, or how, it came to operate within the rules.

A large part of the explanation lies in the comparatively narrow range of conflict American conditions produced and in the rise of the American liberal tradition toward national consensus. The distribution of interests and opinions tended to fall into a curve of dualistic centrality, with most interests and opinions encompassed in two central peaks of concentration which tapered off into much lower measures of extremes, as it were, rather than into a bimodal curve of disruptive extremes or a centrifugal scattering of disruptive drives.[30] Such matters of social fact, prevailing ideology, a relatively limited spectrum of social conflict, and the distribution of interests may be taken as a necessary condition in any explanation of how the American party system came to perform as it did. Yet the explanation as a whole goes beyond such matters and brings us again to the responses of American party leaders to the conditions and loads they faced.

Particularly in a period of national formation, what leaders do and how they do it may have a crucial impact. In the American case the bulk of party leaders were guided by purposes and convictions which included a deep concern for the future of the new nation or the success of its "republican experiment," as well as by concerns for more immediate or particular political goals. Moreover they had before them the example and counsel of Washington, who served far more as a moderator than he did as a mobilizer or dramatizer, as many later prophet-leaders of nationalism have. In the long run American party leaders avoided pushing issues and ideologies to the breaking-point of violence or disruption, as they might have done, and upheld the Constitution and the rules of the polity; and when the test of 1800 came the Federalists as a whole accepted the result rather than resort to force to prevent it. In short, no major party leader was ready to chance the destruction of the new nation in order to gain partisan or factional advantage. The role of leadership in this connection is underscored by the fact that the story might have been quite different if men like the intransigent ultra-High Federalists of Connecticut, for example, had dominated in national party leadership.

Lastly, American party leaders developed unusual skills in inter-group adjustment and combination, in compromise, in aggregating

[30] Cf. Sartori, *op.cit.*, pp. 9-14.

as well as mobilizing interests, and in the practical rationalization of political methods and processes; and through such skills they helped to establish patterns of adjustment as well as of conflict in the party system. These crucial matters of purpose, commitment, and skill became the foundations of the basically pragmatic style the preponderance of American party leaders achieved. It is in important part the lack of such commitments, skills, and styles that has prevented many new nations in Asia or Africa today from establishing a viable measure of national integration and efficiency, and many nations in Latin America from managing peaceful transfers of power by democratic procedures. If there are lessons for developing nations today that may be learned from the early American experience in political development, they lie in large part here—in the area of leadership and in the manner in which leaders conduct politics in general and party politics in particular.

Considered as a whole, the response of American party leaders to the problems of nation-building and party-building was more than a reflex action to social conditions and emerging ideology. It was also a creative element operating in reciprocal interaction with these elements, an active and positive factor itself. It was forwarded by human purposes, modes of behavior, and shared hopes, notably the hope of building a strong nation and making the republican innovation work in a hostile world. Rivals though they were and spokesmen of strongly different points of view, Hamilton the Federalist and Jefferson the Republican were outstanding examples of this creative personal element, one by virtually inventing a program to point the nation toward economic growth, the other by embodying the spirit of American nationhood and liberal democracy. If the total historical process in its groping, its occasional pettiness, and its conflict as well as its creative aspects was by no means all smooth and orderly, it did bring the United States from uncertainty to stable nationhood, from faction politics to working party politics, and to a political system that was cohesive, internally legitimate, and autonomous, in Deutsch's terms.[31] The measure of integration early America achieved was in part a byproduct of underlying forces. It was also in part the result of active responses to conditions and loads by political leaders.

[31] Deutsch, *op.cit.*, pp. 11-12.

CHAPTER 4

THE DEVELOPMENT OF PARTIES IN TURKEY

DANKWART A. RUSTOW

I. The Origin of Middle Eastern Parties

"Wherever a group of equals seeks to arrive at a common decision it is likely to be divided. But only where decisions are weighty and frequent will division crystallize into competitive organization. Political parties, therefore, have generally emerged at two points in the history of modern states. First, as representative bodies secured a prominent share in the government, factions or parties arose in their midst. Later, as large masses of citizens sought and obtained the right to participate in the selection of these governing assemblies, national parties sprang up by the side of those in parliament. The English parliament in 1640 declared itself indissoluble, subdued the king by beheading his chief adviser—and was split into Roundheads and Cavaliers. The French revolutionary assemblies a century and a half later brought Louis XVI to Paris as a captive, forced him to approve a constitution, proclaimed a republic, at length executed him—and found themselves already engaged in the internecine battle of Feuillants, Girondists, Montagnards, and Thermidorians. The events of 1688-1689 in England confirmed not only parliament's right to determine the constitution but also its division into Whigs and Tories. The Reform Act of 1832 called into action the Chartists, the Anti-Corn-Law League, and other popular organizations; that of 1867 the Birmingham caucus. In the United States the unsuspecting constitutional fathers, by vesting the legislative power in a congress and the choice of a president in an electoral college, opened a wide field for partisan activity. National conventions took over the task of presidential nomination after 1832 when manhood suffrage was making rapid gains throughout the states."[1]

THE FOREGOING generalization applies with minor variations to most countries of western, northern, and central Europe and to their

[1] Dankwart A. Rustow, *The Politics of Compromise: A Study of Parties and Cabinet Government in Sweden*, Princeton: Princeton University Press, 1955, p. 9. I am indebted to Bernard Lewis for critical comments on an earlier draft of this essay.

overseas offshoots, such as the United States, Canada, Australia, and New Zealand. Most legislatures in these countries can trace their origins to the medieval estates: lords, burgesses, and knights of the shire in England; nobility, clergy, and commoners in France; noblemen, clergy, burghers, and peasants in Sweden. These early representative bodies asserted and expanded their privileges against royal power, now in long tenacious struggles, now in brief revolutionary convulsions. While the see-saw contest between assemblies and princes was continuing, the territorial boundaries of the European states became solidly established, a feeling of national identity took root among the citizenry, and the great equalizing and unifying instruments of the modern state—universal taxation, public education, and general conscription—created firmer bonds between rulers and subjects. In the end, representation came to be considered a general civic right rather than a corporate class privilege, and the partisan contest spilled over from the chambers of the legislature to the public at large. Throughout the European cultural realm, party organization thus has become a universal and durable instrument of modern politics under democratic and even under totalitarian regimes.

In the Middle East there is no indigenous tradition of representation. Medieval political theory in Islam was preoccupied with the personal qualifications of the ruler and with the precepts of sacred law derived from scripture and precedent. Principles of statecraft were laid down in "mirrors for princes," and rules of jurisprudence elaborated in legal and theological treatises. Ibn Khaldun's *Prolegomena* are rightly considered a forerunner of modern historical sociology. But there were no notions of corporate personality, no practice of majority vote, no claims to legitimate revolution, and no theory of representation. Muslim authors of the classical period agree that any effective exercise of power—even tyranny or usurpation—is preferable to civil war or anarchy; in short, the subject's unconditional duty is to obey the powers that be.

In the Ottoman Empire the absolutism of the sultans was strengthened by a number of drastic devices. At first the brothers of the acceding ruler were killed off, and later his sons were reared in a secluded palace, known as "the cage"—all in a zealous effort to prevent wars of succession and princely rebellions. The soldiers and administrators of the early Empire were largely recruited from among forced converts to Islam who had the legal status of slaves to the sultan and hence could form no ties of family or hereditary property. These strong tendencies toward absolutism were restrained in practice by potent countervailing forces. The government was mainly a palace and an armed camp. Warfare and administration were the privilege of the ruling class of slave-converts. Commerce and industry were reserved largely to Christians (as well as Jews) who lived within their autonomous legal orders under the *millet* and capitulation systems. Tax collection was entrusted to private entrepreneurs known as tax farmers. Islamic law was administered by the *ulema*, a self-perpetuating class of freeborn Muslims. The villages and nomadic tribes preserved their parochial customs with little interference from the government in distant Istanbul. Decline of the Empire's power brought further decentralization. The Janissary elite corps, freed from the rule of celibacy, became an unruly caste of praetorians. In the provinces, governors, Janissary garrisons, landowners, and other notables defied the sultan and established themselves in hereditary power.

In the double revolution of 1807 and 1808 Janissaries, *ulema*, and notables rose up against the Westernizing reforms of Selim III (1789-1807) and forced Mahmud II (1808-1839) upon his accession to sign a Covenant of Union in which central government and provincial magnates pledged mutual respect for their vested rights.[2] That document, like the Magna Carta, signaled a victory for the power of local notables rather than for universal civic rights, but like the Magna Carta it might have laid an indigenous foundation for limited and representative government. The rival factions in the capital in 1807-1808, each with its backers in the provinces, may well be compared to the factions that foreshadowed party developments in sixteenth-century England or eighteenth-century France. Yet in two decades of tenacious struggle Mahmud managed to erode that foundation, bringing most of the local notables and provincial dynasties to heel, and destroying the Janissaries in 1826. The secession of Serbia, Greece, and Egypt and the continual interference of the European powers severely weakened his external position. Internally, within these reduced boundaries, Mahmud's cadre of Westernized bureaucrats and military officers established a system of imperial rule unchallenged by any institutional checks or balances. In Egypt,

---

[2] On the revolutions of 1807 and 1808 see Halil İnalcık's contribution to Robert E. Ward and Dankwart A. Rustow, *Political Modernization in Japan and Turkey*, Princeton: Princeton University Press, 1964, pp. 352-388.

Muhammad Ali (1805-1849) similarly broke the power of the Mamluk aristocracy. Toward the beginning of the Middle East's intensive Westernization autocracy for the first time became firmly established in practice as well as in theory.

The next century brought European colonial rule—outright or in the form of military occupation, protectorates, and mandates—to most of the Arab-speaking Ottoman territories: Algeria 1830, Tunisia 1881, Egypt 1882, Libya 1912, the Fertile Crescent 1920. Colonialism provided even less opportunity for the organic development of representative institutions, and hence of legislative or electoral parties, than did domestic despotism. In Egypt, in fact, the British occupation of 1882 directly thwarted the attempt by military officers and a consultative council to set legislative limits to the Khedive's spendthrift habits.

Despite these basic deviations from the European model, political parties—or at least organizations brandishing that name—have arisen during the last fifty or one hundred years in most Middle Eastern countries (notable exceptions being the traditional monarchies of Afghanistan, Saudi Arabia, and Yemen, and the semi-dependent principalities of the Arabian Coast). But the earliest of these parties, and a good many of the later ones, had their origins in subversive conspiracy or in agitational protest against foreign or domestic absolutism rather than in voting alignments in assembly or constituency. The parties often have been concerned less with seizing power or directing policy within existing political systems than with redefining state boundaries, establishing new national identities, or setting up new regimes. In the countries of Northwest Africa there has been a development of "comprehensive-nationalist" parties[3] not unlike the anti-colonialist movements elsewhere in Asia and Africa. In some countries (e.g. Sudan, Lebanon) party alignments have been a surface reflection of deeper sectarian or religious divisions. Elsewhere (e.g. Egypt, Syria, and Iraq between the World Wars, and Iran in the 1940's and 50's) parties started out as ephemeral cliques within a narrow oligarchy. At other times (e.g. Egypt since 1952) party organization has resulted from a dictator's desire for a semblance of plebiscitary support. Throughout most of the area parties have been feeble instruments for seizing or wielding power when

[3] For that concept see my chapter in Gabriel A. Almond and James S. Coleman, eds., *The Politics of the Developing Areas*, Princeton: Princeton University Press, 1960, pp. 397ff.

compared with such potent forces as traditional monarchy, foreign occupation, bureaucracy, and military conspiracy.

Only two countries provide a sharp contrast to this general picture of atrophy and ineffectiveness of party life—two countries where political parties have become the principal device of competition for public power. One of these is Israel, where parties and their affiliates permeate political and economic life so as to produce a pluralistic *parteienstaat* of even purer form than in the smaller European democracies; but precisely because of the European character of its institutions (and of the dominant element among its immigrant population) Israel must remain outside of our purview. The other country is Turkey, where parties made their appearance a century ago to become a central and even dominant feature of politics after 1908. Turkey thus offers the richest evidence for exploring the impact of historical and social variations in the Middle East on party developments. Although in a later section comparisons and contrasts will be drawn from other Middle Eastern countries, most of the empirical detail of this paper will therefore come from recent and contemporary Turkish history.

II. Major Characteristics of Turkish Party Development

Unlike most other developing countries Turkey never lost her independence. The Turkish Republic, founded in 1923, was the direct heir of seven centuries of Ottoman governmental tradition. As a result the Turks display a sense of governmental responsibility, an organizational talent, and an appreciation of the realities of power that contrast sharply with the more dogmatic and anarchic tendencies among their former Arab subjects and their Iranian neighbors. Turkish parties have produced strong leaders—Enver and Talât Pashas, Atatürk, İnönü, Menderes—because politically active Turks have displayed an instinct for discipline, a readiness to provide followership. Similarly, Turkish political organizations have shown a remarkable ability to survive in adversity. With the introduction of open party competition in 1945 there has been a strong tendency, despite recurrent splits, defections, and expulsions, for political forces to group and regroup themselves in only two major parties. At first this tendency was greatly strengthened by the multiple-member plurality system in effect for assembly elections until 1960 (a system similar in its workings and effects to that in force for the United States electoral college); but the trend of elections in the

Second Republic since 1961 indicates that this tendency continues unabated under proportional representation.

The most notable record of survival is furnished by the Society for Union and Progress, founded in 1889 by a handful of students at the military medical school. After two decades of persecution, exile, and attempts at infiltration by the sultan's agents it came to power through the revolution of 1908 and the coup d'état of 1913. Following the party's dissolution in the wake of the Ottoman defeat of 1918 its provincial branches formed the nucleus of the Society for the Defense of Rights.[4] This group in turn was transformed in 1923 into the (Republican) People's party, which supported the dictatorial regime of Atatürk and İnönü (1923-1945), weathered systematic harassment by the Menderes government in the 1950's, and survives as one of the two major forces on the current political stage.

An equally impressive resilience has been demonstrated by Adnan Menderes' Democratic party (DP). After a decade of increasingly oppressive rule his regime was overthrown in the military coup of 1960, Menderes himself and two close associates were hanged, the party dissolved, and its parliamentary followers jailed and barred from further political participation. Nevertheless the two hastily improvised groups which provided an organizational home for the orphaned Democratic voters, the Justice and New Turkey parties, garnered a total of 49 per cent of the national vote in 1961, exactly as Menderes' DP had in 1957; and by 1963 nearly all the former DP support had concentrated in the Justice party as the more promising successor group. In 1965 that party, under the energetic leadership of Süleyman Demirel, was returned to power by a popular landslide.

Against this background of organizational longevity a secondary theme may be traced, perhaps best described as a rhythm of diastole and systole, of expansion and contraction. During the first phase of each cycle there is a great degree of freedom of organization, at least in comparison with the preceding period; a large number of parties are formed, and in the acrimonious competition among

---

[4] On the history of the Union and Progress movement up to 1908 see E. E. Ramsaur, *The Young Turks*, Princeton: Princeton University Press, 1957; on the Unionist base of the Defense of Rights movement, see Rustow, "The Army and the Founding of the Turkish Republic," *World Politics*, Vol. 13, No. 4 (July 1959). A study, on the basis of primary sources, of the Union and Progress party and its domestic policies during the period from 1908 to 1918 remains a prime desideratum of historiography concerning Turkey.

these a single group wins out and at length establishes its dominance. This victorious group proceeds to suppress its rivals and, during the second phase of the cycle, to rule the country dictatorially; the latent opposition forces now consolidate in a single organization which displaces the dictatorial regime, revokes the repressive measures, and thus starts the first phase of the next cycle. Historical events provide recurrent variations upon this basic theme. The relatively free development of public opinion and incipient political organization from 1865 to 1878 may be seen as the expansive phase of the first cycle, followed by the autocracy of Abdülhamid (1878 to 1908; he reigned from 1876 to 1909). The Young Turk Revolution of 1908 ushered in a phase of party proliferation followed by the Unionist party dictatorship of 1913-1918. There ensued a period of relatively free political expression leading up to the firm consolidation during the dictatorial rule of the People's Party (1923-1945). The years after the Second World War brought a hitherto unknown degree of political freedom accompanied by a great intensification of party activity until Menderes in the late 1950's reverted to earlier authoritarian patterns. The interlude of military dictatorship in 1960-1961 finally gave way to an even freer and more intensive interplay of political forces.[5] Professor Tunaya's compilation of historical data on political parties enables us to establish something of a quantitative index for these cycles by listing the number of parties founded during each successive period:[6]

		Years	No. of Parties Founded
I	a)	1865-1878	3
	b)	1878-1908	13
II	a)	1908-1913	22
	b)	1913-1918	2
III	a)	1918-1923	55
	b)	1923-1945	5
IV	a)	1945-1954 ca.	30[7]
	b)	ca. 1954-1961	?
V	a)	1961-	?

[5] For an elaboration of the cyclical theme see, e.g., Arif Payaslıoğlu's contribution to Ward and Rustow, *op.cit.*, pp. 427f.

[6] My calculations from Tarık Z. Tunaya, *Türkiyede Siyasî Partiler*, Istanbul, 1952, pp. 773-777 and *passim*.

[7] Note that Tunaya's data go only up to 1952.

III. Party Organization, Changing Issues, and the Widening of the Elite

The cycles just distinguished in Turkey's political development are reflected in the impact of party organization on the recruitment of political leadership. During the diastolic or expansive phase of each cycle new social elements crowd upon the political stage; during the systolic or repressive phase power is consolidated in the hands of some of these new elements. Each cycle, however, is not a mere repetition; for the circle of political participants is widened in each diastole far beyond its contraction during the systole. To use a Leninist metaphor, it is a pattern of two steps forward and one step back. As the political elite has widened, party organization has evolved toward greater complexity. The first cycle (1865-1908) was one of conspiratorial organization. In the next two cycles (1908-1945) the parties became instruments for the organization of the ruling elite. In the last two cycles (since 1945) the parties have served as vehicles for the political mobilization of the masses. But politics is not a game played for the mere sake of organization. The continual crowding of the political stage must be seen in connection with the emergence of successive political issues that preoccupied these actors.

THE YOUNG OTTOMANS (1865-1876): MALCONTENTS IN THE NEW BUREAUCRACY

The chief political issue in the Ottoman Empire from the days of Selim III to the 1908 revolution was that of defensive modernization: the attempt to remedy the Empire's weakness in its contest with the rising powers of Europe by introducing European methods first of military training and then of public finance and administration, education, and legislation. Mahmud II's concern, as we have seen, was to reassert imperial authority against the centripetal forces that threatened the extinction of state and dynasty. His struggle, as Selim's before him, may properly be interpreted as one of reform versus tradition; his chief target was the entrenched power of Janissaries, of notables, of *ulema*.

During the Tanzimat period (1839-1876) there developed for the first time an intensive contest between alternative programs of modernization (or more precisely, alternative blended formulas of tradition and modernity); and it was in this contest that Ottoman party organization found its origins. The sultan's reforming ministers proclaimed civic equality and instituted new administrative bureaus and new training centers for civil servants—all on the basis of the ruler's hard-won absolute power. But some of the recruits of this new educational and administrative organization, especially those who had completed their training in Europe, believed that the most urgent reform was some effective check on the despotic powers of sultan and ministers. The earliest spokesman for this protest movement was İbrahim Şinasi (1824-1871), one-time clerk in the artillery corps, who came back from his studies in Paris an ardent admirer of the romantic poetry and the liberal politics of men like Hugo and Lamartine, founded the first Ottoman newspaper, and wrote the first Turkish poems and plays in a European style. Some of Şinasi's literary disciples within the bureaucracy joined in 1865 with other malcontents (some younger military officers, some low-ranking *ulema*, and an exiled Egyptian prince) to form the New Ottoman Society.[8]

Western-style literature, a daily press, the public debate of government policy, and partisan organization thus all had their origin in the same period and within the same circle of men. It was a small circle indeed. It has aptly been observed that the literature of this period was written by civil servants in their spare time for the edification of other civil servants in their leisure hours.[9] Like early political parties in Europe, the New Ottomans were founded by dissidents within the ruling elite; but in the Ottoman Empire the vocal dissidents were to be found within the administrative establishment rather than in a parliament which was yet to be founded. In the narrow official circles of Istanbul the small New Ottoman movement could exercise great leverage. Within a single year (1876), and with the help of some friendly military officers and their units, the New Ottomans engineered the successive deposition of two sultans and the adoption of the first representative, written constitution outside of Europe.

Elections to the first Ottoman House of Representatives in 1877 were hastily improvised, without an election law, without a lengthy campaign, and without party organization. After a little over a year

[8] See Şerif Mardin, *The Genesis of Young Ottoman Thought*, Princeton: Princeton University Press, 1962. For the period generally, see Roderic H. Davison, *Reform in the Ottoman Empire 1856-1876*, Princeton: Princeton University Press, 1963.

[9] Şerif Mardin, "Some Notes on an Early Phase in the Modernization of Communications in Turkey," *Comparative Studies in Society and History*, Vol. 3, No. 3 (April 1961), pp. 250-271.

Sultan Abdülhamid reestablished an autocratic system by adjourning the House *sine die*, banishing the chief draftsman of the constitution, and, at length, having him murdered. Some of the former New Ottomans were involved in abortive plots to restore Abdülhamid's insane predecessor; but the New Ottoman movement as such had come to an end.

THE YOUNG TURKS (1889-1918): WESTERNIZED ELITE AND THE NATIONAL QUESTION

Even during the decades of Hamidian "reaction" many of the reform policies of the Tanzimat were continued. Railroads and telegraph lines (effective instruments alike for the communication of liberal ideas and for their repression) were built at an unprecedented rate, and the newly founded centers of higher education continued to train military officers and civil servants in the European fashion. It was during this period that the Imperial lycée at Galatasaray, with its French-Turkish curriculum, became (together with the graduate school of administration, or *mülkiye*) the chief reservoir for public officials and that the Prussian general Colmar Freiherr von der Goltz became inspector general of the military schools.

Many of the products of this Westernized education embraced constitutionalist ideas with even greater fervor than had the New Ottomans in their day, and Abdülhamid's stern measures of banishment and exile only enhanced the radicalism of the movement. By necessity rather than choice, the exiled constitutionalists left the state service and continued their activities as journalists and pamphleteers. Partisan activity thus shifted from the executive branch to the "free" professions.

The chief aim of the exiles, known to their European hosts as *Jeunes Turcs*, was the restoration of the parliamentary constitution of 1876. In addition the question of the relationship among the nationalities of the polyglot Empire began to haunt them. At the Young Turk congresses held in Paris in 1902 and 1907 a centralist and a federalist faction emerged. The founders of the Society of Union and Progress in 1889 had included one Circassian, one Albanian, one Kurd, one Azeri, and one Turk. Now the Turks were drawn mainly to the centralist faction while the federalists appealed most strongly to various non-Turkish elements, including Arabs and Armenians.

The victory of the constitutionalist program of the Young Turks in 1908 ushered in a full-dress fight between the centralists and their federalist opponents in the restored parliament, in the proliferating press of Istanbul, and in the growing organizational life of urban centers throughout the Empire. The Society of Union and Progress remained the citadel of the centralists, whose Ottoman patriotism turned into an intransigent Turkish nationalism. The coup d'état of January 1913 gave the Unionists full control of the government; through systematic use of patronage and economic regulation they built up by 1918 a strong network of party organization linking all major provincial towns.

The federalists were greatly weakened by their internal divisions and lack of a concrete program. In the Balkan Wars, moreover, the Empire lost most of its Albanian, Bulgarian, and Greek population; by 1916 the Armenians and the more active groups among the Arabs also had opted for secession. With the Turks left as the major ethnic element loyal to the Empire, the federalists' demand for "unity of the elements" had become hollow and illusory.

The Young Turk period marks not only the advent of nationalism but also the adoption of many novel devices in politics: cabinet responsibility to the legislature, periodic parliamentary elections, daily journalism and public oratory in the capital, partisan clubs in the provincial towns, and periodic military interference in politics. Many new social elements entered into the ruling elite, and party organization supplied much of the drive for this social ascent. The Young Turk revolution was brought about through the interrelated activities of journalists in exile and of the secret conspiracy of military officers reinforced by some civil servants. Among military and civilians alike, specialists in communication played a preeminent role: Ahmed Rıza, the leader of the centralist faction among the exiles, began his career as a provincial director of education; among the Young Turk dictatorial triumvirate of 1913-1918, Cemal had been an officer in charge of railroads, Talât a telegraph official. Although a detailed social study of politicians of the Young Turk period remains to be done, it would seem that younger army officers and school teachers were attracted to the centralist Union and Progress movement, whereas other members of the liberal professions (lawyers and physicians) were more strongly represented among the federalist opposition. Each faction included some personages of royal descent—the long-time leader of the federalists was "Prince"

Sabaheddin, a grand-nephew of Abdülhamid; the Unionist grand vezir of 1913-1917 was an Egyptian prince. With the penetration of Unionist organization into the provinces some prominent families of land-owning magnates were drawn into the party. The main branches of the civil service (judiciary, finance, interior) seem to have held aloof from partisan activity. Businessmen were conspicuously absent among both Unionists and federalists, for commercial activity down to the republican period remained largely in the hands of non-Muslims who took little active part in politics.

The career of Talât illustrates the new vistas of social ascent which partisan activity opened up. As a young official in the post and telegraph service before 1908 he had helped to spread the Unionist conspiracy throughout Macedonia. Subsequently he became a member of the House, Minister of the Interior, and Secretary-General of the party; in 1917 he rose to the rank of pasha and grand vezir (i.e. prime minister). The novelty of his career lay not in the rise of a humble man to highest office but in his rise through party organization rather than through the protection of a prominent member of the governing elite. Talât also seems to have been the first politician to be appointed to a ministry without previous experience in the higher public service. It was to be an electrifying example. "After I became Minister," Talât once confided in a friend, "everyone began nursing the same ambition."[10]

The influx of army officers, civilian officials, and professional persons into the political elite which was the chief characteristic of the Young Turk period was further promoted by partisan and governmental action under the Unionist regime, including a purge of older officers in 1913-1914 and the appointment of Union and Progress partisans to provincial governorships and even to the post of Şeyhülislâm. Partisan use of the government's vastly increased powers of economic regulation during the war promoted the rise, for the first time in history, of a Muslim-Turkish business class. Thus Kara Kemal, the much-hated Unionist party chief in Istanbul and Minister of Food, tightly controlled the distribution of bread in the capital. The 1916 annual report of the Unionist party boasts that, through the surcharge of 2 to 3 para per loaf, the "Istanbul city council created a capital fund which enabled it to enter into

[10] Remark to Abdülhak Adnan (Adıvar) quoted in İbnülemin Mahmud Kemal İnal, *Osmanlı Devrinde Son Sadrıazamlar*, Istanbul, 1940-1953, p. 1962.

other commercial ventures" handled through Kara Kemal's Tradesmen's Association.[11]

The calamitous defeat of the Ottoman Empire in the First World War resulted in the eclipse of the Young Turk movement. The most prominent Union and Progress leaders fled the country immediately after the armistice of 1918. Those who stayed behind dissolved the party, hopefully renaming its rump Renewal party. In 1918 and 1919 a great many new parties and associations were founded in Istanbul by anti-Unionists returning from exile or emerging from forced inactivity, by journalists, school teachers, and university professors, by army officers and civil servants—all of them stirred into frenzied activity by the Empire's desperate plight.

But the real renewal took place in the towns of Anatolia and Thrace, especially those most immediately threatened by foreign occupation and annexation. The close timing and the similarity of slogans ("Defense of Rights" and later "Rejection of Annexation") suggested a central impulse; the prominence of Unionists among the leaders indicated its source.[12] In Kars the movement was composed of "local landowners, lawyers, and school teachers, reinforced by some Muslim officers of the former Russian Imperial Army." The Anatolian movement as a whole was characterized by a contemporary as "made up for the most part of military commanders and their staffs, of country notables, and of intellectuals."[13] Over-all coordination was undertaken by Mustafa Kemal (Atatürk), an ex-Unionist who had become one of the few victorious generals in 1914-1918.

As the movement readied itself to assume leadership in the war of independence and to form the de facto government of the coun-

[11] A German translation of the report will be found in *Korrespondenzblatt der Nachrichtenstelle für den Orient*, Vol. 3, No. 2 (21 October 1916), supplement. Ahmed Emin (Yalman) *Turkey in the World War*, New Haven, 1930, p. 125, states that the fund amounted to $1.2 million. Later, Kara Kemal hit upon the even more lucrative scheme of a weekly treasury subsidy for the capital's bread supply in the amount of 140,000 Turkish pounds (*ibid.*, p. 133).

[12] For details see Rustow, "The Army and the Founding of the Turkish Republic," *op.cit.*, pp. 514f. and literature in note 69 of that article. On Kemal's coordination efforts, see *ibid.*, pp. 536ff.

[13] The quotations are from W. E. D. Allen and Paul Muratoff, *Caucasian Battlefields*, Cambridge, Eng., 1953, and from Izzet Pasha, grand vezir in Istanbul in 1918, as quoted in İnal, *op.cit.*, p. 1996.

try, its social image changed significantly. Like any comprehensive-nationalist movement engaged in an anticolonial struggle, the Kemal-ists strove to maximize their appeal to all prominent social groups and to postpone divisive issues. The military character of the na-tionalist leadership and the movement's connection with the dis-credited Union and Progress party were played down; instead, the local roots of the movement in Anatolia and its support among civil servants and religious leaders were prominently displayed. Thus the Representative Committee of August 1919, precursor of the first Kemalist government, consisted of two ex-officers, three former Unionist deputies from prominent Anatolian families, one former governor, one religious shaykh, and one tribal leader. Similarly, the first Ankara cabinets consisted mainly of civilians who had taken a prominent part in non-Unionist or anti-Unionist politics, and fully 17 per cent of the members of the first National Assembly were *ulema*.

The Kemalists' purpose in courting the civilian, local, and re-ligious elements in Anatolia may have been propaganda and even dissimulation; yet the presence of these conservative forces was not without its profound effect on the nationalist movement. The As-sembly of 1920-1923 was the most representative body ever to be selected in Turkey before 1950. The choice of deputies was so hastily improvised at a time of national crisis that Kemal and his followers, with their still embryonic national organization, could do little to influence the Assembly's composition. The sharp debates that ensued in the Ankara parliament bore little resemblance to those in the last Istanbul Houses of Representatives with their Unionist party harmony conjured up in "big-stick" elections. Despite his brilliant military record in the World War, Kemal spent nearly all of his effort during the War of Independence in the fractious, faction-ridden Assembly, assuming command at the front only when the enemy came to within a few miles of Ankara.

THE KEMALIST DICTATORSHIP (1923-1945): PARTY AND BUREAUCRACY

Kemal's political strategy over the next few years was to devise a phased sequence of issues, grouping and regrouping his followers at each turn: military defense of independence (1919-1922), estab-lishment of a new state (1923-1928), legal and cultural reforms (1926-1933), state-sponsored industrialization (1930ff.) If he had announced his total program at the start, he would have stood virtually alone against solid opposition. As it was, he used religious-conservative support to win the War of Independence, the support of liberal modernizers to found the Republic against conservative opposition, and the support of a younger group of professionals and bureaucrats to consolidate his dictatorship over the strenuous objection of the liberals.

The composition of the Grand National Assembly closely reflects the changing power structure within the Turkish government and within Kemal's Republican People's party (RPP)—for, from 1923 to 1946, nomination by the RPP was tantamount to election. A detailed study of the republican legislators by Frederick W. Frey has revealed a number of interesting facets. There were large turnovers in assemblymen in 1923 and 1927, but from 1931 to 1943 roughly two-thirds of the Assembly was renominated in every election. As a result the average age of deputies rose from 43 years in 1920 to 54 years in 1943, and the proportion of deputies born in their constituency conversely went down—from 62 per cent in 1920 to 34 per cent in 1935. The proportion of army officers has declined ever since 1920, that of civil servants increased sharply in 1923 and then gradually declined, that of teachers and professors rose steadily. If the "top leaders" (cabinet ministers, assembly officers, committee chairmen) are considered separately, it appears that public servants—particularly officers and bureaucrats—held an even more prominent position.[14]

In short, as Kemal and his RPP consolidated their dictatorship, the personnel of the regime became stabilized and local influences diminished. Although the party was in control of the state, its leadership ranks were filled largely with civil servants and military officers. The alliance of party, armed forces, and bureaucracy remained intimate throughout the first two decades of the Turkish Republic. The laws that were to be administered by civil servants and upheld by army officers on active duty were drafted by an assembly in which former civil servants and officers held dominant positions. Though the constitution decreed executive responsibility to the legislature, political recruitment patterns subjected the legislature to executive domination.

[14] Compiled (in part calculated) from Frederick W. Frey, *The Turkish Political Elite*, Cambridge, Mass.: The M.I.T. Press, 1965, pp. 161ff.

THE COMPETITIVE PARTY SYSTEM (SINCE 1945): MASS
PARTICIPATION AND SHARPENED ISSUES

Atatürk's party dictatorship continued after his death in 1938 under the leadership of İsmet İnönü, yet a certain loosening was noticeable both in the institutional structure and in governmental personnel. The RPP experimented with an "independent group" within its parliamentary delegation that was allowed to caucus separately; the secondary electors in the constituencies were allowed some limited choice among alternate RPP candidates; former opponents of the regime were restored to parliament and party and some to leading government positions. While the social composition of the assembly changed only slightly, among the "top leaders" the role of ex-army officers declined and that of educators, lawyers, and physicians increased.

These hesitant changes acquired an irresistible momentum when İnönü in the spring of 1945 decided to allow the formation of opposition groups, thus transforming the one-party regime into a democratic, competitive party system. (His decision was prompted in part by the outcome of the war and hopes for Western support against Russia and in part by social unrest due to wartime shortages and profiteering; the respective weight of the two factors is a subject of continuing debate among participants and scholars.) The most successful opposition group, the Democratic party (DP) enrolled many newcomers to the political scene, especially among businessmen, professional persons, and farmers, and it campaigned for a relaxation of government regulation in the economy and a curtailment of Atatürk's secularist reforms. Under the one-party system political activity had been limited to the major cities and elections turned into a perfunctory affair with preordained results. Now the country was stirred into a state of almost continuous political campaign; newspapers, vastly increased in numbers and volume of circulation, engaged in a lively partisan debate; and the "city politicians went to the village in unheard-of numbers, not as petty proconsuls to rule a sullen populace, but as modest visitors to listen to the peasant's grievances and to plead for his vote."[15] Under the new system of direct elections a remarkably high proportion of

[15] Dankwart A. Rustow, "Turkey's Second Try at Democracy," *The Yale Review* (Summer 1963), p. 520. For details of party developments during this period see Kemal H. Karpat, *Turkey's Politics: The Transition to a Multi-Party System*, Princeton: Princeton University Press, 1959.

Turkey's population went to the polls (89 per cent in 1950 and 1954, 77 per cent in 1957), reflecting the intense community spirit of the peasant majority. Although these changes were promoted most actively by the newly founded DP, the RPP thoroughly re-organized itself to meet the new challenge: for example, it moderated its stand on secularism, in 1948 appointed Turkey's first civilian minister of defense, and from 1946 to 1950 opened more local branches than it had in the previous quarter-century.

In their official programs and propaganda the parties tended to state their difference in ideological terms. In organizational and sociological fact the contrast was mainly one between ins and outs, at both the national and local levels. In the capital the DP was founded by RPP members who had been more prominent under Atatürk than İnönü, by younger RPP members whose ambition the party had failed to satisfy, and by lawyers, businessmen, and civil servants who had remained aloof from the RPP. In a given province the leading land-owning clan might continue to support the RPP and its nearest rivals embrace the DP. In a small town the old established quarter would vote RPP, the quarter inhabited by recent migrants for the DP. Ethnic and sectarian differences also came into play. The non-Muslim groups of Istanbul from the start have been staunch DP supporters—the partisan loyalty of the Greeks being unshaken by the Menderes government's role in the 1955 anti-Greek riots. Many of the Kurdish regions went over to the DP in the 1950's. The Alevis (Shiis) in Central Anatolia have re-mained loyal supporters of the RPP, in whose secularism they see a guarantee against Sunni oppression. The tendency toward two-way splits (into what anthropologists call moieties) is strongly engrained in Middle Eastern nomadic and peasant society, although the basis of the split varies from place to place. Pending further empirical study, we may surmise that the two major Turkish parties are nation-wide coalitions of such moieties, the local faction that was dominant in 1945 being the natural supporter of the RPP, its rival of the DP.[16]

The impact of this intense nation-wide party competition on the social composition of parliament has been striking. Among the legis-

[16] On the importance of moieties in the Middle East, see Raphael Patai, "The Middle East as a Culture Area," *Middle East Journal*, Vol. 6, No. 1 (Winter 1952), pp. 1-21, at p. 11. For a specific example of Turkish party division on the local level see Joseph S. Szyliowicz, "The Political Dynamics of Rural Turkey," *ibid.*, Vol. 16, No. 4 (Autumn 1962), and the same author's unpublished Ph.D. thesis (Columbia, 1961), based on a study of Silifke. There is room for many additional studies of Turkish provincial and local politics.

lators the share of civil servants has declined sharply (19 per cent in 1943, 9 per cent in 1954) and that of merchants, farmers, and lawyers has correspondingly increased. Among the top leaders, civil servants have largely held their own, but army officers and educators have been replaced by lawyers, doctors, and engineers and to a lesser extent by farmers and businessmen. It should be noted that the farmers who enter the Assembly are typically well-educated, urbanized owners of large tracts of land who find the transition from estate management to commodity trade and into public affairs easy and natural. The small peasant has been thoroughly activated as a voter but not yet as a candidate for national office.

Menderes' reversion to authoritarian methods in the years after 1953, his overthrow in the 1960 coup, and the interlude of military rule in 1960-1961 interrupted the trend toward democratic party competition but did not halt it. Since 1961 this competition has resumed with redoubled intensity and so have its effects on political participation by ever-wider social groups. "Governmental power in the last two decades has been wielded on behalf of a variety of social groups, and each of these has had its appetites whetted. Farmers want more agricultural development and high prices; businessmen wish to retain their profits and to make the major investment decisions free from government regulation; workers demand guaranteed wages and job security; civil servants look back with nostalgia to the time when a parliament of Kaimakams was the country's unchallenged ruler. To those disillusioned with democracy, the press offers a variety of nostrums from Panturanism and Islamic fundamentalism to fellow-traveling socialism."[17]

Bitterness within the Justice party—the successful claimant of the DP inheritance—over the execution of Menderes sharpens its antagonism toward the RPP and especially the military. Among the latter, some junior officers have indulged their hankering for subversive plots to establish authoritarian reformist regimes, whereas the general staff has served as the protector of the civilian political leaders and occasionally as umpire in their partisan disputes. One striking innovation in Turkish politics is the increasingly active and mature role of organized labor as a pressure group upon all major parties. Another is the prominence of technically trained personnel, signified by Premier Demirel's political apprenticeship not as a party organizer but as the nation's chief water engineer.

[17] Rustow, "Turkey's Second Try at Democracy," *op.cit.*, pp. 535f.

Today, less than one hundred years after six "New Ottomans" on a summer picnic started the first organized political coterie, political parties have become formidable organizations which enlist the support of virtually every adult man and woman in every town and village and which pervade governmental organization and public life at all levels. In this century of growing activity the parties have both shaped and reflected the continuing changes in power structure within Turkish society.

IV. The Dynamics of Parties and Elites in Turkey and the Middle East

To understand the dynamic role of Turkish political parties in the development process it is essential to keep in mind the relation of the parties to major political issues and to prominent social groups. That relation, in Turkey and elsewhere, is always one of interaction, of both cause and effect. Parties, that is to say, are formed in response to issues which the political process confronts, they contribute to resolving—or obstructing and exacerbating—these issues, and they pose new issues. Similarly, parties form among strata already prominent in society and politics, and they provide an instrument for the rise of new groups—or for thwarting their rise. In short, parties must be understood within their political and social context.

The political situation of the Ottoman Empire in the nineteenth century was confused and discouraging. Military reforms had prevented neither defeat nor loss of territory; pronouncements of universal civic equality did not stem the tide of secessionist nationalism; financial reform did not forestall bankruptcy. European statesmen spoke alternately with horror of the "terrible Turk" or with contempt of the "sick man of Europe." The Young Turks' administrative reforms similarly seemed to miscarry. When elections were ordered in parts of the Empire under foreign administration, the final loss of Bosnia, East Rumelia, and Crete resulted; attempts to create schools with a Turkish curriculum and to disarm the hillside tribesmen prompted Albania to rebel and secede; the extension of provincial administration to the Hijaz provoked the Arab revolt; and the ruthless measures taken in response to treasonable Armenian dealings with Russia exacerbated Muslim-Christian relations.[18] The

[18] On developments in Albania see Stavro Skendi, "Albanian Political Thought and Revolutionary Activity, 1881-1912," *Südost-Forschungen*, Vol. 13 (1954), pp. 1-40; on the Hijaz, C. Ernest Dawn, "The Amir of Mecca al-Husayn ibn-ʿAli

liberal constitution, triumphantly restored in 1908, soon gave way to partisan dictatorship; and, worst of all, the reckless entry into the First World War hastened the Empire's total collapse.

The failures of the reformers from Selim III to the Young Turks were due neither to lack of determination nor even to ineptitude. They had set for themselves an impossible task—that of transforming the polyglot, dynastic-religious Empire into a strong, cohesive modern state. In this task neither they nor any other set of leaders could have succeeded. But as heirs to a state that for centuries had been the most powerful and best administered realm since the fall of Rome, they could hardly be blamed for trying. Even as they failed in that larger task, moreover, they were laying the foundations for a more solid and viable nation-state in the Empire's Anatolian rump. Mahmud II reasserted the authority of central government, the Tanzimat created a modern civil and military service based on merit and wide recruitment, the Young Turks' grandiose romantic foreign policy exposed the Empire's fatal weakness more mercilessly and quickly than a cautious policy would have done. The most important legacy of the Ottoman reform efforts was the modernized educational system built from the professional and graduate level down to the high schools and primary grades. It was the products of this education who in the War of Independence turned dismal defeat into Turkey's finest hour.

Turkish political development, despite its many temporary setbacks and difficulties, thus went through a logical and orderly series of overlapping phases: first the reconstruction of central political authority and the creation of a dedicated body of public servants (ca. 1808-1908), then the painful sorting out of the territorial identity of the state and the emergence of a sense of national solidarity within accepted boundaries (ca. 1820-1923), and lastly the progressive involvement of ever larger groups of citizens as active participants in the political process (1908 to the present—and into the foreseeable future).[19]

Within this logical sequence of fruitful tasks political parties came to play an essential and constructive role, particularly in the last

and the Origin of the Arab Revolt," *Proceedings of the American Philosophical Society*, Vol. 104, No. 1 (February 1960), pp. 11-34.

[19] For a more general discussion of the quests for authority and public service, for national identity and unity, and for political participation and equality and of the significance of the sequence of these see my forthcoming study for the Brookings Institution, *The World of Nations*.

phase of broadening participation. The embryonic precursors of the modern parties—the New Ottomans and the early Union and Progress—were small cliques within the bureaucratic-military elite. They began in Istanbul, were forced into exile, but later spread to some of the cities in the more culturally advanced parts of the Empire such as Macedonia and Syria. After 1908 party organization became public, formal, and widespread until it embraced a large part of the educated class—officers, civil servants, lawyers, doctors, teachers, journalists—both in the capital and in the provincial centers. By 1920, party organization spread to the smaller towns where school teachers, administrative officials, and muftis formed the backbone of the Defense of Rights movement. Under the one-party regime of 1923-1945 the dominant position of the central governmental elite (military officers and civil servants) within the party became consolidated. After 1945, lawyers, businessmen, large landowners, and more lately union leaders made their way into the elite, and peasants and industrial workers became active political participants. Violence recurred at various points in this process of development—in contests for control of the central government (1807-1808, 1876, 1908-1913, 1926, 1960), and especially in the struggle for national and territorial identity (the Armenian persecution in 1909 and 1915-1916, the War of Independence 1919-1923, and the Kurdish rebellions of the 1920's and 1930's). Throughout the period of development, however, the widening of the elite and of the circle of political participants proceeded steadily and gradually; there has been so far no tendency to violent social unrest or class revolution.

The other Middle Eastern countries have faced problems of far greater difficulty than those in Turkey, and they have had far slenderer resources at their disposal to solve them. Whereas the Turkish Republic could look back on an Ottoman governmental tradition of more than half a millennium, the Arab countries had had no experience in political responsibility for a thousand years. Whereas Turkey preserved her independence, all the Arab countries (except Yemen and Saudi Arabia) came under European domination. Imperialism came to the area at a time when Western thought had come to consider colonial rule at best a "white man's burden" and at worst a cause of guilt and bad conscience. The system of "temporary occupation" (Egypt, 1882—the last "temporary" units being withdrawn 74 years later), "mandates" (Fertile Crescent,

1920), "protectorates" (Tunisia, 1881; Morocco, 1912), "preferential treaties" (Iraq, 1930; Egypt, 1936) has aptly been described as a "half-hearted, pussy-footing imperialism . . . an imperialism of interference without responsibility, which would neither create nor permit stable and orderly government."[20] This form of imperialist interference, moreover, reached its height after the political elites of the Middle East had been thoroughly imbued with Western ideas of liberal constitutionalism. (Egypt was occupied in 1882 after an army revolt tried to impose parliamentary controls on the Khedive's spending; Britain and Russia agreed to divide Iran into spheres of interest in 1907 just after Iran had adopted its representative constitution; and the French in 1920 established their mandate after bombarding Damascus, where a national assembly had just proclaimed an independent constitutional king of Syria.) Most of the Middle Eastern countries had been ruled by conquest and violence throughout history. The experience of this period seemed to show that Western liberal ideas were not for export, that in the Middle East at least Westerners themselves relied on force and on threat rather than on law and persuasion.

The withdrawal of Western domination also came in response to force—the strains of World War II, violent uprisings or guerrilla fighting in Palestine, Egypt, Algeria. Where a narrow oligarchic group accommodated itself to the foreign power the transition at first was smoother—only to be followed by the revolutionary overthrow of these regimes (Egypt 1952, Iraq 1958) or violent challenges to the old order (Jordan 1955). Force thus has remained a major instrument of domestic politics, and in most Arab countries the armies—as specialists in violence—have been the major powers on the political scene.[21]

The Arab successor states of the Ottoman Empire began their careers with a severe shortage of trained military, political, and administrative leaders. Among the graduates of the Ottoman civil service school who lived in 1920 only 15 per cent went to Syria or Iraq, of the graduates of the military college as few as 7 per cent. At a time when generals and colonels in the Ottoman army were organizing the Turkish War of Independence and founding the

[20] Bernard Lewis, "Democracy in the Middle East," *Middle Eastern Affairs*, Vol. 6 (April 1955), p. 105. Cf. the same author's *The Middle East and the West*, Bloomington: Indiana University Press, 1964, p. 59.

[21] See D. A. Rustow in Sydney N. Fisher, ed., *The Military in the Middle East*, Columbus: Ohio State University Press, 1963, pp. 3-20.

Republic former Ottoman captains and lieutenants were trying to create new states in the Arab-Ottoman territories under the shadow of British domination.

Whereas Turkey has a well-balanced assortment of agricultural and mineral resources, some of the other countries face desperate economic problems. Although Egypt has moved toward industrialization for over a century, there are no mineral deposits of importance and there is virtually no rain. Agriculture therefore is strictly limited to the narrow strip of land over which the waters of the Nile can be made to spread in the middle of the desert. Within these inexorable limitations of resources a staggering rate of population increase has in recent years threatened a decline of per capita income despite the most strenuous development efforts. The rich petroleum deposits are mostly in arid countries (Saudi Arabia, Kuwait, Libya) that lack agricultural resources and advanced social organization for economic development. Only Iran, Iraq, and Algeria combine petroleum income with other essentials of development.

The most serious political problem for the Arab countries has been the uncertainty of national identity—the contrary impulses for preservation of existing states or for merger under a variety of possible formulas for unity. This question has absorbed a staggering amount of political energies, particularly in Egypt and the Fertile Crescent countries. Because of the maldistribution of economic and human resources (the most advanced country having the bleakest economic prospects, the most primitive areas having the greatest petroleum wealth), no Prussia or Piedmont has yet emerged and the problem of unification is likely to remain insoluble for some time.

Within this historical and social setting, party development in most Arab countries and in Iran has not merely lagged half a century behind Turkey; it has also been stunted, thwarted, and diverted into conspiracy and violence. Political organization among young intellectuals in Syria began only in the second decade of this century. In Egypt there was the shortlived National party of Mustafa Kamil (1897-1907) and the Wafd (1918-1952). Both groups were frustrated in their aims by the British occupation and the royal palace. The Wafd began as a comprehensive-nationalist party, but it soon lost its nationalist momentum, yielded to a British ultimatum in 1924, supported the British treaty of 1936, and meanwhile was transformed into an exploitive, corrupt patronage organization. (In the Maghrib, on the other hand, comprehensive-nationalist movements have formed along lines familiar from other ex-colonial countries.)

A more common type of Middle Eastern party has been characterized by groups that are little more than shifting cliques in an oligarchy, held together for a time by fickle loyalties to a particular leader, and easily dissolved by government decree. Such groups emerged in Egypt during periods of royal rule, in Iraq until 1958, and in Iran before the advent of the National Front in 1952.

The National Front and especially the Ba'th party in the Fertile Crescent countries represent a different type of party, with a wide potential of popular support and a clear program. The National Front was suppressed in 1953 and now faces serious competition from the Shah's reform program. The Ba'th has continued to spread its organization from Syria into Iraq and Jordan, but it is perforce involved in the frustrating question of Arab unification on the international scene. Within each of the countries it must contend for power less by parliamentary and electoral methods than by the prevalent techniques of intrigue and violence. In Egypt the Nasser regime has made several half-hearted attempts at founding a government party, but repeated failures indicate that the regime can survive by relying for contact with the populace on such instruments as bureaucracy and police rather than on any party.

Turkey has inherited an ancient political tradition which in the last century and a half brought about an orderly sequence of the major tasks of political development—the quests for public authority, for national identity, and for civic participation. In the Arab countries no early solution to the problem of national identity is in sight, public authority still is precarious, political personnel often still untrained and inexperienced—and this at a time when there is general impatience for political participation by the masses. This historical and social contrast amply accounts for the differences in party development.

V. The Outlook for Turkey: A Test for Democracy in Developing Countries

There is some question whether Turkish political developments will proceed as smoothly and in as much internal peace as they have in the past. To vary the earlier metaphor of systole and diastole, the successive expansion of the political elite in Turkey may be likened to the downward penetration of successive geological layers. Within the softer and more uniform layers the penetration has proceeded smoothly. In the Tanzimat period the new Westernized elite was limited mainly to bureaucrats and military officers; in the Young Turk and Kemalist eras it came to include a growing urban educated class; and in the first democratic period (1945-1960) some of the wealthier rural elements were added. But between times, as harder layers were reached, the movement was first arrested, as by Abdülhamid's despotism and by the party dictatorships of the Young Turks, of Kemal, and of Menderes; at length it broke through, often with violent force, as in the crises of 1908-1909, 1919-1923, and 1960-1961.

There are several hopeful indications of further progress toward political equality and toleration, of a strengthening of democracy and constitutionalism. Menderes' authoritarianism was overthrown in good time by a military regime which, in sharp contrast to most other military juntas throughout the world, restored democracy on a firm constitutional basis after only seventeen months. Since 1961 ideological issues and social contrasts can be fought out that had always been taboo in the past: socialism vs. liberalism, Sunni vs. Alevi Islam, ethnic divisions among Turks and Kurds, land reform, economic redistribution through taxes, workers' rights, and many others. The trade unions, keenly conscious of their newly enhanced power, are displaying their political maturity and building up their internal organization by keeping aloof from the more sterile ideological disputes and the more partisan political quarrels. The growing stream of Turkish industrial workers who go for a few years to West Germany or other European countries for the first time brings members of the lower classes into direct and intensive cultural contact with the West; the political and social influence of these workers upon their return is likely to be enormous. The business community, while pressing for political and economic advantage with all financial and propaganda resources at its disposal, also is beginning to show a new sense of social responsibility in sponsoring research, in philanthropy, and in other civic activity. Village communities are raising private funds so as to obtain priority in the government's school expansion program. In the government itself the coalition cabinets of the Second Republic have given Turkish politicians their first experience in the novel arts of public negotiation and compromise. Finally, all these new tendencies are at work in a setting where specialists in all spheres of economic and political life—economic planners and government administrators, industrial managers and union organizers, university teachers and engineers—are attaining levels of technical competence that are now fully up to international standards, equivalent, for example, to those of southern or eastern Europe.

But there also are opposite, more ominous indications. The wholesale and vociferous airing of pent-up issues is creating an atmosphere of overexpectancy, of spurious excitement, of resentful impatience. The pressing of group demands for advantages in consumption may well slow down the pace of development in production and investment. The commitment to constitutionalism and democracy, which in the past has been well-nigh universal in principle, is now being challenged by a few scattered but strident voices. Neither the Young Turks nor with few exceptions the Kemalists offered any apologia for authoritarianism as such; rather they pleaded the exigencies of national defense or of rapid modernization in their temporary abrogation of constitutional practice. Even Menderes justified his most repressive measures by invoking not only religious symbols but also a theory of unrestrained majoritarianism. Now, however, some impatient military officers (e.g. those expelled from the military junta in November 1960, and those responsible for the abortive coups of February 1962 and May 1963) and some doctrinaire university professors recently rallied to the Turkish Labor Party openly reject party competition and elections as detrimental to the needs of a developing country. It should be kept in mind that any repressive political regime is likely to be more ruthless the higher the level of social organization and the greater the degree of political freedom and participation previously attained. A dictatorship by Alparslan Türkeş in 1960 or by Talât Aydemir in 1962-1963[22] if it had managed to install and keep itself in power would have been far more draconian than was that by Mustafa Kemal in 1923-1938, by Enver Pasha in 1913-1918, or even by Menderes in 1954-1960. Although Türkeş's and Aydemir's bids for power failed, it is far too soon to assume that all such dangers have been weathered.

It seems clear that the latest phase in Turkey's crisis of political participation—the phase that opened in 1960-1961—is also the grav-

[22] On these figures see the two studies by Walter F. Weiker, *The Turkish Revolution 1960-1961*, Washington, D.C., 1962, esp. pp. 125-127; and "The Aydemir Case," *Middle Eastern Affairs*, Vol. 14, No. 8 (October 1963), pp. 258-271.

est; that the geological layer now reached will be the hardest to pierce and penetrate. For what is now at stake is not just a restructuring of a limited political elite; rather the issue now is no less than the admission to full political participation of the lower classes in the cities and of the peasant masses in the Anatolian villages—in short, the breaking of the power monopoly held by the urban educated class since classical Ottoman days. This task must be accomplished even while administrative efficiency must be improved, population growth restrained, and current consumption balanced against the needs for expanded investment. Turkey is fortunate in having restored, by 1965, a clear two-party alignment and a vigorous governmental leadership. There is no doubt however that the social crisis of the 1960's will continue to provide severe tests for the technical competence and the political imagination and integrity of these new leaders.

Western ideas of constitutionalism and representation were naturalized in Turkey by the New Ottomans and Young Turks who as exiles in Europe espoused liberalism and nationalism at a time when their fellow exiles from Russia became anarchists, communists, and revolutionaries.[23] After the First World War Atatürk erected a national republic based on Western legal and parliamentary institutions at a time when the Bolsheviks proclaimed their ruthless dictatorship of the proletariat. The fuller realization of the democratic principles implicit in Kemal's program was attempted under İnönü after 1945 and again under Gürsel and İnönü after 1960. "Pour découvrir les meilleures règles de société qui conviennent aux nations," Rousseau wrote in the *Contrat Social*,[24] "il faudroit une intelligence supérieure . . . qui, dans le progrès des temps se ménageant une gloire éloignée, pût travailler dans un siècle pour jouir dans un autre." Only the actions of the next several generations of Turkish rulers and citizens can determine whether representative institutions will truly have taken root in their country and whether Atatürk's experiment of tutelage and gradualism will go down in history as a success or as a failure. Since Turkey, among all non-European countries, has been one of those most solidly committed to Western political ideas and traditions, the outcome of the experiment will be of the most profound interest to democrats and dictators throughout the world.

[23] On the contrast between the two exile movements, see my essay "The Appeal of Communism to Islamic Peoples," in J. Harris Proctor, ed., *Islam and International Relations*, New York, Praeger, 1965, pp. 42ff.

[24] Book II, Ch. 7.

Part II: Party Systems and their Transformation

CHAPTER 5

EUROPEAN POLITICAL PARTIES:
THE CASE OF POLARIZED PLURALISM

GIOVANNI SARTORI[*]

I. Varieties of Multipartism

IT IS usually assumed that Western-type party systems follow one of two patterns; namely, the two-party and the multi-party; and the usual implied assumption is that the whole spectrum of party pluralism can be covered with a dichotomous *Gestalt*, by using a model essentially based on paired alternatives: Left-Right, majority-opposition, movement-status quo, and the like. In this mood Duverger has gone as far as to suggest a sort of natural law of politics; for according to him dualism is "natural," and while one does not always find a two-party system one almost always finds, all over the world, "a dualism of tendencies."[1]

I shall challenge both assumptions. From a descriptive point of view we are confronted in Western free Europe not with two but with three types of party systems: simple two-party pluralism, moderate pluralism, and extreme pluralism. Moreover, the important dividing line is not so much that between the first and second, but that between the second and third, that is, between moderate pluralism and extreme pluralism. My first point is, then, that we usually misplace the essential border and that it is wrong to deal with multipartism as a single category; for there is a world of difference between the bipolar pattern of moderate pluralism and the multipolar features of extreme pluralism.[2]

This difference has been blurred by the fact that we have been extrapolating a dualistic model far beyond its range of application.

[*] I am pleased to record my gratitude to Joseph LaPalombara for his invaluable assistance in revising and editing this manuscript.

[1] M. Duverger, *Les Partis Politiques*, Paris: Armand Colin, 1954, e.g. p. 245. The dualistic blinkers lead Duverger to astonishing approaches, as when he finds that the two countries in continental Europe which currently "show a marked tendency towards bipartism" are Germany and Italy (p. 241). Actually the German and Italian patterns are the very opposite of one another.

[2] For the over-all typology to which I shall make reference, and for the broad explanatory context, cf. G. Sartori, *Parties and Party Systems*, New York, Harper and Row, forthcoming (1967).

Present-day Western Germany, the Scandinavian democracies, Switzerland, Austria, Belgium, and some other "small democracy" may still be interpreted by means of a dualistic approach (with some additional sophistication). But when we come to the French Fourth Republic, to Italy, or to the Weimar Republic, this is no longer the case. That is to say that a dichotomous *Gestalt* cannot account for the case of extreme pluralism. My second point is, then, that we need another model.

Perhaps the simplest way of illustrating the framework that I shall use is to clarify my terminology by reference to the following table:

TABLE 1: TYPES OF EUROPEAN PARTY SYSTEMS
AND CRITERIA OF ANALYSIS

Party Systems	Poles	Polarity	Drives
Simple pluralism	bipolar	none	centripetal
Moderate pluralism	bipolar	small	centripetal
Extreme pluralism	multipolar	polarized	centrifugal

By *bipolar* I mean that the actual working of the party system pivots around two poles (no matter whether the parties are two, three, or four); for in this case the system has no "center," no center pole. By *multipolar* I mean that the party system pivots upon more than two poles, for in this case the system has a "center."

What matters, however, is not only the number of the poles but the distance between them. When the spectrum of political opinion is extremized, that is, when the Right and Left poles of a political system are literally "two poles apart," then I shall say that the system has polarity, i.e. that we are confronted with a *polarized* party system. Lest there be any doubt,[3] I emphasize that I am using "polarized" as an indicator of distance, and precisely to indicate a situation of lack of basic consensus[4] in which the distribution of opin-

[3] In the wake of Duverger's usage or—I would say—misuse; for he employs "polarization" merely to mean "bipolar"; cf. *Les Partis Politiques*, p. 279. In current usage "polarity" and "polarized" convey the idea of two things which are symmetrically opposed, or have contrary qualities; i.e., they imply an idea of either extreme distance or strong opposition. And these are precisely the properties which do not belong to the two-party systems, which are bipolar but *not* polarized.

[4] Basic consensus is not the consensus at the level of government (or the authorities), but the congruence of basic orientations—especially values and attitudes—at the level of regime and/or of the political community. Cf. D. Easton, R. D. Hess, "Youth and the Political System," in Lipset and Lowenthal, eds., *Culture and Social Character*, Glencoe, Ill.: The Free Press, 1961, pp. 229-237.

ions covers the maximum conceivable distance; and that the term does not necessarily imply that the cleavage is particularly *intense*, for the intensity of a cleavage may decrease and the cleavage (i.e. the distance between the poles) remain: there is no necessary synchronism between the two occurrences.

Finally, one must take into account the drives of the polity. The bipolar systems tend to converge toward the center and are therefore *centripetal*; the multipolar polarized systems tend to be *centrifugal*: they have a center pole, but no centrality, no centripetal drive. If a polity, besides lacking centrality, also displays a centrifugal trend— i.e. a process which is one of growing radicalization—then we may say that polarization prevails over depolarization. When the drive of a political system is centripetal one finds moderate politics, while immoderate or extremist politics reflects the prevalence of centrifugal drives.

In short, I shall analyze party systems according to the number of poles, the distance between their poles, and the centripetal or centrifugal drives resulting from their interactions. Thus "bipolar" and "multipolar" indicate how many are the pivotal points of the system; "polarity" and "polarized" are used as indicators of strong distance; and "polarization" and "depolarization" are defined dynamically to mean a centrifugal process toward disruption of basic consensus and, vice versa, a centripetal process toward reunification of basic consensus. According to the foregoing terminology, simple pluralism, i.e., the English two-party kind of system, is bipolar and not polarized; moderate pluralism, i.e., the systems which operate on a three-four party basis is bipolar and centripetal;[5] whereas extreme pluralism is multipolar, polarized, and also likely to be centrifugal.

My basic suggestion is, then, that the traditional distinction between two-party and multiparty systems could be fruitfully replaced by a model-oriented distinction between bipolar and multipolar party systems which, first, accounts for the positioning and pattern of

[5] Let it be clear that party numbers cannot be taken at their face value; they must be interpreted. A party system does not acquire different properties simply because some splinter party may happen to win a few seats, or because of the existence of very small marginal parties which play no significant role. Thus I consider Sweden, Norway, Denmark, and Switzerland as belonging to the pattern of moderate pluralism, together with Western Germany, Austria, and Belgium. It is true that the full number of parties of the first group of countries which are represented in the legislatures is five or six; nonetheless all these countries display no significant polarization, no anti-system party, and the actual working of the political system remains based on a bipolar alignment of three-four parties.

interaction of the parties (regardless of their number), and, second, breaks down the undifferentiated category of the multiparty systems. And my specific concern with the polarized polities is explained by the obvious reason that, while the working of both the simple and moderate party systems which can be explained by a dualistic model is fairly well known, little is actually known about the mechanisms of the multipolar and extreme type of party system for which we have as yet no satisfactory model.

It will be necessary to start from a concrete illustration, and for this purpose the present-day Italian political system deserves a special hearing. Not only is it less familiar than the commonly cited examples, France and the Weimar Republic, but it is also a purer and more significant illustration in the sense that the Italian experience has been disturbed by neither external nor exceptional intervening variables.[6]

II. The Italian Pattern

THE POLES OF THE SYSTEM

That present-day Italy qualifies as a multipolar polarized system can be easily seen by a perusal of Chart 1. The relevant parties (including the very small but very influential Republican party) which have been running for office from the general election of 1948 to 1963—during four legislatures—have numbered eight: Communist (PCI), Socialist (PSI), Social Democratic (PSDI), Republican (PRI), Christian Democratic (DC), Liberal (PLI), Monarchist, Neofascist (MSI).[7] The Chart shows their electoral support in the general election of April 1963 with reference to the Chamber of Deputies. (The figures are very similar with reference to the Upper House.)

The very number of the durable parties already suggests that we are far beyond the threshold of the bipolar systems and well into the realm of the multipolar ones; and the polarity of the spectrum, with a 25 per cent Communist vote on the extreme left and a Fascist party on the extreme right, is self-evident. The spectrum shows a highly dispersed distribution and covers—in terms of political cleavage—all the possible distance.

---

[6] Such as the French crisis of decolonization and the German crisis of unemployment. In this latter connection cf. K. D. Bracher's interpretation, *Die Aufloesung der Weimarer Republik; Eine Studie zum Problem des Machtverfalls in der Demokratie*, Stuttgart: Ring-Verlag, 1957.

[7] The total number of parties running for office in the Italian general elections of 1963 was actually 26.

Chart 1. Percentage of the total vote cast in the 1963 elections
for the Chamber of Deputies, by party

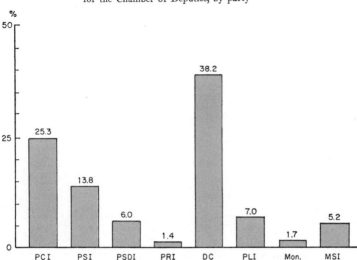

The next question is: What about polarization? That is, over the course of time have the centrifugal drives prevailed over the centripetal appeal? As Chart 2 shows, during the last 15 years the centrifugal tendencies have, if anything, become stronger. There has been an over-all general shift to the left, but the most salient features are: first and foremost, the trend toward a weakening of the center (the Christian Democratic Party has lost from 1948 to 1963 ten percentage points); secondly, the consistent growth of the Communist party (apparently at the expense of Nenni's Socialists); thirdly, that the other extreme pole, or the polarization on the right, the MSI, appears fairly stabilized. Since these trends are not sufficiently counteracted by the progress which has been made in 1963 both by the moderate left (the Social Democrats) and by the moderate right (the Liberals), one is bound to conclude that—despite the very high degree of existing polarity—the Italian trend has been one of polarization rather than depolarization,[8] a conclusion

[8] I shall refer only in passing to the developments which have followed the general elections of 1963 for I am concerned with trends, and it is still too soon to predict the final outcome of the "Opening to the Left" and its bearing on the next general elections. It should be noted, however, that the foregoing diagnosis is apparently confirmed by the split, in January 1964, within the PSI, whose maximalist wing left Nenni's Socialist party and created PSIUP—a party of Marxist orthodoxy which tends to place itself to the left of the Communist party. When the split occurred, 25

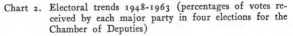

Chart 2. Electoral trends 1948-1963 (percentages of votes received by each major party in four elections for the Chamber of Deputies)

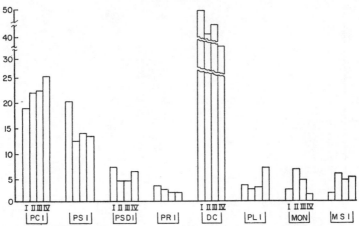

The Roman numbers indicate the legislatures: 1st legislature 1948-53; 2nd legislature 1953-58; 3rd legislature 1958-63; 4th legislature 1963———. The percentages of each party at the four general elections have been: PCI 19.0 (1946), 22.6, 22.7, 25.3; PSI 20.7 (1946), 12.8, 14.2, 13.8; PSDI 7.1, 4.5, 4.5, 6.0; PRI 2.5, 1.6, 1.4, 1.4; DC 48.5, 40.1, 42.4, 38.2; PLI 3.8, 3.0, 3.5, 7.0; Monarchists 2.8, 6.9, 4.9, 1.7; MSI 2.0, 5.8, 4.8, 5.2. The initial percentages of the Communist and Socialist parties are brought back to 1946 (the elections to the Constituent Assembly) because in 1948 the two parties presented a common "popular front" list.

confirmed by the fact that even the parties located in the central area of the spectrum have displayed a centrifugal tendency.

This being the general picture, let us turn to the significant details, beginning with the cleavages. In Italy ethnic and regional cleavages are not relevant at the level of national policy making. There are only two very small ethnic regional parties: the Südtiroler Volkspartei, which elects three German-speaking deputies in Alto Adige, and the Union Valdotaine, which elects one deputy in Val d'Aosta. Some parties are stronger in the North, others in the South,

---

of PSI's national deputies left the party; in subsequent local elections through the end of 1965 one-fourth of PSI's previous electorate supported the new group. It appears therefore that with the center-left governments the polarity of the over-all spectrum has not diminished, and that the centripetal convergence of the PSI has been counteracted by a centrifugal loss. Let it be added that the emergence of the PSIUP, a purely ideological and principled type of party, certainly does not conform to the "decline of ideology" interpretations (see *infra*, section 3).

but the only party which had a definite regional backing (the Monarchists, a typically southern party) is now in the process of disintegrating.

There is no conflict between religions, such as we find for instance in Holland: Italians are all Catholics. There is, however, a religious cleavage between church and state, and perhaps in no Western country as much as in Italy the problem of the place of the church in the society remains a burning issue. The DC is resented as being the "priest's party," and in Italy no less than in France governmental coalitions are blocked—and fall apart—on the traditional issue of state subsidies to private schools (which actually are church schools). However, the comparison with the French cleavage cannot be pushed too far. There are indeed basic differences: that the French MRP is not the leading party of the system, that the French Catholic party is definitely less clerical-minded than its Italian equivalent, and that the Vatican sits in Rome, not in Paris.

Therefore the Italian case cannot be understood in terms of principled or abstract anticlericalism. This is a side issue. What matters more is the very concrete fact that Italians have been ruled since 1948 by a predominant Catholic party[9] that receives a great deal of overt electoral support from the clergy, that would never dare defy a veto of the Vatican, and that permits a very consistent amount of daily church interference at all levels. It is, then, the overbearing and tiresome daily presence of the DC which produces, by way of reaction, a very definite cleavage between Catholic and laical policy orientation, a cleavage which deeply affects the recruitment of political leadership and accounts for many of the paralyzing complications of the party system.

The first consequence of this state of affairs is, then, that Christian Democracy attracts wide electoral support but poor and very inadequate leadership. The DC has more posts than it has competent people to fill them. Its basis for recruitment is indeed narrow[10] for

[9] Let it be pointed out that while the DC is a predominant party, the Italian party system is not a predominant party system. (See the overall classification of party systems in my *Parties and Party Systems, op.cit.*) The only instance, in Europe, of a predominant party system from the end of World War II to 1965 has been Norway.

[10] The major channel being Catholic Action. [E.g. 85 per cent of the DC's members of parliament comes from religious organizations—in substance A.C.I. and/or F.U.C.I. (Catholic University Students Federation): cf. G. Sartori, ed., *Il Parlamento Italiano 1946-1963*, Naples: ESI, 1963, p. 104.] For the shortcomings see G. Poggi, *Il Clero di Riserva*, Milan: Feltrinelli, 1964, *passim*, whose conclusions on the severe drawbacks of the clergy's strict control over the laical

it is open only to the non-secular, or at any rate less secular elements of the society, and otherwise to opportunists who are willing to display religious zeal. Thus a large majority of the intellectuals and of the potential political elites, are either bitterly and radically opposed to the Catholic regime (and eventually sidetracked into the ranks of the Communist party) or not put to use at all.

The second unfortunate consequence of the predominance of a denominational party is that the alignment of the Italian parties reproduces confessional and laical versions of essentially the same political platform. The DC aggregates in one direction—in the sense that it manages to cover, with a multiple appeal, a left, a center, and a right platform—but disintegrates in another direction: for its right wing is resisted by a laical right, and its left wing is equally resisted by the reaction of a secularized left. In the final analysis the DC displays an infelicitous mixture of political polivalency and religious narrow-mindedness, thereby combining the drawbacks of both. The possible brokerage benefits of the DC's flexibility are frustrated by its denominational rigidity, and the net result is that the DC manages to complicate rather than to simplify the party system.

If the Christian Democratic party is the major pole of the Italian party system, the other decisive pole is the Communist party (PCI). The strength of the Italian Communist party is revealed not only by the figures, which place it second, with one-fourth of the total vote; it also is revealed by the fact that the PCI finds a backing among intellectuals, that it attracts the alienated secularized political elites, and that it controls the major worker's union (the C.G.I.L.). Last but not least, the Communist potential for control over the neighboring Socialist party, the PSI, remains strong—this being another distinctive difference between the Italian and the French cases.

The rather obvious socio-economic generalizations which attempt to explain Communist success in countries such as Italy lose much of their significance if the data can be adequately analyzed. Workers in general may well be inclined to vote Communist, but one finds that in some cases this is true only for the low wage earners while in other cases the Communist vote is provided by the highest-paid workers. Regions with high income have either a low or a high Com-

---

Catholic militant implicitly apply to the DC's leadership. For the Catholic Action relationships to the Italian legislature and bureaucracy see J. LaPalombara, *Interest Groups in Italian Politics*, Princeton: Princeton University Press, 1964, Chs. 7-9.

munist turnout. At times a rapid increase in the standard of living breaks Communist allegiance, but in other instances it does not affect it in the least. Moreover, the voting behavior of rural areas defies economic explanations. My own feeling is that the tremendous effort we are making at socio-economic fact-finding is somewhat wasted because we underplay the impact of a crucial variable, namely, of the organizational incapsulation and cultural saturation that a Communist network is capable of producing. Marxist ideology is in itself a formidable communication stopper, for its preliminary tenet is precisely that any external information is untrue, capitalistically biased, and falsified by bourgeois class interest. Thus a stable Communist orientation is closely related to the ability of the party's organizational network to produce a culturally manipulated isolation of given social groups in given areas. This is indeed the key for understanding the success of Communist proselytism. Our socioeconomic data do not fit in any coherent pattern because we lack an organizational map of the physical presence of a Communist network. But the data would fit nicely, I believe, if we devised some index of organizational pressure, and thereby of the cultural and ideological impermeability which it entails.[11]

One can hardly account, for instance, for the success of the Italian Communist party if one forgets that an organizational network requires money, and that the PCI's budget is able to provide that money. Estimates of Communist expenditures in Italy range from a minimum of 12 billion lire to a maximum of 30 billion lire per year.[12] I am inclined to believe that the second estimate is more realistic than the first,[13] but for the sake of compromise let us say

[11] Of course the organizational variable accounts for the magnitude and the lasting success of Communism, not for its existence. For other variables see Erik Allardt's perceptive analysis of Finnish Communism (which provides very challenging comparative queries) in Allardt and Littunen, eds., *Cleavages, Ideologies and Party Systems*, Helsinki: The Academic Bookstore, 1964, pp. 78ff. and 97ff. See also Allardt, "Social Sources of Finnish Communism: Traditional and Emerging Radicalism," in *International Journal of Comparative Sociology*, Vol. 5, No. 1 (1964), pp. 47-70.

[12] The first figure is accepted by Stefano Passigli, "Comparative Political Finance: Italy," in *Journal of Politics*, Vol. 3 (1963), pp. 721-723. A more analytical probing of the PCI's finances is to be found, however, in the review *Il Borghese*, Supplement to Number 49, December 1961, whose estimates rise to 13.5 billion lire. The second figure has been indicated by Seniga (a high echelon ex-Communist), and is also the estimate of Luigi Barzini, Jr., *I Comunisti Non Hanno Vinto*, Milan: Mondadori, 1955, pp. 59-65.

[13] The 12-13 billion lire estimate is actually drawn from a probing of the PCI's party expenditures, while the 30 billion lire estimate is drawn from a probing of the PCI's income, that is, with reference to the party's very large business side-

that the PCI can rely on about 20 billion lire (something less than 33 million dollars).[14] In any case the amount is formidable, especially if one considers that according to current appraisals the DC does not manage to collect in the interelection periods more than half of the amount collected by the PCI, and that all the other parties are by comparison penniless. As for the manpower requirement of an organ-izational machine, it has recently been estimated that out of ap-proximately 20,000-21,000 party employees and professional pol-iticians operating in Italy, more than half, precisely 12,000, belong to the Communist party.[15] With reference to this impressionistic but nonetheless impressive evidence, which indicates that the PCI may more or less equal all the other seven parties put together (in terms of both financial strength[16] and active organizational manpower), it is astonishing that nobody has given much thought to an organiza-tional map as a critical research variable.

The organizational hypothesis seems to be at odds with the fact that while the Italian Communist party has been consistently gaining votes it has also been consistently losing members.[17] However, if one

---

lines (such as the import-export companies which have monopolized the transactions with the East, and the "Cooperative Societies"). To give just one telling example, according to the official figures in 1958 the Communist "Federazione Reggiana delle Cooperative" in the town of Reggio Emilia had 16,000 employees, a working capital of 12 billion lire, and transactions amounting to 32 billion lire. And the over-all network of Cooperative Societies declared in 1960 a volume of business of more than 230 billion lire, more than 370 million dollars (Cf. Table 3 of the statement presented to the 1962 Congress of the "Lega delle Cooperative"). It is from this latter perspective that Barzini reports that "even the Communists are prepared to admit that the commercial cost of all the activities can easily rise to 20-25 billion lire" per year (op.cit., p. 59).

[14] This is also the recent estimate of another ex-Communist, who writes that "according to my direct sources the budget [of the PCI] ranges about 20 billions"; G. Averardi, "La Macchina dei Partiti," in Critica d'Oggi, Vols. 7-8 (1962), p. 21.

[15] Marco Cesarini, L'Uomo Politico, Florence: Vallecchi, 1963, pp. 29-31. Ac-cording to the official data of the PCI, at its IX Congress in 1960 the 113 Federa-tions (plus the central office in Rome) had about 6,000 functionaries, and the number of militant members holding party offices at the local level ranged from 33,000 to 55,000; cf. Tempi Moderni, Vol. I, (1960), pp. 3-42.

[16] While the figures are indeed controversial, the statement that the PCI may well equal all the other parties on a one-to-one ratio makes all the more sense if one recalls that, while the PCI leaders actually spend the money for the party, the leaders of the other parties are very much inclined to employ (and waste) their funds on intra-factional strife.

[17] According to the latest official PCI data (cf. Berlinguer, in Critica Marxista, V-VI, 1963) during the last ten years, from 1954 to 1963, the party members have fallen from 2,145,000 to 1,615,000 and the junior affiliates ("Federazione Giovanile") have fallen from 430,000 to 172,000, with a total loss of 800,000 members. Thus the Communist ratio between voters and members has been 2:8 in 1953, 3:6 in 1958, and 4:8 in 1963. Vice versa, the DC's trend has been to acquire

recalls the dual nature of Communist organization—a party of elite with mass following—and of the distinction between "party" and "movement," this development is hardly surprising, and there is no contradiction in the fact that a Communist party may have less members qua party and more votes qua mass movement. Therefore the expectation that if a Communist party loses membership it will also lose votes is unwarranted whenever the party remains strong enough —in terms of active organizational manpower—to keep the movement going.

Let it be added that the Italian Communist party is also the greatest political employer in the country for all those posts which are below the level of the national government; it is solidly in power in about 1,200 municipalities, including many of the large cities.[18] In this sense it is hardly a party confined to sterile opposition. Quite on the contrary, it has the best trained group of civic administrators in the country, and one could say that the PCI has all the power that it needs below the threshold at which power corrupts. Finally, since the PCI is, on the one hand, a wealthy party with very large business ramifications, while it also controls, on the other hand, the largest trade union, it is the most efficient clientele-based or patronage party in Italy for the workers. And both as business entrepreneurs and as civic administrators the Communists are efficient, realistic, and they pay off.[19]

We thus come to the uncomfortable paradox that the Communist party would make for an excellent opposition if it were an opposition, i.e., a possible alternative government. But since it would replace the system as well as the people, the net result is that the country is deprived of its best potential elites—which fall under the Communist pole of attraction—and cannot really profit from the mechanism of alternation to power. On both accounts the working of the polity is paralyzed to a very large extent.

---

members and to lose voters (the 1963 ratio between members and voters being 7:3). Moreover no correlation appears to exist in the constituencies between the size of party membership and voting turnout; cf. *Tempi Moderni*, Vol. 13 (1963), pp. 99-105. Therefore, even though for different reasons, the data of both the PCI and the DC seem to indicate that mere membership is not a significant variable.

[18] In the local elections of 1960, in the communes having more than 10,000 inhabitants the PCI elected 4,867 city counselors (as against 13,433 elected by all the other parties). Cf. A. Spreafico and J. LaPalombara, eds., *Elezioni e Comportamento Politico in Italia*, Milan: Comunità, 1963, pp. 956, 958.

[19] For additional information, see G. Braga, *Il Comunismo tra gli Italiani*, Milan: Comunità, 1956, who presents a number of interesting maps; and G. Galli, *Storia del Partito Comunista Italiano*, 2nd ed. Milan: Schwarz, 1959, which is a valuable historical introduction.

THE COMPLICATIONS OF THE SYSTEM

Since the underlying logic of the Italian policy-makers is to keep the polity going in a situation in which the very survival of the political system is at stake—as the electoral margins clearly show—it is proper to take a "defense of the system" outlook and to arrange the party spectrum accordingly by dividing the Italian parties into three groups: what we can call the "pro-system" parties; the "half-way" parties (half-way between the defenders and the negators of the system); and the "anti-system" parties. This classification can be represented by three concentric circles, as in Chart 3.

Chart 3. Encirclement of the Italian political system

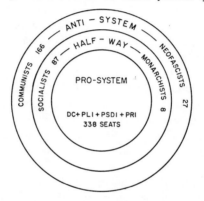

The inner circle indicates the besieged citadel; i.e., the four parties which are committed to saving the system: DC, Liberals (PLI), Social Democrats (PSDI), Republicans (PRI), which obtained respectively—in the 1963 Lower House—260, 39, 33, and 6 seats for a total of 338 seats. The middle circle indicates the half-way parties, which in the last 15 years have been torn between the need to help the system to survive and the need to compete with the extreme parties: the Socialists (PSI) and the Monarchists. We might call this position—with reference to the latest developments—feeble acceptance, or conditional support. The outer circle indicates the position of refusal of the system, the anti-system parties: Communists and Neofascists.[20]

[20] To be sure the coupling of the PSI and the Monarchists is somewhat arbitrary. In fact the Monarchists have always been more available than the Socialists; but the more the Monarchists have come to accept the system, the less they have been acceptable to the system. And the same applies to the coupling of the MSI and the

Given the fact that the total membership of the present Lower House is 630, if all the four pro-system parties managed to form a coalition government, they would have a 23-vote majority. However, such a coalition—which existed during the preceding legislatures—currently appears unlikely because even the pro-system group of parties has developed in a centrifugal direction. Despite the encirclement, and despite the logic of self-defense, the external attraction has prevailed on the centripetal drive, and the left-right polarization has thus become intensified within the pro-system group itself.[21]

Chart 4. Encirclement and cleavages

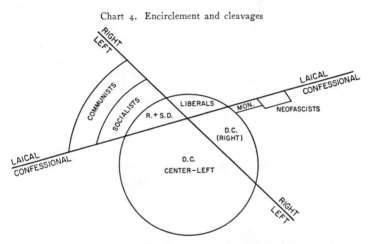

If the situation of encirclement is combined with the cleavages that I have previously mentioned, the full picture of the complications of the Italian political system is as represented in Chart 4,[22] in which the over-all complexity of the pattern is very visibly shown by the crosscutting of four superimposed cleavages: the cleavage between the four pro-system parties and the half-way parties; the cleavage between the half-way and the anti-system parties; the right-left cleavage; the laical-confessional cleavage. Of

Communists: for the more the MSI has agreed to support the system, the less any government has been able to accept its support. Since 1964, a third party, the PSIUP, should be added to the anti-system parties in the outer circle.

[21] That ideological internal splitting is the main obstacle is confirmed by the fact that the 1963 majority of 23 votes is still a better majority than the ones on which the center coalitions relied in the 1953 legislature (barely 5 votes) and in the 1958 legislature (20 votes).

[22] Chart 4 is only a section of the cirles drawn in Chart 3, arranged, or divided, by two ulterior lines of cleavage.

the latter two, the left-right conflict is the more intense one—not because the religious cleavage has lost force, but because the other has increased its strength.

Chart 4 shows a very muddled and complicated pattern. Theoretically, and following the lines of cleavage, five possibilities can be envisaged: 1) a center-left alignment (DC, Republican, Social Democrats, Socialists); 2) a center-right alignment (DC, Liberals, Monarchists, Neofascists); 3) a center coalition; i.e., the "defense of the system" alignment; 4) a laical front (Liberals, Republicans, Social Democrats, Socialists); 5) a Catholic majority (DC, Monarchists, Neofascists).

However, possibility 4—a laical front—would not have a majority (unless it accepted external support from the Communists), and it is unthinkable because of the intensity of the right-left cleavage between the Liberals, which are a conservative party, and the Socialists. Also possibility 5 appears unlikely and would not have a majority in the present-day parliament.

Possibility 1, a center-left coalition, is the "new experiment" attempted in the sixties. But despite the support of an adequate majority, it is a difficult experiment on three counts: the alignment cuts across the DC (i.e., the right wing of the party follows with great reluctance); it is undermined by the confessional cleavage; and it is weakened by the need of relying on a party, the PSI, which exhibits only a feeble acceptance of the system. Possibility 2, i.e., an alternative center-right alignment, would be much worse off, however; it cuts across the DC even more deeply, it is also undermined to some extent by the denominational cleavage, and it would have to accept the votes not only of the monarchists but also of the MSI. As for possibility 3, the "defense of the system" coalition which was the formula *par excellence* of the fifties, I have already pointed out that the left-right cleavage has become so intense within the pro-system parties themselves that this majority currently appears an *ultima ratio*. And it goes without saying that the other element of potential conflict, the laical-confessional cleavage, has troubled the existence also of the center coalitions.[23]

The complications arising at the governmental level should not divert our attention from those that pre-exist at the party level and within the parties themselves. If it is to be expected that the parties of

[23] I have not included the PCI in these majorities because (at least up until the present writing) no government could really accept Communist support as a determining factor.

a two-party system have a nebulous platform, a heterogeneous following, and eventually serious problems of internal cohesion, it would be reasonable to expect, on the other hand, that, when the number of the parties increases, the need for having multi-dimensional parties diminishes. However, this is not what happens in Italy. The disadvantage of having as many as eight parties is not compensated by the advantage of having fairly homogeneous and uni-dimensional parties; most Italian parties are as polimorphic and as internally fragmented as they could be. No simplification has followed from the multiplication of the parties. With the sole exception of the Communist party—whose discipline and hierarchical structure overcome internal dissent—intraparty factionalism is intense and widespread. The DC is actually very close to being a confederation of a variety of sub-parties, and most Italian parties are bitterly divided between a right and a left, with a center that tries to hold the party together.[24]

Why is it that despite the latitude of choice provided by eight parties—which should theoretically offer to everyone the possibility of a congenial home—each party remains polymorphic and heterogeneous? On the one hand, all Italian parties are highly ideological rather than pragmatic. On the other hand, parties cannot live in a purely ideological setting; they must also commit themselves to earthly policy decisions. It follows from this that a member may adhere to a party for reasons which have little in common: either because he accepts the ideology but not the current policy orientation, or because he agrees with the current policy orientation but not with the ideology. Therefore no matter how many are the parties, each party still provides ample opportunity for intraparty disagreement.

Thus, we find in Italy four rights [the right wing of the DC (i.e., a religious right), plus the Liberals, the Monarchists and the Neofascists]; as many as five or six lefts [a religious left in the DC, a historical left (i.e., the Republicans), plus Social Democrats, Socialists, Communists, and the new splinter left-socialist party, the PSIUP]; and a fluid center crossed by several possible lines of cleavage and consensus. In practice this implies that people who could agree on concrete policies are divided by their ideological or religious affiliation; while people who share similar ideological or confessional beliefs do not necessarily agree on concrete policies. The net result

---

[24] Not always successfully, since party splits have been avoided only by the PCI, the DC, and the MSI (and the latter case is a dubious one since the party is practically divided in two).

is a Byzantine and undecipherable party system whose end product is overcomplication and confusion. At least this is how the polity must look to the ordinary voter. The average citizen is surely not in a position to disentangle the mess; and one should not be surprised, therefore, that this state of affairs leads to frustration and alienation. I do not mean a cultural alienation that is a historical heritage; I mean that the complexity of the political system is in itself a powerful agent of alienation.

Whatever the cultural heredity, surely the living actors carry a responsibility of their own. And since the Italian party system is so constructed as to impede rather than facilitate civic integration, there are reasons for speaking of a specifically political alienation which flows directly from the Byzantine nature of that system. Its intricacies alone suffice to explain the confusion and the frustration of the average citizen.[25]

This does not imply that all the blame can be laid directly on the political managers of the system. Of course not. To put it in Weiner's and LaPalombara's felicitous terms, the Italian polity suffers from the load of simultaneous crises of "legitimacy," of "participation-integration," of "distribution," and of "secularization."[26] When a Communist party polls over 7,750,000 votes, and when the parties which are unequivocally loyal to the political system manage only to put together a bare 52.8 per cent of the total vote,[27] the problem of legitimacy, i.e., of acceptance and integration within the constitutional order, is surely an unresolved problem. In addition, the fact that the major Socialist party, the PSI, still adheres, at least at a verbal level, to a Marxist "maximalist" platform, indicates that the country as a whole has neither overcome the crisis of participation nor adopted a realistic approach toward solving the crisis of distribution. Lastly, all the tensions that follow from the laical-denominational cleavage suggest that the crisis of secularization and, in this sense, the crisis of modernization are far from being settled.

Clearly, then, the Italian political system is overloaded. However, this conclusion, which confronts us with the fact that the management

[25] It is apparent that my interpretation diverges from G. Almond and S. Verba, *The Civic Culture*, Princeton: Princeton University Press, 1963, esp. pp. 402-403. The general point will be discussed *infra*, sect. 4.

[26] Cf. the introductory chapter to the present volume, as well as the pertinent general remarks in Daalder's brilliant essay, chapter 2 of this volume.

[27] The figures refer to the 1963 general elections. The situation has not been more impressive from the "defense of the system" point of view at former elections. The percentage of the votes collected by the DC, PLI, PRI and PSDI has been 49.2 in 1953 and 51.8 in 1958.

of the polity is bound to be very difficult indeed, poses the problem but does not tell us whether the polity is well managed or mismanaged; and in particular it does not tell us whether an overcomplicated and Byzantine party system is, under the given circumstances, inevitable or avoidable.

III. The Nature of Polarized Pluralism

ITALY, FRANCE, AND THE WEIMAR REPUBLIC

Besides present-day Italy, at different times Germany and France have also been pluralistic polarized polities: France especially under the Fourth Republic, and Germany during the Weimar Republic.[28] That the three polities belong to the same type can be shown— quickly and somewhat impressionistically—by comparing their respective party and voting distribution at three significant moments. With this end in view, Chart 5 represents the distribution of the Italian electorate in 1963; Chart 6 the distribution of the French electorate in the Parliament of 1956; and Chart 7 the distribution of the German electorate in the critical *Reichstag* of November, 1932.[29]

A first common trait of the three patterns is that the number of relevant parties far exceeds three or four (which is the normal number for the cases of moderate pluralism). While it is difficult to draw any definite conclusion from a numeric criterion either because we may be led astray by a situation of party atomization or because of the existence of small marginal parties, nevertheless I am inclined to believe that, in mature party systems which have bypassed the stage of atomization, a minimum of five parties is required to produce or to reflect a polarized society.[30]

[28] The Spanish Republic (1931-36) could also be a relevant illustration. Although the Spanish experience was too brief and too revolutionary to be meaningfully compared to France, Italy, and Germany, it is significant that the four countries in question exhaust the list of the large European countries. Is a problem of dimension involved, that is, are the successful democracies more likely to be small democracies? I shall argue *infra*, however, that the most relevant variable appears to be the religious dimension and the relationship between Church and politics (cf. also note 40).

[29] I am aware of the methodological difficulties involved in the use of a linear unidimensional space. Cf. e.g. the criticism of the Hotelling-Downs model by Donald E. Stokes, "Spatial Models of Party Competition," *American Political Science Review*, Vol. 57 (June 1963), pp. 368-377. However, I am concerned with polities having a strong ideological focus, and Stokes himself agrees that in this case a spatial right-left scheme of party positioning can be assumed to be a realistic representation (pp. 375-376).

[30] The critical number is apparently related to mechanical reasons in the sense that the very interactions of more than four parties help to explain a centrifugal pat-

Chart 5. Distribution of preferences in the 1963 elections

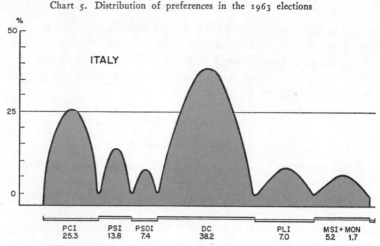

PCI: Communists; PSI: Socialists; PSDI: Social Democrats plus Republicans (1.4); DC: Christian Democrats; PLI: Liberals; MSI: Neofascists plus Monarchists (1.7).

Chart 6. Distribution of preferences in the 1956 elections

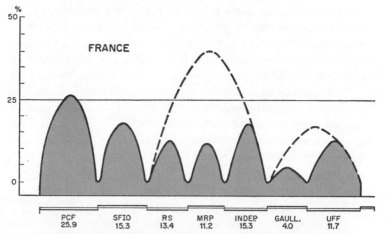

PCF: Communists; SFIO: Socialists; RS: Radical Socialists and Republican Radical party; MRP: Popular Republican Movement (Catholic); Indep.: Independents, Moderates, and Peasants; Gaullists: formerly RPF (Rally of the French People) and subsequently UNR; UFF: Poujadists (Union French Fraternity). The placement of the Gaullists may be questioned, but since most of the 1956 Poujadist votes came from the RPF and returned in 1958 to the UNR, it seems that Gaullists and Poujadists have both been very much bordering protest movements and that the electors perceived the common anti-system attitude of the two movements rather than their differences in economic policy or in style. In this connection, a cumulative curve from 1951 to 1958 would significantly show a consistent 4,000,000 rightist anti-Fourth Republic vote.

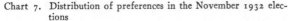

Chart 7. Distribution of preferences in the November 1932 elections

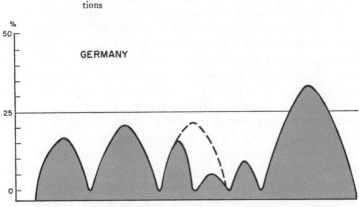

KPD: Communists; SPD: Socialists; Z.: Zentrum (Catholic Center) plus DDP, German Democratic party (0.9); DVP: German People's party (moderate conservatives) plus small parties (3.0); DNVP: German National People's party; NSDAP: Nazis. The Nazi party actually received a higher percentage (37.3) in the July 1932 elections, and rose to 43.9 in the March 1933 elections.

A second similarity is that all three patterns show a polarization at both extremes; i.e., they have both a left and right anti-system opposition. It is true that this polarization is very strong on the right end for the Weimar parliament, very strong at the left end in the Italian parliament, and more balanced at both ends in the French case. This difference, however, is immaterial as long as the "distance clause" applies to the over-all spectrum.

A third common element is that each pattern shows a large area which is unequivocally central despite its center-right and center-left shades and subtleties. There is an important difference, however, in this respect: that whereas the Italian center is occupied basically by one party, the French and the German centers are fragmented. And while this difference does not alter the fact that in any case we must now refer to a triangular model and dismiss the dualistic *Gestalt*, it cannot be denied that the difference between a unified and a divided center may lead to a variety of interpretations.

---

tern of development. This I have tried to show in my forthcoming *Parties and Party Systems* and in my "Modelli spaziali di Competizione tra Partiti" *Rassegna Italiana di Sociologia*, Vol. 1 (January 1965), pp. 25-28. The notion of party atomization will be clarified later.

Let us simply say that a political system is center-based as long as its metrical center is physically occupied. And the core of the matter seems to be that the very existence of a center (qua party) discourages and actually impedes centrality, i.e., the "moderating" drive. This is not to say that under certain conditions a center-based political system does not have its use; it may be, at least at the outset, the only possible working solution. Yet in the long run a center-based political system gives way to a circularity. For a center party positioning is not only a consequence but also, and just as much, a cause of polarization. As a consequence that reflects the existence of a polarized society the center party is mainly a feed-back of the centrifugal drives which predominate in the system. As a causal factor it is precisely the existence of a center party which feeds the system with centrifugal strains—as we shall see later.

THE FEATURES OF THE MULTIPOLAR SYSTEMS

Duverger states that "the center does not exist in politics: there may well be a center party, but there is no center tendency, no center doctrine."[31] But the statement confuses the issue. A "doctrine" is not merely a tendency or merely an opinion, for the term "doctrine" applies to some kind of theorizing. And since it is futile to discuss the spatial positioning of thinking—and therefore to discuss what makes a doctrine a "center doctrine"—we may simply concentrate on the problem of a center opinion or tendency. From the interpreter's point of view this is surely a problem, for it is difficult to decide what a center-located opinion means. It may be understood as being the moderate, mature, and thoughtful opinion which rejects the simplicity of extremism; or as being the equivalent of indifference, the opinion of those who lack an opinion; or as being the algebraic zero of contradictory or multidimensional issue-oriented opinions. Probably a center opinion is nurtured by all these inputs.[32] In any case, and no matter how we wish to interpret a center opinion, the fact remains that Duverger's statement should be reversed. A center opinion, or a center tendency, always exists in politics; what may not exist is a center party.

A first distinctive feature of extreme pluralism is thus the center

[31] *Les Partis Politiques*, p. 245.
[32] Duverger's thesis that the center is a "superimposition of dualisms" (*ibid.*, p. 245), a "lack of coincidence between categories of dualistic oppositions" (p. 262), may well indicate one of these inputs. As it stands it is a further illustration of his dualistic blinkers.

placement of a party or of a group of parties. What matters is neither the name nor the doctrine (whatever a center doctrine may be) but the position. Thus a party may find it profitable to be considered a center party without having a center position. On the other hand, a center-located party may wish to change its position and be considered, for example, a leftist party, but it may nevertheless remain in the center. Since a center is relative to its left and right wings, if the other parties do not accept the overlapping and shift to the same extent in the same direction, the whole spectrum will move leftward, but the center party will not succeed in acquiring a different positioning.

A second distinctive feature of a multipolar polity is that a center-based arrangement affects the mechanics of governmental turnover. Actually "turnover" is too vague, for we are faced with three possible types of turnover. In a two-party system we have *alternative government* (otherwise the system would become in the long run a predominant party system). In a moderate multiparty system we often have *alternative coalitions*, that is, a more limited kind of alternative government; for some parties alternate while others just change partners. However, all the parties have a chance of becoming governmental parties. In the extreme multiparty systems with a leading center party we do not in any proper sense have alternative government; we have only a *peripheral turnover* limited to some of the smaller parties and which cannot be extended to all the parties. As far as the leading center party is concerned, there is no alternation; the party will govern indefinitely. And there is also no alternation for the extreme parties; they are expected *not* to govern indefinitely (as long as the system survives).

This peripheral and limited access to government helps to explain a third characteristic feature of extreme pluralism: the extent and growth of *irresponsible opposition*.[33] Since the turnover of the possible allies of the leading center party is mostly imposed by arithmetic combinations, and since these partners will not have the effective leadership or the major responsibility in the governing coalition, the system provides no real incentive for responsible opposition. An opposition is forced to be responsible if it knows that it may be called to execute what it has promised—to respond. But

[33] For having called my attention to the importance of this point, I am largely indebted to R. A. Dahl. Cf. *Political Oppositions in Western Democracies*, New Haven: Yale University Press, 1966, Chs. 1, 12, 13.

such motivation is tenuous if the opposition knows that at most it may only share some peripheral governmental responsibility behind the smoke screen of discontinuous and shifting coalitions. And no such motivation exists for the parties which oppose the system. Indeed, for the extreme parties irresponsible opposition is both natural and rewarding.

As a rule of thumb, then, centrifugation and irresponsible demands and promises proceed hand-in-hand. And this accounts for the fourth feature of the polarized polities: outbidding becomes the rule of the game. Somebody is always prepared to offer more for less, and the bluff cannot be seen. Can we still speak, in these conditions, of "competitive politics"? I wonder.

Competition occurs, in a given economic market, under two conditions: when monopolistic situations are impeded and, primarily, when the goods are under legal control; no one is allowed to sell any yellow metal for gold or plain water for medicine. Turning from the economic to the political market, political competition is conditioned not only by the existence of more than one party but also, and particularly, by the possibility of keeping fraud under control. Of course one has to be much more tolerant of political fraud than of economic fraud, but there is a threshold of minimal fair competition below which a political market can hardly survive as a competitive market. If some parties compete by promising gold for nothing or heaven on earth, this is no longer a situation which allows the survival of a political system based on competitive principles. Beyond certain limits, the politics of overpromising and of outbidding is the very negation of competitive politics. And this limit is all the more likely to be exceeded the more the party system includes parties which cannot be called to respond by taking on the responsibility of governing.

The fifth and final distinctive feature of extreme pluralism is its ideological patterning. Let it be clear that when using the term "ideology" I am concerned only with an approach, a way of perceiving politics. As here defined, ideology is the opposite of pragmatism; that is, it implies a doctrinaire and somewhat unrealistic way of framing political issues.[34] It is hard to see how a situation of party over-

[34] What matters is the official policy, so to speak. For an ideological approach is not dispelled by the fact that "multiparty systems seem to survive on the principle that the parties keep their ideological principles and their practical politics in separate compartments" (Avery Leiserson, *Parties and Politics*, New York: Knopf, 1958, p. 175). On that principle they may survive, but not proceed; for the practical approach remains confined to the underground dealings and cannot be extended to

abundance can escape an ideological patterning. Beyond a certain limit, the more the number of parties increases, the more their identification becomes a problem; and the remedy to which each party has recourse in order to be perceived as distinct is a punctilious ideological and principled rigidity. The existence of eight or ten parties can hardly be justified in pragmatic terms, and in this connection the rule of thumb appears to be that the more numerous the parties, the less they can afford a pragmatic lack of distinctiveness.

If this is true, the "end of ideology" prediction does not seem to apply to the multipolar polities. Granted that in an affluent society the intensity of ideology will decrease, a lessening of its intensity should not be confused with a withering away of ideology itself.[35] In particular, there is no necessary connection between ideological intensity and ideological approach; for the intensity may vary, and the approach remain the same. The temperature of ideology may cool, but this fact does not imply that a society will lose the habit of perceiving political problems in an unrealistic and dogmatic fashion; and it implies even less that the party system will turn to a pragmatic approach. Even less, because party fragmentation is not merely a reflection of the ideological cleavages existing in a society. The other side of the coin is that a fragmented party system invests a great deal of energy in the effort to disintegrate basic consensus. Since most parties have no prospect of winning a majority, each party—except eventually the leading party—is more interested in securing for itself a stable electorate of ideologically safe believers, than tempted to run the risk of becoming an open party of the non-ideological variety. In other words, the party system as a whole is hardly concerned with conflict resolution and hardly interested in performing the brokerage function. Quite the contrary, it is the very logic of party pluralization in its extreme form that impedes integration and the cohesive function.

To sum up, the distinctive features of a polarized multipolar system are as follows: (1) the lack of centrality indicated by the physical existence of a center, and thereby the likely prevalence of

the major decisions, that is, to the policy which has to be made public. Thus party leaders—even if realistic or skeptical—remain entangled in their outspoken ideological nets, thereby creating for themselves more problems than they can solve.

[35] To put it bluntly, either the "end of ideology" prediction is understood as touching upon a problem of intensity, or it is unwarranted. For the general point, and my criticism, cf. G. Sartori, *Democratic Theory*, New York, Praeger, 1965, pp. 191-193, 195-196.

centrifugal drives; (2) a high degree of ideological rigidity, or in any case a non-pragmatic approach to politics; (3) marked cleavage at the elite level, which in turn deepens the fragmentation of basic consensus; (4) the absence of real alternative government; (5) the growth of irresponsible opposition and thereby of the politics of out-bidding, of unfair competition.

It goes without saying that in every country the relative impact of each of the foregoing features is likely to be different and also to change over time. With this caution in mind, it is my contention that the foregoing characteristics apply not only to present-day Italy but also to the Fourth Republic and to the Weimar Republic. I leave as an open question whether—and with what amendments—the framework of polarized pluralism could also provide some useful insights for countries such as Finland[36] or Israel.[37] The more stim-ulating question is, however, whether the case of polarized plural-ism does not indicate a trend which may somehow materialize in the future in Spain (after Franco), in some South American coun-tries, and also somewhere outside the Western world.

CHANGE, IMMOBILITY, AND CENTER

Thus far I have passed over the problem of development, or change, because the developmental role of parties cannot be given the same importance in a developed as in an underdeveloped area, and because I have been discussing polities which happen to be particularly inhospitable to change.

In principle change is only one of the requirements of a political system, and we should be wary of laying a unilateral emphasis on change and acceleration at the expense of stability, duration, and sequential timing. Furthermore, and in particular, the developmental role of Western parties is a comparatively minor one both because

[36] Finland, with a strong Communist party polling one-fourth of the total vote and an over-all pattern of six parties, apparently qualifies for inclusion under the "five or more" clause, mentioned *supra* at note 30.

[37] Israel is definitely atypical, however. The existence of 9 or 10 parties is ex-plained by a new start based on a polyethnic and polycultural society in which one finds, moreover, an overlapping of very different time dimensions; and this is indeed a unique syndrome—especially for a small democracy—which defies any generalization. Therefore specific cues of comparison are apt to be very misleading: e.g. the "religious party" problem. For the party system cf. B. Akzin, "The Role of Parties in Israeli Democracy," *Journal of Politics*, Vol. 17 (1955); and for the issue of politics and religion, Amitai Etzioni, "Kulturkampf ou Coalition, Le Cas d'Israel," *Revue Française de Science Politique*, Vol. 2 (1958), pp. 311-331. See lastly, L. G. Seligman, *Leadership in a New Nation*, New York: Atherton Press, 1964, Ch. 5.

our parties are specialized agencies operating within differentiated structures, and because party systems came about in the Western area for a basic purpose which is not development in general, but specifically the purpose of developing democracy. This is tantamount to saying that it would be preposterous to ask Western parties to perform the broad tasks of modernization and economic growth that parties elsewhere may have to perform.

My problem can be narrowed down, therefore, to the following question: What are the conditions that tend to make a fragmented, polarized polity an immobile political system badly fitted for the absorption of change? According to my previous analysis the major conditions leading to *immobilisme* appear to be the complexity and intricacies of the party system; poor recruitment of leadership; the inherent drawbacks of the center-based polities.

That extreme pluralism is conducive to governmental deadlock and paralysis is known, and the Italian case provides an interesting illustration of how the complications of the party system are translated into a very difficult decision-making process which is likely to lead nowhere, at least in terms of orderly and constructive change. Let us distinguish three kinds of majorities correlated to three clusters of issues: (1) an economic majority, or a majority concerned with the distribution crisis, i.e., the kind of coalition that would agree on a major redistribution of wealth by means of large-scale *dirigisme* (if not full-scale nationalization and planning); (2) a political majority, or a majority confronted by the crisis of legitimacy, i.e. a coalition committed to the defense of the system, that would unite on basic constitutional issues, and that opposes any shift in international alliances; (3) a religious majority, i.e., the kind of majority that the DC is likely to seek on confessional issues and for the protection of specifically Catholic interests. Accordingly Chart 8 indicates—impressionistically, of course—where the centers of gravity of the parliamentary majorities are likely to be located, and where they would shift whenever we pass from one type of issue to the other. The suggestion is that each cluster of issues finds its point of equilibrium within different majorities. Thus the economic majority lacks adequate support in terms of constitutional policy; the political majority does not abide by the kind of economic program advocated by the economic majority; and a third kind of alliance may always sneak in and, at least provisionally, reshuffle the cards.[38]

[38] It is true that the 1963 Italian parliament no longer provides, *prima facie*,

Chart 8. Majority combinations based on issues

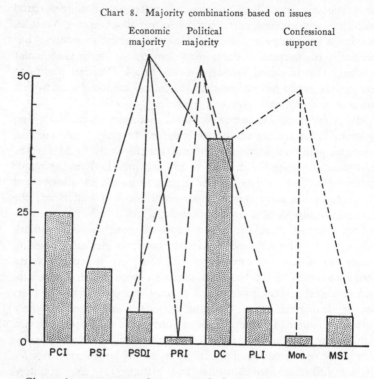

Chart 8 represents, then, a typical situation of governmental fragility and paralysis in the sense that while each coalition can reach an agreement in one sector, it can hardly agree upon the implementation of its policy in the other sector, that is, on a consistent over-all policy. At least until today in Italy the constitutional majority has had no redistribution policy, while the economic majority has no constitutional firmness. The idea put forward by some French scholars that the dynamics of government is related precisely to its rapid turnover is a clever speculation; but it underestimates the importance of a consistent long-range policy, and it also neglects the fact that changing governments are unable to decide a coherent and balanced over-all policy. Hence it remains true that the complexity of party coalition-making (and remaking) leads to govern-

---

a majority supporting confessional issues. It must be recalled, however, that this has always been the case until today, and that the possibility cannot be ruled out, for the DC can still obtain support in exchange for spoils.

mental immobility, at least in the sense that it impedes any coherent and sustained effort of policy implementation.

Whatever the complexity of the party system, immobility is also related to poor leadership, both in the sense that the political elites lack the ability for problem-solving and that they do not provide a generalized leadership. While the lack of generalized leadership is easily explained by the fragmentation of the party system and its ideological rigidity, it is worthwhile to comment on the reason why—at least in Italy, and with particular reference to the DC—the recruiting function is very inadequately performed. It would be wrong to assume that the Italian political system does not allow an adequate mobility toward the higher end of the stratification scale. If one reviews for example the social origin of the Italian decision makers, it appears that the recruitment has not been ascription-based and that vertical mobility has been considerable.[39] The problem is not therefore one of quantitative mobility, but much more a problem of qualitative recruitment and of limited access. While the ladder is there, the main entrance door is too much a denominational side-entrance. Thus the modernizing potential elites of the country tend to adopt a radical protest attitude or are left aside in a wasteful position of estrangement.

However, since this distortion in the recruitment function is clearly related to the special link which ties the Italian DC to the Catholic Church, I leave it as an open question whether the following generalization is permissible: that a denominational requirement is unlikely to be a healthy and adequate criterion of recruitment in a secular civilization.[40] Whether this is generally true or not, the point seems to be that the inability of a political system to respond to change is related to some kind of qualitative recruitment distortion, rather than to the mere rate of political turnover and mobility.

[39] Cf. G. Sartori, ed., *Il Parlamento Italiano 1946-1963*, esp. pp. 168-174 and Figure XVIII; also pp. 316-320. E.g. in the 1958-1963 legislature half of the members of the Chamber of Deputies originated from the middle and low-middle classes, while the upper class was represented by a mere 4%.

[40] In a broader perspective the issue has been raised a number of times. Cf. A. Hauriou, "La Démocratie Parlémentaire Peut-elle Réussir dans les Pays à Comportement Majoritaire Catholique?" in *L'Evolution du Droit Public*, Paris: Sirey, 1956, pp. 321-329; and also S. M. Lipset, *Political Man*, New York: Doubleday, 1960, pp. 83-84. Without entering the discussion, let it be emphasized that the European working democracies have usually been not only "small democracies" but also the democracies which display a religious pluralistic patterning (as aptly observed by Daalder in this volume). In other terms, the democracies which have not yet solved their problems are not only "large democracies" but also "all Catholic democracies": France, Italy, Spain.

Finally, and coming to the third point, it is often argued that the center is by its very nature an immobile position. *Prima facie*, however, it is not very clear why this should be the case. After all, since a center is relative to its left and right wings, it will follow in the long run the general trend of the polity. If history goes to the left, the center can only remain in a central position if it also moves left (and vice versa if history moves to the right). *Immobilisme* should not be confused with *moderatisme* and, therefore, if the charge of immobility is justified, it must be justified more persuasively. According to my interpretation, the crux of the matter is to be found in the relationship between *center* (as a party) and *centrality* (as a drive). The implication of this distinction *vis à vis* the cognitive map of developmental analysis may be pinpointed with reference to the model of the political process suggested in Table 2.

TABLE 2: THE POLITICAL PROCESS

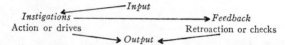

What I call "instigations" indicates the input of the majority of the electorate or of the intense elite minorities, and therefore the prevalent *action* or drive of the system. What I call "feedback" indicates the *retroaction* of the minority of the electorate, or of the inert elite majorities, and therefore the countervailing behavior, the checks, which contextually respond to the instigations.[41] In other terms, the instigations are the input of the "changers," and the feedback is the input, or the counterinput, of the "resisters."

Now if this scheme is referred to party positioning, and more precisely to the query "Why does a center party materialize?", it tends to suggest that in a situation of centrifugal pluralism the center party (or parties) appears to be more than anything else a feedback, or a retroaction, of the centrifugal drives. At least this seems to be the case with the Italian DC. According to this interpretation, then, the center is more a negative convergence, a sum of exclusions, than a positive agency of instigation. And this is why it is likely to be a passive, rather inert, and—all in all—immobile kind of aggre-

[41] It should be noted that my feedback is an input, not an output: it is a counter-input, so to speak. This is to suggest that the output of a political system—which is a historical process—should be viewed as a cumulative output resulting from the interplay between two types of conflicting inputs: the instigations and their contextual feedback.

gation. Of course the center will move if the balance between its left and its right should shift. Nevertheless it will not be the real change agent within the system, for it is not a center of instigations.

Can this conclusion be generalized? That is, can one theorize a somewhat mechanical relationship between center positioning and *immobilisme*, between a center-based political system on the one hand and inertial development on the other? Awaiting further probing I shall leave the question unanswered.

IV. Explanations and Hypotheses

A MANIPULATIVE APPROACH

Why and under what conditions does a situation of multipolar and polarized pluralism occur? In these matters it is always safe to rely on historical explanations. History is liable to explain too much, however,[42] because our reconstruction of the past is guided by our present knowledge, that is, when we write history we already know the answers. Moreover, the problem that concerns us most is—in John Stuart Mill's terms—how much can be done by "invention and contrivance." From this point of view two explanations can be offered, either alternatively or concurrently: that polarized pluralism is a consequence of proportional representation and/or that it reflects the fragmentation of the political culture. Both explanations are valuable, but insufficient in themselves.

That the explanation provided by proportional representation is unsatisfactory, at least in its simple form, is shown by the fact that in several countries proportional representation has led to only moderate pluralism. Is it because we find in such countries a homogeneous secular political culture? This is surely an answer, but it can be challenged by some puzzling and apparently conflicting evidence: the German case, for instance. In the twenties Germany was a multipolar polarized polity, whereas it is currently a bipolar depolarized polity. Thus, according to the political culture approach we could possibly have on record three types of German political culture, namely, fifteen years of cultural fragmentation, ten years of mono-

---

[42] Duverger for example has recently produced a clever explanation of the French "muddle" in a strictly historical key, that is, by deriving everything from the "trauma of 1789" and its dialectic repercussions in 1814-1815, in 1848, and in 1871; cf. "L'Eternel Marais, Essai sur le Centrisme Français," in *Revue Française de Science Politique*, Vol. 1 (1964), esp. pp. 38-42. My question is: how is it that the Italian pattern so closely follows the French one, despite the fact that Italian "traumas" bear no resemblance, either in kind or saliency, to the French ones?

lithism, and now an integrated and moderately pluralistic political culture. Likewise, if a behavioral political scientist had visited Italy in the thirties he would have found, I suspect, a consensual political culture and no anticipation of the fragmentation that was to be discovered in the fifties. The question is: How can a culture change and be reversed so rapidly? And this question leads us back to the importance of manipulation, and in particular to the importance of electoral contrivance.

In the United States, for example, despite the "melting pot" there are a large variety of subcultures and a very serious racial cleavage. Nonetheless the political culture is very homogeneous. We can say that the somewhat surprising fact that the subcultures apparently exert so little influence on the political culture is accounted for by the process of political socialization. Nevertheless let us pose the question: Would the United States remain a two-party polity if it introduced proportional representation (all the other conditions remaining equal)? My guess is that it would not.[43] And my conclusion is, therefore, that the American two-party system is no more a dependent variable of the political culture than a dependent variable of structural and procedural engineering.

My point is, then, that we should pay more attention to the manipulative aspect of politics, whereas we have recently yielded too much to the social-determinist and also to a somewhat cultural determinist point of view.[44] If we attempt to explain everything in terms of the political culture, then we are likely to reach the conclusion that what happens is, or was, inevitable. But we do not need a political science to find that out. If political scientists have something different to say from the historians, and something more to say than the social determinists, this is because we are interested in predictions; and we are interested in predictions not because we advocate an anticipated fatalism but because we want to find out how much of the so-called inevitable is evitable—if we wish to avoid it.

In the abstract one can argue that the party system is an independent variable, a dependent variable, and both, i.e., that party system and political culture interact. If they interact—and everybody

---

[43] Cf. S. M. Lipset, who writes: "It seems likely that if the United States had ever adopted proportional representation . . . it would have developed several main parties" ("Party Systems and the Representation of Social Groups," *European Journal of Sociology*, Vol. 1 [1960], p. 67).

[44] Sociologists aside, this is apparently the case with many political scientists who have adopted, or adapted, the Parsonian "pattern variables" of structural-functional analysis.

seems to pay at least lip-service to this formula—then one of the two actions must be the action of the party system upon the political culture. At any given moment in any given polity the political culture is a datum. But no matter to what extent a political culture is heterogeneous and fragmented (at the regime and even at the community level), there is a manipulative strategic point at which this fragmentation can be neutralized or can be maximized. If this is true, and if we think that extreme pluralism is an unhealthy state of affairs for the body politic, then we should not accept without the benefit of doubt the view that party arrangements and electoral systems only express the deeper determinants of the society and, in particular, we should reconsider the problem of proportional representation.

HYPOTHESES

Since the record shows that proportional representation can be conducive both to moderate and to extreme pluralism, the relevant query is: Under what conditions does it produce i) extreme pluralism and, eventually, ii) centrifugation.

Surprisingly enough we usually discuss the effects of proportional representation as if party systems all belonged to a same phase of development. Now, not only is the number of parties of little significance unless it is related to given stages of structural consolidation of the party system[45] but the point is that the effects of a switch to proportional representation are definitely related to the relative delicacy or maturity of the party system in question.[46] And since all the European countries displaying a record of extreme pluralism underwent a phase of party atomization prior to the adoption of proportional representation, the problem can be approached at this point.

Hypothesis 1: Extreme pluralism is likely to follow a *premature* switch to proportional representation, that is, when proportional representation is grafted on to a situation of party atomization.

By "party atomization" I mean a highly fragmented pattern in which parties are mostly a facade covering loose and shifting coali-

[45] Thus a dozen parties in a phase of party atomization are a relatively low number (for one can find, at this stage, even thirty or forty parties), while the same number appears to be a ceiling in the age of the organizational mass parties.

[46] The remark calls for a historical typology and sequence of party systems (as outlined, e.g., in my *Parties and Party Systems, op.cit.*). For the present discussion, however, the distinction between an initial and a terminal stage appears sufficient.

tions of notables. In this stage the party system is still evanescent qua system: parties have no real platform, hardly a national spread, no centralized or coordinated organization, and even less anything resembling a stable organization.

Hypothesis 2: Extreme pluralism is even more likely when a situation of party atomization is affected *simultaneously* by the introduction of proportional representation and of universal (or quasi-universal) suffrage.

The reason for this appears obvious enough. An atomized party system is still an unstructured party system which cannot be, as such, a system of channelment. In particular an atomized party system has no way of channeling the entry into politics of the new voting strata of the outs.

Hypothesis 3: Extreme pluralism is unlikely, and moderate pluralism is likely, whenever proportional representation is met by an already structured and stabilized party system.

By "structured party system" I mean one in which at least one or two of the existing parties have acquired—at the moment in which proportional representation is introduced—a national platform, a unified symbol, and some stable organization also at the local level, so that they are perceived by the country at large as the natural foci and channels of the political system. Clearly the strong structuring of early parties can in itself be a powerful restrainer or container of party proliferation. Under these circumstances the internally created parties are likely to play a major role also in the mass party era (instead of being ousted by the externally created parties), and the pattern is therefore likely to remain bipolar.

Hypotheses 1, 2, and 3 should be tested against the development of the party systems in Italy and France on the one hand and in Belgium and in the Northern democracies on the other. At least *prima facie*, there is a striking contrast between the atomized pattern of party factionalism which existed during the Third Republic or in Italy in 1913 (when quasi-universal suffrage was introduced) and in 1919 (when proportional representation was adopted) and the corresponding pattern of national "grass roots" parties which existed in Belgium, Norway, or Sweden.

From a manipulative point of view, a structured party system can be considered a "strong" system in that it heavily conditions our very perception of the political arena, whereas an atomized party system has no definite impact on our behavior and can therefore be considered a "feeble" party system. Likewise a plurality system is a "strong" electoral system in that it has a coercive impact on voting behavior, whereas proportional representation is a "feeble" electoral system in the sense that the voting behavior is no longer restrained by the method of voting. Accordingly our former hypotheses can be comprehensively reformulated as follows.

Hypothesis 4: Extreme pluralism follows from a *nonsequential timing* in the adoption of proportional representation and is aggravated whenever enfranchisement and proportional representation are injected more or less simultaneously into an atomized party system. Under these circumstances a feeble party system is combined with a feeble electoral system (proportional representation) and the situation gets out of control.

Hypothesis 4.1: The *sequential timing* which is conducive to moderate pluralism presupposes that the preexisting party system already provides: i) a somewhat stabilized basic pattern of electoral behavior ii) channeled by parties which have acquired a national platform and some local organization and iii) by parties which have acquired the habit and the ability to perform the integrative/aggregative function. Under these circumstances the adoption of a feeble electoral system is counterbalanced by the existence of a strong party system, and therefore the new claimants and the growth of the socioeconomic demands can be kept under control.

Let us now consider the conditions which are conducive not only to extreme pluralism but also to a highly polarized and centrifugal development. Besides the premature introduction of proportional representation, two additional factors become relevant.

Hypothesis 5: A centrifugal development of the political system is likely whenever a religious-confessional criterion of political affiliation is superimposed upon the left-right distribution of the party alignment, and, more precisely, whenever a religious party adopts a clerical policy orientation and affirms itself as a predominant party by means of a special link with the dominant church. Under these circumstances an anticlerical polarization is likely to follow.

Hypothesis 5.1: This centrifugal development will not follow, however, if the religious party does not exploit the confessional appeal and becomes integrated in the spectrum of party alignments by acquiring an inter-confessional dimension in terms of both leadership recruitment and electoral support (e.g. Belgium). Also, an anticlerical polarization is likely not to follow if the religious party is not a predominant party, if it is specifically concerned with the protection of minority rights, or if there is more than one religious party (e.g. Holland).

Hypothesis 6: An extreme centrifugal development is very likely whenever the political system accepts not only as legal but also as a legitimate and somewhat equal and normal competitor a party (or parties) which opposes the very system, such as a Communist party; this very fact fosters irresponsible opposition and gives way to the politics of outbidding.

Hypothesis 6.1: Such a centrifugal development will not necessarily follow, however, if the alienated sections of the population remain isolated by general non-acceptance (e.g. the small democracies in general, with the exception of Finland) and/or if the existence of anti-system parties is legally prohibited. The latter two conditions are not necessarily linked (e.g. Greece), even though legal prohibition is likely to become impossible if not adopted at an early stage.

Hypothesis 6.2: Whenever legal prohibition of the antisystem parties has become impossible because the parties in question have acquired legitimacy, and/or because of their large support, the paralysis of the political system can be remedied at the parliamentary and governmental level by having recourse to a second ballot run-off.[47]

Hypothesis 7: An extreme, polarized, centrifugal development is almost inevitable whenever the conditions set forward in Hypotheses 5 and 6 coexist.

A general confirmation of the points raised in the foregoing hypotheses is provided by the case of the Bonn Republic. With reference to the first point—proportional representation—the Germans have adopted a mixed electoral system and have discouraged party proliferation by denying representation to the parties that fail to achieve 5 per cent of the total vote. On both accounts all the problems raised by the adoption of full-fledged proportional representation have been beheaded (and the contrast with the Weimar development is indeed striking). With regard to the second point—the

[47] Cf. Lipset, who reminds us that: "The French double ballot . . . limited both the participation and strength of the Communists and Fascists in the 1930's. Such a system in Weimar Germany would have obviously kept the Nazis out of the *Reichstag* in the 1920's and . . . would have guaranteed a large democratic majority in the election of 1930, and even in 1932" (*op.cit.*, p. 82). As Lipset implicitly assumes in his reference to Germany, a second ballot can be technically devised also for list systems of proportional representation.

existence of a religious party—the German CDU largely satisfies the conditions of Hypothesis 5.1 concerning the inter-confessional orientation.[48] Regarding the third point—the problems raised by the existence of a Communist party—not only are the conditions set down in Hypothesis 6.1 largely satisfied, but a number of circumstances have actually eliminated the very problem.

The over-all argument can be tested *ex adverso*, that is, with reference to majority systems, as suggested in Hypothesis 8.

Hypothesis 8: Whenever a party system has bypassed the stage of atomization, the maintenance of a majority system is likely i) to impede extreme pluralism; ii) to make the prohibition of anti-system parties superfluous; iii) to discourage both a class or denominational party orientation; and therefore iv) to encourage an inter-class and an inter-confessional integrative approach to politics.[49]

As for the traditional argument that only proportional representation is a truly representative electoral system, let it be noted that this argument holds only under the conditions that are conducive to moderate pluralism. (Cf. esp. Hypotheses 3, 4.1.) For frustration and detachment are the most likely outcome whenever the increase of choices of the voter is detrimental to their clarity and intelligibility; that is, whenever the outcome of party pluralism is an undecipherable and byzantine party system. This is the same as saying that from the voter's viewpoint of feeling represented—or in terms of the subjective perception of representation—it is not necessarily true that a multi-party system is more satisfactory than a two-party system. What is essential for the "tuning," or we may say the empathy between the real country and the legal country, is not whether the voter is offered more than one alternative, but that he be offered clear alternatives. The argument can be resumed as in Hypothesis 9.

Hypothesis 9: In passing from a majority two-party system to a proportional multiparty system, if the increase of alternatives offered to the voter is not detrimental to their clarity, then it is likely that a people will feel better represented. But if the alternatives are increased at the expense of their intelligibility, then the advantages of a wider range of choice are undermined by the drawbacks of a

[48] For instance in the 1953 Bundestag almost 40 per cent of the CDU members were Protestants. Of course the injection of a religious dimension into the political arena remains a complication: despite its openness, the CDU is resented by a Protestant left and by many intellectuals. Yet a comparative appraisal of Germany and Italy shows how different two denominational parties can be.

[49] A similar hypothesis can be formulated with reference to an inter-racial approach whenever this is the problem.

byzantine, ideologized, and highly unrealistic party system. Therefore the more the number of parties increases beyond a certain limit,
the more the effects of proportional representation are self-denying.[50]

My explanation of extreme and polarized party pluralism ends
more or less at this point. This is also to say that I consider of comparatively minor importance the other reasons usually brought forward to explain the troubles of the French or Italian system: such
as the issue of party discipline (or indiscipline), or the problem
of the homogeneity (or heterogeneity) of the party followings, or
the discussion on "partycracy" (*partitocrazia*), that is, on the predominance of party directorates over the constitutional organs of
the state. Also, and in particular, I am unable to follow Almond's
perceptive thinking when he comes to the importance of the "interest
articulation function."[51]

The foregoing should not be taken to mean that the manipulative
approach is confined to the ability of steering electoral systems. For
one thing, once proportional representation is established, this may
well create—electorally speaking—a situation of no return (although
something can still be done about it as suggested in Hypothesis 6.2).
On the other hand, it is obvious enough that other devices can be
fruitfully put to use. For instance, the direct primary is often
deluding from a democratic point of view, but it can be an effective
way of absorbing into the existing party pattern the reform groups or
the "outs," in that it allows them to work their way through the
established channels of political mobility. It is equally obvious,
in the third place, that the keyboard of manipulative devices offered
by the constitutional structures is very wide.[52]

---

[50] Hypotheses 8 and 9 disregard the conditions that allow for the successful performance of a plurality system for the reason that they are germane to my line of
argument only as a checking device. For the same reason I simplistically assume,
here, that a plurality system is conducive to a two-party system.

[51] Cf. especially *The Politics of the Developing Areas*, Princeton: Princeton University Press, 1960. I do not deny, e.g., that in the working multiparty systems "the
relations between parties and interests are more consensual, which makes stable
majority and opposition coalitions possible" (p. 42); but the cause is too small, so
to speak, to account for the consequence. Almond also refers to a more fundamental
property, the "existence of a basic political consensus"; but here again he narrows
the point too much, I feel, by referring the consensus to the party-interest group
interaction (p. 43). The same applies to Almond's statement that in the immobilist
type of multiparty system the existence of a fragmented, isolative political culture
affects primarily "the relations between interest groups and parties" (*ibid.*). I would
say that it affects much more than that.

[52] For this latter approach see notably H. J. Spiro, *Government by Constitution*,
New York: Random House, 1959, which is also one of the few truly comparative attempts in the field of systematic comparative politics.

Yet there are reasons for paying particular attention to the problem of proportional representation. The first *ad hoc* reason is that proportional representation has been consistently discussed under a misleading optic. According to Hermens, proportional representation produces anarchy and pluralistic stagnation; according to Duverger and others, it has multiplying effects. The assumption is, therefore, that proportional representation *does* something. But the plain fact is that proportional representation does nothing: it is a feeble electoral system. If we are interested in the *doing* of electoral systems, then we must study the majority or plurality systems. To say that proportional representation multiplies the parties is wrong and raises a false issue. For it is obvious that whenever several parties are already in existence before the introduction of proportional representation, the number of parties will hardly be affected by its adoption, as has been the case with the transition from the Third to the Fourth Republic in France or from the German Empire to the Weimar Republic. The point is not, therefore, that proportional representation multiplies the parties; it is that it does nothing to prevent the fragmentation of a party system. Better said, proportional representation has, by itself, no impact, aside from the effect of removing a previous impediment (i.e., a plurality electoral system that did serve to impede party fragmentation). And the real issue is under what conditions even a majority system is unable to reduce or to limit the multiplication of parties.

Correctly stated, then, the point is that proportional representation amounts to a loss of control over party proliferation. And this is indeed a vital key, for there are several mechanical consequences that are liable to follow—somewhat like a chain reaction—from the very number of the parties. As we have seen, the more the parties, the more one is likely to find a left-right positioning and a center placement which impedes "centrality"; the more the parties, the more the party pattern will belong to the rigid ideological non-aggregative variety rather than to the pragmatic brokerage variety; the more the parties, the less they can all expect to share governmental responsibility, and the more this creates the conditions for irresponsible opposition; the more the parties, the more the conditions for the politics of outbidding and outflanking.

These are not laws, to be sure. They are merely statements of mechanical tendencies which will display their effect only under given historical conditions; and this is precisely where the historical explanation comes in.[53] In the second place, it must be repeated that the foregoing rules apply only to the mature party systems which have bypassed the stage of party atomization. In the third place, I am not trying to prove that there is a unidirectional relationship between the number of parties and what follows. My rules can also be presented and argued in the reverse. However, even if in principle the number of parties can be said to be no more a cause of everything else than an effect of everything else, the practical point is that the number of parties is subject to electoral control and engineering. My position is, then, that since there is no reason for deciding that one of the ends of the skein is to be preferred, the reason for choosing the manipulative end is that it allows us to disentangle the web.

Lastly a conclusive reason for paying particular attention to proportional representation is that while the conditions that make a majority system inadvisable or hardly applicable are fairly well known, there is a widespread belief that proportional representation can always be applied to any situation with a wait-and-see hopeful attitude. Quite to the contrary there are at least as many arguments for carefully planning in advance the adoption of proportional representation as there may be reasons for hesitating *vis-à-vis* the adoption or the preservation of a majority system.

V. A Summary Conclusion

My purpose has been to show that complex party systems cannot be explained by extrapolating from the two-party systems, and that the case of extreme pluralism actually escapes us if we approach it by using a dualistic model.[54] It also appears that a better and more balanced understanding of the various possible patterns can be obtained by approaching the continuum of party systems from the

[53] Daalder's analysis in the present volume is indeed very relevant in this connection.

[54] Eckstein's recent account of the Italian pattern is perhaps the most convincing illustration of this. According to Eckstein, "Italy today uses PR, but there has occurred in Italy neither any fragmentation nor any radicalization of party life. If anything, the opposite has occurred: the Christian Democrats are a very large multi-interest party . . . the coalition of Communists and fellow-traveling Socialists furnishes a sort of opposition bloc . . ." ("The Impact of Electoral Systems on Representative Government," in H. Eckstein, D. E. Apter, eds., *Comparative Politics, A Reader*, Glencoe, Ill.: The Free Press, 1963, p. 251). It is apparent that Eckstein is led astray, in presenting this optimistic and distorted picture, by the use of Duverger's dualistic blinkers. Let it also be noted, incidentally, that Italy is, if anything, a good illustration of the thesis that proportional representation does fragment and dogmatize party conflict.

complex end of the party spectrum. In this purview, a brief appraisal of the three systems that we have been examining may lead to the conclusions that follow.

Simple two-party pluralism is the most secure working solution—whenever it is an applicable solution, that is, if it is backed by a homogeneous and secularized political culture. On the one hand it benefits from the reasonable stimulation provided by alternative government and responsible opposition, and it obliges the parties to perform an integrative and aggregative function; while on the other hand it discourages the growth of a highly ideologized policy orientation and the polarization of the party system. Under these conditions a realistic and pragmatic process of orderly change, i.e., a gradual change which does not throw off balance the equilibrium of a political system, is probable and is very likely to be successful.

Extreme and centrifugal pluralism is the most insecure and the least viable solution. On the one hand it cannot profit from the stimulation of a responsible opposition, and on the other hand it is largely paralyzed by cabinet instability, by the heterogeneity of the governmental coalitions, and finally by the presence of anti-system parties which replace competitive politics with irresponsible outbidding. Under these conditions the party system is more an agent of disintegration than an instrument of aggregation, and the outcome is either sheer immobility or disorderly change, that is, an ideologically motivated, unrealistic sequence of abrupt changes that are likely to be unsuccessful.

Moderate pluralism is a *via media*. It has the advantage of providing a wider range of choice than simple pluralism and the drawback of being more exposed to some of the inconveniences, not to say the temptations, of extreme pluralism. Yet whenever a situation of moderate pluralism is stabilized, orderly change is likely, and the party system is able to perform a cohesive and integrative function.

Let it be emphasized that while the choice between a majority system and proportional representation is largely conditioned by the "take off" situation of a given country (also because a two-party system can hardly be imposed from above merely through electoral devices), the same does not apply to the choices that are conducive to moderate pluralism rather than to extreme pluralism. That is to say that the alternative between moderate and extreme pluralism is largely under manipulative control if awareness of consequences comes in time. Beyond a certain point of mishandling, once that the jar is broken the chances of successful manipulation are low. But if broken jars cannot be repaired, surely future breaches in new jars can be prevented if a manipulative foresight is applied at the proper time.

In this connection, and with this aim in view, an intensive probing of the experience of the multipolar polarized polities appears to be a vital and very urgent task of present-day political science. We have not learned enough from the fact that a number of Western democratic systems have already crumbled between World War I and II, that democracy has failed in Spain, that it is again insecure in France and in Italy. It would be wise to focus our attention again on the European area, coming back as it were from the developing to the developed areas. For one thing, the concern for the developing areas will take a somewhat ironical flavor if in the meantime the democratic slice of the developed areas grows thinner and thinner. Moreover, if we are not able to master the problems of the Old World, something is also likely to be wrong with the predictive talents that we are now applying to the Third World.

CHAPTER 6

THE TRANSFORMATION OF THE WESTERN EUROPEAN PARTY SYSTEMS

OTTO KIRCHHEIMER *

I. Load Concept and Party Failures

I HAVE BEEN intrigued enough by the LaPalombara-Weiner concept of the load to use it as a point of departure for inquiring into the successes and failures of major European political parties as transmission belts between the population at large and the governmental structure.

The British case has a pristine beauty: national unity brought about in the sixteenth century consolidation of the establishment, followed by a seventeenth century constitutional and social settlement allowing for the osmosis between aristocracy and bourgeoisie. The settlement happened early enough to weather the horrors and concomitant political assaults of early nineteenth century industrialism. The fairly smooth and gradual integration of the working classes was completed late enough so that the unnerving cleavage between the political promise and the social effectiveness of democracy (LaPalombara and Weiner's "distribution crisis") lasted only a couple of Mac-Donald-Baldwin decades. Thus once we omit the 1910-1914 interlude, Great Britain offers a case where problems could be handled as single loads. The time factor thus merges into and coincides with the load factor. The impact of constitutionalism slowly unfolds in the eighteenth century, then follows the acceleration of middle-class and the beginning of working-class integration during the nineteenth century, and the tempestuous combination of the consequences of full political democratization with the demands of a distributionist society after the First World War.

Where do we get if we apply the single-load concept to the French case? If there was a French problem of national identity, it was almost oversettled by 1793, with the revolution only intensifying results in principle reached by 1590. Universal suffrage, that is, political democracy as the constitutional basis of the French state, has

---

* Otto Kirchheimer died suddenly before he could make final changes in this chapter. It is included here with only minor revisions (J. L.).

been almost continuously on the program since 1848 and was definitely achieved in the early 1870's. Whatever the subsequent upheavals in executive-legislative relations, the popular basis of the French regime has not been contested except for the short-lived Pétainist period. But why did political integration, the business of transforming the state apparatus of the bourgeois society into a cooperative enterprise of all social classes, stop so short of success? Why is it that this goal has been reached only now, to some extent at least, as a simple byproduct of increased material well-being and ensuing lessening of social antagonism in the French species of industrial society? How is it that the political parties contributed so little to the end result?

There are reasons why French society in spite of, or because of, the early introduction of universal suffrage could force its working class to accept a position of stepchildren. They were a minority in a society not particularly favoring disruption of the existing social equilibrium by accentuated industrialization. Yet without such industrialization there was little chance of creating a unified party system. Instead there was a dichotomy between parties of individual representation (with their double basis in the local parish pump and the operations of the parliamentary faction) and the incipient mass party of the working class, the Socialist party of the first decade of the century. Most bourgeois parties remained restricted electioneering organizations with loose connections to still looser parliamentary factions having little radius of action beyond the parliamentary scene (Duverger-LaPalombara-Weiner's internally created parties).[1]

Through the courtesy of Alain[2] these parties were equipped with an ultra-democratic theory of eternal vigilance to be exercised by the proverbial small man over his intermediaries in party and parliament. But the reality was far different. Behind the façade of democratic vigilance political fragmentation excluded the party from advancing from the stage of *ad hoc* parliamentary combinations to permanently organized transmission belts between population and government. Party organizations and party conventions were over-sized *Café de Commerce* confabulations of *raisonneurs* without effective man-

---

[1] The internal-external creation dichotomy has to be viewed in the light of presence or absence of a supporting framework of religious or class-motivated parallel organizations. The local committee of the internally created bourgeois party and its financial backers can never serve as such a fool-proof prop of electoral success as can the network of parallel organizations typical of external parties.

[2] Alain, *Élements d'une doctrine radicale*, Paris, 1925.

date.[3] Thus the bourgeois parties and the parliamentary government they carried saw themselves at every turn of events disowned as mere bubbles blown up by the *pays légal* to be confronted with the *pays réel* discovered from the confluence of thousands of discordant voices. Yet neither the *raisonneurs* nor the more or less benevolent intermediaries of the *Comité Mascuraud* watching over the parliamentary performance of rival political clans in the interest of the commercial and industrial community could substitute for the people at large.[4]

As these parties had to face less of a challenge from class-based integration parties than did their German neighbors, they could afford to become inoperative in semi-crisis periods. In such periods they were, as office-holding combinations, bailed out in the 1920's and early 1930's by proconsul saviors, Poincaré and his cheap imitator Doumergue. Yet as opinion-transmitting conveyor belts they had more and more to contend with the welter of anti-democratic organizations.

The last democratically legitimized attempt of the Third Republic to integrate the working class into the political system was Léon Blum's *Front Populaire*. Its failure was in part a failure of the parties, in part a consequence of international events. With its failure the Third Republic, with its juxtaposition of bourgeois parliamentary clans and class-based integration parties, was near its end.

How did it happen that the Fourth Republic failed to integrate the Communist party into its political system and allowed both the SFIO (French Section of Workers' International or Social Democratic party) and the MRP (Popular Republican Movement, or Christian Democratic party) to slip into the habits of the bourgeois parties of the previous periods? Should we single out two load factors: the supervening, mutually exclusive international policy commitments of the majority of the French political parties and the Communists, and the crisis of decolonization? Yet the end of tripartism in 1947 need not have arrested the transformation of French parties into organizations able to integrate major social groups into

[3] For a study of the working of the most characteristic of these parties see Daniel Bardonnet, *Évolution de la Structure du Parti Radical*, Paris, 1960.

[4] *Ibid.* Pages 251-256 contain details about the *Comité Mascuraud* (named after a Senator of the Seine Department), officially called the *Comité Républicain de Commerce et de l'Industrie*, the major agency for distributing commercial and industrial funds to bourgeois parties. For the *Comité Mascuraud* and other channels, more important later, see also Henry W. Ehrmann, *Organized Business in France*, Princeton: Princeton University Press, 1957, pp. 219ff.

the political system and able to work in coalition—collaboration or in alternative shifts. There is no reason why the challenge of *personalismo* in the form of Gaullism and the challenge of the Communist working class opposition of principle had to lead to an atavistic return to the party system of the 1920's. Decolonization was a challenge which the parties might have faced with clear-cut policy propositions. Working-class integration and decolonization, the former on the agenda for virtually half a century, the latter a limited problem, were burdens which an operative party system could have mastered.

Yet the majority of the French political parties had never progressed beyond the stage of local-interest messengers and parliamentary clubs with or without ideological overtones. They were equally unable to make commitments in the name of their voters or to obtain legitimacy through transforming the voters' opinions and attitudes into impulses converted into governmental action. They therefore had little to do with the continuity of the state, which remained the business of the bureaucracy. Major socio-political options were avoided, or, if and when they had to be faced, they became the work of individual politicians temporarily supported by strong elements in the community. It is doubtful whether even such a combination as that of Caillaux and Jaurès, which appeared likely in the spring of 1914, would have been able to establish the party as an effective transmission belt between population and government and a basis for policymaking. It might have failed because of the bourgeois distaste for devices which would transmit and thereby increase popular pressure on political action. In the single-load job of integrating the *couches populaires* into the French polity the performance of the political party remained unimpressive.

The rise of Italian and German political organizations in the middle of the nineteenth century cannot be separated from the history of belated unification. Unification was a competitive effort between the political endeavors of Cavour and Garibaldi and his adherents in Italy and between Bismarck and the Liberals in Germany. The respective statesmen's timing and actions cannot be understood without the urgency of these competitive pressures. But did the more nimble hand of Cavour provide the party system greater chances than the staccato fist of Bismarck?[5] What did Cavour's and Bismarck's

[5] A German author has recently put the case as follows: "Bismarck's policy to the Liberals was unfair in that he achieved what the Liberals wanted to have achieved,

styles of unification mean in terms of party loads and chances?

Could the Italian Left, the *Partito d'Azione*, have tried to find contact with the southern peasant masses?[6] Could it by such contact
have established a basis for national loyalty transcending class and
region? Or was it inevitable that it had to become part witness, part
victim, of a *trasformismo* which remained an essentially commercial
operation rather than an instrument of national integration? The
possibilities may have been slight, but at any rate the attempt was
never even made. In Germany, on the other hand, even the late-
ness and the Little Germany formula involved in the founding of
Bismarck's Reich did not prevent that creation from soon becoming
a socially and economically viable unit. All political forces, whether
friendly or hostile to the Founding Father, accepted his Reich as
a basis of operation. But in terms of the chances of the political
parties the outcome was not much different. Italy had found a
fictitious solution of its national identity problems, workable in constitutional but not in socio-political terms. Bismarck's heirs, the combined forces of bureaucracy, army, industrialists, and agrarians, upheld for about the same time both in Prussia and in the Empire a
constitutional setup which prevented any approach to effective working-class participation in the government. In both Italy and Germany
the mismanagement of the crises of national identity and of participation increased the problem load which the nation had to face at
the end of the First World War. However, it would be difficult
to evaluate the differential impact of these load factors as compared,
for example, with France. Here, without any crisis of national
identity and without constitutional barriers to working-class participation, the long smoldering participation crisis came fully into
the open in the mid-thirties. I would argue that the extent of the
1940 breakdown is clearly related to this crisis of participation.

Is the load concept helpful, then, in analyzing the failure of the
continental parties to assume their appropriate roles in the 1920's?
May we, for example, argue that the belatedness in accepting a constitutional regime which would have allowed political democracy to
become fully effective militated against successful political integration of the working classes into the German political system in the

---

but he gave them neither the chance nor the means to do it on their own." E. Pikart,
"Die Rolle der Deutschen Parteien im Deutschen Konstitutionellen System," in
Zeitschrift für Politik, 1962, pp. 12-15.

[6] The point is discussed in some detail in Antonio Gramsci, *Il Risorgimento, Opere
di Antonio Gramsci*, Vol. 4, 1949, pp. 100-104.

1920's? The acceptance of this argument hinges on some further differentiation. By "political integration" we mean here the capacity of a political system to make groups and their members previously outside the official political fold full-fledged participants in the political process. Many a mass party, however, was neither capable of nor interested in integrating its members into the existing political community. The party might even want rather to integrate its followers into its own ranks *against* the official state apparatus.

II. The Antebellum Mass Integration Party

Socialist parties around the turn of the century exercised an important socializing function in regard to their members. They facilitated the transition from agrarian to industrial society in many ways. They subjected a considerable number of people hitherto living only as isolated individuals to voluntarily accepted discipline operating in close connection with expectations of a future total transformation of society. But this discipline had its roots in the alienation of these parties from the pre-World War I political system whose demise they wanted to guarantee and speed up by impressing the population as a whole with their exemplary attitudes.[7]

During and soon after the First World War the other participants in the political game showed that they were not yet willing to honor the claims of the working-class mass parties—claims based on the formal rules of democracy. This discovery was one of the primary reasons why the social integration into the industrial system through the working-class organizations did not advance to the state of a comparable political integration. Participation in the war, the long quarrels over the financial incidence of war burdens, the ravages of inflation, the rise of Bolshevist parties and a Soviet system actively competing for mass loyalty with the existing political mass organizations in most European countries, and finally the effect of the depression setting in at the end of the decade—all these were much more effective agents in the politicization of the masses than their participation in occasional elections, their fight for the extension of

[7] The German end of this story and Bebel's emergence as commander-in-chief of a well-disciplined counter-army have often been commented upon. It has recently been discussed in Guenther Roth, *The Social Democrats in Imperial Germany*, Ottawa, 1963. Similar observations on the social integration function of socialism are equally valid for Italy. As essentially hostile an observer as Benedetto Croce notes these factors in his *History of Italy, 1870-1915*, New York, 1963; Robert Michels in his *Sozialismus in Italien*, Karlsruhe, 1925, p. 270 *et seq.*, provides ample documentary proof.

suffrage (Belgium, Britain, Germany), or even their *encadrement* in political parties and trade union organizations. But politicization is not tantamount to political integration; integration presupposes a general willingness by a society to offer and accept full-fledged political partnership of all citizens without reservations. The consequences of integration into the class-mass party depended on the responses of other forces in the existing political system; in some cases those responses were so negative as to lead to delayed integration into the political system or to make for its disintegration.

Now we come to the other side of this failure to progress from integration into the proletarian mass party and industrial society at large[8] to integration into the political system proper. This is the failure of bourgeois parties to advance from parties of individual representation to parties of integration, a failure already noted in France. The two tendencies, the failure of the integration of proletarian mass parties into the official political system and the failure of the bourgeois parties to advance to the stage of integration parties, condition each other. An exception, if only a partial one, is that of denominational parties such as the German Center or Don Sturzo's *Partito Popolare*.[9] These parties to a certain extent fulfilled both functions: social integration into industrial society and political integration within the existing political system. Yet their denominational nature gave such parties a fortress-type character seriously restricting their growth potential.[10]

With these partial exceptions, bourgeois parties showed no capacity to change from clubs for parliamentary representation into agencies for mass politics able to bargain with the integration-type mass parties according to the laws of the political market. There was only

[8] Integration into industrial society: while the worker has accepted some aspects, such as urbanization and the need for regularity and the corresponding advantages of a mass consumer society, powerlessness as an individual and the eternal dependence on directives by superiors make for strong escapist attitudes. The problems are discussed in detail in André Andrieux and Jean Lignon, *L'Ouvrier d'aujourd'hui*, Paris, 1960. The ambiguous consequences to be drawn from these facts and their largely negative impact on the political image of the workers are studied in detail in H. Popitz, *et al.*, *Das Gesellschaftsbild des Arbeiters*, Tuebingen, 1957.

[9] For the typology of the denominational party, see Hans Maier, *Revolution und Kirche*, Freiburg, 1959.

[10] Another exception was that of parties such as the German Nationalist party of the 1920's, whose conservative predecessor in the days before World War I had already profited from the ability of the agrarian interest representation (*Landbund*) to funnel enough steady support to its companion organization in the political market. See in general: Thomas Nipperdey, *Die Organisation der deutschen Parteien vor 1918*, Dusseldorf, 1961, Vols. V and VI.

a limited incentive for intensive bourgeois party organization. Access to the favors of the state, even after formal democratization, remained reserved via educational and other class privileges. What the bourgeoisie lacked in numbers it could make good by strategic relations with the army and the bureaucracy.

Gustav Stresemann is the politician who stood at the crossroads of this era, operating with a threefold and incompatible set of parties: the class and the denominational democratic mass integration parties; the opposition-of-principle parties integrating masses into their own fold against the existing order; and the older parties of individual representation. Forever on the lookout for viable compromises among democratic mass parties, old-style bourgeois parties of individual representation, and the powerholders outside the formal political party structure, Stresemann failed. For the party of individual representation from which he came could not give him a broad enough basis for his policies.[11]

Not all bourgeois groups accepted the need for transformation to integration parties. As long as such groups had other means of access to the state apparatus they might find it convenient to delay setting up counterparts to existing mass parties while still using the state apparatus for keeping mass integration parties from becoming fully effective in the political market. Yet after the second World War the acceptance of the law of the political market became inevitable in the major Western European countries. This change in turn found its echo in the changing structure of political parties.

III. The Postwar Catch-All Party

Following the Second World War, the old-style bourgeois party of individual representation became the exception. While some of the species continue to survive, they do not determine the nature of the party system any longer. By the same token, the mass integration party, product of an age with harder class lines and more sharply protruding denominational structures, is transforming itself into a catch-all "people's" party. Abandoning attempts at the intellectual and moral *encadrement* of the masses, it is turning more fully to the electoral scene, trying to exchange effectiveness in depth for a wider audience and more immediate electoral success. The narrower polit-

[11] See the conclusions of Wolfgang Hartenstein, *Die Anfänge der Deutschen Volkspartei, Dusseldorf*, 1962, and H. A. Turner, *Stresemann and the Politics of the Weimar Republic*, Princeton: Princeton University Press, 1963.

ical task and the immediate electoral goal differ sharply from the former all-embracing concerns; today the latter are seen as counter-productive since they deter segments of a potential nationwide clientele.

For the class-mass parties we may roughly distinguish three stages in this process of transformation. There is first the period of gathering strength lasting to the beginning of the First World War; then comes their first governmental experience in the 1920's and 1930's (MacDonald, Weimar Republic, *Front Populaire*), unsatisfactory if measured both against the expectations of the class-mass party followers or leaders and suggesting the need for a broader basis of consensus in the political system. This period is followed by the present more or less advanced stages in the catch-all grouping, with some of the parties still trying to hold their special working-class clientele and at the same time embracing a variety of other clienteles.

Can we find some rules according to which this transformation is taking place, singling out factors which advance or delay or arrest it? We might think of the current rate of economic development as the most important determinant; but if it were so important, France would certainly be ahead of Great Britain and, for that matter, also of the United States, still the classical example of an all-pervasive catch-all party system. What about the impact of the continuity or discontinuity of the political system? If this were so important, Germany and Great Britain would appear at opposite ends of the spectrum rather than showing a similar speed of transformation. We must then be satisfied to make some comments on the general trend and to note special limiting factors.

In some instances the catch-all performance meets definite limits in the traditional framework of society. The all-pervasive denominational background of the Italian *Democrazia Cristiana* means from the outset that the party cannot successfully appeal to the anticlerical elements of the population. Otherwise nothing prevents the party from phrasing its appeals so as to maximize its chances of catching more of those numerous elements which are not disturbed by the party's clerical ties. The solidary element of its doctrinal core has long been successfully employed to attract a socially diversified clientele.

Or take the case of two other major European parties, the German SPD (Social Democratic party) and the British Labour party. It is unlikely that either of them is able to make any concession to the specific desires of real estate interests or independent operators of agricultural properties while at the same time maintaining credibility with the masses of the urban population. Fortunately, however, there is enough community of interest between wage-and-salary earning urban or suburban white- and blue-collar workers and civil servants to designate them all as strategic objects of simultaneous appeals. Thus tradition and the pattern of social and professional stratification may set limits and offer potential audiences to the party's appeal.

If the party cannot hope to catch all categories of voters, it may have a reasonable expectation of catching more voters in all those categories whose interests do not adamantly conflict. Minor differences between group claims, such as between white-collar and manual labor groups, might be smoothed over by vigorous emphasis on programs which benefit both sections alike, for example, some cushioning against the shocks of automation.

Even more important is the heavy concentration on issues which are scarcely liable to meet resistance in the community. National societal goals transcending group interests offer the best sales prospect for a party intent on establishing or enlarging an appeal previously limited to specific sections of the population. The party which propagates most aggressively, for example, enlarged educational facilities may hear faint rumblings over the excessive cost or the danger to the quality of education from elites previously enjoying educational privileges. Yet the party's stock with any other family may be influenced only by how much more quickly and aggressively it took up the new national priority than its major competitor and how well its propaganda linked the individual family's future with the enlarged educational structures. To that extent its potential clientele is almost limitless. The catch-all of a given category performance turns virtually into an unlimited catch-all performance.

The last remark already transcends the group-interest confines. On the one hand, in such developed societies as I am dealing with, thanks to general levels of economic well-being and security and to existing welfare schemes universalized by the state or enshrined in collective bargaining, many individuals no longer need such protection as they once sought from the state. On the other hand, many have become aware of the number and complexity of the general factors on which their future well-being depends. This change of priorities and preoccupation may lead them to examine political offerings less under the aspect of their own particular claims than under that of the political leader's ability to meet general future contingencies. Among the major present-day parties, it is the French UNR (National Republican Union) a latecomer, that speculates most clearly on the possibility of its channeling such less specialized needs to which its patron saint De Gaulle constantly appeals into its own version of the catch-all party. Its assumed asset would rest in a doctrine of national purpose and unity vague and flexible enough to allow the most variegated interpretation and yet—at least as long as the General continues to function—attractive enough to serve as a convenient rallying point for many groups and isolated individuals.[12]

While the UNR thus manipulates ideology for maximum general appeal, we have noted that ideology in the case of the *Democrazia Cristiana* is a slightly limiting factor. The UNR ideology in principle excludes no one. The Christian Democratic ideology by definition excludes the non-believer, or at least the seriously non-believing voter. It pays for the ties of religious solidarity and the advantages of supporting organizations by repelling some millions of voters. The catch-all parties in Europe appear at a time of de-ideologization which has substantially contributed to their rise and spread. De-ideologization in the political field involves the transfer of ideology from partnership in a clearly visible political goal structure into one of many sufficient but by no means necessary motivational forces operative in the voters' choice. The German and Austrian Social Democratic parties in the last two decades most clearly exhibit the politics of de-ideologization. The example of the German Christian Democratic Union (CDU) is less clear only because there was less to de-ideologize. In the CDU, ideology was from the outset only a general background atmosphere, both all-embracing and conveniently vague enough to allow recruiting among Catholic and Protestant denominations.

As a rule, only major parties can become successful catch-all parties. Neither a small, strictly regional party such as the South Tyrolian Peoples' party nor a party built around the espousal of harsh and limited ideological claims, like the Dutch Calvinists; or

---

[12] The difficulties of a party in which the dynamics of personalization substitute completely for agreed-upon goals as well as the style of operations fitting the personal loyalty variant of the catch-all party become readily apparent from the description of the Third UNR Party Congress by Jean Charlot, "Les Troisièmes Assises Nationales de L'U.N.R.—U.D.T.," in *Revue Française de Science Politique*, Vol. 14 (February 1964), pp. 86-94.

transitory group claims, such as the German Refugees; or a specific professional category's claims, such as the Swedish Agrarians; or a limited-action program, such as the Danish single-tax Justice party can aspire to a catch-all performance. Its *raison d'être* is the defense of a specific clientele or the lobbying for a limited reform clearly delineated to allow for a restricted appeal, perhaps intense, but excluding a wider impact or—once the original job is terminated—excluding a life-saving transformation.

Nor is the catch-all performance in vogue or even sought among the majority of the larger parties in small democracies. Securely entrenched, often enjoying majority status for decades—as the Norwegian and Swedish Social Democratic parties—and accustomed to a large amount of interparty cooperation,[13] such parties have no incentive to change their form of recruitment or their appeal to well-defined social groups. With fewer factors intervening and therefore more clearly foreseeable results of political actions and decisions, it seems easier to stabilize political relations on the basis of strictly circumscribed competition (Switzerland, for instance) than to change over to the more aleatory form of catch-all competition.

Conversion to catch-all parties constitutes a competitive phenomenon. A party is apt to accommodate to its competitor's successful style because of hope of benefits or fear of losses on election day. Conversely, the more a party convinces itself that a competitor's favorable results were due only to some non-repetitive circumstances, and that the competitor's capacity of overcoming internal dissension is a temporary phenomenon, the smaller the over-all conversion chance and the greater the inclination to hold fast to a loyal—though limited—clientele.

To evaluate the impact of these changes I have found it useful to list the functions which European parties exercised during earlier decades (late in the nineteenth and early in the twentieth centuries) and to compare them with the present situation. Parties have functioned as channels for integrating individuals and groups into the

[13] Ulf Torgersen, "The Trend Towards Political Consensus: The Case of Norway," in Stein Rokkan, ed., *Approaches to the Study of Political Participation*, Bergen, 1962; and Stein Rokkan and Henry Valen, "Regional Contrasts in Norwegian Politics" (1963, mimeographed), esp. p. 29. For both weighty historical and contemporary reasons the Austrian Social-Democratic party forms a partial exception to the rule of less clear-cut transformation tendencies among major class-mass parties in smaller countries. It is becoming an eager and rather successful member of the catch-all club. For the most adequate treatment see K. L. Shell, *The Transformation of Austrian Socialism*, New York, 1962.

existing political order, or as instruments for modifying or altogether replacing that order (integration-disintegration). Parties have attempted to determine political-action preferences and influence other participants in the political process into accepting them. Parties have nominated public officeholders and presented them to the public at large for confirmation.

The so-called "expressive function"[14] of the party, if not belonging to a category by itself, nevertheless warrants a special word. Its high tide belongs to the era of the nineteenth-century constitutionalism when a more clear-cut separation existed between opinion formation-and-expression and the business of government. At that time the internally created parliamentary parties expressed opinions and criticism widely shared among the educated minority of the population. They pressed these opinions on their governments. But as the governments largely rested on an independent social and constitutional basis, they could if necessary hold out against the promptings of parliamentary factions and clubs. Full democratization merged the opinion-expressing and the governmental business in the same political parties and put them in the seat either of government or an alternative government. But it has left the expressive function of the party in a more ambiguous state. For electoral reasons, the democratic catch-all party, intent on spreading as wide as possible a net over a potential clientele, must continue to express widely felt popular concerns. Yet, bent on continuing in power or moving into governmental power, it performs this expressive function subject to manifold restrictions and changing tactical considerations. The party would atrophy if it were no longer able to function as a relay between the population and governmental structure, taking up grievances, ideas, and problems developed in a more searching and systematic fashion elsewhere in the body politic. Yet the caution it must give its present or prospective governmental role requires modulation and restraint. The very nature of today's catch-all party forbids an option between these two performances. It requires a constant shift between the party's critical role and its role as establishment support, a shift hard to perform but still harder to avoid.

In order to leave a maximum imprint on the polity a party has to exercise all of the first three functions. Without the ability to integrate people into the community the party could not compel other

---

[14] Cf. Sartori's paper, "European Political Parties: The Case of Polarized Pluralism," Ch. 5, above. Cf. Sartori, *Parties and Party Systems*, New York, Harper and Row, forthcoming.

powerholders to listen to its clarions. The party influences other power centers to the extent that people are willing to follow its leadership. Conversely, people are willing to listen to the party because the party is the carrier of messages—here called action preferences—that are at least partially in accord with the images, desires, hopes, and fears of the electorate. Nominations for public office serve to tie together all these purposes; they may further the realization of action preferences if they elicit positive response from voters or from other powerholders. The nominations concretize the party's image with the public at large, on whose confidence the party's effective functioning depends.

Now we can discuss the presence or absence of these three functions in Western society today. Under present conditions of spreading secular and mass consumer-goods orientation, with shifting and less obtrusive class lines, the former class-mass parties and denominational mass parties are both under pressure to become catch-all peoples' parties. The same applies to those few remnants of former bourgeois parties of individual representation which aspire to a secure future as political organizations independent of the vagaries of electoral laws and the tactical moves of their mass-party competitors.[15] This change involves: a) Drastic reduction of the party's ideological baggage. In France's SFIO, for example, ideological remnants serve at best as scant cover for what has become known as *"Molletisme,"* the absolute reign of short-term tactical considerations. b) Further strengthening of top leadership groups, whose actions and omissions are now judged from the viewpoint of their contribution to the efficiency of the entire social system rather than identification with the goals of their particular organization. c) Downgrading of the role of the individual party member, a role considered a historical relic which may obscure the newly built-up catch-all party image.[16] d) Deemphasis of the *classe gardée*, specific social-class or denominational clientele, in favor of recruiting voters among the population at large. e) Securing access to a variety of interest groups. The financial rea-

[15] Liberal parties without sharply profiled program or clientele may, however, make such conversion attempts. Val Lorwin draws my attention to the excellent example of a former bourgeois party, the Belgian Liberal party, which became in 1961 the "Party of Liberty and Progress," deemphasizing anticlericalism and appealing to the right wing of the Social Christian party, worried about this party's governmental alliance with the Socialists.

[16] Ample material to points b) and c) may be found in the interesting study by a practicing German politician: Ulrich Lohmar, *Innerparteiliche Demokratie*, Stuttgart, 1963, esp. pp. 35-47 and 117-124. See also, A. Pizzorno, "The Individualistic Mobilization of Europe," in *Daedalus* (Winter 1964), pp. 199, 217.

sons are obvious, but they are not the most important where official financing is available, as in Germany, or where access to the most important media of communication is fairly open, as in England and Germany. The chief reason is to secure electoral support via interest-group intercession.

From this fairly universal development the sometimes considerable remnants of two old class-mass parties, the French and the Italian Communist parties, are excluding themselves. These parties are in part ossified, in part solidified by a combination of official rejection and legitimate sectional grievances. In this situation the ceremonial invocation of the rapidly fading background of a remote and inapplicable revolutionary experience has not yet been completely abandoned as a part of political strategy. What is the position of such opposition parties of the older class-mass type, which still jealously try to hold an exclusive loyalty of their members, while not admitted nor fully ready to share in the hostile state power? Such parties face the same difficulties in recruiting and holding intensity of membership interest as other political organizations. Yet, in contrast to their competitors working within the confines of the existing political order, they cannot make a virtue out of necessity and adapt themselves fully to the new style of catch-all peoples' party.[17] This conservatism does not cost them the confidence of their regular corps of voters. On the other hand, the continued renewal of confidence on election day does not involve an intimate enough bond to utilize as a basis for major political operations.

The attitudes of regular voters—in contrast to those of members and activists—attest to the extent of incongruency between full-fledged participation in the social processes of a consumer-goods oriented society and the old political style which rested on the primordial need for sweeping political change. The latter option has gone out of fashion in Western countries and has been carefully eliminated from the expectations, calculations, and symbols of the catch-all mass party. The incongruency may rest on the total absence of any connection between general social-cultural behavior and political style.[18]

[17] However, even in France—not to speak of Italy—Communist policies are under pressure to accommodate to the new style. For a concrete recent example see W. G. Andrews, "Evreux 1962: Referendum and Elections in a Norman Constituency," in *Political Studies*, Vol. 11 (October 1963), pp. 308-326. Most recently, Maurice Duverger, "L'Eternel Marais: Essai sur le Centrisme Français," in *Revue Française de Science Politique*, Vol. 14 (February 1964), pp. 33, 49.

[18] This hypothesis is discussed in more detail in Georges Lavau, "Les aspects socio-

In this sense electoral choice may rest on family tradition or empathy with the political underdog without thereby becoming part of a coherent personality structure. Or the choice may be made in the expectation that it will have no influence on the course of political development; it is then an act of either adjusting to or, as the case may be, signing out of the existing political system rather than a manifestation of signing up somewhere else.

IV. The Catch-All Party, the Interest Group, and the Voter: Limited Integration

The integration potential of the catch-all mass party rests on a combination of factors whose visible end result is attraction of the maximum number of voters on election day. For that result the catch-all party must have entered into millions of minds as a familiar object fulfilling in politics a role analogous to that of a major brand in the marketing of a universally needed and highly standardized article of mass consumption. Whatever the particularities of the line to which a party leader owes his intraparty success, he must, once he is selected for leadership, rapidly suit his behavior to standard requirements. There is need for enough brand differentiation to make the article plainly recognizable, but the degree of differentiation must never be so great as to make the potential customer fear he will be out on a limb.

Like the brand whose name has become a household word, the catch-all mass party that has presided over the fortunes of a country for some time, and whose leaders the voter has therefore come to know on his television set and in his newspaper columns, enjoys a great advantage. But only up to a certain point. Through circumstances possibly outside the control of the party or even of the opposition—a scandal in the ranks of government, an economic slump—officeholding may suddenly turn into a negative symbol encouraging the voter to switch to another party as a consumer switches to a competitive brand.

The rules deciding the outcome of catch-all mass party competition are extremely complex and extremely aleatory. When a party has or seeks an almost nationwide potential constituency, its majority

---

culturels de la dépolitisation," in Georges Vedel, ed., *La Dépolitisation: Mythe ou Réalité?*, 1962, esp. p. 198. For some other explanations see Seymour Martin Lipset, "The Changing Class Structure and Contemporary European Politics," in *Daedalus* (Winter 1964), pp. 271-303.

composed of individuals whose relation to politics is both tangential and discontinuous, the factors which may decide the eventual electoral outcome are almost infinite in number and often quite unrelated to the party's performance. The style and looks of the leader, the impact of a recent event entirely dictated from without, vacation schedules, the weather as it affects crops—factors such as these all enter into the results.

The very catch-all character of the party makes membership loyalty far more difficult to expect and at best never sufficient to swing results. The outcome of a television contest is dubious, or the contest itself may constitute too fleeting an exposure to make an impression that will last into the election. Thus the catch-all mass party too is driven back to look out for a more permanent clientele. Only the interest group, whether ideological or economic in nature or a combination of the two, can provide mass reservoirs of readily accessible voters. It has a more constant line of communication and higher acceptance for its messages than the catch-all party, which is removed from direct contact with the public except for the comparatively small number intensively concerned about the brand of politics a party has to offer these days—or about their own careers in or through the party.

All the same, the climate of relations between catch-all party and interest groups has definitely changed since the heyday of the class-mass or denominational integration party. Both party and interest group have gained a greater independence from each other. Whether they are still joined in the same organization (like British Labour and the TUC [Trades Union Congress]) or formally enjoy complete independence from each other (like the German SPD and the DGB [Workers' Federation]), what matters most is the change of roles.[19] Instead of a joint strategy toward a common goal there appears an appreciation of limited if still mutually helpful services to be rendered.

The party bent on attracting a maximum of voters must modulate its interest-group relations in such a way so as not to discourage potential voters who identify themselves with other interests. The interest group, in its turn, must never put all its eggs in one basket. That might offend the sensibilities of some members with different political connections. More important, the interest group would not

[19] See the conclusions of Martin Harrison, *Trade Unions and the Labour Party Since 1945*, London, 1960.

want to stifle feelings of hope in another catch-all party that some moves in its direction might bring electoral rewards. Both party and interest group modulate their behavior, acting as if the possible contingency has already arrived, namely that the party has captured the government—or an important share in it—and has moved from the position of friend or counsellor to that of umpire or arbitrator. Suddenly entrusted with the confidence of the community as a whole, the government-party arbitrator does best when able to redefine the whole problem and discover solutions which would work, at least in the long run, in the favor of all interest claimants concerned.

Here there emerges a crucial question: What then is the proper role of the catch-all party in the arbitration of interest conflicts? Does not every government try to achieve the best tactical position for exercising an effective arbitration between contending group claims? Is the catch-all party even needed in this connection? Or—from the interest viewpoint—can a society dispense with parties' services, as France now does?

A party is more than a collector of interest-group claims. It functions at the same time as advocate, protector, or at least as addressee of the demands of all those who are not able to make their voices felt as effectively as those represented by well organized interest groups: those who do not yet have positions in the process of production or those who no longer hold such positions, the too young and the too old, and those whose family status aligns them with consumer rather than producer interests.

Can we explain this phenomenon simply as another facet of the party's aggregative function? But functionalist phraseology restates rather than explains. The unorganized and often unorganizable make their appearance only on election day or in suddenly sprouting pre-election committees and party activities arranged for their benefit. Will the party be able and willing to take their interests into its own hands? Will it be able, playing on their availability in electoral terms, not only to check the more extreme demands of organized groups but also to transcend the present level of intergroup relations and by political reforms to redefine the whole political situation? No easy formula will tell us what leader's skill, what amount of pressure from objective situations has to intervene to produce such a change in the political configuration.

In this job of transcending group interests and creating general confidence the catch-all party enjoys advantages, but by the same token it suffers from an infirmity. Steering clear of sectarianism enhances its recruiting chances in electoral terms but inevitably limits the intensity of commitment it may expect. The party's transformation from an organization combining the defense of social position, the quality of spiritual shelter, and the vision of things to come into that of a vehicle for short-range and interstitial political choice exposes the party to the hazards of all purveyors of nondurable consumer goods: competition with a more attractively packaged brand of a nearly identical merchandise.

V. Limited Participation in Action Preference

This brings us to the determination of action preferences and their chances of realization. In Anthony Downs's well-known model action preference simply results from the party's interest in the proximate goal, the winning of the next election. In consequence the party will arrange its policies in such a way that the benefits accruing to the individual members of the community are greater than the losses resulting from its policy.[20] Downs's illustrations are frequently, though not exclusively, taken from fields such as taxation where the cash equation of political action is feasible. Yet Downs himself has occasionally noted that psychological satisfactions or dissatisfactions, fears or hopes, are elements in voters' decisions as frequently as calculations of immediate short-term benefits or deprivations. Were it different, the long-lasting loyalty of huge blocks of voters to class-mass integration parties in the absence of any immediate benefits from such affiliation could scarcely be explained. But can it be said that such short-term calculations correspond much more closely to the attitudes connected with the present-day catch-all mass party with its widely ranging clientele? Can the short-term benefit approach, for example, be utilized in military or foreign-policy issues?

In some countries in the last decade it has become the rule for catch-all parties out of office simply to lay the most recent shortcomings or apparent deterioration of the country's military or international position at the doorstep of the incumbent government, especially during election campaigns: thus in the United States the Republican party in 1952 with regard to the long-lasting indecisive Korean War, or in Germany more recently the Social Democrats

---

[20] "It always organizes its action so as to focus on a single quantity: its vote margin over the opposition in the test at the end of the current election period." In A. Downs, *An Economic Theory of Democracy*, 1957, p. 174.

with regard to Adenauer's apparent passivity in the face of the Berlin Wall. In other instances, however, the opposition plays down foreign or military issues or treats them in generalities vague enough to evoke the image of itself as a competitor who will be able to handle them as well as the incumbent government.

To the extent that the party system still includes "unreformed" or—as in the case of the Italian Socialist party—only "half-reformed" class-mass type integration parties, foreign or military issues enter election campaigns as policy differences. Yet even here the major interest has shifted away from areas where the electorate could exercise only an illusory choice. The electorate senses that in the concrete situation, based in considerable part on geography and history, the international bloc affiliation of the country rather than any policy preference will form the basis of decision. It senses too that such decisions rest only partially, or at times nominally, with the political leadership. Even if the impact of the political leader on the decision may have been decisive, more often than not election timetables in democracies are such that the decision, once carried out, is no longer contested or even relevant to voter choices. As likely as not, new events crowd it out of the focus of voters' attention. Few voters still thought of Mendès-France's 1954 "abandonment" of Indo-China when Edgar Faure suddenly dissolved the Assembly in December 1955. While a party may benefit from its adversary's unpopular decisions, such benefits are more often an accidental by-product than the outcome of a government-opposition duel with clearly distributed roles and decisions.

A party may put up reasonably coherent, even if vague, foreign or military policies for election purposes. It may criticize the inept handling of such problems by the government of the day, and more and more intensively as it gets closer to election day. But in neither case is there a guarantee of the party's ability to act as a coherent body in parliament when specific action preferences are to be determined. Illustrative of this dilemma are the history of EDC in the French Parliament and the more recent battles within the British parties in regard to entrance into the Common Market (although the latter case remains inconclusive because of De Gaulle's settling the issue in his own way, for the time being). Fortuitous election timetables and the hopes, fears, and expectations of the public do not intermesh sufficiently with the parliamentary representatives' disjointed action on concrete issues before them to add up to the elaboration of clear-cut party action preference.

The catch-all party contributes general programs in the elaboration of domestic action preferences. These programs may be of a prognostic variety, informing the public about likely specific developments and general trends. Yet prognostics and desirability blur into each other in this type of futurology, in which rosy glasses offer previews of happy days for all and sundry among the party's prospective customers. These programs may lead to or be joined with action proposals in various stages of concretization. Concrete proposals, however, always risk implying promises which may be too specific. Concretizations must remain general enough so that they cannot be turned from electoral weapons to engines of assault against the party which first mounted them.

This indeterminacy allows the catch-all party to function as a meeting ground for the elaboration of concrete action for a multiplicity of interest groups. All the party may require from those who obtain its services is that they make a maximal attempt to arrive at compromises within the framework of the party and that they avoid coalescing with forces hostile to the party. The compromises thus elaborated must be acceptable to major interest groups even if these groups, for historical or traditional reasons, happen not to be represented in the governing party. Marginal differences may be submitted to the voter at elections or, as older class-mass parties do on occasion, via referenda (Switzerland and Sweden). But expected policy mutations are in the nature of increments rather than major changes in intergroup relations.

It is here that the difference between the catch-all and the older form of integration party becomes most clearly visible. The catch-all party will do its utmost to establish consensus to avoid party realignment. The integration party may count on majority political mechanisms to implement its programs only to find that hostile interests frustrate the majority decision by the economic and social mechanisms at their disposal. They may call strikes (by labor or farmers or storekeepers or investors), they may withdraw capital to safe haven outside the country, they may undermine that often hypocritically invoked but real factor known as the "confidence of the business community."

VI. Integration through Participation in Leadership Selection— the Future of the Political Party

What then remains the real share of the catch-all party in the elaboration of action preferences? Its foremost contribution lies in the mobilization of the voters for whatever concrete action preferences leaders are able to establish rather than *a priori* selections of their own. It is for this reason that the catch-all party prefers to visualize action in the light of the contingencies, threats, and promises of concrete historical situations rather than of general social goals. It is the hoped-for or already established role in the dynamics of action, in which the voters' vicarious participation is invited, that is most in evidence. Therefore the attention of both party and public at large focuses most clearly on problems of leadership selection.

Nomination means the prospect of political office. Political office involves a chance to make an impact via official action. The competition between those striving to influence official action puts into evidence the political advantage of those in a position to act before their political adversaries can do so. The privilege of first action is all the more precious in a new and non-repetitive situation where the political actor can avoid getting enmeshed in directives deriving from party action preferences. Much as the actor welcomes party support on the basis of revered (but elastic) principles, he shuns specific direction and supervision. In this respect the catch-all party furnishes an ideal background for political action. Where obtaining office becomes an almost exclusive preoccupation of a party, issues of personnel are reduced to search for the simplest effective means to put up winning combinations. The search is especially effective wherever the party becomes a channel by which representatives of hitherto excluded or neglected minorities may join the existing political elite.

The nomination of candidates for popular legitimation as officeholders thus emerges as the most important function of the present-day catch-all party. Concentration on the selection of candidates for office is in line with an increasing role differentiation in industrial society. Once certain levels of education and material welfare are reached, both intellectual and material needs are taken care of by specialized purveyors of communications and economic products. Likewise the party, which in less advanced societies or in those intent on rapid change directly interferes with the performance of societal jobs, remains in Western industrial society twice removed—through government and bureaucracy—from the field of direct action. To this state of affairs correspond now prevailing popular images and expectations in regard to the reduced role of the party.[21] Expectations previously set on the performance of a political organization are now flowing into different channels.[22]

At the same time, the role of the political party as a factor in the continued integration of the individual into the national life now has to be visualized in a different light. Compared to his connection with interest organizations and voluntary assocations of a non-political nature and to his frequent encounters with the state bureaucracy, the citizen's relations with the political party are becoming more intermittent and of more limited scope.

To the older party of integration the citizen, if he so desired, could be closer. Then it was a less differentiated organization, part channel of protest, part source of protection, part purveyor of visions of the future. Now, in its linear descendant in a transfigured world, the catch-all party, the citizen finds a relatively remote, at times quasi-official and alien structure. Democratic society assumes that the citizen is finally an integral and conscious participant in the affairs of both the polity and the economy; it further assumes that as such he will work through the party as one of the many interrelated structures by which he achieves a rational participation in his surrounding world.

Should he ever live up to these assumptions, the individual and society may indeed find the catch-all party—non-utopian, non-oppressive, and ever so flexible—an ingenious and useful political instrument.

What about the attitude toward the modern catch-all party of functional powerholders in army, bureaucracy, industry, and labor? Released from their previous unnecessary fears as to the ideological propensities and future intentions of the class-mass party, functional powerholders have come to recognize the catch-all party's role as consensus purveyor. In exchange for its ability to provide a clear-cut basis of legitimacy, functional powerholders are, up to a point, willing to recognize the political leadership claims of the party. They expect

[21] See the discussion of political attitudes in Habermas, *et al.*, *Student und Politik*, Neuwied, 1961, and the German preference scale quoted in R. Mayntz, "Loisirs, participation sociale et activité politique," in *Revue Internationale des Sciences Sociales* (1960), pp. 608-622.

[22] See the contribution of S. Mallet, "L'Audience politique des syndicats," in Léo Hamon, ed., *Les nouveaux comportements politiques de la classe ouvrière*, Paris, 1962, esp. pp. 241-244.

it to exercise certain arbitration functions in intergroup relations and to initiate limited political innovations. The less clear-cut the electoral basis of the party's leadership claim and the closer the next election date, the smaller the credit which functional powerholders will extend to unsolicited and non-routine activities of the political powerholders impinging on their own positions. This lack of credit then sets the stage for conflicts between functional and political leadership groups. How does the catch-all party in governmental positions treat such conflicts? Will it be satisfied to exercise pressure via the mass media, or will it try to re-create a militant mass basis beyond the evanescent electoral and publicity levels? But the very structure of the catch-all party, the looseness of its clientele, may from the outset exclude such more far-reaching action. To that extent the political party's role in Western industrial society today is more limited than would appear from its position of formal preeminence. Via its governmental role it functions as coordinator of and arbitrator between functional power groups. Via its electoral role it produces that limited amount of popular participation and integration required from the popular masses for the functioning of official political institutions.

Will this limited participation which the catch-all party offers the population at large, this call to rational and dispassionate participation in the political process via officially sanctioned channels, work?

The instrument, the catch-all party, cannot be much more rational than its nominal master, the individual voter. No longer subject to the discipline of the party of integration—or, as in the United States, never subject to this discipline—the voters may, by their shifting moods and their apathy, transform the sensitive instrument of the catch-all party into something too blunt to serve as a link with the functional powerholders of society.[23] Then we may yet come to regret the passing—even if it was inevitable—of the class-mass party and the denominational party, as we already regret the passing of other features in yesterday's stage of Western civilization.

---

[23] For some recent strictures on slavish party dependence on the results of polls, see Ulrich Lohmar, *op.cit.*, pp. 106-108.

CHAPTER 7

THE DECLINE OF THE PARTY IN SINGLE-PARTY AFRICAN STATES

IMMANUEL WALLERSTEIN

THE POLITICAL history of the colonial period in Africa is in large part that of the demand made by the educated classes for participation in their government—at first for some minimal participation, later for total control; at first in their own name, later on behalf of the whole of the indigenous population. For example, Wight reports: "In 1917 (Joseph) Casely-Hayford founded the National Congress of British West Africa, which sought to unite the four West African colonies in the demand for 'self-determination' and 'no taxation without representation.' Mr. Hayford led a deputation of the Congress to the Secretary of State in 1920-1, to ask for a legislative council one-half elected, a 'house of assembly' containing the legislative council plus six financial members to control revenue and expenditure, municipal corporations with unofficial majorities, the appointment of Africans to judicial offices, and the establishment of a West African university."[1]

Put forward first and with most vigor in British West Africa and French North Africa, this demand came to take essentially the same form everywhere. And everywhere the initial response of the colonial powers was similar to that of Lord Lugard: "It is a cardinal principle of British Colonial policy that the interests of a large native population shall not be subject to the will either of a small European class [N.B. This proviso did not seem equally to apply in settler territories such as Kenya] or of a small minority of educated and Europeanised natives who have nothing in common with them and whose interests are often opposed to theirs. . . . A Council in such circumstances, as Sir C. Dilke observed in Parliament, 'is not a liberal institution, but a veiled oligarchy of the worst description,' and responsible autocracy is preferable. The point is of special importance in Northern Nigeria where the intelligent Emirs are in acute divergence in religion and social status from the natives of

[1] M. Wight, *The Gold Coast Legislative Council*, London: Faber and Faber, 1947, pp. 26-27.

the Coast."[2] As Metternich claimed to defend the "true people" against the middle classes who wished to participate in government in the name of the people, so did the colonial governments claim to protect the natives against the educated classes in Africa.[3]

After the Second World War nationalist movements emerged throughout Africa. Their demands were multiple. Included among them were demands for greater popular participation in and democratic recruitment for government.

The meaning given to popular participation in and democratic recruitment to government tends to vary with the perspective of the observer. Among the things referred to under the heading of political participation are: voting for elected officials (leaving open the question of which officials shall be elected and which appointed); collective militant activity, especially in the form of political parties (including giving of funds, public meetings, demonstrations); discussion of political issues in the public arena; representation of one's interests in the legislative process; negotiation of one's interests at the level of administrative decisions; the continual according of legitimacy and support to a state and its government. Each of these meanings can be discussed in terms of whether the right exists to its exercise, either de jure or de facto. Furthermore each can be discussed in terms of the degree to which the right is in fact exercised. Discussion of democratic recruitment involves a similar confusion. On the one hand, one may inquire whether there exist any ascriptive criteria which debar some people *ab initio* from access to posts of power (either political or administrative). On the other hand, one may inquire into who, as a consequence of the interplay of political forces in a particular society at a particular time, in fact accedes to the positions of power.

The African Nationalist leadership did not distinguish among the many forms such participation or recruitment could take. It was clear that colonial rule was a major barrier to realization of their demands in all its aspects. Thus sooner or later the nationalist movements stated as their explicit goal the achievement of independence.

In most countries of Africa the struggle for independence resulted in the emergence of one political party with a mass, inter-ethnic

[2] *Report on the Amalgamation of Northern and Southern Nigeria and Administration, 1912-1919*, Cmd. 468, p. 19 cited in R. L. Buell, *The Native Problem in Africa*, New York: MacMillan, 1928, Vol. I, p. 738, n.3.

[3] See R. Emerson, *From Empire to Nation*, Cambridge: Harvard University Press, 1960, p. 193.

base (or at least mass, inter-ethnic aspirations) along with other political formations of two main varieties: remnants of, or descendants of, earlier nationalist movements whose present base tended to be inter-ethnic but not mass; and tribal-regional parties that often had mass support in their region but whose appeal was largely to one ethnic group.

The strength of the mass, nationalist movement at the time a country achieved independence was affected by several factors which varied according to the policy of the colonial authorities: the degree of clandestinity of the party, the violence and length of the decolonization struggle, the role traditional chiefs wished to and were allowed to play in the movement, the strength of traditional political structures. In terms of national popular support the movements ranged from extreme strength (Ivory Coast, Tunisia, Tanganyika) to relative weakness (Congo-Leopoldville, Nigeria) with many examples in the middle (Ghana, Sierra Leone, Uganda, Upper Volta, Sudan). The parties ranged also, though not necessarily in parallel fashion, according to strength of internal organization.

The role of the national party in the post-independence era was not the same as that of the nationalist movement in the pre-independence era. The revolutionary conquest of power required different emphases and different programs from those involved in the building of a nation. As the leaders of the movement moved into positions of governmental authority, they became enmeshed in an ongoing machinery which had its own requirements and constraints different from those of a political party. The fact that the personnel of party and government were intermeshed created certain clear strains, which were variously resolved. We can analyze the consequences in terms of three phases, although the time period for some phases in some countries may be short indeed and although it may be very difficult to give dates to the various phases in each country.

Phase number one is the emergence of the one-party state. Faced with the problems of national integration after independence, the people in power tended in almost all cases to feel with Rousseau that "it is therefore essential that if the general will is to be able to express itself, there should be no partial society within the State, and that each citizen should think only his own thoughts."[4] This feeling took form in the drive toward establishing one-party states, a drive which has been more or less successful in some two-thirds of Africa's

[4] J. J. Rousseau, *The Social Contract*, Bk. II, Ch. 3.

independent states as of the beginning of 1964. This political push, and even more its success, has had very important consequences for the mode of political participation in post-independence Africa and for the ways of recruitment into politics.[5]

The primary reason for the tendency to create a one-party state was ultimately to promote national integration, immediately to prevent secessionist movements which existed or might grow up around ethnic-regional parties. This was true even where the dominant nationalist party was historically primarily the emanation of one ethnic group. Corpierre states the situation very well: "The ethnic party, if it wins, loses its ethnic character from the very fact of its victory. . . . This dialectic of nation and ethnic group is the essence of the originality of contemporary black African politics."[6]

If the most pressing concern was that of containing opposition which might find its outlet in the destruction of the nascent state, the second concern was expressed precisely in terms of recruitment and participation. The shortage of cadres at the top level led to a demand that they all be incorporated into the ruling structure in such a way as to maximize technical efficiency and minimize competition among themselves vis-à-vis either the outside world or the peasant masses. As part of the need to build an effective state machinery and to create an aura of legitimacy for it, it was essential both to expand and control the popular participation which the granting of universal suffrage made inevitable for juridical and normative reasons. For both these tasks the single party was seen as the most effective mechanism. These "political" objectives took precedence over, indeed were seen as prerequisites to, economic development. Again, as Corpierre notes: "For Algeria as for China, economic development is not priority number one, but priority number three. The prime objective is the building of the State; the second, the formation of the national ruling class. To achieve them, the second especially, it may be advantageous to regress with regard to the third."[7]

Such an operation seems to require not merely a single party but

[5] It should be clearly noted at the outset that whereas what has happened in terms of political participation can be followed from the general press, knowledge about recruitment patterns is much more difficult to obtain and given both the shortness of time since independence and the difficulties of research very little scholarly (or other) material, reliable or otherwise, is available on this subject.

[6] M. Corpierre, "Le totalitarisme africain," *Preuves*, No. 143, January 1963, p. 16.

[7] *Ibid.*, p. 17.

also a clear leadership principle within the single party. Power has not been shared at the top very long in most states. Collective leadership in Algeria gave way to the primacy of Ben Bella, seconded by Colonel Boumedienne. Ultimately the latter took sole control because of his power over the military. The dual leadership of Senghor and Mamadou Dia in Senegal has ended with the latter in prison.[8] The list of number-two men who have been eliminated from power in African states since independence is indeed very long. The resulting unitary leadership has found expression in the constitutional presidentialism so prevalent today.[9] It is as though so little total power attaches to the central state authority that having less than all of it is insufficient to the maintenance of this authority.

The effort to create a single-party system was most intense immediately following the granting of independence. It is easy to see why. The transfer of sovereignty is a move of major importance, and regional groups whose economic or political interests are threatened by those in control of the new state machinery are most apt to take advantage of this moment—perhaps their last—to attempt to secede or at least to weaken the central authority. Katanga is the classic example, but the cases are legion. However, if on the one hand it is a good moment to attempt secession, it is also the first moment when those who now have the central authority can really crack down. Up to this point the ultimate authority of the colonial government has meant some restraint on the action of leaders of the nationalist party, both for normative and political reasons. Now such interference is no longer legally possible.[10]

The power of the state in this situation is great in two respects: it has force at its disposal as well as a judicial system and can jail opponents. It has money, and is indeed the major source of money, which can be used to support pro-government machinery and propaganda efforts as well as to buy off opponents. In ancient days the state machinery was used to force dissidents to kneel before the king. The modern functional equivalent is to join the party. Perhaps

[8] P. Decraene observes of the late 1963 crisis in Senegal: "Thus, if we seek to draw the lessons of the affair, we observe to begin with—on first sight—that power is no more shared in Senegal than in other states south of the Sahara." "Réflexions sur les récents événements du Sénégal," *Comptes-Rendus Mensuels de l'Académie des Sciences d'Outre-Mer*, Vol. 23 (February 1963), p. 61.

[9] See J. Buchmann, *L'Afrique Noire Indépendante*, Paris: Librairie Générale de Droit et de Jurisprudence, 1962, Ch. 6, "Le présidentialisme negro-africain."

[10] The fact that it was attempted in the Congo after independence by the invasion of Belgian paratroopers accounts for the violence of African reaction to this violation of the essence of independence.

the question might be raised, why the party? But the party has acquired a legitimacy both specifically from the immediate colonial struggle and generically from world history of the past 200 years. It responds to the value of universal participation in government, a value underlined by universal suffrage. In any case, as Apter notes: "The interest of the militants is one of maintaining solidarity and cohesion in society. They intend to make such cohesion a joint concern of party and state."[11]

Toward this end they have sought in most cases the dissolution of other parties, the inclusion of the opposition leadership as members in the governing parties, the crossing of the floor by opposition deputies (usually elected in the last pre-independence election), the enrollment of civil servants and other self-styled non-political elements in the party. The government can give money directly or indirectly to party structures and party newspapers. In many African states the theory of the precedence of the party over the state has become official doctrine.[12] The extreme point of such a process is the proclamation of a one-party state, which has been in the constitutions of Algeria, Ghana, and Tanzania.

This era may be seen as the high-point of the party's importance. With the one exception of Algeria, the single parties have been everywhere defined as mass parties open to all adult citizens; and they have seen in most African states a mass adhesion since nominal membership has often been a prerequisite for the individual of maintaining the neutrality of the state toward him. Recruitment has thus seemed to be optimally democratic and a certain kind of participation has been great. This mass recruitment has not been merely nominal but has been sometimes accompanied by mass mobilization in the sense of widespread activity of local party units in community labor (*investissements humains*) and political education. But mass mobilization has been most effective in states that were under external strain during the post-independence period (in particular, Guinea, and to a lesser extent Mali). In many other states mass mobilization has been a slogan or an objective but seldom a reality.

One-party regimes have not been fully installed in all countries. Where two constitutional units have merged (Cameroun, Somalia) the smaller unit has kept its separate single-party structure as a

---

[11] David E. Apter, *Ghana in Transition*, New York: Atheneum, 1963, p. 358.

[12] This is a well-known feature of the so-called radical states, such as Guinea, Mali, Ghana, Algeria. But it is true of many of the others as well, especially in French-speaking Africa.

bargaining weapon within the state. Where countries have had a federal system (Nigeria, Congo-Leopoldville) no national single-party system has emerged, but single-party systems have developed within most of the constituent units—notably, for example, in Nigeria.[13] But as of the end of 1963, of the 21 provinces of the Congo, 12 (with two more marginal cases) had a single dominant party.[14]

The first post-independence phase, then, was characterized by the growth, at the level of the first governmental unit that controlled force, money and jobs, of a party structure coterminous with that unit. How long this took varied greatly, as we have indicated. The curious phenomenon, however, was not the emergence of a one-party system. It was rather its rapid loss of meaning. As soon as the one-party system reached its peak and thus performed its function of securing at least initial allegiance to the new state, as soon as it became an essential channel of both recruitment and participation, it seemed immediately to become little more than a formal framework despite all the talk about it, unless great effort was placed in maintaining its role as the key center of decision-making. As a Tanzanian report put it, "By a paradox the more support the people have given to [the party] the more they have reduced their participation in the process of government."[15]

In some respects the decline of the party sometimes began while it was still increasing its role in other ways. One basic way in which it declined, the most obvious, was the loss of revolutionary momentum. Enthusiasm for and participation in mass movements can, almost by definition, be maintained at high levels for only relatively short periods of time. The saliency of the private aspects of one's life creates constant pressure toward the reduction of time-commitments to public functions. Crises lead to priority for public functions on the grounds of urgency. Once urgency is no longer felt or felt less, public activities suffer. So it has been clearly the case in the party structures of African one-party states.

The decline in mass interest was reinforced by the decline in cadre interest. In the early stage of the anti-colonial struggle party cadres

[13] See J. P. Mackintosh, "Electoral Trends and the Tendency to a One-Party System in Nigeria," *Journal of Commonwealth Political Studies*, Vol. 1 (November 1962), pp. 194-210.

[14] See M. C. Young, "The Congo's Six Provinces Become Twenty-One," *Africa Report* (October 1963). But this broke down in the Congo because of the lack of sufficient stability nationally to assure sufficient continuity locally.

[15] *Report on the Presidential Commission and the Establishment of a One Party State*, Dar es Salaam Government Printing, 1965, p. 14.

were, if not professional revolutionaries, men who devoted all their possible time to furthering the work of the party.[16] In the late colonial period, when the nationalist movement entered the government, men in key party posts at all levels took on simultaneously governmental responsibilities at all levels. This was even more true immediately after independence. But a governmental appointment, whether political or in the civil service, precludes full-time party work. And the new governments need their cadres. The governmental work has become more and more time-consuming, eating constantly into the time available for after-hours party work. And as a single-party system emerged, less need was seen for party activity.

The number of meetings of the party, whether at the ward level or at that of a national political bureau, has tended to diminish, in extreme cases to virtually zero. Collection of dues has become increasingly difficult as the party increasingly faces no opposition and controls the government (and therefore, in the eyes of its members, funds). Conversely, the party has in fact needed less support in the form of funds from the ordinary member since it could now levy large contributions from the salaries of well-paid ministers and civil servants. The trend has been therefore toward inanition. The Algerian intellectual, Franz Fanon, saw this clearly: "After a few years, the break-up of the party becomes obvious, and any observer, even the most superficial, can notice that the party, today the skeleton of its former self, only serves to immobilise the people."[17]

One way of combatting the decline of mass and cadre interest is to turn to those elements of the masses who have especial interest in the work of the party, who are the most self-interested in change, and to those elements of the cadres who have the most energy and time. Such elements are organized in the auxiliary movements of the party: the youth, the women, the trade-unions, the farmers' groups. Syndical structures appeal to self-interest and have their own activist traditions. International links of these groups serve to spur activities. The youth especially may be less caught up in the administration of the country.

These auxiliaries have been seen by the parties as a way of mass mobilization, of canalizing the desire for participation, of serving as channels to filter recruits into the party and government. Therefore,

[16] Unless, of course, as in Algeria or Angola, they were in armed rebellion. While service in an armed force was perceived as equivalent to party work in other countries, the net consequence of such activity is not necessarily the emergence of a strong party structure per se. Witness Algeria.
[17] *The Wretched of the Earth*, New York, Grove Press, 1963, p. 138.

once brought firmly within the party orbit, they have received financial assistance from party and government. Very quickly after independence the auxiliaries tended to become more active (as measured by numbers of meetings, abilities to raise funds, turnout at mass functions) than the party itself. The auxiliaries, especially the youth and the trade-unions, tended also to regard themselves as a vanguard element, the representatives of revolutionary purity. They often attracted into their leadership dissident elements within the national party.

Thus, while the top leadership of the party by its accession to posts in government inevitably moved out of day-to-day contact with the party's supporters, a second echelon of leaders in the auxiliaries was increasing such contact. Whatever the motivations of the leaders of the auxiliaries, they could not but tend to become the voice of the critics, and critics who were rapidly becoming more solidly entrenched in popular support than the national leadership.

The combination of the auxiliaries' greater activity and their factionalism has tended to bring a reaction from the government. The leadership has been purged, often arbitrarily, sometimes extralegally. Sometimes separate membership cards for trade-unions have been abolished, as in Ghana. Age-limits have been placed on membership in youth organizations, as in Nigeria (thus limiting the ability of dissident party leaders to find refuge there). The national co-ordinating structures of the youth section have been abolished, as in Guinea and Mali, and replaced by a governmental ministry. The objective of reducing these organizations as separate power structures has been realized, but at the price of reducing their activity, sometimes to the level of over-all party activity. Thus success of party and auxiliary activity has been self-defeating in that it has tended to generate counterforces which lead to decline.

There is another way in which the very achievement of a single-party system has militated against the power structure. One of the themes of the new nationalist governments as expressed through the demand for a single-party system has been national reconciliation, the purpose being to contain regionalism, to promote national integration. This has involved bringing into the fold of the party the traditional elements, who were often hostile to the nationalist movement during the colonial period, an objective further reinforced by cultural nationalism, which also tends to revalorize traditional leaders.

At the level of the village this process can effectively transform the function of a party unit from a reformist weapon to a defense mechanism of local interests. In many cases, then, the reformist elements found expression in the youth wing of the village (or sometimes the women's wing). But as the national administration sought more and more things of the village administration, now increasingly in the hands of the elders, it became more prone to make concessions on local quarrels, which meant backing the party unit against the youth wing even if the latter more closely reflected national long-range goals.

What occurred was an increasing merger of government and party at both the national and local levels. It is argued that the party was taking over the government. It often looked like the reverse. There was a trend toward merging the office of President of the country and Secretary-General of the party, lest a separate occupant in the latter post threaten the primacy of the former. High party officials sought ministerial office, as did leaders of auxiliaries—at the very least as ministers without porfolio; for ministers are paid well, have many perquisites, have prestige abroad, and while internal protocol gives precedence to party officials, international protocol does not. There was a trend to place the auxiliaries under the appropriate government ministries. At the regional and local levels the dual structure of party and government became cumbersome and inefficient. Very shortly, therefore, devices to avoid conflict were developed. In Tanzania, for example, the regional and district commissioners now direct and promote the activities of the party structures, as since 1963 do the equivalent officials in Tunisia and Algeria.

Finally, the government demanded increasing technical efficiency. At first civil servants were suspected by party politicians as persons who might sabotage their work. They were supervised by parallel party structures. They were recruited into the party, often under pressure. But as time went on, the loyalty of civil servants became more secure, the attitudes of political leaders less different from their own. Incompetent personnel whose only claim to position was nationalist militance tended to be superseded. Persons whose career-line had been through the civil service came to be recruited into key party machinery, as with the inclusion in 1961 of three senior civil servants in the Central Committee of the Convention People's Party (Ghana). The wheel had turned.

The consequences of this rapid turn of events, occurring in a very few years after independence, have been greater than at first realized.

Wherever the party structure is declining in vitality there seems to be a real decline in popular participation in the governmental process in the sense of the ability of individuals to affect the decisions of the state by communicating their point of view. The succession of coups and attempted coups in African states has revealed a deep public apathy about the parties. The parties have not served as a channel of political action in terms of preventing, starting, or ending the coups, which have seemed to be palace revolutions even when, as in Congo-Brazzaville and Dahomey, they were accompanied by the spectacle of some public rioting. The riots served no immediate ideological objective other than changing personnel, and the rioters seemed more manipulated than manipulators. It is possible of course that such coups may start processes in some of the states which will eventually result in more substantial change.

The one-party system seemed originally to promise a real change in modes of recruitment in the direction of egalitarianism. The decline of the effectiveness of the party seems to have halted such a trend. The degree to which the educational system and governmental structure recruit from non-traditional elites now is not greater than, perhaps even less than, in the late colonial era. The precedence of the party has tended to be more formal than real. If invoked in a crisis situation, it cannot prevail against those who have access to the military, as the attempt in 1963 of Mamadou Dia in Senegal indicates.[18]

Where the powers-that-be have not been split among themselves and are therefore identical with the party executive it has been convenient to recall to the legislators, who tend to speak for local interests, that the party is primary, as, for example, Philippe Yacé did in the Ivory Coast in 1961, when he reminded the members of the National Assembly, over which he presided, that "the comportment of members of parliament, the nature of their speeches must be formulated within the political framework defined by the doctrine of *Parti Démocratique de la Côte d'Ivoire* and by the chief of state."[19]

Nevertheless, the decline of popular participation, the narrowing

[18] Prime Minister Dia argued that the decisions of the Political Bureau of the U.P.S. must determine those of the National Assembly. His supporters had a majority in the former body, those of President Senghor in the latter. When he tried to prevent by force the National Assembly from voting no confidence in his regime, he was bested by Senghor with the support of the Army.

[19] *Afrique Nouvelle* (Dakar), No. 740, October 11, 1961, p. 5.

base of political recruitment, and the inefficacy of party primacy when the party leadership is split have had very serious repercussions on the strength of the central government. The nationalist movements came to power largely as the spokesmen of modernizing elites interested in creating nation-states which would transform their societies into units that were politically and economically strong, measured on a world scale. They are in the process of becoming transformed into coalitions of local elites interested in obtaining a cut of the increased income of a market economy but fearful of more rapid modernization because it may threaten their newly acquired privileges. The national assemblies are becoming in some states revalorized as a gathering of local notables. The member would thus become the direct representative of local electors charged with interceding on their behalf or negotiating with the central authority.[20] In this kind of situation Apter's comment about Ghana probably applies to all of Africa: "The greatest danger . . . is not autocracy, nor socialism, nor neo-traditionalism but simply political cynicism."[21]

The decline of the party has not occurred unnoticed. In some countries those who control the central machinery have sought to revitalize the party, which can be considered the beginning of phase three. The then Prime Minister of Tanganyika, Julius Nyerere, resigned his post in early 1962 in order to reestablish the party as a functioning body. Both the Ivory Coast and Dahomey announced that same year the establishment of special party cells within government ministries to supervise governmental activity. These efforts were in fact desultory. In 1963 a series of steps were taken in some of the states that have the strongest party structures to preserve their strength by a sort of neo-vanguardism. Shortly after the attempted assassination of Bourguiba Tunisia announced such steps involving a closer interpenetration of key administrative and party personnel. Some persons in the party are now advocating an elite party. Mali established special schools for party cadres, and leading cabinet members who were also members of the Political Bureau took six weeks out of their work in the summer of 1963 to supervise

[20] In Ghana, the organ of radical elements in the C.P.P. attacked the National Assembly precisely for playing this role. See "Whither Parliament?" *The Spark*, No. 47, November 1, 1963.

[21] Apter, *op.cit.*, p. 372. *The Spark* argued in an editorial in No. 16, March 29, 1963, that the supremacy of the party over the cabinet could only be assured by "institutional checks and balances," and that "if ministers constitute a majority on the central committee, that body inevitably comes under the control of the cabinet," a condition the editorial deplored.

personally these schools. Guinea, at its Seventh Congress of the *Parti Démocratique de Guinée* in August 1963, reorganized its national conference so that a body of some 200 rather than some 2,000 would be the supreme decision-making body. It also expanded the National Assembly from 60 to 75, allowing 60 as before to be nominated by the regional federations of the party but 15 to be nominated by the Political Bureau. In February 1964 in Guinea the P.D.G. recreated both the *Haut Commissariat de la Jeunesse* and the national executive of the youth organization. In November 1964, the P.D.G. reduced the number of sections so as to end a situation where a section could represent a few families.[22] Algeria, establishing its structure several years after the others and in the light of their experience, opted outright for a vanguard structure. In the wake of the assassination attempt on President Nkrumah in December 1963 party cadres seized the opportunity to try to reassert their primacy over civil servants in governmental decision-making.

In résumé, the single party in Africa has seen an evolution of its role since independence, or rather since a peak point reached in most countries shortly after independence. The party has become much less active, as have its auxiliaries. Since in a one-party system an active party is the only meaningful channel of popular participation in government, this has meant a real decline in participation. Not only does government find it increasingly difficult to mobilize mass action except in international crisis, but also there is less expression of the desires and demands of the ordinary citizens. This is least true where the party structure remains relatively strongest.

Perhaps more important than the decline of participation is the change in patterns of recruitment. While the former is clear to any attentive observer, we have little hard data on the latter phenomenon. But indirect evidence seems to indicate that in most African countries the bandwagon riders (the *"combattants de la dernière heure"*) are acquiring or reacquiring much influence and that the hold of traditional elites is being strengthened by their continued (perhaps increased) preferential access both to education and to political and administrative posts in state and party. This natural tendency to cooptation is encouraged by international pressures for middle-range stability. As this cooptation takes place, the party ceases to be the watch-dog and agent of the central administration on political and economic affairs and becomes the arena of trade among the various

---

[22] See *Afrique Nouvelle* (Dakar), No. 902, November 20-26, 1964, p. 4.

privileged sectors of the population. It ceases to be the major agent of social change. It comes to register whatever changes occur external to it.

The explanations adduced here for the decline of the role of the party apply very widely and would not explain why the party has remained stronger in some African countries than others, or, if we look more widely on the international arena, why it has remained relatively strong in the Communist regimes. The staying power of single parties seems to be a function of the explicitness of an ideology, the degree of national isolation, and the degree to which the party concentrates on mobilizing and training middle cadres as agents of the center. The combination of these variables might suffice to explain why in Africa today the party is an effective organism of power to some extent in some states, for example Guinea, Mali, Tanzania, and Tunisia, and irrelevant in many other states. That is not to deny that it is all-pervasive in many other states and that it is an electoral mechanism in some states. But in many of these states, to some extent indeed in all, status in the party structure is a consequence of status elsewhere and not the reverse. Put another way, if an individual has a key position in both the party and the government hierarchy, he tends to operate in terms of the priorities, exigencies, and pressures of the governmental structure. Position in the party becomes then nothing but the final instrument of legitimation of authority. It remains an important symbol but one that is an instrument in hands external to it. In effect, the one-party state in Africa has become in many places the no-party state.

Part III:
Parties and the Crises of
Political Development

CHAPTER 8

POLITICAL RECRUITMENT AND PARTICIPATION IN EGYPT

LEONARD BINDER

IN THE *Philosophy of the Revolution*, the only book which has been attributed to President Gamal Abd al-Nasser, the leader of the Egyptian revolution expressed his disappointment with the nature of the popular response to the initiative taken by the Free Officers in July of 1952. It had been the assumption of the conspirators that the act of removing the king would be sufficient; they expected that the people would immediately rally behind the revolutionaries and support the reforms which all knew were necessary. But this assumption was doubly naïve, for it presupposed, first, that the amelioration of Egypt's social and economic problems could be accomplished by the negative act of removing the evil-doers of the old regime and; second, that the people of Egypt comprised an integrated and mobilized community.

These two presuppositions define the empirical relationship between party organization and development in the new state. The people of Egypt did not rise as one man to the support of the new regime. Egyptian political and social life was not transformed overnight. The problem of what to do with the supreme authority once it had been attained was not resolved by a self-evident solution. To simplify greatly the problem which faced the new regime, it may be said that it had to find a way to mobilize support and to break down mass indifference while containing elite opportunism. The very difficulty of attaining this end revealed the nature of political underdevelopment in Egypt: the illiteracy and inaccessibility of the peasant masses; the sharp differences in income and styles of life between the urban upper class and the middle classes of both town and country; the inarticulateness of the urban proletariat; and the fanaticism of the lower middle classes, the artisans, and the small-scale bazaar merchants. Gradually it was also learned that mass poverty was not the consequence of exploitation alone, but largely due to limited resources and structural factors that could not be overcome merely by passing laws.

In another context we have discussed the slow emergence of the ideology of Arab Socialism, which currently expresses the development goals of the present government of Egypt and describes the policies by which development is to be achieved. Here our concern is with the more restricted problem of political organization, which is one of the instruments for implementing those policies. The other instruments are primarily bureaucratic and will not concern us. We would note that insofar as enhancing the solidarity of the people of Egypt is an ideological desideratum our distinction between ideology and organization does not hold because political organization is then not merely an instrument for the implementation of policy; it is in some sense a direct realization of the policy goal itself.

The issue of central concern here may be expressed in terms of political participation. The revolutionary government felt that in order to achieve Egyptian development it should increase the political participation of certain groups and restrict the participation of others. In general it has sought to increase the participation of the masses, whom it intended to benefit but who made few concrete demands other than that their government be an Islamic-Egyptian one. It has also sought to limit the political participation of the urban political elite of the *ancien régime*, which was likely to make the greatest demands.

President Nasser has sought to achieve these ends through the establishment of three successive political organizations, the Liberation Rally, the National Union, and the Socialist Union. The government of Egypt has been reluctant to call these organizations political parties although they resemble single mobilization parties in almost every way. Their creation coincided with certain phases of policy orientation. The Liberation Rally was established after all political parties were banned and while revolutionary control of the bureaucracy was still limited. It was meant to fill the gap left by the previous parties and to mobilize support for Nasser immediately after his victory over Naguib, who had been the nominal leader of the revolution and had the support of the Wafd and other groups such as the lawyers and students. The National Union was organized after the Sinai-Suez invasion and represented an attempt at unifying the Egyptian population behind a narrowly preserved regime. The National Union, unlike the Liberation Rally, was not merely meant to block the formation of other parties. The founding of the Socialist Union coincided with the adoption of a Socialist ideology and the growing realization that mass cooperation and not merely moral support would be necessary if development goals were to be achieved.

Each successive organizing effort has revealed new dimensions of Egyptian policy regarding political participation. Each of the three political parties has been organized as a pyramid of committees paralleling the village, district, province, and national levels of government. At the higher levels, as might be expected, members have sought effective rather than merely ceremonial political participation. There has been tension between the various committees of the parties and the parallel levels of the service branches of the bureaucracy. Each successive organization has recruited persons more sympathetic to the aims of the revolutionary regime into its upper ranks; and, as the rationalization of the economy outside of agriculture has proceeded, each successive organization has included more members of the government establishment in its higher echelons.

For purposes of easier analysis we may examine the Egyptian situation retrospectively. From this point of view it is possible to disregard the early confusions and naïvete of the Egyptian revolutionary leadership. Instead we may focus upon the more widely experienced dilemma of all populist regimes bent on development. This dilemma is posed by the need, both ideological and pragmatic, of mobilizing a total population behind the goals of development and by the need at the same time to prevent a premature diversion of resources from development to the satisfaction of immediate popular needs. Complicating this problem of how to stage and control the development process there is the issue of how to cope with existing articulate demands for effective political participation by groups which have already become in some degree modernized—what we would term the participation crisis. In Egypt the old regime did not or could not cope with this or other crises of modernization. But we cannot assume that the emergence of a revolutionary regime will automatically dispose of the forces which created the prerevolutionary participation crisis. Nor need we assume that either the admission of new groups to political participation or the occurrence of new demands for participation will appear as a simple accumulation of undifferentiated pressure for the immediate distribution of benefits.

According to a largely implicit theory of evolutionary democracy, the participation crisis should be resolved by the gradual attainment of universal participation. Recruitment, on the other hand, should be on an achievement basis. Democratic theory does not emphasize distinctions of political achievement, but it has emphasized representation as a means of simplifying the difficulties of implementing universal political participation in more populous states. This pattern of emphasis has resulted in the widespread belief that recruitment by political parties should be directed at permitting wider participation rather than at producing sharply defined policies or highly qualified statesmen. A similar orientation prevails among parties asserting a nationalist ideology. Even though such parties are non-Marxist (though not necessarily anti-Marxist) or at least deny the existence or significance of class distinctions within their own nations, their "national" quality is measured by the degree to which all classes and social segments are represented in their ranks. The participation crisis is therefore often viewed as an historical sequence of demands by groups, ever lower on the social scale than their predecessors, for admission to legitimate participation in the political system. The European and quasi-Marxist basis of this thinking should be obvious. Does it make sense to apply this kind of thinking to modern Egypt?

It is difficult to know whether the participation crisis in Egypt has reached its peak of intensity. Certainly not all social segments have been admitted to political participation in any meaningful sense, although all citizens were considered to be members of the National Union, and the Socialist Union is only slightly more selective. The critical question is: Membership at what level constitutes really effective participation through a mass party such as the Socialist Union?

In creating first the Liberation Rally in 1954, then the National Union (formally announced in the constitution of 1956 but actually organized in 1959), and now the Socialist Union (organized in 1962-1963) it is not at all clear that the purpose of the revolutionary regime has been to resolve a participation crisis. It might as easily be argued that in refusing to permit the continued activity of the pre-revolutionary parties, especially the Wafd, the Revolutionary Command Council was enhancing the participation crisis. Some observers have argued most forcefully that the reason why the National Union failed was that the officers who held no official position with government were not really admitted to participation; that when they learned that their offices and activities were ceremonial only, they stayed home. The situation was, I think, far more complicated, but it may be useful to follow this line of interpretation further. The same point of view holds that at least the former Wafdists and the better educated are still committed to parliamentary democracy and a competitive party system; and that they and the much abused intellectual elite are now biding their time with the wonted patience of a people who outlasted the Pharaohs and will in due course demand their political rights again.

This interpretation suggests that the participation crisis in Egypt is at present invisible or suppressed. That there is no open pressure for increased participation and that only the most harmless of private murmuring goes on is certainly the case. Another observer, reflecting upon the same problem, shrugged his shoulders and said, "Certainly they [the revolutionary government] decide all important questions. And why shouldn't they? They made the revolution and got rid of the old regime, didn't they?" This second view came from a younger and less well educated person, but I think the crucial difference was that he had no connection with the Wafd party. It would appear that many recent graduates in Egypt are not engrossingly concerned with political participation. If this is true, it is in sharp contrast to the prerevolutionary situation.

II

Before 1952 Egypt was beset simultaneously by all of the crises of political modernization. The situation is represented and recognized by Nasser's discussion of the need for simultaneous multiple revolutions. Insofar as participation was concerned industrialists were from the time of the founding of the Federated Chambers of Industry by Tal'at Harb Pasha in the early twenties pressing for a measure of recognition. The lower middle clerical, religious, and artisan classes expressed their protest through the Muslim Brethren. The urban proletariat, though small and relatively weak, found a measure of organization in a few unions and a means of protest in strikes which often involved violence. The legitimate existence of the proletariat was recognized in the early forties, and additional measures favoring labor were passed in subsequent years. Students organized along the lines of the political parties, both officially recognized and not. Student political organization was a training ground for a future political career and also a means of winning a claim to future employment should the party of one's choice attain a measure of power. During the interwar period professional associations were formed or strengthened and generally found representation through the recognized political parties. Of the minorities, only the Coptic Christians sought equality of political participation. They did this by stressing national unity, anti-imperialism, and secularism and by pressing these views upon the recognized parties. The responsiveness of these parties varied more or less with the intensity of the challenge to national secularism from romantic-Islamic-nationalism, as Safran and others have described it. Other members of minority groups either withdrew completely from political life, preferring the traditional "protected" status of non-Muslims or else (in small numbers) joined the Communist party. Many Armenians, Greeks, Jews, and Italians identified only with the political organizations of their own countries or respective national movements.

More important than knowing the immediate details of the participation crisis in Egypt before 1952 is understanding the much broader flow of events into which that crisis fitted. The crucial question for the participation crisis in Egypt is: When and how did Egyptians begin to take part in their own government?

The first important participation of indigenous Egyptians was under the French during the Napoleonic occupation. The French made use of *ulama* and urban dignitaries to govern the populous cities after they had defeated the Mamlukes. The French neither controlled the countryside well nor did they encourage the political assertion of the rural class of notables that doubtlessly existed. This rural notable class was strengthened by the increasing transfer of public and communal lands to private ownership and by the increased authority granted to village headmen (*umdahs*) under the centralizing administrative reforms of the nineteenth century. The most dramatic evidence of the rising influence of this class occurs in the establishment of an advisory council by Khedive Isma'il in 1866. This council, the forerunner of the later parliaments, was comprised for the most part of *umdahs*. The tension and even open hostility which prevailed between the Khedive and the advisory council from its founding to the Khedive's deposition in 1879 is the first confrontation in a sequence which we have referred to as the participation crisis.

The tension between the council and the Khedive culminated in the Arabi revolution when the Khedive attempted to dismiss a large number of indigenous officers from military service. Since it is fairly well established that both the members of the council and these officers were drawn from the same class of rural notables and headmen, our analysis need not be clouded by considering the mixed motives which prevailed. Indigenous (i.e. not Turkish, Circassian, Syrian, Mamluke, or Albanian) rural dignitaries made a bid for political participation and succeeded so well that they undermined the stability of a regime which they were incapable of running and whose security depended upon a very delicate international arrangement among Britain, France, and the Ottoman Empire. The British occupation of 1882 set the entire movement back on its heels.

Advisory councils of somewhat varying responsibilities continued to meet during the ensuing occupation, but no political parties were formed within these bodies. The earliest parties were small ideological or conspiratorial bodies, more like clubs than political parties, comprised of urban groups. It is important to note the significant differences of interest and activity between the very small group of urban radicals and the rural notables. The urban radicals sought a fundamental change of regime and a policy of cultural and administrative reaction to the West. The rural notables mainly sought effective political participation. It is further important to note that during this same period, as a result of irrigation improvements, fiscal stabilization in Egypt, and new administrative regulations, there was created a new class of urban absentee landowners of great wealth. From this time on it is possible to refer to the rural notables as a rural middle class.

The revolution of 1919 will bear much new scholarship and reinterpretation, but the least that might be argued is that all three groups, the urban radicals, the rural middle class, and the large landowners, combined for a time to produce an overwhelming protest against continued British occupation. Since the *ulama* and even the humble *fellah* participated in the revolution, it is not easy to judge whether it had a more modernizing or traditionalizing thrust. The widespread character of the revolution and the near simultaneity of outbreaks throughout the country have raised questions concerning its organization. Two answers have been suggested, the first is that coordination was the product of the communications efforts of the *ulama*; the second is that the countryside was aroused by the newly organized Wafd party. I would not say that the issue must be posed as spontaneity vs. coordination, modernity or political awareness vs. traditionalist obscurantism, or nationalism vs. Islam. We know enough about attitudes in Islamic countries to understand how all groups could agree on protesting the British presence in Egypt even though the crises of modernization had not been resolved. It would seem therefore that, despite the almost universal participation in it, the revolution of 1919 cannot be taken as a critical phase in the participation crisis. It appears to me that its prime significance is expressed in terms of the other crises of modernization, particularly that of legitimacy.

At any rate, the events of 1919 could be taken as an expression of overwhelming national unity, and the Wafd was subsequently able to associate itself exclusively with this expression. The Wafd became the Egyptian equivalent of the Indian National Congress, the Muslim League, and the Convention Peoples Party. Because the image of the party was associated with the revolution, with adamance on the question of British imperialism, and with opposition to the throne, it was able to insist that it alone stood for Egyptian nationalism. Frustrated in its first attempted reform, the Wafd performed magnificently in opposition but haltingly when in power.

The Wafd may have been associated with the idea of comprehensive national unity, but it did not otherwise represent all classes. It might be argued that the Wafd and the Wafd alone in the 1920's and 1930's could have resolved Egypt's participation crisis by expanding its own ranks and interests as did the Indian National Congress. The Wafd was not unaware of these possibilities but did not emphasize the recruitment of peasants or members of the urban lower middle classes and proletariat because of the organizational and tactical problems such a policy would entail. The Wafd was not often in power, and when it was the King constantly harassed it. In struggling to maintain itself the Wafd preferred issues of national unity rather than controversial issues of social and economic reform. Aside from the tactical preference to avoid vulnerability on divisive issues, had the Wafd leaders sought to encourage effective political participation by peasants, workers, craftsmen, and the like, they would have alienated their strongest support. Wafd support might be described as a coalition of the rural middle class and certain high-status urban groups. The predecessors of these urban groups might have been called radicals twenty or thirty years before, but now they are often thought of as conservatives. They were the professionals (lawyers and doctors in particular), non-bazaar business men and financiers, industrialists, and the intellectuals (professors, students, authors, newspaper editors). Under the Wafd, the rural middle class was strongly represented through the regional constituency system; and it was the loyal support of this class which guaranteed electoral success for the Wafd whenever the King was unable to completely control the returns.

From a certain point of view it is possible to see the three-way struggle between the Wafd, the King, and the British as a continuation of the old struggle of the rural notables for political participation. The Wafd rather than the parliament as a whole was the vehicle of the demand for participation. However, it is possible to see other things going on at the same time. In the first place, all that the Wafd could do for the rural middle class was to see to the reelection of loyal *umdahs*, prevent land reform, and extend irrigation facilities. The Wafd did not provide adequate credit facilities; it did not expand the educational system rapidly enough to accommodate the sons of the rural notables; it did not protect the rural middle class from the manipulations of Alexandria cotton merchants and from the fluctuations of the market. Above all, the Wafd did nothing and probably could have done nothing to prevent the gradual breaking up of holdings through inheritance and hence the steady decline in wealth and social status of rural middle-class families.

By contrast, merchants, industrialists, financiers, transporters, professionals, and the newer class of absentee landowners were direct beneficiaries of Wafd policies. The Wafd paid lip service to the need for land reform, for labor legislation, and for expanding the system of rural cooperatives while in fact acting to benefit the urban upper-middle classes by means of administrative action and the use of "influence." The king of course was capable of competing for the support of these urban groups, but his greatest reliance was placed upon a few landowners, industrialists, members of the military, and the *ulama*. His methods, which involved dividing his enemies by doing ad hoc favors, were not conducive to continuous cooperation with the throne. Even though the king's friends were not a negligible group, their influence was intermittent, surreptitious, illegitimate, and insecure. Insofar as members of the same social segments supported the Wafd, their influence was continuous, overt, legitimate, and secure.

At the same time, the demands and frustrations of lower urban classes were growing. Increasingly difficult economic conditions and the pressure of population growth drove many peasants to the cities. Their demands were largely unarticulated except when student riots or similar events gave occasion and outlet to the expression of their plight. Far more important was the growing protest of a new group of urban radicals. This group has sometimes been referred to as a lower-middle class, and it did include teachers, students, journalists, *ulama*, shop keepers, junior army officers, civil servants, and some skilled craftsmen. The distinction between these members of the lower-middle class and the proletariat on the one hand and the urban upper-middle class (the old urban radicals) is crucial. For the most part, this urban lower-middle class was educated, though not so highly as the urban Wafdist elite. They were also immigrants to the city from rural home towns. In other words, there is a strong presumption of kinship links between the rural middle class and the urban lower-middle classes. The kinship links are to be contrasted with the political links between the rural middle class and the Wafd leadership. If we assume, as I think we must, that the downward social and economic pressure upon the rural middle class continued and that there was a consequently steady increase of rural middle-class immigration to the cities, we can conclude that there has been an almost irresistible pressure upon educated members of the urban lower-middle classes to desist from identifying their interests with those of their rural origins and to seek political participation in their own right. It was developments of this kind which led to increasingly frequent demonstrations, to widespread political alienation, to the growth of system-challenging organizations (the Muslim Brethren, the Young Egypt movement, the Communist party, the Ruwwad), to numerous efforts to reinvigorate the Wafd, to the formation of the Free Officers organization, and to the near collapse of the old regime upon the burning of Cairo on January 26, 1952.

Obviously the participation crisis was but one aspect of the difficulties of the Egyptian political system on the eve of the revolution; nevertheless we can conclude that the Wafd had not measured up to the task of resolving or easing that crisis. This conclusion might not be a condemnation of the party leadership, which had troubles enough with the palace, were not the party so well situated to admit both the rural middle class and their related urban lower class to effective political participation. In the meantime there has been a growing shift of emphasis among these rural notable families from their rural branches to their urban branches, and from their agricultural interests to their urban employment interests. Few in this group are engaged in commerce, and few have substantial investments. Most are "farmers" or civil servants, professionals, army officers, bank clerks (employees), teachers, or journalists. Furthermore we are still concerned with a very small group. We have not included the bulk of the peasantry or the urban proletariat because these groups have not yet articulated a demand for political participation. Now as in the past, when anyone purports to speak for the rights of the peasants and workers, it is most likely one who believes he can manipulate their voices.

III

The revolutionary regime of Egypt did not and does not consider that one of its major tasks is to resolve a participation crisis. Certainly many more Egyptians, peasants, workers, civil servants, and teachers feel that this government is more truly Egyptian than any they have known. Many more have come within range of the propaganda network of the government and in this sense have become participants in the political system. In addition we have already noted that under the constitution of 1956 every Egyptian was to be a member of the National Union and hence a participant. Still the first problem faced by the Revolutionary Command Council was not how to admit new groups to the political process but how to break the virtual monopoly which the Wafd was found to hold when the king abdicated.

The purpose behind the establishment of the Liberation Rally and its successors was to block the effective participation of the pre-revolutionary party elites. There has never been any intention of granting an effective voice to the members of the mass party. The purpose of the mass parties has been exploitative in the extreme, since they were means of mobilizing sentiment for the regime and (in Kornhauser's terminology) means of rendering the masses unavailable to alternative leaders. Later, when the security of the regime was better established, additional uses of the mass party were recognized. The development goals of hygiene, education, and agricultural cooperation were all admitted but neglected in fact. Only in the fields of interest group coordination and in the redress of individual grievance did the mass party appear to serve anyone but the government itself.

We can learn a few things about the limits and the possibilities of the use of the mass mobilization party by examining the experience of Egypt. First it should be remembered that Egypt had its mass party with an authentic grass roots base in the Wafd. The National Union (here using the term for its predecessor and successor as well) was an artificial creation based upon a composite of Indian, Ghanaian, Guinean, and above all Yugoslav models. In all of the parallel cases the national mobilization party was organized in pre-independence times and was so influential politically that it has been interesting to discuss the distribution of administrative tasks between party and government in these countries, but not in Egypt. Furthermore, regardless of how tightly the leadership controls these parties, it is apparent that they represent significant power structures that may not be whimsically altered despite superficial organizational manipulation.

The Egyptian mass party differs on all these points. There is no revolutionary aura about it. Loyalty to the state cannot be equated with loyalty to a party which did not create that state but is its creation. The mass party may be changed at will, and it has been changed at times significantly. Its members approach it pragmatically. For those who are not on the inside, membership or, better still, holding office in the mass party is the only way of making one's voice heard. It is not a very effective way, but it is worth a try. For rural dignitaries, officeholding is a necessity if they are to retain their local prestige and function of seeking redress for their aggrieved neighbors. But when none of the really important members of the regime is willing to give the organization much time, when others become suspicious that the party may be used as a means of building an independent power base, when the benefits the regime gets from the party fall below the favors that must be done, or when a new political crisis requires a renewal of enthusiasm, then the whole ceremony of establishing a mass popular political organization may be repeated. If a popular organization is to be the repository of legitimacy, such an organization cannot be frequently or radically changed without mitigating its legitimizing effect. Finally, a mass political organization cannot serve as a legitimizing symbol without also serving as an effective means of popular political participation.

Another point that emerges from the experience of the National

Union is that the effective building up of a mass political organization requires time and skill. The Egyptian government has demonstrated its ability to organize a mass party in a very short time. There have been two important consequences of this procedure. First, because of the rapidity of organization it is clear that effective organization must depend upon exploiting (or subordinating organizational purposes to) the existing social structure; second, the selection of organizational elements from among existing structures is a most direct form of recruitment into political participation. As indicated, membership or even officeholding in the National Union did not convey much political influence, but given the close control over the distribution of political values in Egypt this is the only manner in which participation by outsiders is possible. Redress of grievance, protection of existing rights, retention of social prestige, and attainment of minimal qualifications for cooptation into higher political echelons—these are the benefits of membership in the mass political party.

With the elaboration of these general considerations it is possible to understand the very difficult nature of the participation crisis after the revolution of 1952. The revolutionary regime did not wish to permit the political participation of other system-challenging parties any more than that of the Wafd. The new regime was obviously favorably inclined toward labor because of its assistance against Naguib in 1954; it favored the peasant through its insistence on land reform and the breaking up of the large estates. It was suspicious of students and lawyers because of their support for Naguib. It generally favored (until 1958 at any rate) businessmen, financiers, and industrialists because of the importance of economic development. The rural middle class and the urban lower middle class were otherwise neither especially rewarded nor disfavored by particular policies.

The attitude of the Nasser government toward mass political organization has been governed by the principles of the Marxist-influenced theory of representative democracy which was discussed above. The Liberation Rally was to organize the entire nation. Members of the Revolutionary Command Council toured the country and established branches by investing various notables with responsibility and office in local branches. Offices and clubhouses were opened in existing facilities. The Rally did nothing except express its approval of Nasser's ouster of Naguib, the proposal to postpone elections for three years from early 1954, and similar things. The Rally was not organized systematically, but branches were established in all the major centers. Responsibility for the Rally was borne by Anwar al-Sadat, and his temporary decline in influence coincided with the demise of the Rally.

The Rally was allowed to die after the announcement that the National Union would be founded under the Constitution of 1956. The National Union was made the responsibility of Kamal al-Din Husain, Minister of Education at the time. The National Union was established in more systematic fashion even though in most cases its officers were the same as those who served under the Liberation Rally. Since the National Union was supposed to include the entire nation, it was organized on a regional basis. Every village was presumably included. Elections were held in each village, and National Union committees were chosen for these basic organizational units. In the cities the basic units were wards and city quarters. While elections were free, it would appear that the established notables were returned in the villages while the city lists that were led by members of the Cabinet won everywhere. Regional representation resulted in underrepresentation of the crowded cities. Free elections in which great dependence upon established local elites was expressed confirmed the position of the rural middle class.

The first post-revolutionary parliament was elected in 1957. It was comprised of 350 representatives. After the union of Syria and Egypt in the United Arab Republic (UAR) on February 1, 1958, this parliament was disbanded and a new one met for the first time in 1960. In the parliament of the UAR there were 600 members, of whom 400 were Egyptian representatives. Most of these 400 were drawn from the membership of the earlier parliament, the candidates for which were approved by the government. Since it was produced by the National Union, in a sense the parliament of 1960 represented the highest levels to which recruitment was possible through the National Union. The top leadership and bureau of the Union were members of the government and, in fact, seconded on a part-time basis to the Union.

With the separation of Syria from the UAR in 1961, after the passage of the July Socialist laws, both the old parliament and the National Union were allowed to wither. The need for a new and more vigorous national political organization was declared. In due course that organization would prepare for parliamentary elections.

By the end of 1961 a preparatory committee met and decided upon the representative formula for a Congress of Popular Forces. This Congress, meeting in the Spring of 1962, adopted a new National Charter and decided which groups should be excluded from political participation in the future mass organization, to be called the Socialist Union. In the year following the meeting of the Congress of Popular Forces ordinary members were enrolled wherever organizers went. Only those who made application were to be members of the Socialist Union, in contrast to the National Union, of which every citizen was considered a member.

Two significant changes are to be noted in the recruitment patterns of the Congress of Popular Forces and the Socialist Union. The Congress of Popular Forces was appointed on the basis of a formula for occupational distribution. In other words, the representational theory employed was corporative and not democratically conceived. The corporative principle is at once more Egyptian and more Marxist. A somewhat different emphasis was brought into the organization of the Socialist Union. In addition to the regional organizational units, a large number of institutional units was established providing for the representation of government agencies, of schools, of factories, and other establishments like banks. This innovation, which was foreshadowed in the corporative organization of the Congress of Popular Forces, greatly increased urban representation. On the other hand, occupational representation was now more clearly tied to organizations and institutions under government control. The interests thus represented are not occupational but those of segments of the establishment.

With these developments in mind it is possible to perceive that there was probably some effort to achieve an occupational balance in the National Union. (For example, agriculturalists comprised just about half the members.) This balance has been changed in the Socialist Union, but even more important is the fact that the shift from solely geographical representation has changed the significance of the occupational distribution of the members of the mass party. Nor should it necessarily be thought that this form of representation weakens the ability or will of such persons to participate actively in the Egyptian political process. That process is predominantly administrative, and most of those employed in governmental enterprises and agencies identify with their fellow employees and their own organizations. This is true even for many professionals even though the professional associations continue to exist in apparent independence (but are really quite closely controlled by having leading members of the regime on their governing boards).

For many Egyptians the only important political access they desire is the power to intercede with the directors of their own enterprises. In the past, government employees were not permitted to form unions or independent associations. Hence the official establishment of Socialist Union branches in the various ministries can be seen as a long-awaited legitimation of the interests of those in government employ. The urban lower-middle class will be much better represented even if in terms of the enterprise by which they are employed rather than in terms of a broad class. As we shall see below, many of these people gained membership in the new parliament under the general category of workers. However, it is not at all clear that the access of the rural middle class has been reduced nor that of the related urban lower-middle class increased. Even more surely can it be stated that as yet the interests of neither have been affected. The reduction of the maximum allowable landholding from 200 to 100 feddan in 1961 had no effect on the rural middle class.

Technically both the National Union and the Socialist Union were to be the highest policy-making organs in the country. The Nationalist Union at its sole National Congress of 1959 passed a series of resolutions that were to be the basis of legislation until the subsequent Congress was held. At various times during the short history of the National Union attempts were made to infuse life into the organization by declaring that committees were about to examine whether or not the government had in fact implemented its resolutions. Just before the separation of Syria in 1961 plans were afoot for holding the postponed National Congress that would review government achievements and pass new resolutions for the guidance of Parliament. The 1961 congress was not held. Instead the National Union and the Parliament were dissolved and the resolutions of the congress of 1959 all but forgotten.

The question of the relative importance of the Parliament and the National Congress of the National Union cannot be fully resolved on the basis of so short an experience. Nevertheless it is clear that (despite the weakness of both organizations) membership in Parliament carried much greater prestige. Furthermore it proved possible for members of Parliament, working through legislative committees, as interested blocs such as doctors, lawyers, members of the Chamber of Commerce, and the like, to influence government concerns, if not policy and legislation. In this sense it is possible to conclude that representation in Parliament was the highest level of recruitment into the political elite of Egypt possible by means of the National Union. It is also possible to argue that the groups thus represented in the Egyptian Parliament may not be described by reference to the mass base of the National Union but may more accurately be described in terms of the education, occupation, and family backgrounds of the members of Parliament themselves. In this regard it is worth mentioning that elections to Parliament were from geographical constituencies and by means of universal adult suffrage. Parliamentary elections were not organized through the National Union.

The situation at present under the Socialist Union and the new Parliament is not much different. There has been no National Congress of the Socialist Union. Instead, prior to the recruitment of the mass membership of the Socialist Union a Congress of Popular Forces was held in May 1962. That Congress expressed itself vigorously but accomplished its essential task in the approval of a national charter presented to it by President Nasser. That charter is to serve as the ideology of revolutionary Egypt as well as a guide to policy and legislation. The Congress of Popular Forces was disbanded with some relief after a session of thirty days. Thus the present Parliament is once again the highest representative organization associated with the mass political party. There is of course but one party represented in the Parliament—the Socialist Union. Its members were also elected from geographical constituencies by universal adult suffrage (excepting a few thousand persons barred from political life because of their "reactionary" political activities in the past). A further exclusion which may have considerable significance in political-sociological terms is that no member of Parliament may own more than twenty-five feddan. Members of the present Parliament were elected from two-member constituencies while the previous elections were held in single-member constituencies. The change was made in order to facilitate implementation of the rule that one-half of the members of the new Parliament should be either workers or peasants. It is apparent that the definition of workers and peasants (especially the former) is quite broad, including civil servants, doctors, and other professionals. Despite the resultant difficulty in determining the social and occupational background of elected members of Parliament it will be instructive to compare the social composition of these Parliaments and the intervening preparatory bodies in order to discern the degree to which the Egyptian political authorities have earnestly attempted to recruit particular social elements into this most effective organ of political participation.

Tables 1 and 2 compare the occupational breakdown of the Parliament of 1957, the Parliament of 1960, the Preparatory Committee of 1961, the Congress of Popular Forces of 1962, and the Parliament of 1964. The Parliament of 1957 was elected before the union of Egypt and Syria in 1958. Many of the same persons served in the Parliament of 1960. The Preparatory Committee of 1961 was appointed to determine the representative basis of the Congress of Popular Forces, which was to determine the future political organization of Egypt.

The figures in the tables were derived in the following manner: (1) The totals for 1960 were taken directly from the registration forms of the members of Parliament by the author with the permission of the Secretary-General of the Parliament; (2) the totals for 1957 were obtained by comparing the names of the 1957 members with those of 1960, by checking the remaining names against those listed by village and occupation in the Golden Register of the National Union, and by reference to a breakdown by occupations contained in a note to N. Safran, *Egypt in Search of Political Community*, Cambridge, 1961, p. 291, drawn from *Oriente Moderno* (July 1957); (3) the Preparatory Committee and Congress of Popular Forces figures are taken from *Al-Ahram*, November 19, 1961, a Cairo daily; (4) the figures for the Parliament of 1964 were derived from the three-way listing in *Al-Ahram* as "peasants," "workers," and "others," and by comparing the names of members with those who served in 1960 and with the Golden Register. The results are not complete, but they are reasonably accurate and as complete as available sources allow.

In order to understand the significance of these tables some additional explanation is needed. Over the period from 1957 to 1964 there were some profound policy changes which considerably affected the status and dependence of the educated middle classes. This was the period of the most extensive nationalization, during which the government increased its control and regulation of professional associational groups. The press came under indirect government control. Student and youth activities were brought under authority of the High Council for Youth Welfare and under special bureaus

TABLE 1

	Occupation	1957	1960	Prep.	Cong.	1964
I.	Army	26	24	—	—	13
	Police	8	24	—	—	3
	Army/Police	14[a]				
II.	Provincial Admin.	41[a]	—	56	—	—
	Ministers/Undersec's.	19[a]	—	—	—	—
III.	Govt. Professional	28	48	—	—	12
	Lawyer	37	61	11	—	24
	M.D.	3	8	5[b]	—	4
	Engineer	1	8	9	—	11
	Journalist	1	6	7	—	3
	Teacher	10	9	3	—	13
	Accountant	2	5	—	—	1
	Syndicate Council[c]	3	7	7	—	—
	Professor	5	4	34[d]	105	2
	Miscl. Professional	33	—	—	225	—
IV.	Student	—	—	6	105	—
	Gov't. Employee	7	7	—	155	13
	Managerial-Commerce	7	21	6[e]	75	—
	Managerial-Industry	8	17	—	75	4
	Insurance-Banking	4	13	—	—	4
	Managerial-Gen'l.	—	—	25	—	—
	Educ./Inspector	—	3	—	—	—
	Qadi (Judge)	1	2	—	—	1
V.	Farmer	40	71	20[f]	375	55
	Fellah[g]	—	—	—	—	47
	Umdah	24	30	—	—	29
	Local Council	4	—	—	—	7
VI.	Worker	1[a]	—	28[h]	375	5
	'Amil[i]	—	—	—	—	44
	Entrepreneur	3	2	—	—	2
VII.	Merchant	4	4	—	—	6
	Contractor	2	8	—	—	2
	Transport	—	5	—	—	—
	Private Employee	5	6	—	—	8
VIII.	Miscellaneous	—	7	33[j]	10	47[k]
	Total	341	400	250	1500[l]	360[m]

[a] Based on Safran after *Oriente Moderno*.

[b] Includes 2 pharmacists.

[c] Syndicate Councils are the ruling bodies of recognized professional associations such as the Bar Association or the Society of Engineers.

[d] Includes Directors and Deans and 2 professors from al-Azhar.

[e] Managers of Cooperative Enterprises.

[f] 18 representatives of agricultural cooperatives and two farmers.

[g] Under the 1964 electoral law all candidates were officially designated as farmers (*fellah*), workers (*'amil*) or other (*fi'at ukhra*). It would appear that many so designated had other professions and where these could be ascertained these members have been listed under a more specific category. Those remaining under these headings are the members for whom no additional information was available.

[h] Including 13 union leaders.

[i] See g above.

[j] Includes 10 women and 23 former members of Parliament (i.e., 1960).

[k] These are "others" (*fi'at ukhra*). See g above.

[l] To which was added the total membership of the Preparatory Committee.

[m] Ten members were nominated by the government. Only about 80 were members in 1960 and reelected in 1964.

TABLE 2ᵃ

Table 2, translates Table 1 into percentage terms.

	Occupation	1957	1960	*Prep.*	*Cong.*	1964
I.	Army	7.6%	.6%	—	—	3.6%
	Police	2.3	.6	—	—	.8
	Army/Police	4.1	—	—	—	—
II.	Provincial Admin.	12.	—⎫	22.4	—	—
	Ministers/Undersec's.	5.5	—⎭		—	—
III.	Gov't. Professional	8.2	12.	—	—	3.3
	Lawyer	10.8	15.2	4.4		6.6
	M.D.	.8	2.	2.		1.1
	Engineer	.2	2.	3.6	15.	3.
	Journalist	.2	1.5	2.8		.8
	Teacher	2.9	2.2	1.2		3.6
	Accountant	.5	1.2	—		.2
	Syndicate Council	.8	1.7	2.8	—	—
	Professor	1.4	1.	13.6	7.	.5
	Misc. Professional	9.6	—	—	—	—
IV.	Student	—	—	2.4	7.	—
	Gov't Employee	2.	1.7	—	10.3	3.6
	Managerial-Commerce	2.	5.2	2.4	5.	—
	Manager-Industry	2.3	4.2		5.	1.1
	Insurance-Banking	1.1	3.2		—	1.1
	Managerial, Gen'l.	—	—	10.	—	—
	Educ./Inspector	—	.7	—	—	—
	Qadi (Judge)	.2	.5	—	—	.2
V.	Farmer	11.7	17.7	8.	25.	15.2
	Fellah	—	—	—	—	13.
	Umdah	7.	7.5	—	—	8.
	Local Council	1.1	—	—	—	1.9
VI.	Worker	.2	—	11.2	25.	1.3
	'Amil	—	—	—	—	12.2
VII.	Merchant	1.1	1.	—	—	1.6
	Entrepreneur	.8	.5	—	—	.5
	Contractor	.5	2.	—	—	.5
	Transport	—	1.2	—	—	—
	Private Employee	1.4	1.	—	—	2.2
VIII.	Miscellaneous	—	1.7	13.2	.6	13.
	Total	98.5	99.4	100.	99.9	98.9

of the Ministry of Education and the Ministry of the Interior (Internal Security). Most transport and foreign trade as well as all banking, insurance, and finance were nationalized. Most professionals are now government employees even if not so listed in the tables. Many "farmers" are professionals who own small amounts of land, and whenever this was found to be the case those members were listed as professionals. Students are preparing themselves for entry into government service and are not to be differentiated from other members of the educated middle classes. University professors, including those at the religious institution of al-Azhar, are in government employ.

Thus it is important to read the percentage changes over time in the light of the status changes resulting from government policy. Hence, as we read from left to right, the professionals become more like civil servants and the managerial groups become increasingly high officials, engineers, economists, and retired or transferred army officers. Provincial administrators are for the most part employees of the Ministry of the Interior and often former police officials.

Furthermore it is clear that the three Parliaments and the two special committees represent significantly different bases of recruitment. The Parliaments were elected within the framework of a single-party system and through geographical constituencies. As we have seen, since the single party was not well organized, the elections reflect local power structure and tradition outside of the major urban areas, just as did the elections during the heyday of the Wafd. Hence the professionals (group III) and the rural middle class (group V) have much in common as manifesting local social structure and in that the individuals concerned belong to families whose members fit into both classes; that is, *umdahs* often have professionals or government employees for relatives. Group VII is the most urban and represents the remains of the "private sector" to a large extent. Groups I and II are socially homogeneous and tend to merge with the managerial sections of group IV. These three groups, i.e. I, II, and IV, together with the workers (group VI) represent urban groups that are losing their rural connections rather more rapidly than the rest. Group VIII, which we have been forced to designate as miscellaneous, appears to fit best with group III or group VII, as is revealed by the notes to Table 1. The *'Amil* section of group VI may contain several persons who belong in either group III or group IV; and the same may be said for the *Fellah* section of group V.

TABLE 3

Occupation Groups		1957	1960	Prep.	Cong.	1964
I.	Army and Police	14%	12%	%	%	4.4%
II.	High Administration	17.5	—	22.4	—	—
III. & VIII.	Professionals	35.4	38.8	43.6	22.	32.1
IV.	Managerial and Gov't. Empl.	7.4	14.3	12.4	20.3	5.8
V.	Rural Middle Class	19.8	25.2	8.	25.	38.1
VI.	Workers	.2	—	11.2	25.	13.5
VII.	Urban "Private Sector"	3.8	5.7	—	—	4.8

Hence it is by no means clear that the percentage changes represent a substantial impact of revolutionary social policies. The fact that only about 80 members were reelected in 1964 may indicate no more than that the stratum represented in the Parliament of 1957 and 1960 is a very broad one. On the other hand, the increase in the size of the constituency consequent upon the establishment of two-member constituencies and the limitation on the holdings of candidates to 25 feddan have doubtlessly had their effect. The former change enhances the influence of the stratum-breadth hypothesis, while the latter might involve the entry of new strata into Parliament. Nevertheless it is clear that the election rules, which were only formally applied, led many candidates to put themselves forward as workers or peasants who might see themselves as members of other groups according to more traditional or Western prestige values.

We can get a better idea of the changes involved in these elections if we examine the composition of the Preparatory Committee and the Congress of Popular Forces. The Preparatory Committee was a small group, hastily gathered to determine the composition of the Congress of Popular Forces. In terms of the immediately preceding events of the July Socialist Laws, the separation of Syria from the UAR, and the expropriation of a few Egyptian and many Lebanese families of the *haute bourgeoisie* we can understand that this Committee was meant to mobilize all the loyal and politically influential members of the elite behind the regime at a most critical phase of the Egyptian revolution. With this background in mind we can understand why there was in the Preparatory Committee such strong representation of the top governmental elite, the leadership of the professional associations, managers of government enterprises, directors, deans and professors from the universities, and trade union leaders. The character of the Committee was essentially urban. Rural representation was small. It is also apparent that most members of the Committee were well educated.

If the Preparatory Committee provides a fairly good picture of the kind of people who run the Egyptian polity, the Congress of Popular Forces presents their ideal picture of Egyptian society. The Congress was large and proved itself unwieldy. At times worker and peasant members demonstrated their lack of sophistication (though such manifestations had not been absent from the earlier Parliaments). Nonetheless, the major differences between the Preparatory Committee and the Congress are shown in the relatively larger representation of the universities and professional groups (including both group III and group VIII) and in the lower representation of government employees, farmers, workers, and students in the Preparatory Committee.

It is further clear that the attempt to replicate the "ideal" balance of the Congress of Popular Forces in the Parliament of 1964 did not succeed. This failure was in one sense due to the loose definition of worker and peasant, but in a more significant sense it was due to the persistence of an older pattern of influence structure despite superficial attempts at mass political organization. The ambivalence of the regime toward creating an effective mass organization is revealed in the composition of the Preparatory Committee and particularly in the appearance of fifty-six vice-presidents, ministers, directors-general, undersecretaries, and provincial governors among the members of that body. Thus the Preparatory Committee represents something approximating real power structure at the national level, the Congress of Popular Forces represents a rationalized ideal of a national cross section, the purpose of which would be to ratify elite decisions (and perhaps receive ideological guidance therefrom), and the Parliament represents at once the degree to which Egyptian society has not been penetrated by the revolution and also the measure of support which Egyptian society is willing to give the revolutionary regime. It should also be noted that since the function of Parliament is limited to supportive activities, the lack of representation of high government officials and managers is due to the fact that they have more important things to do. This same consideration applies in explaining the decline in the representation of former military and police officers, for these have increasingly found their places in managing government enterprises. The decline in the representation of professors and students, despite their willingness to serve the government and despite the government's slowly growing willingness to make use of them, is due to their inability to get elected under a system of self-nomination and local constituencies and in which the device of the party list is not employed.

To summarize, it is the firm resolve of the present government of Egypt to restrict popular political participation as much as possible. Despite this resolve, the requirements of legitimacy and national integration in particular have made it advisable to organize a mass party and to give it both a structure of leadership and the responsibility for producing a Parliament. Even though the primary tasks of such an organization are of a plebiscitary nature, and even though many high governmental officials will hold down Socialist Union offices, membership in Parliament is bound to afford unique opportunities for influencing less critical decisions. Hence the participation crisis is being dealt with indirectly and without completely satisfactory results because of the relatively inflexible pattern for the representation of interests and because of the limited influence of those recruited into middle elite positions through the mass party. From quite another point of view, however, the system works well indeed. Despite the wide representation of nearly all classes at the lowest levels of the mass party, the upward recruitment procedure has been selective enough to provide for the predominance of the most supportive element of all, the rural middle class and its urban offshoots.

CHAPTER 9

ELECTORAL MOBILIZATION, PARTY COMPETITION, AND NATIONAL INTEGRATION[*]

STEIN ROKKAN

THE HISTORIES of the Western European polities since the French Revolution have a number of traits in common: all extended the right of political participation to wider and wider circles of their citizens and finally, with few exceptions, introduced universal and equal suffrage for women as well as for men; all developed, some of them quite early, others much more slowly and erratically, nation-wide party organizations based on mass memberships; and all have experienced, largely as a result of the universalization of suffrage and the growth of mass parties, a decline in strictly territorial politics and an increasing emphasis on functional cleavages cutting across the traditional divisions into localities and provinces.

For most countries of the West these trends can be documented statistically, from official electoral counts, from party records, from local newspapers. The introduction of universal suffrage, the standardization of electoral procedures and the equalization of votes led to the production of enormous masses of data for analysis and eventually stimulated the development of a discipline of political statistics. Most of the analyses carried out within this field have limited themselves to single elections and to particular localities and constituencies, but there have been indications in recent years of greater interest in long-term analyses of processes of electoral change and in systematic studies of variations in sequences of change within given nations.[1] The increasing interest in the development of data

[*] I am indebted to Joseph LaPalombara for his critical reading of an earlier version of this chapter. I have also benefited from comments by W. J. M. Mackenzie Richard Rose and Agnes Gustafsson.
[1] These are a few of the recent efforts of quantitative historical analyses of electoral data:

Denmark. Erik Høgh is completing an extensive study of elections before and after the introduction of secret voting in 1901. Poul Meyer and associates have carried out detailed analyses of turnout levels in different types of communities; see J. Jeppesen and P. Meyer, *Sofavelgerne* (Electoral turnout in Denmark), Aarhus: Institut for Statskundskab, Aarhus Universitet, 1964. Jan Stehouwer is currently following up these analyses through an historical analysis of the demography of the vote in Denmark.

Finland. Erik Allardt has carried out extensive correlation analyses of data on the strength of the Finnish Communists and Social Democrats and made imaginative use of data on local political traditions since 1906; see especially his paper "Patterns of Class Conflict and Working Class Consciousness in Finnish Politics," in E. Allardt and Y. Littunen, eds., *Cleavages, Ideologies and Party Systems*, Helsinki: Westermarck Society, 1964, pp. 91-131, and his chapter with P. Pesonen "Structural and nonstructural cleavages in Finnish Politics," to appear in S. M. Lipset and S. Rokkan, eds., *Party Systems and Voter Alignments*, New York: The Free Press, 1965. O. Rantala is engaged in an even more extensive data processing operation for Finnish electoral data and will carry out shortly a number of multivariate regression analyses to pin down factors of change in alignments.

France. The Siegfried school of electoral cartographers has produced thousands of historical electoral maps but has so far rarely engaged in detailed computations of factors making for change. The recent work by statisticians such as J. Klatzmann (chapter in J. Fauvet and H. Mendras, *Les paysans et la politique*, Paris: Colin, 1958), J. Desabie, *J. Soc. Stat. Paris*, Vol. 100, Nos. 7-9 (1959) pp. 166-180, and G. Vangrevelinghe, *Rev. Stat. Appliquée*, Vol. 9, No. 3 (1961) pp. 83-100, may pave the way for the application of computers to the processing of electoral data. Mattei Dogan's extensive work on data on recent elections in France and Italy has stimulated increasing attention to the possibilities of detailed ecological analysis, cf. his chapter in S. M. Lipset and S. Rokkan, eds., *Party Systems and Voter Alignments*. A good introductory presentation of trends in German elections since manhood suffrage can be found in E. Faul, ed., *Wahlen und Wähler in Westdeutschland*, Villingen: Ring-Verlag, 1960; Faul's discussion of "mobilization," pp. 156-163, is of particular relevance. No nation-wide trend analyses have as yet been attempted. The basic data for the *Reichstag* elections can be related to social and religious divisions; thus F. Specht and P. Schwabe, *Die Reichstagwahlen von 1867 bis 1907*, 2 Aufl. Berlin, 1907, give the degree of urbanization and percent of Evangelical and Catholic for each *Wahlkreis*. Analyses such as A. Klöcker's *Die Konfession der sozialdemokratischen Wählerschaft 1907*, M. Gladbach, Volksverein-Verlag, 1913, a pioneering study of the religious factor in German elections, could easily be extended by adding further variables and by tracing trends over time.

Sweden. Swedish official statistics are more detailed than any others in Europe and allow a great variety of analyses. Among recent historical analyses are G. Wallin, *Valrörelser och valresultata. Andrakammarvalen i Sverige 1866-1884*, Stockholm: Christophers, 1961. Of particular interest for their high level of methodological sophistication are the analyses by the statistician C.-G. Janson (*Mandattilldelning och regional röstfördelning*, Stockholm: Idun, 1961) and the sociologist Gösta Carlsson ("Partiforskjutningar som tillväkstprocesser" *Statsvet. ts.*, Vol. 66, Nos. 2-3 (1963), pp. 172-213). The historian Jörgen Weibull is currently completing a statistical analysis of the occupational bases of party strength for the elections from 1911 to 1920.

United Kingdom. The poll books and the returns of the elections of the Victorian era have recently been subject to increasingly sophisticated analyses. See especially N. Gash, *Politics in the Age of Peel*, London, 1953; D. C. Moore, "The Other Face of Reform," *Victorian Studies*, Vol. 5 (September 1961), pp. 7-34; H. J. Hanham, *Elections and Electoral Management: Politics in the Time of Disraeli and Gladstone*, London, 1959; J. Cornford, "The Transformation of Conservatism in the Late 19th century," *Victorian Studies*, Vol. 7 (1963), pp. 35-66. Cornford's work represents a great advance on earlier work in its insightful use of ecological statistics. The possibilities of ecological research in Britain are amply demonstrated in Claus Moser and Wulf Scott's *British Towns*, Edinburgh, Oliver and Boyd, 1961; this is essentially an exercise in factor analysis but happens to include, in addition to a great number of demographic, socio-economic, and health variables, a few basic electoral data for each town. The zero-order correlations calculated between the socio-eco-

archives and in the use of electronic computers in processing historical information can be expected to accelerate the production of diachronic as well as synchronic analyses of political data[2] and the findings of such analyses can again be expected to have a profound impact on current conceptualization and theorizing in the field of comparative politics.

In this chapter I shall describe a few promising lines of developmental analysis and suggest some possible tasks for systematic comparisons across polities. I shall first summarize the results of the studies we have so far been able to carry out on developments in Norway and shall then discuss a few possibilities of systematic comparisons of rates and directions of change after the breakdown of traditional and absolutist systems of rule in the nineteenth century.

---

nomic and the political variables prove remarkably interesting but, curiously enough, were left unanalyzed and uninterpreted: here is clearly a task for secondary analysis. A very interesting attempt at developmental analysis at the local level has been made by J. M. Lee in *Social Leaders and Public Persons. A Study of County Government in Cheshire since 1888*; Oxford: Clarendon Press, 1963. This study focuses on changes in the recruitment of elected personnel and seeks to determine the conditions for a "take off" (p. 215) from the traditional politics of the "county society" ruled by part-time amateurs recruited from the local social elite to the modern politics of full-time professionals recruited through training and service rather than through family status. If statistical studies of such changes in recruitment could be done systematically for a variety of local units we should know much more about the conditions of changes in political style in mass-suffrage democracies.

United States. Historians such as Lee Benson (*The Concept of Jacksonian Democracy*, Princeton: Princeton University Press, 1961) and sociologists such as Seymour Martin Lipset (*Political Man*, Garden City: Doubleday, 1960, Ch. 11) have for years called attention to the rich opportunities for diachronic electoral analysis in the United States. The Social Science Research Council has recently taken an important step in helping this movement forward by giving a grant to Walter Dean Burnham for a detailed inventory of the archival sources for early electoral statistics state by state, cf. W. D. Burnham "The United States of America 1789-1920," a chapter in the forthcoming *International Guide to Electoral Statistics*, to be edited by S. Rokkan and J. Meyriat. A great advance in historical analysis could be brought about through arrangements for central processing of all such data. The Survey Research Center at the University of Michigan has recently taken steps to build up a county-by-county archive of census and election data: this will be based in part on Burnham's work, in part on the collations of electoral statistics established by Richard H. Scammon and his staff. Cf. Lee Benson "The Comparative Analysis of Historical Change," a paper presented at the Conference on Comparative Research organized by the International Social Science Council in April 1965.

[2] The International Social Science Council and the International Committee on Social Sciences Documentation, both supported by funds from UNESCO, have since 1962 organized several conferences on problems of data archiving in the social sciences, see the Introduction by S. Rokkan to Vol. 16, No. 1 (1964) of the *International Social Science Journal*, an issue devoted to "Data in Comparative Research." For further developments see S. Rokkan "Second Conference on Data Archives in the Social Sciences," *Social Science Information*, Vol. 4, No. 1 (1965), pp. 67-84.

I. Four Steps of Change

Our attempt to piece together a statistical history of Norwegian politics is based on data and analyses bearing on four distinct steps in a complex process of change: the formal incorporation of strata and categories of residents kept out of the system under the original criteria; the mobilization of these enfranchised citizens in electoral contests; their activation into direct participation in public life; the breakdown of the traditional systems of local rule through the entry of nationally organized parties into municipal elections, what we call the process of politicization.

For each of these steps we have tried to formulate a series of questions and done some initial work on the sifting of potential data.

One set of questions concerns the process of formal incorporation: What were the original criteria of political citizenship and through what sequences of initiatives, delaying tactics, and compromises were they transformed into universalistic rules of participation? What were the economic, educational, social, and organizational characteristics of the adult residents kept out of the system under the original criteria and what were the characteristics of those first admitted and those last admitted in the subsequent process of universalization? Did the rules affect all communities of the nation in roughly the same way, or did differences in socio-economic structure affect the local balance between the enfranchised and the politically underprivileged?

Another set of questions concerns the electoral mobilization and activation of the last to be enfranchised: How far had they already been organizationally mobilized before they were given the right to vote? How long did it take to mobilize them for electoral participation once they had the vote; and how quickly were citizens from these lately underprivileged strata recruited into organizational work in the political parties, into candidacies and public offices? Did this process of mobilization and activation move forward at roughly the same rate throughout the national territory, or were there marked differences in the rate of change between the central, economically advanced localities and the geographical and economic peripheries?

And a final set of questions concerns the process of politicization after the establishment of mass suffrage: How long did it take the political parties to establish themselves as mass organizations through the recruitment of dues-paying members and to entrench themselves in each locality of the nation, whether through the operation of affiliated branches or through direct participation in contests for municipal offices? How far did the peripheries of the nation lag behind its central areas in this process of politicization? To what extent was this politicization of the periphery accelerated through the development of polarized conflicts between established and underprivileged strata and to what extent was it slowed down through the persistence of local and regional traditions of territorial and cultural defense against the expanding urban centers?

Our analyses are based on six types of sources:

1. Published records of debates, deliberations, and decisions on changes in electoral laws and regulations.

2. Official statistical data, some published, others archived, from elections, referenda, censuses, and other enumerations.

3. Biographical data, from a variety of published and unpublished sources, on the background of candidates and elected representatives at the local as well as the national level.

4. Data from the party press and the party secretariats on the establishment of local branches and the sizes of local memberships.

5. Data from organizations and associations on their local branches and their memberships.

6. Data from sample surveys, some nation-wide, others confined to selected localities.

The initial analyses of long-term trends simply consisted of rearrangements and recomputations of the officially established statistics for elections. We are currently at work on the development of an historical archive of ecological data on Norwegian politics and hope in this way to be able to pursue much more detailed analyses of variations between localities in the rates and directions of change. This punched-card archive was originally built up to allow multivariate analyses of local variations in turnout and party strength for the elections from 1945 onward, but efforts are now under way to extend the time series for each local unit. We are also making efforts to extend the range of data for each unit: we have so far punched on decks for each commune not only data from local and national elections but also data from censuses, from educational, agricultural, industrial, and fiscal statistics, data from a church attendance count, data on local party organizations and memberships as well as on nominees to party lists for parliament. We have found such data archiving an essential tool in our cooperative research work, and we hope in the years to come to expand the scope of our archive both backward to the earliest partisan contests and forward to the oncoming local and national elections. We think our experiences justify us in recommending that similarly conceived archives be set up in other countries of the West, and we are convinced that the greater control of the data masses achieved through such archiving will facilitate systematic comparisons of rates of development in different countries.

II. A Statistical History of Norwegian Politics

Our analysis of the process of political development in Norway concentrates on three phases:

1. The period of initial mobilization from 1879, the first partisan election, to 1900, the first election under manhood suffrage.

2. The period of politicization and polarization from 1900 to 1935, the year the Labor party came to power.

3. The period after 1945, a period of ideological *détente* at the center and continued mobilization and politicization in the periphery.

This is not the place to give details of the findings so far established on each of these points: for further information the reader is referred to a number of articles and reports published under our program of electoral research.[3] Much remains to be done to map the variations within the national territory over all the elections since the beginning of competitive politics, but some results already stand out as significant, whether judged within the context of the history of the one nation or judged in the framework of a comparative analysis of similar time sequences across a variety of nations.

[3] For a general account of the Norwegian program of electoral research see the chapter by S. Rokkan and H. Valen in O. Stammer, ed., *Politische Forschung*, Cologne: Westdeutscher Verlag, 1960. These publications deal specifically with analyses of long-term change: S. Rokkan and H. Valen "The Mobilization of the Periphery," pp. 111-159 in S. Rokkan, ed., *Approaches to the Study of Political Participation*, Bergen: The Michelsen Institute, 1962; S. Rokkan and H. Valen "Regional Contrasts in Norwegian Politics," pp. 162-238 in E. Allardt and Y. Littunen, eds., *Cleavages, Ideologies and Party Systems: Contributions to Comparative Political Sociology*, Helsinki: The Westermarck Society, 1964; S. Rokkan "Norway: Numerical Democracy and Corporate Pluralism," to be printed in R. A. Dahl, ed., *Political Oppositions in Western Democracies*, New Haven: Yale University Press, 1966; and S. Rokkan "Geography, Religion and Social Class: Crosscutting Cleavages in Norwegian Politics," to be printed in S. M. Lipset and S. Rokkan, eds., *Party Systems and Voter Alignments*, New York: The Free Press, 1966. A student working within the program has recently completed a thesis on the politicization of local elections in the rural areas of the Western region from 1900 to 1963: T. Hjellum, "Partiene i norsk lokalpolitikk," Oslo, 1965 (typescript).

THE PROCESS OF FORMAL INCORPORATION

The Constitution of 1814 gave Norway the most democratic system of representation in Europe. All the freehold peasants and most of the leaseholders were given the right to vote. In an overwhelmingly rural nation of small holdings this meant that practically half of all men over 25 were enfranchised.[4] It took decades, however, before the peasants were mobilized to make effective use of their electoral power: they tended to vote for their betters, the King's officials and the local lawyers and teachers, and they were for a long time, in fact up to the 1870's, content to leave the affairs of the nation in the hands of the educated administrators of the realm and the privileged burghers of the chartered cities. There were many signs of incipient mobilization, however: first through religious revival movements against the established state church, subsequently through a variety of cultural movements, not least through the development of a rural "counter-language" against the standard imposed by the urban centers, and, finally, through a general process of monetization and urbanization, a gradual breakdown of the isolated pockets of subsistence communities in the countryside, and the growth of complex systems of cross-local exchange and interdependence. The conditions for rapid and effective political mobilization were there: a literate peasantry, a growing network of voluntary associations, increasing facilities for cross-local communication through the mails and the press, a steady increase in the spread of urban commodities and ideas toward the periphery, a growing flow of migrants at all levels of the social hierarchy from the rural areas to the cities. The decisive thrust toward power came in the 1870's:

[4] The standard treatment of the history of the franchise in Norway gives the figures for registered and for qualified citizen in percent of the total resident population in each election year; cf. most recently Alf Kaartvedt, *Fra Riksforsamlingen til 1869*, Vol. 1 of *Det Norske Storting gjennom 150 år*, Oslo: Gyldendal, 1964, p. 113. By this reckoning 6.7% of the population was registered in 1815 and 7.6% of the population was qualified at the first election for which such calculations became officially available, that of 1859. Such indexes of democratization are highly questionable because of changes in demographic structure over time. A better indicator for the 19th century would be the percent qualified of all men of 25 and over. Exact figures of the totals qualified for the vote in 1814-15 are not available but estimates based on censuses suggest that 40-50% of all men over 25 qualified. Cf. S. Rokkan, "Geography . . . ," sect. I. 3. By comparison, about one out of seven adult males was enfranchised in England and Wales before 1832, about one out of five after the First Reform, one out of three after the Second, and two out of three after the Third. Cf. D. E. Butler and J. Cornford, "Britain," a chapter in S. Rokkan and J. Meyriat, eds., *International Guide to Electoral Statistics*, Paris, International Committee on Social Sciences Documentation, forthcoming, 1966.

an alliance of urban radicals and mobilized peasantry challenged the supremacy of the King's officials and finally won out in 1884.

The decisive thrust toward universal democracy came in the years from 1876 to 1882: the turnout level rose from 55 percent to 83 percent in the cities and from 41 percent to 70 percent in the countryside.[5] This spurt of mobilization produced the first extension of the suffrage: taxable income was added as a new criterion. While the old rules of 1814 had tended to favor the owners of land and real estate in a primary economy, the new criterion reflected the increasing importance of liquid money in a growing economy: the result was that more than half of the working class men in the largest cities were enfranchised as against only a quarter of the landless proletariat in the rural areas.[6] The electoral reform of 1884 eased the most mobilized of the workers into the political system and left the majority of the underprivileged in the countryside still disfranchised. This was a decision of great importance for the subsequent history of electoral mobilization and alignment in Norway.

There was a brief lull in the process of mobilization after the first extension of the suffrage in 1884, but the new entrants soon made use of their rights: by 1894 the turnout level was at an all-time peak of 91 percent in the cities and 83 percent in the rural areas. This second thrust of mobilization again led to an extension of the suffrage: a reform voted in 1898 introduced near-universal suffrage for all male citizens aged 25 and over.

THE LAG IN RURAL MOBILIZATION

The first result of the introduction of manhood suffrage was a distinct drop in the over-all turnout levels: 63 percent in the cities and 52 percent in the rural areas. The statistics do not allow direct calculations of the turnout for the new entrants but it can be estimated that the differences between the entrants and the established electorate were of the order indicated in Table 1.

The rural proletariat clearly lagged behind in the process of mobilization: the over-all urban-rural difference for the men stayed over 10 percentage points until 1909 and remained at the 5 to 10 point level until 1930. The rural lag was further accentuated through the enfranchisement of women. When women were first given the

[5] S. Rokkan, "Geography . . . ," *op.cit.*, Table 1.1 and the discussion in Rolf Danielsen, *Det Norske Storting gjennom 150 år*, Vol. 11, pp. 47-77.

[6] S. Rokkan, "Geography . . . ," sect. 1. 3. These estimates are based on a tax census for 1876.

TABLE 1. ESTIMATED DIFFERENCES IN TURNOUT BETWEEN OLD
ELECTORATE AND NEW ENTRANTS, BY CITIES AND RURAL AREAS,
1900-1903

| | Cities | | | Rural Areas | | |
	1897 %	1900 %	1903 %	1897 %	1900 %	1903 %
The established electorate						
actual (1897) and estimated (1900-1903)	78	78	78	68	68	68
New entrants (automatically registered)						
estimated turnout	—	44	52	—	33	28

vote, in the local elections of 1901, only 9.5 percent of them actually voted in the rural areas. When women first entered national
politics, in 1909 under an income criterion and in 1915 under the
same rules as the men, the rural lag persisted. The discrepancies in
turnout levels between cities and country districts stayed at around
20 percentage points for fully two decades and the decisive breakthrough in rural mobilization did not come until the election of 1930,
a contest fought largely over issues of fundamentalism and secularism. Even in the elections after World War II the turnout of rural
women has remained 8 to 11 percentage points lower than for the
women in the cities. Ecological analyses of differences between communes show persistent differences in turnout between central and
peripheral communes in the countryside: the over-all turnout is
highest in the suburban and the industrialized communes and some
15 to 20 percentage points lower in the primary economy communes
along the coast and in the mountainous fjords. The gap in turnout
levels between men and women has practically disappeared in the
cities and the urbanized countryside but is still very marked in the
peripheral areas.

A number of factors account for the persistence of such differences
in the Norwegian system: the fragmented geography, the dispersed
population and the difficulties of physical access to the schoolhouses
and the other places of voting, the occupational handicaps of the
fishermen and the seasonal workers, the strong rural traditions of
male dominance in community roles.[7] Our analyses indicate marked
territorial differences in the economic and the social costs of political
participation but also suggest concomitant differences in the incentives offered and the pressures exerted to overcome such cost barriers. The turnout in the peripheral areas is low not only because

[7] Rokkan and Valen, "The Mobilization of the Periphery . . . ," *op.cit.*, pp.
114-119, 134-141.

it takes more effort from the average resident to cast his vote but also because the local political leaders, being less directly tied in with the provincial and the national party organizations, will only rarely assign a high marginal value to the last mobilized vote.[8] We cannot study the time lags in the process of mobilization without a detailed mapping of the local entrenchment of party organizations: When were the first members recruited? When was a regular branch set up? When did the party first appear as a distinct unit in the election of local councillors?

THE PROCESS OF POLITICIZATION

Our study of the spread of partisan competitiveness from the central to the peripheral localities has not yet taken us very far toward complete coverage, but even our early findings appear to be of great interest in a comparative perspective.

We have not yet been able to assemble records of the growth of party organizations and party memberships by locality, but the official statistical publications at least allow us to trace changes over time in the number and character of the lists presented at local elections. Under the system in force in Norway after 1896 the first sign of incipient politicization would be a change from the traditional single-list plurality vote to the modern system of competitive lists and proportional representation. This meant that local leaders were no longer certain of their traditional clientèle and had to organize in politically distinct groups to maintain control of municipal affairs. Three-quarters of the cities had reached this initial level of politicization at the very first election under universal suffrage, but only one quarter of the rural districts. By 1910 practically all the urban units of any size had changed to PR but only one-third of the rural ones. There was then a period of rapid rural politicization. The industrialization of a number of isolated localities in the countryside, the sudden increases in the monetization of the primary economy as a result of the war, the spread of socialist and syndicalist ideas into the recently mobilized rural proletariat—all these developments intensified the conflicts within the communes and made it impossible to retain the traditional system of single-list voting. The splits in the working-class movement in the 1920's seem to have halted the process of rural politicization for a while but the gigantic thrust of the Labor party in the crisis years of the 1930's finally reduced the

[8] *Op.cit.*, pp. 125-126.

number of traditionally organized communes to a mere handful. By 1937 only 31 out of a total of 682 communes were still in this "pre-political" state, by 1945 32, by 1951 29, and by 1963 10.

This, however, was only a first step toward full politicization: A commune might have introduced competitive PR elections and still maintain purely territorial contests between lists for its constituent districts. The next step would normally be the introduction of *one* list identified with a nationally registered party, the next again *two* such lists and the final step a completely partisan contest solely between such national lists. A classification of the rural communes (Table 2) for four local elections after the Second World War will demonstrate how far this process of politicization has gone in Norway:

TABLE 2. ELECTOROL LIST ALTERNATIVES IN LOCAL ELECTIONS IN IN RURAL COMMUNES, 1947-1963

	1947	1955	1959	1963
Total no. of communes = 100%	680	680	670	476
One list, plurality election	5.0%	2.8%	2.5%	2.1%
Several lists, all non-partisan	4.9	5.7	6.0	5.2
One party list, one or more non-partisan	9.3	8.5	8.7	5.7
Two or more party lists, one or more non-partisan	26.1	29.0	23.2	31.3
Only party lists	54.7	54.0	59.6	55.7

The process of politicization seems to have reached a plateau in the years from 1945 to 1955. Roughly one-sixth of the communes were still at a very low level of partisan competition, well over a quarter of them were at an intermediate level, and just over half of them were fully politicized. From 1959 onward a new wave of change set in: Under the pressure of increasing demands for administrative efficiency in the operation of communal services a number of rural units were merged into larger ones and these territorial reorganizations set the stage for further changes in the local cleavage systems.

Our analyses of the geographical, cultural, and socio-economic conditions of politicization suggest these conclusions:

a. the communes in the central provinces of the East were first to reach a high level of politicization.

b. the peripheral primary-economy communes of the outer provinces, most markedly the fisheries communities along the western and the northern coast, were the last to reach even the first stage of politicization and the majority of them were still at the first or intermediate stage in the 1950's.

c. the industrializing and urbanizing communes of the outer provinces differ markedly in their levels of politicization from one region to another. In the West, a region of strong traditions of territorial and cultural opposition to the national center, politicization still tends to be low in such communes, while in the North, a region of marked class polarization, it tends to be considerably higher.

d. the contrast between the West and the North (Table 3) is indeed intriguing.

TABLE 3. NUMBERS OF NATIONALLY REGISTERED PARTIES, IN LOCAL ELECTIONS OF 1955, BY TYPE OF COMMUNE

			Nationally Registered Parties		
		No. of Communes = 100%	*None or only one %*	*Two or more, also non-partisan %*	*Only party lists %*
Coastal communes: 16% or more in fisheries					
Peripheral communes[9]	West	16	50	31	19
	North	72	26	51	22
Other communes	West	55	58	27	15
	North	33	18	73	9
Inland communes: less than 16% in fisheries					
Peripheral communes	West	28	39	25	36
	North	20	20	35	45
Other communes	West	108	23	40	37
	North	91	5	27	67

More than half of the coastal communes of the West were in 1955 still at only the first stage of politicization. In the North only a quarter of these communes were at this level and more than half at the next level. The same differences emerge from the analysis of the inland communes: In the West only about one-third had reached the highest level of politicization as against two-thirds in the northern provinces.

These differences reflect a basic contrast in Norwegian politics:[10] The emphasis on territorial representation and cultural defense in

[9] "Peripherality" is here measured by a six-item score originally developed by the Norwegian geographer A. Thormodsæter. For details see S. Rokkan and H. Valen, "The Mobilization of the Periphery," *op.cit.*, p. 117.

[10] Rokkan and Valen, "Regional Contrasts . . . ," *op.cit.*, sect. III.

the West, and the emphasis on functional representation and class cleavage in the North. The territorial-cultural emphasis sets limits to the possibilities of party conflict within localities and tends to reduce politics to questions of external representation. The functional-economic emphasis reflects active alliances across local geographical units, tends to undermine the established leadership structure, and introduces elements of direct interest conflict into community politics.

Comparing the results of local and national elections in communes at different levels of politicization we find marked contrasts between the two regions: In the West the parties in the middle of the political spectrum are strongest in the least politicized communes and considerably weaker in the fully politicized ones; in the North even the least politicized of the communes will be strongly polarized between Socialists and Conservatives.

These differences are also reflected in the data for levels of electoral mobilization. In the least politicized communes of the West the turnout at local elections tends to be markedly lower than the turnout at national elections, while in the North the communes at the same level of politicization tend to mobilize as many or more voters at local than at national elections.[11] This finding requires detailed checking through case studies in selected communities, but the interpretation closest at hand is that it reflects a basic difference in the strategies of mobilization of the local leaders. In a safe local election the marginal utility of mobilized votes is very small, but in the national election each vote delivered to the provincial total serves as a "counter" in bargains for positions and for favors at the next level of the system. In an increasingly polarized community the leaders will be as concerned to mobilize their maximum in local as in national elections. This is typically the case in the peripheral communes of the North where the Labor party is on the verge of establishing firm local allies but has not yet organized itself for direct participation in municipal contests.

THE TWO PERIPHERIES: THE "COUNTER-CENTRAL" AND THE "POLARIZED"

The original lines of cleavage in the Norwegian system were territorial and cultural: the provinces opposed the capital, the peasantry fought the officials of the King's administration, the defenders of

[11] Rokkan and Valen, "The Mobilization of the Periphery," *op.cit.*, pp. 119, 123-125.

the rural cultural traditions spoke against the steady spread of urban secularism and rationalism.

Three developments brought about a decisive change in the cleavage system during the first two decades after the establishment of universal suffrage. First, the entry of the bulk of the peasantry into the national money and credit economy and the concomitant shift from an attitude of negative resistance against the tax-collecting state towards a positive emphasis on the role of the national government in meeting the claims of the rural population.[12] Second, the emergence of a nation-wide movement of working-class protest, not only in the cities and the industrializing countryside but also in the forestry and fisheries communities of the eastern, the middle, and the northern provinces. Third, the transformation of the original Right from an organization for the defense of the established administration of the state to a party essentially defending the claims of the urban middle class and the emerging business community against the encroaching apparatus of the national government.

These functional-economic lines of conflict cut across the earlier territorial-cultural cleavage and produced a complex system of alliances and oppositions. In the cities and the industrializing communities in the countryside the electorates were increasingly polarized between a Socialist left and a Conservative right. In the highly stratified forestry and fisheries communities of the East, the Trøndelag, and the North there was a similar, although slower, process of polarization, even in the extreme peripheries of the outlying provinces. In the more equalitarian primary economy communities of the South and the West the forces of territorial defense remained strong and vigorous and resisted effectively the pressures toward a polarization of local political life.

Our ecological analyses show that these regional differences in the levels of class polarization are most pronounced in the peripheral, economically backward communes and tend to disappear with urbanization and economic growth: as is shown in Table 4.

The striking difference between the southwestern and the northern peripheries essentially reflects a difference in the timing of the crucial waves of mobilization: in the South and the West the breakthrough

[12] Knut Dahl Jacobsen has described the first phase of this process of change in *Teknisk hjelp og politisk struktur*, Oslo: Universitetsforlaget, 1964, especially pp. 172-196. Details about further developments will be available in the forthcoming history of the central administration in Norway 1814-1964.

TABLE 4. POLARIZATION SCORES BY REGION
AND TYPE OF COMMUNES

	Polarization Scores 1957[a]
East and Trøndelag	
Principal cities	.88
Other cities	.85
Central rural[b]	.82
Peripheral	.68
South and West	
Principal cities	.75
Other cities	.68
Central rural[b]	.61
Peripheral	.45
North	
Cities	.84
Central rural[b]	.85
Peripheral	.80

[a] This score simply indicates the relative strength of the "class" parties vs. the "territorial-cultural" parties: the higher the score, the greater the preponderance of the Socialists (CP + Labor) and the Conservatives in the locality; the lower the score, the stronger two offshoots of the old Left, the Liberals and the Christians. A third offshoot of the old Left, the Agrarians, has been disregarded in this context since its contribution to within-community polarization varies considerably from region to region.

[b] This classification is based on a score for "accessibility," an alternative measure of "centrality-peripherality." See the explanation in Rokkan and Valen "The Mobilization of the Periphery," p. 116.

came during the second half of the nineteenth century and found expression in a number of religious and cultural movements of resistance against the centralizing urban forces; in the North the breakthrough came with the introduction of manhood suffrage and took the form of a movement of violent social and economic protest, not primarily against the center of the nation but against the local property owners and employers.

In the South and the West the struggle centered on the symbols of community identification: the religious creed and the language. The mobilized peasantry fought the lukewarm liberalism of the state church and rejected the standard urban language brought into their communities by the clergymen, the officials, the teachers, and the traders. The rural counter-language, the *landsmål*, became the rallying symbol for a broad movement of cultural defense, not only in the South and the West but also in the old peasant communities of the eastern valleys. In the other regions of the country the movement never rallied such decisive community support; in these regions the functional cleavage lines soon emerged as the dominant ones and the earlier territorial contrasts lost in importance.

In the northern periphery there was much less of a basis for such counter-cultural movements of territorial defense. The communities tended to be culturally fragmented and socially hierarchized; the privileged merchant families stood far apart from the crofters and the landless fishermen, and after the introduction of manhood suffrage even very small and peripheral communes soon found themselves politically divided. The smallholders and the fishermen had for centuries depended for their living on the owners of port facilities who bought their produce and controlled their credit. The introduction of manhood suffrage coincided with a number of changes in the primary economy, the installation of processing plants, the motorization of the fishing fleet and the consequent increase in the need for credit. The result was an explosive mobilization of protest against the owners and the controllers. The Labor party had built its initial organizational strength in the metropolitan areas of the East, but the decisive political breakthrough came in the extreme periphery of the North; the first socialist representatives to enter the *Storting* were elected by the fishermen of the North in 1903, at the second election after the introduction of manhood suffrage. This alliance between the rural proletariat and the urban working class proved of the greatest importance in Norwegian politics: it accelerated the development of a national party system and halted the tendencies toward an accentuation of center-periphery contrasts.[13]

III. Implications for Developmental Comparisons

I have summarized the principal findings of our current studies of the process of mobilization, politicization, and polarization in Norway. Some of these analyses are primarily of interest to one-nation historians; some of them, I hope, may provide possible paradigms for detailed developmental comparisons across a number of different political systems.

At a high level of abstraction what we have been concerned to study in our program of developmental analyses is the propagation of waves of political innovation from the centers of the national territory to its peripheries.[14] We have studied the spread of the idea

[13] For further details on the implications of this urban-rural alliance, see S. Rokkan "Numerical Democracy and Corporate Pluralism."

[14] This is the central theme of research in the flourishing school of geography

that everybody, whatever his or her status in the community, is entitled to a vote and should make use of it; we have tried to map the diffusion of party memberships and organizations; and we have described the steps in the spread of polarized party politics throughout the localities of the nation.

Our initial concern with the mobilization of the latest subjects to enter the national political arena led us step by step to a wider concern with the latest communities to enter nationalized party politics: why were some communities politicized and polarized so quickly after the introduction of mass democracy while others remained largely unchanged in their community structure for decades after the decisive extension of the suffrage?

Ecological analyses of the conditions of competitive community politics have been attempted in the United States[15] and could easily be repeated in a number of countries. Such *synchronic* analyses of the relationships between levels of economic growth, politicization and polarization must eventually be fitted into a broader context of *diachronic* studies of sequences of change in communities of different structure.

Two tasks must be clearly distinguished in any such attempt at developmental analysis: the sifting of information on variations in the *initial structural conditions* in the locality, quite particularly in the stratification of the population, the concentration of economic power and the extent of social, cultural and religious cleavages; and the collection of data on the *processes of external and internal change* and their consequences for the equilibrium of forces within each community.

Hans Daalder[16] has persuasively argued the importance of research on the inherited structures of urban and rural societies for an understanding of divergencies and convergencies in the development of European party systems. Our own work on Norwegian de-

---

at the University of Lund, see particularly T. Hägerstrand, *Innovationsförloppet ur korologiskt synpunkt*, Lund: Gleerup, 1951. Attempts to apply this technique to the spread of political affiliations and commitments are still very few. Cf. F. Lägnert, *Valmanskåren på Skånes landsbygd 1911-1948*, Lund: Gleerup, 1952, and the recent article by G. Carlson, *op.cit.*; see also his "Time and Continuity in Mass Attitude Change," *Public Opinion Quarterly*, Vol. 29, No. 1 (1965), pp. 1-15.

[15] Philips Cutright, "Urbanization and Competitive Party Politics," *Journal of Politics*, Vol. 25, No. 3 (1963), pp. 552-564, an analysis of the influence of urbanization, industrialization, and religious divisions on competitiveness in the counties of ten states.

[16] H. Daalder, "Parties and Elites in Western Europe," above, Ch. 2.

velopments adds further evidence of the importance of such research not only for an understanding of regional variations but also for comparative "typing" of the resultant national party systems. The contrasts in electoral alignments between East and West, West and North reflect fundamental differences in inherited socio-economic structure, and the complex crosscutting of cleavage lines in the national system can be understood only against this background.

This, however, is only half the story. The initial structure conditions the process of change toward competitive mass democracy but does not determine its course. Our Norwegian analyses leave no doubt that industrialization and urbanization affected political life in all regions irrespective of inherited traditions: the regional differences have remained in the typical primary-economy communes but tend to disappear in the suburbs and the cities. To study these processes of community change we shall clearly need standardized time series data for as many as possible of the distinct localities. On this point a comparative perspective on processes of nation-building may help us to generate fruitful models for an understanding of our own system. Daniel Lerner[17] and Karl Deutsch[18] have each in his way pointed to important variables in the study of sequences of community mobilization and integration into the national political system.

To account for differences in the rates of political change under conditions of mass democracy it will prove of great interest to collect for each community developmental data for a broad range of cross-local transaction flows:

a. monetization of exchanges and the consequent entry into a wider network of economic relations;

b. entry into the credit market and the consequent increase in the defense of the peripheral units on the central ones;

c. spread of urban commodities, skills, and technologies and the consequent changes in the structure of the local labor force;

d. mobility of works from the primary sector into the secondary and the tertiary and from the peripheral areas to the central;

e. development of cross-local contacts through the schools, the armed forces, the administrative services, and the dominant church;

[17] D. Lerner, *The Passing of Traditional Society*, Glencoe, Ill.: The Free Press, 1957.
[18] K. Deutsch, "Social Mobilization and Political Development," *American Political Science Review*, Vol. 60 (September 1961), pp. 493-514.

f. growth of a membership market for voluntary associations and the establishment of local branches of regional and national organizations;

g. entry into a wider market of information exchange within the nation, partly as an indirect result of the opening up of other channels of exchange, partly through the diffusion of such personal media as the mails, the telegraph, and the telephone, and partly through the spread of locally, regionally, and nationally based mass media.

If time-series data could be established for each of these channels of exchange for large samples of localities, it should be possible to establish with some precision the average thresholds of economic and social mobilization required to trigger processes of within-community polarization and cross-local party development. We are very far from this goal in our developmental studies in Norway, and the many gaps in the sources of historical and statistical information will force us to resort to a variety of short-cuts in the analysis. We hope, however, that as we continue to accumulate such time-series data we shall be able to differentiate our analysis and our conclusions and to develop more complex models of the processes of change.

A theory of political change can never be built on data for a single country, however. What we need to gain further insight and perspective is a series of parallel analyses of developmental sequences in countries of different social and political structure and with different histories of suffrage extensions.

The official records of elections in the countries of the West contain staggering amounts of information for such comparative time series analyses.[19] With the increasing accessibility of large-scale computers it is no longer an impossible task to collate such political data with demographic, socio-economic, and cultural data from censuses and other official statistics and carry out the appropriate analyses of sequences of change. It is true that conditions for such data collection will vary very much between highly centralized nation-states and loosely organized federations. It is vastly easier to assemble such data in a country with a long history of centralized bookkeeping such as

[19] The International Committee on Social Sciences Documentation has taken steps to facilitate comparisons of such data through the preparation in two or more volumes of an *International Guide to Electoral Statistics*. The first volume, to be edited by S. Rokkan and J. Meyriat, is close to completion and will be published in 1966; it will cover 15 countries of Western Europe.

Sweden than in such federations as the United States and Australia. In general, countries emphasizing territorial representation tend to have poorer electoral statistics than countries with stronger traditions of estate representation and PR. The British statistics for national elections allow analyses only at the constituency level, and the statistics for local elections have never been centralized. In Australia and New Zealand research workers such as R. M. Chapman and R. S. Parker have not only had to dig their way through local archives and newspapers but also had to draw up boundaries for the territorial counting units they found data for.[20] Uncertainties and changes in the delimitation of the data units do indeed create headaches in ecological research, but in most cases it will be possible to carry out analyses for several shorter periods of relative stability even if it is not possible to cover the total history of the country's electoral politics within one data sequence.[21] An archive organized by periods of comparable data is vastly better than no archive. Replications of similarly designed analyses at different points in time can often reveal a great deal about factors at work in the process of change even in the absence of continuous time series data.

Once such archives are in operation for two or more countries it should be possible to match localities by their economic structure and the level of social mobilization and to study similarities and differences between political cultures in the character of local political divisions and in the extent of turnout at local and national elections.[22]

Several strategies of comparative analysis suggest themselves. My own inclination would be to focus the initial analyses on the lags in rural political change. Our Norwegian analyses have already demonstrated the importance of a concentration on the politics of the rural periphery for an understanding of regional contrasts within the polity. The differences between the equalitarian South and West and

[20] R. M. Chapman, *et al.*, *New Zealand Politics in Action*, London: Oxford University Press, 1962, particularly Chs. 11-12. R. S. Parker, ed., *Political Handbook of Australia 1890-1962*, forthcoming. I am indebted to Robert Chapman for information on the methodological problems of ecological research in New Zealand and Australia.

[21] W. D. Burnham, *op.cit.*, has studied the available data for 19th-century U.S. elections and reports that analyses at the county level will present very few problems of this kind; the major difficulties occur in the analysis of data for congressional districts and city wards.

[22] To give readers some concrete indications of the types of analysis suggested, I shall include here a few tables comparable to the Norwegian ones. The abundant Swedish statistics have not yet been analyzed along the same lines as the Norwegian but preliminary checks indicate largely similar patterns of development:

TABLE 1. THE LAG IN RURAL MOBILIZATION

ELECTION	TURNOUT IN % OF ELECTORATE			
	Men		Women	
	Urban	Rural	Urban	Rural
1866	40.5	15-16		
1881	45.2	19.5		
1887 (I)	62.9	48.1		
1908	70.0	57.4		
1909 manhood suffrage				
1911	63.0	55.5		
1921 universal suffrage	62.2	61.9	50.5	45.5
1932	74.0	72.7	65.6	60.6
1948	85.7	84.2	82.8	78.7
1956	82.4	80.8	80.0	76.2

Herbert Tingsten, in his pioneering volume on *Political Behaviour*, London: P. S. King, 1937 was the first to call attention to the early lags and the gradual equalization of turnout discrepancies. He found roughly the same patterns in Denmark and Iceland as in Norway and Sweden: gradual decreases both in the rural-urban and in the men-women discrepancies. In Finland the rural population was mobilized as early as the urban in the national elections, but the same basic pattern of change was found for municipal elections and for the men-women discrepancies.

A review of Swedish statistics for local elections indicates the following sequence of change.

TABLE 2. THE POLITICIZATION OF LOCAL ELECTIONS

ELECTION	PARTY DIVISIONS IN RURAL COMMUNES		TURNOUT IN LOCAL ELECTIONS			
	Competitive	Not competitive	Competitive		Not competitive	
			M	W	M	W
1920	69.4%	30.6%	62.4	56.9	27.9	20.1
1930	75.6%	14.4%	59.9	47.2	24.5	12.0
1934	91.8%	8.2%	65.7	53.9	29.3	16.7

ELECTION	LEVEL OF POLITICIZATION			TURNOUT IN LOCAL ELECTIONS					
	I	II	III	I		II		III	
	Political parties only	Several non-political	Only list one	M	W	M	W	M	W
1938	79.3	6.6	14.1	69.7	59.3	62.9	49.3	43.2	27.2
1946	88.5	1.7	9.8	73.9	66.8	63.2	51.8	49.8	34.6

1950 all communes except 6 fully politicized
1954 all communes except 2 fully politicized

A breakdown for 1938 indicates the structural conditions for low politicization*:

	GROUP I	GROUP II	GROUP III
Communes with 75% or more in agriculture	66.7	10.3	23.0
Communes with 50-75% in agriculture	81.7	6.6	11.7
Other communes, not urbanized	92.8	1.0	6.2
Urbanized communes	94.1	2.5	3.4

* Sveriges off. stat. Alm. val., *Kommunala valen år 1938*, Stockholm, 1939, p. 59.

the hierarchically stratified East and North underscore the importance of detailed attention to land tenure systems and rural organization. In a cross-national perspective this concentration on rural politics appears equally promising. Differences in rural social structure not only make for difference in the levels of mobilization and politicization in the countryside but also influence the character of the rural-urban alliances and alignments in the party system and consequently the over-all balance in the polity.

Differences in systems of land tenure and rural stratification were of crucial importance in the early history of suffrage extensions in Europe in the nineteenth century.[23] The First Reform Bill had strengthened the power of the aristocracy and the gentry in the counties in England[24] and the introduction of manhood suffrage had also tended to consolidate the positions of the *Gutsbesitzer* of rural Prussia[25] and the *notables* of rural France.[26] Clearly in many of these rural structures the ingrained hierarchical traditions and the sheer force of economic dependence made voting more frequently an expression of loyal deference than of political protest. By contrast, in Scandinavia the decisive thrust toward democracy and parliamentary rule was brought about through the associational mobilization of the freehold peasantry.[27] Their grievances against the established regimes were not exclusively economic: their rejection of the centralizing nation-state and the dominance of the officials and the

The rapid politicization of local elections in Sweden can to some extent be explained in ecological and socio-economic terms but the institutional links between local and national elections clearly added decisively to the rate of change: representation in the Upper House is based on elections within the provincial and the city councils and there is accordingly a direct incentive to encourage partisanship at the local level. A report on developments toward local politicization in Sweden was published in 1964 (*Rapport och arbetsmaterial från arbetsgruppen för det kommunala sambandet*, Stockholm: S. O. U., 1964, p. 39).

[23] Cursory comparisons of sequences of suffrage extension are given in S. Rokkan, "Mass Suffrage, Secret Voting and Political Participation," *Arch. eur. sociol.*, Vol. 2, No. 2 (1961), pp. 132-152; also in the chapter by R. Bendix and S. Rokkan, "The Extension of National Citizenship to the Lower Classes," in R. Bendix, *Nation-building and Citizenship*, New York: Wiley and Sons, 1964, pp. 74-100.

[24] D. C. Moore, *op.cit.*, and F. M. C. Thompson. *English Landed Society in the Nineteenth Century*, London: Routledge, 1963.

[25] See especially Th. Nipperdey, *Die Organisation der deutschen Parteien vor 1918*, Düsseldorf: Droste, 1961, Kap. V.

[26] For the West of France the basic text on rural politics is André Siegfried's classic *Tableau politique de la France de l'Ouest sous la Troisième République*, Paris: Colin, 1913, esp. Ch. 23. "Influence du régime de la propriété foncière. . . ." For a follow-up analysis of elections under the Fourth Republic see J. Fauvet and H. Mendras, eds., *Les paysans et la politique*, Paris: Colin, 1958.

[27] Summaries of historical information on the developments of the Scandinavian party systems have recently been published in *Problemer i nordisk historieforskning*, Oslo: Universitetsforlaget, 1964, Part II. "Framveksten av de politiske partier i de nordiske land på 1800-tallet."

patricians in the cities was cultural as well. Such counter-movements against the central culture can be documented in all ethnically divided polities: the opposition of the "Celtic fringe" to the dominance of the Tory culture of England is an obvious example. The rapidly increasing strength of the Liberals in the Welsh countryside paralleled the emergence of the Nordic "Left": what counted were not just the grievances against the absentee English landlords but also the cultural and religious mobilization against the influences they represented.[28] What distinguished the Nordic developments was the initial polarization of politics along an urban-rural axis: the central culture was predominantly urban and the movements of cultural protest appealed to essentially rural values. In Britain the central culture had its roots in the English landed estates and the movements of opposition were partly recruited from the non-conformists in the growing cities, partly from the subject peasantry of the Celtic peripheries.

Such contrasts in rural-urban relations have had profound effects not only on the rate and direction of mobilization but also on the level of politicization and the development of cross-local party organizations and the integration of the local leadership into the national network.

In Scandinavia the conflict between urban dominance and rural claims was at the heart of the early struggle over constitutional reform and parliamentary power. The basic dimension of cleavage was territorial, and the internal politics of the peripheral units remained largely unchanged. The move toward nationalized politics was essentially a consequence of the spread of the Social Democrats from the cities to the rural areas and the alliance of the industrial working class and the rural proletariat. Wherever the rural lower class could be mobilized the local elections were increasingly politicized and the local leaders found it essential to establish close cross-local alliances within the provincial and national party organizations.

In England the crucial change from constituency to national politics came after 1885 with the entry of the Conservatives into the boroughs and the gradual merger of the landed interests with the urban and suburban business interests.[29] While in Scandinavia the drive toward nationwide class polarization came from the working class, in England it was the Conservatives who brought about the decisive change from the tradition of cross-class territorial representation to the emphasis

---

[28] See especially Kenneth O. Morgan, *Wales in British Politics*, Cardiff: University of Wales Press, 1963.
[29] Cornford, *op.cit.*

on cross-constituency class representation. In Scandinavia the rural and the urban establishments were never able to merge into one major party of opposition against the Social Democrats; in Britain the alliance of the aristocracy, the gentry, and the urban middle class eventually produced a strong national party destined to govern the polity for decades.

The consequent contrasts between the over-all levels of rural politicization in Scandinavia and Britain are well-known: in Scandinavia on the whole markedly competitive rural politics and high turnout levels in local elections, in England much lower levels of politicization in the primary economy areas and often very low rates of participation in local elections.[30] Obviously the frequency of contested elections and the level of the turnout are to some extent direct

---

[30] J. M. Lee has developed a typology of the counties in England and Wales in an effort to study the conditions for local politicization. His essential finding is that the counties least affected by urbanization and industrialization have the lowest numbers of contested elections both at the level of the district councils and at the level of county councils. This of course is in general conformity with results for Norway and Sweden but the over-all level of competitiveness is much lower. Lee's tables for the average politicization of elections from 1946 to 1958 reveal a great deal about patterns of regional variations in England and Wales. The calculations in the following table are adapted from his *Social Leaders and Public Persons, op.cit.*, Appendix D.

Region	Average % contested seats 1946-58		Range of within-region variation			
	County Councils (% of pop. in R.D.C.s)	Rural D.C.s	County Councils		Rural D.C.s	
			Max. % contested	Min. % contested	Max. % contested	Min. % contested
			(% in parentheses: pop. in R.D.C.s in the country)			
1. Home Counties	72	41	88	51	53	26
	(19)		(11)	(51)	(10 & 30)	(32)
2. North & North Midlands	56	36	74	43	47	27
	(18)		(14)	(20)	(14)	(20)
3. Midlands	44	31	52	37	47	22
	(31)		(33)	(33)	(33)	(22 & 48)
4. Southwest	34	28	45	21	40	14
	(37)		(52)	(45)	(52)	(39)
5. Eastern England	33	27	65	19	47	13
	(43)		(55)	(56)	(38)	(56)
6. Border Countries	39	22	46	26	36	10
	(33)		(13)	(55)	(45)	(55)
7. Wales & Monmouth	27	36	42	13	66	9
	(32)		(18)	(59 & 67)	(18)	(59)

The differences at the regional level are quite clear-cut but they tend to cover up important variations among counties within the regions. In regions such as the Midlands, the Southwest, and Eastern England there is in fact no clear relationship

functions of the system of representation: the Scandinavian PR systems encourage general participation, the British plurality system discourages minorities. But as we saw in our account of developments in Norway, the transition from plurality representation to PR was in itself a first sign of increasing politicization. The triumph of PR in the Scandinavian polities reflects the strength of the pressures for representation from below; the persistence of the plurality system indicates higher levels of local consensus and a stronger tradition of rural territorial representation.

It is interesting to reflect on the similarities and dissimilarities between the rural Southwest of Norway and the rural areas of England: in both cases we find low levels of politicization and polarization, but in the deviant Norwegian regions the rural units are typically equalitarian communities of small freeholders, while in England they tend to be dominated by highly stratified structures inherited from a manorial and feudal past. The paternal rule of the aristocracy and the gentry offered as effective a barrier against class politics as the equalitarian structure of the Norwegian communities but the consequences for rural-urban integration were very different in the two cases. In England the rural leaders could ally themselves to a strong national party of prestige and wealth; in Norway the equalitarian Southwest became the stronghold of a rural counter-culture alienated from the society and the politics of the urban centers of the nation.[31]

Similar analyses of contrasts in rural-urban cleavage structures can be multiplied for country after country. To get beyond the stage of vague speculation and impressionistic generalization so characteristic of much of the current work in comparative history and comparative politics it is essential to get down to detailed analyses of ranges of variations within countries, both at the initial stage of mobilization and in the current phase of development. Only through such efforts of massive data-gathering and analysis can we avoid the Scylla of hasty overgeneralization and the Charybdis of myopic attention to local and national peculiarities.

between the levels of urbanization and the levels of competitiveness. To account for variations county by county it would be necessary to develop a multivariate analysis design and to take into consideration such factors as the size distribution of land holdings, the strength of agricultural unions and farmers' organizations, the strength of the Liberals during the early phases of competitive politics. The work currently undertaken by Michael Steed at Nuffield College on partisanship in English local politics may provide important data for such analysis.

[31] For further analysis, See Rokkan and Valen, "Regional Contrasts . . . ," *op.cit.*, and Rokkan, "Norway: Numerical Democracy . . . ," *op.cit.*

CHAPTER 10

PARTIES AND NATIONAL INTEGRATION IN AFRICA

RUPERT EMERSON

~·~

I

PRECEDED BY all the assumptions of democracy, of popular sovereignty, and of the welfare state, the African masses have been catapulted into the political arena with only the barest minimum of preparation for their new powers and responsibilities. As many commentators have pointed out, there has been in Africa no gradual evolution toward universal suffrage, and all that it implies, such as characterized the history of the West. In Africa the finished product of Western political development, in the guise of an intricate parliamentary system plus a rationalized administration, was presumed to be both valid and viable as the instrument for the self-government of peoples who had as yet experienced virtually none of the revolutions through which the West passed in the last centuries.

In these circumstances the significance of political parties as agencies for political socialization is peculiarly vital. On several counts the task of African parties in promoting national integration in particular is both more difficult and more necessary than it would be in any other major part of the world. Achieving independence with a lower and less stable level of national integration within the existing political units than is generally to be found elsewhere, all the African countries south of the Sahara are in grave need of forces which can actively promote their unity. In a number of these countries political parties have played a central and invaluable role in speeding and consolidating the processes of integration, although it must also be recorded that in some instances parties have impeded rather than advanced integration, notably where their guiding star was tribalism rather than nationalism—a term whose specific meaning is always to be examined with a skeptical eye in the African context.

One of the familiar roots of the problem of national integration in Africa is that the colonial powers imposed upon the continent a set of political boundaries which impinged erratically on the established ethnic and political alignments of the African peoples, creating political entities which each embraced a larger or smaller miscellany of disparate communities and not infrequently cut across tribal lines. The opening moves toward what came to be regarded as national integration within each territory were made under colonial auspices. What took place in the different dependencies varied greatly and moved at different rates of speed, but everywhere the existence of a single colonial government, when such a government in fact came to embrace the whole territory, had the effect of intensifying communications within the territory and of spreading an awareness among at least some of its inhabitants that a new political order had been instituted. The awareness of a new common identity was, however, limited to a relatively small, if constantly growing, new elite, which shortly began to press its claims, first to a share in the management of its own affairs, and then to self-government or full independence. To the ethnic gap was thus added the gap between those who, generally through more or less intimate contact with the Europeans, had moved to a new kind of political participation or a demand for it and the far larger masses of people who lingered essentially within the confines of the traditional communities.

The political party or movement soon emerged as the embodiment of the claim of the rising modern-oriented elite that a new self had come into existence which sought the right to determine its own destiny. The particular form which such parties or movements took and the goals they publicly professed were inevitably strongly influenced, if not determined, by the colonial situation in which they found themselves; but whatever their special attributes, the creation and management of these nationalist organizations and the waging of the struggle against colonialism lent the potential national community a flesh-and-blood reality denied to it up to that point. Since the governmental apparatus, including its military adjuncts, was in the hands of the alien ruler, only the nationalist party could be counted on to undertake the positive promotion of a sense of national identity to which primary devotion was owed. After independence the government as well, now under nationalist control, could be directly enlisted in the processes of nation-building, but the party necessarily had priority as far as overt political action was concerned.

To assess the significance of African political parties in the process of national integration it is neither necessary nor useful in defining the term "party" to draw such fine distinctions as to exclude significant manifestations of African political life. African political organizations have been adapted to African uses, and it is the better part of wisdom not to seek to press too tightly upon them usages which have been derived primarily from the European or American experience. Thus I propose to accept the position taken by Thomas Hodgkin that "There is nothing to be gained by attempting a precise definition of the term 'party' at this point. . . . For the moment it is probably most convenient to consider as 'parties' all political organizations which regard themselves as parties and which are generally so regarded."[1] The loss suffered through looseness of terminology is more than compensated for by the gain in inclusiveness of coverage of African political phenomena.

What is important for the present purpose is that the different types of organizations which the political leaders have brought into being and the different functions which they have performed have all contributed to the growth of political consciousness. It may generally be presumed that in doing so they have also contributed to the spread of national integration save where their focus has been implicitly or explicitly divisive because they rested upon a tribal, religious, or regional basis.

Those who take a purist view of parties may lay their stress on limiting the title of party to those associations which perform their functions of political recruitment and the formulation and representation of interests through the process of electoral competition. This limitation may be carried to the extreme of denying that political associations are parties where electoral competition is absent. The most grievous result of such an approach would be to eliminate from consideration the multitude of African states which have either swung over officially to the one-party system or have one party which has achieved so dominant a position as to deprive its rivals of any share in power. On such terms few African states remain in the running, since it is close to the general rule that elections have ceased to be competitions in any meaningful sense and have been turned into predetermined and glorified plebiscites in which the ruling party spreads its gospel and sweeps the field. Where 99 per cent victories have come to be commonplace the party is no doubt

---

[1] Thomas Hodgkin, *African Political Parties*, London: Penguin African Series, 1961, pp. 15-16. He later suggests the lines of distinction between parties, movements, congresses, fronts, etc., pp. 50ff.

still engaging in political recruitment, but its recruits for elective office need face election day with no concern, save under the uniquely competitive conditions of the one-party election in Tanzania in September 1965.

It is undoubtedly true that African parties ordinarily came into being to compete in the elections which were being introduced into the political systems of their countries. A striking example is the emergence of parties in French West and Equatorial Africa at the close of the Second World War as elections were authorized for the central governing institutions in Paris and for local councils. In this circumstance parties appeared in several instances after the first elections had been held and were built around individual leaders who had stood as independents. In some instances national movements or congresses, looking to a broad-based protest against colonial rule, have emerged to challenge the hold of the alien rulers before any electoral possibilities were opened to them, but they have normally been followed by more tightly organized parties equipped with programs and concentrating in part on the contesting of elections. A contemporary example of political organizations which have come into being despite the denial of African access to the ballot are those foreign-based organizations which seek to take over control in Portugal's African dependencies, where the government has tolerated neither parties nor political activities in which they might engage.

What everyone would concede to be authentic political parties in the sense of being contestants for some share in power were very likely to be preceded in Africa by other groupings, frequently without any direct political bearing, or, at most, of a quasi-political nature. Such proto-political associations do exist in the Portuguese territories and may well come to play a political role when the opportunity opens. The process is well illustrated by what shortly became the National Council of Nigeria and the Cameroons (NCNC), notable as the political vehicle of Nnamdi Azikiwe, which, when it got under way in 1944, had as its constituent elements two trade unions, two political parties, four literary societies, eight professional associations, eleven social clubs, and 101 tribal unions.[2] Here was already a large labor of integration which led to the creation of a Nigerian nation—although it also contributed to the tribalist regionalism characteristic of the country. Its main rival in the south of Nigeria,

[2] James S. Coleman, *Nigeria, Background to Nationalism*, Berkeley and Los Angeles: University of California Press, 1960, pp. 264-265.

the Action Group, of which Obafemi Awolowo was the principal architect, came into being in 1951, building largely on foundations which had been laid by the Yoruba cultural organization, the Egbe Omo Oduduwa. In some of the French territories a distinctive form of predecessor of the political party appeared with the establishment of Marxist study groups which served as one of the sources feeding into the *Rassemblement Démocratique Africain* (RDA), affiliated in its early years with the French Communist party. Other progenitors of parties were the societies formed by the graduates of particular schools or of Western schools in general, such as the Graduates General Congress in the Sudan which led into the National Unionist party, founded in 1949.

It is possible to identify African political parties with only a small margin of error. The same cannot be said of African nations. The core nations around which the national existence is built are usually not open to serious dispute in other continents, but in Africa a number of factors conspire to complicate the situation. The essential element has already been mentioned: the colonial boundaries cut across the traditional ethnic patterns but have been in existence too brief a time to give any assurance that they have served to consolidate nations. The political choices are in process of being made, but no conclusive answer has yet emerged.

The most obvious answer and the one which presumably now has both the widest appeal and the greatest accuracy is that the nations of Africa are to be identified with the former European dependencies. With very rare exceptions it is these dependencies, adhering rigorously to their colonial boundaries, which have asserted their separate sovereignty and taken their place as members of the United Nations. As a current betting matter these are Africa's nations, but they rest on unstable foundations, and other alternatives, including different versions of pan-Africanism, remain open. For the most part African leaders have come to accept the present state structure despite its evident and much publicized inadequacies, in growing awareness that any move for significant change in frontiers might bring the entire structure down in unpredictable confusion. Immanuel Wallerstein has given pithy expression to the underlying fears in pointing out that "every African nation, large or small, has its Katanga. Once the logic of secession is admitted, there is no end except in anarchy."[3]

[3] Immanuel Wallerstein, *Africa: The Politics of Independence*, New York: Vintage Books, 1961, p. 88.

Much of the problem can be easily illustrated by a glance at neighboring territories in the west and center of Africa: Nigeria and the ex-French colonies which were formerly joined in the two federations of West and Equatorial Africa, plus the two French trust territories of Togo and Cameroun thrown in for good measure. Nigeria, endowed with a larger population than all the French territories combined, was preserved by the British and its own leaders as a federation, in which three (now four) regions gave political expression to the great ethnic diversity of the country. Its major political parties tended each to represent the dominant tribe in its region, and, while the parties in varying degree cut across the regional boundaries, their hold in other regions than their home base was likely to reflect ethnic differences and difficulties. The Northern Peoples Congress (NPC) limited itself by its title to the northern region and was dominated by the leading elements in the Hausa-Fulani emirates. The NCNC and the Action Group spoke, respectively, primarily for the Ibos in the East and the Yorubas in the West. In contrast to the bulk of the African states, Nigeria has so far evaded the one-party system (although some observers see the country as now moving in that direction), but it has tended toward a single party in each of the three original regions and it has had no party which could claim undisputed national or Nigeria-wide stature. It is, so to speak, an accident of history that Nigeria has maintained its political unity since it is scarcely open to doubt that the British could easily have seized upon the prevalent tribal suspicions and hostilities to break up their amorphous colony into, say, three to a dozen states on essentially ethnic lines. The nation's continued survival as a single entity, although this seems more likely than not, is still a matter of legitimate political conjecture.

The history of the French territories is almost exactly the reverse of the Nigerian experience. Although the two large African federations had been in existence for several decades, the weight of the French decision at the time of the *loi cadre* of 1956, which greatly extended the sphere of self-government in French Africa, was in favor of a dissolution of the federal bonds and the substitution of direct links between France and each of the dozen territories involved, each of which was to become a self-governing unit. For many African leaders this was a thoroughly undesirable outcome, but a few, for whom Houphouet-Boigny of the Ivory Coast was the outstanding spokesman, welcomed the new autonomy of what have been called the micro-nations, so soon to be accepted as independent states. As Britain might have dissolved Nigerian unity, so France could in all probability have maintained the two federations if it had so chosen, thus creating the presumption of two large French-derived nations in Africa, in some sort of relationship with Togo and Cameroun, instead of the dozen now on the map. The contrast with Nigeria is sharpened when it is remembered that French Africa had one party, the *Rassemblement Démocratique Africain* (RDA), which was dominant or influential in a number of the territories, and other parties, notably the *Parti du Regroupement Africain*, which less successfully reached out to embrace several territories. It is of course true that the RDA was itself a quasi-federal body of which the constituent parts were the parties which developed in each of the territories, but if the accidents of history, represented in this case by the authorities in Paris backed by some African leaders, had swung the other way, the RDA and its rivals might well have become national parties on a grander scale instead of disintegrating into the lesser "national" units which were the successor states of the two federations. With the decline and then demise of French West and Equatorial Africa and the rise of the member territories, the territorial parties now took over as the national parties in their own domains. Given this background it was inevitable that there should have been some confusion on the part of French African leaders as to what constituted the nations they were supposed to integrate, particularly if it is remembered that there was also some talk of an African nation in the large.

What is meant by integration varies significantly from country to country, in part because of the ambiguity as to what constitutes the nation which is to be integrated and in part because of the great differences between the countries in their history and ethnic composition. Even assuming agreement that the nation to be integrated coincides with the former colonial territory, now become independent, there are inevitably diverse interpretations as to what can and should be done. In their different fashions Nigeria and Uganda each seek a national integration which rests upon the continuing and basic fact of ethnic diversity, where other regimes, such as those of Ghana and Guinea, assume the need to achieve a far greater degree of homogeneity through the elimination as far as possible of tribal loyalties and distinctions. The single-party system by itself represents an evident attempt to eliminate diversity or at least to subordinate it to an overriding political unity.

II

ONE-PARTY AUTHORITARIAN SYSTEMS

It is no doubt to be seen as a part of the process of consolidating nations that the new African states have in almost all instances moved into the era of mass parties, replacing the elite or patron parties into which Africa's early political stirrings were often channeled. That the older style has not totally vanished is evidenced by the continued existence of Nigeria's Northern Peoples Congress (NPC) and the *Union Progressiste Mauritanienne*, but these are anachronistic survivals at a time marked by the "crisis of participation" and must surely broaden their base as the forces of modernization penetrate more deeply. The typical African party now is the mass party whose organization is designed to reach not only the constantly growing multitude of city dwellers but the rural peasantry as well. The new-style Western-educated elite, or the single charismatic leader, may in fact be the focal point of decision and action, but the theory brings the mass into the decision-making process, and political prudence makes it advisable that the party have means by which it can communicate with all its constituents, which has come to mean the entire population of the country. The importance of the party is well reflected in the action of Julius Nyerere when, shortly after Tanganyika gained its independence, he resigned as Prime Minister in order to concentrate on the rebuilding of the Tanganyika African National Union into what he called a two-way all-weather road by which the government could reach the people in every village and the people could reach the government.

The mass party which acknowledges no limitations on the potential range of its activities and which seeks to make an operative reality of a sense of national identity is to be found in a number of different guises in Africa. One of the most striking variants is in the three West African countries—Ghana, Guinea, and Mali—which have been joined in the never fully realized Union of African States. Although there are substantial differences between them, all three can be brought together under such adjectives as neutralist, "progressive," left-wing, anti-colonial, and pan-African. All three have felt the attraction of significant aspects of Marxist doctrine and in particular of Communist party organizational methods despite the fact that, precisely as mass parties, they depart from the Leninist conception of the party as a select and close-knit inner core.

The most elaborate rationale of the role of the party has been presented by Sékou Touré, as leader of the *Parti Démocratique de Guinée* (PDG) and president of his country. Although the metaphysics of the relationships may be less than wholly clear, Touré has repeatedly insisted that the PDG is the people of Guinea, that it embodies the thought of the people, that it is the wholly trustworthy guide of the people, and that a clash between the interests of party and people is inconceivable because of the complete interlocking or identity of the two. This identity is established through the virtual universality of membership in the party: "All our people," Touré has said, "are mobilized in the ranks of the PDG; that is to say that the common will derives not from the summit but from a base of the popular will. Authority rests not with the government but with the people."[4] To give solid organizational reality to this merging of people and party the PDG has established more than 7,000 village and urban committees, which, to the extent that the system works as it is supposed to, are utilized to keep up a constant flow of information between the center and the parts and to give to Guineans in the mass a sense of participation in the political life of their country.

One of Touré's major preoccupations has been to break down the tribal divisions which had plagued Guinea's political life until he took firm charge of the PDG in the early 1950's. The immediate postwar years had seen a mushrooming of political groups in Guinea as elsewhere in French Africa, but they had for the most part been limited to particular ethnic communities. Touré regarded this situation as intolerable, and with an explicit aim of achieving national integration he moved to smash the hold of tribalism both in the party and in the society at large. A first step, which got effectively underway in 1957, was to remove the chiefs from political power and to substitute for them a system of elected local councils under the control of the party. Within the party itself Touré turned away from organizing its local units on an ethnic basis, in contrast to the neighboring *Parti Démocratique de la Côte d'Ivoire* (PDCI) (also a section of the RDA), which based itself on ethnic groups

---

[4] Cited by L. Gray Cowan in Gwendolen M. Carter, ed., *African One-Party States*, Ithaca, N.Y.: Cornell University Press, 1962, p. 177.

in urban centers. Similarly PDG organizers and propagandists, and candidates for office as well, were selected on a non-ethnic basis with the expectation both of strengthening the sense of national unity and of establishing a direct relationship with the party, no longer mediated through the traditional ethnic community.

In 1959 it was Touré's optimistic hope that the new monolithic and progressive Guinea would so far succeed in making the country a viable national entity that in "three or four years no one shall remember the tribal, ethnic, or religious rivalries which, in the recent past, caused so much damage to our country and its populations."[5] The attack which he made on tribalism in general and the chiefs in particular was unusually forthright and vigorous, but it is unlikely that he or other Guinean leaders will be able to evade recourse to that "ethnic arithmetic" which has been held to be necessary for all successful African parties in selecting leaders and candidates. It appears to be on the record that in manning the top posts in party and government Touré has had to take ethnic groupings into account as do political leaders everywhere in the world.[6] Sékou Touré has from time to time defended the role of the PDG as the single party in Guinea on several counts, although he has also denied that it has been imposed as the single party from above or in any other sense than that the people at large have brought it into being and sustain it. In an open breach with Marxist tenets he has affirmed the unity of the nation in his insistence that the African society is essentially classless and hence does not require two or more parties to represent the interest of opposing classes. This, it might be remarked, is a view which is frequently repeated in other African countries and appears to be taken as a definitive refutation of the contention that an opposition party is an indispensable feature of a democratic society.[7] In support of the claim that the African society is classless he has also argued that in the

[5] Sékou Touré, *Towards Full Re-Africanization*, Paris: Présence Africaine, 1959, p. 34. Touré contended that "of all West Africa, Guinea was the most deeply divided country during the years 1946-1954. . . . We witnessed the birth of spontaneous movements with religious, tribal, or ethnic bases. These movements divided and subdivided our people." Cited by Martin L. Kilson, "Authoritarian and Single-Party Tendencies in African Politics," *World Politics*, Vol. 15, No. 2 (January 1963), p. 273.

[6] See Ruth Schachter Morgenthau, *Political Parties in French-Speaking West Africa*, New York: Oxford University Press, 1965, Part 6.

[7] One of the rare contrary versions is contained in the "Declaration of Principles" of Nigeria's Northern Elements Progressive Union: Hodgkin, *African Political Parties*, p. 159.

colonial situation all lesser differences fade away in face of the need to overthrow the alien rule which distorts every aspect of African life. What is essential is to safeguard the national unity lest the colonialist or neo-colonialist drive in a wedge of discord. In discussing Guinea's political system Touré has not hesitated to use the word dictatorship, but he sees it as a democratic dictatorship, imposed by the people through the party and intended only to safeguard and develop the liberty and the rights of the people. Certainly it is a dictatorship of the party and not of the government, which is no more than the instrument which executes the decisions taken by the PDG. All power rests with the party: "Without it, the political life of Guinea becomes literally incomprehensible."[8]

The type of national integration which Touré has sought to achieve is singularly close-knit and intimate. He has, indeed, described African life as being essentially *communaucratique*, inspired by a deep sense of social solidarity; no African, as he sees it, can conceive of a life outside that of the family, the village, and the clan. He accuses colonialism of having destroyed Africa's cultural foundations, and in particular of having introduced an individualism, a personal egotism, which is alien to Africa's past and hostile to its unity: "The voice of the African peoples is without face, without name, without a sense of individualism."[9] Through a reconstituted educational system, given a new African content, and by every other means re-Africanization is to be undertaken until all the negative and un-African values of colonialism have been extirpated. (It might be noted in passing that here, as so often in contemporary Africa, the emphasis is on *Africanization* and not on Guinea, but it is difficult to estimate what, if any, bearing this has on the development of a sense of national identification. Touré has been a strong advocate of African unity, and the constitution of Guinea authorizes partial or total abandonment of sovereignty if it will promote such unity.)

As a means of advancing national integration and strengthening the control of the party over all aspects of society the PDG has

[8] Bernard Charles, "Un Parti Politique Africain: Le Parti Démocratique de Guinée," *Revue Française de Science Politique*, Vol. 12, No. 2 (June 1962), p. 345. ". . . behind the State, there is something higher, which is the Party. . . . It is because the Party assumes the leading role in the life of the nation that it has at its disposal all the powers of the nation. The political, judicial, economic, and technical powers are in the hands of the Democratic Party of Guinea. And therefore it is the party which elects the Chief of State by means of direct universal suffrage." Touré, *Towards Full Re-Africanization*, p. 35.

[9] Sékou Touré, *La Guinée et l'émancipation africaine*, Paris: Présence Africaine, 1959, p. 169.

taken over or organized several special groupings of people within its own framework. Of these, presumably the most significant is organized labor, which was the starting point of Touré's own career as a public figure in Guinea. Others which have played a role of some prominence are the organizations embracing women and youth. Under one version of the proper structure of a democratic society the pluralistic existence of a number of autonomous bodies and interest groups is an essential safeguard of popular liberties; for Touré and many other African leaders the more important consideration is that all interests and groups within the society should be closely interlocked with the structure of the ruling party. Touré himself has made it clear that he regards individual and group liberties as having validity only insofar as they promote the realization of the sovereign popular will, again as expressed by the PDG.

Although the union between Guinea and Ghana, joined later by Mali, never became an effective joint enterprise, it is probably correct to see Kwame Nkrumah as being more closely akin to Sékou Touré in some important respects than any other African leader. Both have been highly articulate spokesmen for an aggressive anti-colonialist African socialism, and both have sought the full winning of the political kingdom through the operations of a dominant political party with one key figure as the central source of power around which party and state revolve. With Touré the emphasis has been more heavily on the "communocracy" which he sees as typical of the traditional African society, while Nkrumah has stressed more heavily the pan-African theme, and they have differed significantly in their style of political expression and action; but the points of basic similarity are of greater importance. Touré would surely agree with Nkrumah, as would many other Africans, in the latter's defense of the Preventive Detention Act of 1958 as a product of the need "to consolidate our forces now" with the hope of being able to afford to be liberal later, although Touré would be unlikely to have made even this much of a bow in the direction of liberalism.

In contrast to the early enthronement of the PDG, Ghana did not give official single-party status to the Convention People's party (CPP) until 1961, but the dominance of the CPP in the country's political life was established prior to independence and moved steadily to become a more and more unchallengeable fact. Less stress has perhaps been placed on the identity of people and party than in

Guinea, but no one has been allowed to linger in doubt as to the supremacy of the CPP. On the tenth anniversary of the founding of the CPP, Nkrumah reiterated what he has often said: without the CPP there would be no Ghana; "The Convention People's Party is Ghana."[10] At other times and places he has stressed the theme which is also a favorite with Touré, that the government is only an agent of the party, or even of its Central Committee. The party commands, and the government apparatus fulfills the party's wishes.

According to the official version, by no means wholly remote from the facts, it was the party, under the leadership of the Osagyefo, Kwame Nkrumah, which won Ghana's independence, and the party which preserved the country's integrity and unity despite all the disruptive forces which threatened it. Nkrumah has summed up the role of the party in building the victorious coalition in the following terms: "A middle-class elite, without the battering ram of the illiterate masses, can never hope to smash the forces of colonialism. Such a thing can be achieved only by a united people organized in a disciplined political party and led by that party."[11]

In Ghana as in a number of other countries the most serious threat to unity has been a tribalism which is accused of having drawn its inspiration from the imperialists. The transition from colonial status to independence was gravely complicated by the demand of the Ashanti for a regional autonomy which would preserve their historic identity as a people. Allied with opposition movements in the Northern Territories and British Togoland, they put up a stubborn resistance to the emergence of a unitary Nkrumah-dominated CPP Ghana, and the scars left by the bitter conflicts of those days have still not completely vanished. Nkrumah has habitually attacked federalism, in the Congo for example, as a menace to the solidarity of African nations, and he has cited Nigeria as a country whose national unity was shattered by the tribalism sponsored by the colonialists. In Ghana he was able to break the resistance of the forces arrayed against him, but he did not use his victory to launch a sweeping frontal attack on tribalism and the chiefs comparable to that of Sékou Touré in Guinea. The standard position of the CPP was that it did not intend to destroy chieftainship but rather to adapt it to modern democratic needs, and it was the practice of Nkrumah

---

[10] Kwame Nkrumah, *I Speak of Freedom*, New York: Praeger, 1961, p. 161.

[11] Kwame Nkrumah, *Ghana: The Autobiography of Kwame Nkrumah*, New York: Nelson, 1957, p. 213.

in the past to address himself to the "chiefs and people" of Ghana in public utterances. Even in the republican constitution of Ghana adopted in 1960 the Declaration of Fundamental Principles states that "the office of Chiefs in Ghana, as existing by customary law and usage, should be guaranteed," and the presidential oath specifically reaffirms the guarantee. What has actually been involved has been the gradual elimination of the chiefs as a political force, but without deliberate destruction of their other roles in the society. Each of Ghana's regions still has a House of Chiefs which deals with chieftaincy matters and some questions of customary law.

The CPP has made it plain that it will tolerate no racial or tribal chauvinism and has pledged itself to purge any offenders from its ranks. Illustrating the characteristic intertwining of Ghana-national and pan-African motifs, Nkrumah has stressed the CPP's commitment to work with all nationalist, democratic, and socialist movements in Africa and elsewhere that fight for national self-determination and against any form of chauvinism and oppression. "That is why we insist that in Ghana in the higher reaches of our national life there should be no reference to Fantis, Ashantis, Ewes, Gas, Dagombas, 'strangers', and so forth, but that we should call ourselves Ghanaians—all brothers and sisters, members of the same community—the state of Ghana. For until we ourselves purge from our own minds this tribal chauvinism and prejudice of one against the other, we shall not be able to cultivate the wider spirit of brotherhood which our objective of Pan Africanism calls for. We are all Africans and peoples of African descent, and we shall not allow the imperialist plotters and intriguers to separate us from each other for their own advantage."[12]

For the winning of the political kingdom Nkrumah has laid great emphasis on the need for organization. As early as 1949 he was urging that all men and women should join a political organization or one of the special associations or movements, leaving no individual without membership in some organization. Through organization the country could be unified and the people would then become invincible. From the time of the creation of the CPP in 1949 the party occupied the whole center of the political stage, and it has been constantly reiterated that the party is supreme. The existence of other associations, as for labor, women, youth, and farmers,

[12] Kwame Nkrumah, *I Speak of Freedom*, pp. 167-168.

has been encouraged, but with the express proviso, at least from the time of Nkrumah's dawn broadcast of April 8, 1961, that they were to be totally merged into the structure of the CPP. National unity, finding its operational expression in the party, could tolerate no rifts or rivals. As a result of the plebiscite of January 1964 the CPP was enthroned as the only national party which is now constitutionally recognized as "the vanguard of the People in their struggle to build a socialist society and . . . the leading core of all organizations of the People."[13]

ONE-PARTY PLURALISTIC SYSTEMS

Ghana and Guinea have described themselves, properly enough, as revolutionary states. The Ivory Coast has stood in striking contrast to them as essentially non-revolutionary as far as the intent of its leaders for the last decade and more is concerned—and yet a revolution is in progress there which may transform the society as thoroughly as the PDG and the CPP have been transforming their countries. In a few words, far too summary to do justice to the situation, the differences might be examined in terms of the position of the presidents of the three countries on two significant points. Where Touré and Nkrumah looked primarily to the workers and the lower middle strata as their political activists, Houphouet worked closely with the reasonably well-to-do cocoa planters and with the chiefs, despite the affiliation of the RDA, which he headed, with the French Communist party for parliamentary purposes from 1946 to 1950. The leaders of Guinea and Ghana boasted of the completeness of their breach with colonialism and with the colonial power, although Ghana stayed in the Commonwealth, whereas Houphouet deliberately played it the other way, boasted of the closeness of his connections with France, and assumed that the Ivory Coast would be able to forge ahead faster if it accepted all the aid it could get from France, opening its doors to foreign capital and manpower. The revolution which is taking place is an economic development which, in good part under French auspices, has surged ahead.

Under Houphouet's leadership the *Parti Démocratique de la Côte d'Ivoire* (PDCI) has established itself as the single party in the country but with marked, if often subtle, differences between it and the PDG and CPP. Save at certain limited periods in its history the

[13] The Constitution of Ghana, as amended 5 February 1964, Part I, Section 1A (1).

PDCI has not been a party of militants nor has it had as tight and penetrating an organization as the others although it has always sought to be a mass rather than an elite party. In the mid-1950's, according to Aristide Zolberg, there was a growing gap between the organizational theory invoked by the founders of the PDCI and political reality: "The PDCI emerged as an organization for the masses rather than as a mass organization. The party press and the territorial organs of government, curtailed in 1951 to facilitate strategic manipulation by Houphouet-Boigny, were never reactivated. The basic units seldom met except during electoral campaigns."[14]

The continued survival of the party at the center of the Ivory Coast's political life has been due primarily to the great skill of Houphouet in political maneuvering, his readiness to swing with the changing winds, and his ability to draw opposition leaders into the ranks of the PDCI and of the government. The tribal factions backed by the French in their attack on the PDCI in 1948 and after were skillfully absorbed and brought within the fold, a process which was eased by French acceptance of Houphouet and his party in the mid-1950's. That this line of action involved losses as well as gains is indicated by Zolberg's comment that while the party could develop an effective structure through using the tightly-knit ethnic group as its basic cell, the existence of this structural device over a period of fifteen years "is now perceived by national leaders as a major impediment to the process of national integration."[15]

The readiness of Houphouet and his colleagues to promote the development of the Ivory Coast as an essentially bourgeois regime, relying heavily on France, has carried as its counterpart the lack of any intensive drive to achieve national integration. The national identity of the country has been disturbed to a lesser extent than some others by the competing pull of pan-Africanism because Houphouet has given a low priority to the claims of African unity and has insisted on the need for each of the African countries to achieve first the unity of its own tribes and social strata; but the

[14] Aristide R. Zolberg, *One-Party Government in the Ivory Coast*, Princeton, N.J.: Princeton University Press, 1964, pp. 185-186.

[15] Aristide R. Zolberg, "Poiitics in the Ivory Coast: 3," *West Africa*, August 20, 1960, p. 939. Zolberg adds that while Houphouet has been able to secure political control by including many new elements in the party, "he has only succeeded in shifting the locus of the political struggle from outside the party to inside." See also his "Effets de la structure d'un parti politique sur l'intégration nationale," *Cahiers d'Études Africaines*, No. 3 (1960), pp. 140-149, and his *One-Party Government in the Ivory Coast*, pp. 319-320.

positive drive toward an Ivory Coast nationalism has not been evident. Late in 1957 Houphouet is quoted as saying: "We will not fall into the trap made for us by Great Britain in creating independent states in Africa";[16] and he reversed his stand to demand independence for his country only when confronted by the pledge of independence secured by the Mali federation from de Gaulle.

In part because of his own changes of position and in part because of the situation in which he found himself, it is difficult to define the role of Houphouet as a nationalist. As the leading figure in the RDA he was identified with French Africa in the large, and he spent much of his time in Paris, including service as a member of French Cabinets. He has decried nationalism as being out of tune with the times. Yet he has also fought the Ivory Coast's political and economic battles both within and outside the country. He was the guiding spirit in what came to be the national party, he worked to ensure that the country should not be further milked on behalf of its poorer associates in the former French West Africa, and he yielded, for the sake of national unity, to the demands of his countrymen for a curtailment of the part played in the Ivory Coast by foreigners, both European and African.[17] Yet he and his PDCI, for all the hold which they have had upon the country, have not been a militant force driving toward national integration as have the PDG and the CPP.

Another version of the one-party system can be found on the other side of the continent in Tanganyika, where the Tanganyika African National Union (TANU) stands somewhere between the revolutionary parties of Guinea, Ghana, and Mali and the flexibly adaptable PDCI. In comparison with the former, TANU has a lesser revolutionary zeal and is ideologically less committed, but it lacks the bourgeois complacency which might be attributed to the PDCI in recent years, and it has been more constant to its ideals and purposes. Its predominance in Tanganyika is virtually unquestioned, and Nyerere as its leader has a stature at home and abroad which is not inferior to that of the leaders of the other countries.[18]

TANU was brought into being by Nyerere in 1954 with a con-

[16] Cited by Virginia Thompson, "The Ivory Coast," in Carter, ed., *African One-Party States*, p. 243.

[17] *Ibid.*, p. 267.

[18] The name Tanganyika has been retained since this and the succeeding paragraphs refer almost wholly to the period prior to the creation of Tanzania, and TANU remains a Tanganyikan party.

stitution, modeled on that of the CPP, that pledged it to independence and to fight "tribalism and all isolationist tendencies amongst the Africans and to build up a united nationalism." Membership was open to organizations, tribal and otherwise, as well as to individuals.[19] Tribalism was not on the whole a matter which proved of great concern to TANU, although Nyerere has been frank to admit that Tanganyika does not form a single nation but is a composite of some 120 tribes. One problem, lacking in West Africa, which the country's setting between Kenya and the Rhodesias forced upon it was the effort of the colonial administration to move toward a multi-racial polity in which Asians and Europeans would be given some version of parity with Africans. Again in contrast with the West African countries discussed above, Tanganyika's status as a trust territory gave its leaders an unusual opportunity to place their case before the world in the Trusteeship Council and the General Assembly of the United Nations.

In a somewhat gentler and more moderate fashion Nyerere has taken many of the same positions as Touré and Nkrumah, including advocacy of pan-Africanism and, regionally, the elaboration of an East African federation on the foundations laid by the British. He has been a stalwart champion of the need to create a Tanganyikan nation, but he has also insisted that the nationalism of African peoples must differ from the European in that it is to be an instrument not of division but for the unification of Africa.

Repeatedly Nyerere has laid his emphasis on nation-building as the most urgent task ahead, and he has included in the term the need to achieve both the material and the spiritual attributes required by a free people in the modern world. The attainment of unity has been a first order of business for him—and in that unity he has been prepared to give a larger role to Europeans and Asians, both in the party and outside it, than have his colleagues and opponents.[20]

[19] George Bennett, *An Outline History of TANU*, Oxford University Institute of Commonwealth Relations, Reprint Series, No. 31, 1963, p. 3. Bennett concludes that at least prior to independence TANU was "a nationalist movement rather than a political party. Resembling other 'Congress-type organisations' formed in the struggle for independence, it was a combination of urban workers and village dwellers, educated and illiterate, chiefs and democrats, Muslims, Christians and Pagans" (p. 12).

[20] See, for example, *President's Address to the National Assembly, 10th December, 1962*. Also Margaret L. Bates, "Tanganyika," in Carter, ed., *African One-Party States*, p. 451. This issue presumably was again involved in the somewhat obscure circumstances surrounding the mutiny of Tanganyikan troops in 1964.

As in so many other African countries the party is the primary instrument to be used to win national unity, but, in keeping with his characteristic position, Nyerere has been somewhat more reluctant than Nkrumah or Touré to exalt the party above the government and portray the latter as only the servant of the party. Setting out perhaps a little hesitantly as the defender of the single-party system, Nyerere has become an increasingly ardent advocate and is now inclined to put the idea forward as the one proper expression of African democracy, although since Tanganyikan independence the party has tended to recede in importance as the government has advanced and attracted the party's cadres to itself. The arguments which he has drawn upon are for the most part familiar ones: the absence of classes makes more than one party unnecessary; national unity is embodied in the party, which brought independence and should be preserved; at a time of crisis, represented by Tanganyika's war on poverty, ignorance, and disease, the consolidation of all forces for the common purpose is needed; the one-party system was not imposed from above but was the result of the people's choice freely expressed at the polls. Where there is one party, Nyerere has contended, "and that party is identified with the *nation as a whole*, the foundations of democracy are firmer than they can ever be where you have two or more parties, each representing only a section of the community."[21]

On no count, at least in the African setting, does Nyerere accept the standard defenses of the two- or multi-party system. If it be argued that checks and balances are desirable, he sees them as an admirable means of applying brakes to social change whereas what Tanganyika needs is "accelerators powerful enough to overcome the inertia bred of poverty." The creation of an opposition for the sake of having someone who will oppose, he ridicules as absurd; but he has insisted that it is the job of government "to protect the freedom of the minority—however small—to convert itself into a majority while preventing it from sabotaging the efforts of the existing majority."[22] He has sought to bring trade unions and other associations within the orbit of TANU, but he has not sought to wipe out

[21] Julius K. Nyerere, *Democracy and the Party System*, Dar-es-Salaam, Tanganyika: Standard Limited, n.d., p. 7. A unique series of safeguards for democracy within the one-party system were contained in the *Report of the Presidential Commission on the Establishment of a Democratic One Party State* (Dar-es-Salaam, 1965.) yika: Standard Limited, n.d., p. 7.
[22] *Africa Digest* (October 1961), p. 51.

their separate identity as Nkrumah came close to proposing in the case of the CPP; but he has also attacked the idea that the trade unions should be independent of the party since TANU is the party of the people and hence of the trade unions as well.

At bottom Nyerere's defense of the single-party system rests upon the proposition that "a National Movement which is open to all—which is identified with the whole nation—has nothing to fear from the discontent of any excluded section of society, for there is no such section."[23]

It is an inspiring, if not particularly novel, thought that no section of the people is politically excluded since all are members of the national movement which is indistinguishable from the nation. Perhaps under Nyerere's temperate leadership an approximation of this desirable outcome can be found in Tanganyika, although even there the introduction of a preventive detention act was found necessary after independence. In the ordinary course of events the single leader governing through the instrumentality of the single party is certainly not to be trusted to bear gladly with those who disagree with him. Despite the admirable pretensions of democratic centralism, not much room is likely to be left over for dissenters, within the party or outside it, where there is only a single party dominated by one leader and the party is the government. In such situations the party may work, and work effectively, for national integration, but the danger is always present that disaffected minorities may be festering toward revolt under the enforced surface appearance of unity. The widespread charges of subversion, the overturns and attempted overturns of government, and the successful and attempted assassinations of leaders in Africa in the last couple of years indicate the gap between the political reality and the claims to have achieved national unity under single-party rule. It must be added that the effort to justify the single-party system on the ground that it prevents the dissipation of the limited available high-level manpower among several parties loses much of its persuasiveness when account is taken of the many able men who have been immobilized, imprisoned, or forced into exile by the ruling party or leader, as, for example, in Ghana.

The assumption of the identity of the national movement and the people at large runs into a further difficulty, already noted in the case of Ghana. What is the theory and practice of the relationship

[23] Nyerere, *Democracy and the Party System*, p. 25.

between the masses and the party, particularly as embodied in its top leadership? Both democratic and Marxist, as well as nationalist, theories have an inclination to assume that true wisdom is to be found in the masses, that the "African peasant's common sense" should be the guiding star. As the *Union Soudanaise* in Mali has put it: "We must never forget this eternal truth, *that the people is always revolutionary in its aspirations and that the revolution will be effective if the Party never ceases to identify itself with the masses, to blend into them, to refer without ceasing and forever to their possibilities and to their desires*." [Italics in text][24] But the *Union Soudanaise*, like other African parties, also recognizes its responsibility to give leadership to the people and specifically to create "a national consciousness within the peasant masses." Where development has come to be a matter of prime concern it is evident that the party leaders must take upon themselves the task of guiding their people into the new channels, and the problems which are posed are only partially answered by such assertions as that the party is realizing the inchoate aspirations of the mass. The leaders may bow to the mass as the source of their political inspiration, but it is an easy and familiar transition from following the mass to imposing upon it what it must surely want if it were aware of its own real interest.

PLURALISTIC-COMPETITIVE SYSTEMS

The most evident and omnipresent divisive force in Africa is tribalism, which is regarded by African nationalist leaders as a double threat to the kind of nations they seek to bring into being. Where the new dominant elites want to modernize their societies in order to establish nations on terms of equality with those of the advanced world the pressures of tribalism and of the chiefs tend to be in the direction of a defense and perpetuation of the traditional order. Secondly, the lack of coincidence between the tribes and the existing states, and hence the putative nations, means that any turn toward tribalism threatens the existing structure. Tribalism carried through to a political reordering of the continent implies a further Balkanization, and in a number of instances it may also involve a demand to cut across present frontiers where a tribe has been divided by colonial boundaries. But, whatever the woe which it may cause to nationalists, the continued existence of tribes as basic social entities with which

[24] William J. Foltz, "The Political Theory of an African Mass Party," *Ventures*, New Haven, Conn. (Winter 1964), p. 18.

large numbers of Africans identify themselves means that tribalism is a social-political force which no African political system or leader can ignore.

A generally unforeseen turn of events was that the extension of democratic practices, hailed as a progressive and liberalizing step, often tended in fact to strengthen the hold of tribalism, at least in the first rounds.[25] In the vast expanses of the rural areas the effect of enfranchising the politically unsophisticated voter was in most instances to enhance the power of a chief whose word continued to carry great, and perhaps decisive, influence with his people, and whose inclinations were conservative. As universal suffrage gave a new lease on life to Indian castes, so in Africa the tribes were inevitably seen as built-in constituencies, and, particularly where larger tribal groupings were concerned, parties were likely to rest on a tribal base. It was the conclusion of W. J. M. Mackenzie, after surveying five African elections in detail, that all African parties tend to become tribal parties and that "If tribalism is the enemy, elections are partly responsible for encouraging it."[26] It deserves to be added that although tribalism is inherent in the African traditional scene, further support for tribally based groupings came from colonial administrations which sought to bolster their positions in the face of attack from more radical and colony-wide nationalist parties by throwing their weight behind local parties with a more conservative bias. The coming of independence and the advance of political socialization, in both of which the dominant party plays a central role, are gradually changing the situation, but for the foreseeable future the significance of the tribe as a political factor will generally remain impressive.

In contrast to parties with an ideological, class, or interest base, parties whose essential base is tribal constitute a unique threat to the national existence because they challenge the very existence of state

[25] "The most important consequence of this massive expansion of the electorate (1952) was one that had not been widely foreseen—a transfer of the balance of political power from the more radical urban evolués to the conservative rural inhabitants." Virginia Thompson and Richard Adloff, *French West Africa*, Stanford: Stanford University Press, 1958, p. 60.

Padmore summed the matter up succinctly in his comment that he was hopeful for the future of the Gold Coast "despite all the tribal backwash which the application of democracy there has aroused." *Pan-Africanism or Communism?* London: Dobson, 1956, p. 345.

[26] W. J. M. Mackenzie and Kenneth E. Robinson, eds., *Five Elections in Africa*, Oxford: Clarendon Press, 1960, p. 484.

and nation, proffering another framework of loyalty and identity if they press home their ultimate claims.[27] An alternative possibility, but one which is only marginally more acceptable, is that they express their separate identity through the assertion of a right to rule over other and neighboring peoples; the charge of "black imperialism" has indeed been heard with some frequency in one or another part of Africa as the independent peoples have sorted themselves out. In either event, the unity of the nation comes in as a weak second-best, if it is acknowledged at all. The fear which the Katangan claims of Tshombe roused in the Congo and throughout Africa was that the integrity of the nations-in-process-of-becoming was confronted by a force which might totally shatter them.

This fear that any multiplication of parties would in fact be a multiplication of separatist tribal groups has been one of the major grounds on which the advocates of the one-party system could defend their position. Given the incontrovertible urgency of establishing firm and coherent political entities, it is understandable that there should be reluctance to safeguard the status of an opposition at the price of encouraging tribal dissidence. It is one thing to have parties which are divided by programmatic differences, but something very different to have them follow the lines of ethnic cleavage within the society.

Although the great swing has been in the other direction, a few African countries have retained the multi-party system which was the prevalent pattern under colonialism, and in all of them tribalism has been a key determining factor in shaping the party structure.

The case of Nigeria, which is the leading example of a multi-party system in Africa, has already received some attention in earlier pages. Although some Nigerian nationalists may dispute it, the essence of the Nigerian case is that "national" unity could be preserved only if large-scale concessions of a federal variety were made to the disparate elements brought together under British colonial rule. At the outset no other bond held the country together than the over-arching British presence, and the consequences in the way of inter-mingling of the people of the country were by no means always favorable to the development of a sense of national identity, as witness the dismay of much of the North at Ibo and Yoruba penetration, and

[27] See Clifford Geertz, "The Integrative Revolution," in C. Geertz, ed., *Old Societies and New States*, The Free Press of Glencoe, 1963, p. 111. His entire treatment of the problems involved in the integration of what he calls "the primordial societies" into the new civil state is well worth study.

the low view which each of the latter tended to take of the North and often of each other as well. Aside from the colonial and later the federal government, almost no institutions or organizations existed which operated on a Nigeria-wide basis. As far as political parties are concerned, while the Action Group and the National Council of Nigeria and the Cameroons (NCNC) both aimed at an all-Nigeria coverage and scored occasional substantial successes in regions other than the one which constituted their home (and tribal) base, their firm roots were clearly in the West and East, respectively, and neither was able to cut in any lasting fashion into the hold of the Northern Peoples Congress (NPC) in the North. It might be said that the survival of Nigeria as a political entity was conditioned on the existence of a federalism of parties as well as of constitutional structure. Certainly, however, such national integration of Nigeria as has been achieved cannot be attributed to the work of a political party or parties; nor has there been any single national figure who has occupied the center of the stage as outstanding leaders have elsewhere. The president and ex-NCNC head, Nnamid Azikiwe, comes closest to having attained such national stature, but large segments of the country fail to accord him the kind of recognition which he has received in his own region and among his own Ibo people. The country has its activists who look with envy on the more dynamic and dramatic political life of "progressive" African states that possess one supreme leader who operates through a single party, but these remain a minority. As things now stand they could secure what they speak for only by overthrowing the existing order, and the closer national integration at which they aim might in fact be further impaired by the resentments and suspicions they would arouse. The fragility of the foundations on which Nigerian unity rests has been well illustrated in the controversy over the census, with its implications as to the demographic political balance of power.

A very different kind of picture is presented by Kenya where African participation in the political life of the country, looking to self-government and independence, came significantly later than in Nigeria.

The differences between Nigeria and Kenya in setting, including the white-settler issue, and in extent and maturity of political experience are so great as to make comparison largely meaningless, but one significant point on which the two countries coincide is that Kenya, like Nigeria, had never had a party before independence which was "national" or territory-wide in scope. Parties tended to be formed on a tribal basis and in the earlier stages drew chiefly on the Kikuyu. Where Nigeria's parties have had a relatively long and coherent existence, Kenya's counterparts have been short-lived and swiftly changing. Thus the two major parties of the recent past, the Kenya African National Union (KANU) and the Kenya African Democratic Union (KADU) came into existence in their contemporary guise, respectively, in March and June 1960. It was characteristic of Kenya's political make-up that KANU should represent the larger tribes which have had more contact with the West, notably the Kikuyu and the Luo, whereas KADU was spokesman for the lesser tribes such as the Kalenjin, Baluhya, and Masai. Given their different situations, it was only to be expected that KANU should have demanded a centralized unitary state with a trend toward an authoritarian socialism while KADU held out for a strongly protected regionalism and a looser system of control and development.[28]

The recent political history of Kenya was deeply affected by the Mau Mau affair, which might, if one felt so inclined, be regarded as the work of an authentically *African* "party," organized by the Kikuyu, as contrasted with a party constructed on a Western model. Despite the considerable political advance which came to Kenya in the aftermath of the Mau Mau rising, Kikuyu domination was feared by many of Kenya's peoples who suspected that such domination might be involved in the acceptance of the kind of unitary Kenya nationalism for which KANU was the spokesman. A further feature of the aftermath of Mau Mau was the British restriction of African political parties to local organizations, which tended to guide political life into tribal channels, and which Tom Mboya has characterized as having "harmed national unity immeasurably."[29] It was not until 1960 that territory-wide parties were again allowed.

The bitter controversies over the constitution of Kenya preceding independence also sharply emphasized the tribal divisions that impeded any effort to secure national integration. In the sparring over the constitution tribal leaders within KADU, for example, engaged in threats ranging from the use of spears and poisoned arrows to secession if their demands for autonomy were not granted.[30]

[28] See George Bennett and Carl Rosberg, *The Kenyatta Election: Kenya 1960-1961*, London: Oxford University Press, 1961, particularly Ch. 2.

[29] Tom Mboya, *Freedom and After*, London: André Deutsch, 1963, p. 75.

[30] See, for example, *East Africa and Rhodesia*, January 15, 1962, p. 490 and February 1, 1962, p. 541; *The New York Times*, October 11, 1963; *The Observer* (London), October 20, 1963.

The nearer independence approached, however, the more KANU widened its hold on the country as defectors, reading the handwriting on the wall, left its politically less powerful rival. Less than a year after independence, which came in December 1963, Kenya became a single-party state as the dwindling remnants of KADU joined with KANU. Prime Minister Kenyatta, shortly to become President of the Republic of Kenya, welcomed the move as ending the political division which he saw as a device engineered by the imperialists.[31]

The last example to be looked at in this connection is the Congo, whose internal divisions and catastrophes have been so notoriously spread on the public record since 1960 as to require little comment.[32] If Kenya lagged behind Nigeria in the extent and duration of its political experience, the Congo was far behind both. Up to the last two or three years before the sudden grant of independence Belgium not only allowed nothing in the way of Congolese political organization but also had opened no channels of political activity in the Congo into which the Congolese might at some later time be drawn. For a number of years disaffections and frustrations which might in other circumstances have found political outlets took the form of aberrant religious sects such as Kitiwala and Kimbanguism. At a somewhat later stage tribal associations provided a more "modern" form of organization, and, although these associations were at the outset nonpolitical in intent and operation, they were the precursors of the parties which later competed for control of the country. The leadership of these ethnic groupings was originally drawn primarily from the traditional elements, but in the last decade or so younger men with some measure of Western education began to take over.

Almost everything in the Congo conspired to give a tribal twist to political life. The first overt stirrings of nationalism were to be found in these tribal associations, of which the Abako (*Alliance des Bakongo*), representing the Bakongo people, was perhaps the earliest. It certainly was one of the most important, and the first hesitant Bel-

---

[31] In an election pamphlet issued in 1963, *What a KANU Government Offers You*, KANU asserted it had "no desire to suppress the diverse cultures and communities which go to make up our nation. . . . On the other hand the government will not tolerate the sabotaging of the national effort by those who would play upon tribal or racial differences. We shall not allow the hopes and aspirations which our people have for their independence to be disappointed by such wrecking tactics." It also welcomed those non-Africans who wanted to join in "the noble task of building a Kenya nation" (p. 12).

[32] See, for example, Crawford Young, *Politics in the Congo*, Princeton, Princeton University Press, 1965, and René Lemarchand, *Political Awakening in the Congo*, Berkeley and Los Angeles, University of California Press, 1964.

gian venture into democratic procedures in 1957 involved elections in the municipalities, which meant that the local ethnic forces were called into action with no effective stimulus for operations on a Congo-wide scale. Furthermore the Congo was a vast territory in which the Africans, tribally divided and often with ancient or newly inspired grievances against each other, had scant occasion or opportunity to come to know each other or meet on a national basis. As a tidal wave of political activity began to sweep over the country in 1958 or even later, it was inevitable that it should flow almost exclusively along the lines of the ethnic divisions. In some instances the parties which sprang into existence bore tribal names, as in the case of the Abako and the Balubakat. The outstanding party which sought to cut across tribal ties and look to a national Congo was Lumumba's *Mouvement National Congolais*, and the fame and almost universal support which Lumumba won in Africa—even greater after his murder than before it—derived in substantial part from precisely this effort to achieve a national solidarity which would overcome the centrifugal force of tribalism.

The more recent turn of events in the Congo has set the country on a peculiar and, at least as far as Africa is concerned, a unique path. Where most African states have both a strong party and a charismatic leader, or a reasonable facsimile thereof—Nigeria its strong party system, and Kenya its Kenyatta as well as its two principal parties now merged into one—the Congo has produced no towering national figure, with the possible exception of Lumumba who appears to have had a more wide-spread fame in the rest of Africa than in the Congo and whose removal from political power soon after independence was shortly followed by his murder. Although many parties have risen and declined as the political fortunes of the Congo have changed, no party has come near to playing the kind of role which national parties or movements have played elsewhere and not infrequently they have left behind them little more than the labels under which their heads operated in the parliament or political skirmishes in Leopoldville. It would be difficult to assign to the parties any substantial credit for such glimmerings of Congolese national integration as may have appeared.

III

The heart of the reason why African parties have so speedily risen to preeminence while governments have tended to be downgraded as only one of the instruments through which the parties work may be sought in the fact that the parties were the creation of African nationalists whereas the governments were in the first instance a direct inheritance from the colonial regimes.

The conception of parties was of course a product of the contact with the West, and the African parties were patterned after Western models, including the Communist variant, but they were made and led by Africans and intended to serve African purposes. The colonial-built apparatus of government, on the other hand, had been established to serve the imperial power and was manned in its upper brackets either by Europeans who often stayed on in positions of prominence after independence or by Africans who were frequently regarded with suspicion by the political leaders as too Europeanized, too close to the colonial rulers, and too deeply inbred in the European political-administrative systems.[33] Seen in these terms it is wholly in the realms of nationalist reason that there should have been a subordination to African political parties of the European-derived governmental machinery, even though the constitutions which came into effect on independence were often a product of consultation between the imperial center and African leaders. The party, for all its European origins, was immediately African in a sense that most African states are still only in process of becoming. Furthermore, aside from the government itself, national parties were in many, perhaps in most, instances the only organizations which were "nation"- or territory-wide in scope. It remains to be seen to what extent the reverse implications of this statement will become apparent, i.e. that as governments become increasingly nationalized and Africanized, the parties will come to play a lesser role. There has been some noticeable trend in this direction, but the parties are often so firmly established and offer so usefully flexible an instrument for a number of purposes as to make their being pressed into the background unlikely. However, the effort to achieve an appropriate balance between the agents of the party and of the government has often been a complex and difficult one.

It requires little ingenuity to discern why Africans should have

[33] Nyerere has protested against the "friction and mutual resentment between our politicians, of whom the majority have not had very much education, and the members of our civil service, of whom the majority are very well educated indeed." *President's Address to the National Assembly, December 10, 1962*, pp. 14-15.

utilized political parties as the principal vehicles for the attainment of their political goals. Carl Rosberg has summed the matter up well in his double statement that nationalism's central concern was to maximize social and political support in order to confront the colonial power with a unified people and that, with few exceptions, "there is no alternative organizational instrument available to African leaders except the political party."[34]

The almost universal post-independence swing to the single-party system raises more complex issues. In relation to the problem of national integration it can be explained on either of two contradictory grounds. The explanation which Africans find pleasanter is that national unity was already so firmly embodied in the national party that it would have been outrageous folly to encourage or force an opposition into existence. Even in the case of tribally divided Kenya, Mboya asks the rhetorical question as to whether those who want African states to practice democracy on Western lines will be disappointed "if, having developed a strong nationalist movement and mobilized the whole mass of the people to support a single leader, we do not attempt the impossible task of changing it all overnight."[35] The other explanation covers precisely the reverse situation: national unity was so gravely threatened by parties or movements representing tribal, regional, or religious factions, no doubt alleged to be backed by the neo-colonialists, that it was essential to contain the political life of the country within a single mold in order to check the forces of disruption.

The first of these alternatives appears to be applicable in such cases as those of Guinea, Mali, the Ivory Coast, Tanganyika, and Nyasaland, where a single party had in each instance so far established itself, although it might earlier have had serious rivals, as to make its continuation after independence as *the* national party both appropriate and inevitable. Where this was the situation it was essentially a matter of detail whether the lesser splinter groups which had failed to win national stature were absorbed, abolished, or allowed to linger on. The cautionary word should be added, however,

[34] Carl G. Rosberg, Jr., "Democracy and the New African States," in Kenneth Kirkwood, ed., *African Affairs, No. 2*, St. Antony's Papers, No. 15, London: Chatto and Windus, 1963, pp. 30-31. He adds: "African parties characteristically seek to perform the functions of fostering and establishing a national consciousness and providing a set of national symbols; in short, to establish the very legitimacy of their regimes" (p. 31).

[35] Tom Mboya, *Freedom and After*, p. 88.

that in any of these countries disruptive factions might have emerged as a serious threat if the dominant party had not maintained a strong grip on the country as a whole.

The second alternative of enforced unification following a threat of disintegration is well illustrated by the experience of Ghana, where opposition parties and leaders in Ashanti and the Northern Territories were forced to abandon their claims. Several of the former French territories, such as the Congo, Gabon, Upper Volta, Niger, and Dahomey, have likewise resorted to some form of enforced suppression or absorption of parties, usually tribalist in nature, which sought to rival the dominant party.[36]

Given the diversity of African conditions, it would be hopeless to seek one formula which might be applicable across the board, but it is generally more plausible to see the upsurge of the single-party system as a response to the need for strong clamps to hold the country together than as the expression of a unity so firm and coherent as to make second or third parties redundant. One-man one-party regimes are necessary in Africa precisely because the nations rest on such shaky foundations and are confronted by such urgent and monumental tasks of integration and development. The existence of a single national party is obviously no guarantee of successful national integration, but it is plausible to assume that one party will do a more successful job than two or more, particularly if the two or more spring from a tribal base and have little, if any, comprehension of the proper functioning of a loyal opposition. The example of Nigeria, however, demonstrates that if there is a widespread will for national unity, the existence of several competing parties need not be incompatible with it.

In many countries the mass nationalist party has been the principal instrument working to unite different elements of the population. That this involves not only the breaking down of ethnic differences but also the elimination of other gaps in the society has been asserted by Mali's Minister of Development, Seydou Kouyate, who contended that ". . . the political organization has been the melting-pot where the peasant and the city-dweller have met. It has pulled the former out of his isolation, cured the latter of his disdain for the bush, and achieved the national unity from which it was drawing its strength. Thus, the gap which existed between the city and the countryside

[36] See Jean Buchmann, *L'Afrique Noire Indépendante*, Paris: Librairie Générale de Droit et de Jurisprudence, 1962, pp. 300-310.

has been filled up and the various strata of the population have been unified into one single stream oriented toward the political objectives."[37]

For people still at a low level of political sophistication, success in producing a sense of national identity is presumably much enhanced by the concentration of political attention not only on a single party but on the single leader, the Führer, the Osagyefo, who is the symbol and embodiment of party and nation. The state and its newly achieved independence are made flesh and blood in the familiar and highly publicized figure of the leader who becomes the crystallizing center of the nation. To avoid the confusions and complexities inherent in a more diffuse structure the bulk of the African states have shifted to a presidential system in which the leader is at once the head of party, government, and state, becoming the unmistakable center of authority with no visible rivals to compete with him on the public stage.[38]

The means by which the parties press forward toward national integration are many and varied, although undoubtedly the major service which they have rendered is in their existence as spokesmen for the people against the colonial government and in their active spreading of the gospel of national identity and unity. Before independence their primary function was to stir up national sentiment and enlist as much of the populace as possible in the anti-colonial struggle. After independence similar tasks of agitation and organization are undertaken in an effort to endow the people with a sense of continuing political participation even though the colonial power is no longer so readily available as the enemy to be attacked. Election campaigns and plebiscites are obvious occasions for the party to rally the people, but the active mass party keeps up a more continuous agitation and consultation than periodic elections call for. Where the supremacy of the party is at the heart of the system it has not only the more

[37] *Africa Report* (May 1963), p. 16. "The mass party became the framework within which ethnic, caste, and regional differences among the population at large could be submerged in the search for a common goal. It both embodied and promoted a preliminary sense of national unity and identity." William J. Foltz in Karl W. Deutsch and William J. Foltz, eds., *Nation-Building*, New York: Atherton Press, 1963, p. 121.

[38] The difficulties involved in the existence of a two-headed leadership became all too apparent in the Senegalese crisis of December 1962, when Senghor and Mamadou Dia confronted each other. This crisis also concerned the question of the supremacy of the party over the constitutionally established government. See Victor D. Du Bois, *The Trial of Mamadou Dia*, American Universities Field Staff: West Africa Series, Vol. VI, Nos. 6-8 (Senegal).

specific function of training substantial numbers of people in leadership at all levels and in political and administrative skills but also that of spreading information and keeping the center informed of local opinion. Knowledge as to what is going on and what is at stake, and a sense of what is expected of the individual and the local community and how these latter can play their roles—in brief, the inculcation of a measure of political sophistication—these are functions which the party can perform.

On the 14th anniversary of the Convention Peoples party, President Nkrumah, who is also the party's General Secretary and Chairman, reiterated the party's need to multiply and strengthen its contacts with the masses of the people, ". . . winning their confidence as their defenders against the evils of poverty, disease, hunger, ignorance and squalor to whose elimination we are dedicated . . . the masses of the people form the backbone of our Party and their living conditions and their welfare must be paramount in everything we do. . . . To achieve the foregoing objectives, there is a clear need so to re-organize the Party that it touches every single individual wherever he or she may live in order to bring the entire people into participation in the administration of the country, but also to make it impossible for external and internal reaction to interfere with the security of our State and the progress being made in all spheres of our national life."[39]

The themes touched upon by the Osagyefo in this address indicate the central post-independence sphere of party activity once the fundamentals of maintaining power and the territorial-political integrity of the country have been taken care of. With independence achieved, development comes to be the major concern of the party, which assumes responsibility for inspiring state activity and for rousing the people to their role and stake in it. Thus Mamadou Dia, early in 1962 when he was still Prime Minister of Senegal, portrayed the party in the era of development as having the essential function of mobilizing the entire nation from bottom to top to fulfill its destiny; the party, as he saw it, must play no parasitic or accessory role but must be "the very nerve and muscle, and the conscience" of the new work which is being undertaken.[40]

[39] Ghana Information Service, New York, June 12, 1963.
[40] Cited by Franz Ansprenger "Zur Rolle der Führungspartei in einigen jungen Staaten Afrikas," in Gerhard A. Ritter and Gilbert Ziebura, eds., *Faktoren der*

One phase of development activity in which a number of African parties have engaged may be put under the general heading of community development, the party serving as the crystallizing force to spur the local communities into action to better their own conditions. In some of the former French West African territories such developmental labors went under the name of *investissement humain* and were used by the party concerned as a means of enlisting rural and mass participation as well as of bringing about material improvements. In Tanganyika the Tanganyika African National Union, which had previously embarked on an ambitious program of establishing a network of independent schools to meet the people's educational needs, inaugurated a similar program of self-help projects at a local level. That such programs can make a significant contribution to national well-being and solidarity is beyond question, but it has also been the universal experience that it is exceedingly difficult to sustain the original enthusiasm, to combine coordinated planning with local initiative, and to meet the costs and supply the materials that reach beyond the locally available human investment of labor.

Another quite different and highly important integrating function which African parties have performed is the creation of an effective political tie between the new and the traditional elites.[41] In Northern Nigeria the Northern Peoples Congress has been marked, if not by the virtual identity of the old and new elites, at least by the necessity for the rising new elements to make their peace with the dominant traditional forces. The dual position of the latter is well illustrated by Alhaji Sir Ahmadu Bello, who holds the second most eminent traditional post as Sardauna of Sokoto and is at the same time President of the NPC and Premier of the Northern Region. In the different setting of the Western Region the Action Group brought together the traditional Yoruba rulers and the new Western-educated elements, themselves not infrequently derived from the

politischen Entscheidung, Berlin: Walter de Gruyter and Co., 1963, p. 431. Yacouba Maïga, organizing secretary of the party states that "L'union soudanaise doit assurer le contrôle de tous les organismes économiques, sociaux et culturels de l'Etat." Philippe Decraene, *Tableau des partis politiques de L'Afrique au sud du Sahara*, Paris: Fondation nationale des Sciences Politiques, Serie C: Recherches No. 8, Mai 1963, p. 10.

[41] I am indebted for the bulk of the material in this paragraph to my colleague, Martin Kilson. For illustrations of the way this integrating role has been played in Nigeria, see K. W. J. Post, *The Nigerian Federal Election of 1959*, London: Oxford University Press, 1963, and Richard Sklar, *Nigerian Political Parties*, Princeton: Princeton University Press, 1964.

pre-existing aristocracy. As in many other countries, African political parties in Nigeria have also served to secure the collaboration within a common framework of business groups and political leaders.

More broadly, the mass parties have in varying degree reached out either to replace tribe and clan as the virtually all-embracing centers of a warm and intimate social life or to fill the gap left by their decline or disappearance. Much has been done to override ethnic differences and to introduce a sense of common national identity, but, as has been remarked in relation to the Ivory Coast, "enforced political unanimity is a mere palliative" and fails to carry with it assurance that basic national integration has been accomplished. The latent conflicts deriving from the past may easily again be stirred to break out into open flames.[42] If this is true within the African community proper, it is all the more true of the relations between Africans, Arabs, Asians, and Europeans, where, whatever the pretensions of parties, only a minimal integration has been achieved at the best.

For the Africans the mass parties have often become parties of social integration which Ruth Schachter has well characterized in the following terms: "They and their cultural affiliates were interested in everything from the cradle to the grave—in birth, initiation, religion, marriage, divorce, dancing, song, plays, feuds, debts, land, migration, death, public order—and not only electoral success."[43]

In these many spheres, tending to embrace the totality of life, the party furnishes the symbols and in some part the working reality around which the national unity can cluster; it provides at least some of the focal points of national identity of which the most striking and immediately evident is the party leader himself, the national symbol *par excellence*.

No one can dispute that the role of the parties in national integration is, and presumably will remain, very great; but some reservations must be entered. Up to this time the general populace in most of the African countries has appeared to acquiesce patiently, perhaps enthusiastically, in the exercise of power by their dominant party leaders, but the upheavals and threat of upheavals previously referred to indicate that there are rumblings underground which more probably than not will cause further political earthquakes. Party leaders and government officials are accused, whether with or without

[42] Zolberg, *One-Party Government in the Ivory Coast*, pp. 340-341.
[43] *Op.cit., American Political Science Review* (June 1961), p. 300.

a direct accusation of corruption, of living at a level of expenditure and conspicuous consumption which is quite out of keeping with the way the people at large can afford to live. The men at the top in party and government, Western-educated and in some sense Western-oriented, are a distinct group separated in many ways from the mass of their countrymen and inevitably tempted to regard themselves as an elite above the mass. In such a situation, equally inevitably, there is a strong element of political tutelage or of "guided democracy," which may very easily come to be resented by those who are being tutored or guided; all the more so if the conviction grows, rightly or wrongly, that the superiority of those on top is no longer being exercised in the public interest but in the interest of the leaders themselves. The political tremors and earthquakes which have shaken so many African countries in the last couple of years are certainly not unrelated to this state of affairs. The assertion of national unity as a cloak to cover private manipulation is a worldwide phenomenon, but when it is suspected or caught out, in Africa as elsewhere, the political consequences may be dire. Increasingly, as recent events begin to demonstrate, where rifts open up in the society it is likely to be the military who take on the responsibility of securing national integration, supplanting leaders and parties which have failed to achieve the goals they set themselves.

CHAPTER 11

POLITICAL PARTIES AND THE CRISIS OF SUCCESSION IN THE UNITED STATES: THE CASE OF 1800*

MORTON GRODZINS

THIS PAPER views political parties in democratic states more as consequences than as causes. Parties are conceived as the products of their social and political environment, far more likely to be dependent than independent variables. Except for revolutionary cadres, political parties and party systems fall naturally into the design of the national social fabric. To put the matter bluntly, it is inconceivable that a totalitarian party could characterize the politics of a democratic nation, just as one cannot imagine two-party democratic politics in a totalitarian state.

Dependence of the party system on larger societal forces is particularly great in the early stages of a democratic nation's development. Again with the exception of revolutionary groups, the form of politics can emerge only from the character of the society. Here particularly is the danger of talking about reified names rather than facts, of giving the label "parties" to emerging groups of political activists and then endowing these "parties" with an independent force and importance. For the United States as a new nation the great political events cannot be explained in terms of party politics. When the United States as a mature political system is considered, parties play some independent role, but even then they must be seen as reflecting and making operative more basic factors in the society and the governmental system.[1] The parties then become convenient points at which diagnostic readings of the society can be made, as pulse at the wrist is indicative of heart action. Radical changes in the party system accompany radical changes in the social structure or constitutional practices, or both. But it would be an error to believe that the party changes are the causative force except in relatively modest ways.

---

* Morton Grodzins died before this paper could be revised. It is published here with only minor editorial changes. (J.L.)

[1] I have elaborated the distinction between the functional and causal roles of parties in "American Political Parties and the American System," *Western Political Quarterly*, Vol. 13, No. 4 (1960), pp. 974-98.

What I have said generally about democratic parties being derivative rather than determinant applies specifically to the issue on which this paper is focused: the change of leaders in the United States of America. The United States has never faced the most difficult problems involved in substituting one set of leaders for another, the sorts of problems encountered when republicans attempt to replace monarchists, or communists succeed capitalists, or religious libertarians follow religious absolutes. No such fundamental schisms have divided our society. The only comparable situation was the sectional conflict that led to the Civil War. With that exception, it need hardly be argued that the United States represents, *par excellence*, a society characterized by an easy circulation of elite groups and, no less important, by relatively numerous routes of political recruitment and advancement. The party operates most of the time to encourage both these attributes. But it will be argued that the party system is only a minor cause of them.

In the pages that follow I propose to examine in detail the first great crisis of succession in U.S. history: the peaceful transition from Federalist to Republican rule in 1800. Political parties were at the first stages of their growth, but nevertheless they were organized, easily identified, and the principal institutions through which nominees were chosen and the campaign fought. The question asked is: What role did the parties play in achieving the peaceful transfer of leadership? The conclusion is that the parties were not an important causal factor. If anything, they made the peaceful succession more, rather than less, difficult.

In the last section of the paper I shall attempt briefly to distinguish the role of American parties in the nation's early stages of development from their role today and to argue the unreality of comparing parties in democratic states with those in totalitarian states. I shall also summarize the important ways in which American parties aid in fostering upward mobility for a wide variety of social groups.

I. The Emergence of Parties

The first American parties became visible before the end of Washington's first term. Any brief statement of the doctrinal differences between the two groups—one of which became known as the Federalists, the other as Anti-Federalists, Jeffersonians, or Republicans—inevitably effaces important nuances. The Federalists were the party of mercantile interests, while the Jeffersonians found the Republic's virtue in agriculture. The Federalists believed in the need for a strong and active central government; the Republicans "were almost congenitally sceptical of proposals for governmental action. . . ." They believed "the federal government was to be kept out of the business of the states . . . and the states were to be kept out of the business of the private citizens."[2] From their differing views of the propriety and need for governmental action grew opposing principles of constitutional construction, Federalists urging a broad interpretation of the central government's powers, Republicans holding for a narrow construction of those powers.[3] Federalists believed in the rule of an aristocratic class consisting of "the rich, the beautiful and well-born" (to use a famous phrase of John Adams); Republicans, in Jefferson's words, believed only in an aristocracy of "virtue and talent." "Viewed as a whole, and viewed entire, the Republican philosophy is a series of variations on the theme of freedom."[4] Federalists feared the uses to which the lower classes would put freedom and in some cases denied the validity of the republican form of government itself.

From the founding of the new United States in 1789 until 1800 the government was firmly in control of the Federalists, whose leader was Alexander Hamilton. Federalist policies were based on Hamilton's view that governments had to be ruled by gentlemen, by his distrust of popular majorities, and by his conviction that American progress depended upon bringing the wealthy and well-born to the firm support of the new government. Since during this period farm population ranged from 90 to 95 per cent of the total, Hamilton's party was not exclusively a party of merchants and traders. If it had been, whatever the existing limitations on suffrage, the party could not have maintained itself in office. Nevertheless the principal points of the Federalist program were aimed at promoting the interests of urban mercantile groups and fostering the development of business and industry. The great Hamiltonian measures of the first

[2] Stuart Gerry Brown, *The First Republicans*, Syracuse, N.Y.: Syracuse University Press, 1954, pp. 161-162.

[3] Alas for the theories of limited government and narrow constitutional interpretation, Jefferson as president in 1803 purchased Louisiana from France, a master stroke that more than doubled the size of the United States. At first he did not think he could make the purchase without an authorizing constitutional amendment, but when he realized the amendment process was too slow, he bought anyway—an act that he firmly believed was unconstitutional.

[4] Stuart Gerry Brown, *op.cit.*, p. 171.

years of the republic included the funding and assumption of the revolutionary debts (funding paid off the sharply depreciated debts of the old confederation at their face value; assumption made the federal government responsible for state debts, which were even more depressed). Both policies, and especially assumption, gave enormous profits to speculators who had purchased state securities from their original holders at a fraction of their face value. A protective tariff (the first bill introduced into the first Congress), the establishment of the first United States bank, excise taxes on whiskey, sale of public lands in large tracts, and a strongly pro-English foreign policy were all a part of the Hamiltonian program; and all of them were designed "to bind the moneyed classes firmly to the central government."

Controversy over early Federalist policies was blunted because they were carried out under the presidency of the respected hero of the Revolution, George Washington, who (like a more recent general-president) was largely dependent upon staff work and staff recommendations. Washington, said Hamilton, was an "aegis very essential" for his purposes. Jefferson, who was soon to emerge as the leader of the opposition party, served alongside Hamilton in Washington's cabinet until 1793. He did not oppose the funding of the revolutionary debts, and his scruples about assumption—with Madison he initially wanted a scheme of liquidating state debts that would have prevented or minimized profits by speculators—were overcome by the agreement to put the new national capital in a northeastern corner of his native Virginia. The plan to establish the national bank was the first Federalist measure which Jefferson, and Madison in the House, met with full opposition. As Washington increasingly allowed Hamilton to dominate the policies of the administration, so Jefferson increasingly grew restive in his cabinet position where he found himself "daily pitted [against Hamilton] in the cabinet like two cocks."

II. Discord Between the Parties, 1794-1800

The first scratches of disagreement soon developed into wounds, and the period from 1794 to 1800 seemed to those who lived through it, as it now seems to afterviewers, one in which a growing crescendo of political discord threatened the very existence of the nation. Federalists and Republicans divided on each successive issue. Here, in brief review, are the most important crisis points:

Whiskey Rebellion. In 1794 farmers of Western Pennsylvania and neighboring sections of Virginia took up arms against the federal tax on distilled liquors. Whiskey to those who made it was not the luxury that Hamilton conceived it to be but a basic commodity, more potable and portable than corn, and a medium of exchange on the frontier. The rebellious group had the sympathy of many farmers and tradesmen throughout the country (people who were beginning to think of themselves as Republicans) though Republican leaders had little sympathy with the tactic of armed insurrection. Washington dispatched no fewer than 13,000 troops to the scene (Hamilton accompanied them), and the rebellion collapsed. Jefferson viewed the sequence of events as a gloomy augury that the nation might be breaking up.

The Jay Treaty. Debate over ratification of the Jay Treaty (1795) brought about a deeper and more general division of the nation. The movement of the French Revolution from moderation to violence (and the war between France and Great Britain which began in February 1793) had already separated pro-British Federalists from pro-French Republicans. Washington's course of official neutrality was viewed by Republican leaders as a retreat from the revolutionary spirit of 1776 and, more specifically, as a betrayal of treaties with France that dated back to this nation's period of greatest need. The French-British war produced tensions between each of the combatant nations and the United States. John Jay's mission to London was aimed at reducing these tensions with Great Britain (for example, the harassment of our shipping and impressment of our sailors) as well as at solving long-standing issues between the two nations (for example, the incitement of Indians in American territory by the British in Canada). Even many Federalists, and Washington among them, were unhappy with the treaty as it was finally negotiated. Washington kept the text of the treaty for four months before submitting it to the Senate.[5] It was debated and passed by the Senate

[5] There was nothing in the treaty to protect American seamen from impressment or to stop the incitement of Indians on the frontier. The treaty contained no significant commercial concessions from Great Britain, and the U.S. gave up for ten years the right to levy a discriminatory tariff against British goods and thus the right to give preferential treatment to those nations with whom the U.S. had a commercial treaty. Jay conceded that a mixed commission, rather than the U.S. Courts, would adjudicate outstanding debts owed to British subjects. To many Americans, the only tangible benefit the treaty gave the U.S. was the promise by Great Britain to surrender western outposts which had been maintained on American territory since the end of the Revolutionary War. See Samuel Flagg Bemis, *Jay's Treaty*, New York, 1923.

in secret session, but the text soon leaked to the Republican press, which immediately launched a campaign of criticism. Republicans organized petitions, issued pamphlets against ratification, hanged Jay in effigy, and stoned Hamilton in the streets of New York. Federalists denounced those who took part in the criticism as "the scum of the society."[6] The national debate was prolonged as Washington hesitated over signing the treaty and, subsequently, as the House of Representatives debated at length an appropriation that was necessary to effectuate it. The appropriation carried only under Federalist threats that a failure to do so would cause the dissolution of the country or war with Great Britain. Jefferson regarded the treaty as a betrayal of the Revolution; Federalists responded that the only opposition to the treaty came from those who were the tools of France. Washington admitted that the public mind was agitated over the Jay Treaty "in a higher degree than it has been at any period since the Revolution."[7]

XYZ Affair. If the nascent Republican party gained strength because of popular disapproval of the Jay Treaty, the advantage was all to the Federalists in the XYZ affair of 1798. The five years between the Jay Treaty and the XYZ affair were years of internal political turmoil and steadily worsening relations with France. John Adams replaced Washington as President in 1796, Thomas Jefferson, the leader of the opposition, being selected Vice President as the consequence of disagreement in Federalist ranks and a quirk of the election laws.[8] Even during the election the French minister to the United States openly campaigned for Jefferson and hinted at war between France and the United States if Jefferson were not elected. And from the first day of his administration Adams was caught up

[6] Joseph Charles, *The Origins of the American Party System*, New York, 1956, p. 108.

[7] Washington to Pinckney, May 22, 1796, quoted in Joseph Charles, *op.cit.*, p. 111.

[8] The Constitution (Art. II, Sec. 3) provided no distinction between those running for President and Vice President. Of those nominated the person having the greatest number of votes was elected President, if he had a majority, and the person having the second greatest number of votes was elected Vice President. (Amendment 12 of the Constitution, adopted in 1804, changed the system to its modern form, separate electoral ballots being cast for President and Vice President.) In 1796 Adams and Thomas Pinckney were nominated by the Federalists, it being well understood that Adams was the Presidential candidate. Jefferson and Aaron Burr were the Republican nominees. Hamilton, who feared Adams' independence, intrigued to reverse the Federalist ticket and make Pinckney President. Strong supporters of Adams retaliated by urging Federalists not to vote for Pinckney. The total situation was one that almost lost the election for Adams, whose margin was 71 to 68. Jefferson, not Pinckney, had the 68, and consequently was named Vice President.

in difficulties with France. The Directory refused in an insulting manner to recognize Adams' new diplomatic representative to France, Charles C. Pinckney (brother of Adams' running mate, Thomas Pinckney). An undeclared war at sea broke out between France and the United States. Adams at every turn of affairs was faced by demands from Hamilton, Secretary of State Timothy Pickering, and other High Federalists for an all-out war against France. Instead, Adams asked for and received congressional authorization to increase the size of the army and navy (against Republican opposition). At the same time he dispatched John Marshall and Elbridge Gerry to join Pinckney in Paris for a new round of negotiations in search of an agreement that would lead to peace and a commercial treaty. The French government avoided the new envoys for weeks. Finally they were approached by three unofficial agents of the Directory who demanded, as a prerequisite to negotiations, an American loan to France as well as bribes to certain French officials.[9] The Americans refused, and negotiations were broken off. When the correspondence between the negotiators was laid before Congress in the spring of 1798 (Adams substituted the letters X, Y, and Z for the names of the French emissaries), congressional and popular indignation ran high.

The XYZ affair catapulted Adams to a high point of popularity. Republicans, including Jefferson, who still served as Vice President, were condemned as actual or near traitors, "Frenchmen in all their feelings and wishes." High Federalists went so far as to charge Republicans with being ready to join an invading French army on American beachheads.[10] Hamilton and others were confident that the XYZ affair would "give a most fatal blow to the Jacobins." And Republican opposition was nearly nonexistent as Congress authorized new efforts to strengthen the army, fortify harbors, and build new ships. Jeffersonians speculated that the nation's new military might would be turned against them.

The Alien and Sedition Laws. The XYZ affair allowed Federalists to identify Republicans with France and thus to consider opposition to administration measures as seditious or traitorous. France became the external, Republicans the internal, foe. With national defense and political orthodoxy their main planks, Federalists worked

[9] Pinckney is supposed to have replied, "Millions for defense, but not one cent for tribute," which later became a popular anti-French slogan in the U.S.
[10] William N. Chambers, *Political Parties in a New Nation*, New York, 1963, p. 134.

to perpetuate themselves in power. "Under the guise of patriotic purpose and internal security, [they] enacted a program to cripple, if not destroy, the Jeffersonian party."[11]

The Federalists' principal instruments were four laws passed during the spring and summer of 1798, the Alien and Sedition Acts. Three of the laws were aimed at aliens. (Many Republican converts and pamphleteers were relatively recent arrivals to the United States from Great Britain, Ireland, and France.) The period required for admission to citizenship was increased from five to fourteen years. The President was authorized to deport any alien deemed "dangerous to the peace and safety of the United States," and a failure to obey such a deportation order was punishable by imprisonment. Enemy aliens were subject to summary restraint and removal. The Sedition Act itself was aimed at all residents of the country, not just aliens. It provided heavy criminal penalties for the writing, printing, or speaking of "any false, scandalous, and malicious" words which were judged by a federal court to bring the government, President, or Congress "into contempt or disrepute."

The Alien Laws had the effect of silencing noncitizens and of encouraging the emigration of many, but President Adams was not aggressive in the use of his deportation powers. Though warrants for the seizure of several aliens were signed by the President, not a single alien was deported under the acts. The case was altogether different for the Sedition Law. The foremost historian of the Sedition Act has verified seventeen indictments taken under it (plus three others that were inspired by the act but were returned under the common law).[12] In addition, a number of arrests were made that were not followed by formal indictments. The principal thrust of the prosecutions was against the proprietors, editors, and chief writers of Republican newspapers. Of the five most influential Jeffersonian journals in the country (the Philadelphia *Aurora*, the Boston *Independent Chronicle*, the New York *Argus*, the Richmond *Examiner*, and the Baltimore *American*), only the last escaped a suit. Minor Republican newspapers were not ignored, and several were forced to cease publication. A number of political leaders, including at least one congressman, were prosecuted. Others were frightened and silenced by threats of suits. The wide latitude given the courts in the Sedition Act allowed partisan federal judges to apply it with

[11] James M. Smith, *Freedom's Fetters*, Ithaca, N.Y.: Cornell University Press, 1956, p. 21.
[12] *Ibid.*, p. 185.

severity against Republicans for relatively innocent remarks. Fines or imprisonment, or both, were imposed on all the Republicans actually tried under the Sedition Act.

The principal effort to enforce the Sedition Act was a part of the Federalists' campaign for the presidency in 1800. Although most of the suits began in 1798 or 1799, many trials were not held until the spring and summer of 1800. Secretary of State Pickering, who made himself the chief enforcement officer of the Alien and Sedition Acts, did not scruple in the timing of prosecutions so that either indictments or trials coincided with the presidential campaign of 1800. The campaign of suppression gained strength from the widely held Federalist belief that the Republican press was supported by French money. Federalist leaders saw themselves as true patriots and saw in any Republican opponent "an Anarchist, a Jacobin, and a Traitor."[13]

The Virginia and Kentucky Resolutions. Republicans denied these Federalist changes and were particularly aroused by the Sedition Act. They charged that the act was unconstitutional in the light of the First Amendment and that the Federalists were bent upon destroying democracy and establishing a despotism. It was freely predicted by Republican spokesmen, in and out of Congress, that neither the people nor the states would submit to the tyranny of the Alien and Sedition Laws.

The most important Republican response to the Alien and Sedition Laws were the Virginia and Kentucky Resolutions, drafted by Madison and Jefferson and passed by the legislatures of the two states. Each resolution condemned the Sedition Act and its companion measures on the grounds that they were unlawful exercises of national power. Though steering clear of proposals for secession, the resolutions declared that the states were the rightful judges of the limits of the central government's power. Since the Alien and Sedition Laws exceeded the delegated powers of the central government, those laws (to quote the Kentucky statement) were "void and of no force." It was the duty of the states "to interpose for arresting the progress of the evil." The Virginia legislature added action to words and ordered the state to reorganize and increase its militia and levy taxes for munitions.[14] A number of Federalists took

[13] *Ibid.*, p. 178, quoting the Boston *Sentinal*, October 5, 1798. In the paragraph above I have relied heavily on James Smith's work.
[14] Manning J. Dauer, *The Adams Federalist*, Baltimore: The Johns Hopkins Press, 1953, p. 202.

the resolutions to be portent of civil war. Hamilton himself suggested that Virginia be put "to the test of resistance," and that with regular troops (as opposed to the militia) he would not hesitate "to subdue a refractory and powerful State."[15]

Fries' Rebellion. Subsequent events deprived Hamilton of the opportunity to subdue a state. But for the second time in five years military forces were needed in 1799 to put down an armed rebellion against Federalist policies. In the wake of the XYZ affair Congress was spurred on by High Federalists, seeking an official declaration of war with France, to increase military expenditures substantially. Such measures needed taxes to support them, and Congress levied a direct tax on dwelling houses, land, and slaves. In northern states, where there were few slaves, the burden of the tax fell most heavily on houses and land, the value of the houses being determined by the number and size of windows. (The Federalists neatly exempted from the tax wealth represented by securities, shipping, mercantile establishments, and factories, thus placing the burden primarily on agrarians, who of course were primarily Republicans.) The inquisitorial nature of the survey carried out by federal officials aroused strong opposition among farmers of German descent in southeastern Pennsylvania. This resistance led to a number of arrests by the federal marshals, but the prisoners were rescued by an armed group under the leadership of John Fries. The insurgents marched about the countryside intimidating the assessors and gaining new recruits until Fries led a band of several hundred men. Federal troops were dispatched, and the rebellion immediately put down. Fries was captured and subsequently tried for treason.[16]

III. Party Organization and the Election of 1800

The Federalist party became badly split during the period of national tension between 1794 and 1800. The conflict had its beginnings in Hamilton's defection from John Adams in the campaign of 1796. Nevertheless Adams carried over in his cabinet three High Federalists—the Secretaries of State (Timothy Pickering), Treasury (Oliver Wolcott), and War (James McHenry)—who were each in his own way more loyal to Hamilton than to the President. Hamilton also had great influence in both houses of Congress, and it was

[15] Quoted in *ibid.*, p. 209.
[16] Fries was sentenced to be hanged but was pardoned by President Adams shortly before the end of his term.

often difficult to tell whether the leadership of the country was being exercised by the President or the ex-Secretary of the Treasury. The principal plank of Hamilton's High Federalist policy was war with France and an alliance with Great Britain. The rigors of war, and, consequently, the military forces made available to the central government, would supply at once the occasion and the resources for sweeping away all Republican opposition, already "traitors" in Federalist eyes for their sympathy toward France.

Adams was not altogether unmoved by arguments of the High Federalists: he was enthusiastic in his support of the Sedition Act, for example. But he shared none of the High Federalists' enthusiasm for a French war or for the armed suppression of the Republican opposition. Indeed, before the end of his term he seemed more frightened of Hamilton and his friends than of the Jeffersonian opposition. Issues of policy became intertwined with personal bickerings and animosities, the latter coming to a head in a scheme by Hamilton to have himself appointed Inspector General in the new army which was being raised and which Washington had agreed to lead; but Washington was aged, and Hamilton's position would put him second in command and actual head of the armed forces at least until the recruitment period was over. All this was highly distasteful to President Adams, especially so when he had to agree to Hamilton's appointment on the threat that if he did not appoint Hamilton, Washington would refuse to serve.

Internal strains within Federalist ranks led finally to an open split in the party. While his cabinet and High Federalists in the Congress were calling for formal war with France (the informal war at sea was still being fought), President Adams was exploring the path to peace. Shortly after the XYZ papers had been sent to Congress Adams stated that he would not send a new minister to France without official assurance that the envoy would be "received, respected, and honored as the representative of a great, free, powerful, and independent nation."[17] When the French foreign minister, Talleyrand, gave assurances that these conditions would be met, Adams sent to the Senate (February 18, 1799) a nomination for a new envoy to Paris whose task would be to negotiate a peaceful settlement of French-American affairs. Adams did not even bother to consult with his cabinet, and the nomination "came as a bombshell to the cabinet and to the High Federalists."[18] Adams went so

[17] Adams, *Works*, Vol. IX, p. 159, quoted in Manning J. Dauer, *op.cit.*, p. 230.
[18] *Ibid.*, p. 231.

far as to threaten to resign if the Senate did not approve the new mission to France—a threat the High Federalists would have welcomed if its execution would not have elevated the hated Jefferson to the presidency. In any case, the split in Federalist ranks contributed greatly to Jefferson's becoming President in the election of 1800.

The period between 1794 and 1800 was a period of growth in the organization of both political parties. Each party had recognized leaders and an identifiable press. Though there were no platforms as such, the programs of the parties were well advertised through newspapers, the distribution of pamphlets, and correspondence. By the end of the period well-established communications patterns were developed between central leaders and those on the state and local level, and Republicans and Federalists alike understood the principle of keeping a wavering congressman or senator in line by stirring up pressures from his home constituency. The congressional caucus was used by both parties. As Manning J. Dauer has demonstrated, it is possible to trace party unity by an analysis of congressional votes over time (a high point of party regularity came in 1796 with votes during the debates on the Jay Treaty); and it is also clear that the party of a congressman was closely related to constituency characteristics (for example agrarian vs. commercial, North vs. South, proximity to or safety from Indian danger).[19] By 1796 the election of old revolutionary leaders without regard for their party had practically ceased. "The growth of party feeling had reached the point that the demand was for party men."[20]

Party organization at the grass roots varied greatly from state to state. In the election of 1796, for example, the Republican campaign led by John Beckley in Pennsylvania had all the earmarks of a modern election: a carefully selected "ticket" of electors, a central campaign committee, rallies in populated places, streams of partisan literature, special efforts to turn out voters on election day, and all the rest. In North and South Carolina and New Jersey, on the other hand, party activity in 1796 was virtually nonexistent. Federalist organization at the local level never matched that of the Republicans at their best. The party in power relied primarily on patronage and newspaper propaganda, held infrequent public meetings, and tried to capitalize on its self-advertised status as the party of patriots following in the path of the great Washington.

[19] *Ibid.*, Ch. 1; appendix II.
[20] *Ibid.*, p. 34.

Jeffersonians entered the campaign of 1800 united and on the offensive, while the Federalists were handicapped by the now unbridgeable schism between Adams and the High Federalists. The Republican caucus again nominated Jefferson and Burr. The Hamiltonian faction at first attempted to replace Adams on the Federalist ticket: the aged Washington (who died before the election) was urged to run instead. He refused. Finally a caucus of Federalist members of Congress agreed to back Adams for President and Charles C. Pinckney for Vice President. Hamilton and his friends again tried the tactic of 1796, that is, to induce some Federalist electors to vote for Pinckney and not for Adams. Before the campaign was over, Adams and Hamilton were publicly castigating each other in terms usually saved for the opposing party. Because of the very moderation of his policy, Adams retained the support of most Federalist leaders of the middle and lower rank.

The Republicans did not lack substantive issues. They made the most of an unsuccessful attempt by Federalists in Congress to create an electoral commission whose function would be to declare the Federalist candidates victorious, whatever the electoral count.[21] The Sedition Act was now almost universally hated outside of New England, and its application in an election year made votes everywhere for the Republican cause. Federal expenses had doubled in the four preceding years as a consequence of military expenditures made to defend the country, or to wage war, against France. Adams' decision for peace gave the Republicans an excellent campaign issue. They argued that the new taxes, including the hated tax on land, houses, and slaves, had always been unnecessary. Jefferson vigorously publicized his insistence on "a government rigorously frugal and simple" and free of debt; a drastically reduced navy and dependence for internal defense on the state militias except in case of actual invasion; free commerce with all nations but political connections with none; and freedom of religion and the press, including repeal of the Sedition Act.[22]

Despite Federalist disunity the election returns of 1800 were close. Jefferson and Burr won over Adams and Pinckney by a vote of 73 to 65.[23] (See Table 1.) The sectional alignment was clear: Federal-

---

[21] *Ibid.*, p. 244. Hamilton similarly tried without success to change the system of choosing electors in New York so as to insure a Federalist victory. *Ibid.*, p. 250.

[22] William N. Chambers, *op.cit.*, p. 154.

[23] In fact Pinckney only polled 64 electoral votes, one elector from Rhode Island

TABLE 1ª: ELECTION RESULTS OF 1800

State	Jeffer-son	Burr	Adams	Pinck-ney	Jay	Seventh Congress, 1st session, House of Representatives	
						F	R
New Hampshire			6	6		4	0
Vermont			4	4		1	1
Massachusetts			16	16		8	6
Rhode Island			4	3	1	0	2
Connecticut			9	9		7	0
New York	12	12				3	7
New Jersey			7	7		0	5
Pennsylvania	8	8	7	7		4	9
Delaware			3	3		1	0
Maryland	5	5	5	5		3	5
Virginia	21	21				2	17
North Carolina	8	8	4	4		5	5
South Carolina	8	8				3	3
Georgia	4	4				0	2
Kentucky	4	4				0	2
Tennessee	3	3				0	1
	73	73	65	64	1	41	65

ª Source: Manning J. Dauer, *The Adams Federalists*, p. 257.

ists swept New England, and Republicans won all but four of the southern electoral votes. Maryland split her votes evenly. A clean Republican victory in New York and a partial one in Pennsylvania insured the victory for Jefferson and Burr.

But one more crisis had to be faced. Since Jefferson and Burr had an equal number of electoral votes, the choice of who would be President, who Vice President, fell to the House of Representatives, each state having a single vote. And it was the lame-duck Federalist House, not the new heavily Republican one, that was to make the choice. Though it was clear that the country (and the electors) assumed that Jefferson would be President, High Federalists schemed to turn the highest office over to Burr. Others sought a deadlock until Jefferson would commit himself to the continuation of Federalist policies—the enlarged navy, for example. But Jefferson refused to make any commitment; and the issue remained in doubt for seventeen days and through thirty-five inconclusive roll calls in the House. Finally the majority of the voting states elected

marking his ballot for Adams and Jay, thus insuring that, if the Federalist ticket won, High Federalists in the House would not contrive to make Pinckney president.

Jefferson, but only after Federalists from South Carolina, Vermont, and Maryland refrained from voting. At last and in high tension the first fundamental change of leaders took place in the new American nation.

IV. The Role of Party in the Change of Leadership

"Our first national parties," wrote William N. Chambers, "represented the conflicting forces of pluralism in American politics, while at the same time they worked to harness them. They provided vehicles for political participation, fulfilled to a remarkable extent the capacities of parties for offering effective choices to the electorate, and brought *new order into the conduct of government*."[24] This is the conventional view of the important role played by parties in making possible the peaceful changing of leaders in 1800. The view is persuasive because it supplies a simple answer to one of the most complex and mysterious phenomena in political life: the voluntary, peaceful transfer of vast powers from one set of committed leaders to another who by definition are adversaries. To explain this phenomenon by saying "the party system made it possible"—or to explain the failure of peaceful succession by asserting "the parties were not flexible enough to accommodate the conflicting views"—is to offer explanations that do little explaining. If the path indicated by the Whiskey Rebellion and Fries' Rebellion had been followed, the course of American government would have led to anarchy or tyranny. "At the time of these disorders substantial groups felt that they had no effective voice in the government, while many conservatives wished to see the disaffected areas treated like conquered provinces."[25] The author of these words (Joseph Charles) believed that only the growth of political parties allowed representative government to survive in the United States. In my view the most that can be claimed, especially in the earliest days of party growth, is that the parties were vehicles through which other moderating factors made themselves felt.

The truth of the matter is that the peaceful succession of 1800 could never have taken place if other factors had not been operative. A scholar working on a theory of parties as an independent social force is faced with the fact that party activities exacerbated—and not at all moderated—the claims of the competing social groups. It

[24] *Political Parties in a New Nation*, vii, italics supplied.
[25] Joseph Charles, *op.cit.*, p. 42.

must be recalled that by 1798, following the XYZ affair, the passage of the Alien and Sedition Acts, and the response of the Kentucky and Virginia Resolutions as well as of Fries' Rebellion, the High Federalists were dominant within the governing party. They regarded the total situation as a golden opportunity to erect an aristocratic system on what they considered the ruins of the new republic. So that an army might be raised they worked for war with France, emphasized the danger of invasion, and dwelled upon the likelihood of civil war. They hoped to use the army against France (and possibly Spain) and, just as importantly, use it to whatever extent necessary to suppress internal opposition. "To crush democracy by force," said Henry Adams, "was the ultimate resource of Hamilton. To crush that force was the determined intention of Jefferson."[26]

Extremists from both parties, in short, regarded the election of 1800 as one in which a fundamental change in the regime would occur. It was no simple replacement of one set of leaders for another in the continuing process of governance. Rather the election was one of two nations confronting each other, of political good against political evil, of one design of government competing against an opposing regime. The British Foreign Secretary speculated that this clash of extreme views brought the American government "tottering to its foundations." "I much doubt," he said, "their power of maintaining internal tranquility."[27]

"Regime politics,"[28] which would have indeed made the union totter, were approached most closely by the Alien and Sedition Acts. The Acts must be viewed as a revolutionary effort. They represented an attempt to suppress not a noisome minority but a major (and as it turned out a majority) opposition. Yet this repression was not ruthlessly applied (Republican editors were often more vociferous in jail than out), nor was it followed, despite attempts made in that direction, by any military effort to suppress the opposition by force. If force had been used—if Federalist plans to suppress the "Jacobin traitors" were realized, or if the Whiskey Rebellion and Fries' Rebellion had been scaled up to national dimensions—then the line would have been crossed into regime politics. No peaceful change of leaders would have been possible. Jefferson later called his election "The Revolution of 1800." No blood was shed. It is nevertheless

[26] *Life of Albert Gallatin*, Philadelphia, 1879, p. 170.
[27] Lord Grenville to R. Liston, February 28, 1800; quoted in Manning J. Dauer, *op.cit.*, p. 241.
[28] I am indebted to Professor Martin Diamond for this phrase.

true that partisan politics brought the nation to the brink of a bloody civil war in 1800.

The parties' role in making more difficult the peaceful change of leaders can perhaps be best illustrated by the level of discourse of the campaign of 1800. The language of American politics is rarely polite and often sinks to careless condemnations and name-calling. And it is almost certainly true that American political controversy during the later eighteenth and early nineteenth centuries was characterized by more vituperation than that of the twentieth century. Nevertheless the campaign of 1800 was a period of uniquely vicious contumely. The Republican newspapers made it a commonplace to refer to Hamilton as a bastard and a self-confessed adulterer who schemed to make himself a tyrant. President Adams was also a preferred target. James T. Callender, one of the less restrained of Jeffersonian spokesmen, wrote that "the reign of Mr. Adams has been one continued tempest of malignant passions." The President's "grand object" was "to calumniate and destroy every man who differed from his opinions." Adams was a "hoary headed incendiary." The voters' choice was "between Adams, war, and beggary, and Jefferson, peace, and competency."[29] Federalist newspapers treated Jefferson even more unkindly. He was called a Jacobin and traitor. He was charged with being the father of mulatto children and a mad scientist who practiced vivisection and whose home should be called "Dog's Misery." Jefferson was scourged as an atheist whose election would result in the burning of all Bibles and would excite the just vengeance of an insulted Almighty.[30]

Neither the intention nor the action nor the words of the political parties can in any way be seen as giving "flexibility" or "moderation" or "order" to the American government in the period between 1796 and 1800. Parties, if in any degree an independent source of action, exacerbated differences and sharpened the conflict between the (largely) mercantile and (largely) agricultural segments of the population. What, then, made the peaceful change possible?

The most important immediate cause of the peaceful change was the action of President John Adams. The first priority of Adams' High Federalist colleagues was war with France. The public temper produced by such a war (roughly, new heights of patriotism in the

---

[29] The quotations come from Callender's pamphlet, *The Prospect before Us*, cited in Manning J. Dauer, *op.cit.*, pp. 339-40.

[30] William N. Chambers, *op.cit.*, p. 153.

cities, especially northern cities, and new demonstrations of disapproval in rural areas, especially in the South) would supply ample excuse for the armed suppression of the opposition party. Under such conditions no peaceful change of leaders would have been possible. Adams clearly saw all this. He scotched it completely by sending a new peace-seeking mission to France, and later (in May 1800) by ridding his cabinet of Hamilton's lackeys, Secretary of War McHenry (who resigned at Adams' request) and Secretary of State Timothy Pickering (who was ousted when he refused to resign). Adams fully realized that this splitting of the party would almost certainly result in Jefferson's victory. But this did not deter him. Despite his vanity, quick temper, and general irascibility, and despite his approval of the Alien and Sedition Acts, Adams at base believed in the viability of the Union. He had no taste for either a foreign or civil war. He never wavered in working, according to his own lights, for the preservation of the Union he had helped to establish.

Furthermore Adams could not have given credence to his party's view of Jefferson. Adams then looked upon Jefferson as a political enemy. But the two had been Revolutionary colleagues and coworkers in the establishment of the Constitution; later, after both retired from politics, they would be friends again. Though there seems to be no relevant documentation, Adams even in 1800 must have felt that the union would be safe in Jefferson's hands. He certainly did not regard Jefferson as a traitor. By his very actions Adams showed greater confidence in Jefferson's leadership than in Hamilton's. He thereby brought his party to defeat and set it on the path of ultimate destruction.

If one asks the simple question: Did any activity or consideration of party cause Adams to choose in favor of peace with France and an end to domestic extremism, the simple answer is "No." The important factors were Adams' conviction, courage, stubbornness, and rectitude.

Other forces making for the peaceful exchange of leaders in 1800 are more general in nature. Some importance must be accorded to the fact that the United States is (and was then) a nation of many elected officials serving terms that vary in length and therefore chosen at elections widely scattered in time. Such a system (which is most characteristic of a federal government) makes it highly unlikely that any major party will ever be completely turned out of *all* offices. The Federalists, following their defeat in the presidential election of 1800, still controlled at least four governorships (in Connecticut, Massachusetts, New York, and New Hampshire), the mayor's office in a number of the larger New England cities, 14 Senate seats (as compared with 18 for the Republicans), and 40 places in the House of Representatives (Republicans had 66). There was, then, no complete ousting of one party, no sweeping the leaders of that party into the back alleys where revolutionaries are made. On the contrary, the system of elections in the United States makes defeat ambiguous by leaving the losers with scraps of power and with places of responsibility. So it was in 1800. And so the very electoral system further checked whatever penchant for violence still existed in Federalist ranks.

The untapped wealth of the nation was also a moderating influence. The search for riches was an attractive alternative to the search for political power. There is sound evidence that many leaders of both parties attempted to combine the two efforts. Political defeat in more than a few instances was the occasion for searching with renewed vigor for the wealth that seemed to hang ready for plucking in land speculation, exploration of the great West, schemes for manufacturing and foreign trade, shipping, and privateering. Revolt is less likely when attractive career opportunities exist for the political losers.

Chance—plain luck—must also be given its due. A less resolute President than John Adams, a Hamilton who was more consistently and radically anti-democratic, a less dependent Secretary of War than McHenry, a determined attack by France on our shores—any single one or combination of these contingencies could have prevented the peaceful succession of 1800. The great stabilizing influence of Washington had largely vanished. Parties that would make two nations of the Union, the contingency that Washington so deeply feared, were almost realized in the years between 1798 and 1800. Whatever rational or deterministic reasons one adduces for the avoidance of violence, the element of good fortune must also be counted as important.

In a pat phrase, democracy is viable only if the nation is so fundamentally at one that the parties "can safely afford to bicker." Here one approaches the concept of social consensus, difficult to define and even more difficult to measure. The basic agreements on the nature of the good society and the proper role of government—agreements that constitute the heart of political consensus—were severely strained by the election of 1800 and the events preceding it. Yet the High Federalist leaders of first rank who pushed hardest toward violence seem in retrospect to have been further separated from their political opponents—the Adams wing of their own party as well as the Republicans—than were lesser leaders of the three groups or followers at large. The failure of all High Federalist schemes to defeat Adams as well as Adams' respectable showing in the presidential election demonstrate to what degree High Federalist national leaders lacked popular support. Of course there existed pockets of extreme Federalism and extreme anti-Republicanism—in Congregational communities of Massachusetts and Connecticut, for example. But even New England as a whole supported the moderation of Adams, with Jeffersonians powerful in the hinterlands. There had been faint hints of secession in the Virginia and Kentucky Resolutions, and a few years after Jefferson's election there would be even more powerful separatist tendencies in New England. But despite alarms and damnations from each side, the nation from 1796 to 1800 maintained some basic unities. The party leaders never quite crossed the line that would convert the single nation into two. Whatever else they were, the High Federal radicals were irresolute revolutionaries.

With respect to the people as a whole, they had fought the great revolution together. They were the patriots of 1776. They bickered, sometimes violently, seldom politely; but they showed no disposition for violence on any large scale. They suffered from apathy, the enemy of all political reformers. They were not agreed on any alternate form of government. They had no widespread fear of recrimination by the new administration against its political enemies. They were for the most part willing to accept Jefferson as their President. They did so out of Republican conviction, as followers of the moderate leadership of Adams, as participants in the booming and buzzing business of making a nation, and as beneficiaries of good fortune that prevented the potential coup d'état from becoming a harsh reality. From these elements there was built the modicum of national consensus that helped make possible the peaceful change of leaders of 1800.

V. Some Concluding Observations

As a political system matures, established democratic parties become institutions in their own right. They continue to reflect and implement other aspects of the society such as law, ideology, social conflict, and the distribution of wealth. But to a greater extent than developing parties, mature parties play a causative role. For example, the members of the United States Congress express their own will—not only that of the social groups they represent—in their devotion to the seniority principle for committee assignments and the right of unlimited debate in the Senate. To cite only one more example, the internal dynamics of parties may dominate external pressures in such party functions as nominating candidates, establishing the style and tone of an election, and in the many varied informal ways of establishing cooperation (or making cooperation impossible) between the President's office and Capitol Hill.

The danger in analysis, nevertheless, is more that of overemphasizing than of slighting the independent or causative role of mature political parties. The most accurate picture, I think, is also a complicated one. Party structure and functions must be conceived as the consequence of many overlapping and reciprocal factors, among which are the internal or independent dynamics of the parties themselves. For example, provisions of the United States Constitution intended to prevent even a "majority faction" from completely controlling the national government also clearly militate against the tight organization of the contesting parties. The substantial control over elections given to the states; the electoral college system; the fixed terms for President, senators, and congressmen; and the composition of the Senate are all contained in constitutional provisions that produce party decentralization and disunity. Directly as well as through the function of parties these provisions also produce the situation, so puzzling to Europeans, in which congressional members of the President's own party (even legislative leaders of the party) often and as a matter of course refuse to support the chief executive's program. Thus to constitutional provisions can be traced one reason for the outstanding characteristic of American political parties, their decentralization and lack of unity or discipline. Yet the Constitution is not alone responsible for the character of the parties. For one thing, the simple absence of deeply divisive schisms with respect to basic economic issues in the American society allows the political parties to be only marginally unlike and permits members of one party to support the other on many issues. For another, many social groups find themselves advantaged by party disunity, and, therefore, disunity must be seen as a direct consequence of the rewards that it gives to significant social groups. The constitutional factors are pegs on which such groups support their opposition to more disciplined parties. Finally, there are forces within the parties that have a role in maintaining their undisciplined character. State and local party chiefs and individual members of Congress have important positions that they would not have in a more centralized party system. It is to their personal and professional advantage to maintain those positions. Disunited parties provide numerous routes of upward mobility that might be closed off in more tightly controlled parties. Issues of sociability, of personal ambition, of honest (and dishonest) graft, and of intraparty institutional stability are all involved. In the view of the party functionaries concerned these factors are inseparable from their convictions about the welfare of the nation, however narrow or exalted those convictions might be.

It would be easy to complicate further the picture of causation. The point, however, is clear: constitutional law, social structure, and internal party forces reciprocally affect each other and together fix the nature and functioning of the party system. In my view the role played by parties in the complex chain of causation is not the most important one although it is not negligible.

The recruitment of political leaders further illustrates the point. In the United States there is a bewildering number of paths to political status and leadership positions. For one thing, there are approximately 102,000 organized, tax-levying governments. (Some 50,000 are local school districts.) No one has ever counted the elected officers, including members of commissions or boards, that at any given moment staff the many American governments. It is not unlikely that their number ranges up to 900,000.

Not only the numbers are impressive. So is the variety of social groups whose members are offered a path of upward mobility through the political parties. In the big and medium-sized industrial cities politics has beckoned strongly to otherwise deprived members of ethnic groups. Italians, Poles, Irish, and Jews are prominent among the mayors and other leading officials of Boston, New York, Detroit, and Chicago. (Paul Screvane, a leading Democratic aspirant for the mayoralty of New York in 1965, is said to be a perfect candidate: his father is Italian, his mother Irish, and he speaks Yiddish fluently.) In these and other industrialized places the next wave of leadership will almost certainly come from the newest immigrants to the cities, the American Negro. But this will not occur without protest from the established leaders, whose ethnicity has been attenuated by the passing generations but whose electoral appeal to their own national or religious groups shows surprising tenacity.

Careers in politics for members of disadvantaged groups have been in many cases substitutes for menial jobs and careers in crime. In the earliest days of ethnic politics in the great cities crime and politics often went hand in hand.[31] With the passage of time and the respectability offered to political careerists, the connection between local politics and crime becomes more tenuous, though perhaps never completely broken. Ethnic leaders are increasingly able to exert influence in state and national affairs. They do so partly by using local offices as a point of leverage in nominating state and federal candidates and lobbying at the state and national legislatures. They also move on to posts in the state and national governments. Their names appear in the House of Representatives (among Chicago's twelve representatives to the 88th Congress, 1962-1964, were Congressmen O'Hara, Murphy, Derwinski, Kluczynski, O'Brien, Libonati, Rostenkowski, Finnegan, and Pucinski); in the Senate (for example, Ribicoff of Connecticut, Javits of New York, Pastore of Rhode Island); and in the Cabinet (Celebrezze, Health, Education and Welfare; R. F. Kennedy, Attorney General).

Outside the heavily industrialized areas the disadvantaged are also offered upward social mobility through politics. To cite a single example, Harry S. Truman, a bankrupt haberdasher, started on the road to the Senate and the presidency by serving as a county judge (an elected administrative, rather than a judicial, office). The more frequent route to the presidency has been through the office of governor, long the stronghold of rural politics and only now coming under the influence of the city-suburban vote as industrialization urbanizes state after state.

Even where state and local office does not lead to Washington the officeholders and party functionaries are often given a scope of activity, a sense of power, and a status that would otherwise be lacking in their lives. An observer can sense this even at the board meeting of the most rural county where farmers are part-time legislators for such matters as the disposition of funds for scraping dirt roads. He can also feel the dignity of office when mothers confer about a dangerous school crossing with a small-town mayor in his hardware shop.

[31] See Lincoln Steffens, *The Shame of the Cities*, 1904.

The opportunities offered disadvantaged groups are of course not denied to the advantaged. Wealth and social position are important in politics as they are in other aspects of life. The "silk stocking" mayor, the middle-class reform governor, and the millionaire senator or President are not rare phenomena. The principal effect of wealth in politics is undoubtedly the shortening of the time needed to achieve high office. The long apprenticeship in party ranks may be skipped, as when a leading industrialist (for example, Romney of Michigan) runs for the governor's office in his first try at politics, or as when a relatively young senator (Kennedy of Massachusetts) successfully campaigns for the Presidential nomination.

The party mechanism provides for this varied recruitment of leaders from a wide range of social classes at numerous points of the local-state-federal hierarchy and at positions ranging from precinct worker to presidency. Yet it would be a gross oversimplification to claim that the party system caused this sort of recruitment. For one thing, the way the parties attract new cadres of leaders is a consequence of their decentralized character. As we have seen, this decentralization is itself the consequence, among other things, of constitutional provisions and economic and social forces. Even more important, the antecedent determining factors for the easy access to positions of political leadership are the openness and relative classlessness of the American culture as a whole and the "rags to riches" ethic that is so common in that culture. The upward mobility offered by politics is only one aspect of the ease of social and professional advancement which characterizes the larger society.

As a final postcript it must be emphasized that everything I have said applies only to competing parties in a democratic state. Even then it does not apply to revolutionary parties. By definition they are not a part of the larger society but alienated from it and pledged to the destruction of existing political and social institutions. As for the one-party totalitarian states (in the Weiner-LaPalombara classification I would include in this category the "one-party authoritarian system" and perhaps also the "repressed party" situation), there seems to me to be no justification for considering them comparatively with the several sorts of competing party systems. Rather than existing to put alternatives before the citizens, the single party attempts to repress all competition. Rather than being separate from and less than the government itself, where only the single party exists state and party tend to become merged, one with the other, so that distinguishing their functions becomes difficult. Rather than relying on persuasion, the single party ultimately depends upon threats of violence and violence itself. Fear replaces persuasion for dissident groups.

The single party is of course a prime mover in remaking societies and even in attempting to alter the very personality of its citizens. This constitutes no refutation of my larger point that political parties are more consequence than cause. In my view a single party is an altogether different breed of animal from competing parties. Unless described in rarefied terms that have little political content, their intentions and functions are poles apart. There is, to be sure, semantic confusion in referring to both sets of circumstances as party systems. This should not confuse analysis. Rather it should inspire analysts to find a new label for the one-party system.[32]

[32] After writing the two paragraphs above, I have been cheered by the more elegant, lengthier, and more persuasive statement to the same general point made by Giovanni Sartori in Ch. 5, above, "European Political Parties: The Case of Polarized Pluralism."

Part IV:
Parties and Governmental Performance

CHAPTER 12

POLITICAL PARTIES AND POLICY-MAKING IN LATIN AMERICA

ROBERT E. SCOTT

THE SIGNING of the Punta del Este Charter in August 1961 appeared to promise that the Alliance for Progress would accomplish long overdue social and economic change in Latin America. Since that apparently auspicious beginning a record of failures, frustrations, and delays in nearly every country of the region offers eloquent testimony that other elements required for success in a rapid development program are lacking. One of the most vital of the missing elements relates to governmental decision making: most Latin American states do not have internal political structures appropriate for rationalizing speedy shifts in the society and economy.

The original Charter of the Alliance did not seem to take into account the fact that such political structures cannot be imposed from outside or their evolution accelerated simply by expenditure of funds. Nor is the emphasis on spot grants for fields of activity already proved effective by past performance, which President Johnson seems to prefer, likely to encourage emergence of balancing and integrating mechanisms.

The seriousness of their internal structural weakness is demonstrated by the evident difficulties encountered by most Latin American polities in their attempts to evolve a political process that permits prompt and adequate representation of new and developing interests produced by proliferating change. Almost anyone who has studied Latin American politics will agree that in Latin America, as society and economy become more complex, the policy-making process is characterized increasingly by confusion, immobilism, and a tendency to supply symbolic, affective decisions rather than positions of concrete and positive action. This pattern appears not only in long-range, fundamental, and all-encompassing policy questions but also in short-term, specific, and day-to-day matters of public administration. This essay will suggest that throughout Latin America the absence in most party systems of nationalizing and integrating political parties that can act as auxiliary political structures to bind together the operations of an expanding polity is one of the most important factors contributing to the problem of effective public policy formation.

I. The Operational Environment

Establishing the operational environment is particularly important in the case of the Latin American polities because most theoretical conceptualizations of the functioning of party systems have been presented by Europeans who think in terms of parliamentary government or by North Americans who think in terms of presidential government. In both cases the legislative agencies enjoy at least some recognized role in the policy process (even if only a veto), and the political parties almost invariably perform an essential function in organizing and integrating the legislators' actions. The importance of legislative participation is much less marked in Latin America. Despite constitutional precepts which carefully elucidate norms of separation of powers (or, in a very few polities, of parliamentary relationships), and despite a façade of observance of constitutional formalities in policy making, real political authority resides in the executive, who dominates a personalistic following that calls itself a political party. Although members of this group may—in fact usually do—control a majority in the legislature, they relate to and are dependent upon the executive. As a consequence they often do more to hamper and restrict the policy functions of the formal law-making agency than to strengthen them, as most modal prototypes of parties described in the theoretical literature are supposed to do.

Even more important, the political style of many Latin American countries places a larger share of public policy determination under the control of what might be called "private governments"—chambers of commerce and industry, bankers' associations, commercial agriculturalists' groups, even labor unions. Decisions concerning their particular interests may never reach the formal units of government or, if they do, may be presented as accomplished facts to be ratified rather than considered in terms of a general welfare. Where this occurs, the role of political parties as such is negligible, and all of the traditional panoply of nominations, elections, and congressional maneuvering by party blocs has little real significance for the policy-making process. Formulations which fail to take these factors into account invariably must distort the true role of Latin America's parties in the political decision-making process. This role differs considerably from what one finds in the less rapidly changing new nations of Asia and Africa.

Precisely because the Latin American countries are involved in fast-moving and basic change they are faced with the concerted pressures of development crises which call for the kind of unity and widely based representation in the political process that mass parties of national integration can offer. Evolution from a pattern of traditional values, subsistence agriculture, and primarily local orientation toward a system of more nearly universal values reflecting industrial technology, a national society, and an absorptive central government with increasingly specialized functions seems to evoke similar problems in every country. These crises—of foreign relations, legitimacy, integration, participation, and distribution—appear to affect every people as they pass through the process of nation building.

In those states which modernized in earlier periods the impact of the development crises was less devastating, perhaps because most major adjustment problems came singly and widely spaced. Crises in foreign relations, for example, generally occurred among countries at relatively similar stages of technical competence, so that smaller and weaker states had some possibility of defending themselves, particularly because in the days of crude communications logistics favored the defenders. Similarly, crises of governmental legitimacy were resolved by the gradual adaptation of traditionally accepted authority to the needs of a modern nation, while the crises of physical integration of the country and its people could be spread over centuries until common experience evoked a sense of national identity. This same common experience provided a nucleus of shared understandings around which the debate resulting from demands of new sectors of the populace for participation in the political process could be carried on safely. Moreover, the distribution crisis, during which government is pressed to allocate a larger share of the material benefits of industrialization to the masses, affected the earlier modernizing states only after the spread of technology and the increased productivity of their own citizens made a higher standard of living for the entire population feasible without ruining the established upper classes. Finally, the already developed nations offer a model for the populations of the emerging countries that greatly exacerbates the crises of legitimacy, integration, participation, and distribution through which the political systems of the late-developers must also pass.

Communications and some forms of transportation are among the easiest products of technology to export, but it is precisely a growing knowledge of the material and social-political advantages enjoyed by the masses in the more advanced countries of the world, coupled with a better understanding of the necessity for fuller utilization of all the physical and human resources available in the national territory, that leads a people to question the legitimacy of a political system which fails to satisfy their growing aspirations. That is, looking outward at the high standards of achievement found in the developed countries where they are an end product of a long and sustained process of growth, the emerging peoples seek to telescope the process by insisting that all of their demands be met simultaneously and immediately. When this happens the crises of development come all at once, overwhelming the economic and social systems as well as the political system, so that none of them find the time to reach stable rather than disintegrative solutions.

In a sense, this proliferation of development crises is artificial and unhealthy. Insofar as crises appear in less developed countries, such as most of those of Latin America, not as a natural result of social and economic change but artificially induced by observation of foreign models, the environmental conditions under which effective control devices might evolve do not obtain. The country is not sufficiently integrated physically or psychologically to attain optimum economic output or a national society; the masses who demand political participation and distribution of material benefits are not yet ready to assume the political responsibilities and the work discipline such rights entail; the traditional governing elites are still unable to accept the loss of social status and political influence that must accompany basic structural change. Either the existing government must attempt to dominate the situation, putting down the challenging elements which precipitate the crises, or there must appear some omnibus political structure which can seek to resolve certain of the development crises while holding others in abeyance.

In most parts of the world the political structure that has appeared in response to the crises of development in the late emerging nations has been the mass-based, popular-nationalizing political movement, what Sigmund Neumann termed "parties of integration." In states undergoing rapid social and economic change the operations of a system of integrating-nationalizing parties offer the best hope of closing the gap between the traditional and modern sectors of the population that must be bridged if the political system is to keep pace with the shifting needs of society and economy. These party operations can supply essential two-way interaction between the emerging traditionally oriented masses and the change-motivated elites.

An extra-legal mechanism such as the party system, with no formal and delimited government responsibilities, often is a more efficient means of translating the demands and desires of an unintegrated populace from particularistic and parochial instincts into universalistic and national norms than are constitutionally established, formal agencies of authority. But if this informal political structure is to perform successfully the dual function of integrating the masses into the nation and legitimatizing the activities of a central government for them, it must play a positive and meaningful role in the political decision-making process. Only a political party system that plugs into the critical core of national political power before it sends its interpretation of government policy out and down through an unofficial communications network can speak to the general citizenry in terms that make official actions not only meaningful and acceptable but also, simultaneously, legitimate and binding. If such organizations are not intimately related to public power, they cannot play a strong role in the solution of development crises.

A party system, of course, is by no means the only mechanism for selecting government officials, easing the transfer of power, aggregating interests, or formulating policy alternatives. Indeed in some political systems such varied functions may be handled largely by formal governmental structures. This could badly overload the political process, especially in systems where the legislature has very little real role in policy-making. In such cases the preponderance of decision-making authority falls upon already burdened executive agencies or into the hands of "private governments" with little or no responsibility to society as a whole.

This is the situation in Latin America.[1] For most countries of the region, Neumann's point that this is the century of parties of integration is not yet true, though the polities involved certainly face a need for such parties. The fact is that in nearly every country civilian or military leaders have tried to spark popular nationalizing movements. The *peronistas* in Argentina, Vargas' *estado novo* in Brazil, the so-

[1] The best (and very nearly the only) study of political change in Latin America is Gino Germani, *Politica y Sociedad en una Epoca de Transición*, Buenos Aires, 1962. The author does take into account some of the problems of conceptualizing during a period of rapid change.

called Aprista-type parties—APRA in Peru, Acción Democrática in Venezuela, Liberación Nacional in Costa Rica, MNR in Bolivia, among others—are examples of such attempts. But in virtually every case the attempt has proved ineffectual because, while some change exists to spark the appearance of development crises, the major motivation seems to be mimetic rather than internal evolution. Because this artificially induced condition produces premature pressures, the levels of physical, economic, and social development are not yet really propitious for production of shared values or a spirit of compromise. The masses are not ready to subsume themselves within a national system, and the elites are not willing to go all the way in accepting popular sovereignty.

The few political movements whose activities and goals more nearly resemble those of a popular integrating party—and they very nearly can be counted on the fingers of one hand—generally have suffered the abortive experience of being unable to operate effectively as part of their country's decision-making process on a continuous and peaceful basis. With the possible exception of Uruguay's urban parties and Mexico's PRI, these integrating, mass-based parties and their modernizing activities are unique within their nation's party system, and not eminently successful in their competition for influence and power with the traditional regional, class, and special interest-oriented political parties. The experience of these few and tentative movements in the direction of nation-building and popularizing of the political process suggests that the transition toward parties which can face up to and solve the crises of development will not take place as speedily in Latin America as it may in the ex-colonial states of Asia and Africa. The deeply ingrained patterns of political action that have jelled over a century and a half of independent national life cannot be amended overnight.

For this reason it is safer to discuss Latin America's parties in terms more suited to the environment. We shall speak of traditionally oriented and challenging parties, with the understanding that neither type is mass-based, national-integrating in operation. The few parties which do meet these criteria will be labeled as such.

II. Political Parties

The foregoing suggests that the function of Latin America's political party systems in the political development process is largely negative and scarcely accords with the more constructive aspects of party activity found in some other parts of the modern world. The reason for this condition is apparent to the student of the region's politics; both the political style and the nature of the dominant party types preclude easy evolution of the kind of political structures which could perform the sort of integrating and aggregating functions necessary in a complex political environment.[2]

Today, as traditionally, the political style of the area calls for a weak, even subservient legislature and a strong executive around whom the members of his political party form a personalistic following. Popular participation in politics is highly restricted and sporadic. Little real political party machinery exists at the local level, and what does exist is seldom related directly to a national party. Instead, a few local notables build their own personalistic organizations for each election, allying themselves with national leaders of so-called national parties for reasons of power or material advantage. The principal exception to this rule lies in some of the highly centralized, modernizing parties—the Apristas in Peru, Acción Democrática and COPEI in Venezuela, the Communists in various countries. These may be so rigidly controlled from the national capital that they cease to be very representative of local needs; in the long run this reduces their ability to act as mass-based, integrating parties.

The problem of attracting and retaining active support of the general citizenry is a continuing one. True universal suffrage is not really common, though the constitution may call for it. Even where literacy, sex, and property qualifications have been removed traditional apathy and difficulties of communication restrict the electorate. Moreover suffrage usually means literally voting at elections, with

[2] Few analytical studies of Latin American parties or party systems have been made by Latin Americans themselves. Two examples of what can be done, both from Argentina, are Torquato S. DiTella, "Monolithic Ideologies in Competitive Party Systems—The Latin American Case," a paper presented at the World Sociology Congress, Washington, D.C., September 1962, and a survey studying attitudes of Argentine citizens toward their political parties, the text of which was published by the Instituto de Desarrollo Economic Social during 1962 under the title *Motivación Electoral*. A short version of the latter appeared as "Partidos Políticos" in *200 Milliones*, Buenos Aires, Junio de 1963. The better general sources on Latin America's parties and party systems are found in North American texts. See, for example, Frank Brandenburg's chapter on "Political Parties and Elections" in H. E. Davis, ed., *Government and Politics in Latin America*, New York, 1958, and the chapters on "Political Parties" and "Political Dynamics" in K. M. Schmitt and D. D. Burks, *Evolution or Chaos: Dynamics of Latin American Government and Politics*, New York, 1963. Another interesting commentary is Russell H. Fitzgibbon's journal article, "The Party Potpourri in Latin America," *The Western Political Quarterly* (March 1957). Studies of parties in specific countries will be cited in appropriate places.

minimal sustained participation between campaigns. Political awareness and individual political participation in or outside a political party are rarer still.

In such an ambience the dominant party type is apt to be a carryover of old-style coteries of privileged notables who hide behind a façade of apparently democratic political structures and practices. In order to characterize the area's most common traditional political parties in gross terms, one might say that they are organized horizontally rather than vertically, with class, regional, and functional distinctions rather than integrating and cross-cutting memberships. Many are temporary rather than permanent, personalistic rather than principled, ideological in format but narrowly pragmatic in practice, because their leaders as well as their rank and file are particularistic rather than universalistic in viewpoint, a natural outgrowth of the lack of generally accepted values in the society. Party membership is a concomitant of group membership rather than of individual affiliation more often than is true in most Western-type advanced political systems. Not surprisingly, such parties tend to be monopolistic when they control government and inherently disloyal oppositionist when they do not.

Regardless of the fact that few if any of Latin America's political parties display every one of these characteristics, a sufficient number of parties share enough of them to hinder development of pluralistic democracy as it is known in the West, and to impede the evolution of representative, responsible party systems which can perform integrating and nationalizing political functions.

A preponderance of the most politically effective parties can be classed as traditionally oriented; as in the nineteenth century, they continue to represent the vested interests of small ruling cliques who act as "legislators" in the sense of making government policy although by no means all of the decision makers sit formally in a legal legislative body. The more complex political systems also have produced a number of challenging political parties which are attempting to alter the status quo and end the hegemony of the traditional parties. To date, most of these challengers have not been very successful, but they continue to appear because the inability of the ongoing political system to absorb new interests gives their members little alternative.

The participation and distribution crises have caught the members of the traditional ruling parties unprepared psychologically and organizationally. They are unwilling, perhaps even unable emotionally, to share political power and material wealth with the emergent masses, both because such sharing means a drastic shift in their long-established dominant political roles and because conceivably it could mean loss of their economic power. The traditional parties have failed to expand their strength by broadening their goals to attract a greater number of adherents in the national capital; neither have they modernized in the sense of building effective local organizations throughout the country which could socialize emerging citizens as well as transmit local needs to the center. In the face of recalcitrant refusal to allow them easy access to the existing upper-class and national capital-oriented parties, the awakening but unintegrated masses have begun to organize their own challenging parties based on regional, class, and other particularistic values. These are not necessarily national-izing-integrating parties because the same conditions which preclude evolution of such functions for the traditional parties are at work on the challenging movements.

Unfortunately, the majority of traditional ruling parties and their leaders have reacted to the challenging parties and the crises which produced them in the one way that cannot resolve the problem—by extreme solutions, repression and ignoring the emerging interests. Instead of facing the situation, recognizing and accepting the need for compromise and adjustment, and changing both the operations and the structures of their parties to incorporate both the newly aware individuals and the interests they represent, the traditional leaders tend to reinforce their historic positions, to try to freeze the status quo. This forces the challengers into equally extreme activities, into alienation from the existing political system and, ultimately, into anomic demonstrations and physical retaliation.

In short, the political party systems operating in most Latin American countries today not only fail to resolve the crises of rapid change but actually work to aggravate these crises. Because the traditional-type political parties which dominate the party systems relate to particularistic and specialized interests, competition among them, or between them and challenging parties, builds barriers to fusion and inhibits the inculcation of generalizing norms which reflect the ideal goals of the nation-state. Instead of providing an infra-structure that could assist a smooth flow of political activity, such parties block the upward and downward flow of communications and interfere with easy interaction among regional, class, and functional interest groups.

Because traditional parties represent established positions and vested interests, they discourage political action on the part of the awakening citizen who is just becoming aware of the nation and its government and beginning to consider the role they could play in his life. They therefore interrupt the orderly evolution of patterns of political action which could socialize the individual into a national society, economy, and polity. In so doing the traditional parties deprive the average Latin American of the opportunity to develop a sense of personal identity within the changing environment that might strengthen his role as a competent and competitive participant in the political process, and at the same time they inhibit the polity from developing the sense of national identity that could turn it into a nation in the fullest sense of the word.

HISTORICAL EVOLUTION

A short review of the historical evolution of Latin America's political parties may help explain why the party systems have adopted the particular action patterns they follow. For most countries the story begins some 150 years ago with independence from Spain, but the pattern is not dissimilar for such later arrivals in the world community as Brazil, Panama, and Cuba. Almost immediately upon separation from the metropolitan state political factions reflecting the interests of the great landowners, the military, and the church developed, but the shared values of the upper class precluded open breaks. Instead, the political movements called parties generally were personalistic followings of leading *políticos*. Somewhat later, new groups began to appear, a "service" middle sector aping the ruling class— upward mobile lawyers, physicians, and other professionals, urban intellectuals, small commercial leaders, and still later, incipient industrialists. As the emerging elements began to challenge the established power factors, the political competitors tended to dichotomize into what usually but not universally were known as the Conservative party and the Liberal party. As "new men," the members of the latter attacked the position and the privileges of the incumbent authorities, vocalizing their ambitions in anti-clericalism, anti-militarism, and often in demands for stronger central government which could control the virtually independent landowners. Much of Latin America's political history of the nineteenth century centers on the bitter power struggle between these groups.

By the beginning of the present century a *modus vivendi* had been worked out between these contenders for political control, although for personal and material reasons their heirs frequently continued to oppose each other in elections. In a few cases the Liberals managed to gain political access only by resorting to physical force; in most they obtained entry into effective political life by means of increased economic influence; in all they formed a working alliance with their former opponents to establish a cooperating (if not monolithic) ruling class. This was possible because over the years the Liberals had become socialized into the value system of the landed aristocracy and joined it by acquiring land as a status symbol whenever possible. Equally important, the gradual expansion of the economy, as commercial agriculture, mining, and foreign commerce developed, permitted the challenging Liberals to penetrate the political process without ruining the older, established families.

The new coalition, whether it consisted of a single political organization, dual Liberal and Conservative parties, or a proliferation of personalistic and/or regional factions within the ruling class, represented a monopolistic control over politics by a tiny politically aware and economically dominant portion of the population. It still does in at least eleven of the twenty Latin American countries, although in most of them challenging interests have formed political movements and parties in hopes of attaining access to the political process. Their success has varied, depending on their own size, strength, and organization and on the intransigence of attitude that marks the ruling class. A majority of these countries, but not all, are among the least advanced in the region, socially, economically, and politically.

These eleven countries, in which the dominant traditional parties remain undaunted if not unchallenged, have begun to feel some pressures for broader political participation, but the demand has not yet reached the proportion of a continuing crisis.[3] They can be divided into two very rough categories: those polities in which challenging parties have been unable to make much headway, and those in which the out groups are beginning to make themselves felt politically and,

[3] The parties of some but not all of these countries have been studied. On Central American parties, for example, see Charles W. Anderson, "Politics and Development Policy in Central America," *Midwest Journal of Political Science* (November 1961), and "Central American Political Parties: A Functional Approach," *The Western Political Quarterly* (March 1962). For Colombia, see Pat M. Holt, "Constitutional Development in Colombia," a paper prepared for delivery at the convention of the American Political Science Association, New York, September 1963.

in a very few cases, even have managed to capture the government temporarily, only to lose it to better organized, economically powerful and/or army supported traditionals.

In the first category are such diverse states as Colombia, with its constitutional "arrangement" that divides all elective offices between Liberals and Conservatives, virtually ignoring a few challenging movements, and the Dominican Republic, which has turned full circle from a personalist single-party dictatorship to a reasonably open multiparty system and back to a military-dominated regime that spoke of multiparty politics and most recently to revolution and chaos. One also encounters states such as Paraguay and Nicaragua, in which the free interplay of parties long has been restricted in favor of the personalistic organization of a representative of the established power clique. Finally, one can list Ecuador, Honduras, and Panama, where infighting among the numerous factions of the traditional ruling group periodically is damped down by intervention of the military.

In the second category, where the traditional parties have felt some challenge, are countries like Guatemala, where the short-lived and radical Arbenz regime accomplished little more than to alert the traditional parties to the dangers change might pose to the vested interests they represent, or Haiti, where the attempt of a successful challenging party to popularize government has degenerated into near chaos and the rigged plebiscite that named François Duvalier lifetime president. One also finds here El Salvador and Peru, in which political movements purporting to represent a change from past aristocratic-oligarchic control have taken power, but too recently to demonstrate whether they can indeed break the domination of long-entrenched traditional power factions.

In probably all of these eleven countries in which traditional party patterns still predominate one feels that the crisis of participation is imminent, as is that of material distribution, but that the crises of political legitimacy and integration are not yet resolved. In the face of mounting pressures these states face a problem of inflexibility on the part of the traditional rulers that must lead inexorably and ultimately to bloody and basic revolution such as occurred in Mexico and later in Bolivia and Cuba, or to the less drastic but also less effective evolutionary reform movements that characterize Venezuela and Costa Rica, if effective general participation in national political life is to be achieved and a sense of national identity is to develop. But even such drastic means of inducing change in the established patterns of political authority does not always produce political structures which can help resolve the crises of development.

Of these last five states, only Mexico has been able to develop a reasonably representative, mass-based political party, the PRI, which though firmly dominant provides both stability and a certain degree of access to the political process for most emerging interests.[4] Venezuela's Acción Democrática party has sought to do the same but has been unable to compromise the divergent interests of the urban population in Caracas with those of its rural supporters, leaving the party vulnerable to the attacks of the openly disloyal political movements of both right and left.[5]

Cuba, as the world knows, has been able to promote political change only at the price of driving out large numbers of the traditionally oriented but technically competent portions of its citizenry and by enforcing a kind of *fidelista* legitimacy upon the remainder of the population through the activities of a monopolistic and authoritarian (but not yet totalitarian) party.

Whether or not Castro's party can resolve the legitimacy and national integration crises in light of continuing attacks from the Cuban refugees, it continues to be plagued with an acute crisis of distribution that results from incorporation of large numbers of previously isolated rural Cubans into the national consumption process just as the island's industrial and commercial agricultural production are breaking down. As of this writing, the system has managed to hold together, but sooner or later the crisis of political participation will have to be faced, and this may overload the shaky political machinery. This is particularly so because Cuba has been unable to solve the development crisis resulting from foreign relations. One of the principal factors leading to the downfall of the traditional regime was its inability to handle the other crises of change because of United States pressures; in another sense the same is true today, with Cuba's position further complicated by the addition of Soviet pressures.

[4] For Mexico's party development, see Frank Brandenburg, "Mexico: An Experiment in One-Party Democracy," unpublished Ph.D. thesis, University of Pennsylvania, 1955, and Robert E. Scott, *Mexican Government in Transition*, Urbana: University of Illinois Press, 1959. Brandenburg's more recent *The Making of Modern Mexico*, New York, 1964 plays down the role of the PRI.

[5] On Venezuela's parties, see Stanley J. Serxner, *Acción Democrática of Venezuela: Its Origin and Development*, Gainesville, 1959, Harry Kantor, "The Development of Acción Democrática de Venezuela," *Journal of Inter-American Affairs* (April 1959), and John D. Martz, *Acción Democrática: Evolution of a Modern Political Party in Venezuela*, Princeton, 1966.

In Bolivia the tenuous alliance between agrarian and mining workers that provided the nucleus for a popularly based MNR broke down, leaving the nationalizing political structure vulnerable to the undermining activities of the unreconciled older ruling groups and the uncompromising radical left. When neither accepted the 1964 re-election of Víctor Paz Estenssoro, the military was forced to provide stabilization by ousting the MNR and imposing one of its own leaders in political control. Even Costa Rica, where the crises of political legitimacy and integration as well as that of distribution are more nearly settled, has seen its nationalizing and popularizing movement—the National Liberation Party—lose two presidential elections to a more particularistic and traditional party, the last time early in 1966.

Brazil, for its part, offers an almost classic case study of the difficulties involved in trying to resolve the development crises with political parties which have been unable to make the transition from traditional and particularistic to modern:[6] President Vargas' *estado novo* of the thirties and forties supplied an important impetus toward national integration, but not of a sufficiently sustained nature to provide a viable sense of national identity or of the legitimacy of the political system as it now operates. Part of the problem was that Vargas really did not—could not—develop an abstract and pragmatic nationalizing political party; instead he organized a personalistic movement—a kind of "instant nationalism"—that offered the advantage of supplying a hard core of devoted followers to assist him in his attempts to resolve the development crises. Unfortunately, such a movement also presented disadvantages; its monopolistic attempts to impose the legitimacy of the modernizing *estado novo* created a number of influential and intransigent enemies of national development who continued to sabotage constructive change long after Vargas' suicide marked the declining influence of his particular version of a nationalizing-integrating auxiliary political structure.

Under these circumstances it is hardly surprising that former President João Goulart's Brazilian Labor party, which claims Vargas'

[6] Brazilian political parties have been discussed in Phyllis J. Peterson, "Brazilian Political Parties: Formation, Organization and Leadership, 1945-59," unpublished Ph.D. thesis, University of Michigan, 1962. See also R. H. Fitzgibbon, "Federalism and the Party System in Brazil," a paper prepared for delivery at the convention of the American Political Science Association, St. Louis, September 1961, and Leslie Lipson, "Challenges to Constitutional Government: Brazil," a paper prepared for delivery at the convention of the American Political Science Association, New York, September 1963.

political inheritance, failed to act effectively as a unifying and modernizing political structure. With the crises of political participation and material distribution fast approaching a climax, neither it nor the other Brazilian parties were much more than personalistic and regional political factions which could not perform the auxiliary political functions already discussed. The disruptions of change finally swamped the overloaded political system, practically forcing the authoritarian stabilization initiated by the military takeover of April 1964. It remains to be seen whether the new and artificially imposed two-party system—the government National Renovating Alliance and the tame opposition Brazilian Democratic Movement—can hold together through the 1966 elections, much less act effectively afterward as a nationalizing-integrating mechanism.

THE DILEMMA OF DEVELOPMENT

Perhaps the best way to point up the dilemma of evolutionary political development in the region is to consider the experience of three countries which saw the integration of a new type of citizen into the national political process. Early in this century, because of their essentially European-culture populations, relatively easily utilized natural resources, and other social and economic advantages, Argentina, Chile, and Uruguay developed a politically aware middle-class group that came to be known in Argentina and Chile as the Radical party.[7] This urban, white collar, bureaucratic, small industrialist, and shopkeeper movement differed from the nineteenth-century Liberals in that its members accepted middle-class status and did not pretend to be upper class. This new middle sector managed to seize enough political influence to capture a role in national politics, but once they had assured the position of the still tiny middle class the Radicals seemed uninterested in carrying popularization of the political process down to the masses. Instead, as political initiative passed to the upper middle class, its members appeared to identify their interests if not their way of life with the traditional ruling parties and to support continuation of the status quo. Here again the expansion of economic development made this limited opening

[7] See Robert Potash, "Argentine Political Parties, 1957-1958," *Journal of Inter-American Studies* (October 1959); Federico Gil, *Genesis and Modernization of Chilean Political Parties*, Gainesville, 1961; Roger S. Abbott, "The Role of Contemporary Political Parties in Chile," *American Political Science Review* (June 1951); Peter G. Snow, "The Radical Parties of Chile and Argentina," unpublished Ph.D. thesis, University of Virginia, 1963; and Philip B. Taylor, *Government and Politics of Uruguay*, New Orleans, 1962.

toward the middle sectors possible without too great a cost to the established power groups.

In these three countries this partial solution of the four development crises slightly broadened the membership of the ruling coalition, providing a certain amount of political stability for several decades, but the next great step toward popular and representative government proved difficult to take. In none of the countries where Radical-type parties gained access to the political process did the political reform extend much beyond the middle class. Intransigence on the part of the ruling factions, as well as lack of economic growth, have frustrated the next steps which might have incorporated the masses into national political life. In Uruguay most of the urban population benefited in the sense of winning a greater share in governmental output, such as social services; but the rural population benefited scarcely at all. This was the price paid the landowning faction for not opposing the reform movement. In Chile only the more effectively organized urban elements benefited. The city masses and the agricultural population were and to a large degree still are excluded from effective political participation and material advantages. Much the same situation obtained in Argentina until the Perón regime; now the traditional parties are attempting to relegate the newly emerging popular interests whose principal spokesman is the *Peronista* party to their previous apolitical role, hoping to return to the status quo ante Perón. In none of these countries or in any of the others in which the beginnings of a Radical-type movement have been felt has the reform movement led to nationalizing modern-style parties which are accepted as legitimate by the traditional political actors in the political system.

A priori, one might have teneted that inclusion of the middle sector in politics would have the effect of generalizing the goals of the traditional parties and forcing them into a more modern political mold. This did not happen because the next development crises arose before moderating and integrating bourgeois values could become deeply imbedded in the value systems of the new middle class and, in time, permeate the existing political parties. Moreover, the usual moderating middle-class attitudes were weakened by economic problems. The new middle sectors resulted from social changes wrought by economic development, including industrialization, but in Latin America such growth has been accompanied by a continuing process of inflation that erodes the standards of living of the very middle groups it spawns. Frustration, unrest, and uncertainty mark the attitudes of the very groups which in other circumstances might be expected to provide a nucleus of support for constitutional legitimacy and constructive nation building, including absorption of the lower classes into national political life. For this reason the middle sectors which might spark compromising, integrating, and stabilizing political parties instead provide leadership for extremist movements to the right and left and for authoritarian stabilizing regimes. Only time can demonstrate whether this is a transitional pattern or a more permanent one.

To be sure, in the give-and-take of politics these three countries and a few other of the more complex semi-industrialized polities have seen a tenuous and usually temporary alliance between middle-class politicians and organized labor, with the former supplying leadership and the latter numbers in their disputes with the economically stronger and politically more aware, if much smaller, ruling clique. But this has not produced parties of national integration. Labor generally is more interested in improving its own position than in altering the nature of the political parties to assure representation of the lower classes, either among the unorganized urban masses or in the rural hinterland. In this sense much of labor's political activity falls directly into the pattern of the traditional political parties.

Significantly, neither organized labor nor the labor-oriented parties have become a fully accepted part of the political process. Even for the Radicals this could prove too expensive and politically too dangerous. As John Johnson has pointed up, the alliance between the middle-class reform parties and labor grew up when industry was small and frequently foreign controlled.[8] The middle sectors today find that a larger labor movement, earning somewhat more than previously and often employed by native entrepreneurs, is an expensive source of popular political support. As a consequence some traditional leaders at least are turning to unorganized city masses and even to the rural population to strengthen their political position vis-à-vis the competitive traditional parties.

As the Argentines discovered with Perón's *descamisados*, however, not only labor but unorganized populations, once awakened politically, can precipitate crises of participation and distribution. The one-time pattern of extremely slow evolution of political parties as they

[8] See John J. Johnson, *Political Change in Latin America: The Emergence of the Middle Sectors*, Stanford: Stanford University Press, 1958, *passim*.

resolved minor versions of the participation and distribution crises by absorbing small segments of the population more or less in proportion to the expanding economy of the nation no longer is operable. No longer can individuals be held outside of the political process until they are socialized into its traditional patterns. In virtually every Latin American country economic and social development has brought with it a rapidly snowballing political awareness in portions of the general population. The desirability of material improvement and the first glimmerings of the possibility of utilizing political action to achieve this goal bring citizens into the political arena infinitely more quickly than the economy can expand to absorb them, or than the traditionally political parties can politicize them.

For all of this ferment, one cannot assume that the challenging political parties which emerge from this situation necessarily represent modern, integrating, and nationalizing political structures. The history of Latin America's political parties suggests that there is little direct or permanent correlation between challenging parties and national development goals. The experience of the few popular integrating movements which have emerged suggests why this is the case.

MASS-BASED MODERNIZING PARTIES

Historically Latin America's traditional parties have acted and spoken as though they were national parties seeking members throughout the country and from all ranks of society. In practice such parties have been particularistic, localistic, and more than a little unwilling to set up a grass-root organization that could reach out into the countryside or down into the general populace. If the masses are taken into account by the political elites, it is more in a tutelary or controlling sense than through socialization of parochially oriented locals into the nation via participation in the political process. With this pattern of organization, the traditional parties have been unable to develop any broadly-based and popular source of power that might provide them with a strong or independent role in policy making and implementation. This is particularly true as regards policy situations relating to the crises of development, which almost inevitably involve society- or economy-wide problems.

On the policy-formation side the traditional parties at best share authority with functional-interest associations which at times act like private governments, with the civil bureaucracy, and all too frequently with the military, and with a chief executive whose principal influence is not always dependent upon his political party; most of these appear to have more voice in deciding policy than the constitutionally established legislature. At worst the traditional parties may be excluded completely from participation in policy formation for longer or shorter periods as a result of a military embargo on partisan political activity.

On the policy-implementation side the record is even worse. Because carrying out national policy on a general basis is conditional upon both an organization that can reach large numbers of persons throughout the country and upon the ability to communicate meaningfully with those persons, a system of particularistic and regional political parties must cede this responsibility to other governmental and political structures whose breadth and depth of organization are better suited to the function.

The few Latin American political parties which have played any real role in the public-policy process are those which have attempted (no matter how inadequately) to serve as a bridge between the unintegrated masses and national political life. Such a bridge permits two-way traffic, transmitting and interpreting highly specialized parochial values and felt needs into modern policy alternatives and at the same time translating universalistic governmental decisions applicable to the whole polity into action programs meaningful to isolated traditionals. Performing this kind of function can capture a significant role in the policy process for an informal political structure such as a party.

Not entirely unexpectedly, the Latin American political environment has restricted the number of nationalizing-integrating parties which have appeared and limited the success of most which do exist. One reason for this is that by definition such parties must act as though they were functioning in a national state when in reality they are not. In order to impose common values or at least common action patterns on government and polity the few mass-based (or more correctly mass-oriented) parties that have managed to capture control of government or win acceptance as legitimate contenders in the political process—in Mexico, Bolivia, Cuba, Venezuela, or the like—of necessity often must be semi-monopolistic or even authoritarian.

Surrounded by traditional parties which make the most of the deeply incised divisions which characterize the underdeveloped world, and attempting to incorporate peoples who are congenitally mistrustful of new ideas, the nationalizing party may have little choice. In order to survive to accomplish its nation building goal the party may be forced to dominate a disloyal opposition even though the political style requires a façade of a competitive party system and free elections. And it may find that it operates more as a bureaucratic administrator, acting upon the populace than as a socializer encouraging the citizenry to participate directly and individually in the national political process.

The compelling factor is that a majority of Latin America's societies simply are not sufficiently integrated socially, economically, or politically to support political parties that cut across regional, cultural, or social class lines. It is hard indeed to develop a political program that meets the needs of highly diverse peoples, and still more difficult to sustain it in practice, particularly when the party must operate in competition with more homogeneous groups that have a vested interest in protecting their hegemony over the political process. For that matter, political exigencies may result in competing nationalizing movements very nearly canceling each other out.

The Peruvian experience is a case in point. Despite its long existence and its intensely nationalizing emphasis based on *indiginismo*, the Aprista party has never been able to extend its influence effectively throughout all regions of the country. Neither has it penetrated very deeply into the *mestizo* lower class, much less the Indians, who are scarcely aware of Peru as a legal entity. Its real support lies with some, not all, of the lower middle class in northern Peru and in Lima-Callao. Nonetheless it remains the country's largest single political party and by far the best organized down to the village level in the regions of its strength. Over the years, however, both individuals and interest-oriented sections of the party have defected. Some persons left because the older Aprista leaders, who succumbed in spite of themselves to the need for personalistic control over the rank and file, could not make room for new faces in the party hierarchy; others separated because the party doctrine could not accommodate all sectors of opinion among the opponents to the entrenched governing oligarchy.

The incumbent president of Peru, Fernando Belaunde Terry, is a former Aprista who broke off from the parent nationalizing movement to form his own nationalizing-integrating party, but one with an even clearer pattern of personalistic leadership. In so doing he not only broke into the ranks of Apristas for some of his following but also accepted the campaign support of yet another specialized nationalizing movement, the Christian Democrats, who may or may not be able to continue working with his administration until the next election.

The fact is that in Peru those elements which seek to alter the entrenched political monopoly of the oligarchy do not have enough in common to work as one movement or even to cooperate for very long. This situation leaves the policy-making and implementing process in the hands of the traditional power elements almost by default. Because the competing national-integrating factions disperse their energies in internecine battling, they fail to perform effectively the necessary function of politicizing their potential followers, aggregating the populace's views and channeling their demands into the policy-making mechanism. No more can they transmit and sell national policy decisions to the whole citizenry to enhance the unity of the country by making its governmental activities more comprehensible. Each nationalizing party seeks to sabotage the work of the others, leaving the balance of political power in the hands of the traditional, particularistic parties.

Somewhat the same pattern can be traced among the mass-oriented parties which have enjoyed a slightly greater degree of success. Venezuela's Acción Democrática has been unable to find a common denominator between the urban masses and its rural supporters. The party also finds a potential competitor in another popular nationalizing party, the Christian Socialist-leaning COPEI party. Although the two have acted in temporary coalition to offset right traditionals and left extremists, during the December 1963 presidential elections the COPEI increased its popular support mainly at the expense of Acción Democrática, and it became increasingly evident during 1964 that the two parties were having difficulty working out acceptable divisions of appointive offices at the local level. By the end of that year, with the addition of two small traditional parties to the A.D. coalition, COPEI went into semi-opposition.

A much more obvious split occurred in Bolivia during 1964 because the MNR has been unable to penetrate all of the popular elements which it sought to integrate into the national scene. The party suffered a serious division within its ranks with the defection of Vice President Juan Lechin and his miners over his personalistic desire to be the MNR's presidential candidate for the 1964 election. When Víctor Paz Estenssoro was elected, Lechin began to work with the rightist traditional opposition to undermine his regime leading ultimately to a military take-over of the government.

Under such circumstances the effectiveness of the nationalizing government parties is greatly diminished, and their ability to influence the decision-making process in order to speed up national integration or to maximize economic growth in order to resolve the distribution crisis is weakened dangerously. Worse yet, the pattern of disintegration is likely to grow as the development crises exert more and more pressure on the political systems of the region. A vicious circle could be the consequence, with each new defection weakening the ability of a nationalizing party to reflect the needs of the entire populace as it hammers out policy alternatives. This in turn would cut back on its outlets for transmitting and legitimatizing government policy decisions to the general citizenry, which again could lead to new defections. Little wonder then that the nationalizing party that controls a government is tempted to monopolize the political process in practice if not in outward forms.

THE MEXICAN EXPERIENCE

It is no coincidence that the country in Latin America that has had the greatest degree of success in facing up to and resolving the crises of quick development has been governed by a mass-oriented nationalizing party in uninterrupted, semi-monopolistic control for longer than any other party in the region. For over thirty years Mexico's Revolutionary party, the PRI, has worked diligently to penetrate and politicize the general population. Probably it is fair to say that during this time, given the multiplicity of problems and the speed with which change took place, the PRI has done more than any other party in Latin America to assist government in providing the physical means and the social-economic environment to encourage national integration and resolution of the crises of development.

Though much remains to be done, the Revolutionary party has sought to integrate Mexico through the expansion of communications, the building of schools, the development of a strong interdependent internal economy. At the same time, over the three decades it has imposed a sense of legitimacy for the modernizing goals of the government until few politically aware Mexicans fail to accept these norms. As it dealt with these tasks, the PRI also assisted the Revolutionary regime to handle (if not fully solve) the distribution crisis, expanding the economy and improving the lot of the vast majority of citizens. It also participated in the partial resolution of the political-participation crisis, encouraging emerging elements to enter the political process collectively as they became politically conscious. Some of these groups have affiliated formally with one of the PRI's three sectors—Agrarian, Labor, or Popular; others have not but operate within the same political frame of reference through their relationship with and dependence on the presidency and the government bureaucracy.

In terms of the policy process the PRI plays a markedly different role from most—probably from all—other parties in Latin America. During the years since its formation the Revolutionary party has taken upon itself principal responsibility both for imbuing the government bureaucracy with modernizing values and for infusing the Mexican populace with nationalizing, integrating norms. In doing so the party has acted as the transmission belt between the two, converting parochial, particularistic desires into policy alternatives for policy formation and carrying the decisions of government to the people throughout the country. To do so the PRI has created a kind of Mexican "establishment" of technical and administrative experts who are moved from party-controlled elective positions to appointive governmental posts and even into ostensibly private organizations as the need arises.

In spite of these admittedly great achievements, personal observation, reinforced strongly by other investigation,[9] suggests that even the long and fruitful operation of a nationalizing party offers no panaceas. Mexico still faces a multitude of problems before completing the difficult transition to a fully integrated nation state. If the PRI is a modernizing and nationalizing party it also is semi-monopolistic in the tradition of other Latin American political party systems. If pluralistic democracy as well as representative government and maximum individual political participation are ideal goals of political development, the semi-corporative organization of the "official party" and the domination of its satellites among the functional interest associations are barriers to free interplay among the forces that operate in the society and economy.

With all that the Revolutionary party has done to integrate the individual Mexican into national life, precious few have achieved the sense of personal identity required before a widespread sense of national identity can evolve. Many Mexicans still are suspicious of and some alienated from the present political system, and most are con-

[9] See, for example, Gabriel A. Almond and Sidney Verba, *The Civic Culture*, Princeton: Princeton University Press, 1963.

fused or uncertain about their personal political competence. Study of popular attitudes toward both government and PRI demonstrates that the average Mexican finds it very difficult to conceive of himself as an effective participant in political action and still harder really to act. Individual membership in the Revolutionary party is minimal despite efforts to increase it during recent years.[10]

The reason for a lag between development of the physical and material attributes of modernization and the mental cast of many Mexicans may lie in the fact that the relationship of individuals to the functional interest groups which make up the PRI does not meet the psychological needs of persons involved in quick transition from parochial and rural life to more nearly universalistic and urban conditions. Faced with the insecurity of speedy change, such persons need to be able to identify with leaders they feel can be trusted (*hombres de confianza*). This is the reason that every six years the official party's presidential candidate is given such an overwhelming campaign build-up although everyone knows that his nomination is tantamount to victory over the nominal opposition candidates. The president provides a personalistic link between the citizen who still is seeking his identity in a strange new world and an impersonal and inadequately understood political system. Related to this is the fact that no matter how substantive and operational governmental programs may be, an important emphasis of the related publicity is affective or symbolic in nature, so as to immerse the average Mexican into the mainstream of national life as painlessly as possible.

This is not to suggest that no Mexicans have become active participants in the political process or that nearly none share in the policy-making function. A small but ever expanding portion of the population has made the transition into effective national life, with a constructive sense of both personal and national identity. Neither does it suggest that most government output is framed to afford emotional rather then empirical satisfaction; of all the countries in Latin America Mexico seems to have produced the highest portion of rationally based governmental action programs.

The Mexican experience suggests that many of the divisive factors which underlie Mexico's social and economic systems and which have so profound an impact upon the evolving political system may have

---

[10] See Robert E. Scott, "Mexico: The Established Revolution," in Lucian W. Pye and Sidney Verba, eds., *Political Culture and Political Development*, Princeton: Princeton University Press, 1965.

their counterparts throughout the rest of Latin America. I submit that this is the case and point out that if such devices as an official party, a personalistic president, and large doses of affective propaganda are required in a country where the PRI has labored for over three decades to socialize the citizens to national politics, the need must be infinitely more pressing in those states where no nationalizing-integrating party has performed its functions on a sustained basis.

THE NATIONALIZING PARTY

The historic environment in Latin America is not conducive to widely based individual participation in policy making that could perform the function of rationalizing the dislocations which accompany accelerated change. Given the Iberian tradition of strong governmental intervention in all aspects of social, economic, and political life, as long as authority remained in the hands of a tiny ruling elite that did not concern itself with development this did not constitute a problem. Once the factors which had to be considered in decision making became too complex for the major families to settle over the dinner table, however, a new system had to be evolved. The government's police power over the individual continued, and its responsibility in supplying public services expanded; but in certain spheres of activity policy making was left tacitly to private functional interest associations, with little or no participation by government agencies to protect the general welfare or to assure a degree of balanced growth. Nor did the particularistic and unrepresentative traditional political parties provide the kind of national common denominator needed to counteract this highly specialized influence.

Despite the façade of legislative hearings, administrative controls, and well-publicized formal electoral activities of political parties, to a large degree this situation continues to obtain in most countries today. Proponents of such interests as commercial agriculture, commerce, industry, organized labor, the Church, and of course the military are in many aspects of their activities nearly independent of government, leaving them little opportunity to learn the discipline of political compromise or the responsibility of subordinating private advantage to a national welfare. They tend to view all opposition as illegitimate, all controls for a general interest as unacceptable, because they have not yet accepted the concept of universal values which might limit their freedom of action.

As a corollary to this set of attitudes, when any faction captures control of government and the political process, it attempts to turn the functional-interest groups into captive "protective associations," as Pye has termed them.[11] This again practically eliminates the role of the political party as an intervening aggregating structure unless the ruling faction so dominates the situation that party and government are nearly identical, as in the case of Mexico. Especially when dealing with highly particularistic parties which provide no mechanism for compromise and adjustment in policy formation, the very nature of their relationship with the government forces the protective associations to concentrate their political activities on the output side of the decision-making process, attempting to influence the manner in which government applies regulations to their particular operation in order to avoid the inconvenience of having public policy apply unmitigatedly to it. In so doing the interest associations preempt the attention of their incompletely politicized members, sidetracking individuals from participating in general political affairs as party members and encouraging them to think primarily in terms of the specific goals of the association.

Although this pattern of relationships apparently inhibits development of independent voluntary associations for whose support competitive political parties can bid, much the opposite is true. On the face of it, each political movement seeks to organize its own captive functional associations, but these are merely hollow shells unless the interests involved are truly dependent. Because traditional parties have no broad base of individual support they have little leverage in their dealings with the specialized groups; so it is much more expedient for such parties to support affective policies which exercise minimal influence over the interests of the group, leaving it to act as a private government in its own field.

Again as a corollary, the traditional party-interest association relationship weakens the party's ability to reach down to and penetrate its own membership in universalistic terms because a high proportion of members belong on a group rather than an individual basis; like some Gresham's law of politics, the specialized goals of the group drive out the generalizing goals of the party. Equally important, the tendency to structure parties around groups interferes with the party's attempts to recruit and socialize individuals from the masses because the group leadership is not anxious to bring in large numbers of new

[11] Lucian W. Pye, *Politics, Personality and Nation-Building*, New Haven: Yale University Press, 1962.

members who do not share their particular goals, and the potential individual members are unwilling to accept special interest-oriented programs which do not meet their personal interests.

Despite these difficulties, some political structure must perform the integrating and rationalizing functions. As the pressures of development multiply, the nationalizing party has sprung into being as the structure best suited to the task. Taking into account the clear evidence that existing nationalizing parties cannot pass miracles and that the impediments to a smooth transition toward the nation-state take the form of certain political values and patterns of action which are component parts of the operational political system, the fact remains that some means of easing and, hopefully, ultimately solving the recurring crises must be found. No other political structure, constitutional or extra-constitutional, has demonstrated sufficient success in this matter to displace the nationalizing party from its task. When one considers the differences of organization and function encountered among the party systems of the twenty Latin American republics, however, it is extremely difficult to forecast how speedily any given political system will adopt this solution for its problems, much less how successful it will be.

III. Latin American Party Systems

In light of the relatively restricted role played by individual parties, one might legitimately question whether analysis of party systems is likely to be as helpful in describing the decision-making process in Latin America as in some other world regions. Certainly plenty of evidence can be adduced to show that the function of the party system in most countries' political processes is considered by the Latins themselves as something less than indispensable. Nonetheless a short discussion of party systems may prove enlightening, both to underline the difficulties inherent in attempting to utilize concepts evolved to describe political phenomena under very different circumstances and to point up why Latin America's party systems have less influence over the political process than do their counterparts in many developed countries.

In view of the lack of integration throughout Latin America one would hardly expect many two-party systems and even less that they might act as representative and aggregative mechanisms in the manner of the classic British-United States prototypes. Only Uruguay and Colombia have dominant two-party systems, and in each case the principal parties are traditional in organization and outlook so that the dialogue between them is limited to a very restricted sphere of policy questions. In both countries challenging parties or movements representing dissatisfied interests are seeking access to the political process and soon may break into the charmed circle, by force if necessary. In a third country, Brazil, only time can tell whether the military government's attempt to impose a two-party system upon the traditional multiparty system will work. The remainder of the Latin American states have either single-party or multiparty systems, in a majority of cases shifting from one to the other as the influence of a given party rises or ebbs. As we have seen, the tendency toward monopolistic parties is deeply rooted in the mores of the political culture and based upon the imperatives of the political environment.

Perhaps it would be more accurate to speak of oligopoly rather than monopoly in the party system, for the political mores also call for the appearance of party competition and contested elections. Most governments try hard to preserve a semblance of opposition, preferably tame parties which will not disturb the status quo. In this connection George Blanksten coined the term "one and a half party" system. During the 1964 Mexican presidential campaign one might even have spoken of a "one and three eighths" party system, with the "one" representing the PRI, the "three" enumerating the opposition parties, and the "eighth" summing up the total opposition share of the presidential vote.

In any event, the nature of the functions performed in the political process changes markedly as a party system composed mainly of traditional parties shifts to a mixture of traditional and nationalizing parties, or is dominated by one or more national-integrating movements. Equally, the operation of one, two, or more parties in the party system affects the degree to which a particular type of party can influence the political process. The total permutations of type and number in a party system seems astronomical; in dealing with twenty systems, most of which are in a state of flux, the possibilities are endless. For that reason I retreat into my previous observation that proportionately Latin America's traditional party systems have had less positive influence than elsewhere and that with the exception of Mexico the modernizing parties have not really had a chance to demonstrate patterns of influence. For its part, the operations of Mexico's PRI have been analyzed so widely that this study is not the place to do so again.

The tendency for parties and party systems to shift functions makes conventional typologies based on stable political systems more deceptive than informative. As of this writing (1966), only six of the twenty party systems have been consistent enough over any length of time in the nature of their political function to fall into a single definite cell. The remainder tend to alternate between two categories, probably because power factors other than party activities themselves exercise a decisive influence over party function. The six more consistent party systems are found in countries where the pressures of change are not yet very compelling (Paraguay), where the crises have been weaker or partially resolved (Chile, Costa Rica, Uruguay), and where the party-government structures are strong enough to satisfy or to repress the demands of the populace (Mexico, Cuba). The other fourteen range from countries just beginning to feel the effects of fast-moving change to those deeply involved; they have in common a weakness in the political structures with which they attempt to face the crises of development.

Shifting our frame of reference from functions associated with the problems of development to somewhat more conventional power factors, and again inserting the caveat that Latin American party systems at best share their authority with other political structures, we can review the nature of the party systems of the various countries of the region. When one considers the strong emotional identification with democratic aspirations found throughout the region and the general weakness of communications with which to enforce a common dictate, it is not surprising that no one-party totalitarian system is found. Now that Generalissimo Trujillo has disappeared, only two one-party authoritarian systems exist, in Cuba and Paraguay. Mexico stands alone as a one-party pluralistic system of the "pragmatic-pluralistic" rather than the ideological monolithic type under the Coleman-Rosberg terminology. Uruguay, Costa Rica, and Chile's party systems are quite pure examples of the pluralistic-competitive variety, and all three seem to fit the subclassification "turnover systems," with the qualification which will be discussed below, as will the question of whether Latin American parties can easily be divided into ideological and pragmatic types.

The remainder of the party systems alternate between an intermittent repressed party system and a pluralistic-competitive system. In the fourteen countries included here the military (at times in conjunction with traditional power factors) establishes restrictive boundaries on freedom of party activity, usually in terms of prohibiting certain kinds of social and economic policies but sometimes going so far as to bar the seating of certain parties' elected candidates, as occurred with the Apristas in Peru and the *peronistas* in Argentina during 1962. On the other hand, military intervention may take the form of requiring political parties to observe the formal constitutional norms, or what the army leaders interpret as the spirit of the constitution, as it did in Brazil in 1945 when Vargas was ousted and ten years later when the seating of President-elect Kubitschek was assured. From time to time the military may prohibit party activity altogether, as has happened for longer or shorter periods of time in all these countries, frequently because the traditional, interest-oriented parties themselves refuse to observe norms that would make a system of civil government workable.

These suspensions suggest the low esteem in which political parties often are held; indeed they demonstrate only too graphically that the Latin American political process is not very dependent upon the auxiliary functions provided by the party system. Obviously the degree to which the military sets limits on the freedom of the party system to participate in policy formation and the frequency and duration of full military intervention in the political process depends upon a multitude of factors which affect each country differently. As a rule of thumb, the greater the amount of popular participation in political life and the more effective the role of the political party system in the governmental process, the less likelihood there is for interdiction. But this is simply another way of saying that the military is less impelled to step in if the civilian politicians are facing up to the problems of rapid change. As we have seen, in most cases they are not, so that often the military is forced to act to provide the authoritarian stabilization that can preserve a deteriorating situation. In recent years a much higher proportion of military take-overs have been of this sort than of the old fashioned *golpe de estado* in which one general replaced another as president of the republic. Whatever the source of military action, during the past decade every one of these fourteen countries has experienced some form of military intervention or the immediate threat of it. So have Cuba and Paraguay, where military force remains in control.

Nonetheless the Latin American political culture places a premium on elected civilian government and a certain amount of onus on military rule, which encourages a fairly quick return to civil government. This military solicitude has been enhanced recently by a growing recognition that easing the pressures of the development crises requires certain technical and political skills the army does not possess. Rather than face failure, the military returns authority to the civilian politicians, who can at least attempt to use the parties to organize public opinion, channel the demands of the most politically aware citizens to the center of political power, and transmit government decisions to the people. Generally after a political hiatus during which a military junta or so-called apolitical cabinet governs the civilian political parties accept a pluralistic-competitive system that observes the formal constitutional provisions, limited only by rules of acceptable policy enforced by the military through its potential veto power. This system gradually breaks down as party in-fighting and the pressures of change cause the participants in the party system to lose the respect for constitutional norms that was engendered by the extra-legal military rule. In time the military finds it necessary to provide authoritarian stabilization again, and the whole cycle begins anew.

In speaking of the pluralistic-competitive systems, however, we must recognize that they often are neither as pluralistic nor as competitive as the model suggests. We already know that the relationship of both traditional and nationalizing parties to voluntary associations in Latin America is very different from that in most Western party systems. In the Latin American systems either economic and social groups act independently of government as private governments, or the government dominates these forces by making them protective associations, leaving the political party little function in the transaction. This is hardly democratic pluralism in the normal sense of the term.

Much the same is true of competition, for where effective competition exists within a party system it is primarily among traditional parties representing the higher classes; even the challenging parties seldom represent any real attempt to bring the masses into the party system. Competition between traditional and nationalizing parties may take place of course, but unless the latter dominate the situation the struggle will be outside the operating party system.

At the level of functional interests, however, competition among parties can be intense. Because party strength depends so highly on group rather than individual support, a party's success in capturing control of a regime may mean life and death for its leaders and to some extent for the incumbent leaders of the voluntary associations as well. At an earlier date the need for success was less pressing because the most active participants in the game of politics had land and status, making them less vulnerable to government decisions. Today businessmen, industrialists, mining and oil operators, and the lawyers or other professional men who service these activities are much more dependent on political favor because they cannot count on government neutrality without it. Future competitiveness within the party systems will be made even more intense by the expansion of the development crises. Ever-growing demands upon government for social and economic benefits by the awakening masses whose political awareness and influence may develop far faster than the ability of the political structures to absorb or discipline them will force the parties in a bidding spree to capture these new resources of political power.

In this situation it is highly doubtful that a competitive party system made up of traditional parties will be able to provide the kind of fusion necessary to encourage development of a sense of national identity out of the conflicts of old and new values. Only nationalizing parties which really provide two-way communication between the center and the periphery, between the masses and the leaders, can perform this function. And even these can do it only if the traditional parties do not sabotage the effort and if the material conditions work out well—in short, if they have the gift of time.

Another conventional classification of party systems that needs special interpretation for the Latin American environment is the dichotomy between hegemonic (semi-permanent) and turnover types of pluralistic-competitive party systems. In nearly every one of the seventeen pure or intermittently competitive systems in which traditional parties predominate "party" changes take place quite regularly. But this does not result in basic policy shifts so much as in changes among the upper- and middle-class individuals who benefit from maximum government cooperation. A true turnover system presupposes broad popular participation in free elections, in a party system that recognizes the legitimacy of challenging parties. Unless these conditions obtain, one wonders whether changes in the government party really represent turnover or simply continued hegemony of the same ruling class and interests. The only real turnover in such a situation may result not from party competition but from the military intervention already discussed.

As regards the ideological-pragmatic dichotomy in competitive party systems, the lines in Latin America are blurred. Most political parties and movements—be they traditional or nationalizing—cloak themselves in statements of formal and universalistic ideologies. As we have seen, this may be a means of avoiding the specific policy commitments that could ruin a movement trying to attract highly particularistic persons. Or perhaps it is a recognition of the felt need of formerly isolated parochials in transition toward a more modern life to find a new frame of reference, a new and established set of relationships, to replace the lost sense of security that was provided by a traditional society that clearly delimited each individual's status. In operation, however, most Latin parties are personalistic and/or pragmatic in their approach to government, economics, and society, with ideology conveniently ignored or amended by exegesis that would make a Soviet revisionist of Lenin red with envy.

This is a special kind of pragmatism reflecting the limited and particularistic interests of the elite traditional party membership. Because these parties do not have roots in the masses, it is possible for their leaders to be as intransigent as they are. They can speak in universalistic ideological terms, appearing to translate the party's program into policy by enacting symbolic and affective government legislation, but in practice they refuse to compromise the interests of a select and particularistic membership because the party's position is not tempered by the necessity of satisfying a broad cross-section of the population.

IV. Party Systems and Policy-Making

As in most parts of the world, development has become an important symbol in Latin America. Not simply the dominant elite parties but also the political movements which represent the emerging masses seek change and look to government both for the impetus to change and for rationalization of it. In the case of the elite this represents a present ability to manipulate government, to cause the regime to act or, in some matters, not to act. In the case of the masses the private sector often is identified with the ruling clique and with foreign influence; so the challengers look to government to control the activities of the established social and economic forces and, simultaneously, to institute new patterns of action and production to satisfy growing popular demands.

In both cases, however, the present and potential leaders look on government, not on political parties, as the modernizing agency. The political style that plays down the role of the party system has crystallized over the decades so that neither decision making in general nor those aspects of the process relating to solution of the development crises are likely to be left to the operations of the political parties. Given the weaknesses of party organization and activity, there can be little hope that this attitude will change without major political upheaval.

For the most part the parties themselves have done little to strengthen their role. One scarcely can speak of effective participation in policy making by the party system when that system exercises hardly more than intermittent and negative influence. If personalistic and particularistic bickering and in-fighting among the traditional parties makes a shambles of the constitutional norms, annuls the meaning of elections, and inhibits the efficient operation of the legislature, policy initiative ultimately must fall from the damaged political structures into the hands of the executive or of private governments.

In Latin America the traditional parties do little to politicize the general population, to organize public opinion, to communicate, to aggregate and integrate, or to build a sense of national identity. Some of the challenging parties might attempt to perform a few of these nationalizing-integrating functions if it were not so difficult to break into the charmed circle of legitimate participation in the political process. As it is, only those nationalizing parties which capture and hold the government itself—in Mexico, Cuba, and a few countries, like Bolivia, where the permanency of their influence is less secure—become part of the political system. In fact, for practical purposes they become most of the political system, for the tendency of these parties too has been monopolistic, usually with the explanation that the progress of the Revolution, of reform, of nationalization—read "modernization" if you will—must not be sabotaged by a recalcitrant and reactionary opposition. But the very concept of party monopoly weakens the ability of the whole political system to face and resolve the crises of development.

Nonetheless in the search for progress the great majority of Latin American leaders, both traditionalists and modernizers, seek to avoid the disruptions they identify with competitive party politics and the participation of parties in policy making. Particularly as they begin to feel the dual pressures of the political participation and the material distribution crises, to paraphrase Weiner's observation on Indian politics, for the Latin *politico* the best politics of scarcity is a scarcity of politics.

As a consequence the response of Latin America's political systems to the demands imposed on government by increasing economic and social complexity has not been expansion of party responsibilities. Instead, the integrating and rationalizing functions have been pushed off on already over-burdened governmental structures which are not suitable to perform them. Throughout the region the growing need for structural differentiation to carry on ever more specific administrative duties has led to a proliferation of governmental agencies and multiplication of activities by existing structures. Adding the political responsibilities involved in handling the development crises cannot help but weaken the functional specificity of the government units. Apparently, however, the political leadership is willing to pay the price of inefficiency and ineffectual solution of both administrative and political problems as long as the power to act is retained by political structures over which it feels a degree of control.

Some of these acceptable agencies are non-governmental structures—interest associations ranging from such traditional power factors as agrarian societies representing large landholders and commercial export agriculture, chambers of commerce, bankers, and employers' associations to emergent forces such as labor unions, small shopkeepers groups, and peasant organizations—which relate to government as protective associations. Other acceptable political structures are the government agencies, usually the civil bureaucracy, both the traditional service agencies and the newer multifunctional ones like the national planning commissions and development banks, but sometimes the military extends its activities into administration. The one kind of political structure that could perform these general integrating and politicizing functions without loss of administrative efficiency—the nationalizing political party—has found it extremely difficult in the Latin American environment to gain and hold responsibility for these functions. Nor have the traditional parties done much better in capturing influence over policy.

The real consequence of this short-range solution to development problems is that constructive and consistent adjustment to political change is inhibited in the long run. Unquestionably the multifold dislocations of social and economic development require prompt and positive rationalization, and harassed political leaders must seek the answers to their problems where they can—in action by government units, by private organizations, or wherever else. Certainly the need for national integration and the building of a sense of national identity cannot wait until political parties get around to organizing themselves to do the job. But the constant allocation of nation-building tasks to government agencies which have other functionally specific responsibilities and to non-governmental structures which by their very existence represent specialized and particularistic interests makes the transition to a modern political system doubly difficult. Not only is political policy making frozen into its traditional forms, but the political parties which might thaw it out are further impeded from breaking their historic action patterns to assume the auxiliary political functions which might allow them to play a decisive role in the vital decisions associated with the crises of change.

In this connection it should be mentioned that Ronald Dore has suggested that in the face of the development crises there is nothing inherently sacred about democratic pluralism or the type of popular representation that a working nationalizing party system offers. He raises the possibility that a well-developed authoritarian system based upon an efficient bureaucratic structure might succeed in carrying out the reforms proposed at Punta del Este and accomplish the economic development of Latin America where a liberally elected, uncontrolled democratic political system depending on free interplay of parties could not.

To my mind Latin America's experience proves just the contrary. We have seen that throughout the region the ability to convert to monopolistic and even authoritarian governmental practices is by no means unknown. Despite this reserve of power, and with very little help or hindrance from either the formal legislative bodies or the political parties, the bureaucracy already is engaged in the principal task of policy planning; and it is not doing it well, least of all as regards the problems of development. How could it when the upper bureaucrats come from the traditional ruling class and reflect its rigid, particularistic, and elitist views? Even if a bureaucracy better attuned to the exigencies of change could be recruited, the peculiar demands upon a political system undergoing rapid development are such that without some sort of auxiliary political structure to perform the nationalizing-integrating function the bureaucratic agencies are swamped. Under such circumstances to speak of "an efficient bureaucratic structure" is a contradiction in terms.

My contention is that the political structure best suited to perform this auxiliary function—though by no means the only one theoretically possible—is the nationalizing-integrating political party. As of now, in most of Latin America the extent of its utility as an integral part of the political decision-making process is limited by the role allocated in the political system to political parties in general and to challenging parties with this specialized function in particular. But the imperatives of the crisis conditions growing out of development may change this, as they did in Mexico after its revolution.

Even today the logic of the problems facing the political structures involved in government policy formation calls for the kinds of services nationalizing parties can provide. An integrating and aggregating party system, for example, could do much to bring the other governmental and non-governmental political structures into constructive relationship with each other, allowing each set to concentrate upon its primary functions in the political system. More important, because the inadequacies of the present party systems and the other informal auxiliary political structures overload a decision-making process that must depend on formal governmental agencies, Latin America's political systems are not keeping up to date with the demands heaped upon them by the burgeoning crises of development. Inexorably, therefore, throughout most polities in the region pressures which are not being eased by the Alliance for Progress are mounting so alarmingly that if a nationalizing party system does not exist one must be invented.

CHAPTER 13

PARTY SYSTEMS AND NATIONAL DEVELOPMENT
IN ASIA

LUCIAN W. PYE

I. Party Systems on the Current Scene

IN OCTOBER 1958 General (now Field-Marshal and President) Ayub Khan interrupted Pakistan's political life in order, in his words, "to clear up the mess." One of the first acts of the new regime was to abolish all political parties. In the Sandhurst-trained general's vision of the just—and stable—society there was no provision for such unruly organizations, for, again in his words, "We are not like the people of the temperate zones; we are too hot-blooded and un-disciplined to run an orderly parliamentary democracy."[1]

In May 1963 President Ayub Khan joined a political party and with his customary candor said sadly: "Someone asked me the other day, 'Why have you joined a political party?' The reason is simply that I have failed to play this game in accordance with my rules, and so I have to play in accordance with their rules—and the rules demand that I belong to somebody; otherwise who is going to belong to me? So it is simple. It is an admission of defeat on my part."

President Ayub's frustration with political parties is the frustration of all Asian political systems. Asian politics are caught in a profound dilemma: they can neither get along well without political parties nor work well with them. Historically the introduction of political parties has seemingly created as many problems as it has solved; and although by now Asians have had considerable experience in proclaiming, inaugurating, and living off political parties, Asia has had pathetically little experience with working party systems.[2]

Only in the Philippines has there been a general and easy accept-

[1] *The Times* of London, August 14, 1963.

[2] For general surveys of the development of political parties throughout Asia, see: Rupert Emerson, *Representative Government in Southeast Asia*, Cambridge: Harvard University Press, 1955; George McT. Kahin, ed., *Governments and Politics of Southeast Asia*, Ithaca: Cornell University Press, 1959; Robert E. Ward and Roy C. Macridis, eds., *Modern Political Systems: Asia*, Englewood Cliffs, N.J.: Prentice-Hall, 1963; W. H. Morris-Jones, *Parliament in India*, New York: Longmans, Green, 1957; Gabriel A. Almond and James S. Coleman, eds., *The Politics of the Developing Areas*, Princeton: Princeton University Press, 1960.

ance, without serious and lingering reservation, of the efficacy of the party system as the appropriate mechanism for dealing with the problems of transferring power and changing the personnel (if not the policies) of the government. Since independence the Filipinos have accepted with considerable grace and a modicum of violence the dictates of national elections which have thrown out the party of the power-holders and brought in the party of opposition. The remarkable stability and capacity of the Philippine party system is also attested to by the fact that this extremely unprepossessing and flamboyantly self-critical country could endure the jolting shock of having its most popular and charismatic leader die in office and accept the constitutionally defined transferral of power to a nondescript Vice President without the slightest tremor or break in stride.[3]

India, the most self-proclaimedly democratic country in Asia, has demonstrated the capacity to transfer power and office from party to party at the state and at lower levels but not so far at the center of affairs. Indeed, much of the conventional wisdom about Indian politics holds that the duration of Congress's near monopoly in national affairs is likely to be coterminous with the lifespan of democracy in India. And some people still hold their breath in anxiety when contemplating how long Indian democracy will survive the death of its charismatic leader, Nehru.[4]

The Japanese, in creating a workaday democracy, have, as is their habit, defied the conventions of Western classification and produced a one-and-a-half party system. Japanese political theorists, in their desire to prove that at least they as individuals are respectfully Westernized, frequently protest that Japan has no party system at all. In their view the Liberal Democrats have none of the attributes of a political party except an unaccountable propensity for winning all elections and managing governments while the Socialists, in form a reasonable facsimile of a modern Western party, seem to be talentless in winning elections or managing public affairs. These Japanese thinkers are presumably impressed with the Socialist's capacity to find meaning in ideological dogma, a capacity foreign observers often find hard to distinguish from mere pig-headedness.[5] In spite of these objections the fact remains, however, that the Japanese

[3] For an excellent over-view of Philippine politics see: Jean Grossholtz, *Politics in the Philippines*, Boston: Little, Brown, 1964.

[4] The best summary of the divisive forces in India is Selig S. Harrison, *India: The Most Dangerous Decades*, Princeton: Princeton University Press, 1960.

[5] The best analysis that balances objectivity with understanding for the feelings

parties, through inordinately frequent general elections, have developed a competitive party system.

The fourth country in Asia in which political parties have played a significant and sustaining role in furthering nation development is the Federation of Malaysia, where much of the miracle of Malayan stability and progress can be attributed to the extraordinary political maturity and farsightedness of the Alliance party. Composed of the United Malay Nationalist Organization (UMNO), the Malayan Chinese Association (MCA), and the Malayan Indian Congress (MIC), this holding-company political party has been able to bring together for the purposes of advancing judicious and rational national policies the three racial communities that otherwise deeply divided the country. However, in spite of this amazing feat it cannot be said that Malaya as yet has a fully developed party system. Indeed, the split between Singapore and the Federation which has threatened the future of Malaysia can be traced directly to the inability of the Malaysian party system to integrate within itself the People's Action Party (PAP) which dominates Singapore's political life.

Aside from these four countries—and possibly Ceylon might be added—the story of political parties in Asia becomes either increasingly depressing or utterly trivial. The ceaseless scheming and cynical skulduggery of the Pakistani politicians, the tragi-comical wheeling and dealing of Indonesian parliamentarians, and the airy illusions of the Anti-Fascist Peoples Freedom League (AFPFL) leaders in Burma have never constituted the work of political parties except in the minds of the most charitable Westerners who have allowed their fears of ethnocentrism to overcome their good sense. And as for the fragile and bizarre groups in Thailand, Laos, Cambodia, and Vietnam, nothing is advanced by trying to stretch that all too elastic term "party" to cover them. The sects, cliques, and government-sponsored associations of mainland southeast Asia need to be understood in the light of the traditional form of politics of the region and not confused with any presumed emergence of modern party systems.[6]

---

of the Japanese Socialist is Robert A. Scalapino and J. Masumi, *Parties and Politics in Contemporary Japan*, Berkeley: University of California Press, 1962.

[6] For a vigorous statement that the cliques and sects so often found in transitional societies should not be confused with modern parties and interest groups but recognized as a distinctive phenomenon, appropriately called "clects," a portmanteau word formed by combining sounds from the words "clique" and "sect," see Fred W. Riggs,

From this brief tour of the Asian scene it might be tempting to race to the conclusion that the degree of development of a party system can serve as a useful indicator of the relative level of general political and social development. But let us resist this temptation to rank and grade political systems and instead merely conclude for the moment that the party systems in Asia are closely linked with the Western impact and that their futures are bound up with the fundamental issue of the fusion of the old and the new, the traditional and the modern, in these countries. It could be argued that of all the political institutions the political party has the most intimate and direct connection with the basic problem of the reintegration of Asian societies; for, on the one hand, the political party is uniquely the child of the modern political system—whether democratic or totalitarian—and yet, on the other hand, the political party must also be the most sensitive political institution in reflecting the distinct and peculiar sentiments of each particular political culture. The floundering of the party systems of Asia is thus a reflection of the persisting difficulties of these societies in achieving a workable balance between traditional and modern, between the parochial and the universal.[7]

The relationship between parties and the making of national policies is in turn conditioned entirely by this fundamental problem of fusion that invokes crises of identity and integration. For political parties to perform the dynamic role in effecting national policies they must be capable of serving as a two-way communication channel, processing the demands and interests of the population upward to the centers of power, and simultaneously passing downward to the people as a whole a better understanding of the absolute restraints and the ultimate requirements of the polity as a whole. Yet these processes of communication are constantly being interrupted and fading out because of the unsureness of people about the blending of the old and the new.[8]

"The Theory of Developing Politics," *World Politics*, Vol. 16 (October 1963), pp. 147-171.

[7] For general discussions of the problems of fusion and integration in the transitional Asian societies see: Rupert Emerson, *From Empire to Nation: The Rise of Self-Assertion of Asian and African Peoples*, Cambridge: Harvard University Press, 1960; Ralph Braibanti and Joseph J. Spengler, eds., *Traditions, Values and Socio-economic Development*, Durham: Duke University Press, 1961; and the theoretical discussion in Leonard Binder, *Iran: Political Development in a Changing Society*, Berkeley: University of California Press, 1962.

[8] For a study of many aspects of the communication function in the developmental

Our main concern, however, is not with the performance of individual parties in Asian societies. Although from time to time the requirements of analysis will make it necessary to deal with internal characteristics of Asian parties, our primary focus will be on total party systems and on how the processes of interaction among parties may influence the prospects for national development. Often in the Asian setting political parties have emerged and mobilized considerable power with almost no regard to the performance and claims of other parties; but, while these examples would be significant in recounting the story of political parties in Asia, they would not for our purposes represent significant developments in the building of party systems.

It is useful at times to stress the importance of the development of party systems in the context of analyzing the problems of political development. The emergence of individual parties may have a very important effect on the course of national development, as for example when nationalist parties capture an independence movement, or when a single party after independence comes to dominate the nation's entire political life. In such cases, however, the political party tends to serve the functions of a mass movement or another public institution, such as the bureaucracy or the formal government. Parties can, and often do in Asia, govern a society. At the same time, however, parties can perform other political functions, and one of the most important of these is to engage in mutual competition with respect to ideas, policies, and popular power. In this sense a party system is important to the process of national development because it provides the basic form and structure for the emergence of a distinct and integrated polity.

In all human societies there is political power, and some people and groups will have more than others; but it is in the modern nation-state that we find the development of an integrated and responsive polity which is distinct and somewhat removed from the general structure of society on the one hand, and from the formal processes of government on the other. In the Asian scene political systems have not generally been sharply differentiated from other social processes. Consequently there has not been an intervening level between society and government which might have been filled by the operations of a party system and which might thus have

---

process see: Lucian W. Pye, ed., *Communications and Political Development*, Princeton: Princeton University Press, 1963.

provided some cushioning for the total system against the shocks of historical change. Without the interplay of a party system the fragile public institutions of Asia are either pathetically vulnerable to any tremor that might run through the society, or they are compelled to apply power directly and crudely in the day-to-day workings of all aspects of the society.

We must delay for a moment any further discussion of the relationships between party systems and national development and first examine briefly the historical conditions which have affected the development of party systems in Asia. This is necessary if we are to appreciate how deeply rooted are the various factors inhibiting the development of modern party systems.

II. Historical Background of Asian Political Systems

TRADITIONAL ASIAN POLITICS

One striking and paradoxical conclusion which emerges from a survey of traditional Asian political systems is that the very attitudes and practices which have provided a receptive environment for the creation of individual party organizations have been the major factors inhibiting the development of effective party systems. Certainly within limits the existence of particular attitudes and values in the traditional politics of some of the Asian societies has facilitated the development of more modern party structures. In India, for example, the interplay of caste and community leadership with the cliques of officialdom has produced skills in the calculations essential to party organization and strategy.[9] Traditional Japanese sentiments about mutual obligation and the relationships between superiors and inferiors have certainly eased the tasks of building party loyalties.[10] Yet in spite of these traditions in support of group allegiance and a collective striving for power the traditional Asian systems tended on balance to create attitudes incompatible with the effective operation of a competitive party system. It now seems that these traditional attitudes are of central importance in explaining why Asians,

[9] For a perceptive analysis of the role of traditional attitudes in supporting modern political behavior and group organization see: Myron Weiner, *The Politics of Scarcity: Public Pressure and Political Response in India*, Chicago: Chicago University Press, 1962; and his "Traditional Role Performance and the Development of Modern Political Parties: Reflections on the Indian Case," paper presented at the annual meeting of the American Political Science Association, New York, September 1963.

[10] See Edwin O. Reischauer, *The United States and Japan*, Cambridge: Harvard University Press, 1957.

in spite of their overriding desires to modernize their societies, have been most hesitant in fully supporting the development of modern party systems.

There were great differences among the traditional Asian systems. China was a model example of an ancient empire; Japan was a complex system of centralized feudalism not too dissimilar to some of the early European systems; India was a mixture of petty king-doms and grand dynasties of conquest; Southeast Asia presented an array of aspiring empires such as those of Indo-China and Java, a series of unstable kingdoms as in Burma and Thailand, and a col-lection of cultures which never developed structures of government much above the immediate community level as in the Philippines. To facilitate our discussion it would be helpful to simplify the diversity of ancient Asia and speak in terms of three general cate-gories or types of systems. We can do this by treating as one group the *traditional imperial systems* of which China would be the arche-type but which would also include the aspiring empires of South and Southeast Asia; then feudal Japan in a category by itself; and finally the *competitive parochial systems* of the Philippines, Malaya, and much of the outer islands of present-day Indonesia.[11]

The imperial systems produced the least congenial environments for the emergence of voluntary associations capable of articulating public policies. The chasm between the world of the elite and that of the masses was so great that the demands and interests of the common people could be communicated to the rulers only under extreme conditions and usually only with the support of violence. The elite world itself was mobilized in a hierarchical form, which when it achieved its highest expression became a bureaucracy. In the less developed systems the hierarchical arrangement became merely the status gradation among the officials and the nobility.[12]

[11] Some question might be raised as to whether India properly belongs in the category of imperial states. It is true that India only had two nearly nationwide or culture-wide periods of central government before the advent of the Moguls and the British. These were the empires under Chandragupta, who died in 298 B.C., and his grandson Asoka, who ruled from 273 to 232 B.C.; both empires disintegrated after the death of their founders. On the other hand, Indian history revolves around lesser dynasties and regional centers of power which were of the imperial tradition. Com-pared with the political units that made up the parochial competitive systems of Southeast Asia, the Indian states were clearly massive bureaucratic empires.

[12] Our political and sociological understanding of the dynamics of traditional imperial systems has been greatly advanced by the masterful analysis of S. N. Eisenstadt, *The Political Systems of Empire: The Rise and Fall of the Historical Bureaucratic Societies*, New York: The Free Press of Glencoe, 1963.

We could not possibly give justice here to the extraordinarily complex and ingeniously devised Chinese imperial system, which produced the longest enduring and the most stable form of rule known in all human history. The interrelationships among the Confucian world view, the literati-mandarinate, the emperor, the gentry, and a powerful family system created a remarkably closed system which proved to be stubbornly impervious to change, either domestic or foreign inspired. The system had its weaknesses, which were most apparent during periods of crisis when dynasties might fall, but on balance it was as integrated and as stable a political system as was known to the world of traditional societies.

Possibly the most vulnerable point in the imperial system was the link between formal government and common citizen. The Chinese never acknowledged the need for explicit institutions for bringing together the interests of government and those of the population, whether high-born or low. It was assumed that the government had a monopoly of all the relevant wisdom necessary for the just and successful ruling of a society. Magistrates and officials might listen to the complaints or petitions of private individuals, but there was no assumption that the world of private affairs could generate significant social demands which should be systematically related to the operations of a somewhat separate and distinct political system. Officials were taught the art of playing off private groups and factions against each other so as to ease the burden of government; but there was never any suggestion that government should ever be responsive to the outcome of power struggles among autonomous groups. To allow the open interplay of interests would be the same as abdicating the responsibilities for ruling and permitting affairs to get out of hand.

The basic instinct in the imperial system was one of monopoly. Rulers sought to maintain complete control over the world of the elites, and the government vigilantly sought to prohibit the emergence of any autonomous sources of power.[13]

At the same time independent groups and highly organized associations did exist, and they contributed to the stability of the entire system. There were, for example, in traditional China well-recognized clan and kinship associations, strongly disciplined guilds in most of the important trades, and above all secret societies that

---

[13] On the relationship of polity to society see S. N. Eisenstadt, *op.cit.*, and Karl A. Wittfogel, *Oriental Despotism: A Comparative Study of Total Power*, New Haven: Yale University Press, 1957.

had the power of life and death over their membership. Such groups existed throughout the society, and in terms of their individual organizations they were as developed and professional as any voluntary groups known to the modern world. Among the secret societies the loyalty of the membership was complete, and the leaders certainly had a greater range of choice over what they could do with their organizations than do leaders of modern interest groups and parties.[14] In India we find that much the same situation existed with respect to the caste panchayat, and that in the pre-British cities there was considerable capacity to build organizations.[15]

Yet these associations and societies, largely because of the assumptions about the rights of monopoly of the rulers, were in no way prototypes of modern political parties and interest groups. Their operating styles were entirely those of protective associations that might shelter their members from the worst effects of government but would not bring pressure on government, and certainly never in any open fashion. The dynamic forces which shaped public policy were assumed by all to lie entirely within the domain of the formal government and of officialdom. It would have been the height of impropriety and folly for mere citizens, no matter how wealthy and influential, to strive openly to place demands on government.

The refusal to recognize the need for explicit and institutionalized links between private associations and governmental offices meant that all contacts between the two worlds tended to follow the lines of personal associations and to fall into a shadow world of impropriety, corruption, and petty scheming. Everyone could assume that any attempt at influence between citizen and official was bound to be an immoral and politically disruptive matter.

It is profoundly significant for the history of Chinese political development that these feelings about the proper restrictive relation-

[14] Chinese secret societies and even guilds and provincial associations have been little studied. The most useful information on them is to be found in: John Stewart Burgess, "The Guilds of Peking," doctoral dissertation, Columbia University, 1928, published in *Studies in History, Economics and Public Law Series of the faculty of Political Science*, No. 308; Sidney D. Gamble and John S. Burgess, *Peking, a Social Survey*, New York: George D. Doran, 1921. T. T. Meadows, "The Chinese and Their Rebellions," London, 1856; J. S. M. Ward and W. G. Stirling, "The Hung Society or the Society of Heaven and Earth," London: Baskerville Press, 1926, 3 vols.; and Lean Combs, *Chinese Secret Societies in Malaya*, Locust Valley, N.Y.: J. J. Augustin, 1959.
[15] For a discussion of the political and economic roles of certain associations in pre-British India see: George Rosen, "The Urban Overlay," Ch. 3 in *Democracy and Economic Change in India*. Berkeley: University of California Press, forthcoming.

ship between government and private circles survived the fall of the Manchu dynasty and continued to dominate Chinese political thinking during the early republican era. Even without the direct impact of colonialism the Chinese displayed remarkable capacity for building many types of Western institutions and structures. Yet the one area in which they displayed almost no interest in emulating the West was in the building of independent parties and pressure groups. It is noteworthy that during the 1920's and 1930's, when the Chinese were translating and reproducing on a massive scale material from nearly every field of modern knowledge, the Commercial Press in Shanghai, apparently indiscriminate in reproducing pirated editions of all manner of Western books for the Chinese market, conspicuously ignored the entire literature of American political science in the field of parties and interest groups. The open society which might have emerged from the republican era had no attraction for most educated Chinese, who in their fears about disorder and competition wanted only unitary rule and a government by monopoly. If there had to be political parties in response to modern fashions, then the Chinese were nearly unanimous in agreeing on the desirability of a one-party system in which the one party would be as nearly undistinguishable from the formal government as possible. This was the spirit behind the Kuomintang rule, and it is the spirit behind the rule of the Communist party.

It is indeed sobering to remember that during the 1920's and 1930's the Chinese intellectuals and politicians advanced with great cogency—and, we must assume, deep sincerity—precisely the same sets of arguments about the need for one-party rule and the disruptive dangers of competitive politics that now one hears in so much of the former colonial world. The Kuomintang, hypersensitive to the divisive forces of warlords and contending cliques within its fold, became fixated on the dangers of competition and blinded to those of excessive authoritarianism. In so doing it established a pattern of behavior that to a disturbing degree seems now to be well on the way to becoming the widely, albeit unconsciously, shared model for many of the new states.

Within China the victory of the Communist party has, for this moment in history at least, closed the book on any prospect for the development of a party system. It would take us beyond the scope of this analysis to investigate further the relation of the Chinese Communist party to Chinese national development; that party is not a participant in a party system but is in a sense the revival in contemporary guise, and in the most extreme form, of the old tradition of monopolistic politics. Its functions are not those of competitive political parties but rather those of bureaucracies and governments.

In looking elsewhere in Asia we find the monopolistic tendencies of the imperial and aspiring imperial systems were given reinforcement by the experiences of colonialism and the emergence of diffuse but monolithic nationalist movements. However, before examining the colonial impact on party development in Asia we must first survey the feudal Japanese tradition and the parochial competitive systems of archipelagic Asia.

In many respects traditional Japan was closer in structure and organization to feudal Europe than to imperial China. Although the Tokugawa regime created many of the trappings of a centralized government, the various *daimyos* or lords with their independent fiefs, their separate household regulations, and, above all, their loyal samurai followers gave an essentially competitive framework to Japanese politics. The clash among the contending lords—whether in the form of direct military adventures of the earlier Japanese history or through the strange contests of conspicuous consumption in the social life of Edo, the Tokugawa capital city—established the enduring Japanese tradition that politics legitimately involves the interplay of interests of principal figures each of whom has his independent basis for power and autonomous organization. The spirit of Japanese politics was thus a blend of intense and absolute loyalties to particular orders of ranking and a high regard for skills in alliance building, in accommodation and bargaining, by the leaders of these groupings.[16]

In the late Tokugawa period very explicit economic interests were brought into the competitive politics, and the leaders accepted the idea that politics might be appropriately used to advance and safeguard the economic well-being of individual groups and enterprises. This occurred when the various feudal domains or estates began to specialize in making various distinctive products and to sell their unique goods on ever larger markets. As the feudal units moved from a state of near self-sufficiency to increased specialization and thus to a form of division of labor, the political strategies and ma-

[16] The classic descriptions of traditional Japan are those of Sir George Sansom, *Japan: A Short Cultural History*, New York: Appleton-Century, 1931 and 1944; and *The Western World and Japan*, New York: Alfred A. Knopf, 1950.

neuvering of the lords had to become increasingly sensitive to the need to support and protect their economic interests.[17]

In this process of historical development the Japanese power-holders not only learned the appropriateness of using politics to back economic interests, but, more important, they also learned that the economic sphere is in some respects distinct, that it has rules of its own which if violated will cause severe economic hardships to all concerned. Thus in the emerging Japanese tradition of competitive politics there developed the strong belief that politics had to be held in check, and that there was an appropriate limit to the political because economic values had to be respected and deferred to on their own terms.[18]

This recognition of the legitimacy of separate bases of power and of the need to respect technical specialists was established well before the Meiji Restoration and helps to explain the rapid pace at which Japan was able to modernize its political and economic institutions. This is not the place to engage in a detailed examination of all the factors which contributed to the speed of Japanese modernization, but it is significant to note that the recent work of historians has been all in the direction of pushing back into ever earlier periods the establishment of the social and economic prerequisites for Japanese modernization. Thus we have learned that the process involved a longer sweep of time than earlier scholarship indicated. It seems likely that as more work is done on the fascinating history of Japanese transition into the modern world we are also going to have to revise our impressions of the extent to which the Japanese experience was a case of simple authoritarianism. In the past when Japan was largely being contrasted with the Western democracies and when she was being analyzed as an enemy of the international order there was an understandable tendency to highlight her authoritarian qualities and to classify the discipline and orderliness of her people as being counter-democratic attitudes. Yet when we compare this earlier Japan with the later, post-colonial developing countries we are immediately struck with the fact that there was relatively a greater dispersion of power in even the immediate post-Meiji period.

[17] E. H. Norman, *Japan's Emergence as a Modern State*, New York: Institute on Pacific Relations, 1940.

[18] Edwin O. Reischauer, *Japan, Past and Present*, 2nd ed., New York: Alfred A. Knopf, 1953; Charles P. Sheldon, *The Rise of the Merchant Class in Tokagawa Japan, 1600-1668*, Locust Valley, N.Y.: J. J. Augustin, 1958; and Thomas C. Smith, *Political Change and Industrial Development in Japan*, Stanford: Stanford University Press, 1955.

Japanese politics from an early stage involved several power centers, including in particular the bureaucracy, the military, the court, the *zaibatsu* or the financial and industrial leaders, the party politicians, and the leading government figures. Although all of these groups might work together, each also had its separate interests and its particular demands on the system, and no group could operate without respecting to some degree the rights of the others. This was a far more open and competitive circle of leadership than is common in the authoritarian systems in the currently developing countries.

This pattern of Japanese development was completely contrary to that of the imperial systems of Asia. In the latter, politics and government were supreme, the merchant was suppressed and controlled, and neither separate economic interests nor the integrity of the market and the economy as a whole were respected. Thus in Japan politics was legitimately seen as the competition among power groupings, each with its separate economic and social interests, and it was recognized that while politics might marginally advance these interests, the total sphere of politics should not be allowed to disrupt the more fundamental structure of the economy and of the society at large. In the imperial tradition politics was monopoly, there were no legitimate interests acknowledged except those of the rulers, the government could properly dominate the economy, and any change in rulers could be expected to bring violent changes in the economy and in those who held wealth and social status. Significantly the Chinese term for "economics" is expressed by ideographs which mean "the management of wealth through the use of political power." Indeed, in classical Chinese thought the closest approach to economic theory was the discussion of how rulers and officials might most effectively curb the activities of any people with inordinate talents for making money so as to prevent them from becoming a nuisance and interfering with the free play of politics and government. Bluntly put, the Chinese official view was that the concept of free enterprise should at best belong only to the realm of government and politics and most decidedly not to economics.

In the remainder of Asia where parochial competitive systems abounded the aspiration for political development was certainly that of the imperial tradition, but the realities were closer to the spirit of the Japanese system. In much of the Malay world all local leaders, whether headmen, *datus*, sultans, or earlier potentates, desired to achieve the security of a monopoly of all powers and to arrange their societies as a hierarchy with themselves at the pinnacle. But their impotence left them as competitive, feuding rulers who had to be constantly engrossed in struggles with other petty leaders whose strategic ambitions similarly exceeded their organizing abilities. For example, in the pre-Spanish Philippines social and political life was organized in terms of small autonomous local communities, whose leaders, called *datus*, had great pretensions of importance and grandeur but whose security depended entirely upon their skill in coping with the threats of neighboring communities.[19]

In these cultures there emerged not empires but vaguely defined systems of competitive power. Leaders were expected to give security and protection to their loyal followers, and all subjects knew the dangers of being raided and the advantages of plundering others. Out of interminable petty warfare came a tolerance for the need of appropriate limits to political competition and the acceptance of rules for alliance and of the existence of mutual self-interest. The process of politics was thus the acknowledged jockeying and scheming for power and influence among autonomous leaders. The spirit of politics was competitive; the purpose of politics was instrumental to the advancement of separate interests.

CONDITIONING INFLUENCES OF COLONIALISM

So much has been written on the colonial experience in producing political parties in Asia that we need only touch very briefly on the colonial period. The principal point we would make is that colonialism, and its natural product of nationalist movements, tended to strengthen and reinforce the essential spirit of politics basic to imperial traditions wherever such traditions had significantly developed during the pre-European period. Thus the dual forces of colonialism and nationalism inspired powerful latent urges toward politics of monopoly. Colonial rulers and bureaucratic administrators understandably distrusted political competition and opposed any tendency to allow conflict of interests to become fused with open competition for power. Their attitudes were not just the normal human reaction of those on top preferring not to be annoyed; they also reflected a powerful rationalistic and technocratic outlook on public affairs. That is, the colonial officials often felt that their highest

[19] The traditional systems of Southeast Asia are well described in: Cora DuBois, *Social Forces in Southeast Asia*, Cambridge: Harvard University Press, 1959; D. G. E. Hall, *A History of Southeast Asia*, New York: St Martin's Press, 1955; and Brian Harrison, *Southeast Asia, A Short History*, New York: St Martin's Press, 1954.

obligation should be to the ideals of technical proficiency, administrative efficiency, and sound, if not scientific, sense. As dedicated champions of rationality trying to overpower the myriad forces of irrationality, colonial officials might happily defend and publicly justify their decisions, but as long as their frame of reference was foreign to the masses of their subjects their reasoning must have seemed as arbitrary as that of the most autocratic of traditional rulers. Only gradually did the practice, as in India, of the government publicly justifying its decision provide a basis for open debate of public policy. In the main, however, the spirit of colonial rule was one of treating government as all-knowing, all-wise, and possessed with a monopoly of grandeur, pomp, and power. Whole generations of Asians grew up to believe that there could be nothing more wonderful than to find one's way into the reaches of government.

The colonial tradition was also at heart a bureaucratic tradition, which in its full potency readily infected all organizations, whether public, semi-public, or even private, with its distinctive ethos and style of operations. Thus all groups tended to become bureaucratized; their offices generally replicated governmental procedures, and their officials copied the style and official mannerisms of bureaucrats. And thus at this late date after independence political parties and governmental departments seem often to share a common heritage, and their officials to share an equal interest in insuring for themselves all possible perquisites of office. This tendency to bureaucratize all forms of organizational life in the manner of governmental offices has meant that private organizations and quasi-public groups, such as political parties, trade unions, and other interest associations, have adopted the basic attitudes and practices of governmental offices which were informed by the monopolistic spirit. Aside from attitudes of superiority toward non-officials and private citizens, these supposedly political associations often display a brittle quality in that they prefer autonomy and petty empire-building to the challenge of competitive politics and the demands of alliance-building through accommodation and bargaining.

In most of Asia the most significant direct impact of colonialism was in the realm of public administration, law and order, and the introduction of some social welfare measures. Constitutional development and the encouragement of political parties generally lagged behind the building of civil services. In all the significant colonial countries some scope was given to the creation of political parties, but in most of the countries the Asians were reluctant to exploit such opportunities, particularly after nationalist movements appeared and contended that as long as colonial rule continued it was divisive to the oppressed people to have competitive elections.

In British India, for example, there was a remarkably long history of local elections dating back to the 1840's and 1850's. Various groups and factions began to compete in these elections, and possibly they might have formed in time significant political parties. However, in spite of British intentions, the traditions which emerged from these starts in local government were largely pushed aside by the later nationalist movement. Thus, although India does have a long tradition of local elections, and in the Congress party, founded in 1885, she has one of the four or five oldest significant political parties in all the world, there was no effective fusion of the two traditions during British rule. Although Congress competed in local elections, it focused its main energies on the need to articulate a mission of a new and de-Hinduized India and to preach more modern attitudes to the people generally. Much of this ideological ferment of the Congress party was distant from the immediate demands and interests of the different segments of Indian society of that time, and indeed the principal link between Congress and the Indian people was in terms of the general demand for independence and the more specific concerns for Indianizing the government services. Thus was established that unique blend that increasingly, especially after independence, became the hallmark of Congress: a mixture of moralistic exhortation and unabashed job-seeking and job-giving.[20]

The gap between local and national politics which was not well bridged during the colonial period still remains a dominant feature of the Indian political system. Since independence Congress has had increasingly noticeable fits of ambivalence about its proper role in Indian developments. Under the unassailable leadership of Nehru, Congress leaders had little trouble in thinking of themselves as the administration and government of India, and they apparently convinced themselves that the future unity and progress of India as a nation was absolutely dependent upon Congress's remaining in power. Congress thus, while professing a modernizing and socialistic ideology, has tended to act in many ways in the spirit of monopolistic

[20] A. B. Keith, *A Constitutional History of India*, 2nd ed., London: Methuen, 1936; M. V. Pylee, *Constitutional Government in India*, Bombay: Asia Publishing House, 1960.

politics of the traditional imperialistic and the colonial administrative regimes. At the national level Congress leaders have tended to give the appearance that they actually believe that the emergence of opposition parties might disrupt the unity of the country and retard the modernization of the Indian economy and society.

It should be pointed out, however, that some careful observers of the Indian scene are less convinced of the essential role that Congress is to play in modernizing India. These observers note that India is developing a functioning party system and that at the state and local levels there at least appears to be significant fusion of distinctly parochial Indian interests and the collective requirements for Indian development as a modern system. At these levels Indians have demonstrated the ability to peacefully transfer power from one party to another as indicated by a succession of elections since independence. Myron Weiner has brilliantly argued that the stable and democratic development of India lies largely with the continued spread of the process of competitive politics at the lower levels; but in the meantime the dominant spirit of national politics is that of monopoly and of anxiety over dissent and competition.[21]

Colonial policies differed elsewhere in Asia, but in the main the outcome was the same reinforcing of monopolistic tendencies wherever they had existed before in the traditional imperial system. Both the French in Indo-China and the Dutch in Indonesia sought to incorporate into the constitutional development of their colonies special roles for the functional interests basic to the economy and society of their colonies. In both colonies there were advisory councils and quasi-legislative bodies composed of representatives of all important functional interests, ranging from the rubber plantations and the chambers of commerce to the various professions and minority communities. Nationalist leaders in both colonies denied the relevance of such functional representation and insisted upon the need for competitive political parties as the only appropriate vehicle for articulating and aggregating local interests. It goes without saying that, once in power, the nationalist leaders found the instinct for monopolistic politics irresistible and have abolished all parties; and in Indonesia Sukarno even reverted to the old Dutch concept of functional representation.

It is appropriate to dwell a bit longer on the experience of the

[21] See both Myron Weiner, *Party Politics in India: The Development of a Multi-Party System*, Princeton: Princeton University Press, 1957, and his *Politics of Scarcity*, *op.cit.*

Philippines, for not only is that country a model example of the competitive parochial system of traditional Asia but also it was able to emerge from its colonial experience not with strong, bureaucratized political parties but with a remarkably adaptable competitive party system.

During the Spanish period the Philippines were to some degree transformed into the traditional imperial pattern of monopolistic politics, and this tendency was reflected in the type of political parties which were organized: they were essentially secret societies such as Rizal's *La Liga*, the Free Masons, and Bonifacio's *Katipunan*. The American occupation brought competitive politics and the creation of open parties organized to compete within an electoral system. The spirit of the emerging party system and indeed the temperament of the Philippine nationalist movement were conditioned by the fact that the *Partido Federalista*, the first party, organized in December 1900, championed as the ultimate goal of Philippine development statehood within the United States, an objective which the occupying powers would in the end have had to oppose. In the general elections of 1907 the Federalista party was opposed by a variety of groups which combined to form the Nationalista party, which argued that the more appropriate goal for the Philippines was self-government and independence. Thus public debate about the future goals for the Philippine nation from the beginning revolved around the issue of how close a permanent tie should be maintained with the United States. The initial presence of the Federalista party had a moderating influence to the extent that the early Nationalista leaders, in seeking to win away the support of the Federalistas, argued that even with complete independence it would be possible to preserve an intimate association with the United States.

The Nationalista party became in time not only the oldest party in Southeast Asia but also the main vehicle for the independence movement and the political interests of the wealthiest groups in the islands. With the landlord interests monopolizing the nationalist movement, the tenant farmers, laborers, and even the emerging urban middle classes had either to follow docilely along or turn to sporadic anomic movements. The result would no doubt have been a highly cynical pattern of development had it not been for the fact that with the Jones Act of 1916 power was being transferred to elected Filipino officials at a rapid enough rate so that they could

aspire to achieve autonomy by finding a balance between the economic
oligarchy and the popular electorate.[22]

The emergence of this limited degree of autonomous political
activity was greatly facilitated by the dramatic series of personal
power struggles between the two foremost Filipino politicians,
Sergio Osmeña and Manuel L. Quezon. In endeavoring to take the
leadership of the Nationalista party away from Osmeña, who had
been the autocratic Speaker of the House since its inception in 1907,
Quezon began to argue in 1921 that all important decisions should
be made solely within the framework of legally constituted authorities and not in a private forum, whether that of a political party
or the oligarchy. Osmeña was compelled to defend the proposition
that caucus rule was consistent with the spirit of democratic politics.
Like most historically important issues, the question was never
neatly resolved, but the debate did have the significant effect of
making the oligarchy move one step back from the political area and
thus leave the politicians as clearly the middlemen between formal
government and private interests in the society. The result was a
tradition of ever increasing freewheeling politics with individual
politicians aspiring to grandeur, power, and wealth and striving
to accumulate various combinations of interests. Gradually even before independence certain fundamental understandings were reached
in Philippine society: the political game should never be allowed
to go to the extreme of violently threatening the basic social and
economic structure of the society, and in return the important social
and economic interests were prepared to allow the politicians their
freedom in following the logic of their internecine struggles.

Thus with independence there emerged in the Philippines a competitive party system composed not of rigid, bureaucratically organized parties but of two loosely structured coalitions of factions. In
the continuing struggles between the Nationalista and the Liberal
parties both have had to balance a variety of conflicting demands and
restraints. Both parties have vacillated between dependence upon
the established interests and an urge toward unfettered populist
sentiments. The need for financing—Philippine elections tend to have
the highest per capita costs in the world—compels the politician to

[22] For the best general analysis of party development in the Philippines see:
Jean Grossholtz, *op.cit.*; Joseph R. Hayden, *Philippines*, New York: Macmillan, 1942;
Dean C. Worcester, *The Philippines: Past and Present*, New York: Macmillan, 1930;
Robert Aura Smith, *Philippine Freedom 1946-1958*, New York: Columbia University
Press, 1958.

accept some backing from the managers of the economy; while the need for votes demands dramatic if not radical programs. Both parties appreciate the potentialities of the "pork-barrel" in giving financial independence, and both realize the dangers of being charged with "anomalies," the Philippine euphemism for corruption.

The Philippine party system, by seeking to aggregate and accommodate as many interests as possible and by striving to make government serve very particular and concrete interests, is constantly in danger of appearing excessively corrupt and lacking in principle. Its spirit of pragmatic politics is, however, balanced by the propensity of Filipino politicians to express themselves in flamboyantly idealistic forms that have little relationship to realities. In many respects contemporary Philippine politics resembles American urban politics shortly before the First World War. Strong reformist urges periodically creep up, and there is a diffuse expectation that some day the muckrakers will be able to clear out the sordidness; but in the meantime the Filipino politicians continue to give vigor to democracy by faithfully serving as brokers among all the interests of the society as a whole. In conducting their spirited campaigns as highly individualistic leaders they are acting in the tradition of the parochial competitive politics of the pre-Spanish era. Now, however, they carry on their contests of power within the framework of a party system which in turn is related to a relatively centralized structure of bureaucratic government, and thus their struggles tend to give unity and integration to the Philippine polity. Moreover in seeking to optimize the interests of their constituencies they are able to bend public policies to the goals of community and national development. Indeed in the Philippines the community development program for improving life in the barrios is of prime interest to the politicians; in India, by contrast, community development was long a concern mainly of the administrators and the civil service.

III. Parties and Policies for Development

In surveying traditional and colonial Asia we have sought to emphasize the factors which might contribute to or hinder the development of party systems capable of influencing policies of political and national development. In several Asian countries individual parties are or have been extremely important in making policy, but in doing so they have acted more as administrative hierarchies in the tradition of imperial monopolistic polities than as aggregating political parties functional to a party system. Indeed, in ruling their peoples some of the Asian national leaders have almost arbitrarily opted to rely upon either their party bureaucracies, which they inherited from the nationalist movement, or their civil bureaucracies inherited from the colonial administration. Party bureaucracies in some situations have thus been the functional equivalent of the instruments of rule and of policy control.

From our review of Asian history it is apparent that the emergence of competitive party systems has in all cases depended upon at least minimum separation of the political sphere from the social and economic spheres of life. The monopolistic traditions, whether imperial or colonial, involved very intimate ties between political power and the control of social and economic behavior. Where the calculus of politics is uninhibitedly sovereign over the rationale of economic performance it is impossible to have a competitive system of politics. Unless there is some separation between the dynamics of politics and the ordering of social and economic life it would appear that the stakes of political controversy can easily become too high for the acceptance of a competitive party system. Under such conditions any shift in the political realm can become a major threat to the security of all with social and economic interests; hence the tendency to control and freeze the political, at least as far as any substantive change in the personnel and policies of government.

When the political realm is not somewhat divorced from the rest of society, the politicians themselves are likely also to feel threatened and strive to freeze the political process. The difference between having power and not having power becomes so absolute as to affect the total well being of the individual. It is true that at present in Asia the loss of power does not involve the same catastrophic decline in income, status, and welfare as it does, say, in Africa, for unemployed Asian politicians display an amazing survival ability as they apparently defy all economic laws by spending their days with their entourages of cronies in interminable discussion about the sorry state of affairs. Yet as long as the penalties for defeat are so out of line with the rewards for victory the instincts of Asian politicians have understandably been to keep the game as monopolistic as possible.

It is a universal proposition of politics that power holders have a deeper appreciation of the status quo than most people and that they are quick to sense the dangers of rocking the boat; therefore, for the reasons we have just mentioned, many Asian politicians display a fine sensitivity to the dangers of national disintegration which they feel is certain to follow upon any disintegration of their personal power position. The more positive argument for retaining power that is frequently advanced by Asian leaders is that rapid national development demands centralized and unitary control of the society in the tradition of monopolistic politics. Leaders of countries that are not in the slightest danger of becoming democracies will still proclaim that their countries cannot "afford the luxury" of democracy until they have developed their economies.

Even after recognizing the propensities of politicians to rationalize their own indispensability the question remains as to whether in fact an authoritarian system may not be more effective than a party system in facilitating economic and national development. Unfortunately there does not seem to be any easy answer to this question, and the more we learn about the processes of development the more we are impressed with the wide variety of factors which seem to be relevant in determining the pace of national development. Many of these factors are little related to, or affected by, the type of party system within the country. There is, for example, the fundamental question of whether the basic cultural values of a people are conducive to supporting the kinds of behavior essential for modern life and economic growth. There are places in Asia about which it is fair to speculate, given the values of the people, whether any form of government could influence their capacity to modernize. Closely related to the matter of basic values is the problem of the availability of the necessary skills and knowledge. Again no form of government can overcome basic deficiencies in human resources. Indeed, this question of skills applies directly to the political realm in that there is all the difference in the world between effective, competent, and honest politicians and bureaucrats and ineffectual, bungling, and corrupt ones; and such differences in ability may have little relationship to the form of the polity.

In the light of these and other equally important qualifications it is impossible to make any sweeping assertions about the overriding advantages of either authoritarian or competitive systems for national development. The most that can be done is to indicate, first, the conditions which favor the emergence and the effective performance of both authoritarian and more competitive systems—something we have touched on in our historical analysis of Asian systems—and, second, the relative advantages and disadvantages for development of either form of polity when all other factors are "more or less equal."

One of the conditions which frequently confuses debates over these issues is that within the Asian context the political and the administrative spheres have not been historically sharply differentiated and thus standards of behavior appropriate to the functions of one sphere become mixed with those of the other. For example, public administration in all situations calls for clear lines of authority, uncompromising efficiency, rapid and unambiguous decision making, and an unconfused structure of authority; but in the Asian context administration is often characterized by slothful bungling, arrogant ignorance, and petty, if not grand, corruption. Yet in diagnosing the problem many would prescribe for the political, rather than the administrative, a clearer sense of hierarchy and of command. In theory of course it is possible to have competitive politics coupled with either rigorously efficient and decisive or incompetent and corrupt administrative processes; and, conversely, authoritarian politics can be linked with either form of administration.

Unfortunately for the prospects of development in Asia there has not only been little differentiation between appropriate standards to the two spheres, but there also has been a positive reversal, producing the odd result that in the minds of many Asians incompetence, laziness, and corruption are associated with democracy—a concept basic to the political and not the administrative realm—while efficiency, decisiveness, and competency are related to authoritarian rule. In some of the countries this attitude is so firmly established that shameless leaders can point to the existence of corruption and mismanagement in their societies as evidence of the "democratic" nature of their rule. In part this attitude is related to the phenomenon of the general decline in administrative efficiency which accompanied the termination of colonial rule and the initiation of popular politics; and in part it comes from the ideology of independence movements in which it was argued that self-rule was justified even if it meant misrule.

Unquestionably economic and political development depends upon the work of effective bureaucracies and competent administration. Yet the story of Asian development overwhelmingly points to the conclusion that administration is not enough. If it were, colonial rule might not have ended as it did, for several of the colonial administrations in Asia were near models of rational and efficient government which was not unmindful of the welfare of the people. Monopolistic politics in Asia, at present as in the past, has tended to produce stagnant rule even when the vocabulary of the rulers has been that of radical slogans. For rule by oligarchy, even when disguised in the language of revolution, remains the sterile rule of oligarchy.

Once it is recognized that there is an appropriate difference between the functions and hence the standards of politics and those of administration, and that a highly orderly and efficient bureaucracy, such as Japan had during the end of the nineteenth and the beginning of the twentieth centuries, is fully compatible with a competitive political system, as was Japan's when measured against Asian standards, there still remains the question of whether or not even within the political realm there may not be some inherent advantages of authoritarian practices for facilitating development. Respect must be given, for example, to the more sophisticated argument than that commonly advanced by Asian politicians which contends that authoritarian rule is more capable of compelling a society to postpone immediate gratifications and to make the necessary investments for development which generally are not popular and do not coincide with the present interests of any particular element in the society. There is no question that development calls for heavy investments and that thus in the broadest sense consumption must be held back in relation to potential income. In practical terms this means that the present generation must deny itself advantages in favor of later generations and that a society must accept the burdens of a tax structure that can extract the necessary savings and provide the necessary revenues for investing in the forms of social overhead— such as roads, schools, and the like—which will make future development possible. Granted that these are the essential policies for rapid development, the question becomes the empirical one of whether in Asian societies authoritarian rule has in fact displayed any noticeable advantages over more competitive systems.

If we survey the record of the last two decades in Asia, we must conclude that it is hard to find any striking advantages for authoritarian rule. In Indonesia, for example, the pattern has been a contrary one in that, with the destruction of the forms of competitive politics and the rise of one-man rule, there has been a dramatic decline in the ability of the government to make long-range investments. The insecurities inherent in Sukarno's rule have forced him to shy away from any painfully unpopular developmental policies. In Burma, military government has led to the expropriation of many forms of economic life, but this has resulted only in the government living off a form of capital while the army in the meantime has found it impossible to make even as heavy a demand upon the peasantry as the previous civilian politicians had. In contrast, India, Malaysia, and the Philippines have the most extensive and penetrating tax structures of all the newly independent states in Asia, and these are the countries making the most effective investments in development. In fact it is precisely the dynamics of popular politics which makes such investments acceptable in these countries.

There is, however, evidence in support of the advantages of authoritarianism. Taiwan has been one of the most rapidly developing areas in all of Asia during the last decade, and it manifestly does not have competitive politics. But Taiwan represents a somewhat abnormal situation, and some authorities would insist that greater popular involvement, particularly of the native Taiwanese, might produce significantly greater rates of development. And of course there is the example of Communist China, which at one time was assumed to have many advantages as a result of its totalitarian one-party rule. More recently the policy failures of the Peking government have raised some justified doubts as to how impressive the Chinese record will be, given the perspective of a few more years. It is certainly clear that Peking has far from realized the potentials inherent in Chinese society.

This is not the place to seek to total up the balance sheets of relative rates of development among the various Asian countries. For our purposes it is enough that the record suggests that authoritarian rule in Asia has not generally brought all the advantages for development which theoretically might be expected. The capacity of governments to ask their people to postpone gratifications in favor of investing for development seems less related to the simple matter of authority and more to such complex questions as the environment of confidence and faith in the relations between leaders and followers. If a people lack the essential trust in their leaders, they are likely to feel that they are being exploited whenever it is suggested that they should deny themselves and provide more for the government's use. Historically, very few authoritarian rulers in Asia have been able to make heavy extractions from the people for investing in development because of this problem of appearing merely to be exploiting their peoples for their own whims and their private policy interests. Thus the record seems to suggest that authoritarian systems have their peculiar problems in making effective demands upon an Asian population.

If we now move on and look at the positive side of the question, it seems that in the Asian setting of limited competitive party systems there is considerable evidence to support many of the classic arguments for democratic practices. The notion that the electorate might throw out their rulers does make the Indian politicians run a bit faster and display some sense of urgency. In Japan the constant threat of the Socialist opposition has certainly made the Liberal Democratic leaders more sensitive to popular needs and demands. In both Japan and the Philippines government officials are demonstrably kept on their toes and diligently made to revise and improve upon their plans and policies because of their fears of criticism by opposition politicians.

The Asian experience of the last decade suggests, moreover, some even deeper reasons why competitive politics has some special advantages in facilitating national development. We would dwell on two of these. First, it seems that the degree of competitive party politics which has emerged in Japan, the Philippines, Malaya, and India has helped the people of these countries to sense not only the need for a gap between the political and the other realms of life but also the distinction within the political realm between partisan and nonpartisan institutions. It is this distinction which makes it possible for people to grasp the realities behind such abstractions as the "nation," the "national economy," and the "national interest." In all the Asian societies political development has involved the need to encourage people to look beyond the parochial horizons of the family, the clan, the village, and the ethnic community; and it makes a considerable difference for the future stability of the society if in developing these broader commitments people can sense the legitimacy of essentially nonpartisan institutions. Where the spirit of monopolistic politics exists under the aegis of a dominant nationalist movement people may fail to distinguish between a national identity that transcends partisan interests and the nationalist sloganizing of partisan leaders. What is Indonesia today beyond the personality of Sukarno; and what was Burma yesterday except the will of the Anti-Fascist Peoples Freedom League (AFPFL) and U

Nu? In contrast, where partisan politics is explicitly recognized the people can readily sense the existence of objective considerations against which the performance of the competing factions can be measured. In the Philippines all politicians are constantly being judged against higher standards of national interests which provide the basis for the spirit of muckraking and the constant appeals for reform and improvement.

The traditions of colonialism and nationalist movements in most of Asia blurred the distinctions between the partisan and the non-partisan spheres of public life. Both colonial administrations and nationalist leaders tended to adopt a totalistic view toward public affairs, and neither allowed much room for the concept of autonomous state and public institutions. Consequently entire generations of Asians received their basic instructions in politics from, and were first politically awakened by, highly partisan sources.

In the transitional societies of Asia the need for an appreciation of the differences between the partisan and the nonpartisan in politics and government is particularly important because so much of contemporary life is a source of frustration and humiliation. National ideals and self-respect can be better built if there is a distinct partisan realm of competing leaders who can be criticized and held accountable for the failures of the day. Cynicism and scorn will then not be directed at the vital sense of national identity and of pride in the potentialities of a people.

The prevalence of frustration in much of Asia brings us to a second major role that competitive politics seems better capable of performing than monopolistic politics. This is the function of fusing a new sense of national identity out of the tensions between the old and the new, the parochial of the indigenous culture and the universal of the modern world. Where we find competitive politics in Asia we observe politicians striving to associate themselves with the interests and concern of concrete groups and segments of the society on the one hand and with the problems of national or community-wide management on the other. Filipino politicians have increasingly sought to acquaint themselves with the very real but limited aspirations of farmers in particular communities, of workers in specific enterprises, of businessmen in definite lines of trade. This Filipino capacity to relate specific interests and the national concern is reflected in many aspects of public policy and legislative actions, not the least being the remarkable blending of political and administrative considerations in the community development program and the belated land reform act. When monopolistic politics prevails, as in Indonesia, the national leaders seek to combine the old and the new through abstract formulations and the generalities of ideologies. A competitive party system can accept the existence of parochial and communal differences and seek to build a larger unity out of a respect for the legitimacy of such traditional diversity. Monopolistic national leaders tend to be embarrassed by manifestations of traditional life and give respect to the validity of the old culture only in the abstract.

THE DISCIPLINE OF ELECTIONS

The ability of a party system to relate concrete interests to public policy depends upon the ultimate disciplining effects of popular elections. In some Asian countries the political class has engaged in the extraordinary experiment of trying to operate a party system without the benefit of a reasonable threat of elections; and not surprisingly these are precisely the countries in which the leaders have arrived at the conclusion that representative government is unworkable. In Asia there is a direct correlation between the effectiveness of the party system and the frequency of general and local elections. Since the end of the Second World War Japan and the Philippines have had the most frequent and regular elections, followed by India and Malaya. In these countries the politicians do not have to indulge in fantasy and imagination to believe that they have a popular mandate and that they might in the reasonably near future lose their jobs if they do not maintain contacts with their constituencies.

In contrast, Indonesia and Pakistan made a shambles of parliamentary government as their politicians engaged in endless inter- and intra-party maneuvering with almost no expectation that their decisions and behavior would be effectively judged by the test of the polls. In Indonesia from independence until 1955 there were no elections; but the self-appointed politicians and their self-proclaimed parties engaged in a spirited game of musical chairs as they formed and overthrew and re-formed new governments. When the life expectancy of new governments became hardly four months, the politicians finally decided to hold an election in 1955. As such affairs go in Asia it was a crude first approximation, but it demonstrated that the Indonesian people, with more experience, could readily manage the process. However, it was apparently too much for the

Indonesian politicians, and they have never tried another. Finally Sukarno decided, as the Dutch had earlier, that parliamentary democracy was not for the Indonesians; and he replaced the spectacle of scheming Indonesian politicians with the equally bizarre spectacle of one-man rule by Bung Karno himself. What in fact happened was that Sukarno replaced the game of balancing off political parties with the much more dangerous one of balancing the army and the Communists. The short-run effect of this was that Indonesian propagandists were kept busy producing an extensive literature on the inherent limitations and the corrupting influences of democracy for countries that are in a hurry. It might be possible to take more seriously the Indonesian arguments about the potential efficiencies of "guided democracy" if the Indonesian leaders had the minimum dignity necessary for even autocratic rule.[23] Finally, however, when Sukarno's delicate balancing act came tumbling down in the Fall of 1965, the weakness of representative democracy seemed to be on a par with that of authoritarianism Indonesian style.

While in Indonesia the lack of elections left the politicians free to wheel and deal with each other, meanwhile ignoring the economy and the society, in Pakistan the absence of elections freed the politicians to peddle their influence and to make a good thing for self, friends, and relatives out of their access to the bounties of a shabby government and a sorry economy. Close observers of the Pakistan scene might question whether that breed of conniving politician could ever have been effectively disciplined by mere elections, since they were hardly fazed by the efforts of two "strong men" and could be checked finally only by the authority of the men in uniform. But as we noted at the beginning of this essay, even the benevolent general has finally concluded that Pakistan cannot get along without its politicians and its parties. As the country gradually returns to civilian rule it is to be hoped that this time the experiment with democracy will be built upon much more intimate ties between the electorate and their representatives. Such at least is the most positive hope for what may come out of the program of "basic democracies" and community development.

There is already considerable evidence that in Pakistan, as everywhere else in Asia, whenever the common people have been asked to make their choices as to what the government might best do to

[23] For a sober account of the limitations of Indonesian politics, see: Herbert Feith, *The Decline of Constitutional Democracy in Indonesia*, Ithaca: Cornell University Press, 1962.

improve the conditions of their daily life, they have come up with remarkably sober, restrained, and responsible suggestions—a bridge here, a new road there, a new village school this year, and a delay until next year for the new well. It is precisely these choices within the context of the immediate realities of Asian society which may prove to be far more important in generating sustained economic and social development than the showpiece projects, such as new airports and the like, which fascinate the more insecure nationalist politicians who would avoid the test of popular preferences.

In conclusion we may observe again that the mixed record of party development in post-colonial Asia reflects the uncertain course of national development in the region. The prospect for stable and vigorous modern political systems depends upon the success of the various countries in passing through the phase of nationalist movements and into a time when they can experience the benefits of organized party systems. For the foreseeable future most of the Asian systems will not be able to escape from the restraints of the monopolistic traditions. Those that can, however, are already showing remarkable potential for vigorous development, for they are the countries which will in fact be able to build upon the strengths of both their historic cultures and the modern world without unnecessarily compromising the integrity of either.

CONCLUSION

The Impact of Parties on Political Development

MYRON WEINER AND JOSEPH LAPALOMBARA

THE PRECEDING essays treat both the conditions affecting the emergence of political parties and the impact which political parties have had upon various aspects of political development. In this concluding chapter we shall attempt to draw together what the papers in this volume suggest regarding the role played by parties and party systems in political development.

It is customary to view parties as institutions or organizations for the expression of social and economic interests and as mechanisms involved in both the expression and the management of conflict. The literature on parties, especially on American and British parties, assumes that the political system in which parties operate is accepted by most of the population as legitimate, that the public is loyal to the national state, and that there are more or less accepted relationships between political participants and the state and among the participants themselves. These assumptions are not valid in most of the developing areas today. Moreover, there were points in the evolution of modern states at which such assumptions were not valid there either. It is with such considerations in mind that the contributors to this volume have explored the impact of parties themselves on the development of the political system in which they operate.

The term "political development" remains elusive, and we have not attempted any systematic definition. Several preceding volumes in this series suggest preliminary conceptualizations, and it is our hope that the series' concluding volume will provide a definition that confronts most of the conceptual pitfalls that many scholars have noted. In this volume, we have sought to isolate selected problems of development concerning which political parties appear to be particularly relevant. Four such problems have received detailed attention from our contributors: national integration, political participation, legitimacy, and the management of conflict. These problems or crises often arise before political parties emerge and, as we have noted earlier, may be significant in shaping the types of parties and party systems established. But here our concern is with the impact of existing parties and party systems on the handling of these problems. This concern with parties and party systems as independent variables reflects our understanding that they are not only the product of their environment but also instruments of organized human action for affecting that environment.

I. Political Participation

This independent influence of parties on their environment is clearly revealed in the study of political participation. Movements or demands for political participation are a characteristic feature of political development. Many of the factors which first lead entrepreneurial classes and the urban middle classes to seek power from aristocratic elites and colonial rulers soon affect the rural classes and the urban working class. Even in developed countries the patterns of participation change as technological innovation destroys some occupations and creates new ones, diminishes the economic and political role of some regions and increases that of others.

Authoritarian governments, by achieving large-scale economic growth while preventing any massive political participation, demonstrate that there is nothing inevitable about the expansion of political participation. But increased urbanization, the growth of mass communications, and the spread of education appear to be accompanied by an increased desire for some forms of political participation; and the amount of force needed by an authoritarian regime for maintaining control over its population is often in direct proportion to the development of this desire.

The establishment of the first party government often creates a wide-spread expectation that individuals can now share in the exercise of political power not by birth but through political skill. Individuals who had been denied opportunities for participation during the pre-party era may now attempt to enter party politics. If, as is typical, the first party government is created after an era of violence, governmental repression and pent-up hostilities, then it is likely that popular demands for participation will increase, not diminish. In recent years one need only point to Viet Nam after the overthrow of President Diem or Japan after 1945 for dramatic examples of participation movements at the close of dictatorial eras. A similar pattern is apparent in many of the political participation movements that characterized Continental Europe in the late nineteenth and early twentieth centuries.

The response of party government to the desire for participation is often erratic as a government wavers between repression and accommodation. Some regimes pursue the dictum that repression employed early will reduce the need to exercise force later. Other regimes may at first be accommodating and then, as they become concerned with the growth of violence or the threat new groups make toward the regime, turn to a policy of repression. The style of the response, the tone of day-to-day pronouncements, the cohesion or lack of cohesion within the government or among the new groups are all important considerations in the outcome. One can, however, discern four over-all patterns of response by party governments to the demands of groups for greater political participation: repression, mobilization, limited admission, and full admission into the party system.

REPRESSION

The emergence of party systems does not in itself guarantee that governing elites under party systems will welcome expanded political participation. Motivations underlying such resistance undoubtedly vary and it is not easy to isolate what may be the dominant factor. In Europe, for example, it is clear that resistance to participation of the lower classes and religious dissenters was based on motives as wide-ranging as a crass desire to preserve existing economic stratification systems to lofty ideals concerning the "inalienable" right of the religiously elect to control the reins of power. The great debates on representation that date back to Putney and involve momentous intellectual encounters during the Wars of Religion, the advent of Liberalism and several revolutions in the West cannot be explained away by any single-factor formulation such as the mode of production or desires to maintain intact existing stratification systems.

It seems to us, however, that three sets of factors may be associated with tendencies toward repression, whether they occur historically in the West or presently in the developing areas. The first of these may be identified with the system of values held by the dominant elite that exists when the party system materializes. Whatever the economic, religious, social or other nature of these values, if additional participation is viewed as a threat to their maintenance, one can expect to find a heavy incidence of resistance to additional participation.

The second, and related factor would involve the degree of consensus in the society concerning the place which the maintenance of a representative system itself would have in a hierarchical system of values. Where the idea of representative government is accorded low priority, as compared to other values held by the elite, we might expect considerable reluctance to accept demands for increased participation. Where, indeed, such demands are viewed as actual threats to superior values, repressive measures would seem to be a natural response. Similarly, where representative government is articulated as the highest value held by the dominant elite, we might expect repression to occur regarding participatory demands made by groups that could be defined as anti-system. This is true not merely of the attitudes of developed countries toward parties of the extreme left or right, but also of many developing countries toward "traditional" groups such as tribes, communal aggregates, religious minorities, etc.

A third factor would be purely psychological: it involves the hypothesis that new elites operating under a party system find it difficult to share with new claimants the political powers they themselves have been able to wrest from preexisting systems. This is a classic pattern about which a great deal has been written. It would include the reactions to additional participation by middle-class groups in a number of European countries. It surely must now include the reactions to participatory demands by Western-educated urban elites in Asia and Africa who are manifestly not prepared to act on the very premises that presumably governed their own thrusts against colonial or other indigenous political powers.

In a very rough way, we might say that the probability of resistance is associated with the proximity between the creation of a party system and increased demand for participation. Where the new elites are immediately challenged by others who wish to share in the exercise of power the probability of repression is much higher than in those places where the waves of demand are spread over a longer time span. One of the unfortunate problems of the developing areas is that the first generation of elites operating under party systems are confronted with participatory demands long before they have had a reasonable opportunity to institutionalize party government.

MOBILIZATION

One-party governments typically handle the demand for political participation differently from parties in a competitive system. It would be historically incorrect, however, to assume that all one-party systems simply cope with participatory demands through repression. Quite often the one-party state welcomes, even encourages, political participation but does so under carefully controlled and prescribed limits. Some scholars have suggested that the term "participation" is inappropriate here and that alternatively one should speak of "controlled participation" or "mobilization." The notion, whatever term is used to describe it, is that the one-party leadership is concerned with affecting the political attitudes and behavior of the population as a whole and uses the instrument of the party, along with the state's repressive powers and a controlled mass media, to achieve this goal. It is equally concerned with providing the appearances of participation without at the same time giving up the control of power generally associated with admitting additional actors into the political system.

As we have seen, the party may seek to develop a sense of national identity and loyalty. The party may also be used by government—and here we are speaking of one of the central functions of the dominant party in a one-party state—as an instrument for legitimizing authority. The governing oligarchy may also seek popular support to ensure its own security, to enhance its image abroad, or simply because it has a populist ideology and believes that popular "participation" is good for its own sake.

The one-party government is therefore typically a device for facilitating mass mobilization while preventing—reverting now to the conventional use of the term—mass "participation." To put it another way, the regime may be concerned with developing a subjective sense of participation while actually preventing the populace from affecting public policy, administration, or the selection of those who will in fact govern.

It is important to note that with respect to actual participation the mass single party is generally quite different from the cadre party found in the Soviet Union, Eastern Europe, and China. The cadre party may actually recruit individuals into government, while membership in the mass party of a one-party state may only marginally increase, if at all, a member's political influence and political career opportunities. In short, some one-party governments may use the party as an instrument of political recruitment as well as a device for the management of the public. These two functions are not always compatible. The mobilist party may open its doors to mass membership as a device for increasing popular support and thereby diminish the need for large-scale repression. But the more mass the party becomes the more it risks the possibility of being "taken over," if you will, by the masses and the elite's commitment to sacrifice the present for some future goals is in danger of being subverted. This dilemma—whether to open membership to mass participation and risk ideological subversion or to keep membership small and emphasize ideological purity at the risk of losing popular support— is inherent in the mobilist single party and helps explain why such parties often fluctuate from one position to another. Thus periods of mass recruitment and free discussion are often followed by purges and ideological tightening as the party elite fears—paradoxically—that mass participation threatens to destroy the revolution.

LIMITED ADMISSION

Governments may permit social groups to organize their own parties but deny them access to national power and restrict their participation in the system. Frequently parties are permitted to organize after a period of government repression, but it is clear to all that under no circumstances will the government allow them to assume power even if they win elections. Throughout the nineteenth century several European countries permitted the organization of socialist parties under such restrictive conditions. Similarly, linguistic and regional parties with separatist demands have been allowed to organize with the understanding that government will neither allow them to take office nor accede to their demands. Throughout Western Europe today communist, fascist and monarchist parties are aware that, at least at the national level, they will not easily be allowed to exercise power. The degree of limited admission of course varies. In some countries (e.g. West Germany) fascist and communist parties are presumably outlawed and splinter parties impeded by electoral legislation. In others, however, extreme parties are free to hold power at the local level but effectively barred nationally. In view of "popular front" and similar thrusts by the French and Italian Communist parties, it will be of great interest to observe the conditions under which these parties are permitted to share in the formal exercise of national power. It may be that the price extracted for such participation is an abandonment of millennial goals; it may also be that threats to effective participation on the part of other parties will eventuate in a new combination of forces aimed at dislodging existing elites. In such circumstances, limited admission might well be transformed into some form of repression, and, indeed, there are those who, for the very reasons we discussed above (i.e. the preservation of the representative system itself) would counsel such repressive measures.

It is precisely in prolonged situations of limited admission that we find the development of alienated parties. This pattern, typical of several European countries, may be described as permitting the formation of parties without allowing the meaningful participation in government that the formation of the party itself would imply. Thus the alienated political party which integrates the individual into the party rather than into the society at large is a frequent phenomenon in European politics. Such parties of "social integration," to use Sigmund Neumann's felicitous phrase, publish their own newspapers, provide maternity care, medical attention, funerals, and death benefits for party members and their families. Songs, slogans, and literature are directed at cultivating a sense of loyalty to the party, a social class, or religious group rather than to the nation or to the political system under which they are governed. Forged during an era of political repression, the alienated class, ethnic-or regional-based party develops its own myths and legends. It thus alienates its members from the society at large and may institutionalize such alienation.

FULL ADMISSION INTO THE PARTY SYSTEM

The dominant elite may grant individuals and groups demanding political participation the rights of full participation either through existing parties or through newly formed parties. Among well established democracies, this is the typical response. Precisely how new participant groups are absorbed is conditioned very much by whether the governing party, like the Chinese Communist party, is an ideological or, like the Indian Congress party, an electoral instrument. If the governing party is ideologically oriented, that is, if it is concerned with restructuring the values and behavior of its members and its citizens, then it often restricts its membership to those who share a well-defined outlook. Alternatively, when the party's leadership is primarily concerned with winning elections, its program is likely to be pragmatic and it is likely to modify its program to attract the largest number of people. New participation demands are thus more readily handled by electorally oriented rather than ideologically oriented political parties.

Among some democratic parties the desire for electoral victory is so great that ideological commitments will be reduced in order to achieve victory. The toning down of the ideological elements of British Labour party policy in the 1960's in order to win greater support among the middle classes is well known. The willingness with which the Democratic (and in a few instances the Republican) party in America's urban centers eagerly organized and socialized immigrants from Europe during the early part of the twentieth century is also quite familiar. The competition of American political parties for working-class support eliminated opportunities for distinctively ideologically oriented working-class parties. In contrast the reluctance of the Conservative and Liberal parties of the nineteenth century to appeal to the working class—putting, if you will, ideological concerns over electoral calculations—made it possible for the British Labour party to grow.

In all cases where full participation is permitted, we may assume either that additional participation is not perceived as a serious threat to system maintenance or that the commitment to participation itself is so overriding as to supersede any concern for threats to the system or to highly held values of the dominant elite. It is because neither of these conditions is likely to materialize very often that most of the historical and contemporary examples we can point to fall short of achieving this mode of adaptation or response to the crisis of participation.

We have focused at some length on the crisis of participation because the manner of its resolution strongly influences the nature of the parties and of the party systems that emerge. If the impetus to participate comes from a social class, such as the industrial workers or agricultural peasants, and it is opposed or repressed, we can expect class-based parties to emerge; if the demand for participation is geographically based, or reflects a desire for previously denied participation on the part of a religious or ethnic minority, the failure to gradually absorb leaders of such groups into the prevailing system will almost certainly give rise to political parties that reflect these narrow impulses to organization. Moreover, the organization of one party with a relatively narrow base often leads to organizational countermeasures and a proliferation of parties. Socialist parties spur the conservatives and middle class to greater organizational activities; the crystallization of one religiously based party will give rise to others of the same general variety; and workers' parties serve to activate the farmers. As these groups successfully vie for a place in the seats of power and policy they devise electoral systems that facilitate rather than impede this kind of proliferation. Thus, while proportional representation does not *cause* a multi-party system, it most certainly both reflects political fragmentation and helps to maintain it intact. Given the basically unlimited number of ways in which a society can be divided in conflict, it is the two-party system that seems to represent the logical aberration. Whether a two-party arrangement is to have any chance at all of materializing depends in strong measure on the manner in which the participation crisis is handled.

II. Legitimacy

The early phases of party development are almost always accompanied by a problem of legitimizing authority. The first party government in a nation, typically replacing an aristocratic oligarchy, royal authority, a colonial bureaucracy, or a military praetorian rule, must find some basis for legitimizing its new authority in order to win popular support not only for the new government but also for the new *system* of government. While the colonial regime justified its authority on the basis of efficiency and order, royal authority on the basis of religious sanction, longevity, and sheer pomp, and a military government on the basis of its masculine prowess or the charisma of its leader, a party government typically seeks to sanctify popular government and to associate itself with the populace. In fact even the one-party state typically claims the mantle of democracy—that is of popular rule—though a small oligarchy unaccountable for its actions may be in actual control of government.

The early phase of any new system of government, always a period of uncertainty and instability, is especially problematical for party systems if only because the number of participants, and therefore the number of people who must learn the rules, is so much greater than in other kinds of political systems. The instabilities commonly found in the developing areas therefore are not simply a concomitant of rapid social and economic changes but rather the result of establishing new political systems that involve new patterns of political participation. Many new nations experiencing no significant economic or social changes are in the throes of political uncertainty while countries with well established political systems are experiencing rapid socio-economic changes with little political turmoil.

It is for this reason that there is a lack of commitment to newly established governments in most of the developing areas today. There is some evidence to suggest, however, that systems without parties and those with a multiplicity of parties have been among the least successful in establishing a sense of legitimacy.[1] Thus far one-party regimes have been more durable than competitive party systems, but we need a longer time period before we can draw any definite conclusions. Multiparty systems have also experienced a substantial number of coups, but we would suggest that the proliferation of parties in most of the multiparty systems is an indication of the lack of consensus, not a cause. One-party dominant systems (such as the noncompetitive Mexican system and the competitive Indian system) or competitive two-party systems (such as the Philippines and Ceylon) have thus far proved somewhat more durable.

The difficulty which newly established competitive party systems have had in establishing their legitimacy is strongly attested by attempts, successful or otherwise, to overthrow such systems. Instabilities, such as attempted coups, are of course not unknown in the West, as eloquently illustrated by the histories of France and Italy in the nineteenth century, and of Eastern Europe following the breakdown of the Hapsburg and Ottoman Empires. This fragility of party systems, nevertheless, is much more evident in the turbulent histories of Latin American countries in the nineteenth and twentieth centuries and particularly in the more recent evolutions of Asian and African countries that have moved from colonial to independent status.

During the early phases of party development it is common for preexisting political groups—a landed aristocracy or a military elite—to continue to exercise a considerable emotional hold on large sections of the populace. This is especially common in political systems in which parties are largely outgrowths of changes in urban areas, are based primarily on urban support, and are confronted by rural support for the military or landed oligarchy (Japan in the 1920's). But there are also instances in which a rural-based party sys-

---

[1] Some evidence, based upon an analysis of coups among different types of political systems in the developing nations, is suggested by Fred R. von der Mehden, in *Politics of the Developing Nations*, Englewood Cliffs, N.J.: Prentice-Hall, 1964, p. 65.

tem, as Bulgaria had in the 1920's and Turkey in the 1950's, is overthrown by an urban supported military. Perhaps the fundamental issue is how widely accepted is the party system throughout the society? To what extent does each major social group view one or more parties as appropriate and adequate vehicles for satisfying their interests? In short, is the party system legitimated?

As we have noted, some parties are themselves not committed to the maintenance of representative government but participate in competitive politics only in order to overthrow the system. Such parties may in fact be associated with the military, the aristocracy, or insurgency groups seeking to destroy the system. Under such circumstances a fundamental issue in many representative governments is whether to admit non-democratic parties into government (in coalitions, for example) with a high risk that the system may be subverted, or deny them the opportunity for sharing or influencing power, thereby ensuring that such groups will continue to remain alienated and that they will strengthen their efforts to convince supporters that the system does not work precisely because it does not permit them to share power.

The task of establishing a sense of legitimacy for a competitive party system is still further complicated by the general lack of cohesion found in most newly established party governments. While the colonial and aristocratic governments which they displaced may have been unpopular, they often presented to the outsider at least the appearance of cohesiveness. Thus the ideal of united authority that does not publicly bare its disagreements and that masks from the public elements of personal ambitions, corruption, and shabby behavior persists into an era when politics becomes competitive and seems to the public to be disorganized. The shift in public attitudes thus typically lags behind the shift in the nature of the political system. Legitimacy is thus impeded because, in becoming more visible, representative government appears to be a step backward from the image of government associated with colonialism. Thus, since parties often establish themselves through the use of patronage, the opponents of competitive politics can often win popular support for steps to return to oligarchical authority by denouncing unpopular patronage politics.

The problem of legitimacy is further complicated by the fact that the early founders of party systems are not themselves necessarily committed to representative government. In many instances parties were created as a device solely for rallying large numbers of people against a foreign government or one dominated by a small social class. The urban middle class that created the parties (or the nationalist movement which precedes parties) was often more concerned with expelling the colonial rulers than in establishing open, competitive, representative government, or in rallying popular support for such a governmental system. The new government may thus take no steps to persuade the public as a whole, or the army, that representative government per se is desirable. Newly formed parties in a newly established party system may be reluctant to test their popular support through free elections; they may take steps to prevent certain social groups from participating in party politics, thereby forcing such groups to find extralegal ways of winning influence or power. Many early party governments are unable to provide leadership which can sustain support within their own party or in the country at large; the qualities which make men effective militant leaders of a nationalist movement are not necessarily the qualities making for effective leadership of a parliamentary government. Moreover, since there may not be a second-string leadership capable of running ministries and effectively making the governmental machinery work, relations between the new party government and the old bureaucracy—particularly if there is a well-established bureaucracy at work—may be strained, and the bureaucracy itself may undermine efforts to make the system of representative government work.

However, with all of these difficulties, parties have been an important and on the whole successful instrument for establishing legitimate national authority. In general they are more flexible instruments for winning popular support than are armies and bureaucracies—a principal reason why an authoritarian government often organizes a political party. A government-supported party can give government credit for successes while blaming the bureaucracy for its failures. Without responsibility for day-to-day administration, party cadres have more flexibility than bureaucrats for organizing the populace to support government.

The mobilist single party is often as concerned with its image abroad as it is with developing a sense of legitimacy at home. The populist ideologies of Nkrumah and Nasser serve to strengthen the efforts of Ghana and Egypt to extend their influence through Sub-Sahara Africa and the Middle East. Popular demonstrations against foreign "imperialists," attacks against embassies, mass rallies to which the foreign press is invited, and popular plebiscites serve to enhance foreign policy goals as well as to create a sense of popular support at home which intimidates would-be opponents.

But the fundamental issue is not whether government wins popular support, but whether legitimacy with respect to the system is established. After all, an unpopular government may hold power in a system widely accepted by the populace as legitimate (kingship may not be challenged, but a particular king may). Alternatively, a government may be so concerned with its own popularity that it fails to take measures to make the system itself legitimate. A charismatic leader may successfully retain popular support but fail to take steps to institutionalize a new political system.

Perhaps one useful way of observing the legitimacy of a system, in the absence of either full elections or survey data, is to observe the succession process. How is leadership transferred from one man to another, from one generation to another, and most difficult of all, from one party to another? The succession process is a useful checkpoint for looking at the question of legitimacy because when power is transferred, individuals within the system are forced to decide whether their loyalties are confined to those who, up to that point, have exercised authority or to the system of government itself.

The first test of the system often takes place when power is transferred from one leader to another within the same political party— the transference of authority from Washington to Adams, from Lenin to Stalin, from Nehru to Shastri, and from Ataturk to Inonu. The problem of transferring leadership from one individual to another is especially acute in political systems where charisma plays an important role. The attention given by the founding father to the institutionalization of his authority—what Weber referred to as the routinization of charisma—may be a critical factor in how legitimate the party and governmental system becomes. In the Indian case, for example, Nehru chose to work within the framework of parliamentary rule even when it did not suit his immediate needs and however much he dominated the Congress party. The result was that, though his successor could not be predicted with great confidence only months before his death, the procedures for selecting a new Prime Minister were well known and accepted. The problem of transferring authority from charismatic to non-charismatic leaders, or, to put it another way, the problem of learning how to exercise power without charisma, depends very much upon the establishment of accepted procedures within the governing party. One can find a similar pattern in Turkey when power was transferred from Ataturk to Inonu.

The transference of power from one party to another, especially the first such transfer that occurs within a party system, is often the critical testing point for the legitimacy of the system. In the United States, the election of 1800 provides a striking example of peaceful transition. It was facilitated by an underlying consensus—implying a very high place for the representative system itself in the elite's hierarchy of values. Similar patterns are very rare in other parts of the world, as Rustow's discussion of Turkey attests. The notion of representation, which underlies the behavior of American parties, appears to be absent through most of the Middle East. In 1945, Ataturk's successor Inonu agreed to transform Turkey's one-party state to a competitive system. In the absence of a near universal commitment to representative government—irrespective of the policies pursued by the winning party—the attempt failed. A victorious rural-based Democratic party (later the Justice party) was overthrown by a military coup as the educated, secular, urban middle classes found unacceptable a party which sought to modify secularism, was rural based, and appeared to lack a commitment to full-scale modernization.

As far as the new nations are concerned only a few have thus far been confronted with the issue of transferring power, and it is not clear yet whether those with parties will be more successful than those without, and whether countries with only one party will be more successful than those with several. The data on coups, however, suggest that new nations totally devoid of parties rarely reach the point where succession is an orderly process. There is moreover a prima facie case for suggesting that countries with at least one effective governing party are more likely to deal successfully with the problem of succession than are countries where parties are not present. Parties, even in totalitarian systems, are experienced in the art of internal elections while bureaucrats and military officers are accustomed to a process of selection and promotion by higher officials. Governing juntas of bureaucrats and military men are thus rarely prepared for the politics of peacefully electing their own leader or of having leadership peacefully pass from one person to another.

How well the new nations can handle the transfer of power from one party to another is even more a matter of conjecture. There is reason to think that as difficult as the transfer is from one party to another during the early phases of a competitive system, it may prove to be even more difficult if the transfer must be made from a party in an authoritarian state to a party in a competitive system. For in the first instance the transfer of power involves legitimizing an existing system, while in the second, it simultaneously means establishing a new political system. The Turkish case thus raises the fundamental question of how a tutelary system can "prepare" a nation for democratic rule. That a tutelary government can be an instrument for establishing effective central authority there can be little doubt; but whether the attitudes of mind, the tolerance for widely divergent views, and the readiness to see one's opponents in office can be cultivated seems unlikely in the atmosphere of an authoritarian regime.

III. National Integration

The concept of integration has been variously treated in this volume. For some it involves primarily the amalgamation of disparate social, economic, religious, ethnic, and geographic elements into a single nation-state. This kind of national integration implies both the capacity of a government to control the territory under its jurisdiction as well as a set of popular attitudes toward the nation generally described as loyalty, allegiance, and a willingness to place national above local or parochial concerns. For other scholars integration means the regularization of structures and processes whereby the discrete elements in a given national territory are brought into meaningful participation in the political system. Whether these processes are regularized and understood by participants to be legitimate can be defined as process integration as opposed to national integration.

Although these forms of integration are closely related, they can and should be analytically separated because empirical cases suggest that one can have one form of integration without the other. Kirchheimer points out, for example, that France achieved national integration several centuries ago, but that process integration still remains imperfectly established. And Rokkan's analysis of Norway shows that long after the nation-state has come to be accepted by a population there may still remain the task of establishing a national political process involving the rural as well as urban population.

The striking thing about several European countries is that the crisis of national integration was reasonably resolved sometime before political parties made their appearance. British political parties of the nineteenth century did not have to confront the issue of nationhood. Nor did the parties of France, Sweden, Norway, and Holland. This was not the case with Germany, Belgium, Switzerland and even less so with Italy where the crises of nationhood and national identity were mismanaged by elites at the time of unification and remained loads the party systems of these nations had to face at the end of the First World War.

An important justification for single-party systems in many new nations, especially in Africa, is that they are essential for the establishment of national integration. There is some historical evidence from Europe to support this position. German unification was achieved largely under the aegis of the Iron Chancellor and the Liberals, often at the cost of dealing rather ruthlessly with religious and social groups, and Italy was "Piedmontized" under Cavour and his successors in the Liberal party. But in both instances a national bureaucracy and army were the major instruments for national unification. One could argue that parties were complementary, perhaps even necessary elements, but not sufficient conditions for national integration.

In most new nations of Asia and Africa, governing political parties are concerned with two elements of national integration—the issue of control over the nation's territory and the issue of subjective loyalties. In one-party authoritarian states, the government generally justifies the suppression of tribal, religious, and regional parties on the grounds that their very existence constitutes a threat to the nation's territorial integrity. And in competitive as well as in authoritarian party systems, the governing party tends to be concerned with evoking national symbols so as to facilitate the development of a sense of national loyalty. As one leader of Italy's Risorgimento put it after national unification had been achieved, "Fatta l'Italia, bisogna fare gli Italiani"—having made Italy, we must now make Italians. The same refrain can be found in Ghana, Nigeria, Pakistan, and a host of other new nations with heterogeneous cultural and social systems.

It is certainly understandable why single-party patterns grow out of protracted movements for independence and the associated need for a sense of national identity. Where African parties are not narrowly based on tribe, religious, or regional foundations they have helped bring about a sense of national consciousness, if not in the countryside, at least in the urban centers and if not among peasants, at least among large segments of the educated elite. Moreover, one can point out that countries without a single national party reaching geographically into all corners of the territory have often bordered on internal disintegration and violence. Nigeria and Ceylon come readily to mind. Were the Congo, for example, to have a single national party the prospects for national integration would be considerably enhanced. Reflecting on the proliferation of political parties with anti-national loyalties in Africa, Emerson is moved to conclude that while a one-party system is no guarantee of national unity, it is likely in most instances to be better adapted to this mission than would be two or more parties.

There are, however, some shortcomings of one-party systems as an integrating force. In one-party systems the government and party tend to become indistinguishable. As Wallerstein puts it, the party becomes "governmentalized," party work diminishes as leaders assume bureaucratic roles, the party itself loses its effectiveness as an instrument of political participation and recruitment, and party leaders may even become aligned with traditional elites at the price of sacrificing the goals of modernization. Where the party and government are indistinguishable, there tends to be no buffer between the formulation of public policy and its application. The mediating influence of the party is lost, and in the process the party loses much of its ability to interpret government to people and people to power holders. Loyalty to the nation is equated with loyalty to the party and disaffection from the party may mean disaffection both from the national state and from the political process itself. The difficulties of achieving any kind of integration beyond the territorial is enormously complicated by such a pattern.

Which kind of party system exists may affect (and in turn be affected by) the strategy pursued by government in its quest for national integration. Governments may seek to merge the distinctive cultural traits of minority communities into some kind of "national" culture, usually that of the dominant cultural group, or alternatively, may seek a policy of "unity in diversity," politically characterized by "ethnic arithmetic" with the aim of establishing national loyalties without eliminating subordinate cultures. Where this policy of political unity and cultural diversity is pursued, government is more likely to be tolerant of minority parties than when an assimilationist policy is pursued.

The possibilities of the emergence of a single unifying party which reaches into all portions of the country depend too upon the nature and extent of cleavage within the social system. We must look for the scope and intensity of religious differences, ethnic fragmentation, hostility between traditional and modernizing groups, conflict between urban and rural centers, and opposing ideologies. Where a great number of cleavages such as these exist, without the mitigating element of overlapping and cross-cutting cleavages, then it is particularly difficult for any one party to recruit on the basis of appeals that cut across the country. Indeed, frequently political parties associated with such fragmented cultures have no intention of facilitating integration but aim instead at reinforcing the subcultures with which they are identified.

Striking examples of the negative consequences of extreme party pluralism in Europe, based upon religious, regional, class, and ideological cleavages, would be the French Fourth Republic, Weimar Germany, and contemporary Italy. In France neither the Socialists nor the Communists sought to integrate their followers into the existing system. The trauma experienced by the Socialists when a few of their leaders joined a bourgeois government needs no recounting here. It is typical of this hostility toward existing institutions that in Italy it was fully seventy years before Italian Socialists voted to join in the responsibility of government—and only after an emotional appeal by Pietro Nenni, who asked that the madness of 1922 which helped bring the Fascists to power not be repeated.

Whatever integration these mass parties intended was restricted to their own ranks. Their goal was to provide—through auxiliaries—for all of the occupational, social, recreational, professional, associational, and religious needs of their members. Even when such parties have sought to expand their membership to other social or religious groups, the deep cleavages we have noted have proven to be an impediment. Thus, the ability of Italy's Christian Democratic party to expand its base is strongly limited by the party's essentially denominational character. Similarly, Socialist party prospects for expanding in Catholic countries are inhibited by disagreements over such issues as public support for parochial education. Where secular attitudes might appear to be a basis for uniting non-Catholic parties, violent ideological disagreements over economic systems inhibit such a fusion of forces.

Even within some parties organized at a national level there remain manifestations of parochialism that tend to make the party a disintegrative and paralyzing influence in politics. The widespread Latin American pattern is one in which parties impede communications, continuing to serve as instruments of notables who use the parties not to achieve integration but to preserve the status quo. It is significant that the generally most effective parties on that continent are those created and designed to preserve traditional interests and to impede modernization. Thus far cleavage has been relatively contained since parties and government have often been controlled by restricted elites associated with great families, church, military, and bureaucracy. But the increase in political participation now taking place in much of Latin America suggests that further party development will not cut across the existing lines of cleavage but will rather exacerbate and rigidify them, perhaps along patterns typical of southern Europe. We might expect similar fragmentation and proliferation of parties to occur in Africa and Asia where the forces of tribalism, casteism, traditionalism, parochial autonomy, religious variations, and diverse social and economic affiliations are particularly powerful.

It is partly the awareness of the fragility of nationhood and of the centrifugal forces now held in precarious check that leads many leaders of Asian and African countries to advocate single-party rather than competitive-party solutions. When the bureaucratic and military establishment is not well developed or united on a national basis, it is quite common for the nationalist movement to assume what are customarily thought of as governmental functions. But beyond the task of guaranteeing territorial integration—no small matter in many new nations—the single-party pattern, as we have noted, may make attitudinal integration difficult. It may be, as some African leaders claim, that some one-party formulas can be evolved which will facilitate attitudinal integration and a sense of political efficacy. It has been suggested, for example, that factional conflicts within parties may serve the same functions as inter-party competition.

The argument for competition, either within or between parties, has rested largely on the case for democratic values, but competitive-party systems may also facilitate national integration. In competitive systems, political leaders must pay more than lip service to the need for national integration and must do more than seek national symbols, for they must also formulate policies which will amalgamate parochial and national interests. The ruthless adoption of a single language, for example, in a multilingual country may be a successful long-term device for national integration if all dissident elements can be held in check until they, or their descendants, learn the new language. But alternatively, national integration may also be achieved through complicated language formulas arrived at through elaborate negotiations and bargaining. One way of coping with social diversity is to use forceful means to suppress and eradicate it; another is to search out institutional arrangements that will encourage dialogue, unblock communications channels, keep political and governmental leaders on their toes, facilitate the articulation and aggregation of conflicting interests and in these ways create a sense of political efficacy while building national unity out of ethnic diversity.

IV. Conflict Management

Parties as independent factors influencing political participation, legitimacy, and integration direct our attention to problems that are generally viewed in long-range perspective. On a day-to-day basis, however, the essence of politics seems to us to be the management of conflict, that is, the ability of a political system to manage constantly shifting kinds and degrees of demands that are made on it. It seems appropriate, therefore, to examine the role of political parties in handling this vital and universal standard against which any political system should be judged.

How well parties relate to the problems of conflict management will obviously be affected in part by some of the conditioning variables we have already explored. Societal cleavages, for example, may be so basic and intense as to make open and peaceful conflict by political parties difficult. Since this is particularly the case where cleavages are ideological and translated into competing parties that are fundamentally anti-system, it is reasonable to suggest that ideological parties are less able than pragmatic or "brokerage" parties to handle conflict effectively. Following from this would be the suggestion that in competitive systems the ideological-hegemonic and the ideological-turnover systems are less able to cope (short of repressive measures) with conflicts than either pragmatic-turnover or pragmatic-hegemonic systems. From the vantage point of political stability, the ideal situation would appear to be one of pragmatic-turnover.

We should not exclude the possibility that parties reflecting ideo-logical or other societal cleavages cannot effectively manage conflict. A federal structure such as in Nigeria, for example, may facilitate national-level bargaining—and even toleration of hegemonic con-trol at that level in exchange for political power exercised by minority parties over territorial subdivisions. In Austria there is an accom-modation between Catholics and Socialists who are divided on both religious and ideological grounds. In Holland religious cleavage dividing Calvinists and Catholics was eventually reflected in political parties that reached a working accommodation at the national level.

Even where the formal structure is unitary, the prospect of sharing in the exercise of power may moderate the rigidity of ideological parties—even anti-system parties—and make them more willing to participate in bargaining relationships at the national level. Note in this regard Sartori's remark that the Italian Communist party has all the power it needs below the level at which power corrupts. The fact is that Italian Communists have not had to face with frustra-tion and despair the prospect of never sharing in the exercise of political power. Below the national level thousands of Communist leaders hold elective and appointive office. While this has not served to make the P.C.I. a willing participant in national conflict resolution it has dulled the cutting edge of the party's anti-systemic drive.

It may be, therefore, that when basic societal cleavages lead to the creation of ideological or sectional parties, one way to cope with this problem (and therefore to facilitate conflict management) is to provide some means whereby power may be shared. One does not have to predicate a decline in ideology in order to see the ap-plication here of the familiar observation that there is more in com-mon between two deputies one of whom is a revolutionary than between two revolutionaries one of whom is a deputy.

There are of course alternative ways of coping with the multi-plicity of parties that emerge from deeply fragmented societies. Government can prevent the appearance of more than one party. When carried to its typical conclusion, this response involves not merely a repression of opposition parties but also establishing tight party control over (or eliminating) secondary associations. In a few pluralistic one-party systems in Africa secondary associations under the aegis of the dominant party are tolerated. But typically, secondary association leaders are under extreme cross-pressure and tend to identify with the unit—in this case the single party—that is more powerful. Evidence also shows that few single-party leaders practice the toleration of dissent that they may preach. Witness on this point Wallerstein's comments about the second thoughts of African leaders regarding the degree of autonomy to be accorded party auxiliary organizations.

The quality of political party leadership or, more precisely, the attitudes and skills of party leadership are an important element in how conflict is managed. As we reflect on the early history of the United States, political leadership skills loom as critically important in the management of conflict; even then it is well to remember that several decades of bargaining and compromise were followed by a civil war. Nonetheless, it is important to note in the developing areas that a handful of men concerned with finding solutions to apparently intractable disputes can maintain a stable system. The success of Malaysia's Alliance party in hammering out a working relationship among the three major ethnic groups must in some measure be attributed to skilled leadership, even if the successful experience proved unfortunately to be temporary. In attempting to assess the probable impact of any party system on the management of conflict, it is essential to know something of leadership style, the degree of tolerance, the measure of trust, and the degree to which leaders are capable of making realistic assessments of the behavior of other people in the system.

The background and experience of party leadership in dealing with conflict is of course important. The memories of past conflicts often condition current behavior. Individuals brought up in a political system in which coups, assassinations, political arrests, and underground movements have existed will not readily move to a political style emphasizing peaceful and rational discussion. Violent nationalist movements—particularly where the violence was directed at competing countrymen as well as against colonial rulers—do not generally produce a bargaining, pragmatic leadership style. With few exceptions the party leaders of the developing states seem ill-prepared to respond in peaceful ways both to pressures from below and to pressures from potential counter-elites.

Broad-based parties which openly recruit are often most likely to be torn by internal conflict, for the more open the party is the more it mirrors the cleavages within the society at large. On the other hand, by penetrating to regional and local levels and by admitting ethnic minorities and dissident elites, the governing party opens the possibility of providing satisfactions to divergent groups and providing opportunities for the settlement of disputes at lower levels within the system. Insofar as disputes are settled at the level of local government or within the local unit of the party, the loads on the national party and national government for the settlement of dispute are thereby reduced. In India for example, the presence of a decentralized broad-based Congress party functioning in a federal system has meant that disputes could be fought out at the local and state level without endangering the stability of the central government. In contrast, the absence of an acceptable procedure for the settlement of inter-island conflict within Indonèsia culminated in the eruption of a civil struggle.

The costs of failure are still another factor affecting the capacity of parties to reconcile conflicts. If a defeated politician has no alternate occupation, no alternate source of income, no alternate rewards than politics, there may be an uncompromising desperate style to his politics. In contrast a politician who knows that if he is defeated within the party, or defeated by the opposition, he may move into the House of Lords, become an Ambassador, run for a lesser office, or return to a lucrative law practice, can afford to accept political defeat with some grace. These differences may help account for the violence which characterizes politics in many of the new nations. In this connection it is important to note the function played by honorific positions of status without power as an outlet for defeated politicians. Powerless upper houses in bicameral systems are not without their purpose.

The role of parties and party systems in conflict management will also be affected by their relationship to governmental structures. One will want to know therefore whether a single party—or the governing party or parties of a competitive system—does in fact control other sectors of government such as the bureaucracy, and whether or not such control is balanced. For both too little and too much party control would appear to be a defective situation in so far as conflict management is concerned.

On the lack of control side, the Latin American situation is particularly striking. In some instances the short- and long-range policy processes are hamstrung by the absence of a party system capable of performing certain input functions. Thus the party system may be unavailable either for articulating and aggregating interest or for assisting in the legitimation of public policy output. However, the separation of parties from governmental elites such as the executive, bureaucracy, and military is such that the latter groups can operate pretty much as they choose, unchecked by the need to come to terms with the wishes or demands of parties.

Western political systems, however, provide some strikingly dissimilar examples of the consequences incident to a failure of the party system to achieve adequate control over the bureaucracy. Weimar Germany is often cited as a telling case of the disruptive impact of a bureaucracy opposed to a particular political system and more or less committed to undermining it. Similarly, major crises in the history of the French Third Republic revealed situations in which the threat of political disintegration grew out of the lack of political party attention to the need for taming the military and the civil bureaucracy.

Theoretically, party control of the bureaucracy in competitive systems can also go too far, thus impeding effective conflict management. The typical situation would be a hegemonic system (ideological or pragmatic, although more so when ideological) in which extended control by one or several parties results in a colonization of the bureaucracy. In party coalition situations, the hegemonic group members tend to cut up the national bureaucracy into so many feudal holdings. Recruitment and promotion in each of these feudal sectors then tend to rest on particularistic party criteria. The application of policy in each sector then tends to rest on party rather than national considerations and apparent decisions, and compromises reached among coalition members in the legislative arena are subjected to distortion and fragmentation in the administrative sector.

Where a single party enjoys hegemonic control in competitive systems, the threat of political colonization is even greater. Where it occurs—as in Italy since the Second World War under the Christian Democrats—the ability of the bureaucratic sector to aggregate demands on the basis of a national interest is severely curtailed. Loyalty to, even membership in, the hegemonic party becomes a critical determinant of bureaucratic promotion. Interest groups outside the party's pale will have less opportunity to articulate their views to bureaucratic decision-makers; indeed, outside groups may even be denied access to these latter. Such groups, and the general public, come to view the bureaucracy as indistinguishable from the dominant party and therefore unable or unwilling to act as an impartial implementer of public policy or arbiter among conflicting groups. Rather than serve to reduce tensions (particularly in societies of deep cleavage) this pattern intensifies them. The hobbling effect on parties and conflict management engendered by extreme governmental autonomy is matched by extreme politicization. Needless to say, the problems incident to this second configuration are greatly augmented when single-party alternatives emerge in the more developed systems.

In colonial areas where the state apparatus was strong, nationalist parties often developed as parallel governments, taking on at the local level certain functions of police, administration, education, and welfare. The party might continue to perform some of these functions following independence but it could not in fact become a substitute for government. If the inherited administrative structures left by colonialism are extremely weak—Guinea is a good example—the line between party and government may be quite blurred and the party will take on almost the whole spectrum of activities that in most societies are considered to be governmental functions. An invariable consequence is that the existing bureaucratic structures become politicized by the dominant party—and possibly that the full force of governmental apparatus can be used to prevent further democratic development.

However, the question of proper balance is not an easy one to deal with. The legacy in many ex-colonial areas is clearly that the strongest unit within the political system turns out to be an entrenched civil and military bureaucracy with its own elite, its own views regarding the new nation's destiny, its own wishes regarding both the priorities and tempo of national development. Where the bureaucracy is strong, while the executive and legislative branches are new and not yet deeply entrenched, and the political parties are essentially weak, ideal conditions exist for the domination of the new states by the public bureaucrats. Such bureaucracies are capable of stifling the growth of a democratic infra-structure by making interest groups deeply dependent on the bureaucracy for survival and therefore little more than the bureaucracy's instrumentalities.

Strong bureaucrats, then, can become significant competing elites to the political party leadership. In many of the newly independent areas the bureaucracy has been hostile to the ideology and program of political parties and has often tried to undercut governmental programs or in extreme cases taken steps to destroy the party system. The bureaucracy, as was the case of Japan after the restoration, may see itself as the bearer of economic modernization, national integration, and political order and view political parties as expressions of parochial loyalties, personal ambition, and disorder. Its trenchant opposition to the parties may seriously impede pluralistic political development or actually bring about one variety or another of the one-party systems discussed earlier.

In a sense a strong bureaucracy (including the military) may set standards for the performance of the party system, and if the latter drastically fails to come up to these standards the bureaucrats—military and/or civil—may move to take control of the system. It is this pattern of political development that now characterizes places such as Libya, Egypt, the Sudan, Burma, and Pakistan. If the potential for military take-overs appears greater in the Middle East and Southern Asia than in sub-Sahara Africa, perhaps it is because in the former instances a legacy of strong military establishments was left by the colonial rulers, while in the latter areas the military was very small or almost totally non-African.

Finally, since we are speaking of balance of power among emergent parties and authoritative governmental structures, it is necessary to note that in many developing areas a dominant or single party may well succeed in politicizing the bureaucracy. Whether, where such fusion occurs, the party has absorbed the bureaucracy or vice versa is an open question. The point is that here too party and government are not very distinguishable, and this confusion may work to undermine rather than fortify the party's capacity for handling conflict.

V. Political Socialization

By suggesting that parties have an important effect on the integration of a nation, the pattern of extended participation, the legitimacy of its political framework, and the management of political conflict, we are in effect implying that parties are an instrument for political socialization. Though parties have always played a role in affecting the attitudes of their members and supporters, parties may play an even more important socializing role in the developing areas today than they did during the early phases of party development in the United States, Great Britain, and the European continent in the eighteenth and nineteenth centuries.

In the contemporary scene a distinction is often made between the mobilist party and other kinds of parties. The term "mobilization" is frequently used to refer to the use of the party as an instrument for effecting attitudinal and behavioral changes within a society. The mobilist party can be contrasted to the adaptive party whose primary concern is its adaptation to the attitudes of the public in its quest for electoral support.

In practice the distinction is not so clear-cut. The mobilist party which typically functions in a one-party state is also concerned with winning and maintaining support even while it seeks to change its public, and the adaptive party is often concerned with influencing public attitudes even while it is primarily concerned with winning elections.

It is often argued in new states that the mobilist party is more conducive to the needs of developing societies than is the adaptive party since adaptation in effect means pandering to the parochial, traditional, conservative attitudes in the society, while mobilization means working toward the establishment of new attitudes concerning national integration, secularism, economic development and a more rational view of life. The mobilist party wages campaigns between elections (if it permits elections at all) and is typically concerned with arousing a sense of public participation, not in decision-making, but in carrying out the goals established by the elite. The adaptive party may be active between elections too, but typically it is concerned with providing services and rewards to individuals so as to gain greater support, financially and in votes, for the party. In short, while the goal of the adaptive party is victory, the goal of the mobilist party is social reconstruction.

Among scholars there is much controversy over the effects, or presumed effects, of mobilist single-party systems on political development. Some scholars have suggested that while mobilist one-party systems facilitate national integration they inhibit effective participation and thereby facilitate the development of oligarchical systems primarily concerned with political survival, national aggrandizement, or personal gain rather than, say, economic growth, social welfare, or democratic political values. Much depends upon how effective the single party is in developing a sense of popular support even while effective political participation is absent.

There is some doubt too as to how effective the so-called mobilist party is at actually mobilizing people. There is often much exhortation that people should appear at work on time, strive to increase agricultural productivity, or produce steel in backyard furnaces, but relatively little is known of the effects of such campaigns either on people's behavior or on their attitudes.

There is some evidence to suggest, moreover, that in practice the electorally oriented adaptive party actually plays an important role in affecting attitudinal and behavioral changes, and is often more effective in doing so than so-called mobilist parties. In its effort to win electoral support from conflicting ethnic and class groups the adaptive party may have greater success in achieving national integration than a party which relies more heavily on coercion and exhortation. Similarly while a mobilist party (particularly in a one-party state) may be more compatible with the establishment of the minimum central authority necessary for economic development, the adaptive party is often more effective in providing government with information essential for carrying out economic development programs.

It should be noted that the controversy in this area is not simply between those who favor one-party (or no party) authoritarian regimes and the advocates of competitive democratic politics. There are many one-party governments whose party is merely the instrument for maintaining authoritarian rule, and there are some competitive systems in which the dominant party actively seeks to change public attitudes. Moreover, many one-party governments justify their authoritarianism by claiming to be concerned with mobilizing for change, but recent reports from one-party states in West Africa suggest that there is a considerable gap between governmental (and party) claims and performance.

Whatever the conclusions one draws on such issues, it is clear that parties are instruments for political socialization, especially so during the early phases of political development when they are among the few institutions concerned with affecting political attitudes. In highly developed systems where there exist widely read newspapers, effective educational systems, and well established adult political attitudes, parties play a relatively minor role in inculcating feelings of being a national or being a citizen. Moreover, in such systems the attitudes which parties inculcate are generally congruent with those generated by the family and by the school. In the developing areas, however, parties seek to inculcate attitudes which are often different from those which adults have learned as children. Indeed, the clash between national and regional (or tribal, linguistic, caste, or religious) parties involves fundamental questions of loyalty and identity which in most developed systems have been resolved by most people before they are adults and political participants.

The result is that parties during the early phases of development are far more concerned with the political socialization of their membership than are established parties in well-developed systems where other institutions assume this role. In the new nations, for example, it is often the party which takes primary responsibility for holding independence day rallies and for celebrating the birthdays of national heroes. It is the party that organizes extensive social services for its members, that helps find employment and provides medical care. It is the party which organizes political training programs, teaches the national (or class, or regional) history, and propagates the government's economic development program and its international aspirations.

But if recent European experience is any guide we may expect the socializing role played by parties to decline as other institutions assume this function. Kirchheimer reports that among the parties of Europe which had once been ideologically oriented, political socialization is no longer as important as it once was. The parties of Germany, Austria, and the Low Countries are increasingly concerned with gaining the electoral support of all social classes, not with the transformation of the political attitudes of the population or of a single social class. The "catch-all" party is too concerned with catching to be concerned with ideological conversion. It tends to take men's attitudes as they are and to try to persuade the voter that the party will serve these attitudes. From the point of view of the socialization role of the party, the transformation that Kirchheimer describes means that parties are now less likely to be malintegrative than before, that the role parties once played in inculcating in members and voters a sense of the inefficacy of politics and a sense of alienation from existing authority may no longer be played. It is important not only to note whether parties play an important role, as against other institutions, in socializing citizens but also to ask what it is that individuals are being socialized into.

THE "LOADS" ON NEWLY-CREATED PARTY SYSTEMS

One of the great paradoxes of political development is that newly formed governments, that is governments with the least experience, are typically faced with the severest loads. A small ill-trained bureaucracy is often called upon to implement planning programs that would stagger the capacity of some of the world's most developed administrative systems. Newly established armies which often have never been engaged in combat are often called upon to deal with the most complex and difficult military situation, an internal war launched by an insurgency movement. And elites which had once been united by a common hostility to a reigning aristocracy or to colonial rulers must now suddenly cope with decades of pent-up conflict, and fundamental disagreements over what constitutes or ought to constitute the national framework of government.

Thus far we have discussed the role parties have played in responding to particular crises of political development but have said little about the relationship of these crises as they affect the behavior of political parties. We have noted, for example, that once political parties come into existence they are often confronted by demands for broader participation. Frequently the crisis of participation is accompanied by crises in legitimacy and of national integration. In what is now the classic British case, parties were compelled to cope with the issue of constitutional order (a legitimacy issue) but *before* the working class sought access into the political system and before the additional crisis of socio-economic distribution arose. Where the issue of legitimacy is settled and there is throughout the society a general agreement on what constitutes the appropriate rules for seeking and exercising power, then the system tends to be capable of handling further demands for political participation or for socio-economic distribution. Where the demand for participation and distribution materializes before the prior crises of legitimacy and national integration have been laid reasonably to rest, great instabilities are introduced into the political system and extreme solutions are, more often than not, resorted to by the groups or parties in power.

Italy provides an excellent example of this latter point. Italians are fond of remarking that one basic problem for the country is that the "social question" had to be shunted aside while almost exclusive attention was paid the "political question." The overriding concern of Italian political leaders of the late nineteenth and early twentieth centuries was the national integration of the country. The greatest need was for political parties to overshadow older parochialism and to build a sense of national identity in a population that had just achieved nationhood and with considerable reluctance.

However, providing a sense of national identity was only one of several problems the Italian political leadership faced simultaneously. The legitimacy of the House of Savoy and of new national political institutions had to be established in places where it simply did not exist at all prior to unification; new strata had to be politically socialized and inducted into a national political system; a great cultural gap reflected in the dual European-Mediterranean nature of the country had to be bridged; and the great problem of Church-State relations had to be confronted. It was while the traditional parties groped unsuccessfully for solutions to these problems and crises that the nation's political leadership was confronted with the additional participation and distribution crises. The "load" proved too heavy; the national leadership responded with repression and violence, institutionalizing fragmented politics and setting precedents for the kind of violence that led to a one-party solution under Fascism.

Although the fact is often obscured by the great emphasis placed on the nationalism that characterized Japan following the Meiji Restoration, a similar pattern could be detected there. The first anti-Tokugawa forces were interested primarily in effecting certain reforms in the older quasi-feudal system. The later modernizers, those who sought completely to discard feudalism and to make Japan an industrial and military power, were immediately confronted with the crisis of integration, of asserting the identity of Japan as a nation against strong sectional loyalties. However, before that crisis could be fully resolved—indeed it was severely aggravated by the fact that the earliest parties were largely sectional—Japan was confronted with the additional crises of participation and distribution. The agrarian elements, for example, made demands that the entrenched elite failed to meet; proletarian-based groups emerged in large numbers making essentially similar demands. The elite responded first with violence and later with a system of legal repression, corruption, and collusion between the dominant parties and the bureaucracy and eventually, military domination. As Robert Scalapino puts this, those who held power under Meiji were greatly in fear of political parties on the grounds that they were both disintegrative for the nation and greatly disruptive of developmental plans. In some measure it was the inadequate way in which the party leadership responded to a pyramiding series of historical crises that led to the collapse of the party system and to the suicidal steps Japan took in the 1940's.

In most of the Asian and African states today there is an extraordinary pile-up of loads for the party system. In most places the problem of national integration—of asserting and legitimizing the priority of the nation-state over tribal and traditional loyalties—is overwhelming. For those parochial and traditional elements who are the objects of legitimizing and integrating activities by party elites, as well as for some elements of the elite itself, what has been characterized as the "crisis of identity" is of paramount importance.

Long before any real integration has occurred, and certainly before the new political institutions have been able to penetrate the outer, rural reaches of these new states, some social groups attempt to enter the political process through the instrumentality of political parties and interest groups. Demands for social justice, in the form of a more equitable distribution of society's wealth and more consumer as opposed to capital goods, and a desire for greater social and economic opportunities are voiced before substantial economic growth has occurred. The margin of growth, which made it possible in the United States and in some European countries to satisfy the demands of the working class without substantial reduction in the wealth of the upper classes is absent in Africa, and this is a reality that party leaders cannot escape. Yet, despite this reality, the clamor for participation and distribution is raised to a deafening pitch. Party elites in power are often under enormous pressure to respond in some fashion that will permit them to retain power. It is the exceptional emerging-nation elite today that adheres to democratic practices in responding to this challenge, that does not ban or severely restrict parties, that does not attempt to make of interest groups abject instrumentalities of the party or bureaucracy, that does not attempt to ride roughshod over tribal, ethnic, communal, or otherwise traditional groupings in the society.

These examples suggest that the roles political parties play in handling the problems of national integration, political legitimacy, participation, and distribution depend upon (a) the sequence and (b) the clustering of issues. Closer examination may show that, among the independent variables that affect the kind of party system and party-system capabilities that develop, great attention must be paid to these two factors. It may be that there is an "appropriate" or "optimum" timing of issues or crises as distinct from a malsequential pattern. It seems obvious, for example, that if the issue of distribution arises before economic development has moved considerably beyond the "take-off" stage, parties will clearly have a more difficult time managing such demands than they would if the problem did not materialize until the country experienced a period of rapid economic growth. Similarly, the demand by the new groups to enter the political system can be much more effectively managed when the constitutional order and the procedures for influencing government have been clearly defined and accepted as legitimate by the general population. If the governing party is asked to handle the demand for distribution before governmental power itself has penetrated to all portions of the territory, and before disparate and preexisting centers of power have been integrated into a larger national framework, then clearly government will have a low capacity to carry out its decisions. Under such circumstances party personnel are likely to become more concerned with influencing existing local bureaucratic and political structures than with formulating and implementing the public policies of a national government.

We are certainly mindful of the fact that emergent party elites cannot wholly dictate either the sequence or the clustering of the types of crises we have enumerated. One does not issue a proclamation and thereby solve the crisis of identity, turning Bengalis into Indians, Hausa into Nigerians, Tamils into Ceylonese, and Chinese into Thais. Nor does one create a sense of legitimacy by promulgating a new constitution and electing national leaders under it. In the historical European cases, emergent parties were confronted with certain inescapable facts concerning the degree of integration and legitimacy that the political system had already achieved. However, parties have been more or less sensitive to these problems and more or less adept at handling them. There seems little doubt, for example, that Bismarck and the National Liberals were ill-advisedly heavy-handed in their efforts to weld a homogeneous nation out of the conglomeration of geographic, ethnic, religious, and social groups that existed prior to German unification. Similarly, we have already suggested that there are certain predictable consequences that derive from the way in which the crisis of participation is managed. A more systematic look at the performance of parties regarding these crises in various settings and at differing points in history may tell us something of value about how the party elites of the newer states might approach similar problems.

Moreover, to some extent at least, emergent party elites can influence both the sequence and clustering of other types of crises. In those societies where popular demands for greater economic distribution are not well developed, the dominant elite can choose to arouse expectations or restrain them. Where economic growth is limited and the governmental machinery is itself underdeveloped and has not penetrated into all sections of the country, a distribution-minded elite may find that it has aroused expectations which it is incapable of satisfying.

We cannot leave this point without emphasizing that the attitude of the dominant party toward economic development can and usually will have important implications for the kind of political system that is viable or democratic. Because, for example, economic development goals are often accompanied by an ideological commitment to the role of the public sector, steps are often taken to harass or impede the private sector, thereby preventing it from becoming an important source of countervailing power. A single-minded commitment to economic growth often leads the dominant party to be intolerant of opposition and predisposed to legislate or otherwise force it out of existence. Trade unions are viewed not as bargaining instruments for the working class, but as groups whose demand for increased wages reduces funds available for capital investment. A commitment by the dominant elite to use the power of the state to speed the process of economic development need not mean repressive policies. There are many policies which development-minded governments may pursue to hasten economic growth which do not require co-ercion. That many governments of the new states choose to stress controls and sanctions rather than incentives is a matter of choice, not a logical or functional prerequisite or consequence of a development-oriented policy.

Moreover, there is neither historic evidence nor theoretical justi-fication for the argument that economic growth can be speeded by authoritarian regimes. Although the experience of the Soviet Union is often cited as evidence that an economically modernizing society cannot afford the luxury of a democratic infra-structure, one can also point to the rapid growth rate of many democratic political systems and the stagnation of many historical and contemporary authoritarian and totalitarian systems. There is no evidence either that among the new states, those that have opted for authoritarian regimes—either one-party systems or military rule—have had any greater success at achieving high growth rates than those that have maintained competitive pluralistic polities. Thus, even if one were to accord to economic growth the highest priority—putting aside for a while all other human values—there is no evidence that mono-lithic systems can move more rapidly than pluralistic ones.

The question of political tutelage can be viewed in this context. Those who advocate a policy of tutelage—and it is invariably advocated by those who exercise power, not those in opposition—argue that it is not only a prerequisite for economic development but also a necessary stage in political development. It is argued that authoritarianism is necessary to prevent opposition elements from exploiting an illiterate and politically unsophisticated peasantry and it is also argued that the integration of parochial groups, such as tribes and castes, can best take place under authoritarian auspices. It may be that authoritarian regimes do prove more skillful in coping with the crisis of integration than pluralistic, competitive systems, but at this stage there is no clearcut evidence one way or another. There is even less reason to believe, however, that viable democratic systems can be constructed on undemocratic foundations. The evolution of some Western democracies out of absolutist systems is clearly not analogous if only because many of the tutelary systems of Asia and Africa are already experiencing crises of participation. Confronted by such crises, moderately authoritarian regimes must either widen the bases of their power or turn increasingly toward the ruthless instruments of mass control we associate with totalitarianism.

Conclusion

Some scholars have suggested that the differences between the party exercising power in an authoritarian or totalitarian state and the parties which compete for power in a democratic system are so great that comparisons are meaningless. They have suggested that the one-party state be dropped from discussions of party systems (indeed, they rightly point out that one cannot speak of a one-party state as a party system, since by definition a system refers to the interrelationship of several units) and should instead simply be looked at as one form of oligarchical systems.

In this volume we have chosen to treat parties, whether in totalitarian or democratic systems, as a generic phenomenon. We have done so on the grounds that parties, of many kinds and in many differing contexts, seem to be a feature of politics in both the developed and developing nations. The need for linking the individual citizen to the state, either by allowing him to participate in the selection of governmental personnel or by controlling him, is a greater need among modern and modernizing nations than among traditional political systems, and it is parties which typically provide this linkage. Moreover, in the ways in which they are organized, the problems with which they are confronted, and the functions they perform, there is much similarity in the single party of an authoritarian system and the dominant party of a competitive system. Strong national parties, whether in an authoritarian or democratic context, appear to be playing an important role today in providing stable and legitimate government and often in laying the foundations for national integration. Certainly in Nigeria and in India the viability of the party system has been an important factor in the continued viability of these countries. And in Ghana, Guinea, Mali, the Ivory Coast, and many other one-party states in Africa, the governing elite often attempts to use the party (with what success is another matter) as an instrument for affecting attitudes and behavior concerning economic activities, the legitimacy of government and its popularity, and in cultivating a sense of national identification.

Given the crucial role parties have often played in the establishment of (or failure to establish) viable political systems in which the framework of government, whether authoritarian or democratic, is widely accepted as legitimate, it is important to note that U.S. aid programs aimed at the development of the military or bureaucracy can sometimes be politically destructive. Where the bureaucracy, for example, is the outstandingly strong institution and political parties are first being organized, a program to strengthen the bureaucracy through technical assistance or to enlarge the military may serve to undermine a frail party system. Thus in the interests of maximizing economic development, technical assistance to "modernize" the bureaucracies of Africa and Asia that neglects the problems of political development may fail to create a viable political framework without which government-sponsored economic development programs are likely to have little success.

It may very well be that from the standpoint of long-range democratic political development a bureaucracy subject to party patronage, even to a certain amount of political corruption, is to be preferred to one which, while it nicely conforms to the Weberian requisites of a legal-rational authority system, is also by this very reason in a position to distort the development of political parties and interest groups and even to subject them to bureaucratic domination. This may be particularly the case in the early stages of national development. Generalizations about the neutrality and objectivity of British and American bureaucracies often fail to take account of the relative recentness of these patterns.

It is by no means sure that political parties, operating either in an open competitive environment or as the single party of a one-party system, can find solutions to the central problems of political development confronting most of the new nations. After all, parties may become the entrenched instruments of powerful elites primarily concerned with resisting efforts of other groups to participate in the political process. Or parties may be so closely identified with parochial ethnic groups and so unconcerned with a larger national identity that they facilitate political disintegration. Or, finally, parties may become such effective instruments for expressing local sentiments and so concerned with converting demands for distribution into administrative acts that they fail to serve the larger public purpose of mobilizing the population for the broader aims of modernization.

We do not know yet which types of parties or party systems will prove capable of dealing with the central tasks or crises of political development in the developing areas. We have tried to suggest here that these crises and problems—such as integration, participation, legitimacy, and conflict management—existed in the West as well and that the types of party systems, one might even say types of political systems, that ultimately emerged grew in large measure out of the sequence and clustering of these crises and the ways in which they were responded to. How well governments deal with the crises of political development in the majority of the developing nations that now live under party governments (approximately 65 out of 83 countries) is in part affected by the character and performance of parties. In turn, the future of parties depends upon how successful they and their governments are in coping with the crises of political development.

A Selected Bibliography

Contributors

Index

A Selected Bibliography

NAOMI E. KIES

Introduction

The literature relevant to the study of political parties and political development is extensive if disproportionately weighted toward certain topics and approaches. A wealth of descriptive material relates the conditions of origins of parties and party systems in developed as well as developing areas. Few attempts have been made at a systematic analysis and comparison of the conditions for emergence, growth patterns, and effects of party development. The following bibliography is intended to indicate the variety of existing studies relevant to such analysis. It tries to bring together propositions relating social, economic, political, and ideological patterns of societies with the parties and party systems which have developed. Descriptions of political parties, per se, or of the specific political situations in developing countries have not been included except where they contribute significantly to the elaboration of a general framework. Similarly, foreign language works were included only if their content appeared unparalleled in the English literature. Obviously, the demands for selectivity preclude listing all important works on a single subject, though many of the books have extensive bibliographies on particular countries or problems. Hopefully, all possible approaches are represented, and, as a result, the selection will prove suggestive as well as informative.

A. GENERAL BACKGROUND

Classification of political parties and party systems.

Relevant methodological studies. Analytical frameworks for the analysis of parties and party systems.

Systematization of the literature on parties in general as well as for particular areas.

1. Almond, Gabriel A., and James S. Coleman, eds. *The Politics of the Developing Areas.* Princeton: Princeton University Press, 1960.
2. Cassinelli, C. W. "The Totalitarian Party," *Journal of Politics,* Vol. 24 (February 1962), pp. 111-141.
3. Duverger, Maurice. *Political Parties: Their Organization and Activity in the Modern State.* New York: John Wiley and Sons, 1954.
4. Eckstein, Harry. *A Theory of Stable Democracy.* Princeton: Center of Inter-

national Studies, Princeton University (Research Monograph No. 10), 1961.

5. Engelmann, Frederick C. "A Critique of Recent Writings on Political Parties," *Journal of Politics*, Vol. 19 (August 1957), pp. 423-440.

6. Golembiewski, R. T. "A Taxonomic Approach to State Political Party Strength," *Western Political Quarterly*, Vol. 11 (September 1958), pp. 494-513.

7. Hodgkin, T. L. *African Political Parties, an Introductory Guide*. Harmondsworth: Penguin Books, 1961.

8. Hume, David. "Of Parties in General," in Hume, *Political and Literary Essays*. London: World's Classics Editions, 1963.

9. Key, V. O. *Politics, Parties and Pressure Groups*. New York: Crowell Publishers, 1958.

10. Lavau, G. E. *Partis Politiques et Réalités Sociales: Contribution à une Étude Réaliste des Partis Politiques*. Paris: Colin, 1953.

11. Leiserson, Avery. "The Place of Parties in the Study of Politics," *American Political Science Review*, Vol. 51 (December 1957), pp. 943-954.

12. Leys, C. "Models, Theories, and the Theory of Political Parties," *Political Studies*, Vol. 7 (June 1959), pp. 127-146.

13. Lipset, S. M. *The First New Nation*. New York: Basic Books, 1963.

14. McClokie, H. D. "The Modern Party State," *Canadian Journal of Economics and Political Science*, Vol. 14 (May 1949), pp. 139-157.

15. McDonald, Neil A. *The Study of Political Parties*. Garden City, New York: Doubleday, 1955.

16. Michels, Roberto. *First Lectures in Political Sociology* (translated by Alfred De Grazia). Minneapolis: University of Minnesota Press, 1949.

17. Michels, Robert. *Political Parties*. New York: Collier, 1962. (Introduction by S. M. Lipset.)

18. Moore, C. H. "The National Party: A Tentative Model," *Public Policy*. Cambridge: Harvard University Press, 1960.

19. Neumann, Sigmund, ed. *Modern Political Parties*. Chicago: University of Chicago Press, 1956.

20. Ostrogorski, M. I. *Democracy and the Organization of Political Parties in the United States and Great Britain*. Garden City, New York: Doubleday-Anchor, 1964 (abridged).

21. Pye, L. W. "The Non-western Political Process," *Journal of Politics*, Vol. 20 (August 1958), pp. 468-486.

22. Ranney, Austin. *The Doctrine of Responsible Party Government: Its Origin and Present State*. Urbana, Ill.: University of Illinois Press, 1954.

23. Riggs, Fred W. "The Theory of Developing Politics," *World Politics*, 16 (October 1963), pp. 147-171.

24. Rudolph, Lloyd. "The Meaning of Party: From the Politics of Status to the Politics of Opinion in Eighteenth Century England and America." Ph.D. Thesis: Harvard, 1956 (unpublished).

25. Weiner, Myron. "Traditional Role Performance and the Development of Modern Political Parties: The Indian Case," *Journal of Politics*, Vol. 26 (November 1964), pp. 830-849.

26. Wildavsky, Aaron B. "A Methodological Critique of Duverger's "Political Parties," *Journal of Politics*, Vol. 21 (May 1959), pp. 303-318.

See also: E42, E45, E48, H20, H23, I40, J1, J12, J40, J47, L25, L27, L34, L44.*

Conditions of Origin and Development of Parties and Party Systems

B. TRADITIONAL SOCIAL AND POLITICAL ORGANIZATION

Anthropological and sociological studies of traditional patterns of social and political organization and their effect on the types of parties and party systems.

Traditional factors which contribute to or delay the growth of mass parties.

The significance of tradition in Europe and America: historical, ethnic, and religious factors important in the patterns of political organization and behavior.

Studies of the relative adaptiveness of various systems to modernization.

1. Albert, Ethel M. "Socio-political Organization and Receptivity to Change: Some Differences Between Ruanda and Urundi," *Southwest Journal of Anthropology*, Vol. 16 (Spring 1960), pp. 46-74.

2. Almond, Gabriel A. "The Resistance and the Political Parties of Western Europe," *Political Science Quarterly*, Vol. 62 (March 1947), pp. 27-61.

3. Apter, David E. "The Role of Traditionalism in the Political Modernization of Ghana and Uganda," *World Politics*, Vol. 13 (October 1960), pp. 45-68.

4. Austin, Dennis. "Parties and Tradition in Ghana." London: Institute of Commonwealth Studies, University of London (seminar paper), 1959.

5. Bailey, Frederick George. *Tribe, Caste and Nation: A Study of Political Activity and Political Change in Highland Orissa.* Manchester: Manchester University Press, 1960.

6. Barth, Fredrik. *Political Leadership among Swat Pathans.* London: Athlone Press, 1959.

7. Bin Sayeed, Khalid. "Religion and Nation Building in Pakistan," *Middle East Journal*, Vol. 28 (Summer 1963), pp. 279-291.

8. Binder, Leonard. *Religion and Politics in Pakistan.* Berkeley and Los Angeles: University of California Press, 1961.

9. Brenan, Gerald. *The Spanish Labyrinth.* London: Cambridge University Press, 1960.

10. Drake, St. Clair. "Representative Government and the Traditional Cultures and Institutions of West African Societies." (Paper presented to the Ibadan Conference on Representative Government and National Progress, March 16-23, 1959.)

11. ————. "Traditional Authority and Social Action in Former British West Africa," *Human Organization*, Vol. 19 (Fall 1960), pp. 150-158.

12. Eberhard, Wolfram. *Conquerors and Rulers: Social Forces in Medieval China.* Leiden: Brill, 1952.

13. *Journal of Politics*, Vol. 26 (February 1964), special issue on "The American

* Letters refer to sections of bibliography in which additional citations may be found.

South: 1950-1970." See especially William H. Nicholls, "The South as a Developing Area," pp. 22-40; Donald R. Matthews and James W. Prothro, "Southern Images of Political Parties: An Analysis of White and Negro Attitudes," pp. 82-111; Samuel Du Bois Cook, "Political Movements and Organizations," pp. 130-153; and O. Douglas Weeks, "The South in National Politics," pp. 221-240.

14. Krebhiel, Edward. "Geographic Influences in British Elections," *The Geographical Review*, Vol. 2 (December 1916), pp. 419-432.

15. Lambert, Richard D. "Hindu Communal Groups in Indian Politics," in Park and Tinker, eds. *Leadership and Political Institutions in India.* Princeton: Princeton University Press, 1959, pp. 211-224.

16. Litt, E. "Ethnic Status and Political Perspectives," *Midwest Journal of Political Science*, Vol. 5 (August 1961), pp. 276-283.

17. Mednick, M. "Sultans and Mayors: The Relation of a National to an Indigenous Political System," *Il Politico*, Vol. 26 (March 1961), pp. 142-147.

18. Mitrany, David. *Marx Against the Peasant: A Study in Social Dogmatism.* New York: Collier Books, 1961.

19. Price, J. H. "The Role of Islam in Gold Coast Politics," *Proceedings of the Third Annual Conference of the West African Institute of Social and Economic Research.* Ibadan: University College, 1956.

20. Robinson, Geroid Tanquary. *Rural Russia under the Old Regime* (A History of the Landlord-Peasant World, and a Prologue to the Peasant Revolution of 1917). New York: The Macmillan Company, 1957.

21. Rudolph, Lloyd I., and Susanne Hoeber Rudolph. "The Political Role of India's Caste Associations," *Pacific Affairs*, Vol. 33 (March 1960), pp. 5-22.

22. Schapera, I. *Government and Politics in Tribal Societies.* London: Watts, 1956.

23. Sakai, Robert. "Feudal Society and Modern Leadership in Satsuma-han," *Journal of Asian Studies*, Vol. 16 (May 1957), pp. 365-376.

24. Singer, Milton B., ed. *Traditional India: Structure and Change.* Philadelphia: American Folklore Society, 1959.

25. Tinker, Hugh. "Authority and Community in Village India," *Journal of African Administration*, Vol. 12 (October 1960), pp. 193-210.

26. Trager, Frank N. "The Political Split in Burma," *Far Eastern Survey*, Vol. 27 (October 1958), pp. 145-155.

27. Vaughan, James H., Jr. "Culture, History and Grass-Roots Politics in a Nigerian Chiefdom." (Paper presented at the meetings of the American Anthropological Association; Chicago, December 1962.)

28. Von der Mehden, Fred R. "Burma's Religious Campaign Against Communism," *Pacific Affairs*, Vol. 33 (September 1960), pp. 290-299.

29. Wilson, David A. *Political Tradition and Political Change in Thailand.* Santa Monica, Calif.: The RAND Corporation, 1962.

30. Wright, Gordon. *Rural Revolution in France* (The Peasantry in the Twentieth Century). Stanford: Stanford University Press, 1964.

31. Young, Roland, and Henry A. Fosbrooke. *Smoke in the Hills: Political Tension in the Morogoro District of Tanganyika.* Evanston, Ill.: Northwestern University Press, 1960.

NAOMI E. KIES

See also: C3, C13, D5, D24, D27, D32, E3, E5, E15, E38, E39, H19, I3, I4, I5, I7, I14, I15, I16, I32, I51, J19, J28, J44, L25.

C. SOCIAL STRUCTURE AND POLITICAL PARTIES

General relationships between political organizations and society.
Social stratification, social mobility, and political attitudes.
Social composition of societies with different types of parties and party systems.
Impact of social organization on party growth and general political change.

1. Alexander, Robert J. "The Latin American 'Aprista' Parties," *Political Quarterly*, Vol. 20 (July-September 1949), pp. 236-247.
2. Alford, Robert R. *Party and Society: The Anglo-American Democracies.* Chicago: Rand McNally and Co., 1963.
3. Allinsmith, Wesley, and Beverly Allinsmith. "Religious Affiliation and Politico-economic Attitude: A Study of Eight Major U.S. Religious Groups," *Public Opinion Quarterly*, Vol. 2 (Fall 1948), pp. 377-389.
4. Brotz, Howard M. "Social Stratification and the Political Order," *American Journal of Sociology*, Vol. 64 (May 1959), pp. 571-578.
5. Dahrendorf, Ralf. *Class and Class Conflict in Industrial Society.* Stanford: Stanford University Press, 1959.
6. Doggan, M. "Le Vote Ouvrier en Europe Occidentale," *Revue Française Sociologie*, Vol. 1 (January-March 1960), pp. 25-44.
7. Eulau, Heinz. *Class and Party in the Eisenhower Years: Class Roles and Perspectives in the 1952 and 1956 Elections.* New York: The Free Press of Glencoe, 1962.
8. Filley, Walter O. "Social Structure and Canadian Political Parties: The Quebec Case," *Western Political Quarterly*, Vol. 9 (December 1956), pp. 900-914.
9. Fitzgibbon, Russell H. "The Social Basis of Changing Political Structures in Latin America," *Social Science*, Vol. 34 (April 1959), pp. 63-71.
10. Glantz, Oscar. "Class Consciousness and Political Solidarity," *American Sociological Review*, Vol. 23 (August 1958), pp. 375-383.
11. Guttsman, W. L. "Social Stratification and Political Elite," *British Journal of Sociology*, Vol. 11 (June 1960), pp. 137-150.
12. Landecker, Werner. "Class Crystallization and Class Consciousness," *American Sociological Review*, Vol. 28 (April 1963), pp. 219-229.
13. Lenski, Gerhard. *The Religious Factor.* New York: Doubleday and Co., 1961.
14. Lipset, S. M. *Agrarian Socialism: The Cooperative Commonwealth Federation in Saskatchewan; A Study in Political Sociology.* Berkeley: University of California Press, 1959.
15. ———. "The Changing Class Structure and Contemporary European Politics," *Daedalus*, Vol. 93 (Winter 1964), pp. 271-303.
16. ———. "Party Systems and the Representation of Social Groups," *European Journal of Sociology*, Vol. 1 (1960), pp. 50-85.
17. ———. *Political Man: The Social Basis of Politics.* New York: Doubleday and Co., 1960.
18. Lipson, Leslie. "Party Systems in the United Kingdom and the Older

Commonwealth: Causes, Resemblances, and Variations," *Political Studies* (Oxford), Vol. 7 (February 1959), pp. 12-31.

19. Madge, Charles. "Caste and Community in India and Thailand: a Contrast," *Indian Journal of Adult Education*, Vol. 19 (October 1958), pp. 13-15.

20. McKenzie, Robert T., and Allan Silver. "Conservatism, Industrialism and the Working Class Tory in England." (Paper prepared for the Fifth World Congress of Sociology; Washington, D.C., September 1962.)

21. Park, George K., and Lee Soltow. "Politics and Social Structure in a Norwegian Village," *American Journal of Sociology*, Vol. 67 (September 1961), pp. 152-164.

22. Parsons, Talcott. "Social Structure and Political Orientation," *World Politics*, Vol. 13 (October 1960), pp. 112-128.

23. Rose, Richard. *Politics in England*. Boston: Little, Brown and Co., 1964.

24. Van der Kroef, Justus M. "Indonesia's First National Election; a Sociological Analysis," *American Journal of Economics and Sociology*, Vol. 16 (April-July 1957), pp. 237-249, 407-420.

25. Wright, Gordon. "Peasant Politics in the Third French Republic," *Political Science Quarterly*, Vol. 70 (March 1955), pp. 75-86.

26. Yang, Ch'ing-k'un. *The Chinese Family in the Communist Revolution*. Cambridge, Mass.: Technology Press, M.I.T. (distributed by Harvard University Press), 1959.

See also: A10, A16, B1, D2, D8, D14, D33, E30, I16, I35, I37, I54, J5, J29, J53, L31.

D. SOCIAL AND ECONOMIC CHANGE AND PARTY GROWTH

Social and economic conditions necessary for the emergence and continuation of parties and party systems.

Dependence of mass party growth on economic and social changes which make "national" rather than sectional or particularistic parties feasible.

Effects of the simultaneous occurrence of industrialization and urbanization on nineteenth century political change.

The association of particular patterns of social and economic organization with types of parties and systems, distinguished by structure, ideology, and relationship to other groups in society.

The emergence of new classes. The significance of the components of "mass society" for political developments in the twentieth century.

Relationship between parties and particular social arrangements as well as to large-scale societal changes.

1. Berg, Elliot J. "The Economic Basis of Political Choice in French West Africa," *American Political Science Review*, Vol. 54 (June 1960), pp. 391-405.

2. Binder, Leonard. *Iran: Political Development in a Changing Society*. Berkeley: University of California Press, 1962.

3. Blackton, Charles S. "The Dawn of Australian National Feeling, 1850-1856," *Pacific Historical Review*, Vol. 24 (May 1955), pp. 123-132.

4. Boorman, Howard I. "The Study of Contemporary Chinese Politics: Some Remarks on Retarded Development," *World Politics*, Vol. 12 (July 1960), pp. 585-599.

5. Braibanti, Ralph J. D., and Joseph J. Spengler, eds. *Tradition, Values and Socio-economic Development*. Durham, N.C.: Duke University Press, 1961.

6. Brown, B. E. *Middle-class Democracy and the Revolution in Massachusetts, 1691-1780*. Ithaca, N.Y.: Cornell University Press, 1955.

7. Deutsch, Karl W., and William J. Foltz, eds. *Nation-building*. New York: Atherton Press, 1963.

8. ―――. "Social Mobilization and Political Development," *American Political Science Review*, Vol. 55 (September 1961), pp. 493-514.

9. Dore, R. P. "Japanese Politics and the Approach of Prosperity," *World Today*, Vol. 17 (July 1961), pp. 289-299.

10. Fitzgibbon, Russell H. "The Party Potpourri in Latin America," *Western Political Quarterly*, Vol. 10 (March 1957), pp. 3-22.

11. Gil, Frederico Guillermo. *Genesis and Modernization of Political Parties in Chile*. Gainesville, Fla.: University of Florida Press, 1962. (Latin American Monograph Series No. 18.)

12. Glade, William P., Jr., and Charles W. Anderson. *The Political Economy of Mexico: Two Studies*. Madison: University of Wisconsin Press, 1963. ("Revolution and Economic Development"; "Bankers as Revolutionaries: Politics and Development Banking in Mexico.")

13. Gold, D., and J. R. Schmidhauser. "Urbanization and Party Competition: The Case of Iowa," *Midwest Journal of Political Science*, Vol. 4 (February 1960), pp. 62-75.

14. Goldthorpe, J. H., and D. Lockwood. "Affluence and the British Class Structure," *The Sociological Review*, Vol. 4 (Autumn 1963), pp. 133-163.

15. Gusfield, J. R. "Mass Society and Extremist Politics," *American Sociological Review*, Vol. 27 (February 1962), pp. 19-30.

16. Hanham, Harold John. *Elections and Party Management*. London: Longmans, Green and Co., 1959.

17. Hottinger, Arnold. "Zúamá and Parties in the Lebanese Crisis of 1958," *Middle East Journal*, Vol. 15 (Spring 1961), pp. 127-240.

18. Hudson, Geoffrey, *et al. The Chinese Communes*. Stanford, Cal.: Institute of Pacific Relations, 1960.

19. Hyman, Herbert. "Mass Media and Political Socialization: The Role of Patterns of Communication," in Lucian W. Pye, ed. *Communications and Political Development*. Princeton: Princeton University Press, 1963, pp. 128-148.

20. Johnson, J. J. *Political Change in Latin America: Emergence of the Middle Sectors*. Stanford: Stanford University Press, 1958.

21. Johnston, Scott D. "Election Politics and Social Change in Israel," *Middle East Journal*, Vol. 15 (Summer 1962), pp. 309-327.

22. Kantor, Harry. "The Development of Acción Democrática de Venezuela," *Journal of Inter-American Studies*, Vol. 1 (April 1959), pp. 237-252.

23. Kautsky, John H., ed. *Political Change in Underdeveloped Countries*:

445

Nationalism and Communism. New York: John Wiley and Sons, 1962. (See especially "An Essay in the Politics of Development.")

24. Kilson, Martin L., Jr. "Land and the Kikuyu: A Study of the Relationship Between Land and Kikuyu Political Movements," *Journal of History,* Vol. 60 (April 1955), pp. 103-153.

25. Kornhauser, William. *The Politics of Mass Society.* Glencoe, Ill.: The Free Press, 1959.

26. Macpherson, C. B. *Democracy in Alberta: The Theory and Practice of a Quasi-Party System.* Toronto: University of Toronto Press, 1953.

27. Mercier, Paul. "Political Life in the Urban Centers of Senegal: A Study of a Period of Transition," *Prod Translations,* Vol. 3 (June 1960), pp. 3-20.

28. Palmer, R. R. *The Age of the Democratic Revolution.* Princeton: Princeton University Press, 1959.

29. Pye, Lucian W. "Communication Patterns and the Problems of Representative Government in Non-western Societies," *Public Opinion Quarterly,* Vol. 20 (Spring 1956), pp. 249-257.

30. ————. *Communications and Political Development.* Princeton: Princeton University Press, 1963.

31. Rosenberg, Morris. "The Meaning of Politics in Mass Society," *Public Opinion Quarterly,* Vol. 15 (Spring 1951), pp. 5-15.

32. Rustow, Dankwart. *Politics and Westernization in the Near East.* Princeton: Princeton University Press, 1956.

33. Schweitzer, Arthur. "The Nazification of the Lower Middle Class and Peasants," in Maurice Baumong, *et al.* eds. *The Third Reich.* New York: Praeger, 1955.

34. Scott, Robert E. *Mexican Government in Transition.* Urbana, Ill.: University of Illinois Press, 1959.

35. Singh, Jitendra. "Communism in Kerala," *Political Quarterly,* Vol. 31 (April-June 1960), pp. 185-202.

36. Sondermann, Fred A. "Political Implications of Population Growth in Underdeveloped Countries," *Colorado College Studies,* No. 5 (Fall 1961).

37. Spengler, J. J. "Economic Development: Political Pre-conditions and Political Consequences," *Journal of Politics,* Vol. 22 (August 1960), pp. 387-416.

38. Stedman, M. S., Jr., and S. W. Stedman. *Discontent at the Polls, A Study of Farmer and Labor Parties, 1827-1948.* New York: Columbia University Press, 1950.

39. Stokes, William S. "The 'Revolution Nacional' and the M.N.R. in Bolivia," *Inter-American Economic Affairs,* Vol. 12 (Spring 1959), pp. 28-53.

40. Sutter, John Orval. *Indonesianisasi* (An Historical Survey of the Role of Politics in the Institutions of a Changing Economy From the Second World War to the Eve of the General Elections, 1946-1955). Ithaca, New York. Cornell University Press, 1959.

41. Tannenbaum, Frank. *Mexico: The Struggle for Peace and Bread.* New York: Knopf, 1950.

42. Taylor, Norman W. "The Effects of Industrialization—Its Opportunities

and Consequences—Upon French-Canadian Society," *The Journal of Economic History*, Vol. 20 (December 1960), pp. 638-647.

43. Ward, R. E. "The Socio-Political Role of the Buraku (Hamlet) in Japan," *American Political Science Review*, Vol. 45 (December 1951), pp. 1025-1040.

44. Watson, Richard A. *The Politics of Urban Change.* Kansas City, Mo.: Community Studies, Inc., 1963.

See also: A1, B13, B20, B30, C2, C5, C9, C15, E1, E8, E16, E36, E48, I1, I8, I18, J9, J34, J35, J41, J67, K1, K8, K11, K12, K14, K15, L3, L25.

E. POLITICAL CULTURE AND IDEOLOGICAL CHANGE

Changes in value systems involved in society experiencing rapid social and economic development.

Ideological components of the conditions for the development of political movements and party organizations.

Ideological change as a consequence as well as a precondition of party growth.

Differences in party systems according to the differences in value systems of social systems or subsystems.

1. Almond, Gabriel A. *The Appeals of Communism.* Princeton: Princeton University Press, 1954.

2. Almond, Gabriel, and Sidney Verba. *The Civic Culture.* Princeton: Princeton University Press, 1963.

3. Apter, David E. "Political Religion in the New Nations," in Clifford Geertz, ed. *Old Societies and New States.* New York: Free Press of Glencoe, 1963.

4. ———, ed. *Ideology and Discontent.* New York: The Free Press, 1964.

5. Badgley, John J. "Burma's Radical Left: A Study in Failure," *Problems of Communism*, Vol. 10 (March-April 1961), pp. 47-55.

6. Barbu, Zevedei. *Democracy and Dictatorship; Their Psychology and Patterns of Life.* New York: Grove Press, 1956.

7. Beck, J. M., and J. D. Dooley. "Party Images in Canada," *Queen's Quarterly*, Vol. 67 (Autumn 1960), pp. 431-448.

8. Bell, Daniel. *The End of Ideology.* Glencoe, Ill.: The Free Press, 1960.

9. Bernard, J. "Parties and Issues in Conflict," *Journal of Conflict Resolution*, Vol. 1 (March 1957), pp. 111-121.

10. Bittner, Egon. "Radicalism and the Organization of Radical Movements," *American Sociological Review*, Vol. 28 (December 1963), pp. 928-940.

11. Blanksten, George I. *Peron's Argentina.* Chicago: University of Chicago Press, 1953.

12. Bretton, Henry L. "Current Political Thought and Practice in Ghana," *American Political Science Review*, Vol. 52 (March 1958), pp. 46-63.

13. Briggs, A. "Middle Class Consciousness in English Politics, 1780-1846," *Past and Present*, Vol. 1 (April 1956), pp. 65-74.

14. Brzezinski, Zbigniew. *Ideology and Power in Soviet Politics.* New York: Praeger, 1962.

15. Burks, R. V. "Catholic Parties in Latin Europe," *Journal of Modern History*, Vol. 24 (September 1952), pp. 269-286.

16. Cantril, Hadley. *The Politics of Despair*. New York: Basic Books, 1958.
17. Clark, S. D. "The Religious Factor in Canadian Economic Development," in *Economic Growth: A Symposium*, Supplement VII, *The Journal of Economic History* (1947), pp. 89-103.
18. Corpuz, O. D. "The Cultural Foundations of Filipino Politics," *Philippine Journal of Public Administration*, Vol. 4 (October 1960), pp. 297-310.
19. Daniels, Robert V. "The State and Revolution: A Case Study in the Genesis and Transformation of Communist Ideology," *American Slavic and East European Review*, Vol. 12 (February 1953), pp. 22-43.
20. Davis, M., and Sidney Verba. "Party Affiliation and International Opinions in Britain and France, 1947-1956," *Public Opinion Quarterly*, Vol. 24 (Winter 1960), pp. 590-604.
21. Di Tella, Torquato S. "Monolithic Ideologies in Competitive Party Systems—The Latin American Case." (Paper presented at the World Sociology Congress; Washington, D.C., September 1962.)
22. Einaudi, Mario. *Communism in Western Europe*. Ithaca, N.Y.: Cornell University Press, 1951.
23. Fallers, Lloyd. "Ideology and Culture in Uganda Nationalism," *American Anthropologist*, Vol. 63 (August 1961), pp. 677-686.
24. Ferkiss, Victor C. "Political and Intellectual Origins of American Radicalism; Right and Left," *Annals of the American Academy of Political and Social Science*, Vol. 344 (November 1962), pp. 1-12.
25. Froman, Lewis A. "Personality and Political Socialization," *Journal of Politics*, Vol. 23 (May 1961), pp. 341-352.
26. Geertz, Clifford, ed. *Old Societies and New States*. New York: Free Press of Glencoe, 1963.
27. Hirschman, Albert O. "Ideologies of Economic Development in Latin America," in Hirschman ed. *Latin-American Issues; Essays and Comments*. New York: Twentieth Century Fund, 1962.
28. Lane, Robert. *Political Ideology*. New York: Free Press of Glencoe, 1962.
29. Lasswell, Harold D., Daniel Lerner, and Ithiel de Sola Pool. *The Comparative Study of Symbols*. Stanford: Hoover Institution Studies, 1952.
30. Leggett, J. C. "Working-Class Consciousness, Race, and Political Choice," *American Journal of Sociology*, Vol. 69 (September 1963), pp. 171-176.
31. Lerner, D., I. Pool, and H. D. Lasswell. "Comparative Analysis of Political Ideologies: A Preliminary Statement," *Public Opinion Quarterly*, Vol. 15 (Winter 1951), pp. 715-733.
32. LeVine, Robert. "Political Socialization and Culture Change," in Geertz, ed. *op.cit.*, pp. 280-303.
33. Malenbaum, W., and W. Stolper. "Political Ideology and Economic Progress: The Basic Question," *World Politics*, Vol. 12 (April 1960), pp. 413-421.
34. Mannheim, Karl. *Ideology and Utopia*. New York: Harcourt, Brace and Co., 1936 (1940).
35. Mardin, Serif. *The Genesis of Young Ottoman Thought: A Study in the Modernization of Turkish Political Ideas*. Princeton: Princeton University Press, 1962.
36. Matossian, Mary. "Ideologies of Delayed Industrialization: Some Tensions

and Ambiguities," *Economic Development and Cultural Change*, Vol. 6 (April 1958), pp. 217-228.

37. McCully, Bruce Tiebout. *English Education and the Origins of Indian Nationalism*. New York: Columbia University Press, 1940.

38. Micaud, Charles A. *Communism and the French Left*. New York: Praeger, 1963.

39. Moody, J. N., ed. *Church and Society: Catholic Social and Political Thought and Movements, 1789-1950*. New York: Arts, Inc., 1953.

40. Moore, B. *Soviet Politics: The Dilemma of Power*. Cambridge: Harvard University Press, 1950.

41. Nisbet, Robert A. *The Quest for Community*. New York: Oxford University Press, 1953.

42. Pye, Lucian W. "Communist Strategies and Asian Societies," *World Politics*, Vol. 11 (October 1958), pp. 118-127.

43. ———. "Personal Identity and Political Ideology," *Behavioral Science*, Vol. 6 (July 1961), pp. 205-221.

44. ———. *Political Personality and Nation-Building: Burma's Search for Identity*. New Haven: Yale University Press, 1962.

45. ———, and Sidney Verba, eds. *Political Culture and Political Development*. Princeton: Princeton University Press, 1965.

46. Stern, Fritz. *The Politics of Cultural Despair*. Berkeley and Los Angeles: University of California Press, 1961.

47. Ulam, Adam. *The Unfinished Revolution*. New York: Random House, 1960.

48. Watnick, Morris. "The Appeal of Communism to the Underdeveloped Peoples," *Economic Development and Cultural Change*, Vol. 1 (March 1952), pp. 22-36.

49. Weiner, Myron. "Struggle Against Power: Notes on Indian Political Behavior," *World Politics*, Vol. 8 (April 1956), pp. 392-403.

See also: B3, B4, B18, B19, B27, C6, C10, C12, C20, C23, D4, D5, D15, F17, H16, I10, I43, J20, J55, J61, L15.

F. EXTERNAL ORIGINS: NATIONALISM, INDEPENDENCE, AND THE EMERGENCE OF PARTY SYSTEMS

Nationalist movements and party organizations.

The peculiar conditions of colonial rule and the attainment of independence.

External, rather than internal, factors determining party origin.

Comparison of different types of systems in relation to colonial history and nationalist development.

The coincidence of ideological, traditional, and socio-economic problems and their impact on party growth.

1. Ansprenger, Franz. *Politik Im Schwarzen Afrika*. Cologne and Opladen: Westdeutscher Verlag, 1961.

2. Apter, David E., and Carl G. Rosberg, Jr. "Nationalism and Models of Political Change in Africa," in Wallerstein, *et al. The Political Economy of Contemporary Africa*. Washington, D.C.: National Institute of Social and Behavioral Science, 1959.

3. Carter, Gwendolen, and W. O. Brown. *Transition in Africa: Studies in Political Adaptation.* Boston: Boston University African Research Studies No. 1, 1958.

4. Coleman, James S. "The Emergence of African Political Parties," in Haines, ed. *Africa Today.* Baltimore: Johns Hopkins University Press, 1955, pp. 225-255.

5. ———. "Nationalism in Tropical Africa," *American Political Science Review,* Vol. 48 (June 1954), pp. 404-426.

6. ———. *Nigeria: Background to Nationalism.* Berkeley and Los Angeles: University of California Press, 1960.

7. Emerson, Rupert. *From Empire to Nation: The Rise to Self-Assertion of Asian and African People.* Cambridge: Harvard University Press, 1960.

8. Hartenstein, Wolfgang. *Die Anfaenge der Deutschen Volkspartei, 1918-1920.* Dusseldorf: Droste Verlag, 1962.

9. Hobsbawn, E. J. *Primitive Rebels: Studies in Archaic Forms of Social Movement in the Nineteenth and Twentieth Centuries.* New York: Praeger, 1963.

10. Hodgkin, Thomas L. *Nationalism in Colonial Africa.* New York: New York University Press, 1957.

11. Lee, Chong-Sik. *The Politics of Korean Nationalism.* Berkeley: University of California Press, 1963.

12. Leys, Colin. "Tanganyika: The Realities of Independence," *International Journal,* Vol. 17 (Summer 1962), pp. 251-268.

13. Mair, L. P. "Independent Religious Movements in Three Continents," *Comparative Studies in Society and History,* Vol. 1 (January 1959), pp. 113-135.

14. Payne, Stanley G. *Falange: A History of Spanish Fascism.* Stanford: Stanford University Press, 1961.

15. Piper, R. *The Formation of the Soviet Union: Communism and Nationalism, 1917-1923.* Cambridge: Harvard University Press, 1954.

16. Pye, Lucian W. *Guerrilla Communism in Malaya, Its Social and Political Meaning.* Princeton: Princeton University Press, 1956.

17. Snow, Peter G. "The Political Party Spectrum in Chile," *The South Atlantic Quarterly,* Vol. 62 (Autumn 1963), pp. 474-487.

18. Vali, Ferenc A. *Rift and Revolt in Hungary: Nationalism Versus Communism.* Cambridge: Harvard University Press, 1961.

19. Von der Mehden, Fred R. "Marxism and Early Islamic Nationalism." *Political Science Quarterly,* Vol. 73 (September 1958), pp. 335-351.

20. Wallerstein, Immanuel. *Africa: The Politics of Independence.* New York: Vintage Books, 1961.

See also: A1, A7, A18, B31, D3, D7, D23, D39, E11, E35, H7, I56, J48, J58, L4, L5, L30.

G. INTERNAL ORIGINS: PARLIAMENTS, CLIQUES, FACTIONS, AND COALITIONS

Political parties originating within formal institutions of government, rather than from broad social movements.

Works specifically tracing the emergence of factions from informal groupings and parties from factions in parliamentary bodies.

Divisions and opposition in pre-party or one-party situations; coalitions in multiparty systems.

1. Braunthal, G. "The Free Democratic Party in West German Politics," *Western Political Quarterly*, Vol. 13 (June 1960), pp. 332-348.

2. Butterfield, Herbert. *George III and the Historians.* London: Collins, 1957.

3. Chambers, William Nisbet. *Political Parties in a New Nation: The American Experience, 1776-1809.* New York: Oxford University Press, 1963.

4. Charles, Joseph. *The Origins of the American Party System.* Williamsburg, Va.: Institute of Early American History and Culture, 1956.

5. Crandall, A. W. *The Early History of the Republican Party, 1854-1856.* Gloucester, Mass.: P. Smith, 1960.

6. Jennings, William Ivor. *Party Politics.* Cambridge, England: Cambridge University Press, 1962.

7. Johnston, S. D. "Party Politics and Coalition Cabinets in the Knesset of Israel," *Middle Eastern Affairs*, Vol. 13 (May 1962), pp. 130-138.

8. Livingston, William S. "Minor Parties and Minority M.P.'s, 1945-1955," *Western Political Quarterly*, Vol. 12 (December 1959), pp. 1017-1037.

9. Loewenberg, Gerhard. "Parliamentarism in Western Germany: The Functioning of the Bundestag," *American Political Science Review*, Vol. 55 (March 1961), pp. 87-102.

10. Matthews, Donald R. *United States Senators and Their World.* Chapel Hill, N.C.: University of North Carolina Press, 1960.

11. Menzel, W. "Parliamentary Politics in the German Federal Republic from 1957-1960," *Parliamentary Affairs*, Vol. 13 (Autumn 1960), pp. 509-519.

12. Ostry, B. "Conservatives, Liberals, and Labour in the 1880's," *Canadian Journal of Economics and Political Science*, Vol. 27 (May 1961), pp. 291-296.

13. Parsons, M. B. "Quasi-Partisan Conflict in a One-Party Legislative System: The Florida Senate, 1947-1961," *American Political Science Review*, Vol. 56 (September 1962), pp. 605-614.

14. Patterson, Samuel C. "Dimensions of Voting Behavior in a One-Party State Legislature," *Public Opinion Quarterly*, Vol. 26 (Summer 1962), pp. 185-200.

15. Riker, W. H., and D. Niemi. "The Stability of Coalitions on Roll Calls in the House of Representatives," *American Political Science Review*, Vol. 56 (March 1962), pp. 58-65.

16. Salomone, William. "Italian Democracy in the Making: The Political Scene in the Giolittian Era, 1900-1914." Philadelphia: University of Pennsylvania, 1955 (unpublished Ph.D. dissertation).

17. Sharabi, H. B. "Parliamentary Government and Military Autocracy in the Middle East" (bloc parties; single party dictatorships; two party systems; dominant party systems; sectarian and doctrinal parties), *Orbis*, Vol. 4 (Fall 1960), pp. 388-455.

18. Smiley, D. V. "The Two Party System and One-Party Dominance in the

Liberal Democratic State," *Canadian Journal of Economics and Political Science*, Vol. 24 (August 1958), pp. 312-322.

19. Southgate, D. *The Passing of the Whigs: 1832-1886.* New York: St Martin's Press, 1962.

20. Stokes, Donald E., and Warren E. Miller. "Party Government and the Saliency of Congress: To What Extent do Public Reactions to the Legislative Records of the Major Parties Influence Voters' Choices Among Party Candidates at Mid-term Congressional Elections?" *Public Opinion Quarterly*, Vol. 26 (Winter 1962), pp. 531-546.

21. Tarr, F. De. *The French Radical Party from Herriot to Mendes-France.* London: Oxford University Press, 1961.

22. Wahlke, J., *et al. The Legislative System: Explorations in Legislative Behavior.* New York: John Wiley and Sons, 1962.

23. Wildavsky, Aaron. "Party Discipline Under Federalism: Implications of Australian Experience," *Social Research*, Vol. 28 (Winter 1961), pp. 437-458.

24. Zariski, Raphael. "Party Factions and Comparative Politics: Some Preliminary Observations," *Midwest Journal of Political Science*, Vol. 4 (February 1960), pp. 27-51.

See also: A22, A24, C16, C18, H14, H28, J50, J54, K9, K56, L4.

H. POLITICAL PARTIES: ORGANIZATION AND LEADERSHIP

Parties as managers and recruiters.

Internal organization, particularly the relationship between leaders and followers, party elite and rank-and-file. Leadership as it effects aspects of internal organization.

Comparative studies of party organizations.

Analysis of patterns of party growth in terms of the recruitment or admission of new groups into the organization.

Participation at different levels of politics from the perspective of party organization.

General studies of organizations and organizing theory.

1. Armstrong, John A. *The Politics of Totalitarianism: The Communist Party of the Soviet Union from 1934 to the Present.* New York: Random House, 1961.

2. Ashford, Douglas E. *Perspectives of a Morrocan Nationalist: An Analysis of Istiqual Party Militants.* Totowa, N.J.: Bedminster, 1964.

3. Barnard, Chester. *The Functions of the Executive.* Cambridge: Harvard University Press, 1938.

4. Bradley, C. Paul. "Mass Parties in Jamaica: Structure and Organization," *Social and Economic Studies*, Vol. 9 (December 1960), pp. 375-416.

5. Brzezinski, Z. K. *Permanent Purge.* Cambridge: Harvard University Press, 1956.

6. Chao, Kuo-chun. "Leadership in the Chinese Communist Party," *Annals of the American Academy of Political and Social Science*, Vol. 321 (January 1959), pp. 40-50.

7. ———. *The Mass Organizations in Communist China.* Cambridge: M.I.T. Center for International Studies, 1953.

8. Friedrich, Carl, and Zbigniew Brzezinski. *Totalitarian Dictatorship and Autocracy.* Cambridge: Harvard University Press, 1956.

9. Gerth, Hans E. "The Nazi Party: Its Leadership and Composition," in Merton, *et al. Reader in Bureaucracy.* New York: The Free Press of Glencoe, 1952.

10. Glaser, H. "Einige Unterschiede im Partei- und Staatsaurbar Zwischen der Sowjetunion und der Volksrepublic China" (some differences between the party and state organizations of the Soviet Union and the People's Republic of China), *Europa-Archiv,* Vol. 15 (January 5-20, 1960), pp. 1-12.

11. Gosnell, H. F. *Machine Politics: Chicago Model.* Chicago: University of Chicago Press, 1937.

12. Gourlay, Walter E. *The Chinese Communist Cadre; Key to Political Control.* Cambridge: Russian Research Center, Harvard University, 1952.

13. Grodzins, M. "American Political Parties and the American System," *Western Political Quarterly,* Vol. 13 (December 1960), pp. 974-998.

14. Herring, Edward Pendleton. *The Politics of Democracy: American Parties in Action.* New York: Norton, 1940.

15. Hollnsteiner, M. R. "The Development of Political Parties on the Local Level: A Social Anthropological Case Study of Hulo Municipality, Bulacan," *Philippine Journal of Public Administration,* Vol. 4 (April 1960), pp. 111-131.

16. Houn, Franklin W. *To Change a Nation: Propaganda and Indoctrination in Communist China.* East Lansing: Michigan State University, Bureau of Social and Political Research, 1961; and New York: Free Press of Glencoe, 1961.

17. Hsiao, Tso-Liang. *Power Relations Within the Chinese Communist Movement, 1930-1934.* Seattle: University of Washington Press, 1961.

18. Katz, D., and S. J. Eldersveld. "The Impact of Local Party Activity Upon the Electorate," *Public Opinion Quarterly,* Vol. 25 (Spring 1961), pp. 1-24.

19. Koehl, R. "Feudal Aspects of National Socialism." *American Political Science Review,* Vol. 54 (December 1960), pp. 921-933.

20. LaPalombara, Joseph, ed. *Bureaucracy and Political Development.* Princeton: Princeton University Press, 1963.

21. Leiserson, Avery. *Parties and Politics: an Institutional and Behavioral Approach.* New York: Alfred A. Knopf, 1958.

22. Liebman, C. S. "Electorates, Interest Groups and Local Government Policy," *American Behavioral Scientist,* Vol. 4 (January 1961), pp. 9-11.

23. Lipset, Seymour Martin. *Michels' Theory of Political Parties.* Berkeley: Institute of Industrial Relations, University of California, 1962 (Reprint No. 185).

24. Lowell, A. Lawrence. *Governments and Parties in Continental Europe.* Boston: Houghton Mifflin, 1896.

25. March, James G., and H. A. Simon (with H. Guetzkow). *Organizations.* New York: John Wiley and Sons, 1958.

26. McCloskey, Herbert, *et al.* "Issue Conflict and Consensus Among Party

Leaders and Followers," *American Political Science Review*, Vol. 54 (June 1960), pp. 406-427.

27. McKenzie, R. T. *British Political Parties*. New York: St Martin's Press, 1955.

28. Meynaud, Jean, *et al*. "The Parliamentary Profession," *International Social Science Journal* (UNESCO), Vol. 13 (1961), pp. 513-640.

29. Nemzer, Louis. "The Kremlin's Professional Staff: The 'Apparatus' of the Central Committee, Communist Party of the Soviet Union," *American Political Science Review*, Vol. 44 (March 1950), pp. 64-85.

30. North, Robert Carver (with Ithiel de Sola Pool). *Kuomingtang and Chinese Communist Elites*. Stanford: Stanford University Press, 1952.

31. ———. *M. N. Roy's Mission to China; The Communist-Kuomingtang Split of 1927*. Berkeley: University of California Press, 1963.

32. ———. *Moscow and Chinese Communists*. Stanford: Stanford University Press, 1953.

33. Rose, Richard. "Complexities of Party Leadership," *Parliamentary Affairs*, Vol. 16 (Summer 1963), pp. 257-273.

34. Selznick, Philip. *The Organizational Weapon*. Glencoe, Illinois: The Free Press of Glencoe, 1959.

35. Sklar, Richard L. *Nigerian Political Parties*. Princeton: Princeton University Press, 1963.

36. Staar, Richard. *The Communist Party Leadership in Poland: A Study in Elite Stability*. Washington: Institute of Ethnic Studies, Georgetown University, 1961.

37. Stern, Carola. *Portrat Einer Bolschewistischen Partei: Einwichlung Funktion und Situation der S.E.D.* Cologne: Verlag fur Politik und Wirtschaft, 1957 (analysis of origin and role of the S.E.D., methods of preventing anti-Communists from exercising influence).

See also: A2, A3, A17, A20, D16, E4, J24, L8, L37, L39, L43.

Political Parties and Political Development

I. PARTIES AND POLITICAL INTEGRATION

Ethnic and religious cleavages, regional differences in social and economic levels of organization, competing political subsystems associated with these elements.

One-party tendencies as related to attempts at achieving integration through the party organization.

Parties and the representation of various social groups in decision-making or decision-implementing structures.

Party organizations and conflict management between groups or between population and authority.

Types of party systems and the conditions for system stability.

Nationalism, communalism, and their consequences for the party system.

1. Agar, Herbert. *The Price of Union*. Boston: Houghton Mifflin, 1950.

2. Allardt, E., and Y. Littunen, eds. *Cleavages, Ideologies and Party Systems*. Helsinki: Westermack Society, 1964.

3. Apter, David E. *The Political Kingdom in Uganda*. Princeton: Princeton University Press, 1961.

4. Biebuyck, Daniel, and Mary Douglas. *Congo Tribes and Parties*. London: Royal Anthropological Institute, 1961.

5. Binchy, D. A. *Church and State in Fascist Italy*. London: Oxford University Press, 1941.

6. Bondurant, J. V. *Regionalism Versus Provincialism: A Study in Problems of Indian National Unity*. Berkeley: University of California Press, 1958.

7. Bosworth, William. *Catholicism and Crisis in Modern France*. Princeton: Princeton University Press, 1962.

8. Brennan, Tom, E. W. Cooney, and H. Pollins. *Social Change in Southwest Wales*. London: Watts, 1954.

9. Campbell, Jane. "Multi-racialism and Politics in Zanzibar," *Political Science Quarterly*, Vol. 77 (March 1962), pp. 72-87.

10. Carnell, Francis G. "Communalism and Communism in Malaya," *Pacific Affairs*, Vol. 16 (June 1963), pp. 99-117.

11. Carter, Gwendolen, ed. *African One-Party States*. Ithaca, N.Y.: Cornell University Press, 1962.

12. Coleman, James S., and Carl Rosberg, eds. *Political Parties and National Integration in Tropical Africa*. Berkeley: University of California Press, 1964.

13. Cornwell, E. E. "Party Absorption of Ethnic Groups: The Case of Providence, R.I," *Social Forces*, Vol. 38 (March 1960), pp. 205-210.

14. Crow, Ralph E. "Religious Sectarianism in the Lebanese Political System," *Journal of Politics*, Vol. 24 (August 1962), pp. 489-520.

15. Crowley, Daniel J. "Politics and Tribalism in the Katanga," *Western Political Quarterly*, Vol. 16 (March 1963), pp. 68-78.

16. Davidowicz, Lucy S., and Leon J. Goldstein. *Politics in a Pluralist Democracy: Studies of Voting in the 1960 Election*. New York: Institute of Human Relations Press, 1963.

17. Deutsch, Karl W. "The Growth of Nations: Some Recurrent Patterns of Political and Social Integration," *World Politics*, Vol. 5 (January 1953), pp. 168-195.

18. ————. *Nationalism and Social Communication: An Inquiry into the Foundations of Nationality*. New York: John Wiley and Sons, 1953.

19. Duverger, Maurice. "L'Eternel Marais Essai sur le Centrisme Français," *Revue Française de Science Politique*, Vol. 14 (February 1964), pp. 33-51.

20. Einaudi, Mario, and François Goguel. *Christian Democracy in Italy and France*. South Bend, Ind.: Notre Dame University Press, 1952.

21. Eisenstadt, S. N. *The Absorption of Immigrants*. New York: The Free Press of Glencoe, 1955.

22. Fallers, L. A. *Bantu Bureaucracy: A Study of Integration and Conflict in the Political Institutions of an East African People*. Cambridge, England: Heffer and Sons, 1956.

23. Friedrich, P. "Language and Politics in India," *Journal of the American Academy of Arts and Sciences* (Daedalus), Vol. 91 (Summer 1962), pp. 543-559.

24. Geertz, Clifford. "The Integrative Revolution: Primordial Sentiments and Civil Politics in the New States," in Geertz, ed. *Old Societies and New States, op.cit.,* pp. 105-158.

25. Glazer, Nathan, and Daniel Patrick Moynihan. *Beyond the Melting Pot: Negroes, Jews, Italians, and Irish of New York City.* Cambridge: M.I.T. Press, 1963.

26. Graebner, Norman A., ed. *Politics and the Crisis of 1860.* Urbana, Ill.: University of Illinois Press, 1961.

27. Grodzins, Morton. *The Loyal and the Disloyal.* Chicago: University of Chicago Press, 1956.

28. Gutmann, Emanuel E. "Some Observations on Politics and Parties in Israel," *India Quarterly,* Vol. 17 (January-March 1961), pp. 3-29.

29. Harrison, Selig. "Caste and the Andhra Communists," *American Political Science Review,* Vol. 50 (June 1956), pp. 378-404.

30. ————. *India: The Most Dangerous Decades.* Princeton: Princeton University Press, 1960.

31. Hudson, G. F. "The Stability of Mao's Regime," *Chinese History,* Vol. 39 (December 1960), pp. 327-332.

32. Jansen, Marius B. "Takechi Zuizan and the Tosa Loyalist Party," *Journal of Asian Studies,* Vol. 18 (February 1959), pp. 199-212.

33. Karpat, Kemal H. *Turkey's Politics: The Transition to a Multi-Party System.* Princeton: Princeton University Press, 1959.

34. LaPalombara, Joseph. "Political Party Systems and Crisis Governments: French and Italian Contrasts," *Midwest Journal of Political Science,* Vol. 11 (May 1958), pp. 117-142.

35. ————. "The Italian Elections and the Problem of Representation," *American Political Science Review,* Vol. 47 (September 1953), pp. 676-703.

36. Leys, Colin. *European Politics in Southern Rhodesia.* Oxford: Clarendon Press, 1959.

37. Lieberson, Stanley. "A Societal Theory of Race and Ethnic Relations," *American Sociological Review,* Vol. 26 (December 1961), pp. 902-910.

38. Low, D. A. *Political Parties in Uganda, 1949-1962.* London: Athlone Press (for the Institute of Commonwealth Studies, University of London), 1962.

39. Mack, R. W., and R. C. Snyder. "The Analysis of Social Conflict—Toward an Overview and Synthesis," *Journal of Conflict Resolution,* Vol. 1 (June 1957), pp. 212-248.

40. Mackintosh, J. P. "Electoral Trends and the Tendency to a One Party System in Nigeria," *Journal of Commonwealth Political Studies,* Vol. 1 (November 1962), pp. 194-210.

41. Mahajani, Usha. *The Role of Indian Minorities in Burma and Malaya.* Bombay: Vora and Co. (for the Institute of Pacific Relations), 1960.

42. Matthews, Donald R., and James W. Prothro. "Social and Economic Factors and Negro Voter Registration in the South," *American Political Science Review,* Vol. 57 (March 1963), pp. 24-44.

43. Morton, W. L. *The Canadian Identity.* Madison: University of Wisconsin Press, 1961.

44. Padgett, L. Vincent. "Mexico's One-Party System: A Re-Evaluation," *American Political Science Review*, Vol. 51 (December 1957), pp. 995-1008.

45. Potter, David M. *Lincoln and His Party in the Secession Crisis*. New Haven: Yale University Press, 1942 (rev. ed., 1962).

46. Roth, Guenther. *The Social Democrats in Imperial Germany: A Study in Working-Class Isolation and National Integration*. Totowa, N.J.: Bedminster Press, 1963.

47. Schachter, Ruth. "Single Party Systems in West Africa," *American Political Science Review*, Vol. 55 (June 1961), pp. 294-307.

48. Silverstein, Josef. "Politics in the Shan State; The Question of Secession From the Union of Burma," *Journal of Asian Studies*, Vol. 18 (November 1958), pp. 43-57.

49. Skinner, G. W. "Chinese Assimilation and Thai Politics," *Guardian*, Vol. 4 (August 1957), pp. 11-14.

50. Taft, R. "The Assimilation Orientation of Immigrants and Australians," *Human Relations*, Vol. 16 (August 1963), pp. 279-294.

51. Totten, George O. "Buddhism and Socialism in Japan and Burma," *Comparative Studies of Society and History*, Vol. 2 (April 1960), pp. 294-304.

52. Vallee, Frank G. *et al.* "Ethnic Assimilation and Differentiation in Canada," *Canadian Journal of Economic and Political Science*, Vol. 23 (November 1957), pp. 540-549.

53. Whiteley, W. H. "Language and Politics in East Africa," *Tanganyika Notes*, Vols. 47-48 (June-September 1957), pp. 159-173.

54. Wilson, James Q. *Negro Politics*. Glencoe, Ill.: The Free Press, 1960.

55. Wriggins, W. H. "Impediments to Unity in New Nations: The Case of Ceylon," *American Political Science Review*, Vol. 55 (June 1961), pp. 313-320.

56. Zolberg, Aristide R. *One-Party Government in the Ivory Coast*. Princeton: Princeton University Press, 1964.

See also: A1, A19, B5, B7, B8, B15, B16, B17, C8, C19, D30, D42, E30, E41, I13, L44.

J. POLITICAL PARTIES, ELITES, AND OTHER POLITICAL GROUPS

Ability of party systems to coexist with or absorb potentially competing centers of influence.

The development of patterns of consensus and cleavage.

Traditional elites; whether powerless chiefs or opponents of innovation.

Bureaucracy, legislature, and executive roles in relation to party organization.

Relations between political parties; the development of political opposition.

Relations with interest groups: organized labor, business, military elites, and religious organizations.

The emergence of methods for conflict resolution with the party system and between parties and other subsystems of society.

1. Almond, Gabriel A. "A Comparative Study of Interest Groups and the Political Process," *American Political Science Review*, Vol. 52 (March 1958), pp. 270-282.

2. Almond, Gabriel A. "The Politics of German Business," in Speier and Davison. *West German Leadership and Foreign Policy*. Evanston, Ill.: Row, Peterson, 1957, pp. 238-239.

3. Apter, David E. "Some Reflections on the Role of a Political Opposition in New Nations," *Comparative Studies in Society and History*, Vol. 4 (June 1962), pp. 154-168.

4. Armstrong, John. *The Soviet Bureaucratic Elite; A Case Study of the Ukrainian Apparatus*. New York: Praeger, 1959.

5. Ashford, Douglas E. "Labor Politics in a New Nation," *Western Political Quarterly*, Vol. 13 (June 1962), pp. 312-331.

6. Ashford, Douglas E. "Patterns of Consensus in Developing Countries," *American Behavioral Scientist*, Vol. 4 (April 1961), pp. 7-10.

7. Bachrach, Peter. "Elite Consensus and Democracy," *Journal of Politics*, Vol. 24 (August 1962), pp. 439-452.

8. Benda, Harry J. "Non-Western Intelligentsias as Political Elites," *Australian Journal of Politics and History*, Vol. 6 (November 1960), pp. 205-218.

9. Berger, Morroe. *Military Elite and Social Change: Egypt Since Napoleon*. Princeton: Center for International Studies, Princeton University (Research Monograph No. 6), 1960.

10. Bhambhri, C. P. "The Role of Opposition in the House of the People, 1952-1956," *Modern Review*, Vol. 101 (June 1957), pp. 441-458.

11. Bonham, John. *The Middle Class Vote*. London: Faber and Faber, 1954.

12. Booth, David A., and Charles R. Adrian. "Simplifying the Discovery of Elites," *American Behavioral Scientist*, Vol. 5 (October 1961), pp. 14-15.

13. Brady, O. R. *Business as a System of Power*. New York: Columbia University Press, 1943.

14. Brandenburg, Frank. "Mexico: An Experiment in One-Party Democracy" (unpublished Ph.D. dissertation, University of Pennsylvania, 1955).

15. Crane, Robert I. "The Leadership of the Congress Party," in Park and Tinker, eds. *Leadership and Political Institutions in India*. Princeton: Princeton University Press, 1959.

16. Daalder, H. *The Role of the Military in the Emerging Countries*. The Hague: Institute of Social Studies, 1962.

17. Dahl, Robert A. "Business and Politics: A Critical Appraisal of Political Science," *American Political Science Review*, Vol. 53 (March 1959), pp. 1-34.

18. Ehrmann, Henry W. *Interest Groups on Four Continents*. Pittsburgh: University of Pittsburgh Press, 1958.

19. Fallers, Lloyd. "The Predicament of the Modern African Chief: An Instance from Uganda," *American Anthropologist*, Vol. 57 (April 1955), pp. 290-305.

20. Goldrich, Daniel. *Radical Nationalism: The Political Orientations of Panamanian Law Students*. East Lansing, Mich.: Michigan State University, 1962.

21. Graham, David L. "The Rise of the Mexican Right," *Yale Review*, Vol. 52 (Autumn 1962), pp. 102-111.

22. Guttsman, W. L. "The Changing Social Structure of the British Political Elite," *British Journal of Sociology*, Vol. 2 (June 1951), pp. 122-134.

23. Hinton, H. C. "The 'Democratic Parties': End of an Experiment?" *Problems of Communism*, Vol. 7 (May-June 1958), pp. 39-46.

24. ————. *Leaders of Communist China*. Santa Monica, Calif.: The RAND Corporation, 1956.

25. *International Social Science Bulletin*, special issue on "African Elites," Vol. 8, No. 3 (1956), pp. 413-457.

26. Johnson, John J., ed. *The Role of the Military in Underdeveloped Countries*. Princeton: Princeton University Press, 1962.

27. Johnson, Pricilla. "The Regime and the Intellectuals: A Window on Party Politics," *Problems of Communism*, Vol. 12 (July-August 1963), special supplement.

28. Jumper, Roy. "Mandarin Bureaucracy and Politics in South Viet-Nam," *Pacific Affairs*, Vol. 30 (March 1957), pp. 47-58.

29. Keller, Suzanne. *Beyond the Ruling Class: Strategic Elites in Modern Society*. New York: Random House, 1963.

30. Khadduri, Majid. "The Role of the Military in Middle East Politics," *American Political Science Review*, Vol. 47 (June 1953), pp. 511-524.

31. Kilson, Martin L. "Authoritarian and Single-Party Tendencies in African Politics," *World Politics*, Vol. 15 (January 1963), pp. 262-294.

32. Kirchheimer, Otto. "Majorities and Minorities in Western European Governments," *Western Political Quarterly*, Vol. 12 (June 1959), pp. 492-510.

33. Kling, Merle. "Towards a Theory of Power and Political Instability in Latin America," *Western Political Quarterly*, Vol. 9 (March 1956), pp. 21-35.

34. Lamb, Helen. "The Indian Business Communities and the Evolution of an Industrial Class," *Pacific Affairs*, Vol. 28 (June 1955), pp. 101-116.

35. Lane, R. E. *The Regulation of Businessmen: Social Conditions of Government Economic Control*. New Haven: Yale University Press, 1954.

36. Langdon, Frank C. "Organized Interests in Japan and Their Influence on Political Parties," *Pacific Affairs*, Vol. 34 (Fall 1961), pp. 271-278.

37. LaPalombara, Joseph G. *The Italian Labor Movement: Problems and Prospects*. Ithaca, N.Y.: Cornell University Press, 1957.

38. ————. *Interest Groups in Italian Politics*. Princeton: Princeton University Press, 1964.

39. Lichtblau, George E. "The Politics of Trade-Union Leadership in Southern Asia," *World Politics*, Vol. 7 (October 1954), pp. 84-101.

40. Macridis, R. C. "Interest Groups in Comparative Analysis," *Journal of Politics*, Vol. 23 (February 1961), pp. 25-45.

41. Millen, Bruce H. *The Political Role of Labor in Developing Countries*. Washington, D.C.: The Brookings Institution, 1963.

42. Morris, I. I. "The Significance of the Military in Post-War Japan," *Pacific Affairs*, Vol. 31 (March 1958), pp. 3-21.

43. Neumann, Franz L. *Behemoth: The Structure and Practice of National Socialism*. Toronto: Oxford University Press, 1944.

44. Park, Richard L., and Irene Tinker. *Leadership and Political Institutions in India*. Princeton: Princeton University Press, 1959.

45. Rapoport, David. "A Comparative Theory of Military and Political Types," in Huntington, ed. *Changing Patterns of Military Politics*. New York: The Free Press of Glencoe, 1962, pp. 71-100.

46. Rudolph, Susanne Hoeber. "Consensus and Conflict in Indian Politics," *World Politics*, Vol. 13 (April 1961), pp. 385-399.

47. Runciman, W. G. "A Method for Cross-National Comparison of Political Consensus," *British Journal of Sociology*, Vol. 13 (June 1962), pp. 151-168.

48. Rustow, Dankwart A. "The Army and the Founding of the Turkish Republic," *World Politics*, Vol. 11 (July 1959), pp. 513-552.

49. ―――. "The Military in Middle Eastern Society and Politics," in Fisher, ed. *The Military in the Middle East*. Columbus: Ohio State University Press, 1963, pp. 3-20.

50. ―――. *The Politics of Compromise: A Study of Parties and Cabinet Government in Sweden*. Princeton: Princeton University Press, 1955.

51. Schapiro, L. *The Origin of the Communist Autocracy: Political Opposition in the Soviet State; First Phase, 1917-1922*. London: London School of Economics and Political Science, 1956.

52. Scigliano, R. G., and W. W. Snyder. "Political Parties in South Vietnam Under the Republic," *Pacific Affairs*, Vol. 33 (December 1960), pp. 327-346.

53. Scoble, Harry M. "Organized Labor in Electoral Politics: Some Questions for the Discipline," *Western Political Quarterly*, Vol. 16 (September 1963), pp. 666-685.

54. Secher, H. P. "Representative Democracy or 'Chambers State': The Ambiguous Role of Interest Groups in Austrian Politics," *Western Political Quarterly*, Vol. 13 (December 1960), pp. 890-909.

55. Shils, Edward. "Intellectuals in the Political Development of the New States," *World Politics*, Vol. 12 (April 1960), pp. 329-368.

56. Smythe, Hugh H., and Mabel M. Smythe. *The New Nigerian Elite*. Stanford: Stanford University Press, 1960.

57. Soukup, James R. "Labor and Politics in Japan: A Study of Interest-Group Attitudes and Activities," *Journal of Politics*, Vol. 22 (May 1960), pp. 314-337.

58. Spreafico, Alberto and J. LaPalombara. *Elezioni e Comportamento Politico in Italia*. Milan. Edizioni di Comunità, 1963.

59. Stammer, Otto. "Gesellschaftsstruktur und Politische Dynamik in der Sowjetzone," *Gewerkschaftliche Monatshefte*, Vol. 3 (1952), pp. 330-334.

60. Sturmthal, Adolf Fox. *The Tragedy of European Labor, 1918-1939*. New York: Columbia University Press, 1943.

61. Szczepanski, Jan. "The Polish Intelligentsia: Past and Present." *World Politics*, Vol. 14 (April 1962), pp. 406-420.

62. Tedjasukmana, Iskandra. *The Political Character of the Indonesian Trade Union Movement*. Ithaca, N.Y.: Cornell University Press, 1958.

63. Vianello, M. "Rapporto tra Sindacati e Partiti in Italia e in America." *Studi Politici*, Vol. 7 (July-December 1960), pp. 474-496.

64. Von der Mehden, Fred R., and Charles W. Anderson. "Political Action by the Military in the Developing Areas," *Social Research*, Vol. 28 (Winter 1961), pp. 459-479.

65. Ward, Robert E., and Dankwart A. Rustow, eds. *Political Modernization in Japan and Turkey*. Princeton: Princeton University Press, 1964.

66. Weiner, Myron. *Party Politics in India*. Princeton: Princeton University Press, 1957.

67. ———. *The Politics of Scarcity: Public Pressure and Political Response in India*. Chicago: University of Chicago Press, 1962.

See also: B6, B9, B10, B23, C11, C23, H5, H6, H17, H31, K4, K7, L18, L20.

K. POLITICAL PARTIES: THE POLICY PROCESS, AND THE PUBLIC ADMINISTRATION

The often-exaggerated role of parties in policy-making.
Parties and the implementation of public policy.
Types of party systems and success in administration of promulgated policies.
Parties and development policy: initiators, makers, or implementers.
Totalitarian parties and social control.

1. Braibanti, Ralph, and Joseph Spengler, eds. *Administration and Economic Development in India*. Durham, N.C.: Duke University Press, 1963 (published for Duke University, Commonwealth Studies Center).

2. Einaudi, Mario. "The Crisis of Politics and Government in France," *World Politics*, Vol. 4 (October 1951), pp. 64-84.

3. Engelbert, Ernest A. "Political Parties and Natural Resource Policies: An Historical Evaluation, 1790-1950," *Natural Resources Journal*, Vol. 1 (November 1961), pp. 224-256.

4. Fainsod, Merle. *How Russia is Ruled*. Cambridge: Harvard University Press, 1953.

5. Firmalino, T. C. "Political Activities of Barrio Citizens in Iloilo as They Affect Community Development," *Philippine Journal of Public Administration*, Vol. 4 (April 1960), pp. 151-159.

6. Heberle, Rudolf. "Parliamentary Government and Political Parties in West Germany," *Canadian Journal of Economics and Political Science*, Vol. 28 (August 1962), pp. 417-423.

7. Hinton, H. C. "Intra-party Politics and Economic Policy in Communist China," *World Politics*, Vol. 12 (July 1960), pp. 509-524.

8. Hirschman, Albert O., and Charles E. Lindblom. "Economic Development, Research and Development Policy Making: Some Converging Views," *Behavioral Science*, Vol. 6 (April 1962), pp. 211-222.

9. Kayser, J. "The Radical Socialist Party as a Party of Government in the Third French Republic," *Parliamentary Affairs*, Vol. 13 (Summer 1960), pp. 318-328.

10. Meisel, John. "The Stalled Omnibus: Canadian Parties in the 1960's," *Social Research*, Vol. 30 (Autumn 1963), pp. 367-390.

11. Needler, M. C. "The Political Development of Mexico," *American Political Science Review*, Vol. 55 (June 1961), pp. 308-312.

12. Opler, Morris E. "Political Organization and Economic Growth: The

Case of Village India," *International Review of Community Development*, Vol. 5 (1960), pp. 187-197.

13. Schapiro, Leonard. "The Party and the State," *Survey: A Journal of Soviet and East European Studies*, No. 38 (October 1961), pp. 111-116.

14. Smith, Thomas C. *Political Change and Industrial Development in Japan*. Stanford: Stanford University Press, 1955.

15. Van Der Kroef, Justus M. "Agrarian Reform and the Indonesian Communist Party," *Far Eastern Survey*, Vol. 29 (January 1960), pp. 5-13.

16. Williams, Oliver P., and Charles R. Adrian. *Four Cities: A Study in Comparative Policy Making*. Philadelphia: University of Pennsylvania Press, 1963.

See also: D12, D18, D36, D37, E26, E39, H20, H21, J4.

L. PARTICIPATION AND RECRUITMENT

Conditions for participation in mass parties; originating either within the party organization or from external factors.

Effects of types of party organization on extent of participation required and/or encouraged.

Electoral studies: electoral systems as determinants of participation, as indicators of the congruence between party organization and population.

Elections, especially in newly independent countries, as stimulants to accelerated party development and political activity in general.

General theory of participation; types of participation possible and desirable in different systems.

Controlled participation (i.e., recruitment) versus "voluntary" participation (i.e., enlistment) as two perspectives from which to analyze any situation.

1. Almond, Gabriel, and Sidney Verba. *The Civic Culture*. Princeton: Princeton University Press, 1963.

2. Anderson, Bo. "Some Problems of Change in the Swedish Electorate," *Acta Sociologica*, Vol. 6 (fasc. 4), pp. 241-255.

3. Ashford, Douglas E. *Political Change in Morocco*. Princeton: Princeton University Press, 1961.

4. Beer, Samuel H. "Great Britain: From Government Elite to Organized Mass Parties," in S. Neumann, ed. *Modern Political Parties*. Chicago: University of Chicago Press, 1956.

5. Bennett, George, and Carl Rosberg. *The Kenyatta Election: Kenya, 1960-1961*. New York: Oxford University Press, 1961.

6. Berelson, B., Paul F. Lazarsfeld, and William N. McPhee. *Voting*. Chicago: University of Chicago Press, 1954.

7. Burdick, E., and Arthur J. Brodbeck. *American Voting Behavior*. Glencoe, Ill.: The Free Press, 1959.

8. Burks, R. V. *The Dynamics of Communism in Eastern Europe*. Princeton: Princeton University Press, 1961.

9. Butler, D. E., and R. Rose. *The British General Election of 1959*. New York: St Martin's Press, 1960.

10. Campbell, Angus, Philip Converse, Warren Miller, and Donald Stokes. *The American Voter*. New York: Wiley and Sons, 1960.

11. Campbell, Angus, and Henry Valen. "Party Identification in Norway and the United States," *Public Opinion Quarterly*, Vol. 25 (Winter 1961), pp. 505-525.

12. Campbell, Ian. "Parties and the Referendum Process," *Australian Quarterly*, Vol. 34 (June 1962), pp. 74-80.

13. Campbell, Peter. *French Electoral Systems and Elections, 1789-1957.* London: Faber and Faber, 1958.

14. *Citizen Participation in Political Life.* Special Issue of the *International Social Science Journal*, Part I, Vol. 12, No. 1 (1960).

15. Converse, Philip E., and Georges Depeux. "Politicization of the Electorate in France, and the U.S.," *Public Opinion Quarterly*, Vol. 26 (Spring 1962), pp. 1-23.

16. Duverger, Maurice. "Electoral Systems and Political Life," in Macridis and Brown. *Comparative Politics: Notes and Readings.* Homewood, Ill.: Dorsey Press, 1961, pp. 245-258.

17. Edinger, L. J. "Continuity and Change in the Background of German Decision-Makers," *Western Political Quarterly*, Vol. 16 (March 1961), pp. 17-36.

18. Eldersveld, Samuel. *Political Parties: A Behavioral Analysis.* Chicago: Rand McNally and Co., 1964.

19. Encel, S. "The Political 'Elite' in Australia," *Political Studies* (Oxford), Vol. 9 (February 1961), pp. 16-36.

20. Fisher, Margaret W. "The Indian Experience With Democratic Elections," *Indian Press Digests.* Berkeley: University of California, Institute of International Studies (Monograph No. 3), 1956.

21. Gokhale, B. G. "The Communist Party of India and the Ballot Box," *Asian Studies*, Vol. 1 (Summer 1957), pp. 185-191.

22. Gorshener, A., and I. Chelyapor. *The Soviet Electoral System.* Washington, D.C.: Joint Publications Research Service, 1962 (JPRS 12931).

23. Lane, Robert. *Political Life: Why People Get Involved in Politics.* Glencoe, Ill.: The Free Press, 1959.

24. Lerner, Daniel. *The Passing of Traditional Society.* New York: The Free Press of Glencoe, 1958.

25. Lipset, S. M. *Political Man.* New York: Doubleday and Co., 1960.

26. ———, and S. Rokkan. *Party Systems and Voter Alignments.* New York: The Free Press of Glencoe, 1965.

27. Lunev, A. E. *Forms of Participation of Masses in Activity of State Organs of Chinese People's Republic.* Washington, D.C.: Joint Publications Research Service, November 18, 1958 (JPRS 374).

28. McDill, Edward L., and Jeanne Clare Ridley. "Status, Anomia, Political Alienation, and Political Participation," *American Journal of Sociology*, Vol. 68 (September 1962), pp. 205-213.

29. Mackenzie, W. J. M., and Kenneth Robinson, eds. *Five Elections in Africa.* Oxford, Clarendon Press, 1960.

30. Marshall, T. H. *Citizenship and Social Class.* London: Cambridge University Press, 1950.

31. Marvick, Dwaine, ed. *Political Decision-Makers: Recruitment and Performance*. New York: Free Press of Glencoe, 1961.

32. Milbrath, Lester W. *Political Participation*. Chicago: Rand McNally and Co., 1965.

33. Radkey, Oliver Henry. *The Election to the Russian Constituent Assembly of 1917*. Cambridge: Harvard University Press, 1950.

34. Rokkan, Stein, ed. *Approaches to the Study of Political Participation*. Bergen: Christian Michelsen Institute, 1962.

35. ―――. "Mass Suffrage, Secret Voting and Political Participation," *European Journal of Sociology*, Vol. 2 (1961), pp. 132-152.

36. ―――, and A. Campbell, et al. "Citizen Participation in Political Life," *International Social Science Journal* (UNESCO), Vol. 12, No. 1 (1960), pp. 7-99.

37. Rose, Richard. "The Political Ideas of English Party Activists," *American Political Science Review*, Vol. 56 (June 1962), pp. 360-371.

38. Schwartz, Benjamin. "Totalitarian Consolidation and the Chinese Model," *China Quarterly*, Vol. 1 (January-March 1960), pp. 18-21.

39. Seligman, L. G. *Leadership in a New Nation*. New York: Atherton Press, 1964.

40. ―――. "Political Recruitment and Party Structure: A Case Study," *American Political Science Review*, Vol. 55 (March 1961), pp. 77-86.

41. Siegfried, André. *Tableau des Partis en France*. Paris: B. Grasset, 1930.

42. Sorauf, Frank J. *Party and Representation: Legislative Politics in Pennsylvania*. New York: Atherton Press, 1963.

43. Tingsten, Herbert. *Political Behavior: Studies in Election Statistics*. London: P. S. King, 1937.

44. Tinker, I. "Malayan Elections: Electoral Pattern for Plural Societies?" *Western Political Quarterly*, Vol. 9 (January 1956), pp. 258-282.

45. Valen, Henry, and Daniel Katz. *Political Parties in Norway*. Oslo: Universitetsforlaget, 1964.

46. Vedel, Georges, ed. *La Depolitisation: Mythe ou Réalité?* Paris: Armand Colin, 1962.

47. Williamson, Chilton. *American Suffrage: From Property to Democracy, 1760-1860*. Princeton: Princeton University Press, 1960.

See also: B21, C24, D19, D21, D28, D29, D30, E20, E25, E37, E43, H2, H12, H16, H18, I36, I41, J11, J57, K5.

CONTRIBUTORS*

LEONARD BINDER, born in Boston, Massachusetts in 1927, is Chairman of the Department of Political Science at the University of Chicago. He has specialized in the study of Middle Eastern politics and Islamic thought and has done field research in Pakistan, Iran, Egypt, Lebanon, and Tunisia. His publications include *Religion and Politics in Pakistan, Iran: Political Development in a Changing Society*, and *The Ideological Revolution in the Middle East*.

WILLIAM NISBET CHAMBERS, born in Joplin, Missouri, 1916, is Chairman of the Department of History at Washington University. He has also been Professor of Political Science there, has taught at Harvard and Columbia, has received a Senior Research Award in Governmental Affairs from the Social Science Research Council and a Research Award in Constitutional Democracy from the Rockefeller Foundation, and has been Visiting Scholar at the Center for Advanced Study in the Behavioral Sciences. He is author of *Political Parties in a New Nation: The American Experience, Old Bullion Benton: Senator from the New West*, and *The Democrats 1789-1964*, as well as other volumes in collaboration, and has contributed to professional journals.

HANS DAALDER, born in Bergen, North Holland in 1928, is Professor of Political Science at the University of Leiden. He previously taught in the University of Amsterdam and in the Institute of Social Studies at The Hague. In 1954 he spent one year as a British Council Scholar at the London School of Economics and Political Science, and in 1960-61 he visited Harvard University and the University of California at Berkeley on a Rockefeller Foundation Fellowship. He will be a Fellow at the Center for Advanced Study in the Behavioral Sciences during the academic year 1966-67. He has worked mainly in the field of European politics and has published a study in English entitled *Cabinet Reform in Britain 1914-1963* with Stanford University Press. He is currently engaged in an extensive project on the smaller European Democracies in collaboration with Robert A. Dahl (Yale University), Val R. Lorwin (University of Oregon), and Stein Rokkan of the Christian Michelsen Institute, Bergen, Norway.

* This list gives the accomplishments of the contributors only at the time of this book's original publication.

CONTRIBUTORS

RUPERT EMERSON, born in Rye, New York, 1899, is Professor of Government and Research Associate of the Center for International Affairs, Harvard University. He has been a visiting Professor at Yale, the University of California at Berkeley, and UCLA. From 1940 to 1946 he served in several government agencies in Washington, and he has undertaken research in both Southeast Asia and Africa. In 1952-53 he was President of the Far Eastern Association (now the Association for Asian Studies), and he is presently President of the African Studies Association. Among the books which he has published are *Malaysia: A Study in Direct and Indirect Rule*, *Representative Government in Southeast Asia*, and *From Empire to Nation*.

MORTON GRODZINS, born in Chicago, 1917, was Professor of Political Science at the University of Chicago at the time of his death in 1964. He received his Ph.D. from the University of California at Berkeley in 1944 and had since served as Dean of the Division of Social Sciences as Assistant to the President and as Chairman of the Department of Political Science at the University of Chicago. He was a Fellow at the Center for Advanced Studies in the Behavioral Sciences during the academic year 1958-59. He was the author of *Americans Betrayed, The Loyal and the Disloyal, Government and Housing in Metropolitan Areas* (with Edward C. Banfield), and was editor (with Eugene Rabinowitch) of *The Atomic Age*. He also published in the professional journals. His writing on the federal system is now in the process of being edited for posthumous publication.

OTTO KIRCHHEIMER, born in Heilbrenn, Germany, 1905, was before his death in 1965, Professor of Government at Columbia University. He was Professor at the Graduate Faculty of the New School of Social Research in New York City from 1955 to 1961. Previously, he had been associated with the European research division of the State Department. He held fellowships from the Rockefeller Foundation, the Social Science Research Council, and the John Simon Guggenheim Foundation. His main interest was in the field of comparative public law and political institutions. His publications in recent years comprise: *Political Justice* in 1961, an enlarged German edition in 1965, and *Politik und Verfassung* in 1965.

JOSEPH LAPALOMBARA, born in Chicago, 1925, is Professor of Political Science at Yale University. He was Chairman of the Department of Political Science at Michigan State University from 1958 to 1963. In 1957-58 he was a visiting Professor at the University of Florence, and in 1963-64 he spent a research year in Italy on a Rockefeller Foundation Award. In 1961-62 he was a Fellow at the Center for Advanced Study in the Behavioral Sciences. His main research interest is the field of comparative political institutions and behavior. He is editor of *Bureaucracy and Political Development*, co-editor of *Elezioni e Comportamento Politico in Italia*, and author of *Interest Groups in Italian Politics*, *The Italian Labor Movement: Problems and Prospects*, *Italy: the Politics of Planning*, and other works. He has also published in the professional journals of the United States, Italy, Germany, and Spain.

LUCIAN W. PYE, born in China, 1921, is Professor of Political Science at the Massachusetts Institute of Technology, and a Senior Staff Member of its Center for International Studies. He is Chairman of the Social Science Research Council's Committee on Comparative Politics, a former Fellow of the Center for Advanced Study in the Behavioral Sciences, and a member of the American Academy of Arts and Sciences. He has done field work in Southeast Asia and Hong Kong and has served in various capacities in scholarly associations and governmental agencies. He is author of *Aspects of Political Development*, *Politics, Personality and Nation-Building*, *Guerrilla Communism in Malaya*, and co-author of *The Politics of the Developing Areas* and *The Emerging Nations*.

STEIN ROKKAN, born in Northern Norway in 1921, is Director of Research with Professorial rank at the Michelsen Institute in Bergen. He has carried out research on political behavior and electoral arrangements in Norway and a number of countries of Western Europe. In 1949-50 he held a fellowship from the Rockefeller Foundation for study and research in the United States and in 1959-60 was a Fellow of the Center for Advanced Study in the Behavioral Sciences. He has held Visiting Professorships at Yale and Manchester and is on the Executive Boards of the International Social Science Council and the International Political Science Associations. He is co-author of *Democracy in A World of*

Tensions, Approaches to the Study of Political Parties, Regional Contrasts in Norwegian Politics, Party Systems and Voter Alignments and *International Guide to Electoral Statistics.* He has also edited the volumes *Comparing Nations* and *Data Archives for the Social Sciences.*

DANKWART A. RUSTOW, born in Berlin, Germany in 1924, is a Professor of International Forces at Columbia University. From 1952 to 1959 he taught at Princeton University. He has been a visiting Professor at Yale, Heidelberg (Germany), and the London School of Economics and has held grants from the Social Science Research Council, The Fund for the Advancement of Education, and the John Simon Guggenheim Foundation. He was a member of the Senior Staff of the Brookings Institution from 1961 to 1963 and is serving as a member of the Board of Governors of the Middle East Institute and as a consultant to the Department of State and the RAND Corporation. His research interest is in the fields of political change and modernization, and he has done extensive field work in Sweden as well as in Turkey and other Middle Eastern countries. He is author of *The Politics of Compromise* and *Politics and Westernization in the Near East,* co-editor of *Political Modernization in Japan and Turkey,* co-author of *The Politics of the Developing Areas,* and a contributor to the *Encyclopedia of Islam* (second edition), to scholarly symposia, and to journals in the United States, Europe, and Turkey.

GIOVANNI SARTORI, born in Florence, Italy, 1924, is Professor of Political Science at the University of Florence. During the Fall term 1964-65, he was a visiting Professor at Harvard University. He is author of *Democrazia e Definizioni, A Teoria da Representasno no Estado Representativo Moderno, Democratic Theory* (also published in Mexico and Brazil), *Il Parlamento Italiano 1946-1963* (in collaboration), and co-author of several other volumes. He has published in the professional journals of Italy, the United States, England, France, Germany, and Belgium. He also contributes the articles "Democracy" and "Representational Systems" in the *International Encyclopedia of the Social Sciences.*

ROBERT E. SCOTT, born in Chicago, 1923, is Professor of Political Science at the University of Illinois. Since 1948 he has conducted extensive field work in Spain and many Latin American countries. During his career he has held fellowships and grants from the Carnegie Foundation, the Rockefeller Foundation, the Social Science Research Council, and the U.S. Office of Education. In 1962 he was a visiting Professor at Yale University, and in 1963-64 he acted as Senior Staff Member of the Brookings Institution, Washington, D.C., during which time he prepared the study of "Political Parties and Policy Making in Latin America." He is author of *Mexican Government in Transition*, and co-author of *Nation-Building*, *Political Culture and Political Development*, *Government and Politics in Latin America*, and other works.

IMMANUEL WALLERSTEIN, born in New York City, 1930, is Associate Professor of Sociology at Columbia University. He has done extensive field work in various parts of Africa since 1955. He has held fellowships from the Ford Foundation, the U.S. Office of Education, and the Columbia Council for Research in the Social Sciences. He is author of *Africa: The Politics of Independence*, *The Road to Independence: Ghana and the Ivory Coast*, and the forthcoming *Africa: The Politics of Unity*, and editor of *Social Change: The Colonial Situation*. He has also published in the professional journals of the United States, France, Canada, and Africa.

MYRON WEINER, born in New York City, 1931, is Professor of Political Science at the Massachusetts Institute of Technology and a Senior Research Associate at its Center for International Studies. He has done extensive field work in India since 1953. During his career he has held fellowships from the Ford Foundation, the Rockefeller Foundation, the Social Science Research Council, and the John Simon Guggenheim Foundation. In the past he has been a consultant to the Ford Foundation and is now serving as a consultant to the Department of State. He is author of *The Politics of Scarcity*, *Party Politics in India*, *Political Change in South Asia*, and the forthcoming *Party Building in a New Nation: The Indian National Congress*, and co-author of *The Politics of the Developing Areas*. He is also editor with Rajni Kothari of *Indian Voting Behaviour* and editor of the forthcoming Voice of America Forum Series on *Modernization*.

INDEX

Abbott, Roger S., 345n
absolutism, in the Middle East, 108-09
accelerated history, as factor leading to one-party system in new nations, 32
Acción Democrática (Costa Rica), 336; (Venezuela), 337, 343, 351
accommodation, of elites to participation demands, 19
action preference, 195-200; role of catch-all party in, 198-200
Adams, Henry, 318
Adams, John, 6, 81ff, 101, 305ff, 411; role in early integration of U.S., 312; role in peaceful succession, 319-20
adaptive party, 424-25
Adenauer, Konrad, 196
Adıvar, Abdülhak Adnan, 118n
Adloff, Richard, 288n
administration, and development, 391-92; and politics in Asia, 391. *See also* bureaucracy, bureaucratization
Africa, changing nature of leadership, 210-11; coalition of elites, 212; crisis of integration, 204-05, 267-301; crisis of legitimacy, 206; crisis of participation, 201-02; decline of party, 201-14, 285; definition of political parties, 268-69; leadership, 206-11, 275-91, 297-98; multi-party systems, 289-90; nationalism, 292-93; nationalist movements, 202-14 *passim*, 267-301 *passim*; one-party systems, 274-87; origins of parties, 270-71; political power, 205-06; role of parties, 267-301; pluralistic party systems, 287-93; and tribalism, 277-93 *passim*; types of parties in, 274-93
  political parties: Convention Peoples (Ghana), 210, 212n, 224, 287ff, 298; KADU (Kenya), 291-92; KANU (Kenya), 291-92; Nationalist Union (Sudan), 22, 271; Northern Peoples Congress (Nigeria), 272, 274, 290, 299; PDCI (Ivory Coast), 211, 275, 281-83; PDG (Guinea), 213, 275-78; RDA (French Africa), 273, 275, 281, 283; TANU (Tanganyika), 274, 283-86, 299
Agar, Herbert, 81n, 98n
aggregation of interests, 86, 172, 196-98, 388

Akzin, B., 160n
Alain, 178, 178n
Alien and Sedition Acts, 93, 100, 309-11
alienation, from party system, 63-65; of political parties, 405
Allardt, Erik, 145n, 242n, 246n
Allen, W.E.D., 119n
Alliance for Progress, 331, 366-67
Alliance Party (Malaysia), 371, 420
Almond, Gabriel A., 4n, 28n, 43n, 68n, 87n, 93n, 99n, 110n, 152n, 172n, 353n, 369n
American liberal tradition, 85, 102, 105
Ames, Fisher, 91
Anderson, Charles W., 341n
Andrews, W. G., 191n
Andrieux, André, 183n
Ansprenger, Franz, 298n
Anti-Fascist Peoples Freedom League (Burma), 22, 371, 394
Anti-Federalists (U.S.), 8, 304
anti-system party, 148-50
Aprista Party (Peru), 336, 337, 350, 359
Aprista-type parties, 336
Apter, David E., 18n, 174n, 206n, 212n
Arbenz regime, 342
Argentina, 345-48
aristocrats, types of, 55-56
Aron, Raymond, 70n
Asia, ambivalent attitude toward parties, 369; countries in which significant party systems have developed, 369-71; impact of colonialism on political development, 382-88; importance of elections, 396-98; origins of parties, 374-88; party role in development, 388-96; policy making role of parties, 388-96; separation of administration and politics, 391
  political parties: Alliance Party (Malaya), 371, 420; Anti-Fascist Peoples Freedom League (Burma), 22, 371, 394; Chinese Communist Party, 378-79, 405; Federalista Party (Philippines), 386-87; Liberal Party (Japan), 10; Nationalista Party (Philippines), 386-87; Progressive Party (Japan), 10

Atatürk (Mustafa Kemal), 111, 112, 119-23, 131-33, 411, 412
atomization of political parties, 167-68
attitudinal integration, 417
authoritarianism, arguments for, 433; and development, 390-94; and modernization in Japan, 380; and modernization in Latin America, 366-67
authoritarian party system, 37-38
authority, rejection of as cause for party formation, 18
autocracy, as incompatible with political development, 51-52
auxiliaries, of political parties, 208-09
Averardi, G., 146n, 147n
Awolono, Obafemi, 271
Aydemir, Talât, 132
Azikiwe, Nnamdi, 270, 290

Bache, Benjamin Franklin, 91
Bagehot, Walter, 49n
Baldwin, Stanley, 177
Banfield, Edward C., 21n
Bardonnet, Daniel, 179n
Barzini, Luigi, Jr., 145n, 146n
Bates, Margaret L., 284n
Ba'th Party (Syria, Iraq, and Jordan), 130
Bayley, David, 11n
Bebel, August, 182n
Beckley, John, 92, 314
Beer, Samuel H., 6n, 88n
Bello, Alhaji Sir Ahmadu, 299
Bemis, Samuel Flagg, 307n
Ben Bella, Mohammed, 205
Bendix, Reinhard, 56n, 262n
Bennett, George, 284n, 291n
Benson, Lee, 243n
Berlinguer, M., 146n
Binder, Leonard, 5n, 372n
Binkley, Wilfred E., 81n, 91n, 98n
Bismarck, Otto von, 180n, 181, 431
Blanksten, George, 358
Blum, Léon, 179
Bodley, John E. C., 55n
Bonger, W. A., 72n
Bonifacio, 386
Bottomore, T. B., 56n, 60n
Boumedienne, Houari, 205
Bourguiba, Habib, 212
Boutmy, Emile, 60n
Bracher, K. D., 140n
Braga, Giorgio, 147n
Braibanti, Ralph, 372n
Brandenburg, Frank, 337n, 343n
Brazilian Labour Party, 344
Breton Club, 8
Britain, Conservative Party, 10, 87,

263, 406; historical crises, 177; Labour Party, 10, 185-86, 193, 406; Liberal Party, 6, 10, 87, 406; Tories, 15; Whigs, 15
Brown, Stuart Gerry, 305n
Buchmann, Jean, 205n, 296n
Buell, R. L., 202n
bureaucracy, and democratic development, 434-35; and party control, 421-23; and policy-making, 366; and political domination, 423-24; relation to rise of parties, 60-61; role in political development in Turkey, 118, 121
bureaucratization, under colonialism, 383-84; in Europe, 50
bureaucrats, as competing elites, 423-24
Burgess, John Stewart, 377n
Burke, Edmund, 67
Burks, D. D., 337n
Burnham, Walter Dean, 243n, 260n
Burns, James MacGregor, 98n
Burr, Aaron, 93, 100, 308n, 315, 316
Butler, D. E., 247n
Butterfield, Herbert, 15n

Caillaux, Joseph, 180
Callender, James T., 319n
Campbell, Angus, 28n
Carlsson, Gösta, 242n, 257n
Carter, Gwendolyn M., 275n, 283n, 284n
Casely-Hayford, Joseph, 201
Castro, Fidel, 38, 343
catch-all party, 184-92; and competition, 92-94; and ideology, 187-88; as interest aggregator, 197; national policies of, 196-97; role of as arbitrator, 194-95; tactics of, 196-97
Catholic Church, as factor in political development, 47
Cavour, Count Camillo, 180, 414
Cemal Pasha, 117
center opinion or tendency, 157
Center Party (Germany), 17, 183
centralists, in Turkey, 116-18
centralization, as factor in political development, 45-46
centrifugal drives, in party systems, 140-41; in U.S., 306-12
centripetal drives, in party systems, 141-42
Cesarini, Marco, 146n
Ceylon National Congress, 16
Chambers, William N., 6n, 79n, 81n, 82n, 84n, 88n, 89n, 93n, 96n, 98n, 309n, 315n, 317, 319n
chance, as factor in succession, 321-22

change, *see* political development

Chapman, R. M., 260n

charisma, 411-12

Charles, Bernard, 277n

Charles, Joseph, 81n, 93n, 308n, 317n

Charlot, Jean, 187n

Chile, 345-48

China, imperial systems in, 375-78; Kuomintang, 12, 13, 378

Chinese Communist Party, 378-79, 405

Christian Democratic Party (DC, Italy), 36, 61, 74, 140-54, 164, 185, 187, 416, 422

Christian Democratic Union (CDU, Germany), 187

citizen, and relationship to party, 199

class, *see* social class

cleavages, between early parties in U.S., 80-81; consequences of, 143-44, 161-62; factors affecting changes of in Norway, 254-56; in France, 143; and integration, 416; in Italy, 142-43; in Italy and France compared, 143; in Norway, 253-56; and party encirclement, 149-50; religious, and impact on development, 169-70; role of parties in, in U.S., 100-101; tribalistic, in Africa, 289; urban-rural, in Norway, 264-65; varying importance of, 67

clientele, relationship of political parties to, 188

coalition, in Latin America, 341-42, 351; problems of in Italy, 149-50

Coleman, James, 39n, 40, 87n, 93n, 99n, 110n, 270n, 359, 369

colonialism, administration of, 32; and attitudes toward competition, 382-83; contribution to formation of parties, 12-13; and dyarchy, 31-32; impact of on national integration problems, 267-73; impact of on political development, 382-88; and parallel nationalist parties, 423; and political parties, 297, 383-84; response to participation demands, 31, 201-02; and tribalism, 288; types of, 32

Combs, Lean, 377n

communications, and political development in Turkey, 117; relationship of to political parties, 20; and traditional-type parties, 339

Communism, and monopolistic politics in China, 378-79

Communist Party, and decline of ideology, 191

comparative analysis, strategies of, 260-62

competition, antagonism toward in Turkey, 132; among catch-all parties, 192-94; arguments for, 417-18; conditions facilitating, 158; in dual party systems, 95-96; in early Japan, 379-81; and ecological analysis, 257-58; impact of on legislature in Turkey, 123-24

competitive parochial system, 381-82

competitive party, conditions for, 25-29; as expression of ethnic rivalry, 34; ideological type, 36; pragmatic type, 37

competitive party systems, and anti-system parties, 409; limitations of in Latin America, 362; and orderly administration, 392; requisite for in Asia, 389; role of in development, 394-96

  types of: hegemonic, 35; ideological, 36-37; pragmatic, 36-37; turn-over, 35-36

competitive politics, arguments for, 394-95; in the Philippines, 386-87

conciliar government, in Europe, 47

conflict, importance of, 69; inherent nature of in competitive systems, 100; in Latin America, 340-41, 355-56; management of, 100-101, 419-24; among parties in U.S., 306-12; relationship of political party to, 95; religious, in Italy, 143; role of in integration, 100-101; role of parties in moderating, in U.S., 103-04

Congo, 292-93

congressional caucus, 314-15

Congress of Popular Forces, 231ff

Congress Party (India), 35, 36, 384-85, 405, 411, 420; and modernization, 384-85

consensus, meaning of, 321-22; political party as purveyor of, 199-200

Conservative Party (Britain), 10, 87, 263, 406

Conservatives, in Latin America, 340-42

conspiracy, as cycle in party development, 114; and party origins in Middle East, 110-11

constitutionalism, 323-24

Convention Peoples Party (CPP, Ghana), 210, 212n, 224, 278-81, 283, 298

COPEI (Venezuela), 337, 351

Cornford, J., 242n, 247n, 263n

Corpierre, M., 204n

coups, and legitimacy, 408-09

Cowan, L. Gray, 275n

crises, *see* historical crises

crisis loads, 177-82; clustering of, 428-32; in Egypt, 221-22; in Italy, 152, 180-81; in Latin America, 333-35; and levels of government, 421; and party systems, 427-32; and political development, 79-80; sequencing of, 99, 430-32; in U.S., 90-94, 99-100, 306-17

Croce, Benedetto, 182n

Cunningham, Noble E., Jr., 81n, 92n

Cutright, Philips, 257n

Daalder, Hans, 63n, 152n, 163n, 174n, 257n

Dahl, Robert A., 62n, 70n, 157n, 246n

Dallas, Alexander, 91

Dallinger, Frederick W., 81n

Danielsen, Rolf, 248n

Dauer, Manning J., 81n, 91n, 93n, 311n, 313n, 314, 316n, 318n, 319n

Davis, H. E., 337n

Davison, Roderic H., 115n

Dawn, C. Ernest, 125n

deadlock, causes of, 161-65; role of parties in creating, 161-63

decision making, degree of elite freedom in, 70-71; lack of apparent structures for in Latin America, 331-67 *passim*

Decraene, Philippe, 205n, 299n

De Gaulle, Charles, 23, 187, 196, 283

de Jouvenel, Bertrand, 64

demands, of interest groups, 361-62; nature of, 430

    for participation: 48-50; accommodation of elites to, 19; of nationalist movements, 202; and political party development, 400-407; values determining response to, 401-02; by working class, 182-83

Demirel, Süleyman, 112, 124

democracy, favorable argument for, 354; meaning of in Asia, 391; and tribalism, 288

democratic ideals, as means of differentiating political parties, 59-60

Democratic Party (Turkey), 112, 122-24, 412

Democratic Party (U.S.), 10, 80

Democratic Socialists (Norway), 35

democratic theory, 219-20

Desabie, J., 242n

Deutsch, Karl W., 80n, 82n, 99n, 106n, 258n, 297n

development, and authoritarianism, 390-94; and dominant parties in Mexico, 352-53; and governmental response to demands, 430; impact of political parties on, 399-435; indexes of, 250-53; negative role of parties in, 336-37; problems of, 345-48; requirements of, 218-20; role of Asian parties in, 388-96; role of parties in establishing attitudes toward, 426-27; types of activity in Africa, 298-99; varying roles of government and parties in, in Latin America, 363-67. *See also* political development

Dia, Mamadou, 205, 211, 211n, 297n, 298

dialectic, in party formation, 406-07

Diamond, Martin, 318

dictatorship, Kemalist, in Turkey, 120-22; rationale for, 277; in Turkey, 131-32

Diem, Ngo Dinh, 38, 400

differentiation, as factor in political development, 87-88; in U.S., 83-84

Dilke, Sir C., 201

distribution crisis, 29; in early U.S., 92-93; in Turkey, 132

Di Tella, Torquato S., 337n

Dogan, Mattei, 71n, 242n

Dore, Ronald, 366

Douglas, Elisha P., 81n

Doumergue, Gaston, 179

Downs, Anthony, 195n

dualism, as inadequate model for explaining party systems, 68, 137-38, 174

dual-party system, 98

DuBois, Cora, 382n

DuBois, Victor, 297n

Duvalier, François, 342

Duverger, Maurice, 8n, 9n, 10, 12, 15, 29, 68n, 72n, 73, 86n, 94, 97, 137n, 138n, 156n, 165n, 173n, 174n, 178, 191n

dyarchy, 31-32

Easton, D., 138n

Ebenstein, William, 5n

Eckstein, Harry, 8n, 174n

economic development, consequences of, 55-58; as factor in political development, 46; impact of on agricultural development, 57-58; political and social consequences of, 55-56; relationship to political development, 52-58

economics, and voting, 261-62

Egypt, and attitudes of elites toward

political participation, 217-20, 239-46; Congress of Popular Forces, 231ff; historical crises in, 218-21; mass organizations in, 239-40; nature of elites in, 234-37; origins of parties in, 223-25; participation in, 217-40; patterns of political recruitment in, 217-40; role of Wafd in, 223-27

political parties: Liberation Rally, 218, 222, 227ff; National Union, 218, 220, 227ff; Socialist Union, 218-220, 231-32, 240; Socialist Union, 218, 220, 231-32, 240; Wafd, 129, 218ff, 237

Ehrmann, Henry W., 179n

Eisenstadt, S. N., 375n, 376n

elections, and effectiveness of party systems, 396-97; effects of outlawing or postponing, 396-98; impact of political parties on, 312-17; results of in early U.S. history, 316; turnout in Norway, 249-50

electoral committees, as precursors of political parties, 9

electoral statistics, difficulties in obtaining, 259-61

elites, and antagonism toward parties, 22-23, 26-27; attitude toward economic development, 432; attitude toward parties, 199-200; bureaucratic type, 423-24; coalition of in Africa, 212; composition of in Egypt, 234-39; and crisis loads, 32-33, 227-28, 338-39, 364-65; degree of freedom in decision making, 70-71; factors affecting influence of, 75-76; factors conditioning reactions to participation demands, 401-02; importance of to early political development in Europe, 45-52; influence of party types as opposed to others, 75-76; and parties in Western Europe, 43-77; and party development in Middle East, 125-30; and party development in Turkey, 125-30; patterns of recruitment into, in Egypt, 232-33; reactions to participation crises, 48-54, 219-20, 239-40, 401-07; role of in U.S. history, 303-27; and sequencing of historical crises, 431-32; traditional type and party systems, 59-61; varying influence of, 73-74

Emerson, Rupert, 29n, 32n, 202n, 369n, 372n, 415

encirclement, concept of, 148-50; relationship to cleavages, 149-50

Enver Pasha, 111, 132

equalitarianism, in Norway, 265

Esher, Viscount Reginald, 47n

Estenssoro, Victor Paz, 344, 351

ethnic diversity, and integration; 273-74; and party organization, 276

Etzioni, Amitai, 160n

Europe, classification of states in, 44; future of political parties in, 198-200; impact of industrialization on, 55-58; origins of states in, 45-46; parties and elites in, 43-77; parties as outcome of conflict in, 59; political cleavages in, 67-69; political integration in, 192-94; relationship between parties and elites in, 69-77; role of parties in, 50-52, 160, 177-97; varying penetration of parties in, 64-66

party systems, types of: extreme pluralism, 137-38; moderate pluralism, 137-38; multiparty, 137-40; multipolar, 137-40; simple two-party pluralism, 137-38

executive power, in Latin America, 332

expressive function, of parties, 189

externally created parties, and appeal to masses, 25-26; ideology of, 27-28; and opposition, 27-28; and radicalization, 27; as threat to status-quo, 27-28

factions, in early U.S. politics, 83

Fainsod, Merle, 5n

Fanfani, Amintore, 36

Fanon, Franz, 208

Faul, E., 242n

Faure, Edgar, 196

Fauvet, J., 242n, 262n

Federalista Party (Philippines), 386-87

federalists, in Turkey, 116-18

Federalists, in U.S., 80, 81, 86-97, 100-104, 106, 305-22; disintegrative impact of, 101; leadership of, 91-92; reaction to crisis loads, 96

Federation of Malaysia, 371

Federation of National Liberation (FLN, Algeria), 24

Feith, Herbert, 397n

Fenno, John, 91

Ferguson, Russell J., 84n

feudalism, 45; attacks on, 279

feudal political system, 379-81

finances, as source of political party strength in Italy, 145-46

Fisher, Sydney N., 128n

Fitzgibbon, Russell H., 337n, 344n

Foltz, William J., 8on, 82n, 99n, 287n, 297n

force, as political instrument, 128

fragmentation, and proportional representation, 173

France, and disparity between political and socio-economic development in, 54-55; historical crises in, 28-29, 177-78; role of intellectual in, 56; types of cleavages in, 143

political parties: Communist, 24, 154, 178-80, 191, 404, 416; National Republican Union, 187; Popular Republican Movement, 143, 154, 179; Social Democracy, 178, 179, 190, 416

Franco, Francisco, 38, 160

French Communist Party, 24, 179-80, 191, 404, 416

French Revolution, 49-50

Freneau, Philip, 91

Frey, Frederick W., 121n

Fries, John, 312n

Fries Rebellion, 90, 104, 312

functions, of political parties, 3-4, 89-90, 93-94, 100-101, 186-90, 297-300, 358, 372-73, 394-96

Gallatin, Albert, 91, 318

Galli, Giorgio, 147n

Gamble, Sidney D., 377n

Garibaldi, Giuseppe, 17, 180

Gash, N., 242n

Geertz, Clifford, 289n

generations, as they effect party systems, 33

geography, as factor in political development, 47

Germani, Gino, 335n

Germany, Center Party in, 17, 183; Christian Democratic Union (CDU), 187; historical crises in, 180-82; National Liberal Party, 10, 431; parties in, 155, 171n; Progressive Party, 10; Social Democratic Party (SPD), 185-86, 187, 193

Gerry, Elbridge, 309

Gerth, Hans, 8n, 86n

Ghana, 278-281

Gil, Federico, 345n

Goltz, Colmar Freiherr von der, 116

Goulart, João, 344

government, and ability to respond to demands, 430; concept of under colonialism, 383; deadlock in, 161-63; fusion with parties in Africa, 210-11; and integration activities, 415-16; as modernizing agency, 363;

reasons for weakness of in Africa, 293-95

governmental intervention, in Latin America, 355

Gramsci, Antonio, 181n

Grenville, Lord, 318n

Grossholtz, Thelma Jean, 370n, 387n

Guinea, 274-78

Gürsel, Cemal, 133

Guttsman, W. L., 71n

Hägerstrand, T., 257n

half-way party, 148-50

Hall, D.G.E., 382n

Hamilton, Alexander, 6, 81ff, 305ff

Hamon, Léo, 199n

Hanham, H. J., 242n

Harlow, Ralph Volney, 81n

Harrison, Brian, 382n

Harrison, Martin, 193n

Harrison, Selig S., 370n

Hartenstein, Wolfgang, 184n

Hartz, Louis, 85n

Hauriou, A., 163n

Hayden, Joseph R., 387n

hegemonic control, 422-23

hegemonic party systems, definition and examples of, 35

Hermens, F. A., 173

Hess, R. D., 138n

Higginbotham, Sanford W., 84n

High Federalists (U.S.), 309, 312-16, 318-19

historical crises, causes of 14; as causes of emergence of parties, 13-19; clustering of, 99, 428-32, 346-47; as they effect party systems, 32-33; as functions of exogenous influences, 334-36; and party evolution in Latin America, 340-45; problems of solution of, 345-48; response of elites to, 227-28, 338-39, 364-65, 401-07; response to in U.S., 90-96; role of parties in resolving, 90-94; sequencing of, 99, 221, 346-47, 430-32

in: Africa, 201-06, 267-301 *passim*; Britain, 177; Egypt, 218-21; Europe, 48-50; France, 28-29, 177-78; Germany, 180-82; Italy, 28-29, 152, 180-81, 428-29; Latin America, 342-43, 346-47; Middle East, 129; Norway, 246-50; Turkey, 126, 131-33; U.S., 85, 91-93, 96, 98-104, 303-27

type of: distribution, 92-93, 132; identity, 129, 297, 395-96, 414-15, 428-29; integration, 17, 98-104,

126, 204-05, 267-301, 413-19; legitimacy, 102-03, 206, 342-43, 407-13; participation, 16-19, 85-96, 131-33, 201-02, 219, 221, 400-407; succession, 303-27
Hjellum, T., 246n
Hodgkin, Thomas, 29n, 87n, 94n, 269n, 276n
Hogh, Eric, 241n
Holt, Pat M., 341n
Houphouet-Bougny, Félix, 272, 281, 282n
Hugo, Victor, 115
Hume, David, 67n
Husain, Kamal al-Din, 230
hypotheses, regarding impact of parties on development, 167-172

identity crisis, 129, 297, 395-96, 414-15
ideological party, characteristics of, 36
ideological party system, 36-37
ideology, in colonial India, 384-85; and conflict management, 418-19; decline of, 187-88; of externally created party, 27-28; as factor in extreme pluralism, 158-59; impact of decline of on parties, 190; impact of on one-party systems, 214; and integration crisis, 101-02; and Latin American parties, 362-63; misconceptions concerning, 159; and participation, 405-06; and political conflict, 101-02; and political parties, 11, 12, 187; and political party development in U.S., 85-86, 103; of single parties, 410-11
immobilism, see deadlock
imperialism, in Middle East, 127-28
imperial systems, meaning of politics in, 381
Inal, İbnülemin Mahmud Kemal, 118n, 119n
İnalcık, Halil, 109n
India, 12, 17, 20, 370
Indian National Congress, 12, 20, 224
industrialization, consequences of in Europe, 55-58
Industrial Revolution, impact of on party development, 52
İnönü, İsmet, 111, 112, 123, 133, 411, 412
instability, as function of party repression, 24; as result of repression of opposition by externally created party, 27-28; sources of in Africa, 271-72; tribalism as source of, 279
integration, crisis of, 17, 98-104, 413-

19, 204-05, 267, 301; and ethnic diversity, 273-74; impact of political party system on, 102-04; meaning of, 182-83, 273, 413-14; and national parties, 290-91; and one-party systems, 204-05, 295-96; and political style in U.S., 105-06; role of leadership in, in U.S., 105-06, 312-17; role of parties in, 192-94, 331-32, 354-56; role of parties in, in U.S., 79-80, 98-104, 303-27; threats of tribalism to, 279; threats to in early U.S. history, 306-12; and tribalism, 288-89; views of African leaders regarding, 275-77
integrationist party, 17
intellectuals, role in France, 56
interest aggregation, 172; role of parties in, 86, 196-98, 388; and Asian parties, 393-96
interest articulation, and Asian parties, 393-96
interest groups, in Latin America, 332-33, 355-57, 361-62; legitimation of, 232; and national integration in U.S., 103; in one-party systems, 285-86; and party systems, in general, 419-20; political functions of, 193-94; and political parties, 124, 193-94, 278
internally created party, 8-10, 73-74
internal political structure, weakness of in Latin America, 331
Iron Law of Oligarchy, and parties, 69-73
Isma'il (Khedive), 222
Italian Communist Party (PCI), 24, 140-54, 191, 404, 419; finances of, 145-46; loss of membership, 144; membership of 146-47; number of employees, 146-47; organization as source of strength of, 145; sources of strength of, 144
Italy, anti-system party type, 148-50; basic political trends since World War II, 141-42; characteristics of political parties in, 143-47; church-stage cleavages in, 143; crisis loads in, 152, 180-81; as example of polarized pluralism, 140-52; half-way party type in, 148-50; party membership in, 146-47; problems of identity in, 428-29; pro-system party type in, 148-50; types of cleavages in, 142-43; types of party systems in, 140-52
  political parties: Christian Democracy, 36, 61, 74, 140-54, 164,

185, 187, 416, 422; Communist, 24, 140-54, 191, 404, 419; Liberal, 10, 140-54, 148-54, 414; Monarchist, 140-43, 148-51, 154; Neo-Fascist, 140-42, 148-51, 154; Republican, 140-42, 148-52; Social Democratic, 140-42, 148-52, 154; Socialist Party of Proletarian Unity, 141n, 142n; Socialist, 140-42, 148-52, 154, 196, 416

Ivory Coast, 281-83

Izzet Pasha, 119n

Jackson, Andrew, 6

Jacobsen, Knut Dahl, 254n

Janissary, in Ottoman Empire, 109

Janson, C. G., 242n

Japan, 370-71; early political patterns in, 379-80; as example of feudal political system, 379-81; Liberal Party, 10; Progressive Party, 10

Jaurès, Jean, 180

Jay, John, 91, 307n, 316n

Jay Treaty, 101, 307-08

Jefferson, Thomas, 6, 81ff, 305ff

Jeppesen, J., 241n

Johnson, John J., 347n

Johnson, Lyndon B., 331

Justice Party (Turkey), 112, 124, 412

Kaartvedt, Alf, 247n

Kahin, George McT., 369n

Kamil, Mustafa, 129

Kantor, Harry, 343n

Karpat, Kemal H., 122n

Kautsky, John H., 20n, 87n

Keith, A. B., 384n

Kemalists, 119-20, 132

Kemal, Kara, 118, 119n

Kemal, Mustafa, see Atatürk

Kentucky and Virginia Resolutions, 93

Kenya, 290-92

Kenya African Democratic Union (KADU), 291-92

Kenya African National Union (KANU), 291-92

Kenyatta, Jomo, 292, 293

Key, V. O., Jr., 6n, 86, 87n

Khaldun, Ibn, 108

Khan, Ayub, 22, 369

Kilson, Martin L., 276n, 299n

King, P. S., 261n

Kirchheimer, Otto, 58, 76n, 413, 427

Kirkwood, Kenneth, 295n

Klatzmann, J., 242n

Klöcker, A., 242n

Kornhauser, William, 227

Kouyate, Seydou, 296

Kubitschek, J. de Oliveira, 359

Labour Party (Britain), 10, 185-86, 193, 406

labor unions, in Latin America, 347-48

Laboulaye, E., 54

Lägnert, F., 257n

Lamartine, 115

land tenure systems, and participation, 262-63

Lane, Robert E., 20n

LaPalombara, Joseph, 5n, 74, 79n, 99n, 144n, 147n, 152, 177, 178, 326

Latin America, crisis loads in, 333-35; decision making in, 331-67; elite reactions to historical crises, 338-39; evolution of parties in, 340-45; interest groups in, 332-33; lack of integrating parties in, 331-67; mass based parties in, 348-52; mass politics in, 334-36; nationalizing parties in, 354-57; origins of parties in, 340-45; party systems in, 357-67; political style in, 332, 337, 363; role of military in, 359-60

  political parties: Acción Democrática (Costa Rica), 336; Acción Democrática (Venezuela), 343, 351; Aprista (Peru), 336, 337, 350, 359; Brazilian Labor, 344; COPEI (Venezuela), 337, 351; National Liberation (Costa Rica), 344; National Liberation (Venezuela), 336; Perónistas (Argentina), 335, 346, 359; Radical Party (Argentina and Chile), 345-47; Revolutionary (Mexico), 336, 343, 352-54, 358

Lavau, Georges, 192n

leadership, in Africa, 206-11; changing character of in Africa, 210-11; characteristics of in early U.S. history, 92; and conflict management, 420-21; constraints on, 192; co-optation of in Africa, 206-08; in Ghana, 279-81; in Guinea, 275-77; importance of in political development, 105-06; and integration in U.S., 312-17; intermeshing of in Africa, 203; and legitimacy, 410; nature of in Egypt, 220-21; in Nigeria, 289-91; role of party in change of, 317-22; role of party in selection of, 198-99, 298; skills of, 105-06; training of, in Africa, 297-98

Lechin, Juan, 351

Lee, J. M., 243n, 264n

legislative behavior, party role in disciplining, 92-93
legislature, occupational composition of in Egypt, 234-37; origins of, 108; social composition of in Egypt, 234-39
legitimacy, as affected by leadership qualities, 410; crisis of, 15-17, 206, 342-43, 407-13; and coups, 408-09; differing bases for, 407; problems in measuring, 411; role of parties in, 335; role of U.S. parties in furthering, 102-03; varying success of party systems in achieving, 408-09
Leiserson, Avery, 158n
Lemarchand, René, 292n
Lenin, N. V., 363, 411
Lerner, Daniel, 4n, 20n 258n
Lewis, Bernard, 128
Liberal Democrats (Japan), 370, 394
Liberal Party, in Italy (PLI), 10, 140-42, 148-52, 154, 414; in Britain, 6, 10, 87, 406; in Canada, 10, 35
liberals, in Latin America, 340-42
Liberation Rally (Egypt), 218ff
Lignon, Jean, 183n
Link, Eugene Perry, 92n
Lipset, Seymour M., 15n, 22n, 26n, 57n, 80n, 90, 93, 99n, 138n, 163n, 166n, 170n, 192n, 242n, 243n, 246n
Lipson, Leslie, 344n
Liston, R., 318n
Littunen, Y., 145n, 242n, 246n
Livermore, Shaw, Jr., 91n
localism, 348-49
local government, and development, 258-60
Local Registration Societies, 6
Locke, John, 85, 97
Lohmar, Ulrich, 190n, 200n
loi cadre (1956), 272
Lorwin, Val R., 57n, 61n, 190n
Lowenthal, Leo, 138n
Louis XVI, 107
Loyalists (U.S.), 80
Leutscher, George D., 81n
Lugard, Lord, 201
Lumumba, Patrice, 293

MacDonald, Ramsay, 177, 185
MacKintosh, J. P., 207n
Maclay, William, 92n
Macridis, Roy C., 369n
Madison, James, 6, 81ff, 306
Mahmud II, 109, 114, 126
Maier, Hans, 183n
Maïga, Yacouba, 299n
Mallet, S., 199n

Mardin, Şerif, 115n
Marshall, John, 309
Marshall, T. H., 26n
masses, importance of in evolution of political parties, 91; need for mobilizing in Egypt, 217-19; relationship to parties, 189-90
mass integration party, 182-85
mass movements, conditions for maintaining, 206
mass organizations, in Egypt, 239-40
mass party, 177-84; as alternatives to tribal organization, 300; in Egypt, 227-29; in Latin America, 335-36, 348-52; nature of, 274-75
Masumi, J., 370n
Mayntz, R., 199n
Mazzini, Giuseppe, 17, 51n
Mayer, George, 98n
Mboya, Tom, 291n, 295n
McCormick, Richard P., 86n
McDonald, Forrest, 81n
McHenry, James, 312, 320, 321
McKenzie, R. T., 6n, 73
McKenzie, W.J.M., 288n
Meadows, T. T., 377n
Mehden, Fred R. von der, 408n
Meiji Restoration, 6, 380-81, 429
Menderes, Adnan, 111ff
Mendès-France, Pierre, 196
Mendras, H., 242n, 262n
Merritt, Richard L., 82n, 99n
Metternich, Klemens von (Prince), 202
Mexico, 352-54
Meyer, Poul, 241n
Meynaud, Jean, 71n
Meyriat, J., 243n, 247n, 259n
Michels, Robert, 12, 70, 72n, 73, 182n
Middle East, historical crises in, 129; origins of parties in, 107-10; role of elites in, 125-30
militarization, in Europe, 50
military, and political development in Turkey, 117-21, 124; as political power in Middle East, 128; role of in Latin America, 359-60; role of in Turkey, 124
Mill, John Stuart, 165
Mills, C. Wright, 8n, 86n
minorities, as organizers of political parties, 17
MNR (Bolivia), 336, 344, 351
mobilist parties, effectiveness of, 425-26
mobilization, conditions for in Norway, 244; as elite reaction to participation demands, 402-04; meaning of, 403,

424-25; periods of, 246; regional variations in Norway, 252-56

mobilization party, in Egypt, 228-29

moderation, in U.S. politics, 103

modernity, impact of tribalism on, 287-90

modernization, and authoritarianism, 366-67; defensive type of in Turkey, 114; and government, 363; and nationalizing parties, 366-67; as related to emergence of parties, 19-21; role of parties in, 352-54

Monarchist Party (MON, Italy), 140-43, 148-51, 154

Monroe, James, 91, 95

Moore, D. C., 242n, 262n

Morgan, Edmund S., 85n

Morgan, Kenneth O., 263n

Morgenthau, Ruth Schachter, 276n, 300

Moro, Aldo, 36

Morris-Jones, W. H., 369n

Mosca, Gaetano, 72

Moser, Claus, 242n

Mouvement National Congolais, 293

Muhammad Ali, 110

multi-party systems, in Africa, 289-90; impact of, 68; in Latin America, 358ff; types of, 137-40; ways of coping with, 419-20

multipolar system, features of, 156-60

Muratoff, Paul, 119n

Muslim League, in India, 17; in Pakistan, 22

Naguib, A., 218, 229

Namier, Sir Lewis, 15

Nasser, Gamal Abd, 130, 217ff, 410

national development, and party development, 398

National Front (Iran), 130

national identity, *see* identity

national integration, *see* integration

National Liberal Party (Germany), 10, 431

National Liberation Party (Costa Rica), 344; in Venezuela, 336

national political arenas, importance of in U.S., 82-83

National Republican Union (UNR, France), 187

National Union (Egypt), 218-20, 227ff

nationalism, in Africa, 292-93; conflicts over in early U.S. history, 306-12; in Turkey, 117

nationalist movements, 382ff; in Africa, 202-14 *passim*, 267-301 *passim*;

characteristics of, 10-11; conditions affecting, 31; demands of, 202; factors affecting strength of, 203; and legitimacy crisis, 16; in Turkey, 119-20

nationalist organizations, in Africa, 267-301; Ceylon National Congress, 16; Indian National Congress, 20; Muslim League, 17, 244

Nationalist Union Party (Sudan), 22, 271

Nationalista Party (Philippines), 386-87

nationalizing parties, and modernization, 366-67

nation building, difficulties of, 125-26; in early U.S. history, 303-27; importance of leadership in, in U.S., 106; importance of political style in, in U.S., 106; problems of in U.S., 89-90; resolution of problems of in U.S., 90-94; role of parties in, in U.S., 79-106

nations, difficulty identifying, 271-73; as threatened by tribalism, 288-89

Negri, Guglielmo, 13n, 51n

Nehru, Jawaharlal, 370, 384, 411

Nenni, Pietro, 141n, 416

Neofascist Party (MSI, Italy), 140-42, 148-51, 154

Neumann, Sigmund, 6n, 9n, 49, 68, 74n, 334, 335, 406

Nevins, Allan, 81n

new nations, conditions for party development in, 30-33; limited nature of power in, 32-33; party development in, 87; U.S. as first of, 79

New Ottoman Society (Turkey), 115-16, 127, 133

New Turkey Party, 112

Nichols, Roy Franklin, 101n

Nigeria, 272-73, 289-91

Nipperdey, Thomas, 183n, 262n

Nkrumah, Kwame, 38, 213, 278ff, 298, 410

nobility, effect of economic development on, 55-56

non-competitive party system, conditions for, 29-33; one-party authoritarian type, 37-38; one-party pluralistic type, 38-40; one-party totalitarian type, 40-41

non-party systems, 22-24

Norman, E. H., 380n

Northern Peoples Congress (NPC, Nigeria), 272, 274, 290, 299

Norway, cleavage lines in, 253-56, 264-65; Conservative Party, 253, 254;

Democratic Socialists, 35; factors accounting for differences in turnout, 249-50; Labor Party, 253, 256; mobilization in, 244-48; origin of parties in, 250-51; phases of political development in, 244-46; polarization in, 263-65; political participation in, 246-50; politicization in, 250-53; regional variations in mobilization in, 252-56; regional variations in politicization in, 251-56; representation in, 247; Socialists in, 253, 254; urban-rural cleavage in, 264-65

notables, in Egypt, 226-27; in Latin America, 338

Nyerere, Julius, 212, 274, 283ff, 294n

Oligarchy, Iron Law of, 69-73; false tests of, 70-72; tests of, 70-72

one-party system, authoritarian type, 37-38, 275-81; conditions favoring, 24-25, 30-31; consequences, 326-27; defense of, 285; impact of on participation, 204-05; and integration in Africa, 295-96; as justified by integration crisis, 414-15; limitations of as instruments of integration, 415-16; loss of meaning of in Africa, 207; and participation demands, 402-04; pluralistic type, 38-40, 281-87; rationale for, 203-04, 275-87, 285-86; role of ideology in, 214; totalitarian type, 40-41; in Turkey, 121-22

opposition, acceptance of in U.S., 93; attitudes toward, 285-86; in Latin America, 355-56; irresponsible form of, 157-58; in Latin America, 339; nature of in two-party system, 95; patterns of in U.S., 306-17; reaction of single parties to, 204; repression of in Africa, 206, 209

organization, as impediment to integration, 282-83; and national integration, 103-04; of political parties in U.S., 96-97; of political parties in early U.S., 89; as source of party strength, 145

origins of parties, and bureaucracy, 60-61; as efforts to break oligarchical control, 13; as influenced by systemic needs, 86; and institutional sequence, 60; and participation demands, 400-07; as related to political power, 19; as result of systemic crises, 13-18; role of modernization in, 19-21

in: Africa, 270-71; Asia, 374-88; Egypt, 223-25; Europe, 17, 51-52; Latin America, 340-45; Middle East, 107-110; Nationalist movements, 10-11; Turkey, 107-110; U.S., 80-84

Osmeña, Sergio, 387

Ostrogorski, Michael, 12, 72, 73n, 81n, 86n

Ottoman Empire, 107-133 *passim*; government of, 108-110

Padmore, George, 288n

Palmer, R. R., 12n

Pareto, Vilfredo, 72

Parker, R. S., 260n

Parliamentary Clubs, 183-84

parliaments, as cradles of political parties, 8-13

participation, conditions for in Norway, 244; crisis of, 16-19, 48-50, 85-96, 131-33, 201-02, 219-21, 246-50, 400-407; decline of in Africa, 211-12; dimensions of in Egypt, 220-21; full variety, 405-07; early forms of in Egypt, 222-23; kinds of, 63-64, 65, 404-05; and land tenure systems, 262-63; limited variety, 404-05; at local levels, 258-60; meaning of, 202; as opposed to power sharing, 404-05; relationship of to legitimacy, 207; restricted nature of in Latin America, 337; and rural lag in Norway, 248-50; under colonialism in Asia, 384-85

demands for: In Africa, 201-02; in early U.S., 18-19; by elites in Egypt, 218; and one-party system, 402-04; and party development, 400-407; reactions to, 401-407; reasons for, 400-401; response of elites to, 48-50, 54, 239-40; response of parties to, 61-63; response to in U.S., 96

Parti Démocratique de la Côte d'Ivoire (PDCI, Ivory Coast), 211, 275, 281-83

Parti Démocratique de Guinée (PDG, Guinea), 213, 275-78

Parti du Regroupement Africain (RDA, French Africa), 273, 275, 281, 283

party of integration, 182-84

party systems, in Africa, 203-14, 287-93; concept of encirclement in, 148-50; conditions affecting type of, 21-33; and conflict management, 418-24; definition of, 138-39; as dependent or independent variable,

166-67; differing impacts of, 94; dualism in, 137-38; dualism in, challenged, 137-38; in Europe, 137ff; and historical crises in Latin America, 339-40; impact of traditional elites on, 59-61; importance of leadership in, 105-06; importance of style in, 105-06; and interest groups, 419-20; in Latin America, 357-63; and management of demands, 335; means of measuring permeation of, 64; and national integration, 98-104, 413-19; and party roles, 94-98; permeation of, 58-67; and policy making in Latin America, 363-67; and political socialization, 424-27; role of in transfer of power, 317-22; timing as a factor in development of, 169; in Turkey, 121-24. *See also* political party, origins of parties

types of: authoritarian, 37-38; competitive, 35-37, 122-24; dual, 98; hegemonic, 35; ideological, 36-37; multiparty, 68, 137-40, 160, 289-90; multipolar, 156-60; noncompetitive, 29-33; non-party, 22-24; one-party, 121-22, 203-14; one-party authoritarian, 37-38, 275-81; one-party pluralistic, 38-40, 281-87; one-party totalitarian, 40-41; pluralistic-competitive, 287-93, 359; pragmatic, 36-37; repressed, 359; structured, 168; turnover, 35-36; two-party, 94-95

Passigli, Stefano, 145n
Patai, Raphael, 123n
Patriots (U.S.), 80
Paysalıoğlu, Arıf, 113n
peasants, mobilization of in Norway, 247-48; and participation lag in Norway, 248-50
permeation of party systems, 58-66
Peronistas (Argentina), 335, 346, 359
Perón, Juan, 346, 347
personalism, in Latin America, 340ff
Peru, 350-51
Pesonen, P., 71n, 242n
Peterson, Phyllis J., 344n
Philippines, 370, 386-88
Pickering, Timothy, 309, 311, 312, 320
Pikart, E., 181n
Pinckney, Charles C., 309, 315
Pinckney, Thomas, 308n, 309
Pizzorno, Alessandro, 190n
pluralism, in African party systems, 287-93; as characteristic of single

party systems, 281-87; extreme form of, 156-60; extreme form of, and hypothetical conditions determining or inhibiting, 167-72; factional politics in U.S. as type of, 88; importance of in U.S., 83-84; and interest groups, 103; in Latin American politics, 360-62; nature of, 153-56; and relationship to political and economic development, 40; as threat to integration, 303-27

types of: polarized, 94, 153-56; religious, 46-47; religious, and political stability, 163; two-party, 94

pluralistic-competitive party system, 287-93

Poggi, G., 143n
Poincaré, Raymond, 179
polarization, hypothetical factors facilitating or inhibiting, 169-71; in France, 153-55; in Italy, 140-55; in Norway, 263-65; in party systems, 138-39; in Weimar Republic, 153-55

polarized pluralism, nature of, 153-56
policy making, in Latin America, 331-67; role of parties in, in Asia, 388-96; and party systems in Latin America, 363-67; role of parties in, in Latin America, 348-49

political center, as inherently immobile, 164-65
political change, *see* political development
political clubs in England, 8
political community, role of parties in promoting in U.S., 102-03
political culture, 165-67
political development, balanced relationship to socio-economic development, 53; centralization as factor in, 45-46; and crisis loads, 79-80 (*see* historical crises); cycles of in Turkey, 112-14; disparity with socioeconomic change, 54-55; economic development as factor in, 46; effect of political parties on, 87-94; factors conditioning, 44-47; geographic factors in, 47; hypothetical impact of parties on, 167-72; impact of colonialism on, 382-88; impact of ideology on in U.S., 85-86; impact of Industrial Revolution on, 52; importance of political style in, 105-06; importance of leadership in, 105-06; and modernity, 4; phases of in Norway, 244-46; phases of in Turkey, 126; rates of, 258-59; re-

lationship to socio-economic development, 52-58; religious wars as factor in, 46-47; role of elites in, in Middle East, 125-30; role of parties in, 160-65; and social stratification, 84-85; timing as a factor in impact of, 169

political innovation, 256-57

political modernity, *see* political development

political party, *see also* ideology, origin of parties, party systems and acceptance of democratic ideals, 59-60; alternative roles in political development, 435; alternatives to in Latin America, 364-66; ambivalent attitude toward in Asia, 369; attempts to revitalize in Africa, 212-13; auxiliaries of, 208-09; causative role of in U.S., 323-24; changing functions of, 186-87; and colonial experience, 383-84; as competitors of African governments, 293-95; concessions to traditional forces, 209-10; conditions affecting development of, 82; conditions favoring emergence of, 18-22; conditions leading to alienation of, 405; and conflict resolution in U.S., 103-04; conflict among in U.S., 306-12; and crisis loads, 427-32; decline of in Africa, 201-14, 285; decreasing need for, 194-95; as dependent variable, 41; developmental role of, 160-61, 398-435; as distinguished from factions, 87-88; early forms of in U.S., 80-81; effect of mimetic elements on, 87; as essential control instruments, 294; as essential to authoritarian and totalitarian regimes, 23; evolution of in Asia, 374-88; factors causing break-up of, 208-09; finances of, 145-46; and historical crises in U.S., 90-94, 303-27; impediments to development of, 378; as independent variable, 41-42; as influenced by participation demands, 400-407; impact of on legislative behavior, 92-93; as instrument of integration, 98-104, 192-94, 209, 413-19; and integration, 179-81; and Iron Law of Oligarchy, 69-73; leadership of in early U.S., 92; legitimacy of, 206; limited role of in Latin America, 363-67; low status of in Latin America, 360; and national elections in U.S., 312-17; nature of leadership of, 207-08; as not essential to political systems, 22; as obstacles to integration, 416-17;

and political socialization, 424-27; predecessors of, 270-71; proliferation of, 173; as purveyor of consensus, 199-200; reaction of to new demands for participation, 61-63; reasons for emergence of, 3-4; reduced role of, 199; as related to certain systemic needs, 86; as related to modern political systems, 3-42; and relationship to bureaucracy, 60-61; representation of social class in, 71; role in conflict management, 418-24; role in crisis management in Mexico, 352-54; role in Europe, 50-52; role of ideology in, 158-59; role in political development, 126-27; schism in U.S., 313-20; and social mobility in U.S., 324-26; sources of strengths of, 144-47; style of in U.S., 97; as targets of new elites, 26; varying ideological position of members of, 151-52; varying influence of elites in, 73-74; varying role of, 58

definition of: 5-6, 29, 51, 87-88, 268-69, 338-39, 371

development of: 86-87, 185-86; basic conditions for, 80-87; impact of external factors on, 87; relationship of suffrage to, 8-9

functions of: 3-4, 89-90, 93-94, 100-101, 186-90, 297-300, 372-73, 394-96

organization of: in Africa, 275-76; articulation of, 314-15; in early U.S., 89; in Italy, 144ff; in Middle East, 127; problems of, 229-30; in U.S., 96-97

origins of: in Africa, 270-71, 294; developmental theory of, 19-21; in Egypt, 223-25; in Europe, 17; historical-situational theory of, 14-19; importance of masses in, 91; institutional theory of, 8-14; in Latin America, 340-45; in Middle East, 107-11; in Norway, 250-51; theories of, 7-21; in Turkey, 107-10; in U.S., 303-06

types of: adaptive, 424-26; anti-system, 148-50; catch-all, 184-92, 192-200 *passim*; competitive, 33-37; denominational, 143-44; externally created, 10-11, 74; half-way, 148-50; integrationist, 17; internally created, 8-10, 73-74; mass, 177-84, 274; mass integration, 182-84; mobilization, 425-26; nationalist movement, 10-11; non-competitive, 37-

41; party of notables, 91; party of patronage, 74; party of politicians, 86, 91; party of principle, 74; popular, 91; social integration, 74; prosystem, 148-50; total integration, 74

political power, its historical diffusion, 54

political process, model of, 164

political recruitment, declining base of in Africa, 211-14; in Egypt, 217-37 *passim. See also* recruitment

political style, conditions affecting, 421; in Latin America, 332, 337, 363; of parties in U.S., 97; in U.S., 105-06

political system, competitive type, 24-29; competitive-parochial type, 381-82; complexity of as agent of political alienation, 152; feudal type, 379-81; groups outside of, 63-65; non-party type, 22-24; one-party type, 24-25; traditional imperial type, 375-78

politicization, 182-83; conditions for in Norway, 244; regional variations in, in Norway, 251-56; role of parties in, 364

politics, characteristics of in Turkey, 111; as conflict management, 418; early views of in Asia, 378-80; homogenization of, 66-67; nationalization of, 64-66; role of ideology in, 103

polities, types of in Latin America, 341-43

Popitz, H., 183n

Popular Front, 179, 185

Popular Republican Movement (MRP, France), 143, 179

Populist movements, 37

Post, K.W.J., 299n

Potash, Robert, 345n

power, factors affecting, 205-06; sensitivity to in Asia, 389-90

power sharing, as opposed to participation, 404-05

pragmatic party system, 36-37

pragmatism, in Latin American political parties, 363

"private governments," 332, 335

Proctor, J. Harris, 133n

proportional representation, 165-73; as explanation of party impact, 165; as feeble electoral system, 173; in Norway, 250-51, 264-65; as it produces centrifugation, 169-72; as it produces extreme pluralism, 167-72

pro-system party, 148-50

proto-parties, 51

Punta del Este Charter, 331

purpose, and political development, 105-06

Putney Debates, 401

Pye, Lucian W., 5n, 14n, 353n, 355n, 372n

Pylee, M. V., 384n

Quezon, Manuel L., 387

radicalism, in Europe, 57

radicalization, as encouraged by externally created party, 27

Radical Party (Argentina and Chile), 345-47

Ramsaur, E. E., 112n

Rantala, O., 242n

Rassemblement Démocratique Africain (RDA, French Africa), 273, 275, 281, 283

recruitment, in Africa, 202, 217-37 *passim*; changing patterns of in Egypt, 231; of leaders in U.S., 324-25

reform, limited nature of in Latin America, 346

Reischauer, Edwin O., 374n, 380n

religious cleavages, and impact on political development, 169-70

religious pluralism, and political stability, 163

religious wars, as factor in political development, 46-47

representation, in Egypt, 231-33; in Norway, 247

representative government, and anti-system parties, 409

repressed party system, 359

repression, as elite reaction to participation demands, 401-02; impact on subsequent party systems, 24; as ineffective against parties, 30; and instability, 24; in Latin America, 339; of opposition by externally created parties, 27-28; of opposition in Africa, 206, 209; of parties, 23-24

Republican Party (PRI, Italy), 140-42, 148-52

Republican Party (U.S.), 6, 10, 80ff, 195, 305-22, 406; leadership of, 91-92; reaction to crisis loads, 96

Republican Peoples Party (RPP, Turkey), 112, 113, 121-23, 132

revolution, in Egypt, 222-24

Revolutionary Clubs, 7, 8

Revolutionary Command Council (Egypt), 220, 227, 229

Revolutionary Party (PRI, Mexico), 336, 343, 352-54, 358
Riggs, Fred W., 371n
Ritter, Gerhard A., 298n
Riza, Ahmed, 117
Robinson, Edgar E., 81n
Robinson, Kenneth E., 288n
Rokkan, Stein, 62, 76n, 188n, 242n, 243n, 246n, 247n, 248n, 249n, 252n, 253n, 255n, 256n, 259n, 262n, 265n, 413
Rosberg, Carl, 39n, 40, 291n, 295n, 359
Rosen, George, 377n
Ross, J.F.S., 71n
Roth, Guenther, 182n
Rousseau, J. J., 133n, 203n
rural politics, 262-65
rural politicization, compared, 264-65
Rustow, Dankwart A., 5n, 15n, 68n, 107n, 109n, 112n, 113n, 119n, 122n, 124n, 128n, 412

Sabaheddin, ("Prince"), 117-18
Sadat, Anwar, 230
Safran, H., 222, 234, 235n
Salisbury, Robert H., 88n
Sansom, Sir George, 379n
Sartori, Giovanni, 22n, 34, 48n, 63n, 71n, 74, 94n, 105n, 137n, 143n, 159n, 163n, 189n, 327, 419
Scalapino, Robert A., 6n, 9n, 370n, 429
Scammon, Richard H., 243n
Schachter, Ruth (Morgenthau), 276n, 300
Schlesinger, Arthur, Jr., 101n
Schmitt, K. M., 337n
Schumpeter, Joseph, 50n
Schwabe, P., 242n
Scott, Robert E., 343n, 353n
Scott, Wulf, 242n
Screvane, Paul, 324
secret societies, 376-77
Sedgwick, Theodore, 91
Seligman, L. G., 160n
Selim III, 109, 114, 126
Senghor, Leopold S., 202, 297n
"service" sector, 340
Serxner, Stanley J., 343n
Shastri, Lal B., 411
Sheldon, Charles P., 380n
Shell, Kurt, 11n, 188n
Siegfried, André, 262n
Şinasi, İbrahim, 115
single-party system, see one-party system
Skendi, Stavro, 125n

Sklar, Richard, 299n
Smith, Denis Mack, 5n, 9n
Smith, James M., 310n, 311n
Smith, Robert Aura, 387n
Smith, Thomas C., 380n
Snow, Peter G., 345n
social class, in Africa, 276-77; as a cleavage line, 67-68; as diminishing basis for party organization, 190; in early U.S., 84-85; and economic development, 55-58; and participation demands in Egypt, 225-26; and party development in Middle East, 125-30 *passim*; and party representation, 71; and voting patterns, 262-65
Social Democratic Party (SFIO, France), 178, 179, 190, 416; (SPD, Germany), 185-86, 187, 193; (PSDI, Italy), 140-42, 148-52, 154
social integration party, 74
socialist parties, in general, 10, 26, 182
Socialist Party (PSI, Italy), 140-42, 148-52, 154, 196, 416
Socialist Party of Proletarian Unity (PSIUP, Italy), 141n, 142n
Socialist Union (Egypt), 218ff; organization of, 231; origins of, 230-31
socialization, and party systems, 424-27; by political parties, 182-83
social stratification, in early U.S., 84-85
Society for Union and Progress (Turkey), 112-13, 116-20, 127
socio-economic development, impact of on political development, 52-58
Sorel, Georges, 72
Specht, F., 242n
Spengler, Joseph J., 372n
Spiro, H. G., 172n
Spreafico, A., 147n
stability, impact of cleavages on, 161-62; relationship of two-party systems to, 94-95; and religious pluralism, 163; role of national parties in, 434
Stalin, Josef, 41, 411
Stammer, O., 246n
Steed, Michael, 265n
Steffens, Lincoln, 325n
Stehouwer, Jan, 241n
Stirling, W. G., 377n
Stokes, Donald D., 153n
Stresemann, Gustav, 184
structure, as affecting process of change, 258
structured party system, 168

Sturzo, Don Luigi, 183
succession, factors affecting, 317-22; as an historical crisis in U.S., 303-27
suffrage, expansion of as condition for party development, 8-10; factors in extension of, 262; in France, 177-78; impact of extension of, 76; in Latin America, 337-38; and mobilization in Norway, 248-49; and voter turnout, 249-50
Sukarno, Achmed, 385, 393, 394, 397
Sweden, parties in, 15-16
Szyliowicz, Joseph S., 123n

Tal'at Harb Pasha, 221
Talât Pasha, 111, 117, 118
Talleyrand, Charles M. de, 313
Talmon, J. L., 49n
Tanganyika, 283-86
Tanganyika African National Union (TANU), 274, 283-86, 299
Tanzimat, in Turkey, 114-15
Taylor, Philip B., 345n
Terry, Fernando Belaunde, 350
theory, of party systems, 68-69; of political party development, 7-21, 69-73, 82
Thompson, F.M.C., 262n
Thompson, Virginia, 283n, 288n
Tingsten, Herbert, 261n
Tinkcom, Harry Marlin, 84n
Torgersen, Ulf, 188n
total integration party, 74
totalitarian party system, 40-41
Touré, Sékou, 275-85 passim; political philosophy of, 275-78
trade unions, in Africa, 285-86; as instrumentalities, 432; role of in Turkey, 131
traditional imperial systems, 375-78
traditionalism, persistence of in Africa, 209-10
traditionality, in Latin America, 338-39; in Asia, 374-82
traditional society, impact of elites on party systems, 59-61
transaction flows, as dimensions of change, 258-59
transfer of power, as test of legitimacy, 411-12
trasformismo, 181
tribalism, attacks on in Africa, 275; in the Congo, 292-93; efforts to overcome, 275-76, 279-80; in Ghana, 279-80; in Guinea, 276-77; impact of democracy on, 288; and modernity, 287-90; in Tanganyika, 284

Trujillo, Rafael L., 359
Truman, Harry S, 325
Tshombe, M., 289
Tunaya, Tarık Z., 113n
Türkeş, Alparslan, 132
Turkey, early parties in, 112; Kemalist dictatorship in, 120-22; major characteristics of party development in, 111-24; origins of parties in, 107-10; role of elites in, 125-30 passim; role of military in, 117-21, 124; role of trade unions in, 131; varying number of parties in, 113
    political parties: Democratic (DP) 112, 122-23, 412; Justice, 112, 124, 412; New Turkey, 112; Republican Peoples (RPP) 112-13, 121-24, 132; Society for Union and Progress, 112-13, 116-20, 127
Turner, H. A., 184n
turnover party system, 35-36
tutelary government, and transfer of power, 412-13
two-party system, central characteristics of, 94-95; in early U.S., 303-27; in Latin America, 357ff
typology of political parties and party systems, limitations of in Latin America, 358, 361-63. See also political parties, types of; party system, types of; historical crises

unification, and impact on rise of parties, 180-81
Unionist Party, see Society for Union and Progress
Union Progressiste Mauritanienne, 274
United Arab Republic, 230
United States, causes of early conflict in, 306-12; and crisis of integration, 306-27 passim; and crisis of succession, 303-27; early role of elites in, 303-27; early party characteristics, 95-97; early transfer of power in, 317-22; early two-party system in, 303-27; historical crises in, 91-104; impact on of first political parties, 88-93; intermediate conditions affecting party development in, 82-86; origins of parties in, 80-84, 304-06; party organization in, 89, 96-97; party style in, 97; role of parties in, 79-106; role of parties in succession crisis, 303-27; role of party in fostering upward social mobility, 324-26
    political parties: Anti-Federalists,

8, 304; Democrats, 10, 80; Federalists, 80ff, 105-06, 305-22; High Federalists, 101, 105, 312-19 *passim*; Republicans, 6, 10, 80ff, 195, 305-22, 406
Uruguay, 345-48

Valen, H., 188n, 246n, 249n, 252n, 253n, 255n, 265n
values, and response to participation demands, 401-02
Vangrevelinghe, G., 242n
Vargas, G., 335, 344, 359
Vedel, Georges, 192n
Verba, Sidney, 4n, 14n, 28n, 152n, 353n
Virginia and Kentucky Resolutions, 311-12
visibility, as impediment to legitimacy, 409
voters, volatility of, 192-93
voting, factors affecting, 262-63
Wafd (Egypt), 129, 218ff, 237; failures of, 224-27; origins of, 224-25
Waline, M., 72, 73n
Wallerstein, Immanuel, 87n, 99n, 271n, 415, 420
Wallin, G., 242n
war, as factor in political development, 47
Ward, J.S.M., 377n
Ward, Robert E., 5n, 109n, 113n, 369n
Washington, George, 86, 100, 105, 306ff, 411

Weber, Max, 8n, 14n, 29, 56n, 86n, 91, 411
Webster, Noah, 91
Weibull, Jörgen, 242n
Weiker, Walter F., 132n
Weimar Republic, *see* Germany
Weiner, Myron, 74, 79n, 99n, 152, 177, 178, 326, 364, 374n, 385n
Whigs (Britain), 15; (U.S.), 80
Whiskey Rebellion, 90, 104, 307
Wight, M., 201n
Wildavsky, Aaron B., 8n
Williams, Phillip, 54n
Williamson, Chilton, 85n
Wittfogel, Karl A., 376n
Wolcott, Oliver, 312
Worcester, Dean C., 387n
working class, reactions of elites to, 62; reactions of parties to, 62
Wriggins, Howard, 16n

XYZ Affair, 308-09

Yacé, Philippe, 211
Yalman, Ahmed Emin, 119n
Young, Crawford, 207n, 292n
Young Ottomans, *see* New Ottoman Society
Young Turks, 116-19, 125-26, 132, 133

Ziebura, Gilbert, 298n
Zolberg, Aristide, 282n, 300n